THE ADVENTURES OF THE CONSTITUENT POWER

Constitutions are made in almost all transformations of regimes. What are the dangers and the hopes associated with such a process? What can make constitution making legitimate? *The Adventures of the Constituent Power* explores the democratic methods by which political communities make their basic law, arguing that the most advanced method developed from Spain and South Africa. The first part of this book focuses on history of the idea of constitution making, before and during the democratic revolutions of the eighteenth century. The second part traces the notion of the constituent power in recent regime transitions that were consciously post-revolutionary, from Spain to South Africa. With the return of revolutions or revolutionary patterns of constitution making, the book examines the use and potential failure of the new ideas available. The third part then proceeds to consider the type of constitution that is likely to emerge from the post-sovereign process.

ANDREW ARATO is Dorothy Hart Hirshon Professor in Political and Social Theory at the New School for Social Research. He has held Fulbright, Humboldt, and NEH Fellowships, and has lectured in France, Germany, Toronto, South Africa, Nepal, and Zimbabwe. He is the author of several books, most recently *Post Sovereign Constitution Making: Learning and Legitimacy* (2016).

COMPARATIVE CONSTITUTIONAL LAW AND POLICY

Series Editors

Tom Ginsburg *University of Chicago*
Zachary Elkins *University of Texas at Austin*
Ran Hirschl *University of Toronto*

Comparative constitutional law is an intellectually vibrant field that encompasses an increasingly broad array of approaches and methodologies. This series collects analytically innovative and empirically grounded work from scholars of comparative constitutionalism across academic disciplines. Books in the series include theoretically informed studies of single constitutional jurisdictions, comparative studies of constitutional law and institutions, and edited collections of original essays that respond to challenging theoretical and empirical questions in the field.

Books in the Series

Courts and Democracies in Asia Po Jen Yap
Constitutions, Religion and Politics in Asia: Indonesia, Malaysia and Sri Lanka Dian A. H. Shah
Canada in the World: Comparative Perspectives on the Canadian Constitution Richard Albert and David R. Cameron
Proportionality: New Frontiers, New Challenges edited by Vicki Jackson and Mark Tushnet
Constituents Before Assembly: Participation, Deliberation, and Representation in the Crafting of New Constitutions Todd A. Eisenstadt, A. Carl LeVan, and Tofigh Maboudi
Buddhism, Politics and the Limits of Law: The Pyrrhic Constitutionalism of Sri Lanka Benjamin Schonthal
Assessing Constitutional Performance Tom Ginsburg and Aziz Huq
Engaging with Social Rights Brian Ray
Constitutional Courts as Mediators Julio Ríos-Figueroa
Perils of Judicial Self-Government in Transitional Societies David Kosař
Making We the People Chaihark Hahm and Sung Ho Kim
Radical Deprivation on Trial Cesar Rodríguez-Garavito and Diana Rodríguez-Franco
Unstable Constitutionalism edited by Mark Tushnet and Madhav Khosla
Magna Carta and its Modern Legacy edited by Robert Hazell and James Melton
Constitutions and Religious Freedom Frank Cross
International Courts and the Performance of International Agreements: A General Theory with Evidence from the European Union Clifford Carrubba and Matthew Gabel
Reputation and Judicial Tactics: A Theory of National and International Courts Shai Dothan
Social Difference and Constitutionalism in Pan-Asia edited by Susan H. Williams
Constitutionalism in Asia in the Early Twenty-First Century edited by Albert Chen
Constitutions in Authoritarian Regimes edited by Tom Ginsburg and Alberto Simpser
Presidential Legislation in India: The Law and Practice of Ordinances Shubhankar Dam
Social and Political Foundations of Constitutions edited by Denis J. Galligan and Mila Versteeg
Consequential Courts: Judicial Roles in Global Perspective edited by Diana Kapiszewski, Gordon Silverstein and Robert A. Kagan
Comparative Constitutional Design edited by Tom Ginsburg

The Adventures of the Constituent Power

BEYOND REVOLUTIONS?

ANDREW ARATO

New School for Social Research, New York

CAMBRIDGE
UNIVERSITY PRESS

CAMBRIDGE
UNIVERSITY PRESS

University Printing House, Cambridge CB2 8BS, United Kingdom

One Liberty Plaza, 20th Floor, New York, NY 10006, USA

477 Williamstown Road, Port Melbourne, VIC 3207, Australia

314–321, 3rd Floor, Plot 3, Splendor Forum, Jasola District Centre, New Delhi – 110025, India

79 Anson Road, #06-04/06, Singapore 079906

Cambridge University Press is part of the University of Cambridge.

It furthers the University's mission by disseminating knowledge in the pursuit of education, learning, and research at the highest international levels of excellence.

www.cambridge.org
Information on this title: www.cambridge.org/9781107126794
DOI: 10.1017/9781316411315

First published 2017

Printed in the United States of America by Sheridan Books, Inc.

A catalogue record for this publication is available from the British Library.

ISBN 978-1-107-12679-4 Hardback

Contents

Preface

Andrew Arato

For the last four decades, constitutional politics has been a major terrain of contemporary struggles. Contestations around designing, replacing, revising, and dramatically reinterpreting constitutions have proliferated worldwide. Starting with Southern Europe in post-Franco Spain, then in the ex-Communist countries in Central Europe along with Latin America, moving on to post-apartheid South Africa, followed by Nepal and the Arab world, constitution making has become a project not only of radical political movements, but of liberals and conservatives as well. Even populist politics, both on the left and right, once opposed to constitutionalism, has now integrated constitution making into its political projects as well as claims of legitimacy. Wherever new states or new regimes will emerge in the future, whether through negotiation, revolutionary process, federation, secession, or partition, the making of new constitutions will likely be a key item on the political agenda.

Intellectual developments have, in part, kept pace with the rebirth of constitutional politics. We now have an increasing series of excellent comparative and single-country studies concerning constitution making, as well as a few large N monographs seeking to discover the common elements of the constituent process, constitutional contents and arrangements that foster stability. While theoretical deepening has lagged behind somewhat, we do have important new works on the constituent power, both from various radical (Negri, Colon-Rios, Kalyvas) and constitutionalist (Ackerman, Dyzenhaus, Loughlin and Walker) perspectives. What is missing are serious synthetic works linking theory and comparative analysis that are capable of prudentially orienting actors engaged in constitution-making processes all over the world. This volume, combining historical reflection, constitutional theory and comparative analysis, purports to make a contribution to that end.

My book is different than Bruce Ackerman's influential work, *We the People* (vols. 1 and 2) not only theoretically, but also because of its strongly comparative orientation. Moreover, I deal with several country cases, rather than just one, in contrast to many important works on recent constitutional politics, such as Peter Russell's book on Canada (*Constitutional Odyssey*) or T. Moustafa's on Egypt (*The Struggle for Constitutional Power: Law, Politics, and Economic Development in Egypt*). As against most of the comparative and large N literature, e.g., the work of Tom Ginsburg and his collaborators (*The Endurance of Constitutions*), I stress normative theory. Yet my work differs from the works of Negri (*Insurgencies: Constituent Power and the Modern State*) and Kalyvas ("Popular Sovereignty, Democracy, and the Constituent Power," *Constellations*, 2005), by combining theory with case studies, and through a more consistent critique of the framework of Carl Schmitt than is to be found either in their work or in Colon-Rios' *Weak Constitutionalism*. While closer to the approach adopted by the authors in the edited volume by Loughlin and Walker, *The Paradox of Constitutionalism*,[1] I introduce a new paradigm that is not found in the work of any of their contributors. Compared to David Dyzenhaus and Hans Lindahl in that volume, I think the concept of the legitimate constituent power freed of populist fictions remains important, and that it should not be imputed to a process merely on the bases of its outcome. As against the many authors who have written on the important South African process, I draw out its universal implications that they rarely recognized. In comparison to other criticisms of recent constitution making in Hungary, I have a much more critical perspective with respect to the previous, more liberal period of development. Finally, next to the literature on the new constitutionalism (Said Arjomand, *Constitutionalism and Political Reconstruction*) and "juristocracy" (Ran Hirschl, *Towards Juristocracy*) my work is not court-centered, though I do recognize the important and often-positive role of constitutional courts in the development of the new paradigm. I take law and politics in the life of constitutions equally seriously, and I reduce constitutions to neither, taken alone. Thus, hopefully, this book, informed by recent scholarship, has entirely new contributions to make.

Based on a long period of interdisciplinary work in law, political science, intellectual history, and political sociology, as well as following my previous book,[2] it remains my overall thesis that a new paradigm of "post-sovereign" "post-revolutionary" "multi-stage" constitution making has emerged and is increasingly important today. Although path-determined, the new paradigm

---

[1] For my critique of these authors, see the Introduction to *Post Sovereign Constitution Making. Learning and Legitimacy* (Oxford: Oxford University Press, 2016).

[2] Ibid.

promises nonetheless to have great significance wherever constitution making has become salient. Born in processes of relatively recent democratic transitions from authoritarian rule, the normative achievements of this paradigm have now made their appearance during reform attempts, as well as under revolutionary ruptures. There is no question that a veritably international discussion, stressed by Heinz Klug,[3] has played a role in the dissemination of the new ideas. At the same time, those who advocate them in various settings have run into strong competition from older ideas of constitution making. The results have been mixed, as the competing cases of Tunisia and Egypt show. We still do not know enough concerning the conditions under which the new ideas can be successfully transplanted. I aim to present not only the new paradigm, but also some of the necessary conditions for its implementation.

I have three aims in this volume. First, I seek to reinterpret the historical background of the new "post-sovereign" paradigm of constitution making, contrasting it with the main democratic alternatives: the French sovereign model and the American one that I see as antinomic or dualistic (i.e., internalizing the tension between the sovereign and the post-sovereign notions of agency). Second, I wish to reconstruct the new paradigm that has emerged first in Spain, then in Central Europe, and, finally, in the most developed form, in South Africa. I shall do so in terms of theoretical considerations and the analysis of cases. In particular, I am interested in reconstructing what appears to a developmental logic, at least from the Spanish forerunner, to the South African version that I regard as the most complete and coherent. Third, I explore the relevance of the new principles of legitimacy in contexts significantly different than the original Central European and South African settings that established their possibility. Finally, I end with an extended chapter considering the type of democratic constitutionalism that is likely to emerge from the post sovereign paradigm, as well as from more revolutionary forms that have incorporated some of its lessons.

I use three or four related terms to describe the new paradigm of constitution making. I call it "post-sovereign," to focus on the key theoretical issue of the exclusion of any single agency, institution or individual that claims to embody the sovereign power and authority of "the constituent people." But I also refer to it as "post-revolutionary," in that radical changes are accomplished beyond the old antinomy of reform or revolution. Focusing on the central institution of the paradigm, I speak of roundtable-led constitution making.

---

[3] Heinz Klug, *Constituting Democracy: Law, Globalism and South Africa's Political Reconstruction* (Cambridge: Cambridge University Press, 2000).

Finally, concentrating on the process and the key role of interim constitutions, I also use the adjective "multi-stage." Each of these terms highlights a different feature of the paradigm.

My previous book focuses on the great gains of the post-sovereign paradigm in the domains of legitimacy and learning. Yet, in spite of its great advantages, in my still earlier book I had already come to recognize the path-determined aspects of post-sovereign constitution making.[4] Upon further reflection, first on the case of Turkey, and later when comparing Egypt and Tunisia, I have nevertheless come to the conclusion that aspects of the post-revolutionary, post-reformist model are also applicable in revolutions, as well as under comprehensive reform attempts. After previously considering reform scenarios, this book, focusing on the return of revolutionary forms of change, explains how this is possible. I argue that, given the international dissemination of many of the new principles, they are inevitably present in both reform processes, such as Turkey, from the 1990s, and in genuine revolutionary conditions, as in Tunisia and Egypt after 2011. Under all these settings, there seems to be a veritable horse race between paradigms, one in which the older models of sovereign constitution making would have the advantage, and where the presence of elements of the new may play a destabilizing rather than a constructive role. Focusing on issues of time and sequence, and relying on comparisons between Colombia and Venezuela, as well as Tunisia and Egypt, allows me to analyze some of the preconditions under which what has been learned from the new method could be productively utilized even in revolutions.

The purpose of my analysis is not only descriptive. It is rather to intervene in intellectual, ideological, and political problem complexes. As those involved in the relevant processes well know, constitution making and remaking pertains to the highest level of lawmaking, political design of, and allocation of power within a polity. How one understands the process, its structure, participants, and purpose matters a great deal and the stakes are high indeed.

STRUCTURE OF THE BOOK

The book is divided into three main sections. These are preceded by an Introduction developing my understanding of three concepts that are crucial to the intellectual effort here: legitimacy, sovereignty, and constitution. This will be followed by a preliminary introduction of the conception of sovereign constitution making, and the project of transcending it by an alternative democratic paradigm.

---

[4] *Constitution Making Under Occupation* (New York: Columbia University Press, 2009).

Part I focuses first on historical, then on theoretical issues that will help me locate the new paradigm, and explicate the need for it given the problems of its forerunners. Its two chapters reconstruct the origins of the concept of sovereign constitution making in the history of political thought and practice. I stress throughout the almost simultaneous emergence of post-sovereign conceptions, both in theory and practice, which remain, however, a minor chord in the history of constitutionalism till our own time. Chapter 1 focuses on the history of ideas, discussing the intellectual foundations of the sovereign theory (along with anticipations of the post-sovereign one) in early modern political philosophy. Chapter 2 analyzes the complex and contradictory carrier of the idea of the sovereign constituent power during the first democratic revolutions. Particular attention is paid to the earliest attempts in both France and America to move beyond the sovereign conception. In France this happened mostly on the level of theory, while in America it was the practice of "conventions" in their post-1780 version pioneered in Massachusetts that anticipated elements of the post-sovereign idea.

Part II of the volume turns to cases. After presenting an ideal typical reconstruction of the post-sovereign paradigm, Chapter 3 will present its development as a nonlinear learning process from Spain to Central Europe, and from there to South Africa. Moving from case to case, the focus will be the depiction of a process whereby greater institutional elaboration and political democratization were achieved. I call the learning process involved non-linear because there were also losses both on the normative and institutional levels, and indeed successes as well as failures, as we move from country to country. In particular in its existing form, the post-sovereign paradigm never solved the problems of state formation or re-organization where the inherited structure of the state came to be untenable, whether because of voluntary partition as in Czechoslovakia, or through mutually agreed upon incorporation, as in the case of the German Democratic Republic. As in the case of Hungary, however, the process could fail even in an intact unitary state where its inherent logic toward completion in a second stage was not properly followed.

Chapter 4 focuses on cases with three types of scenarios more revolutionary than associated with the post-sovereign paradigm. It examines the cases of Iraq and Nepal where there were clear breaks with existing legality, and where nevertheless something close to the post-sovereign paradigm was adopted. I consider the deformations caused by these breaks, as well as the negative role of external occupation in the case of Iraq. Next, through a brief discussion of India, followed by a comparison of Colombia and Venezuela, I examine the possibility that even where the classical option of revolutionary constituent assemblies is utilized, elements of the post-sovereign conception can play a very positive role. Finally, in the case of two nearly classical revolutions in the Arab world, Tunisia and Egypt, I consider not only such a positive role in the first, but also the destabilizing role of post sovereign norms in the second, where the institutional translation of normative principles of inclusion and consensus was very deficient.

In Part III, Chapter 5 turns to the type of constitutional structure that has the greatest affinity with the post-sovereign process, what I call multi-track constitutionalism involving a differentiated structure for options of change and replacement. In my view the strong constitutional jurisprudence that is required for the working of such a model is a likely consequence not only of the international dissemination of ideas, but the structure of the post-sovereign paradigm. While I derive the constitutionalist component from an insurance model that is highly applicable to the post-sovereign cases, I propose that the democratic dimension follows normatively from the paradigm's main assumptions. I thus revive a project insisted on by Hannah Arendt, but as old as some famous texts of Jefferson and Condorcet, to preserve the spirit of democratic constitution within the new constitutions themselves. I believe that the post sovereign paradigm is a more favorable context for the actualization of such democratic affinity than previous revolutionary models.

Finally, I end with an epilogue on a generally neglected case of the dissolution of the All Russian Constituent Assembly in 1918. In my view this case remains important not only to indicate the moment when the Russian Revolution began to disappoint all the democratic hopes associated with it, but also as a decisive moment in the adventures of the constituent power that took a new turn with the disassociation of constitution and revolution, that were previously united in European history, and even beyond, as in China, Iran, Turkey. In my view the assumptions of the sovereign constituent power played almost as great role in this misadventure as the dictatorial propensities of the Bolsheviks.

A word on the title. It represents conscious borrowing from Merleau-Ponty's great work, *Adventures of the Dialectic*. Ever since my early studies of Lukács, I have felt genuine affinity for Merleau-Ponty's perspective, but more as a political thinker than for his philosophical works. The present work borrows part of Merleau-Ponty's title for reasons that go beyond my longstanding political sympathy for his work of 1955. First, I fight against the conceptual mythology of the popular sovereign of the constituent process, much as he fought against the myth of the subject of history.[5] I focus on the resulting but inevitable

---

[5] On this, and the continuity of my work, see the very generous introductory essay by Enrique Peruzzotti and Martin Plot in *Critical Theory and Democracy* (New York: Routledge, 2013).

antinomies of such an assumption, as did Merleau-Ponty. The two mythologies are internally related, and while the first is a more modest version of the second, the attraction to populist "reason" that brings them together often reveals disappointment in historically generated or self-generated proletarian class consciousness as once articulated by Lukács. Nowhere is this clearer than in the theory of populism of the recently departed Ernesto Laclau, whose whole train of argument closely resembles what Merleau-Ponty depicted as Sartre's ultra-bolshevism.[6] And, second, I am persuaded, and I hope to persuade the reader, that the historical experience in the case of constitutional politics and theory "with all its false starts, its omissions, its disparities, and with the possibility of revisions at a later date"[7] can be just as much an exciting if dangerous "adventure" as the political history of dialectical thought treated by the French philosopher sixty years ago. Of course, with so many years more hindsight concerning Merleau-Ponty's own topic, we are in a better position to give contents to his call for a new left that would also be a new liberalism. Both his own student Claude Lefort, as well as Jürgen Habermas, have contributed a great deal to the realization of this regulative idea. With respect to my topic, the combination of "new left, new liberalism" entails the insistence on constitution-making procedures beyond both radical democratic mythologies of the actor, and equally mythical liberal imputation from result to process. The post-sovereign model of constitution making presented here is liberal as well as radical, but its highest virtue is critical self-reflection on what has been the historical position of liberals and radical democrats in light of their negative experiences. That critical self-reflection must also be directed at the paradigm itself, and aim at "the possibility of revisions at a later date." We can hope for many such revisions because the adventures of the constituent power are exciting enough to continue, and I believe will continue, as long as modern society and politics survive.

[6] See Chapter 6 of *Post Sovereign Constitution Making*.
[7] Merleau Ponty, *Adventures of the Dialectic* (Evanston: Northwestern University Press, 1973) p. 3.

Introduction

Basic Concepts

The idea of post-sovereign constitution making[1] emerged out of the adventures of the revolutionary and populist idea of the sovereign constituent power. Theoretically, it is an important alternative to the conception of the constituent power of a unitary, embodied popular sovereignty. Nevertheless, in spite of premature obituaries, the idea of the *pouvoir constituant* of "the people" is still very much alive. Its presumed viability and vitality are underwritten by the return of populist and revolutionary forms of constitution making, first in the Andean republics of Latin America, and then in the Middle East. All the same, the conceptual foundations of this now-traditional notion have been shaken. In the midst of political competition between constitution-making forms, whose several venues will be explored in this book, there is also a struggle over concepts. In order to understand the main intellectual stakes involved, I begin by presenting my interpretation of the main concepts presupposed by both sides: constitution, legitimacy, and sovereignty. How these notions are interpreted, and especially how they are to be combined, represents a main stake of the debate. Through a preliminary presentation of the idea of sovereign constitution making, I will try to show the special way in which constitution, legitimacy, and sovereignty converged in the traditional idea of the constituent power. I will argue that it is exactly on this level that sovereign constitution making reveals its fundamental weakness, or even danger, namely an elective affinity to dictatorship. The political dangers have been well illustrated by the history of revolutions. It is this weakness and this history that represents the background motivation for immanent criticism, as well as for the construction of the alternative paradigm of the post sovereign constituent power, one more faithful to the values of both democracy and constitutionalism.

---

[1] See my *Post Sovereign Constitution Making: Learning and Legitimacy* (Oxford: Oxford University Press, 2016).

I CONSTITUTION

There are many possible definitions of "constitution." At issue here, first, is whether we are to understand the category as referring to a simple reality like a document with the relevant name, or to a complex set of institutions. Related to that question is another, namely whether we think of the origin of the constitution in terms of a single localizable act, such as a decision by an identifiable agency, or rather as the result of several interrelated processes, and possibly stages of development. While there is no one-to-one relation between the stress on the documentary constitution and a foundational decision, there is an elective affinity between these options that together are at the foundations of the sovereign theory. The case is similar with the alternative, the many-leveled concept, multi stage process, and the post-sovereign paradigm.

Unlike others, I think it is a grave error to simply treat the documentary constitution of countries as the only object of a study on constitution making. That choice, motivated by what is easily operationizable for large-scale empirical study, would avoid the question of definition.[2] The constitution would be simply what a political order has defined as such, by putting a set of norms into a document called "constitution" or "basic law." One could argue for this position by stating, partly incorrectly, that it is only this meaning of constitution that refers to something "made."[3] What is certainly true, however, is that there is a significant relationship between reducing the constitution to the documentary legal text, and the idea of a constituent power whose decision, localizable as an event,[4] produces it. This affinity is both historical and logical. The concept of the constituent power was developed in the three great

---

[2] Z. Elkins, T. Ginsburg and J. Melton *The Endurance of National Constitutions* (Cambridge: Cambridge University Press, 2009). After distinguishing between formal and functional constitution (p. 38ff), the authors simply go on to deal with the former. The book is valuable nevertheless, though it would have been more so if the authors focused on constitutions where there is a significant overlap between the formal and the material (or: the functioning). That would leave the communist constitutions out, for example. Keeping them in leads to strange results. For example, treating the important question of the structure of the amendment rule, the authors forget that in the one party authoritarian systems 50 percent of the legislature and 99 percent amount to the same thing. As in the Central European cases, the structure of such an amendment rule begins to matter only in the context of regime change leading to pluralization.

[3] The term unwritten (and: "not made") is correct only with reference to the conventions of the constitution. As is well known, the supposedly unwritten British constitution contains many written statutes and legal precedents that were made, often with a clear constitutional object in mind. That these should largely work as a protected second order law is admittedly itself a convention, one that is at times violated.

[4] See Robin Wagner Pacifici's forthcoming *What is an Event?* (Chicago: The University of Chicago Press, 2017).

revolutions, each of which has experienced significant episodes of documentary constitution making.

Here I am interested only in those documentary constitutions that become to a significant extent *the* "real" or actual or material one, and will certainly pay attention also to the making of rules that are constitutional but are outside the documentary text. These can emerge at different time periods, involving a multiplicity of events and sometimes no important or even noticeable events at all. In the United Kingdom, for example, the constitution of the state is rightly said to consist of statutes, precedents and conventions.[5] Of these, parliamentary statutes and judicial precedents are "written" and "made" during a plurality of localizable events. The conventions of the constitution are unwritten, however, and can be said to be the results of an evolutionary development. In principle, no event could produce a convention, only long-term, repeated practice. As many interpreters have noticed, all polities with documentary constitutions also rely on statutes, judgments and conventions of constitutional significance. These considerations require a definition of constitution that thus becomes a complex matter.

I begin my analysis with the conceptual distinctions of Hans Kelsen who, in my view, put the topic on entirely new foundations even as he systematized earlier notions. He starts with the distinction of constitution in the formal and material senses,[6] and considers the latter as the more fundamental category.[7] I find highly significant the contrast between Kelsen's scheme and that of Carl Schmitt's definition (also in two parts), one that makes an analogous but much less clear distinction between constitution identified in terms of a fundamental decision of the constituent power and constitutional laws.[8] It is extremely

---

[5] Dicey, *The Law of the Constitution*, 8th ed. [1915] (Indianapolis: Liberty Publishers, 1982).

[6] J. E. Fossum and A. J. Menendez attempt something similar, also derived mainly from Kelsen, in their recent book *The Constitution's Gift* (Lanham, MD: Rowman and Littlefield, 2011), pp. 19–26. While I am hardly an orthodox follower of "the pure theory of law," in this context I do not think the philosophical supplementation in terms of a third concept of the constitution, the normative one, helpful as the authors themselves admit that there are as many such concepts as normative theories. I prefer to discuss what they have in mind in terms of constitutionalism and democracy. Nor do I think that adding a sociological dimension in the sense of Hart's rules of recognition is needed. In the case of the formal meaning of the constitution, this addition either moves the concept into the material domain, or requires only a minimal practice that is always at hand like the ritual meetings of the required bodies, or the celebration of the document on a special day, as in Communist Hungary, always on August 20.

[7] *General Theory of Law and the State* (Cambridge: Harvard University Press, 1945), p. 124ff. and 258–259. See recently Julian Arato, "Treaty Interpretation and Constitutional Transformation: Informal Change in International Organizations," (August 5, 2012) *Yale Journal of International Law*, 38(2), 2013.

[8] *Verfassungslehre* (Berlin: Duncker & Humblot, 1928), pp. 21–25. When criticizing Kelsen, Schmitt inexplicably leaves the material constitution out of consideration. The idea that Kelsen

difficult to identify the contents of this fundamental decision, and which constitutional laws form its parts or its essential legal scaffolding. As in the case of Weimar in Schmitt's own presentation, the same constitution could be interpreted differently by opposing political sides. The decisionist conception does, however, have the advantage of thematizing the relationship of empirical-existential *political* structures and *legal* norms within a constitution. This is unfortunately excluded by Kelsen's *pure* theory. What is significant here, however, is that while Schmitt's decisionist concept identifies *the* constitution as the product of an event, and of a unitary agency, Kelsen's two-part definition focuses on the emergence of structures that can have multiple sources, acting in multiple historical contexts. The decisionist concept of the constitution allows no development on the most fundamental level. The Kelsenian concept of the constitution is, on the contrary, developmental.

According to Kelsen's analytically clear, if not entirely convincing presentation, constitution is interpreted as an entirely legal institution. But it has two senses. In the *formal* sense, the constitution is the "solemn document" ordinarily called by that name. This definition is not complete, however, since Kelsen adds that the completion of its formalization requires entrenchment, a codified rule of change (amendment or revision) more difficult than the rule of legislation in the same document.[9] Thus, the formal constitution establishes the dimension of higher law in the sense that it is only this dimension that has the procedural protections that formally elevate it above all other norms in the legal hierarchy.[10] In Kelsen's spirit and following some of his texts,[11] I would add that the real completion of formality would require some kind of enforcement mechanism that would help maintain the differentiation between constitutional and ordinary legislation, classically judicial or constitutional review. Functional substitutes for both entrenching rules and judicial enforcement, like the checks and balances in the separation of powers, or established conventions, however, are, and have been historically, possible. Their stability ultimately requires political sanctions and political enforcement. It may be that the stability of amendment rules, and in the end even the enforcement of judicial or constitutional review, requires political sanctions

identified the constitution with what is protected by the amendment rule is fallacious. *Verfassungslehre*, chapter 2.

9 Again I disagree with Fossum and Menendez (*The Constitution's Gift*, p. 21), who claim versus Kelsen that entrenchment by an amendment rule does not belong to the formal concept of the constitution. Precisely the same goals are served by entrenchment as by producing a documentary constitution in the first place.

10 Indeed one would think that the Kelsenian hierarchy, with constitution at its pinnacle is only established if a formal constitution establishes a differentiated, higher order, and thus relatively difficult rule of constitutional change.

11 *General Theory*, p. 157.

as well. A court that is not backed by public opinion would ultimately be incapable of policing entrenched provisions and the rules that entrench them, to see that they are not transgressed, derogated from or bypassed through other political mechanisms.[12] I think, however, it makes a great deal of difference, on the level of politics as well as law, whether ultimate political intervention is the only device guarding the formal constitution, or there are other mechanism doing so with legal authority.[13]

Constitution in the *material* sense, according to Kelsen, refers to the legal rules of legal rule making, of legislation, in his own words to the "the rules that regulate the creation of general legal norms" [124]. This is the most important dimension, but not the whole, of what H.L.A. Hart would later call secondary rules.[14] Kelsen's definition identifies constitution as reflexive or meta-law, but it is incomplete. He himself has added fundamental rights constraining legislatures that can still be understood as rules of legislation, and on the level of "political theory," rules defining and regulating "the creation and competences" of other (the highest executive and judicial) organs of government, whose full differentiation from legislation he was unwilling to accept.[15]

---

[12] See D. Davis for an interesting South African illustration of this from the 1950. Davis, D. and M. le Roux. Precedent and Possibility. The (Ab)use of Law in South Africa. Capetown: Double Storey Books, 2009.

[13] It could be maintained that a formal constitution can be relatively well protected by public opinion, as was supposedly the case of the Third Republic in France, and conversely, that not only is judicial review not a full proof defense against informal constitutional change in Jellinek's sense of *Verfassungswandlung* -see *Verfassungsänderung und Verfassungswandlung* (Berlin: Häring, 1906) – but it can also be ultimately the instrument of just such change through reinterpretation. This has been considered from Jellinek to Ackerman and others recently. In particular, the second argument should be taken really seriously, and will be in this book. With this said, structurally judicial review nevertheless strengthens the power of entrenchment, and its own role in bypassing occurs on a constitutional channel higher than the legislative one. Thus, for important cases Ackerman speaks of an informal constitutional *amending* process. This has the same implication as having a second, more flexible amending power in a multi-track scheme.

[14] Secondary rules "specify the ways in which primary rules may be conclusively ascertained, introduced, eliminated, varied, and the fact of their violation conclusively determined." *The Concept of Law* (Oxford: Oxford University Press, 1961), p. 92.

[15] See *General Theory*, pp. 258–259. Kelsen's adjustments open the road to other, legal definitions: Dieter Grimm, in *Die Zukunft der Verfassung* (Frankfurt: Suhrkamp. 1999), to take a particularly sophisticated version, identifies constitution as that "complex of norms which fundamentally regulates the setting up and exercise of state power and the relationship of state and society" [11]. This definition has the advantage that it includes the domain of fundamental rights along with political institutions more directly than it is possible through Kelsen's or Hart's conception. But through a slight change of focus the secondary–primary division is upheld: Grimm speaks of "a group of basic norms for the making of political decisions, aiming at the possessors of power, and a group of politically generated norms aiming at its subjects" [14]. The constitution is thus differentiated from ordinary law by the fact that "it has the highest power itself as its object."

While he paid little attention to conventions of the constitution, presumably because of their nonlegal nature and their diffuse and merely political form of enforcement, the reflexive conception must include them as well to the extent they regulate the process of lawmaking, application, interpretation, and enforcement. Hart's notion of secondary rules, rightly freed from the sanction model through his notion of an "internal relation" to legal obligation, would allow the conceptualization of the laws and conventions of the constitution on a continuum.[16] Conventions are certainly norms that regulate lawmaking. Conversely, even codified, secondary rules are often enforceable only on the political level.[17] Conventions should be included in the concept of the constitution, not only because they are normative with some kind of enforcement attached to them, but also because they can be easily legalized. This has indeed happened with many British norms of parliamentary government when they became parts of documentary constitutions elsewhere, with the 22nd amendment in the United States, as well as important conventions of the Canadian constitution.[18]

The relationship of the material and formal constitutions is very important. Kelsen's idea that the formal is created for the sake of the material, in order to strengthen and stabilize it, can be accepted only as a structural rather than a historical point, not applicable to non-*constitutionalist* or minimally *constitutionalist* constitutions. Many formal constitutions are made for ideological reasons and sometimes primarily for external consumption. But if there is a significant overlap between the formal and material constitution the latter is indeed strengthened and stabilized by becoming public, and is potentially enforceable. When the material structure that is formalized includes limitations on the holders of the most important powers of government, we can speak of *constitutionalism* in more than a minimal sense. Thus, the authors of the French Declaration of Rights were right in the normative sense in claiming that without separation of powers and fundamental rights (art. 16[19]) we cannot speak of constitutions, only the meaning here is that of a *constitutionalist* constitution. Kelsen neglected this dimension in his definitions, in his attempt to

---

[16] *The Concept of Law* (Oxford: Oxford University Press, 1962).

[17] I. Jennings, *The Law and the Constitution*, 5th ed. (London: University of London Press, 1959). This text has been canonical for the Canadian constitutional judges, who have developed the most significant legal doctrine dealing with the conventions of the constitution.

[18] In one well-known group of cases, a constitutional court may try to adjudicate if not yet strictly enforce conventions. Canadian Supreme Court Patriation Reference (1982); Quebec Veto Reference (1982). See P. Russell, *Constitutional Odyssey: Can Canadians Become a Sovereign People?* 3rd ed. (Toronto: University of Toronto Press, 2008), chapter 8.

[19] http://avalon.law.yale.edu/18th_century/rightsof.asp.

keep law purified of ideological elements. But it follows from his scheme that the idea of adding a normative constitution as a third dimension to material and formal, as desirable as it may be politically, is either theoretically superfluous or too demanding.[20] A nonconstitutionalist constitution is possible, but we should be clear about the sense in which we would use this term, and whether or not we are referring to merely symbolic or ideological constitutions that do not involve an overlap between the formal and the material, or also look to include constitutions without fundamental rights and separation of powers.[21] Each of these options is possible independently of the other: rights and separation of powers can be formally present in mere paper constitutions, and formalized material constitutions can exist without the features that liberal theory would insist on.[22]

It is elements of material limitation and documentary protection that together create a two-track structure of constitutional government.[23] Even law that involves documentary entrenchment genuinely separates the two tracks: legislative and constitutional[24] only if the material constitution itself limits power holders by separation of powers, or fundamental rights or other disabilities of the legislature.[25] Such limits conversely require formal entrenchment,

---

[20] As by Fossum and Menedez, *The Constitution's Gift.*

[21] See the taxonomy of types of constitution of Karl Loewenstein, "Reflections on the Value of Constitutions in our Revolutionary Age" in A. Zurcher, *Constitutions and Constitutional Trends Since World War II*, 2nd ed. (New York: NYU Press, 1955), pp. 204–206. His distinction, which still remains relevant, is between normative (i.e., constitutionalist), nominal (nonconstitutionalist, but to be applied) and semantic (or, ritual, namely paper constitutions, not to be seriously applied). Said Arjomand, however, is entirely justified in adding ideological constitutions to this list, meaning constitutions that incorporate a strong substantive project, even if this category can cut across Loewenstein's typology. See, e.g., his "Constitutions and the Struggle for Political Order" 1992 in European Journal of Sociology 33.

[22] See Nathan Brown's interesting book *Constitutions in a Non-Constitutional World* (Albany, NY: SUNY Press, 2002) for examples of both in the Arab world.

[23] Stressed by Ackerman, *We the People* I (Cambridge, MA: Harvard University Press, 1991), following the *Federalist* and J. Marshall in *Marbury* as well as *McCulloch.*

[24] Kelsen (*General Theory*, p. 258) speaks of two stages of the legislative process: "the creation of general norms which is usually called legislation... and the creation of general norms regulating this process of legislation." For this latter, more fundamental stage of legislation producing the constitution, he has in mind the constitution-making and -revising process. As to the latter we can derive from Kelsen the idea that revision or amendment procedures embody the idea of constitution as reflexive law to the highest degree since they apply legal procedures not only to legal procedures, but also on the higher level still to the procedures themselves that regulate the procedures of lawmaking. We find in Kelsen (even less than in Schmitt) no rules for original constitution making, paradoxically in line with the continental European idea of the unlimited constituent power.

[25] While an amendment rule does place the constitution at the highest level of a normative hierarchy, if the constitution itself had no other limits on legislative power, entrenchment would only have the meaning that the legislature cannot abolish or reduce its own absolutism.

otherwise the legislative track can derogate from its material limitations.[26] A three- and multi-track structure is possible when there are formal limits to the amending power (absolute entrenchment), or, preferably, when the amendment rule itself contains several hierarchical rules of possible amendments dealing with different parts of the constitution.[27] It is possible, if not in my view desirable, to add absolute entrenchment to a differentiated set of amendment rules, as was done without the benefit of codification by the creators of the basic structure doctrine in India. But as the Indian judges probably assumed, and as the Turkish judges have explicitly stated, absolute entrenchment can mean only recourse to an original and constituent power to create a new constitution. In turn, that assumption is legalized[28] by being built into constitutions that propose special procedures for replacement, like the Spanish, Bulgarian, Colombian and, we once assumed, the German Federal Basic Law with its article 146 in its 1949 version.

An important reason why analysis should not focus solely on the formal, documentary constitution is because there are very important constitutional elements in almost all political regimes, or norms that significantly determine norm creation that can be, and often are, left out of documentary constitutions. Thus, they lack the benefit of entrenchment against purely legislative alteration or derogation. This is usually the case for electoral rules, and in the USA was and remains the case for both the key institution of judicial review and for determining the makeup and jurisdiction of the federal courts. Some of these material constitutional provisions, like judicial review, can be formally constitutionalized by interpretation. In other words, the protection of existing formal elements, like constitutional supremacy, can be extended to them so that they cannot be abolished by simple statute, at least not without the unlikely agreement of a supreme or constitutional court. Other provisions continue playing a materially constitutional role, even as they become objects of legislative challenge and alteration in various court packing and

All else would be open to the legislative track. A superlegislature would be needed only to introduce a genuine two-track or multi-track structure.

[26] Elster identified the connection between the two forms of precommitment, e.g., separation of powers and entrenchment. See *Ulysses Unbound* (Cambridge: Cambridge University Press, 2000).

[27] See Arato "Multi-track Constitutionalism Beyond Carl Schmitt," *Constellations*, Vol. 18, No. 3, 2011, and especially Chapter 5 below.

[28] On the contrary, the Decision of the Turkish Constitutional Court on the so-called head-scarf amendments in 2008 appealed to an extralegal revolution as the only modality able to alter the eternity clauses of the constitution. See my "Democratic constitution-making and unfreezing the Turkish process." *Philosophy & Social Criticism* 36.3–4 (2010): 473–487. There is no such reference in the Indian Basic Structure doctrine.

unpacking as well as jurisdiction removal schemes. These are vivid reminders that very important provisions like any given composition and jurisdiction are not entrenched and may not be formally part of a US constitution.

The converse is also true. The formal constitution, as Kelsen recognized, may contain many provisions that are not materially constitutional. These can be of very different types. Some may highlight different aspects of the identity of the polity, as preambles often do. In spite of Schmitt's views to the contrary, only when they affirm and point to materially constitutional provisions should they be regarded as fundamental parts of the constitution. Thus, for example, the importance of a statement that "X country is a republic or a democracy" must be confirmed by entrenched provisions having to do with rule of law and elections. When some of these provisions, such as republic, democracy, federalism, fundamental rights, and secularism, are absolutely entrenched as variously in France, Germany, and Turkey, the symbolism of preambles can gain great material importance, with respect not only to the legislative but also to the amending power. However, in the case of ordinary laws, "primary rules" in Hart's sense of regulating citizens directly rather than aiming at the lawmaking and interpreting processes, constitutional formalization can often represent the usurpation of power by a temporary dominant political power or a supermajority wishing to protect its own political decisions against easy alteration and to bind its successors.[29] This has happened in the Chilean Constitution enacted in 1980, and the new Hungarian Basic Law of 2011. It may not be always easy to distinguish between primary and secondary rules, or Dworkin's partly parallel policies and principles. But these lines do exist, even if at an abstract theoretical level, and can therefore be abused. Thus, just as in the case of the abuse of the legislative power, it may be an important task of courts to pay attention to the abuse of the amending power as well.[30]

Finally, the idea of a material constitution raises the question of regime, and the empirical structure of political systems. Historically, earlier

[29] I do not consider such binding per se usurpation, as Elster tends to in a second version of his argument about pre-commitments. See *Ulysses Unbound*. Throughout this book, however, I will argue that the manner of original constitution creation is what distinguishes the legitimate binding of future generations. In this sense I accept the originally British assumption that a parliament should not bind a future parliament exactly like itself, even if such binding could be considered legally binding, as in Hart's argument. Admittedly, omnipotence could be interpreted this way as well as by the traditional British position that would deny such binding of the future. But the legitimacy, if not the legality of binding the future remains a fundamental problem. Both sovereign and post sovereign paradigms address it, in my view the second much more successfully.

[30] Balanced budget amendments, which may make ordinary policy decisions by new governments much more difficult, is one such abuse. Prohibition may have been a successful case of the same.

meanings of constitution (Aristotle's *politeia*; Machiavelli's *modi e ordini*) referred to the empirical structure of regimes that could be distinguished by empirically observable characteristics.[31] Schmitt, who thematized this history or pre-history, still understood constitution on the most fundamental level as referring to a regime rather than a law. Given the requirements of not only "pure theory," but also the pattern of historical development, Kelsen was more right in focusing on normative, legally binding structures when defining the two meanings of constitution. But when he maintained that every political regime must have a material, though not a formal, constitution (125), he was conflating the new eighteenth-century normative concept of an "unwritten" constitution with empirical regime. As has been shown,[32] this claim is misleading even where normative and empirical regularities are not yet differentiated from one another. Moreover, as important German interpreters like Dieter Grimm and E.W. Böckenförde strongly imply, the empirical structure of regimes represents a third dimension of the constitution even if in modern times it is in significant part structured by the normative-legal dimension of the overall political order.[33]

One important example that shows why we cannot neglect the empirical dimension of the constitution is the two- or multi-party system of modern democracies. These can indeed be determined in part by a materially constitutional rule, the electoral law. But only in part. The same law mandating first-past-the-post elections or proportional representation can produce different party systems in different democracies, and also at different times in the same democracy.[34] Conversely, changing electoral laws may not actually transform party systems. The outcome in each case depends also on a number of different factors: demography; the intensity of political cleavages; the character of the actual parties that compete; and the experience of previous elections.[35] The concept of the regime is the proper level where the old empirical meaning

---

[31] Schmitt, *Verfassungslehre*, chapter 1; Grimm, *Zukunft*, p. 12ff; 17ff.

[32] Hart, *Concept of Law* (Oxford: Oxford University Press, 1961), p. 89ff.; and especially Roberto Unger, *Law and Modern Society* (New York: Free Press, 1976), pp. 48–58.

[33] Böckenförde, *Staat, Verfassung, Demokratie* (Frankfurt: Suhrkamp, 1992), chapter 2; Grimm, *Zukunft*.

[34] For a highly interesting example, see S. Ruparelia, *Divided We Govern* (Oxford: Oxford University Press, 2015), showing how even a first-past-the-post (FPTP) electoral rule can have the consequence of extreme fragmentation of parties, in a federal and pluralistically divided society.

[35] G. Sartori, *Parties and Party Systems* (Cambridge: Cambridge University Press, 1978); superseding Duverger, *Political Parties* (New York: Wiley, 1959). For the relevant distinction between electoral rule and system, see M. Shugart and R. Taagepera, *Seats and Votes* (New Haven: Yale University Press, 1989).

of constitution reappears, where empirical elements can be thematized in their interaction with the material constitution. Anticipations about empirical outcomes can, and usually do, play an important role during the making of documentary constitutions, as well as constitutionally material statutes.[36] Thus, the legal theory of constitutions cannot aspire to be entirely pure. What cannot be sustained, however, are two of Schmitt's ideas: that the essence of the constitution is an empirical structure, and that the constitution in this sense is produced by a fundamental decision of a single, unified actor. These ideas are not only highly misleading as interpretations of constitution-making processes, but they also deflect from the consideration of the legitimacy of acts of the constituent power. It is the normative structure of modern constitutions that always raises the question of the authority by which they are made.

II LEGITIMACY

We commonly assume that one purpose of constitutions is to bestow legitimacy on politics practiced under their terms, or to *authorize* political officials and at times *legitimate* other actors, sometimes in opposition to those who rule and administer. But what is the source or what are the sources of a constitution's own legitimation? What is legitimacy? Is it different from legality on the one hand and authority on the other, and, if so, how? Are legitimacy in the sociological-empirical and philosophical-normative senses different? If they are, is there nevertheless a relationship between them?[37] After analyzing the term, we will face the question of whether the identity of the constitution-making agent or agents is a sufficient source of the legitimacy of the constitution-making process, or, alternately, whether the timing, the procedures, and the results of a process are all important for its legitimation. The answer will depend on our concept of legitimacy.

---

[36] A documentary constitution, or a materially constitutional law, may mandate an outcome that would be left to merely empirical phenomena elsewhere. For instance, to stay with my example, a two-party structure could be mandated by giving seats only to the first two parties in electoral competition. While this has rarely happened (the Argentine Lex Sáenz Peña of 1912 may be the one case that comes close) an electoral threshold like the 10 percent one in Turkey moves in exactly this direction. Conversely, a multi-party structure could be mandated by giving minority groups guaranteed representation. These examples do not vitiate the point that in most competitive democracies a party system is the result of a combination of legal rules, and empirical givens as well as processes.

[37] Many have asked these questions of course: See Habermas, *Legitimation Crisis*; J. Weiler, *The Constitution of Europe* (Cambridge: Cambridge University Press, 1999), pp. 77–85; T. Franck, *The Power of Legitimacy Among Nations* (Oxford: Oxford University Press, 1990).

Despite their common etymology and identification in positivist theories,[38] a distinction should be made between legality and legitimacy. Legality is one of the normative orders of society, being distinguished from the others by the existence of external and not merely symbolic sanctions, exercised in the modern world by the centralized enforcement of norms.[39] Not all legal rules require sanctions; rules that regulate other rules commonly rely only on an internal attitude of obligation, or indirect sanctions that are not strictly legal.[40] But as Kelsen rightly, albeit confusingly, noted, sanctions are necessary parts of the interlocking normative order of legality.[41] The "internal attitude" all laws must nevertheless to an extent rely on links legality to legitimacy. According to Hart, as well as the common sense expressed in Napoleon Bonaparte's famous quip about the limits of mere bayonets, no legal order could function without some sense of obligation being present in at least some sectors of the population. Hart distinguished legal functionaries in this regard, and Max Weber the administrative staff, two overlapping categories. That sense of obligation can be present only if the legal system as a whole, or certainly its main political principles, are considered justified or at least valid. To derive that validity from the order itself, as its transcendental condition of possibility, in Kelsen's famous *Grundnorm*, for example, is deeply question begging, or circular. Such attempted derivation only poses the question of legitimacy, without at all solving it.[42]

Legitimacy is impossible to reduce to a single source or type.[43] The fundamental author here remains Max Weber, who established the basic sociological definition: "the legitimacy of a system of domination may be treated sociologically only as the probability that to a relevant degree the appropriate

---

[38] E.g., Kelsen, *General Theory*, p. 117.

[39] Kelsen, *General Theory*, chapter 1, especially pp. 20ff; 28ff.

[40] Hart, *Concept of Law*, Chapter II.2, and chapter V. Therefore, the attempt to describe as "legitimacy" rather than "legality" any rule, such as the rules of international "law," is based on an Austinian (i.e., command of the sovereign, enforced by sanctions) rather than Hartian concept of law (i.e., union of primary and secondary rules). On this subject, see the very interesting book of T. Franck, *The Power of Legitimacy Among Nations*, especially chapters 1–3. Franck's attempt to recover the normative "pull" of international law is nevertheless very important, and comes close to my emphasis on the normative structure of moments between constitutions. What is common here is the demonstration that a Hobbesian stress on a "state of nature" in either the international domain (realism), or the time of constitution making (Schmitt and his followers) is equally wrong.

[41] *General Theory*, op. cit.

[42] E. W. Böckenförde, "Die verfassunggebende Gewalt des Volkes – Ein Grenzbegriff des Verfassungsrechts" in *Staat, Verfassung, Demokratie*, pp. 92–93.

[43] As does even Frank, inconsistently, *The Power of Legitimacy Among Nations*, pp. 18–19, 25, and 34.

attitudes will exist, and the corresponding practical conduct will ensue."[44] These appropriate attitudes do have to do with normative validity, but only as the presence of empirical beliefs in or "ascription of" such a validity or justification.[45] Weber's idea of legitimate domination has often been translated as legitimate authority or, less redundantly, as authority alone, and this is justified by a significant overlap between the concepts of legitimacy and authority in a sociological sense. Indeed, in everyday language these categories are often used interchangeably. Nevertheless, a distinction should be made between legitimacy and authority. Even in the political sense legitimacy can pertain to institutions and even impersonal systems, such as the "state," whereas authority must pertain to concrete persons, such as "the government." Allen Buchanan makes this distinction, but nevertheless seeks to define the difference between legitimacy and, what he rightly understands as its special case, authority, by the presence or absence of an obligation to obey.[46] There is accordingly such an obligation in authority, and it is possibly absent in legitimacy, that only entails the right to rule.[47] Of course, this way of making the distinction could not be made regarding the sociological meaning of legitimacy, which even Buchanan treats as the belief in the rightness of commands issued by rulers or officials. But it is also extremely artificial with respect to the normative or philosophical meaning in which he is interested. Since Buchanan denies the existence of an obligation to obey as a general matter, whether based on consent or any other relationship, it is unclear what authority is still doing in his scheme. But getting rid of obligation leads to a serious difficulty: we will not be able to explain or justify the sanctions applied in the case of disobedience. He sees authority as a special case of legitimacy, and we should stay with that partial definition.

Within a broad concept of legitimacy that can **refer to the** quality of institutions, systems and actors who have no automatic claim to obedience, I think

---

[44] *Economy and Society* (Berkeley: University of California Press, 1968), III i. 1(214).

[45] Ibid., pp. 36–37; and passim.

[46] *Justice, Legitimacy, and Self-Determination* (Oxford: Oxford University Press, 2004), p. 237; 239f.

[47] The idea that authority entails obligation is supported by J. Raz, *The Morality of Freedom* (Oxford: Clarendon Press, 1986) in a somewhat overly rationalistic and inconsistent account that focuses primarily on the normative meaning of authority as it ought to be. Raz interestingly associates legitimate authority with the pre-emption of the obedient's own reasons, and the need for normative justification. Even when an authority is mistaken, Raz upholds the obligation or duty to obey, arguing that this does not exclude challenges to authority and especially independent reflection on the grounds of authoritative commands. Yet authority, as in its theoretical version but not only that, can mean only influence, and one that need not "pre-empt" the reasons of the hearer, nor carry an obligation to obey.

it is better, as did Hannah Arendt,[48] to focus on the strongly personal dimension of authority. Admittedly, in the famous Roman distinction between the *potestas* of the people, and the *auctoritas* of the Senate evoked by Schmitt and Arendt, both power and authority referred to a specific order of Roman society.[49] But the modern concept of power has become impersonal, indeed primarily a factual matter, whether in Parsons, Luhmann, or Foucault. The ability to exert power, however, and especially to do so by issuing commands, can be normatively right or wrong, just or unjust. It is in relation to the right to exercise political power and issue commands (Weber's *Herrschaft*: rule or domination) that the term legitimacy (and illegitimacy) is rightly applied. On the contrary, unlike *potestas*, *auctoritas* has retained some of its classical meaning. Significantly, there is no negative of authority like there is "illegitimacy." Illegitimate rule is still rule by someone, but when authority is absent, the term "unauthorized action" may not have a hierarchically placed subject. Making the distinction in this way, we understand also why systems cannot have authority but can be legitimate, even as they cannot carry obligations to obey, but at best the obligation to protect or defend.

The possible absence of the obligation to obey is relevant for both legitimacy and authority. With Buchanan we can indeed consider claims to rule

[48] "What is Authority?" in *Between Past and Future* (New York: Penguin, 1954). Admittedly, Arendt also says authority always demands obedience (p. 92) and her example of childrearing seems to confirm this. But she later adds "obedience in which men retain their freedom" that may not exclude an absence of obligation. Yet, the authority of a great author, or of a text, or, more importantly, Rousseau's *legislateur* (see chapter 1 below) demands only respectful consideration. Elsewhere she cites Mommsen's interpretation of authority, defined as "more than advice, less than a command" (122), is close to the conception offered here. Raz, *The Morality of Freedom* (chapter 4) is even more inconsistent. He seems to define legitimate authority by the realization of reasons and motives that an obedient person already has, and then specifically exempts authority in the state from this requirement in favor of an authority limited by fundamental moral principles, and justified through consent. All these bind authority. In general, political authority is the solution of co-ordination problems, though relevant only where large number or at least a plurality is the object of commands. However, Arendt's distinction of authority from both force and persuasion can be sustained. A similar three-part distinction has been made, if in a more conservative version, by Bertrand de Jouvenel in *Sovereignty* (Chicago: University of Chicago Press, 1957), chapter 2, between domination, authority, and association, also based on the Roman concepts of the founder of cities and the etymological meaning of augmentation. However, it was already there in the much earlier theory of Alexandre Kojève in *The Notion of Authority* (London: Verso, 2014).

[49] C. Schmitt, *Verfassungslehre*, pp. 9; 75–76. This work systematically conflates the question of whether in the *verfassungsgebende Gewalt* (or: *pouvoir constituant*) both authority and power must be present, or whether the constituent power of the people is only *Macht*, whereas that of the monarch is primarily *Autorität*. See pp. 205ff., where the text contrasts identity and representation, parallel to the distinction of power and authority. I develop this critical point in chapter 1 of *Post Sovereign Constitution Making*, along with Arendt's attempt to restore the duality of power and authority, based on the American experience.

or act politically legitimate, or justified, on, e.g., democratic grounds, without carrying at least the moral obligation to obey, e.g., by aristocratic or religious enemies of democracy, or for those who disobey because of the presumed injustice of a specific rule or an authorized command as in civil disobedience. The actions of the civil disobedient too can be legitimate, without any corresponding obligations to obey their demands. Not all religions declare "render to Caesar what is Caesar's, and to God what is God's," and even that saying derives the obligation to obey from a different source than Caesar's (then) republican legitimacy. However, contrary to the assertions of Buchanan as well as Raz, we can and generally do use the term authority or political authority for an "author" having influence rather than power, while also carrying no obligation to obey. In this sense, authority is based on the presumption of the superior knowledge or judgment of individuals to issue either commands or at least opinions that should be prudentially followed. It implies the ability to get proposals freely accepted because of the personal qualities of an author, whether a founder or an augmenter, rather than by force or persuasion.[50]

Having made the distinction, we can see why it was nevertheless possible for Weber, operating on the sociological level, to treat authority and legitimacy as conceptually very close. He did this by making the personal more important by far in traditional and charismatic forms of legitimate domination, or authority, than in the legal rational version. Generally for him, the forms of legitimate domination or rule (*Herrschaft*) are forms of authority in the sense of their providing prestige and justification for those holding political office to issue commands that will be obeyed wholly or in significant part because of a sense of obligation. Weber's stress here is on the presence on a large scale of subjective attitudes, as against the intrinsic worth of ideas that are believed. But the attitudes *are* understood in terms of belief in the validity, obligatory character, and justification of a system of rule and subordination, where rulers or officeholders justify their decisions and commands on the bases of their relevant authority or legitimacy claims. Such beliefs are not equivalent to momentary opinions recorded in surveys, and they are also supposed to be distinguished from mere rationalizations of interest and fear.

As a whole tradition of discussion indicates, Weber's approach remains very important, but needs to be supplemented and improved on several points. First, the sociological meaning, based on an observer's perspective, has to be linked to a normative one that presupposes a participant's attitude. That opens the way to systematic and ideology critical analyses of legitimacy. Second,

---

[50] This is discussed in detail by Kojève, *The Notion of Authority*. But see also the cited texts of Arendt and de Jouvenel.

the three fundamental types he outlined, namely traditional, charismatic and legal,[51] need to be supplemented. Revolutionary legitimacy is not exhausted by the charismatic type, just as democratic legitimacy is more than the rather unclear combination of the legal and the charismatic.[52] Finally, the legitimating role of legality needs to be solved differently than Weber attempted, and the possible conflict between legality and legitimacy needs to be explored.

While Weber has been criticized along these lines by many theorists, I think Habermas has made the most important contribution, showing the relationship of the three points made here. His first concern was the exclusion of normative notions of legitimacy implied by Weber's cautiously value-free approach. In terms of Weber's own theory of understanding meaning, according to Habermas it is not possible to empirically identify present claims of validity, or reconstruct and evaluate their strength without interrogating the legitimating ideas as to their depth, coherence and relationship to other **ideas**. These steps presuppose an evaluative attitude that questions the validity, in both normative and logical senses, of legitimacy claims.[53] Without exploring the nature of validity we cannot understand belief in it. Going beyond Habermas here, this approach implies that normative validity matters also for beliefs in validity, at least in the relatively long run. This cannot mean normative validity from any one contemporary philosophical point of view, as Habermas tended to imply. While it is certainly not true, even in the modern world, that only ideas that withstand the most rigorous critical scrutiny can play a legitimating role, it is probably true that over time legitimating ideas require elaboration, systematization, and grounding in developed schemes of thought. This is the one of the key roles of religion, or rather of theology and ideology in its broad sense. (Ideology in a narrower sense also has the role of disguising the relationship of a form of legitimation to reality.) All of Weber's legitimating principles are at least historically linked with religion, or with religious ideologies elaborated by various intellectual strata. Therefore, if we wish to understand what he meant by legitimation, it is important to turn to his sociology of religion for a treatment beyond the chapters on political domination.

The variety of forms of intellectual systems that pertain to the validity of forms of rule and social ordering indicates the implausibility of a reduction

---

[51] *Economy and Society*, I: iii; II: x.   [52] *Economy and Society*, I. 1127.

[53] *Legitimation Crisis* (Boston: Beacon, 1975), pp. 97ff. The argument ultimately comes from Gadamer, according to whom only where horizons are fused in interpretation, can a symbolic expression be understood. *Truth and Method* (New York: Continuum, 1975).

to the famous three-term framework (tradition, charisma, and legality) or even to a four-term one, if we add Weber's grab-bag of substantive or value rationality.[54] While it is true that charisma is a revolutionary principle with respect to tradition and law, revolutions and revolutionary elites also gain their justification from other sources. Weber explicitly mentions natural law as his key example of value rationality, but even together with charisma this seems insufficient.[55] One important element he neglects is the critique of old regimes, and the leadership of liberation struggles against them. Such a form of validity may be temporary, but no more so than charisma itself in Weber's analysis. Where charisma gains its stability from an institutionalization that preserves it partially, liberation continues to validate only if it is linked to ideas of a better future. Thus, Hannah Arendt moved from liberation to the notion of constitution as the second stage of revolutionary ideology.[56] However, her concept of authority was ambivalent: on the one side she tended to think of it as only traditional and therefore apt to erode in the modern world, while on the other she posited the need for a new form of authority, one that would occur in revolutions, without being clear about its nature or contents.[57] Given her thesis about the erosion of authority in the modern world, she should have perhaps sought these new principles out at the level of legitimacy. Social development and justice in the sense of equality and democracy can all supply the content of future oriented, secular revolutionary ideologies. As we now know after the Islamic Revolution of 1979, radically reinterpreted traditional or religious ideas can play the same role.

Democratic ideology does not appear only in the context of the future-oriented revolutionary legitimacy, but indicates another possible pure type of legitimation. Weber's reduction of democracy to either rule of law or to charisma, or even a combination of the two, cannot be considered successful. Nor is Schmitt's interpretation of democratic legitimacy in terms of the identity of an actor or agent, "the people," that is especially implausible where the demos or the plebeians do not constitute a distinct order of society as in the ancient world. Arendt's and Habermas' analyses in terms of communication and discourse models remain, to me at least, more convincing.[58] Thus, the key claim of democratic legitimacy rests on the politically influential role of public discussion of all **important** matters of collective significance, and the existence of institutions that permit this. So interpreted, democracy does not

---

[54] *Economy and Society*, I: 33 and 36.   [55] *Economy and Society*, II: viii, section 7.
[56] *On Revolution*, pp. 19–22; 214–215 and passim.   [57] "What is Authority?," p. 141.
[58] See Arendt, *Human Condition* (Chicago: University of Chicago, 1958), chapter v; *On Revolution*, pp. 166–167; and Habermas, especially in *Between Facts and Norms* (Boston: Beacon, 1996), chapter 7 and Appendix I.

reduce to majority rule, and countermajoritarian practices, as demonstrated by a great deal of legal theory from Hamilton and John Marshall to J.H. Ely and Ackerman, can rely on democratic legitimacy. The existence and enforcement of a set of fundamental rights, of assembly, association, communication, electoral franchise and officeholding, as well as the protection of the rights of minorities, may be more important than majority rule. Indeed, there is good justification for constitutionally entrenching these presuppositions of democracy against mere majority decisions. Beyond the rather aristocratic version of republicanism as represented by Arendt, democratic legitimacy presupposes the widest possible and justifiable inclusion under these rights and in the life of political institutions, as facilitated by not only the existence of rights but also substantive requirements like public education.

Finally, the legitimating role of *mere* legality is questionable, and has indeed been repeatedly questioned. The implicit assumption behind this Weberian notion is Hobbesian, implying that any rule-governed order secures civil peace, and peace is always preferable to war. Both the history of international relations and the domestic histories of resistance, rebellion, and revolution make these claims not only normatively weak but also empirically implausible. If the laws themselves are considered unjust, it is doubtful that formal and strict adherence to them or to the secondary rules of their production alone will produce beliefs in the validity of an order or a form of rule.[59] Peace is a value only if linked to some other values. Strictly rule-governed behavior becomes a secondary value if the order regulated is itself considered valid or obligatory on other grounds. Tradition, institutionalized charisma, social solidarity, revolutionary origins, and democracy can all supply what is missing. The matter can also be partially handled within the rule of law, becoming thereby a different and richer idea than that of mere legality. Accordingly, the value of rules is enhanced when the rulers themselves submit to – and are constrained by – the same rules. In turn, however, this process cannot legitimate, unless the rules themselves involve substantive constraints. For example, absolutism can be legitimated by religious ideas of divine right but not by the notion that the ruler is constrained to follow rules that allow him not be constrained at all. To be legitimating ideas, the rule of law, or *Rechtsstaatlichkeit*, thus require separation of powers, independent judiciaries and the protection of fundamental rights. It is these principles that can be expanded as constitutionalism. Rule of law or *Rechtsstaatlichkeit* or constitutionalism thus may be the real secret of Weber's legal rational legitimacy, one that should be so understood if it is given the benefit of a doubt.

---

59 On this see Raz, *The Morality of Freedom*.

Even when reconceptualized in this way, the conflict of legality and legitimacy certainly remains possible, that is excluded in positivist theories such
as Kelsen's that identify the two categories. This possible clash would already
exist on Weberian grounds, where the conflict could be between legal and
other forms of legitimacy – e.g., where the adherence to existing rules is contested by a charismatic dispensation. The enactment of new rules, fully legal,
could also be opposed on traditional grounds. Beyond Weber, even modern
democracy and existing rules could also enter into deep conflict. While the
rules can be a product of democratic enactment, they also can be such as to
exclude or invalidate democratic legislation, not to speak of diminishing other
requirements of democratic legitimacy like many fundamental rights. Equally
important, legislation and legal rules can be used to attack the supports of
constitutionalism, bringing genuine legal legitimacy and mere legality into
conflict as well. This would happen, in the case stressed by Schmitt,[60] where a
mere parliamentary majority, perhaps even a qualified one, is used to abrogate
judicial independence or diminish fundamental rights. When the aim of such
action is to protect incumbents from future challenge and replacement, the
conflict would be with democratic legitimacy as well.

What happens when legality and legitimacy are in conflict? The issue is crucial for constitutionalism, as the British phrase "legal, but unconstitutional"
indicates. Assuming that mere legality has little legitimacy on its own, something that cannot be universally assumed, legality can trump legitimacy under
only two conditions: when it is backed up by sufficient repressive force, or
when alternative forms of legitimation do not give rise to political conflict and
mobilization. These two factors can be, and generally are, combined. Mere
legality ultimately rests on forms of organized, and in modernity monopo-
lized, forms of coercion. The sources of legitimacy are much more diffuse, as
Weber's theory and its supplementation even more indicates. But legitimacy
can challenge mere legality only by taking political forms, whether in the societal public sphere or in forms of social mobilization. Of course, mere legality
is rare, and legal legitimacy is possible when assuming forms of legitimate
enactment and especially rights-oriented adjudication. Moreover, assuming
the latter two options, a previous repressive form of mere legality can be challenged on the legal level by new enactment and new judgment. In these cases
the conflict is between mere legality and legal legitimacy in the wider sense,
and can be resolved by either the increase of repression, as in South Africa in
the 1950s, or the expansion of legality, as in the United States slightly later in

---

[60] See *Verfassungslehre*, pp. 16ff; 102; *Legalität und Legitimität* (Berlin: Duncker & Humblot, 1932), pp. 46ff; 56.

time. Whenever the latter happens, as the history of the American civil rights movement shows, societal political discussion and mobilization generally play important roles, and the new legislation and judicial decisions themselves are widely, and correctly, seen as political.

Given a plurality of forms of legitimacy, it is historically clear that almost any of the forms can play a role for constitutions. As in the case of international law, even where there is no legality in the strict sense constraining the actors, the pull of legitimacy can and almost always does play an important normative role.[61] At issue between sovereign and post-sovereign constitution-making paradigms is whether a single form, like democratic legitimacy interpreted as an identity, can play such a role, or whether genuine legitimation requires a plurality of forms. If the latter choice is made, the question becomes which forms are the most important. On the level of the content of constitutions, legality is the most relevant, both in the sense of legal rational legitimacy, or a coherent, generally hierarchical order of rules, and constitutionalism, providing for legal limitation on all forms of power, through rights, separation of powers and, at times, their division. Legal rational legitimacy, as the term indicates, is the result of rationalization, both in the sense of formal technical development, as well as in the differentiation of a legal sphere organized around a specialized profession as well as bodies of knowledge and discursive forms.[62] The forms of constitutionalism can, however, be based on tradition, and its evolution, as in the United Kingdom, as well as revolutionary enactment, as in France, at least initially. Today, we increasingly encounter claims that legality in both these senses, legal rationality and constitutionalism, is also highly relevant to constitution making. Here lies an important point of contention between post-sovereign and sovereign forms, with advocates of the latter maintaining that legality is impossible in the constituent process.

Less controversial is the requirement of democratic legitimacy with respect to both process and results. Here only its interpretation is different in the case of advocates of the alternative paradigms. Today it is almost universally accepted that legal and constitutionalist rules should provide for a democratic system capable of periodically refurbishing democratic legitimacy. Few would contest even that the making of constitutions should be, in some sense, democratic. At

---

[61] See Franck's important insistence on this point for international law, *The Power of Legitimacy Among Nations*. I do not, however, fully share the idea that in moments between constitutions, or in the international terrain there is no law, only legitimacy. With Hart (*Concept of Law*, chapter 10) I would rather say, that in both settings there is no unified legal order. See my *Post Sovereign Constitution Making*, chapter 1.

[62] Weber, *Economy and Society* (Berkeley: University of California Press, 1968), vol. II.; R. Unger *Law in Modern Society* (New York: Free Press, 1976).

issue is only the controversy between advocates of populist as against procedural democrats.[63] Finally, sociologically, tradition, charisma, and revolutionary legitimacy can all matter for the legitimacy of constitutions, though these forms pertain generally to their origins rather than contents.

Theorists who impute legitimacy to constitutions purely on the bases of a desirable result often contest the premise that origins do matter for the legitimacy of constitutions. This view is supposedly sustainable on factual *historical* grounds, as well as the untenable *conceptual* thesis that the constituent power is in a (Hobbesian[64]) state of nature. The empirical evidence is based not only on the large variety of imposed (*octroyée, oktrojierte*) constitutions, but also on the fact that some constitutions that have emerged in ways impossible to legitimate, e.g., the current Japanese Constitution, now enjoy wide legitimacy in the sociological sense. Nevertheless, even that constitution's legitimacy long remained questionable from a normative point of view. While in normal times this critical normative perspective may be dormant, it comes into play, especially during moments of crisis, or when there is a determined attempt, as in Germany in 1991 and currently in Japan, to replace a constitution. Critiques of origins in 1949 and 1982 have recently justified efforts at replacement in countries such as Hungary and Turkey.[65]

The democratic principle of legitimacy requires also that we examine the related term, namely popular sovereignty. In the modern world, against republican forerunners, the one shared principle of justification of constitutional origins *seems to be* popular sovereignty. "Popular sovereignty is expressed in the act of constitution making," argues Dieter Grimm, who even goes so far as to claim that popular sovereignty is a relevant concept only for constitutional beginnings.[66] It is hard to see, nevertheless, if popular sovereignty cannot mean actual rule by the people, how in the case of constitutional beginnings such direct rule can nevertheless be asserted. However, Grimm articulates only the common claim of many constitution drafters who are usually undeterred by the political passivity of the population or even its partial absence during the process.

---

[63] For my take on this, see chapter 5 of *Post Sovereign Constitution Making* (Oxford: Oxford University Press, 2016).

[64] Sieyes, who may have had the Lockeian concept of natural rights also existing in the state of nature in mind, originated this thesis. See P. Bastid, *Sieyès et sa pensée* (Paris: Hachette, 1939).

[65] Which have been treated in *Post Sovereign Constitution Making*, chapters 4 and 5.

[66] Grimm, *Sovereignty* (New York: Columbia University Press, 2015), pp. 94ff. and 72ff. where it is then admitted that this can be true only through imputation, which for some reason is then denied to acts of EU bodies. For a similar conception, see Ackerman, *We the People* I (Cambridge: Harvard University Press, 1992).

This can be best seen when examining the preambles of constitutions even where, as in (West) Germany and Japan, the origins are empirically difficult or impossible to explain in terms of the principle thereby articulated.[67] These examples point to three possible uses of popular sovereignty as the principle of legitimacy supporting projects of constitution making. In Japan, the reference to the popular sovereign had no content at all, as it was the American occupying authority that imposed its constitution on the defeated population.[68] In Germany, where the occupation authorities have played only a minor role, two types of largely autonomous assemblies were responsible for the drafting and ratification of the *Grundgesetz*, the provincial legislatures and the Parliamentary Council. Yet collectively these bodies claimed to be speaking on behalf of the parts of "the people" under Soviet occupation who were unable to take part.[69] Even the category of "fiction," as eloquently introduced by Edmund Morgan, papers over the differences.[70] Popular sovereignty can be an empty signifier, whose motivational power depends on either overwhelming power behind it, as in the case of Japan, or the rhetorical skills and personalities of leaders, generally a leader.[71] The sovereignty of the people can be embodied in institution or even a group or leader that can make some valid procedural or sociological claim to "represent" the political community. These versions all point to what is called here patterns of sovereign constitution making, one populist and the other (supposedly) formally democratic. But the same

---

[67] The current text of the *Grundgesetz* says "the German people, in the exercise of their constituent power, have adopted this Basic Law", this after a series of 1990 amendments (including the unification act) under the amendment rule art. 79. The original 1949 text, already using the fiction of the constituent power of the German people, admitted more or less in parentheses that such constituent power could be exercised only by the part of the *Volk*, only in the Western *Bundesländer*. The same 1949 text, along with its original art. 146, projected the full use of the people's constituent power for the future, a future whose actual procedures were never articulated and which did not arrive during re-unification. See D. Murswiek, *Die verfassunggebende Gewalt nach dem Grundgesetz für die Bundesrepublik Deutschland* (Berlin: Duncker & Humblot, 1978, for the original text: 23–24). And for the official English translation in A. Zurcher, *Constitutions and Constitutional Trends Since World War II*, sec. ed. (New York: NYU, 1955), p. 289. The Preamble of the Japanese Constitution of 1947 produced in substance by the American military command's team, and formally enacted according to the rule of amendment of the undemocratic Meiji constitution, uses the phrase we the Japanese people at least four times, and begins thus: "We, the Japanese people, acting through our duly elected representatives in the National Diet, . . . do proclaim that sovereign power resides with the people and do firmly establish this Constitution."

[68] Koseki Shoichi, *The Birth of Japan's Post War Constitution* (Boulder: Westview, 1997).

[69] Peter Merkl, *The Origin of the West German Republic* (New York: Oxford University Press, 1963).

[70] *Inventing the People* (New York: Norton, 1988).

[71] E. Laclau, *On Populist Reason* (London: Verso, 2005) and my article "Political Theology and Populism," *Social Research* 80, no. 1 (2013).

concept, of popular or national sovereignty, can also mean the very denial of any part's claim to embody the whole. While this last version brings us to the threshold of post-sovereign constitution making as a *negative* principle close to that of polyarchy, it is insufficient to legitimate political projects, especially democratic ones. In order to understand the legitimacy of post-sovereign constitution making we must then examine popular sovereignty more closely, and the question as to its possible versions that can be the source of the normative legitimacy of constitutional origins.

III SOVEREIGNTY

The concept of sovereignty is central to this study, both in its traditional meaning established by Bodin and Hobbes, and a new version pioneered by the German *Staatslehre* followed in some respects by **a few** representatives of French public law. Schmitt's idiosyncratic synthesis of these traditions is important as well. His version corresponds to the classical idea that *genuine* sovereignty must be exercised by an identifiable, unified organ, but he believes that it is only moments of the exception that the sovereign can appear and be identified. As indicated by his concept of sovereign dictatorship, constitution making easily qualifies as an exceptional break within political time. It is this idea of organ sovereignty that will be interpreted here as a main foundation of the theory of constitution making I call sovereign. The modern theory, whose foundations go back to nineteenth-century German and French public law, will open the way to the post sovereign conception.[72] In order to present the concept, in its two major forms, let me start with what is common to all these approaches.

From the sixteenth century onwards and in the synthesis of Jean Bodin, the modern concept of sovereignty affirms two things: first, that there is a supreme center of authority in the territorial state that has no domestic equal, nor, secondly, an international superior. Earlier, as many have narrated, domestic supremacy has been vitiated by the complex relations within feudal sub and super-ordination,[73] and later by the dualistic system of ruler and estates;[74] while international equality has been opposed by various claims of imperial

---

[72] For a more comprehensive history of the different forms of the concept see, most recently, Dieter Grimm, *Sovereignty*, chapter B. For the analysis from which I have learned the most, Jean Cohen, *Globalization and Sovereignty* (Cambridge: Cambridge University Press, 2012), chapter 1.

[73] Dieter Grimm, *Sovereignty*, chapter B.

[74] Gianfranco Poggi, *The Development of the Modern State* (Stanford: Stanford University Press, 1978).

and papal supremacy. With the medieval foundations of rule in persons rather than territories, the very distinction between internal and external, crucial for classical sovereignty, could not exist. Sovereignty is the active principle behind the notion of the modern state as an organization that monopolizes the legitimate (here = legal) forms of violence within a territory and over its inhabitants. Since all states capable of mutual recognition were as such supposed to have the same monopoly they were legally equal. Evidently that does not mean and has never meant equality in power, in military capacity, in prestige, or economic potential. As it is clear from the above definition of the state, sovereignty is a legal, rather than an empirical concept. No factual monopoly is possible empirically, indeed even legitimate monopoly is possible only if we identify legal and legitimate. Sovereignty, as Kelsen explained, cannot mean supremacy in the domain of causality and, in Weber's sense, power.[75] It exists only in the realm of legitimate domination, or commands that have authority. Nevertheless, as the same Kelsen showed, for all law, in order to be and remain legal, a norm must have some effectiveness. From an empirical point of view such as Weber's, sovereignty would then mean the high probability that superiority claims at home over all contenders, and equality claims abroad can be made effective. Beyond supremacy, most, if not all, serious doctrines assert the indivisibility of sovereignty itself, but only the classical theory assumed the same indivisibility for its many powers.

Classical theory, most importantly Bodin and Hobbes, could only conceive sovereignty as embodied in a fully identifiable person, institution or group actually capable of decisions, whose ultimate authority could not be shared with any other individual, institution or group.[76] Following or anticipating the model of absolute monarchy, sovereignty, whether monarchical or republican had to accordingly be embodied in a single, unified decision maker.[77] While there are differences in the degree of radicalism among the founders of the classical theory, they all argue that the sovereign is *legibus solutus* (not bound by at least positive, enforceable law, ultimately even his own laws, undermining, I think, a strong notion of legal legitimacy as developed above). Again with different degrees of radical emphasis it is asserted that law is the command of the sovereign. Since in international society there is no supreme power of

---

[75] Hans Kelsen, *Das Problem der Souveränität*, 2nd ed. (Tübingen: J.C.B. Mohr, 1927), pp. 6–7.

[76] For Hobbes, see Grimm, *Sovereignty*, 28–30. Ultimately, the state is said to be sovereign in Hobbes, yet must be embodied. Hence the distinction as Grimm admits makes no difference.

[77] Julian Franklin in *John Locke and the Theory of Sovereignty: Mixed Monarchy and the Right of Resistance in the Political Thought of the English Revolution* (Cambridge: CUP Archive, 1981). As he shows this contradicted living traditions of mixed government, and even the composite parliamentary sovereignty emerging in England.

command, the most consistent version (Hobbes) posits that this order is in a state of nature, a real, rather than the hypothetical domestic one. There are multiple powers of sovereignty that can be prioritized differently (for Hobbes, peace and war are definitional; for Bodin, legislation), but since all powers must be possessed and controlled by the undivided supreme authority the rank order is not supposed to be crucial, at least in the classical notion.

Modern theories of sovereignty from the nineteenth century particularly contest these assumptions on several points. In order to achieve supremacy at home and equality abroad, sovereignty need not be embodied in an undivided, single actor. Its powers can be divided, even if the idea that sovereignty itself can be divided was never successfully established (see Grimm). And, according to almost all modern arguments, sovereignty need not, and even cannot, be free of all law and legal limits. According to three versions of ultimately the same argument, it is the state, an abstract entity (German *Staatslehre*), the nation, an organic entity that has no will or decision-making capacity (Carré de Malberg) or the people, a fictional actor (Franklin, Morgan) that is sovereign. In any of the three versions this idea entails the possibility of several equal powers of government, as long as in each issue area there is a clear hierarchy of decision among them.[78] Thus the powers of sovereignty can be divided, and jointly exercised, as under mixed government or the separation or the division of powers (Madison). Importantly, however, persons, institutions that share in that division, or joint exercise are not themselves sovereign. Their sovereign claims (sometimes made) amount to usurpation. They are moreover beholden to the laws they may have participated in devising. According to one line of criticism (H.L.A. Hart) the command model of law is wrong, and the idea of a legal system, even an entirely coherent one, does not assume a supreme, undivided commander as its source.[79] In the most extreme version (Kelsen), the unified, hierarchical legal order (identified with the state) is itself pronounced as sovereign. Thus ruler or organ sovereignty is replaced by rule sovereignty.

International affairs present a difficulty for the modern conception. Even in the American version of the *Federalist*, the decomposition of organ sovereignty is coupled with its implied reassertion in the international domain.[80] As Hart saw the problem, to fully debunk the classical theory, one had to contest the possibility of states acting as unified, equal centers of power, supermen under

---

[78] Ibid.   [79] *Concept of Law*, chapter IV.
[80] The *Federalist* #9. "Reconciling the advantages of monarchy with those of republicanism [Hamilton's words, followed by Montesquieu's:] . . . the internal advantages of republican, together with the external force of monarchical, government."

no enforceable obligation. He succeeded in showing that equality of sovereigns presupposes international law, and also that external sovereignty as a legal concept cannot emerge without international law. But he failed to dislodge the unified subjects that he managed to discredit on the domestic level. As Hamilton perceived, citing Montesquieu, and later explicitly maintained,[81] in the international field governments, or their executive branches, are unified centers of decision and action. They embody the sovereignty of the state even if under law.[82]

A critique such as that of Hart shows that there is no need for unified organ sovereignty for the sake of the unity of the domestic legal order. However, it is only in the British case that he shows that all supposed organ sovereigns (parliament, or the electorate, following John Austin) are under law, despite the doctrine of *legibus solutus*. While the argument can be extended to other cases, Hart has not shown that organ sovereignty, unified and legally absolute, is not possible. Carl Schmitt has called our attention to unified organ sovereigns in two exceptional situations: radical emergencies and constitution making after legal rupture. This claim represents a synthesis of the classical and modern approaches. Under constitutional normalcy sovereignty cannot accordingly be located in an organ, as he admits. But sovereignty proper must be so located, and Schmitt finds it in the dominant subjects of emergency rule and constitution making.

This now-famous conception is riddled with contradictions. First, two very different sovereigns emerge in the exception and in the constitution-making process, the executive lord of the exception and the popular sovereign endowed with constituent power.[83] As these terms already reveal, the status of the two theories that come up with the two different sovereigns is very different. The theory of the exception appears to be highly realistic, without necessarily relying on a legitimating ideology. (Of course, the judgment that a state of exception exists can be ideological, but it can also be based on actual grave emergencies.) It posits an easily identifiable subject of sovereignty, one that can act and decide. The theory of the constituent power is ideological, or rather

---

[81] The Pacificus–Helvidius Debates 1793–4: http://oll.libertyfund.org/titles/1910.

[82] This creates options for internal organ sovereignty, at least in emergencies. See Andrew Arato and Jean Cohen, "Banishing the Sovereign? Internal and External Sovereignty in Arendt," *Constellations*, Vol. 6, No. 2, 2009.

[83] Perhaps misled by the avoidance of the term sovereignty in Schmitt's *Verfassungslehre* most interpreters see only one of these sovereigns, the lord of the exception, and thus not a key contradiction in Schmitt's theory. This is curiously the case even for Grimm, because he himself is inclined to the view that in the domestic sphere the last refuge of popular sovereignty is in the process of original constitution making.

political theological at least in its supposedly democratic version. It posits a subject that even in Schmitt's presentation is impossible to identify, a subject that cannot on its own act or make decisions.[84] Yet in spite of this difference, both involve similar confusions. The theory of the exception confuses the question of who is sovereign in an emergency, whether it is the one who declares it or the other who exercises its powers. The realistic implication (not admitted) must be that it is the same agency, namely the executive of the state, since only that agency can actually exercise emergency power in all modern conceptions. But it must be the regular executive that has this role. Even the dictator of the Roman type, an exceptional executive, cannot by logic declare anything, including an emergency, when not yet in office. Thus the traditional dictator, as against the modern one, is not sovereign.

A parallel division seems to appear in constitution making, between the popular sovereign that has the constituent power and authority supposedly, and the sovereign dictator that is said not to be sovereign. Here the conception is ideological, however, as against either a realistic one, or, if examined more closely, an antinomic one combining both realistic and mythological elements. Without any critical reflection present in other works when dealing with "the people,"[85] Schmitt's constitutional theory contains the most developed version of the myth that an entity that cannot be sociologically or procedurally identified nevertheless is a legitimate source of both power and authority in making constitutions. The body that exercises the actual role, rather than a fictional body that serves as its principle of legitimation, remains the one that embodies sovereign power of the state, at least provisionally. This body, however, is not generally the lord of exception either as identified by constitutions or having a de facto or implied emergency power under them, though it may choose, as the French Convention Nationale did, to assume emergency powers to strengthen or even try to perpetuate revolutionary power. Yet even in that historical case the actual powers of emergency rule were delegated to another actor, namely the largely executive Committee of Public Safety of the legislative body.

Finally, Schmitt implies that in grave emergencies and in revolutions, entirely unconstrained sovereignty in one of the two embodied forms *must*

---

[84] See *Verfassungslehre* p. 83; *Die Diktatur* second. ed (Berlin: Duncker & Humblot, 1927), pp. 142–143.

[85] See, e.g., *Die geistesgeschichtliche Lage des heutigen Parlamentarismus*, 2nd 1926 ed. (Berlin: Duncker & Humblot, 1957), a text that frankly admits both the sociological emptiness and the political theological status of the concept of the people in popular sovereignty: "The belief that all power is derived from the people, has similar meaning to the belief, that all hierarchical powers stem from God" (pp. 34–41).

return. Here he disregards his own occasional statement according to which the lord of exception can be constrained by at least procedural rules.[86] The same error can be shown in the case of the so-called sovereign dictatorship, and it will be the burden of my analysis to demonstrate this error, the possible as well as highly desirable absence of organ sovereignty in the case of radical constitutional change.

Thus, my definition of sovereignty follows a modern rather than a classical, or Schmittian, theory, but yet not entirely. I recognize the possibility but certainly not the necessity of organ sovereignty, a question even Hart confused. Thus I recognize the *possibility*, if not the *necessity*, and even less the *desirability*, of sovereign constitution making. Following Schmitt, I do think that organ sovereignty, while not the only possible form of sovereignty at all, has the strong implication of dictatorship. Following Clinton Rossiter and C.J. Friedrich,[87] I would argue that organ sovereignty, and therefore dictatorship, are avoidable even in well-regulated emergency government, among other provisions by differentiating the one who declares and the one who exercises declarations under some relevant continued separation of powers including prior and posterior judicial review. Thus, rules enforced through some separation (and also "division") of powers can be applied even to emergency government. That is not the theme of the present book, however. Here it is my thesis that organ sovereignty can be avoided even in the radical democratic making of constitutions.

Where does this leave "popular sovereignty"? As an actor, the people are fictional[88] (Morgan), unless they are redefined in legal terms as the collectivity of citizens or the electorate in which case they become an entity produced by law, rather than the ultimate source of law.[89] The theory of imputation,

---

[86] "Die Diktatur des Reichspräsidenten nach Art. 48 der Weimarer Verfassung," 1924, in *Die Diktatur*, a text that admittedly contradicts earlier passages in the original edition of the larger work. In English, in *Constellations*.

[87] C. Rossiter *Constitutional Dictatorship* [1948] (New Jersey: Rutgers, 2002); C.J. Friedrich *Constitutional Government and Democracy*, 4th ed. (Waltham, MA: Blaisdell, 1968). Both authors battle the sovereignty concept developed by Schmitt in context of the exception. Friedrich also tries his hand at the critique of the sovereign constituent power, but this effort is notably unsuccessful.

[88] E. Morgan, *Inventing the People* (New York: Norton, 1988) is still the best treatment, as long as the concept of "fiction" is properly understood. While Margaret Canovan, in *The People* (New York: Polity Press, 2005), seeks to refute the concept of the fiction, her deconstruction of the concept supports rather Morgan, than her own conclusion that is an astonishing claim for the need of mythology in radical politics.

[89] Kelsen, *General Theory*, p. 261; most recently, János Kis in *Constitutional Democracy* (Budapest: CEU Press, 2004), pp. 133–141. I agree with the critical analyses of both, but want to avoid the different forms of imputation they practice, transcendental-logical in Kelsen, and liberal

according to which the unified people as a collective origin can be ascribed to constitutions as long as they make the claim of acting *as* or in the name of *the* people, or, more demandingly, if they realize democratic aspirations on the institutional level and in terms of rights, is also a myth, a liberal myth.[90] It is especially problematic however when it is democratic origins that are ascribed.[91] Moreover, it has the great disadvantage that it not only implicitly treats actual origins as irrelevant or arbitrary, but, unlike legal positivism (e.g., Kelsen and Carré de Malberg), tends to terminologically or ideologically disguise this politically harmful assumption.[92]

At the same time, I find it difficult to admit, at least normatively, the need for mythical group constructs of supposedly real as against imputed origins, which cannot be sociologically identified. Such myths repeatedly constrained theorists from Rousseau to Lenin and Lukács to differentiate the will of all from the general will, trade union consciousness from class consciousness, false from genuine consciousness. Yet exactly such lack of sociological identity characterized the concept of the people, from the very moment of the invention of popular sovereignty.[93] Under law and legal definition there are

democratic in Kis. Unlike Kelsen, Kis is interested in actual origins, and even their legitimacy or illegitimacy, but as a result cannot square this with his reformulation of popular sovereignty. Democratic legitimacy, even in his own conception, cannot be indifferent to the process of making. See his "Between Reform and Revolution: Three Hypotheses About the Nature of Regime Change," *Constellations* 3 (1995): 399–419.

[90] Thus, I was especially surprised when Habermas, after his many critiques of embodied or reified popular sovereignty, finally also took refuge in a theory of imputation. See *Crisis of the European Union* (London: Polity, 2011), pp. 14ff, 28ff, and especially 31. In the European context, the imputation of popular sovereign origins to a double concept, the citizens and the peoples of Europe is doubly unconvincing. Among other things it sustains illusions of a fully democratic refounding of Europe.

[91] Hans Lindahl, "Constituent Power and Reflexive Identity," in M. Loughlin and N. Walker, *The Paradox of Constitutionalism* (Oxford: Oxford University Press, 2007).

[92] In Grimm's version, imputation has the further disadvantage that it sets up an unrealistic standard for constitution making and constitutional development under federations, specifically the EU. By the standard of popular sovereignty that has retreated to constitution making in a country such as Germany, majority acts of the European Council or the ECJ that can effect even local constitutions are seen as undemocratic. There is indeed a democracy deficit in the EU. But it is unfair and misleading to measure it by the fictional or imputed popular sovereignty expressed in constitution making, especially but not only when in a given country, constitution making was in part exposed not just to international influence as is commonly the case, but to external power as well. See Merkl, *The Origin of the West German Republic*.

[93] Made clearest by Claude Lefort [e.g., in "The Revolutionary Terror" in *Democracy and Political Theory* [DPT] (Minneapolis: University of Minnesota Press, 1988), p. 79; and Pierre Rosanvallon in *Le Peuple Introuvable* (Paris: Gallimard, 1998) the relevant section now translated as chapter 3 of *Democracy Past and Future* (New York: Columbia University Press, 2006)], but implicitly admitted by Laclau [*On Populist Reason* (New York: Verso, 2005), and see my chapter 6 in *Post Sovereign Constitution Making*] who tries to make a virtue of it.

indeed loosely held together groups such as citizen electors, or participants in referenda, but their action cannot ever be described as sovereign in either the classical or modern theory.[94]

There is fortunately a third alternative, against liberal and democratic mythologies. Popular or national sovereignty can be treated as a negative principle deliberately referring to entities that cannot act, but that block the claim that those with political power have the right to act with the plenitude of power, as if they were the people or the nation. One can, however, go further than those who originated this conception, who as legal positivists thought that the constituent process therefore operates in legal black hole, not accessible to juridical analysis or critique.[95] Accordingly, since the actors are not the people, valid action on behalf of the people should be seen as satisfying demanding conditions having to do with principles, possibly legality, but generally legitimacy. Thus, if we are to keep popular sovereignty at all, it is best to treat the concept as referring not to a form of power, but as equivalent to democratic legitimacy, incorporating electoral legality and legal representation as its principles, that are always desirable though not always available, and rarely sufficient. Deprived of the unitary dimension of popular sovereignty, democratic legitimacy is best seen in terms of a plurality of principles. Aside from legal representation, other principles as the existence and participation of a viable public sphere of communication, fundamental and enforceable political rights, associational freedom, and the widest possible social and political inclusion are also important. If the fiction of popular sovereignty is to be translated into desiderata which we can demand and monitor in actual political processes, it is some combination of these principles that we must seek instead of a collective actor or even combination of actors. To put this differently, popular sovereignty is both a negative principle denying embodiment and usurpation, and a positive one, a stand-in for an always complex set of principles constitutive of democratic legitimacy.[96]

---

[94] Hart, Concept, chapter 4.

[95] Carré de Malberg, who repeatedly violated his own positivist principles by examining the French and American constituent processes, the first critically, the second affirmatively. See Contribution à la générale Théorie de l Etat (1920) (Paris: Dalloz, 2004).

[96] I say at best, because using the concept of sovereignty even when modified by popular, has the implication according to both the classical and modern concept that legitimate constitution making is and must be a purely domestic affair. Accordingly, an international role in domestic constitution making and interpretation should be rejected, and this assumption is reflected in The Hague and Geneva conventions. Empirically, the assumption has of course been a problematic one, ever since the French Revolution and Napoleon. But that is true for all sovereignty claims. After a large variety of experiences in this area, especially in our own period, ranging from military occupations and UN involvement to the use of soft power through

IV SOVEREIGN CONSTITUTION MAKING

As the term indicates, post-sovereign constitution making as interpreted and advocated in this book presupposes the concept and theories of a sovereign version.

What is sovereign constitution making? Is it possible?[97] What are its forms? These are the issues I want to address in the remainder of this introduction, to provide needed background for the post-sovereign paradigm. Subsequent chapters will deal with the historical development of the sovereign theory, its versions and institutional forms in detail. They will also present and analyze the problems, and dangers, conceptual and political of all these versions and forms.

In a single, if preliminary definition, *sovereign constitution making involves the making of the constitution by a constitutionally unbound, sovereign constituent power, institutionalized in an organ of government, that at the time of this making unites in itself all of the formal powers of the state, a process that is legitimated by reference to supposedly unified, pre-existing popular sovereignty.*[98] Thus, theories or ideologies of sovereign constitution making, even when they distinguish between authority and power, consider the power of the popular sovereign to be authorized by definition to give itself a constitution. In the words of Hannah Arendt, they derive power and authority from the one self-same source. Or: they derive legitimacy from identity, the "who" of constitution making, disregarding the justified occasion, outcome as well as the procedures involved, the "when," the "what" and the "how."

NGOs and civil society organizations, we need to ask however whether there is a legitimate external role in constitution making, what it is and what its limits are. The complex concept of democratic legitimacy may help us in this effort, potentially blocked by the concept of popular sovereignty. This topic will be explored in my next book project together with Julian Arato.

[97] This question was raised by Janos Kis, and answered negatively, in response to an early draft of mine, several years ago. See his own already cited text on popular sovereignty.

[98] In Carl Schmitt's theory there are versions of the constituent power compatible with the three great Aristotelian forms: democracy, monarchy and even aristocracy. But he considers monarchical constituent power to be a late and inconsistent imitation of the popular type. Chapter 8.II.3. As to the aristocratic types, the Bolsheviks and Fascists, he stresses that their ultimate reference to popular constituent power must remain open. 8.II.4. I think these considerations rightly moved E.W. Böckenförde to consider the constituent power of the people as the only genuine type that emerges from the theory of Schmitt that he fundamentally follows. Op. cit., 94ff. 96. When a stratum like the proletariat is said to play this role as in Leninism, he rightly notes that it is supposed to represent the people not unlike the third Estate in the French Revolution. While the Sieyès–Marx link is clear, I would contest the assimilation of the two types of representation to one another, which is possible on non-democratic grounds only, unfortunately shared by Marx and Schmitt. In Sieyès, despite his renunciation of democracy, the electoral and deliberative elements are never absent.

The definition of sovereign constitution making offered here as against the self-understanding of its advocates clearly presupposes a contrast between two sovereigns, the governmental one that exercises legally unlimited powers, and the popular one, in the name of which the governmental exercise is legitimated. Given that it is a constitution that is to be made, governmental sovereignty by its definition is supposed to be temporary or provisional, since government under the constitution will be a new one. While that expectation can be disappointed, and could be seen as ideological, it is from a legal point of view realistic to focus on the exercise of sovereign power by government during many, perhaps most, processes of constitution making. The popular **dimension of** the same definition, as already argued, is based on a fiction. This has been long recognized for the concept of popular sovereignty, with the people, originally a corporate concept of societies of distinct orders,[99] becoming impossible to identify from the very moment it was attributed sovereignty.[100] The attempt to locate it as an identifiable actor, capable of willing and acting has proved impossible even where it was to be its last refuge, the constituent power.[101] Nevertheless the distinction between constituent and constituted power survives, should survive, and it is presupposed not only by my definition of sovereign constitution making, but will be used also for the post sovereign paradigm.

A distinction between constituent and constituted powers was already present in the English Revolution, even if many scholars still insist on accepting the word of Sieyès that the distinction was originally his own. In fact, he only popularized a strong contrast between *constituant* and *constitué*. The latter type of power represents the powers of the constitution while the former is supposed to be the constitution's maker or creator, antecedent to its creation, even if some contemporary writers, based on the notion of imputation or ascription reverse the temporal order, and even the causal connection.[102] In any case, the distinction brings the focus of analysis to the formal or written or documentary constitution. While it is not entirely true, as already indicated,

---

99 J. McCormick's essay in *Paradox of Constitutionalism* (Oxford: Oxford University Press, 2007); and his book on *Machiavellian Democracy* (New York: Cambridge University Press, 2011).

100 See the already cited texts of Lefort, Morgan, and Rosanvallon.

101 As Grimm reluctantly admits in *Sovereignty*, p. 73, noting that the people are no more possible to identify as ruling or dominant during the constituent than during the constituted process. The recognition, however, does not stop him from treating the retreat of popular sovereignty to the constituent power as a standard, which can be validated through ascription (or imputation), although he does not say on what bases.

102 As a challenge see Derrida, "Declarations of Independence" in *Negotiations and Interviews* (Stanford: Stanford University Press, 2002); explicitly and affirmatively Lindahl, op. cit. and implicitly, if reluctantly, jurists like Grimm.

that only the formal constitution is in a strict sense made or, put more clearly, *designed*,[103] it is only the solemn document called the constitution that can be imagined as the object of a unified and temporally localizable act of design.[104] Within the formal constitution it makes sense to regard some elements as more essential or fundamental or basic than others, whether Kelsen's material constitution, Schmitt's "constitution in the positive sense" or Hart's most important secondary rules, all including the form and the powers of government as well as their limitations, along with the meta-rules regulating constitutional change. It is these elements above all that the constituent power is supposed to create in sovereign constitution making.

In this paradigm, the differentiation of the constituent and the constituted is supposed to be absolute even if it is impossible to fully deliver on this claim.[105] Since all the powers of the state's coercive mechanism are to be constituted or reconstituted, no pre-existing state power, whether executive, legislative or judicial, ought in the pure theory of sovereign constitution making limit the constituent power.[106] Admittedly, the territorial and demographic dimensions of the state implicitly limit the constituent power even within the sovereign theory, even if this is rarely admitted. A constitution in the sense of a set of

[103] Rousseau says: "a man's constitution is the work of nature. That of the state is a work of art" (Social Contract book III.11). Hamilton speaks of establishing government "from reflection and choice" (*Federalist* # 1). Neither evidently has in mind the evolutionary development of a constitution in the material sense, and Hamilton explicitly contrasts the priority of the American innovation to the development of institutions through "accident and force." Rousseau as is well known was the author of two constitutional proposals, one for Corsica and another for Poland.

[104] It is even less true that the making of constitutions in the strict sense presupposes a revolutionary process. See J.E. Fossum and A.J. Menendez, *The Constitution's Gift* (Lanham, MD: Rowman & Littlefield, 2011), the same authors who start out by reducing the universe of constitutional development to revolutionary making, and evolutionary process, then repeatedly violate their claim by admitting federal contracts and imposed (*octroyé*) constitutions. The argument that these latter types need to be developed in constitutionalization and even legislation holds also for supposedly revolutionary constitutions just as much.

[105] See Ackerman volume II of *We the People* (Cambridge, MA: Harvard University Press, 1998). The insight regarding participation of already constituted organs is hardly new: see Raymond Carré de Malberg *Contribution à la Théorie générale de l'État 1920–22* (Paris: Dalloz, 2004).

[106] It is another matter whether there is a pre-existing state or not. In Schmitt's version there is one (*Verfassungslehre*, 21 and 47), while in that of Sieyès there is only the nation as a political community. Schmitt's version is the historically accurate one for France, as Tocqueville already confirmed. Sieyès relies on Rousseau, occasionally in a slightly historicized version ("What is the Third Estate" in *Political Writings* (Indianapolis: Hackett, 2003), pp. 136f). Rousseau in the Social Contract, as we will see in chapter 1, did differentiate state and constitution making, but for him the priority of an ideally contractual state (= people) could not constrain the acts of constitutional lawmaking. All prior self-limitations, even the social contract, are said to be without constraining effect on the sovereign people. The authority of the *législateur* is only soft influence, and in any case Sieyès dropped that construct.

provisions with legal effect can be made only for a given territory and a population defined by that territory. While one can imagine (and, unfortunately it has been imagined) a state belonging to a population beyond its territory, its constitution or legal order can regulate only the people within the territory, including those who are not imagined to be part of the state's people.[107] Aside from this limitation, the constituent power of the sovereign conception is conceived or imagined as an unlimited one, in the sense of being able to create any logically and empirically possible form of government and system of laws.

Thus as should be obvious, the reference of the sovereign model to *revolutionary* constitution making is fundamental, even if it has been often used in otherwise non-revolutionary situations. In spite of this clear historical reference, its very possibility has been doubted, because of the very role of the category of sovereignty in it. It must be assumed that there will be empirical influences on the constitution makers and the constitutional process, and there will be empirical limits to what the constituent power can ordain is as usual no objection to the use of this disputed concept. As already seen, sovereignty belongs to the world of law, not causality, even if in order to count as law a relatively high degree of empirical effectiveness.[108] But in the revolutionary theory of sovereign constitution making from Paine to Schmitt, the people are understood as the antecedent source of sovereign power and authority, and, as already argued in the path of many others, it is notoriously impossible to find the people before the (or rather "a") constitution itself that legally institutes and minimally organizes it. Accordingly, a case can be made that sovereign constitution making could not exist because it is a logical impossibility.

My definition has not made the concept hostage of popular sovereignty, in the structural and especially logical sense. Of course, I recognize the ideological or fictional role of popular sovereignty in the emergence of the paradigm, and will even demonstrate this through many references, starting with Lawson, Locke and Rousseau. But I make the existence of the paradigm dependent on a sovereign practice that relies on a species of *state* sovereignty, one that in the tradition of the 19th century German *Staatslehre*[109] the French author Raymond Carré de Malberg is depicted and analyzed as *organ* sovereignty.[110]

---

[107] For how this could happen in the most famous case, Israel, see. S. Sand *The Invention of the Jewish People*. The reluctance to adopt a definitive documentary constitution helped to create what is a constitutional anomaly, the non-convergence of people and territory. See, most recently, Hanna Lerner, with her rather different stress Making Constitutions in Deeply Divided Societies, Cambridge CUP, 2011.

[108] Kelsen, *General Theory* on efficacy; 39–42.

[109] Peter Caldwell, *Popular Sovereignty and the Crisis of German Constitutional Law* (Durham, NC: Duke University Press, 1997), chapter 1.

[110] *Contribution à la Théorie générale de l'État.*

This type of sovereignty, as already defined, exists when an individual, a group, an institution, and, in the most democratic versions, an assembly or a single electoral body in a referendum is said to incorporate all of the sovereign powers of what is said to be "the people" on the ideological level, but in reality the complex organization of the modern state. As already shown, while organ sovereignty is not a necessary foundation of law, as Hobbes thought, it is indeed possible, and involves no self-contradiction. Organ sovereignty is the key to modern dictatorship, and it is not by accident that the first and only name previously given the general category of sovereign constitution making has been Carl Schmitt's "sovereign dictatorship."[111]

Let me make clear, constitution making processes legitimated in terms of the sovereign theory are not automatically dictatorships in the loose, contemporary sense of the term that has made it more or less a synonym of despotism, and tyranny, terms that were clearly differentiated from it, until modern times.[112] They are dictatorships only in the classical sense of referring to a temporally bound form of authoritarian rule, by a person or a group, suspending divisions and separations of power, whose aim is supposed to be constitutional or perhaps democratic (e.g., in the case of Bolsheviks) government rather than its own self-perpetuation. In classical terminology, a Caesar, Sulla or the Roman *decemviri* become tyrants, whatever their legal title, when they aimed to permanently establish their rule. Sovereign dictatorship was distinguished from commissarial, classical forms first by Schmitt in that their aim is the creation of a new constitution rather than the preservation or restoration of the old one.

As Machiavelli already noticed for the early forerunners, the probably mythical *decemviri*, the danger of self-perpetuation is greater in the case of the sovereign law making dictatorship than the preservationist commissarial type.[113] This is so because a future constitution, to be made by an agent, cannot bind it as would an existing constitution, and it is furthermore always possible for that agent to produce a constitution institutionalizing its own power, the

---

[111] I don't insist on an identity here, only an elective affinity, because the paradigm has been often practiced in empirical forms that were not dictatorial. In particular, a sovereign assembly can and often does enact at the moment of its beginnings preconstitutions or little constitutions that will involve any number of liberal protections. I note only that any authoritarian ruler may do the same, without structurally changing the arbitrary foundations of the form of rule.

[112] Still the best treatment is Schmitt's own *Die Diktatur*. I have written three essays on this subject "Good-bye to Dictatorships?" *Social Research*, Vol. 67, No. 4 (Winter 2000); "Dictatorship Before and after Totalitarianism" *Social Research*, Vol. 69, No. 2, 2002; and "Conceptual History of Dictatorship (and its Rivals)" E. Peruzzotti & M. Plot, eds., *Critical Theory and Democracy: Civil Society, Dictatorship and Constitutionalism in Andrew Arato's Democratic Theory* (London: Routledge, 2012).

[113] See chapter 1 below.

power of dictatorial incumbents. Some constitutions, such as that of Bonaparte's first consulate, and General Evren's 1982 document in Turkey, can
even incorporate a personal incumbent by name. Moreover, the making of a
future constitution and the process of guaranteeing its success may be a more
time consuming activity than the maintenance of an emergency, especially
since the people for whom the new constitution is made has been socialized
under a previous different, and presumably unjust one. This is indeed the
reason for sovereign dictatorship, but it is also an argument for its long-term
transitional nature as in Bolshevik theory and practice.

In the case of a commissarial version there are not only rules to return to,
but there are (various) rules possible also for the operation of the dictatorship.
There are things that cannot be done, like (constitutional) lawmaking usually;
there can be time limits; and there may even be supervising authorities left
in place. When the emergency is based on an actual state of affairs, its passing is indicated by events themselves. Admittedly, in a coup defining itself as
commissarial there may not be limits, or, if there are, these may be readily
transgressed. But when the old constitution is abolished with a legal rupture
ensuing, there can, supposedly, be no such limits in principle. In my view there
can be normative limits, but unfortunately the adherents of the sovereign theory can and generally will disregard them. Moreover, the new could be one that
institutionalizes the same authoritarian rule, or even a permanent emergency.
Bringing emergency government together with the idea of a sovereign constituent power makes dictatorship unlimited, and that means self-perpetuation
is not only empirically possible, but theoretically it becomes difficult to deny.
Commissarial dictatorships are however guilty of usurpation, violating both
legality and legitimacy when they declare themselves permanent in word or
action. I should note, however, that when they do so, they convert themselves
into sovereign dictatorships since they have replaced the goal of the protection
of the constitution by the implicit or explicit (by emergency decrees) institution of a new one. This happens frequently, of course, making commissarial
dictatorships too, without adequate institutionalization, unsafe from the point
of view of constitutionalism and democracy. I believe, however, with Rossiter
and Friedrich and against Carl Schmitt, that such institutionalization is possible, and compatible with the concept, as even Schmitt occasionally was forced
to recognize. In terms of the sovereign theory (as against the post sovereign
one), such institutionalization would be a contradiction in terms for constitution making. Ultimately then sovereign dictatorship has an elective affinity to
dictatorships in the loose modern sense.

Sovereign constitution making is a theory. It is an ideological theory (in the
narrow, critical sense of ideology) to the extent it disguises organ sovereignty by

references to a popular sovereign, one that even when referring to some kind of agent or agents cannot commission, authorize or control the constitution-making organ. Indeed the latter often defines what the people mean already during the process, e.g. in organizing referenda according to specific rules, and a determined franchise. While it is true, as Schmitt argued, that logically it is impossible to tie this theory to one specific institutional form, historically it has been linked to a finite set of models. There are four of these: sovereign constituent assemblies, constituent assemblies with ratificatory referenda, plebiscites under the aegis of executive power, and at times ordinary parliaments claiming sovereign powers.[114] The fifth model, the American convention in a multi-stage process with "double differentiation" of legislative and constituent powers too has been interpreted in terms of the sovereign theory, but the logic of this process, as I will show in chapter 2, contradicts the theory, producing an antinomic conception of constitution creation.

Relying on both the classical theory of unitary popular sovereignty and the realistic idea of a sovereign organ, the sovereign constituent assembly has been the preferred form for sovereign constitution making, especially one with serious claims to democratic legitimacy.[115] It has also been specifically identified with democratic constitution making even by Kelsen, stepping for the moment outside of the pure theory in describing a process supposedly in a legal vacuum.[116] Nevertheless it is worth asking Schmitt's question, namely, if a part of the people, namely an elected group can embody the popular sovereign, why can't another part, namely a single, elected leader? The question is logically sound if we openly recognize not only the aristocratic element in the form dominated by an assembly, but, unlike Schmitt, also the monarchical one in the model of the single leader. Historically, Schmitt's suggestion, anticipated as well as followed by Caesarist leaders, has had its main influence on twentieth-century populist leaderships, and even these tended to work through a mixed model where the plebiscitary leader dominated a constituent assembly

---

[114] For Schmitt's list, see *Verfassungslehre*, pp. 85–87; see also Böckenförde, "*Die verfassungebende Gewalt des Volkes*" pp. 102–103, who changed the list by eliminating the creation of a federal union, as in 1787, that Schmitt included inconsistently given his later remarks on the constituent power under federations, and by including democratic as well as plebiscitary democratic referenda that Schmitt seemed to consider the same.

[115] See Karl Loewenstein, "Reflections on the Value of Constitutions in our Revolutionary Age" 191–192, where he calls this the classical democratic pattern, largely prevalent after World War II, a period with over 50 cases in his presentation. He describes Israel as an exception, having supposedly made only an interim constitution. That characterization however is incorrect for the open-ended gradual process of that country, and had very negative consequences Loewenstein could not yet suspect.

[116] *General Theory*, p. 259.

or a normal parliament. Nevertheless in terms of the logic of my definition his idea of plebiscitary constitution making, namely when a popular leader's draft is ratified in a referendum or plebiscite is indeed one version of sovereign constitution making, though the most ideological one given the nature of many constitutional referenda.

The distinction between a leader organizing a referendum around his own draft and a constituent assembly does indicate that there are potentially differences among the types of procedures that fall under the sovereign model, and this difference can be the basis for reducing the propensity for dictatorship in the ordinary sense of the term. That is the case because it has been long understood that the minimum requirement of popular elections can better satisfy the principle of democratic legitimacy, hiding within popular sovereignty, than can those assemblies that are put together in some other way. At the same time, elected assemblies can be more fully emancipated from their convener(s) and constituencies who can control a co-opted body more successfully than an elected one. Reference to the people establishes a gulf between the original convener and the constituent assembly. This is a plus in comparison with co-opted assemblies, but a minus from the democratic point of view. The electorate itself cannot in any way control these assemblies, unless another element is added, "the shadow" of popular referenda. Thus the second model developed by some followers of Rousseau in the French Revolution relying on a constituent assembly (then called Convention in France,[117] later merely as the *Constituante*) added referenda, even as they were open to charges by other Rousseauians that they wished to double the sovereign will.[118]

In any case, empirically the unity of the will in an assembly is an ideological claim, because there is always a provisional government that may very well control both the elections, the elected body as well as referenda. This will not mean genuine separation of powers. Once the body is in existence, the dictatorship can be exercised by the provisional government through the assembly, or by the assembly that generates its own, new provisional government. The French National Convention of 1793–1795 (as against its doubly differentiated American forerunners in the 1780s – see chapter 2) indeed shows that a provisional government may also emerge from the assembly itself. The more obvious doubling of sovereign powers between the drafters, based on a

---

[117] Both Schmitt and Böckenförde accept this terminology, even though it violated the meaning that emerged in America in the 1780s that implied double differentiation between legislature and convention, neither of which was to usurp the functions of the other. On this see Carré de Malberg op. cit. and chapter 2 below.

[118] Keith Baker, "Fixing the French Constitution" in *Inventing the French Revolution* (Cambridge: Cambridge University Press, 1990).

strong provisional government and the ratifying instance, in both this assembly-referendum model and the plebiscitary-referendum one, open both up to the charge of ideology, and the claim that, in reality, only the government is sovereign. In theory, this charge is almost always handled by the insistence that it is the people in a plebiscite or referendum that has the highest and ultimate sovereign power. The drafting instance, convention, one-person or constituent assembly only recommends accordingly, in line with the developed American idea of a constitutional convention, and even the last version of the idea of a lawgiver as in Rousseau. The reality, however, tends to be the reverse of the latter conception, confirming the skepticism of the critics. The draft submitted by an assembly or one man cannot be altered by the ratifying instance. The actual power of the people in plebiscite or referendum is very limited, even if in recent times the power to say "No" has become more significant. Classically, if the voting is not actually constrained or manipulated, the choice will be between continued emergency rule without any constitution at all, possibly disorder and long-term legal uncertainty, and the acceptance of the constitution offered, as it is. Yet both models fully belong to sovereign constitution making, since there is a sovereign organ, and popular sovereignty plays a fundamentally legitimating role. This legitimation admittedly seems to have more content when referendum is used, rather than in the case of the constituent assembly without external ratification. How much actual effect this legitimation has would depend on the democratic qualities of the organization of the referendum process as a whole, and even more on the empirical force that can back up decisions of the majority. If genuinely participatory referenda could be organized, and the way was left open to the rapid election of a second assembly in the case of failure to ratify, the assembly-referendum version at least would transgress the limits of the sovereign theory.[119]

The reverse is true in terms of constitution making through ordinary parliaments that come under the aegis of the sovereign theory.[120] I note that this tends to happen when the executive fully dominates the legislature, but in principle the reverse is also possible. This model is hardly possible under American type of separation of powers, though both cabinet government and hyper-presidentialism allow it. Parliaments that undertake constitution making

---

[119] A boundary case is therefore represented by the French constituent assemblies of 1946, where the first ratificatory referendum rejected a constitution, and where a second assembly was immediately elected. Interestingly, this version in its founding act incorporated a minimal interim constitution, which is a feature of post-sovereign models.

[120] This possibility is entertained by neither Schmitt nor Böckenförde, though Carré de Malberg was forced to discuss it in light of the national assembly formula of the Third Republic, which united the two chambers for purposes of constitutional legislation.

generally begin as non-sovereign instances, operating under an existing amendment rule, or a rule of total revision. When elected under an old constitution,
whatever the amendment and revision rules may say, there is a presumption,
in terms of legitimacy if not legality, that changes will be legislated while
preserving the inherited constitutional identity, which means, in the language
of the Indian Supreme Court, the Basic Structure of the constitution, that (as
Schmitt's fundamental constitutional decision) of course raises interpretive
problems. Transgressing such limits is especially problematic from the point
of view of legitimacy if during the elections constitutional replacement was
not promised and campaigned around by the eventually victorious party. If a
constitution amending majority is then attained (especially as the artifact of a
disproportional electoral system created for the purposes of governability), if it
is used for the creation of a new constitution, and if the resulting legitimacy
problems are dealt with through an appeal to the sovereignty of the people
or the electorate, we get very close to a marginal case of the sovereignty model.
If the parliament in such a case would actually transgress the amendment rules
of the system we would have a more distinct case of sovereign constitution
making, involving the (illegitimate) conversion of a normal parliament into a
constituent assembly. We get close to that conversion, with all of its attendant
legitimacy problems, when before creating the new constitution parliament
uses its legal powers to disempower the institution there to police the legal use
of the amending powers, by court packing or jurisdiction removal.[121]

Again, only strong elective affinities are involved here between models and
the sovereign theory, as in the related case of sovereign theory and modern types
of dictatorship. Some of these models, with the exception of the executive-
plebiscitary version, may involve informal mechanisms of self-constraint and
pluralistic participation. A sovereign organ can limit its sovereignty by voluntarily restraining it, even if some theories imply that the limitations (say a
qualified majority decision rule) could always removed as they were adopted
(by simple majority). That is only one interpretation of the paradox of omnipotence, and the other is consistent with self-limitation that accordingly cannot
be lacking in the case of a *really* omnipotent instance. In such a case we could
have many instances participating in a rule-governed process, and no sovereign
dictatorship. Thus model and theory should not be entirely identified with one
another. Yet the sovereign theory has disturbing implications, because of its

---

[121] Here contemporary developments in Turkey and Hungary are astonishingly similar, as I argue
       in chapters 4 and 5 of *Post Sovereign Constitution Making*. The most recent amendments to
       the Turkish Constitution, in 2016, establishing presidential government, brought the cases
       even closer together. Admittedly, the level of repression and manipulation in the Turkish case
       was much higher.

link to dictatorship, and the elective affinities involved in the case of the four models presented here represent good reasons to avoid each and every one of them. That may not be possible in revolutions and processes of radical reform. But in that case the dangers involved should be made conscious, and attempts should be made to compensate for them. Based on the post sovereign model, this study will suggest two forms of this compensation. The first is an institution like a round table, bringing all major political forces into the drafting process and, most importantly, into the process of drafting the rules for that process as in Colombia in 1991 and Tunisia more recently.[122] In theory, the same could be done under newly elected parliaments or elected constituent assemblies irrespective of their composition. As I will argue, in this latter case the task of full inclusion and pluralistic representation would be more difficult, sociologically because of the problem of sequencing, and legally because of the problem of self-binding of the assembly. For these forms of limitation or self-limitation to be effective a second and very likely prior step seems to be necessary, namely the adoption of a post-sovereign theory of legitimate, democratic constitution making. My effort here is both to contribute to such a theory, and to conceive of legal as well as political devices by which it could be made truly effective.

[122] See chapter 4 below.

PART I

ON THE HISTORY OF THE IDEA OF THE CONSTITUENT POWER

1

The Idea of the Sovereign Constituent Power

The sovereign paradigm is not the first historical understanding of constitution making. Before the modern notion of documentary, normative, positive-legal constitutions emerged in the period of the great revolutions, republican thought, ancient and early modern has famously insisted on the foundation of polities by the veritable figure of the extra-ordinary lawgiver or legislator.[1] I believe that the eclipse of this figure by the notion of the people as the constituent power had to do with four notions linked to the modern age, namely concepts of the social contract, sovereignty, the people understood as the unity of the whole rather than a part of the population, and the separation of powers. This can be clearly seen through the contrast of Machiavelli and Rousseau, who were otherwise close on many issues having to do with the foundation and preservation of republican government. Rousseau, relying on contract and the modern sovereignty doctrine, without even the complete differentiation of

[1] The origin of this conception is in a real institution, the Greek *aisymnetes*, which has often (since Dionysius of Halicarnassus) been compared to the Roman dictatorship, while Aristotle thought of it as an elective tyranny. Neither understanding is useful because of the legal nature of an office that had mainly the function of lawgiving. Max Weber's ideal typical placement of the category between the tyrant and the prophet remains in my view more plausible (*Economy and Society* I. (Berkeley: University of California, 1987), pp. 442–444; II. 1313–1316.) The religious-traditional foundations distinguish the *aisymnetei* from sovereign dictators treated here. The role of religion survives in the conception, even down to Machiavelli and Rousseau, who, because of the Roman tradition are forced to separate foundation of the state and creation of the law-cum-religion as two steps. Jumping forward, while traces of the lawgiver conception, in a completely secularized from, survive to this day in notions of extra-ordinary, expert commissions (appointed by the executive or international instances) that recommend constitutions to a drafting or ratifying assembly, this is already a heritage of the mixed Rousseauian version at best, and is, normatively at least, unsustainable, even if some UN agencies retain a soft spot for it as long as it is dressed up with schemes of popular participation. Alas, it is mostly in Africa that this model has been used, almost always linked to executive dominance, and certainly not in Europe or Latin America. Commissions should, of course, not be confused with parliamentary committees.

constituent and constituted powers, is the founder of the theory of sovereign constitution making.[2] He anticipated its ideological version, one which makes "the people," created by a hypothetical and imaginary contract, an actor before and outside the constitution without legal limitations of any kind. But Machiavelli too can be seen as a founder, because he *has* already imagined the sovereign conception, though without using the concept of sovereignty, only to reject this approach to foundations with its link to "dictatorship" (in his language: tyranny). So it is with these two fundamental authors that my analysis will begin.

MACHIAVELLI AND ROUSSEAU: THE ORIGIN OF THE CONCEPTION

The striking thing about Machiavelli's theory of foundations is that he resolutely defends foundational violence, the act of one man, even as he reinterprets the old (and certainly ahistorical) Livian story of the production of the Twelve Tables by the *decemviri*[3] in terms that come close to sovereign (in the sense of unlimited, thus "tyrannical"!) law or constitution making. He thus glimpses at the sovereign model in the name of the people only to decisively, and I think incisively, reject it. The original foundation must be by one man only, the founder or lawgiver (*Discourses*, I.ix), to avoid the likely opposition of the willful few and the unavoidably ignorant dissension of the many. He is supremely conscious of the resulting legitimacy or authority problem. Because the initial act will be inevitably violent and highly disruptive, the wisdom and self-restraint of the first founder (Romulus sharing power with the Senate) is essential for success (I.ix), as is the support given by religion to the enterprise. In the Roman case thus there was said to be a second founder or rather lawgiver, Numa Pompilius, applauded both by Machiavelli and Rousseau. Thus, the incoherence and arbitrariness of initial violence requires

---

[2] I am not disputing important anticipations by the Levellers (Morgan), Lawson (Franklin, Kalyvas, Laughlin) and Locke (Russell), all of whom had a clearer distinction of the constituent and constituted powers than Rousseau. Before Sieyès, it was Rousseau who applied the sovereignty doctrine most radically to the problem of the origins of the legal, constitutional order. Characteristically, he then shrank back from its implications, as did Sieyès. This is clearly visible in his brilliant, reformist essay *[Considerations on] The Government of Poland* [1771–1772] (Indianapolis: Hackett, 1985), a failed attempt at constitutional engineering, which opts for federalism, mixed government and checks and balances. Willmoore Kendall's highly interesting introduction makes Rousseau more conservative than he was (vis-à-vis serfdom, e.g.) but is right on the attempt to develop an alternative to the large territorial (authoritarian) state.

[3] *decemviri consulari imperium legibus scribendi*, a ten-man commission with consular imperium in order to write the laws, according to Livy's (Titus Livius) *Early History of Rome* (London: Penguin, 1960).

both cognitive rationality and normative legitimacy to yield solid foundations. Even if in Rome these characteristics came together only in successive acts of foundation and re-foundation, Machiavelli imagines that they could be – and were – unified in a single lawgiver, such as Lycurgus.[4] All genuine lawgivers must resort to divine authority: a good law is not enough, the authority of the law, given popular ignorance and gullibility, must also be established (I. xi). This can apparently be done only by religion.

What Machiavelli seems to decisively reject is the possibility that the people (in Rome: a corporate body or order), acting through an elected body should or could safely become the main protagonist in an act of foundation or refoundation.[5] The celebrated case of the decemviri is his case in point (I.xl). According to legendary history, uncritically retold by historians such as Livy, a commission of ten was popularly elected for a year (452 BC is the traditional date) to reform the laws of a Rome endangered by civic strife. They, or rather another nine plus one original member, were subsequently elected for a further year. The decemviri became, in the classical view that Machiavelli radicalizes, the first tyrants of Rome following the foundation of the republic even as their product, the 12 Tables, was accepted, preserved and even celebrated. It was not the documentary result, but its process of production that was wrong and led to a brief period of tyranny.

Machiavelli attributes the tyrannical outcome to two features of the episode, both compared unfavorably to the institution of dictatorship that he defends (I. xxxiv–xxxv). During the tenure of the decemviri all other magistracies, in particular the consuls and the tribunes, were fully suspended. And, Romans consented to the election of another ten after the initial year, and in particular to the re-election of the leader during the first term, Appius. Thus, a temporary institution was allowed to become a more permanent one. While both "errors" are attributed to the mutual jealousies of plebeians and patricians, who wished to see the officers of the other put out of commission, Machiavelli notes or at least implies important justification as well. Extra-ordinary legislation could

---

[4] I leave aside his view that two different types of republics are likely to emerge from these two types of foundation, unitary and sequential. In his view the founding of Rome is never completed; popular insurrection and political strife leads to constitutional reforms (including the 12 Tables episode) and only imperial expansion of the republic stabilizes this type of self-formation, before it creates insoluble problems for the republican institutions themselves.

[5] The repeated constitutional reforms of the Romans are, I believe, no exception here. It is true that in a highly imaginative conception that deserves to be better known, Machiavelli gives a kind of constituent role to the conflict, in which plebeians through their assemblies and tribunes, along with patricians through their Senate and consuls pay important roles. *Discourses* I. iii–vi. But here it is exclusively the question of reform of continuous republican institutions, none of which are the conscious work of a lawgiving or institution making subject.

not proceed with ordinary legislative authorities simultaneously making and changing laws left in place; thus, not only the officers but the judicial processes under them including the famous appeal to the people had to be suspended. The decemviri were able to do "everything the Roman people were competent to do," and thus there was presumably no need for another role for the people outside of them.[6] Secondly, during their first year, in the description both in Livy and Machiavelli, the decemviri acted anything but tyrannically. In their judicial role they were mild, and tended to side with the people. More importantly, as to their lawmaking, before final enactment, they exposed the first ten tablets to general public scrutiny, discussion and possible alteration or amendment. One could thus hazard the claim that even within the terms of the legend the body earned re-election against the consuls and tribunes who kept Rome in previous civil strife, through a form of dual government. We would then still have a good argument here against re-eligibility of an elected official like Appius, for "term limits," especially for those involved in constitution making, an argument that will occasionally make its appearance (with generally bad results!) for constituent assemblies: in France in 1791 and as recently as Columbia in 1991. But in that case there would be still nothing wrong with the decemvir model for a single term, or when coupled with non-re-eligibility.

Machiavelli's critique is more sweeping, however. The right way to read his story of the election of lawmaking magistrates with unlimited power is to understand that he rejects this mode of foundation altogether; such is the point of the unfavorable comparison with the classical dictatorship, one that left the other magistracies in place and was denied law making powers or the ability to use the people's authority to alter the fundamental institutions (I.xxxv). While a quasi-dictatorial power without these limits can choose to be beneficent and even seek the population's consent in decisions (the first decemvir term), the same power, by its very nature tyrannical, is just as likely (to Machiavelli more likely, since he interprets the first term as a ruse) to have tyrannical consequences. This is confirmed by the second decemvir term's arbitrary acts and especially by its end, when the decemviri refused to give up power altogether, now a well-known possibility for constitution-making agents! Unchecked power in the refoundation of republics in Machiavelli's view is not the right replacement for a conflictual model of transformation, whose positive sides he often stressed (I.ii–vi), Note, however, that all this

---

[6] This argument is partially at odds with Livy's presentation, where the Comitia of the people can still be assembled, and indeed are needed to ratify the laws drafted by the decemviri. Rousseau will return to this depiction.

lands him in a contradictory position with respect to the merits of popular role in constitutional change and his view of original foundings. He has not in the end drawn a conclusion against either elected magistracy, or dictatorship, only against electing magistrates whose power would be unchecked by other magistrates or the people themselves, and against dictators given any legislative power. It is easy to see Machiavelli's contradiction. The remedies he has in mind in the case of "constitutional reform" cannot apply in the Machiavellian scheme to initial constitution making, where the violent founder[7] is to be checked only by the traditional instrumentarium of wisdom and religion, both conspicuously missing in the leader of decemviri, Appius. What is the guarantee that self-appointed founders would be different than Appius?

Rousseau[8] no longer leaves the matter of a tyrannical outcome up to the founders themselves. His theory, in spite of its traditional elements, takes a gigantic leap from the tradition to modernity with respect to the foundation of republics. In secure possession of the modern doctrine of *sovereignty*, the classical republican doctrine fundamentally changes in Rousseau's hands. Now even the work of the lawgiver is reinserted within the workings of *popular* sovereignty.[9] Strikingly, Rousseau, expressing admiration for his predecessor, repeats many of Machiavelli's arguments, notably stressing the role of religion in foundings. He even seems to have the same comparative judgment concerning dictatorship and the decemviri as Machiavelli (IV.6). But here his reinterpretation of the making of the Twelve Tables provides an important clue to his different approach, as well as to its ambivalence. He does not re-narrate the full story, and tells us two almost contradictory things about it. On the one hand he repeats Machiavelli's charge of tyranny,[10] that he now attributes, entirely originally, to *legislative authority* and *sovereign power* having been put in the same hands, that of the decemviri.[11] On the other, he states, partially following Machiavelli but extending the claim to the whole episode, that:

---

[7] Admittedly, these are not dictators. But the classical figure of the lawgiver is close to the Greek *aisymnetes* often considered to be close to the Roman dictator.

[8] Meaning throughout this text the Rousseau of the *Social Contract*, where his influence lies, and omitting the federalist texts on Corsica, Poland, and Europe.

[9] Anticipating thereby the variant whereby the drafting assembly only recommends, the manner in which the convention formula was adopted in France in a strongly sovereign version in 1792–1793.

[10] Strictly speaking, he should have said despotism, according to his own definitions: "I call the usurper of royal authority a tyrant, the usurper of sovereign power a despot" (III.11)

[11] This old Roman theme of the separation of *auctoritas* and *potestas* (in the senate and the people), and their unification in *decimvir* rule played no role in Machiavelli's critique. It will return in Hannah Arendt's critique of Sieyès and defense of the American model.

... the decemvirs themselves never claimed the right to pass any law merely on their own authority. "Nothing we propose to you," they said to the people, "can pass into law without your consent. Romans, be yourselves the authors of the laws which are to make you happy." He, therefore, who draws up the laws has, or should have, no right of legislation, and the people cannot, even if it wishes, deprive itself of this incommunicable right, because, according to the fundamental compact, only the general will can bind the individuals, and there can be no assurance that a particular will is in conformity with the general will, until it has been put to the free vote of the people. (II.7)[12]

Thus the decemviri themselves seemed to have separated authority (their own) and power (the Roman people's), thereby apparently contradicting Rousseau's very charge against them. It seems in other words that in spite of the terms of their delegation uniting the Senate's *auctoritas* and the people's *potestas*, they made an effort in again separating the two dimensions, if in a new way, contradicting also Machiavelli's idea that the decemviri "could act as if they were the Roman people."

The retelling by Rousseau throws light on the difficulties of his own particular conception. What the modern reader should notice is that the new separation of power and authority had its foundation only in "self binding," while the jurisdiction of the decemviri gave them the competence to decide between separation and reunification. The fundamental error was made by the Roman people, in having delegated something that is not to be delegated, namely their sovereignty, including the constituent power. Having done so, the error was compounded by not having set up safeguards against the likely usurpation of that power by government.[13] In any case, the apparent contradiction between his two positions seems to disappear as Rousseau later re-interprets what the decemviri did in their second term. Accordingly, after having stressed popular consultation regarding the first 10 Tables, he now seems to explain this (as did Livy much more explicitly) in terms of the continued role of the established

---

[12] *Cependant les décemvirs eux-mêmes ne s'arrogèrent jamais le droit de faire passer aucune loi de leur seule autorité. Rien de ce que nous vous proposons, disaient-ils au peuple, ne peut passer en loi sans votre consentement. Romains, soyez vous-mêmes les auteurs des lois qui doivent faire votre bonheur.*

Celui qui rédige les lois n'a donc ou ne doit avoir aucun droit législatif, et le peuple même ne peut, quand il le voudrait, se dépouiller de ce droit incommunicable; parce que selon le pacte fondamental il n'y a que la volonté générale qui oblige les particuliers, et qu'on ne peut jamais s'assurer qu'une volonté particulière est conforme à la volonté générale qu'après l'avoir soumise aux suffrages libres du peuple....

[13] "Government [he says, implying all government) mounts a continual effort against sovereignty... the prince [the center of government] is bound to sooner or later oppress the sovereign and break the social treaty" [III.10].

popular assemblies, the Comitia. Only when they no longer allowed the Comitia to assemble, did the decemviri become guilty of the actual usurpation of sovereign power, i.e. the actual unification of authority and power.[14] Both for Machiavelli and Rousseau at issue was ultimately usurpation, that of rival governmental powers in one case, and that of the fundamental power of the people in the other.[15] But it should be insisted on that for both of them the usurpation was made possible by a deed first ascribed to the Roman people who established the office of the 10, in effect a constituent assembly without any limitations.

Thus, in Rousseau's general conception, which is different from Machiavelli's, the fundamental lawmaking or constitution-making power, even at the origins, is supposed to belong to the people. In Rousseau this is possible because, as should be well enough known, he distinguished between the social contract that is the origin of the people (= sovereign = state in his view) and the making of the laws, namely the constitution of the state that produces government along with the separation of powers.[16] The latter is not a contract in his view, but is the legislative act of the sovereign people (III.1; 16–17). The original foundational act is now no longer seen as inevitably violent (the figure of the voluntary contract replacing foundational violence) but is doubly bifurcated. Founding the people or the state is one act, and making a constitution is a second one.[17] This second act itself has two main actors, as should be obvious to the readers of *Le contrat sociale*. In rehabilitating the idea of popular power Rousseau has not entirely left the ancient lawgiver figure behind. This

---

[14] III.18 see Livy Book 3: 35; 3:37 where it was the Centuriate Assembly to which the laws were submitted, after thorough informal discussion by all the citizens enabled to propose amendments. Livy does not clearly say whether the last 2 Tables were ratified by the Assembly. Machiavelli who does not mention the Assembly implies that they were not (I:40), and so does Rousseau, speaking of the Comitia directly. Many of Livy's details are however neglected by Rousseau and even more by Machiavelli, regarding the manner of ratification. There is no justification to consider them more apocryphal than the story as a whole.

[15] One can interpret the decemvir's original reliance on the Comitia as informal recognition of the impossibility of the delegation of "sovereignty," and their dismissal of the popular bodies as an act of usurpation – even if it was a possibility entailed in the original institutional design of their powers. This would a way of making Rousseau's two statements consistent with one another.

[16] Inevitably partial in Rousseau given his view of legislature and the absence of a judiciary power in his theory [III.1] See M.J. C. Vile's *Constitutionalism and the Separation of Powers* (Indianapolis: Liberty Fund, 1998).

[17] Indeed divided into three parts, because aside from making a constitution the people must also produce a government, itself a governmental function because of the elections involved that have to be organized. To overcome the circularity, Rousseau quite presciently formulates the notion of a democratic provisional government (the sovereign temporarily taking on the form of a democracy) (III.17) an important corollary of the type of sovereign constitution making involving a rupture.

is the idea behind the reference to legislative authority as distinguished from sovereign power. The need to distinguish authority and power, accomplished by Machiavelli with the help of religion, goes both ways. If the authoritative body assumes popular power, i.e., when the decemviri would no longer allow the Comitia – the centuriate assembly – to meet and ratify their product, they became tyrants.[18] But for the original acts of constitution, popular power is not enough, as demonstrated by the error of the Roman people who gave the decemviri an unlimited jurisdiction. A lawgiver is still needed, now in the guise of an expert, non-violent authoritative adviser.[19] This is because, as Rousseau claims, while the general will is always right, and tends to the public advantage

> . . . it does not follow that the deliberations of the people are always equally correct. Our will is always for our own good, but we do not always see what that is; the people is never corrupted, but it is often deceived, and on such occasions only does it seem to will what is bad.[20]

The issue is deeper than the question of mere information and expertise, although they matter. Even with the problem of factions and partial wills we do not reach the most fundamental problem. As in Machiavelli, the inevitable circularity of forming a free people, where the people are not yet free is still solved by Rousseau with the venerable figure of the lawgiver.[21]

Rousseau does recognize the dangers involved in returning even partially to the tradition of great founders. Instead of the figure of Romulus, he tacitly returns to Moses, Lycurgus and Solon, all of whom, through various fictional devices, were prevented in making or recommending laws to their advantage as incumbents. The *législateur*, the legislator or lawgiver, poor translations of

---

[18] Livy does not mention a formal assembly, but says only the following: " . . . every citizen should quietly consider each point, then talk it over with his friends, and, finally, bring forward for public discussion any additions or subtractions which seemed desirable" (cf. Livy: Early History of Rome III 34).

[19] I find the idea that the *législateur* anticipates the notion of the constituent power untenable. (Beaud, La puissance de l'état (Paris: PUF, 1994) pp. 234ff.) Rousseau explicitly stresses that this figure has no power. We can therefore say at the most that this move anticipates a part of the concept of the constituent power that absorbs power and authority. But Rousseau has a clearer connection to constituent power in his notion of sovereignty. The sovereign legislature establishes the fundamental laws of the state, and is able to re-establish them every time in session. It is a constituent power that absorbs the legislative one, or the other way around. See book III. 16–18.

[20] . . . *il ne s'ensuit pas que les délibérations du people aient toujours la même rectitude._On veut toujours son bien, mais on ne le voit pas toujours: jamais on ne corrompt le peuple, mais souvent on le trompe, et c'est alors seulement qu'il paraît vouloir ce qui est mal.* (II.3).

[21] This element is captured by Beaud, *La puissance de l'état* (Paris: PUF, 1994) 235.

an already misleading original,[22] is not only forbidden violent means, but has *aucun droit* legislative, no legislative right strictly speaking, since that right belongs to the assembly of the whole, the sovereign (II.7). The lawgiver is a combination of an expert draftsman and an authoritative advocate on behalf of his draft, preferably an outsider who is not a magistrate of any kind, and has an extra-ordinary, one-time office in the state (*dans l'État*) that constitutes the republic but remains entirely outside the constitution ("*constitue la république, n'entre point dans sa constitution*"), one with no power except that of persuasion and influence – this is where the instrumental use of religion turns up in a way identical to the recommendation of Machiavelli. It is with this device, Rousseau applies, for the first time as I can tell, the original Roman distinction between *auctoritas* and *potestas* to foundations.[23]

While in relation to the *législateur* the element of the distinction of constituent and constituted authority (if not power) is glimpsed at, this seems to disappear with respect to the second, the actual legislative function, exercised by the sovereign to whom the initial recommendation of the lawgiver is made. The people, the general will is said to be always right (or "in the right") even if in need of enlightenment, given that their judgment is not always enlightened (II.6). Yet he also states that the moment the sovereign legislative body assembles (as it should, lawfully, both at regular and extra-ordinary occasions) all jurisdiction of government ceases, all governmental structure and authority is suspended (III.14). At these moments the assembly must pose and vote on two fundamental questions, the first of which is: "Does it please the sovereign to preserve the present form of government?"[24] If the answer is no, it becomes entirely unclear whether recourse would still be had to a double structure of law-making involving a *législateur*, or the assembly would produce a new constitution as part of its legislative activity. While the assumption of the power by an extra-ordinary lawgiver has been pronounced as usurpation, in Rousseau the reverse would not be illegitimate. The most one could say about the absorption of authority in popular power is that it can be possibly unwise. Even that would *not be the natural way to think of it*, after the rejection of a previous constitution, drafted by an expert, authoritative, disinterested figure who any case has not retained any authority in the state.

The way was thus open to both dualistic (bifurcation of authority and power) and monistic interpretations of Rousseau's scheme, where the dualistic version

---

[22] Schmitt rightly points out that the *législateur* has no legislative competence or even a formal legal initiative of some executive magistrates (p. 125).

[23] Hannah Arendt *On Revolution* (New York: Viking, 1963).

[24] III.18. the second question: "Does it please the people to leave the administration in the hands of those who are presently in charge of it?"

could easily be identified with a traditional, unenlightened age in which the people needed external, authoritative tutelage before they could act wisely. It is on this point that both the authors of the *Federalist* and Sieyès decisively break with traditional Republican thought. They are proud to be able to do without the lawgivers and founders of the past. Yet they chose two different roads. As Hannah Arendt argued,[25] the Americans could rely on the authority of already constituted small republics. But Sieyès, she rightly claimed, did indeed merge original power and authority in the same source, in *Quest-ce que le tiers état?* We might add: a fictional source, not under any positive law, unlike the small republics in America. It is true: in this analysis Sieyès was a stand-in for Carl Schmitt. Yet, in the present context, by adding representation to the Rousseauian scheme, and denying the need for popular ratification, by positing that the constituent assembly "replaced the nation in its independence of all constitutional forms" Sieyès the author of the *Tiers État* did seem to return to the much-criticized decemvir model, at least in the main and most famous line of his argumentation.

As Keith Baker has nicely shown, there were different types of Rousseauians in the great constituent assembly of 1789.[26] Because of the problems entailed by representation,[27] some insisted on the need for popular ratification of their product by the only agency capable of legitimate enactment of a constitution, the people, in something like a referendum. They thereby recovered, at least partially, the distinction between authority and power, just as Rousseau did for the first year of the decemviri. Others, focusing on the unity of the general will, opposed testing its decisions by what they called, following Rousseau, "the will of all."[28] Having fewer doubts concerning the issue of the unification of all power and authority in a single body than even Sieyès, as we will see, these radicals had the authority of Rousseau on one important point at least.[29] For the political philosopher, too, all assemblies of the sovereign in an already constituted order fully possess the power that he did not yet

---

[25] Or should have argued, since she speaks only of their constituent power. This is not, however, a reduction of power and authority to the same source, since the small republics where all under law. They had independent authority to authorize representatives at a convention.

[26] Keith Baker, *Inventing the French Revolution* (New York: Cambridge University Press, 1990).

[27] Confined by Rousseau only to the executive power.

[28] Baker, *Inventing the French Revolution*, Chapter 11.

[29] It was however highly contestable whether Rousseau could have supported the idea that no popular ratification needed. The full transference of the powers of the people to the assembly had this implication. But the assembly could be treated as the *"législateur"* recommending merely to the true sovereign that would have to ratify the product. On this, defenders of the model of a unitary assembly and model of drafting always disagreed, from 1789 to the twentieth century.

call "constituent", and "provisionally" unite in themselves all powers in the state, including the governmental magistracy. To put it in modern terms: the power of constitutional revision or replacement in Rousseau is not only a fully sovereign constituent one, but, has no room for a separated executive, nor, arguably, the need for either the expert counsel or the authority of a *législateur* (III.14). This is the sovereign conception of the constituent power, coupled with the idea of a provisional government.

CONTRACT, POPULAR SOVEREIGNTY AND SEPARATION OF POWERS

In my reconstruction, the eclipse of the figure of the lawgiving founder and its replacement by the modern notion of the constituent power had to do with four highly innovative notions, namely modern concepts of the social contract, sovereignty, "the people" and the separation of powers. Interestingly, however, each of these notions had internal possibilities that could justify two funda-mental interpretations, potentially leading to both what I call the sovereign conception of the constituent power, and also the post-sovereign one. The fact that initially, and for a long time subsequently, the sovereign conception was dominant I would ascribe to a widely prevalent political theology, with the people's two bodies replacing that of the king. It was in the name of the ideal, non-empirical "body" of the people that the sovereign conception was first formulated. Nevertheless, as the next chapter will argue, even in the first great democratic revolutions there was a confrontation of the two interpretations, and the intellectual development of both the dominant conception as well as elements of its alternative. This battle, or antinomy, had its foundations in the intellectual history of the concepts of contract, sovereignty, people and separation of powers.

I *Contract*

The figure of the social contract seems to contain all that is needed in the journey from Machiavelli to Rousseau. It seems to get rid of the necessity of violence in foundings, present in Machiavelli, absent in Rousseau. It appears to replace the deed of one man by that of the collectivity. And, in its modern version,[30] it tends to replace both a heteronomous, traditional legitimacy, as

---

[30] After Quentin Skinner's important reconstructions, I will not go back to the earliest versions of the contract metaphor. There is no need to seek out all the forerunners of the ideas of popular sovereignty and the constituent power, either. The role of sixteenth-century thought in the formation of that of the seventeenth on which I concentrate here is undeniable. *The Foundations of Modern Political Thought* (Cambridge: Cambridge University Press, 1978).

well as a prophetic-charismatic one by a democratically centered form. Unfortunately only the last of these statements is strictly true. In addition, however, it is also true and important, if less commonly understood, that the construct of the contract begins to place the differentiation of the foundation of the state and constitutional law making on solid foundation. That differentiation was admitted by Machiavelli only implicitly and only for Rome according to its own tradition of multiple-foundings and re-foundings.

It is true that contract does *formally* exclude violence in the origins of the state (classical terminology speaks of commonwealth, republic, community, political society, civil society or just society). As everyone knows, however, for the most consistent thinker in this tradition, Hobbes, the state of nature and the contract itself came to be seen as hypothetical, rather than historical.[31] and its importance lies in the fact that its justification by an outcome can be used to *impute legitimacy* to empirical forms of the origin of the state, what Hobbes in general calls sovereignty by acquisition.[32] That outcome is centrally enforced civil peace. Both imputation and legitimacy are important here. The reason that rule by conquest according to Hobbes, and its likely result, absolute rule by the conqueror, can be justified is because the reason for accepting both on the part of the ruled can be fully transferred, hence: imputed, from what would be the case for sovereignty by covenant or "by institution." That imputed reason is fear of death, and for Hobbes it is immaterial that in one case it is fear of one another that is at play, and in the other it is fear of the conqueror.[33]

It has been often pointed out, of course, that the Hobbesian argument[34] justified something very much like a protection racket. This valid criticism

---

[31] See already Blackstone *Commentaries on the Laws of England* (Chicago: University of Chicago, 2002) v. I. 47 but compare to Locke. It seems that in earlier texts than the Leviathan, Hobbes too had a historical understanding similar to that of Locke's later. See Skinner's *Hobbes and Republican Liberty* (Cambridge: Cambridge University Press, 2008).

[32] What is certainly wrong is the reverse: interpreting, as does Schmitt (cited in the previous note), "institution" by "acquisition," as if the power to whom the multitude cedes sovereignty already existed before the contract. That is true only in the case of paternal and despotic forms, i.e., sovereignty by acquisition. In the contractual form, the power is generated, in other words the state is first created. Schmitt is right to regard that as mythological. But he is wrong not to see that he is not dealing with history, but a normative model of justification – however realistic.

[33] *Elements of Law*, I:19.11; *Leviathan*, II.20.

[34] Fallacious because in the one case the trust of the multitude is given to a third, who, whether one person or assembly, exercised no constraint in the choice, while in the other to a second, constraining party. Locke is moreover correct in claiming that in the second case, the original state of nature problem is not resolved, since the source of fear remains in the state of nature in Hobbes' model vis-à-vis the rest. *Second Treatise* VII.93.

spares the notion of imputation, that was transformed from an argument based on fear and peace to one based on constitutional contents, whether the presence of fundamental rights (Locke) or the conditions of justice as fairness (Rawls).[35] It is interesting to note that this very gain that involves the deepening and development of the concept of constitutional legitimacy, already there in Machiavelli, does not destroy one of the main points of Hobbes, namely that legitimacy is possible even on the bases of violent beginnings.[36] This means that the idea of the one founder is only partially replaced by contract models. As a matter of actual history, the lawgiver is in effect replaced in Hobbes by a conqueror, a distinction that may not make much of a difference in many pre-state societies. For Locke, who toyed with the idea of some contractual beginnings in empirical history, beginning through a conquest that can be made legitimate remains possible, even if not necessary. He at least leaves the door open to a more democratic process indicated by the demanding contents of his model of legitimacy.

While the space of a violent founder is still preserved, the scope of the initial lawgiving activity is transformed in contract theories, if less completely by Hobbes than by Locke. In neither Hobbes nor Locke does the formation of the state amount to legislation. For legislation, including the enactment of fundamental laws (*leges fundamentalis*) one must first establish a sovereign (Hobbes) or a legislature (Locke), and have the power to bind the minority. In the Hobbes of the Leviathan,[37] however, the form of the state is determined by the social contract, while in Locke initially only a community, society or people emerge that is now in the position to determine the form of the state. In either case we have a differentiation, partial or complete, of constitution making from state making.[38] This differentiation will be fundamental for the post-sovereign model relying on two stages of state and constitution making,

---

[35] Most recently, see H. Lindahl, for whom the relevant result is unity of the polity or the legal system, which allows imputation to a unitary constituent power.: H. Lindahl, "Constituent Power and Reflexive Identity: Towards an Ontology of Collective Selfhood" in Martin Loughlin and Neil Walker, *Paradox of Constitutionalism* (Oxford: Oxford University Press, 2007).

[36] Admittedly, there is good reason to think that legitimate contents of the type desired by Locke or Rawls (as against Hobbes) are most likely achieved on the bases of legitimate process, defined either in terms of broad participation and/or fair negotiations.

[37] The Hobbes of the *Elements of Law* II.20.2–3 has an intervening democratic stage, as in Locke and Rousseau after him, necessary because of the needed transition from unanimity to majority. But this can be true only for sovereignty by covenant, not "by institution," namely conquest.

[38] I leave aside theories of the two contracts, which seem a remnant from *ständestaatliche* conceptions. Gierke ascribes the full abandonment of the second, governmental contract [*Herrschaftsvertrag* as against *Gesellschaftsvertrag*] to Rousseau. *Natural Law and Society* (Chicago: University of Chicago Press, 1942) cit. 48, 149. I think this was already achieved by Hobbes, even if he was not universally followed.

implying moreover the possibility of contractual rather than electoral begin-ning, which had to be fictional given individualist assumptions, but could possibly be actual in the formation of federations and, in unitary states, agree-ments among important political forces.[39]

The outcomes of the contract concept have an uneasy relation to one another. One gain, the differentiation of state making, may cancel the other, the deepening of the legitimation problem. Strictly speaking, the perspective of contractual legitimacy, however it is understood, applies only to state, not constitution making.[40] The two are now differentiated, and what applies to one does not automatically apply to the other. The road is open to considering the making of the constitution as unbound activity by the new sovereign, still in "the state of nature" (as in the Sieyès of *Tiers état*) or, alternatively, to consider it bound by the terms of the social contract (the same Sieyès in *Exposition raisonée*[41]) implying, for example, equality, that would have to apply to the process as well as the result of constitution making.[42] Such was the gist of Rousseau's legitimacy argument, in spite of his denial that constitution making was a contract. Beyond earlier contract theories, and even later ones, the details of his analysis show that the question "What can make it legitimate?"

---

[39] See Carl Schmitt *Verfassungslehre* (Berlin: Duncker & Humblot, 1928) Ch. 7 and 29. I extend this conception of "federation" to round tables. For a wider concept of constitution making by contract, see: E.-W. Böckenförde in "Die verfassunggebende Gewalt des Volkes – Ein Grenzbegriff des Verfassungsrechts" in *Staat, Verfassung, Demokratie* (Frankfurt: Suhrkamp, 1991).

[40] I leave out of consideration explicit theories of the two contracts, linked to the tradition of the Ständestaat that will no longer be relevant in the age of absolutism. Admittedly, the derivation of legitimacy from the idea of contract came to apply to constitution making too. An important evidence of this is the terminology of constitutional politicians in the American and French revolutions who often regarded constitution making as a contract in spite of Rousseau's, Hobbes' and more ambiguously Locke's denial of this thesis that seems to presuppose the older two contract theories of the origin of society and government. (Amazingly enough, Carl Schmitt seems to buy into this interpretation in his 1938 Hobbes book, *The Leviathan in the State Theory of Thomas Hobbes* (Chicago: University of Chicago, 1996), entirely inconsistent with his view of the relation of contract and constitution in the much more sophisticated 1928 pre-Nazi *Verfassungslehre*, as well as that earlier book's strong differentiation of state and constitution making.) As federalist theories of natural law already anticipated on the historical bases of the Ständestaat that they wished to modernize, only in the case of the making of confederal or federal constitutions, and, more recently, in terms of recent round table agreements can one speak of a genuine contractual element. Both of these "contracts" or horizontal agreements among parties are however under existing law, international or national, and thus are not the famous social contract or covenant of the classical theory.

[41] Both in R. Zappieri ed. *Écrits politiques* (Basle, Switzerland: Gordon & Breach, 1994).

[42] Note that Hobbes and Locke differ on the question whether the sovereign could alter the social contract itself. Rousseau goes with Hobbes on this question in the *Social Contract*, though it remains open whether such a radically constituent activity of remaking the state itself is then under the authority, if not the power, of the lawgiver.

could be applied to constitution making as well as to the founding of a state. As many followers in the revolution assumed, even the representation Rousseau denied could be utilized with the help of this, his most fundamental question. Two roads were thus opened for followers of Rousseau. The differentiation of authority and power raised the question of legitimacy as an independent problem of justification. Yet the notion of sovereignty Rousseau inherited from Hobbes, interpreted in terms of the famous, willfully misread "*auctoritas non veritas facit legem*" *seems* to make the same notion of legitimacy superfluous for the foundations of the constitutional law, or at least reduce it to the identity of its carrier: the people.

II *Sovereignty*

The classical doctrine of sovereignty, ascribed to a "body" or an "organ" within the political community, seems to point directly and tautologically to the sovereign as the maker of the constitution.[43] Once the idea of law as enacted or positive law became established (and this did not happen before the age of absolutism) the older idea of the sovereign as the *legibus solutus*, the source of law not bound by law, seemed to include not only the constitution, but the very process of making it. The sovereign appeared to have an unlimited authority and power to control both the contents of the constitution and the process of its enactment. Thus, the concept of sovereignty seems to be the origin of the concept and theory of the constituent power. Yet there are two problems with this view. The first is that given the classical concept of sovereignty, it becomes difficult to differentiate constituent from the legislative power. And second, even worse, there seems to be no stable, settled constitutional law at all when a sovereign is said to be above and beyond all positive law, unless we identify the constitution with Bodin's "divine and natural law," that, however, could not be enforced against the sovereign. Whether an absolute monarch or the states in J.C. Calhoun's theory or "the people" in Schmitt, the sovereign is an always alive will that can arbitrary enact and retract constitutional law. Lawmaking itself then can be bound to any higher law, only as long as it is the work of subordinate legislators, as for example the American colonies in Dicey's reconstruction.[44] For the highest, sovereign legislator there is no distinction between law and constitutional law, as well as between lawmaking

---

[43] For a much more detailed development of the concept, see the Introduction above. As I argued there, organ sovereignty is fundamental to both the conception of Bodin as well as Hobbes.

[44] Dicey, *The Law of the Constitution* 8th ed. [1915] (Indianapolis: Liberty Fund, 1982) chapter 3, esp. 93.

and constitution making, both potentially subordinated to an arbitrary will. This consequence, already explicit in Hobbes, is well illustrated by notions of parliamentary sovereignty as in Blackstone, popular sovereignty as in Rousseau, and partially even the constituent power as in Schmitt. While leading to obvious contradictions in attempts to differentiate constituent and constituted powers, an all-absorbing constituent power seems to be a logical implication of absolute sovereignty, and the theory of sovereign constitution making based on it. Conversely, it will take attempts to limit absolute sovereignty, whether by dualism as in Lawson, or the alternative concept of supremacy, under limits, as in Locke, to fully differentiate constituent and legislative powers.

But the classical notion of sovereignty suffered from internal problems from the beginning. Namely, it is very difficult to identify the carrier or agent of sovereignty if we hold on to the notion of the absence of limitation and of any law that limits. Omnipotence in the legal sense is paradoxical, as H.L.A. Hart has shown.[45] If an omnipotent power was really omnipotent, it could bind itself and from then on would be all-powerful no longer. Sovereignty would then be a one-time thing in the history of a polity. If the sovereign could not bind itself, however, as in British theory, then it would not be omnipotent in the first place. If there were an original omnipotent power, omnipotent except to the extent that it could not bind itself, we would still have the problem of identifying this power. In the human world this cannot be done without law. Jean Bodin recognized this, as his monarchical sovereign is identified by the terms of the so-called Salic law, the law of succession in France. That law cannot be abandoned without compromising the identity of the sovereign organ, and in the classical model sovereignty itself.[46]

The founder of the classical doctrine, Bodin also considered "divine and natural law" as a significant limitation of sovereignty itself. This implied that even without external enforcement, the law- or constitution-making power of the sovereign amounted to the discovery of law already in existence. Thus, Bodin could not yet posit a sovereign constituent power, in the modern sense of the creator of the fundamental law. Nevertheless, from the point of view of legitimacy, he was on stronger grounds than Hobbes, whose legal positivism could make no sense of normative limits without apparatus of enforcement. Thus, he understood the system of states to be "in the state of nature" – but this was never the dominant view. With the development of international law

---

[45] H.L.A. Hart, *The Concept of Law* (Oxford: Oxford University Press, 1961).

[46] Hobbes famously denied that the law of succession cannot be altered or replaced by the sovereign. Neglecting the problem of legitimacy, he counted thereby on a kind of reconquest, whose success would of course be an empirical matter.

contemporaneous with the modern state system a new notion of limitation was to emerge, and, from the outset, the modern notion of sovereignty was also a category of international law. Unlike God, the sovereign of the state was not the one and only possessor of supposedly unlimited power; the existence of juridically equal other sovereigns implied limitation on each, at the very least limitation to a specific territory.[47] Recognition by other sovereigns depended on each adhering to limits, and violating them could lead to the sanctions of non-recognition or war. The sovereignty of each was thus dependent on and limited by the rules of international affairs in a system of states. Violating these rules was of course very possible (as is crime in the domestic sphere) but not without possible consequences.

Today we in any case consider sovereignty itself to be under law, and constituted by law.[48] The recognition could lead to what is called here the post-sovereign constituent power. That this is not automatic is shown by the ambivalence of authors such as Lawson and Locke. The former, in clear violation of the orthodox sovereignty doctrine played with the notion of *two* sovereigns within the state. This, however, raises exactly the question whether either can be then sovereign in terms of the classical doctrine, and whether the term is being misused for either or both. Lawson[49] relying entirely on Bodin's formulation defined *sovereignty* or *majesty* as 1. Absolute; 2. As the lawgiver not bound by his own laws; 3. Having universal power within the state; 4. Supreme with respect to all within the state, and equal to other sovereigns (also: inferior to God); 5. Having powers that are not and cannot be divided or transferred; 6. Having perpetual powers under fundamental law.[50]

Given this level of orthodoxy, Lawson came to the entirely amazing unorthodox conclusion: there are two such sovereigns in the state, the *real* and the *personal* one.[51] The personal one embodied in a single institution, in England the mixture of three (at the cost of a contradiction in his theory and with Hobbes as well as Bodin), is responsible for all the tasks assigned by the classical theory to it, interpreted all as *constituted* powers. The "real"

[47] D. Grimm *Sovereignty* (New York: Columbia University Press, 2015).

[48] See Jean L. Cohen *Globalization and Sovereignty. Rethinking Legality, Legitimacy and Constitutionalism* (Cambridge: Cambridge University Press, 2102); D. Grimm *Sovereignty* (New York: Columbia University Press, 2015).

[49] *Politica Sacra et Civilis* 1660, corr. in 1689 C. Condren ed. (Cambridge, Cambridge University Press, 1992).

[50] Ibid., 4:14.

[51] As emphasized by Andreas Kalyvas, Julian Franklin, Edmund Morgan, and Martin Loughlin. This double structure will reappear in Dicey, in the form of legal and political sovereigns. Interestingly it is the legal sovereign, parliament that is assigned the constituent power. But the political sovereign has the connotation of "the real" one with respect to all powers in the state.

sovereign or majesty has only one task: to exercise *constituent* powers.[52] Unlike Locke, who mostly, if inconsistently, tried to make the activity of the people's constituent power dependent on the prior self-dissolution of government (understood rather loosely), Lawson made the constituent power much more self-activating potentially, though requiring justification, the famous "just and necessary cause." Depending on the interpretation of that phrase, the two powers may cross. A legislature exercising its specific powers can easily enter into the terrain of the real sovereign by making what amounts to a constitutional change, and vice versa, whatever body represents the real sovereign can start legislating in the guise of resuming its constituent activities. They can each pass laws regarding the powers of the other, and so on. It is obvious that constitutional conflict among actual political bodies can lead to civil war, exactly in the sense that the Monarchomachs anticipated, and Bodin and Hobbes warned concerning dualistic arrangements and mixed governments. Thus Lawson's use of the category of sovereignty for the absolute constituent and the similarly absolute constituted powers runs into fundamental difficulties. In spite of Lawson's influence on him, Locke could here see another model that was worthwhile to avoid, or at least recast in different conceptual terms. That understanding brought him to the threshold dividing sovereign and post sovereign conceptions, a threshold that he did not clearly cross.

One step beyond Lawson was Locke's attempt to delimit the spheres of operation of his two "supreme" powers in such a way that they were not supposed to ever meet as such.[53] I do not think it was accidental that Locke avoided the concept of sovereignty and replaced it with supremacy.[54] He meant to say, very plausibly if not entirely certainly, that neither is unlimited, neither is

---

[52] These terms were already introduced in the Puritan Revolution, and Lawson uses them. See op.cit E. Morgan.

[53] This notion is closer to the medieval rather than the modern concept of "sovereignty." See op. cit Grimm's *Sovereignty* 14ff.

[54] Grimm op.cit agrees. The least important, but probably not unimportant reason behind Locke's choice seems to be that the term sovereignty suggested at the time the absolutist doctrines of Filmer as well as Hobbes, and Locke wished to establish his distance from both. This is suggested by the distinct difference in terminology between the First and Second Treatises. The *First Treatise* uses the concept of sovereignty to refute Filmer's claim of the divine origin of absolute, patriarchal and patrimonial forms of kingly rule, as the only legitimate and viable form of government. In this context Adam's supposed and disputed sovereignty, refers to absolute and entirely unlimited rule: "*monarchical, absolute, supreme, paternal power*" (124) and Locke implicitly included "patrimonial" as well, because Filmer's sovereign, Adam was owner all of material things. Supremacy here is a dimension, but not a synonym of sovereignty. The highest does not have to be absolute, or paternal or patrimonial. Arguing against Hobbes as well as Filmer, Locke goes on to suggest that controlling or disposing over marks of sovereignty such as the power of judgment, and that of peace and war, does not entail absolute sovereignty in the sense of either of his opponents (*First Treatise* pars. 129; 131–132).

quasi-divine. Yet he tried very hard to avoid the possibility of a clash between his two supreme powers. As long as government or the constitution exists, context one, the legislative power is said to be supreme. When it dissolves, the people are supreme. The two cannot be supreme (or, by implication, even assemble) at the same time and in the same context. However, Locke's effort, in its attempt to avoid Lawson's dilemmas, conscious or not, also runs into difficulties. This is so because in a second version of his argument, involving the loss of trust, one supremacy does challenge the other, and before the decisive judgment by God or the sword, two powers, each supreme from its own point of view, do exist in one setting. His solution in this case had already been anticipated by Lawson: to act as a constituent power the people must have a just and necessary cause.[55]

Nevertheless, as already stated, Locke sought to make both of his supreme powers limited. He clearly had in mind challenging not only Bodin's and Hobbes' absolutism, but also what was to become the English theory of parliamentary sovereignty, Blackstone's absolute and arbitrary power, or the power of despotism that supposedly must lie somewhere in the state.[56] It is significant however that his argument works better in the case of the legislature, than in the case of the seventeenth-century concept of popular sovereignty.[57]

As Hart later explained, there is no higher legislative power in Great Britain than parliament, but this fact does not mean its omnipotence, since it comes into being under legal rules that it itself cannot violate. For Locke, it is moreover deprived of the powers of peace and war, that Hobbes had good reason to think was even more central than legislation. These remain parts of the united executive, and federative powers. Granted, Locke seems at times to think of this as a narrow delegation.[58] The legislative has moreover several very important limitations. While interestingly, the federative power that retains other aspects of Hobbesian sovereignty is said to be (not entirely consistently) absolute in

[55] To deny for this reason that either had a constituent power beyond mere right of resistance is untenable, unless we read the category through Carl Schmitt alone, and insist that the constituent power must be by definition unlimited. See J. Colon-Rios, *Weak Constitutionalism* (London: Routledge, 2012), 80–83.

[56] According to Blackstone: "It [the sovereign parliament] can change and create afresh even the constitution of the kingdom and of parliaments themselves; as was done by the act of union, and the several statutes for triennial; and septennial elections" op. cit. I. 156. Thus, in our language both state making (act of union that transforms the territory, population and ruling organization of the state) and constitution making (the election laws that change the relation of parliament and its electors) are within the powers of the legal sovereign, without any legal limit, while in turn the element of sovereignty conceded to the electors ("the people") and even the crown is legally limited, though in different ways, by parliamentary statutes.

[57] See op.cit. Morgan   [58] op.cit. *First Treatise*, para. 132.

its own sphere,[59] in the domain of lawmaking there is no unlimited power.[60] Thus according to Locke, "the legislative is the supreme power: for what gives laws to another must be supreme to him" (*Second Treatise*[61] XIII para. 150). Yet this does not mean *altering* the constitutional status of the other. In Locke's proposal, parliament's legislative power is a lot more limited than that of the modern body analyzed by all the classics from Blackstone, and Dicey to Hart. It cannot "alter" the legislative power itself, and therefore by strong implication the executive and federative powers, without usurpation [paras 134; 149]. The legislative power is said to be sacred and unalterable in the hands that the community placed it. It cannot transfer the power of making laws into other hands [141]. The legislature can only "make laws, not legislators." Moreover, it cannot control its own dissolution or prorogation or reconvening, nor by implication take over that control without altering its powers and that of the executive. The executive's power of dissolution is seen as a fiduciary trust on behalf of the people [156]. The legislature cannot have absolute or arbitrary control over property, or indeed govern by arbitrary and non-public decrees [135–136, 137; 138].[62] Finally, by very strong implication, and given the eventual remedy, the legislature is banned from altering the rules of choosing a legislature, namely electoral rules, even where these are as deficient as in the England of the seventeenth and eighteenth centuries [157]. Here, in amending the constitution, understood as a dimension of the prerogative, the executive again appears as the people's trustee [158]. Thus in the crunch, when constitutional *reform* is needed, when there is a serious constitutional flaw in a system such as the English rotten boroughs, Locke turns not to the most powerful, but to what he takes theoretically at least to be the less dangerous branch, understood as a trustee.[63] In other words, he partially disempowers the one

---

[59] Thus calls the executive "in a very tolerable sense . . . supreme" op. cit. p. 78.

[60] While the legislative's law-making is referred to, I think inconsistently, as the all supreme power, Locke has not said that this is an unlimited power outside the law. The royal prerogative in fact (XIV) seems to be the only dimension of government (the people are not an institution of government) outside the law. Thus the legislature is the author, but under the law, while the executive is not the author, but is partially outside of it.

[61] I am using the edition of C.B. Macpherson (Cambridge: Hackett, 1980) and refer to paragraphs in the text.

[62] As far as I see, Waldron in *The Dignity of Legislation* takes up only the question of property and the natural law argument in which it is embedded, and not the other examples including the issue of the constituent power, rooted in democratic theory. Having made things thus a bit easier, he comes to the conclusion that "consent" is satisfied in the case of property issues by the fact of election. Things are much more difficult in relation to the other issues, most of which would allow the transformation of the parliament-people, or parliament-electorate relationships. Here Locke's problem was not distributive justice-injustice, but freedom-tyranny.

[63] I deliberately use this language to indicate both the missing of something like judicial review in Locke and the fact that he was indeed concerned about the differentiation of two levels of

branch, the legislative, which would be more likely to usurp the constituent power.[64]

To be sure, in Locke amending by a trustee is not the same as original constitution making. The people, while not yet understood as having a higher form of legislative power, establish what Hobbes called the fundamental laws (or their political substratum) for the legislature; and implicitly it is its command, establishing a limited legislature, that bars legislative alteration of these laws. While Locke rather grudgingly admits that in a "very tolerable sense" the monarch too is supreme, it also has limits. The head of state also cannot alter fundamental rules dealing with the executive function. He can change the mode of election, but not the structure and powers of the legislature. Whatever he orders, his officers can be tried and impeached by the parliamentary chambers, and there is no pardon in the case of impeachment. While he can go to war in principle, parliamentary command can deprive him of the funds to be able to do so.

In spite of the repeated use of the term popular sovereignty when commentators speak about Locke, the term supremacy ("*a* supreme power," "in this respect... *always the supreme power*" 149) here also does not mean sovereignty even in the case of the people, who indeed retain what was already then called the constituent power. "The constitution of the legislative being the original and supreme act of the society, antecedent to all positive laws in it, and depending wholly on the people, no inferior power can alter it" (157). Thus, from one point of view the legislature itself is understood as an inferior power, which, however, does not make the constituent power unlimited. While this is not said clearly, the limitation here is exactly the reverse than in the case of parliament; the people without a government, not having a coercive power,

---

power, constituent and constituted. Note however that Lawson, unlike Locke, has a notion of judicial power as the third dimension of "personal sovereignty," though he of course does not rely on it to guard the constitution (Ch.4:13).

[64] Thus, without offering an amendment rule, in a tradition not used to entrenchment, under the principle "*Salus populi suprema lex*," he goes so far as to assign the royal prerogative, a partial survival of absolutist fiat, the task to correct constitutional anomalies (para. 158). Aside from the highly questionable scope he otherwise leaves the prerogative, a clear regression from the Machiavellian theory of dictatorship, with respect to a dimension of the amending power this assignment leads only to self contradiction, since elsewhere in the same text Locke denies that the executive can, anymore than the legislative, change the electoral scheme without risking tyranny (XIX: 216). In Blackstone, the full sovereignty, famously "the despotic power" of parliament will be asserted instead, and this will allow in turn the attempt to bring the royal prerogative, including emergency and habeas suspension powers belonging to the earlier despotic power within the law. Electoral reform will be then located where it actually lay in England, among the powers of parliament (I: 156).

cannot truly legislate nor control the other defining features of sovereignty if we stay with Hobbes: the power of peace and war.

Thus, for once the otherwise not exactly rigorous Locke has chosen his terms well, better than the many interpreters who ascribe to him a doctrine of popular sovereignty the full development of which will have to wait for Rousseau and the special devices he needed to invent to make sense of that notion. Finally, to the extent that the corporate body of the people remains intact also under settled government (and this seems to be the Lockeian view), that body can certainly be given laws and legal orders by its superior(s), both the legislative power and the monarch using his prerogative. To say that the people's constituent power is sovereign in Locke, or that it is the true locus where he locates sovereignty does not seem correct, especially because he denies on both normative and actually strong empirical grounds the people's ability to activate that power merely at will. Only acts of government that mean either the dissolution of government or the beginning of such a process of dissolution can legitimate the people taking all political matters in their own hands, leading to the restoration or transformation of political institutions. Yet a sovereign whose power is activated only by the acts of others is not a sovereign at all. Beyond this, any attempt to provide an organizational form of popular sovereignty is missing as well, as against Lawson's discussions of another expanded assembly or convention having the powers denied to parliament (Ch. 4: 8), or Sir Henry Vane's parallel proposal. These crucial omissions all have to do with the difficulty of making sense of the concept of the people as the supreme body in the state.[65]

---

[65] Julian Franklin in *John Locke and the Theory of Sovereignty* (Cambridge: Cambridge University Press, 1978) gives us a picture of a more radical Locke, who would have preferred the Convention Parliament of 1689 to assume a constituent role, and who developed his theory to justify a revolutionary dissolution in which the people as organizationally distinct from the ordinary parliament would reassert their sovereignty (117–122). I must hesitantly admit that since Locke, unlike Lawson and others gives no textual clue to any such "popular" organizational alternatives, I am more inclined to accept Morgan's interpretation that he gives a conservative turn to inherited ideas (255–256). What neither Franklin, nor Morgan explains is the far greater role the monarch's prerogative has in the scheme to limit the power of parliament. It is however consistent with the general argument of Franklin, even if less stressed in the case of Locke, that the role of the distinction of constituent and constituted powers was the stabilization of the powers of mixed government, and the independence of the king. Granted, in 1689 this could be interpreted as dissolution of government, re-assertion of popular power, and re-confirmation of the "mixed and balanced" constitution but under a new king. It seems to me that Locke has made the conditions of such a scenario coming into play almost as difficult as the fiction of "abdication" used by the Whigs. That he did not satisfy Whigs of his own time or Blackstone later is no proof of his radicalism; only of their even greater fear of revolution.

III *The People, Popular Sovereignty and the Differentiation of the Constituent Power*

The concept of the people referring to the whole rather than a particular part of the political community represents a fundamental distinction between liberal, individualistic and earlier republican-corporate concepts.[66] It also points to an important difference between Hobbesian[67] and Lockeian theories, and thus an "achievement" in Locke's version of the contract theory.[68] This is so even if there are good grounds for treating "the people" as a "fiction," and preferring Hobbes' analytically (if not historically[69]) superior refusal to place a category between "multitude" and legally determined political status.[70] Both Hobbes and Locke use the same concept of the disorganized, atomized multitude [*Leviathan* XVI e.g.] from the legal, if not the anthropological point of view. Both assume unanimity before majority rule begins, and must, I think, for logical reasons if obligation is to be entirely general (*Leviathan* XVI; XVIII). But in Locke, unlike in Hobbes, unanimity, the horizontal and mutual agreement of all does "constitute" a body, variously referred to as the community, society, political society and the people. The different terms merely indicate sociological and political, passive and active perspectives on the same body of the whole. "People" represents an active, political perspective.

[66] M. Canovan, *The People* (London: Polity, 2005); J. McCormick, *Machiavellian Democracy* (Cambridge: Cambridge University Press, 2012).

[67] In Gierke's felicitous phrasing: "Hobbes dealt a death-blow to the idea, that the People possessed a separate personality (op. cit., 44)" " . . . the personality of the people died at its birth" (60). This may have been true in logic, but certainly not historically if we think of his successors, e.g., Sidney and Locke for starters.

[68] Again, this achievement was that of the publicists of the English Revolution, on various sides, as documented by Morgan. Indeed, it was anticipated by Monarchomach theorists in France (Morgan, op. cit., 56), building on late medieval theory and the related Staendestaatliche identification of estates and people (Franklin, op. cit., 1–7; Skinner, *The Foundations*, vol. 2), that the early parliamentary position documented by Morgan recovered. But in England the next steps were taken, as both Franklin and Morgan show, denying the identification between people and representatives. This is what Locke inherits and preserves, as well as makes into a more conservative principle than it was at the height of the English Revolution.

[69] Historically, before the emergence of a differentiated state power capable of legislation and coercion, there are indeed forms of society where even without positive law self-organization is possible. These regimes represent the rule of custom, customary law and diffuse enforcement, where unanimity concerning rules can be more or less assumed.

[70] It remains foundational for legal positivism: Cf. Kelsen, *General Theory*. Hobbes anticipated this argument in his double concept multitude/people in Elements 21: 11, curiously enough in a text that did put something between multitude and ruler/ruled differentiation, namely democracy, a form of sovereignty where the differentiation was not made. 21: 3 But even a democracy has an institutionalized "people" against which the members of the multitude would have only the very limited rights the Hobbesian theory allows under all forms of sovereignty.

For Hobbes, any such entity for which he generally uses the term commonwealth arises only through establishment of a form of unification endowed with
the power of the sword, or sanction. With respect to Locke and his own earlier
Elements of Law, there was therefore a stage missing in his analysis.[71] Thus
Hobbes will also treat the problem of resistance beyond single individuals as
that of the multitude,[72] whereas in Locke the possible struggle of society or
community against the government becomes a fundamental problem.

That difference admittedly is weakened by the fact that Locke very often
used the concept of the people without referring to any imaginable form of
organization, thus as a multitude concept. But the roots of Locke's conception
in authors such as Lilbourne, Overton, Lawson, Vale and Sidney[73] indicate
that "the people" in his theory could imply more than just another name for
the multitude, and it was this *more* that allowed him to restate, if in a more
conservative version, the already existing distinction between constituent and
constituted powers. That distinction itself, during the Puritan Revolution, was
already based on a concept of the people.

In Edmund Morgan's powerful analysis: 1. The claim of popular sovereignty,
a fictional authorization derived from a fiction, the whole united people,
was made by the English Parliament to counterpose an equal principle of
legitimation for a representative body to ideas of divine right monarchy, insisted
on by the first Stuarts.[74] 2. That claim of the representative body was challenged
by more radical elements in the revolution, arguing that the will of the people
is more convincingly embodied, variously, in the electorate, the counties,
the armies or new popular assemblies than in a parliament based on a very
distorted form of representation. 3. The Levellers, George Lawson, Sir Henry

---

[71] This stage was still there in *Elements*, ch. 21 in the form of democracy, out of which aristocracy
and monarch were said to emerge. This democratic beginning, gone when the contract was
made fully hypothetical, was not said to constitute any rights against aristocratic or monarchical
sovereigns. Leviathan was to make the argument more consistent, leaving only the multitude,
already presented in *Elements*, 21: 11, as the only foil facing the sovereign, whether democratic,
aristocratic or monarchical, now all on the same level.

[72] Schmitt, *The Leviathan in the State Theory of Thomas Hobbes* (Chicago: University of Chicago
Press, 2008).

[73] And Protestant and Catholic theorists of resistance, who mostly relied on distinctions among
the action of estates, legal magistrates, the people as a whole, and single individuals. In fact,
the resistance of established political bodies and officials dominated most conceptions still
informed by ständestaatliche constitutions, and when considering the resistance of the people as
a whole authors tended to have in mind representative estates. Skinner, *Foundations*, vols 1 and
2; Franklin, *John Locke and the Theory of Sovereignty* (New York: Cambridge University Press,
1978). There were some exceptions like Buchanan who seemed to foreshadow the Lockean
view, one actually more paradoxical than the earlier conceptions referring to organized forms.

[74] A similar logic in the case of the French Revolution is confirmed in M. Gauchet's excellent
book: *La revolution des pouvoirs* (Paris: Gallimard, 1995).

Vane, and even some followers of Cromwell himself then proceeded to work out various versions of the distinction between the constituent power of the people (organized in alternative, concrete forms) and the governmental power of parliament, the latter being forbidden to make constitutional changes even when based on a reformed representation.[75] 4. Locke adopted the conception to the outcome of the Glorious Revolution retroactively, justifying the results of the revolution as the work of the people, but making future revolutions of the same type very difficult to imagine.[76]

I find the highly suggestive concept of fiction in this context a bit misleading,[77] in that it could have the meaning of a purely imaginary, sociologically unreal entity used as rationalization, or legitimation in the most manipulative sense, as in the concept of "empty signifier" used by populist ideologists.[78] The concept works best if re-interpreted either narrowly (as in Gierke's "legal fiction"), or broadly, in terms of what I referred to as a principle of legitimation, always counterfactual, but not without referents in the political world that can justify its use to various degrees. The latter becomes possible, especially because of the structure noted by Morgan: a politically *workable* fiction cannot be so concrete as to be linked with a single, contestable form of organization (the case of Locke's forerunners) or so abstract that it could be applied to anything in an instrumental and fully undemanding manner (Locke comes close to this). Morgan thus implicitly understood fictions in terms of the normative requirements of legitimation, when he thus implies that the fiction cannot be too distant from reality to be a convincing source of support and obligation.

What is important for the moment however, is that the concept of the people as a principle of counterfactual legitimacy, historically and logically both, was the key to discovering an alternative source of institution creation, constitutional lawmaking, new not only with respect to divine will, tradition and custom, but also to governmental positive lawmaking. This was not possible, historically without the emergence of the modern notion of sovereignty.

---

[75] Following Julian Franklin's interpretation, in *John Locke and the Theory of Sovereignty*, we should not treat these options as parallel. It is obvious that the Levellers wanted to institutionalize popular sovereignty in some organizational form outside of parliament. And it may be that Lawson wanted to achieve both that goal, and the goal of protecting the stability of mixed government, goals, that could be seen after all as consistent and mutually re-enforcing.

[76] For a different, only slightly less plausible view of Locke see Franklin in *John Locke and the Theory of Sovereignty*.

[77] I have however no problem when the concept is restricted to law and juridical fictions as in the case of Gierke's four fictions.

[78] Laclau, *On Populist Reason* (New York: Verso, 2005) and my critique "Political Theology and Populism" *Social Research* 80.1 (2013).

Yet the strong, unlimited concept of sovereignty of Bodin and Hobbes, as *legibus solutus*, as we have seen, tended to absorb the legislative in the constituent power, or vice versa, it does not matter. Based on the concept of the people, the constituent could however be differentiated from the constituted, because the people could not easily be conceived, pace Rousseau, as an ordinary assembly or a legislature. As it is clear in Locke's forerunners, especially George Lawson,[79] the concept of the people allowed the carving out from state sovereignty, as understood in the path of Bodin and Hobbes, another dimension of at least equal, and possibly superior power, one that supposedly did not need to interfere with the normal functions of government.

It is worth reconstructing the Lockeian version that is formative for a tradition in America at least, with an eventual influence also on the continent via France, one that Rousseau was tempted to transform and adopt for his purposes.[80] Locke, in theory at least, allows agreement, or rather imputed agreement, sometimes diminished by his notion of consent, to be the only source of the legitimate political order. As in Lawson, it is this act that pre-constitutes, ideally speaking, a community-society-people as the *constituent power*. While he does not use the term, he does assign the body of the whole, acting by its majority, the original task of *"the constitution of the legislative"* (paras 149; 157) the highest (however, as already argued: not sovereign!) power in the state. What is constituted is referred to as a constitution even if not in the full modern sense that includes the dimensions of legal, and documentary. (The primary focus on the constitution of the legislature is however modern, anticipating Sieyès and Kelsen among others.) Locke assumes that the desirable outcome of this "constitution" would be a representative system with separation of powers, involving important limits on what even the government as a whole can do.

Equally important, as already argued, the body, or (as in England's tripartite scheme) the conjoined bodies, assigned the legislative power are forbidden to alter the legislative power itself (and, by implication, the other powers of government: the executive and the federative) (Lawson: ch. 4:8; ch. 8:9; *Second Treatise* paras 149; 157). This would be usurpation of the constituent power, and an abuse that could lead to tyranny by abolishing other powers in the state, extending terms and length of sessions, reducing franchise etc. Thus the idea of

---

79 *Politica Sacra et Civilis* 1660, corr. In 1689 C. Condren ed. (Cambridge, 1992).

80 While pride of place in terms of originality belongs to Lawson, it is Locke whose version was to influence posterity. The contrasts with Lawson made below will attempt to both clarify some aspects of Locke's theory, and indicate both some losses and gains with respect to the theorist whose conception of the people's constituent power seemed to decisively influence him (see Franklin op.cit.)

attributing to Locke the classical later idea of a British omnipotent legislature found in Blackstone e.g. is clearly erroneous.[81] This does not mean that Locke had any unambiguous theory of enforcement of these limits, and, even more crucially given the nature of the limits, that he could really make clear how the constitution could be significantly transformed, revised, or replaced.

Here we arrive at Locke's notion of the constituent power, though he does not literally use this term. Instead of reducing it to a mere right of resistance,[82] we should note its ambivalent nature. Admittedly it is not an arbitrary form of power, and its activation requires justification, as in Lawson's "just and necessary cause" (Ch. 4:8). Merely wanting a different or new constitution to make the people happier, or in order to get rid of unpopular personnel in government, or even to establish a preferable organization of power will not do, and the conservative psychology of the people (*Second Treatise* para. 223) will not allow rebellions for insubstantial reasons. There are, however, three differences with Lawson, and they are not entirely consistent with each other. First, unlike Lawson who seems to be silent on this issue, the constituent power is not an amending power. That would have required finding an institutional form for it, there in Lawson but not in Locke. Second, unlike in Lawson, the just and necessary cause is not understood merely as normative justification, but is related to empirical phenomena, in particular the self-dissolution of government. Third, self-dissolution itself is understood variously in empirical and normative terms, which seem to carry different implications. Indeed, the forms of normative justifications offered seem to represent a spectrum from the permissive to the highly constraining.

Locke clearly does not recognize any kind of less than revolutionary amending power inherent in the people or the community. Most likely, a careless reference to the people here would have, in his eyes, exposed the state to rebellion and constitutional instability every time the amending or reforming power came into play, even though he considers genuine and grave acts of usurpation and tyranny the major causes of rebellion, rather than diffuse dissatisfaction.[83] Thus, it is not the dissatisfied people themselves, nor especially the legislature, that can change the conditions of election. If there are relevant flaws, they can be dealt with by the people's trustee or the executive. Apparently, the well-known flaws of the English constitution and electoral system were not serious

---

[81] See Waldron's *the Dignity of Legislation* (Cambridge: Cambridge University Press, 1999) who confuses the matter of enforcement, as by judicial review, with the idea of lack of limitation – see Ch. 4.

[82] Colon-Rios, op. cit.

[83] Paras 224–226 [157]: Blackstone therefore relocated the power in the legislature, and thus drew the inevitable conclusion, given that amendments are legislation.

enough to Locke to be remedied by a solution that could lead to even greater problems, namely popular rebellion and the dissolution of government.

What clearly and unambiguously requires the activation of the constituent power in Locke is the self-dissolution of government, which initially seems to mean its collapse as an institution capable of functioning. When such conditions pertain there is neither an actual nor a legitimate authority, as under the hypothetical conditions established by the social contract but before the establishment of a form of government. Society in this case still preserves its corporate status, and must act to re-found government for the sake of its long-term survival and flourishing (para. 211). But problems arise already with this conception. First, governmental collapse may threaten the survival of the corporate body of the people (as a Hobbes would certainly predict). It is unconvincing to largely confine *societal* rather than state dissolution to foreign conquest alone, as does Locke. Intervention after actual governmental collapse however may come too late. Locke does seem to admit the possible legitimacy of pre-emptive action on the part of society, but is unable to show when it can be justified by impending governmental collapse. He seems to variously imply that loss of trust (para. 221) represents the most plausible time for pre-emptive activation of the constituent power, but does not clearly distinguish loss of trust in the stability as against the acceptable moral or political quality of a government. Indeed one could easily conclude from his presentation that tyranny is a cause for loss of trust, even though a tyrannical government can be unfortunately perhaps very stable.

Tyranny, whether of one man or a group, is defined by Locke in traditional terms, as lawless rule in the private interest of the ruler. As against "usurpation" (paras 197, 199) seen as the unlawful acquisition of power, tyranny seems to refer to an illegal and self-seeking transformation of originally legitimate power. Locke seems to be surprisingly skeptical concerning acts of collective (as against individual) acts of resistance to even such a power, detailing their likely negative consequences (paras 203, 204, 207 and 209) It is here that he first introduced the requirement of self-dissolution (205), initially interpreted in terms of a war of the tyrant or his officers against the people. It is the only context where Locke unambiguously consents to collective resistance against tyranny, and not only to usurpation. But he will not remain consistent on this subject when he turns to examine in detail the problem of dissolution of government.

As it will turn out, governmental (self-)dissolution as a war against the people is only its most obvious form, one that would not raise the question of pre-emption at all. When either the legislature or one of its parts reintroduces an internal state of war, in that case the rebels are not the people, but the relevant parts of government (paras 226–227). Thus, those who resist require no additional justification for their actions of armed rebellion or "liberation" and the refoundation of the polity or "constitution." Locke, however, lists several other meanings of dissolution, and unfortunately he oscillates between grave and lesser violations, often conflating therefore the meanings of factual and moral dissolution. While he defines the dissolution of the government as that of the "constitution of the legislative," it is clear that only some of his many examples are consistent with that definition (para. 212). Even in the very passage that provides it, complete collapse, alteration, being bypassed by unauthorized persons (including the executive) all seem to mean dissolution, and justify the people constituting a new legislative power. The most serious examples of an impermissible alteration of the legislature are the corruption of its members by the executive, and the alteration of the structure of the legislative power, by the body itself, namely the usurpation of the constituent power (paras 222, 227). Focusing on the tripartite structure of the legislature in England, he calls the subversion of that structure by any one of its parts, especially the prince or the ruler, also a form of dissolution (214). When the prince does not allow the assembly of the commons or the lords, or, inconsistently with his theory of amendment, changes their mode of election without their consent, that too counts (216). So does his unwillingness to execute the laws of the legislature (219), or, aiming at Catholics, the delivery of the commonwealth to subjection to a foreign power (217). In all these cases the people are free to change either the personnel or the form of government, as they see fit (220). But the same is said to be the case with a formally intact legislature that acts to take away the property or the personal freedom of the subjects (222). This is what is called a form of the violation of trust.

The point of this enumeration, and even more all the caveats attached to it, may have been to show that society or the people do not have the right to dissolve or initiate the dissolution of government, or to activate their constituent power unless there is very significant justification, and that therefore rebellions will not be frequent. Nevertheless, one is justified to think that a list like this provides many opportunities already known from the English history of the preceding century to justify rebellion and the refounding of government. Still it is not unfair to conclude that in the main argument, under normally functioning governments, the constituent power of the people seems to be quiescent in the Lockeian scheme. The people as a corporate body of the whole have an active status primarily in extra-ordinary situations. This is what gives a rise to an interpretation of Locke in terms of parliamentary omnipotence, one that is nevertheless incorrect, given the many limits on legislative power he clearly asserted. While the exclusion of the people in their corporate

capacity from government comes close to Blackstone's view, this position does
not exhaust Locke's perspective.

While for Hobbes, whom Blackstone follows, there is nothing outside government but a shapeless multitude composed of individuals, in Locke as well
as Lawson there is *something*: society, community or the people and it does,
contrary to Hobbes and Blackstone, have a corporate existence even without
the sword of government. Otherwise it would be incapable of majority vote,
a problem that Hobbes solved with the notion of democracy in the *Elements*,
a solution the Leviathan disregards. This means that it must have a kind of
constitution, a kind of organization (not necessarily one type or one kind, a
popular constituent assembly, as Toennies and Schmitt assumed,[84] wrongly
for Hobbes) and is capable of collective action unlike the mere multitude.[85]
Locke even goes so far as to make the corporate body of the people the judge
in fundamental controversies between the prince and a part of the people,
where the laws are silent (242). However inconsistently, this claim also allows
the activation of the constituent power without the dissolution of government,
or even without the need for pre-emption. Sieyès will find in Locke, or independently rediscover this relation of the constituent power to constitutional
judgment.[86] Indeed, many of the enumerated instances of the supposed dissolution of government by Locke, are occasions for constitutional judgment
and invalidation, rather than for the refounding of the constitutional order as
a whole.

But if it is a question of judging, who is to judge exactly when trust is lost
and it is legitimate to resist and to rebel and to make a new constitution? In
these cases, Locke seems to say that one of the parties will have to be judge on
behalf of its own cause, and only God and the people can be legitimately such
a judge (para. 242). As to the people, Paul Kelly is right to point to a paradox.
On the one hand the people as a whole can only do so as a majority, but outside
the legislative structures themselves that may be precisely in question, there is
no way in Locke at least to count up such a majority.[87] Yes, individuals, and
minorities can resist, on much broader grounds than in Hobbes e.g. but this
is not the same as reasserting the constituent power. The right of resistance is

---

[84] Schmitt, *The Leviathan in the State Theory of Thomas Hobbes* (Chicago: University of Chicago
Press, 2008).

[85] This dimension of Locke's thought is disregarded by Waldron who assimilates Locke therefore
entirely to Hobbes in this respect. The difference is only that Locke's prudential preference
for assembly supremacy is the reverse of that of Hobbes.

[86] First in *"Dire sur la question du véto royale"* in *Écrits politiques*, later in his post Thermidor
proposal for a constitutional jury ("Opinion de Sieyes" *Oeuvres*, III).

[87] Paul Kelly, *Locke's Second Treatise on Government* (New York: Continuum, 2007), pp. 133–134.

liberal. The right to exercise the constituent power is democratic. If a minority tries to exercise it, in Locke's scheme it too would be guilty of usurpation.

Thus, there are two trends in Lockean thought. One posits the existence of two supreme powers, and the unlikely activation of the second, the people's constituent power only when government collapses. Here the amending power to the extent that it exists at all falls to the royal prerogative. The other adds to this the people's judgment that there is a real danger of dissolution or perhaps also tyranny, in which case the constituent power, the truly supreme power is activated. This trend is potentially directed against misuse not only of the legislative, but also the prerogative power (para. 168). The theory, from the point of view of the classical theory of sovereignty is doubly antinomic, because it has two (even three) supreme powers, and two alternative scenarios of the conflict between them.

Locke's two achievements, the full differentiation between constituent and legislative power, and the conceptualization of both as limited i.e., non-sovereign, could have led directly to the theory of post sovereign constitution making. That it did not has a lot to do with the concept of the people as a collective actor. Once he adopts this notion, and he makes it hierarchically superior to the other powers that it can command, the idea that it cannot activate itself accept on special occasions and with sufficient cause, and that it must confine itself to generating a form of government but not laws, becomes unconvincing. The notion that in moments of constitution making, even when government has collapsed, the people do not have the powers of peace and war is even more so.

One interpretation of the concept of the people in Locke, relying on its corporate existence, and potentially pre-emptive, anti-tyrannical function points in the direction of Rousseau, and the idea of a sovereign constituent power. All that is missing is an organizational form, and that too could be said to be implicit in the form of mobilized, direct democracy. This notion would lead back to the sovereignty doctrine, as embodied in a direct democratic organ or set of organs. A second interpretation, based on the notion of a limited form of supremacy, and intervention only in the extreme case of government dissolution or open tyranny, would yield a collective right of resistance. This would amount to a conservative interpretation of Locke, closer to English ideas of parliamentary sovereignty than he probably wished to be. With Locke's own concept of the people, one cannot easily take the step to a third interpretation, post-sovereign constitution making, where institutionally developed forms of extra-ordinary democratic politics would receive a role in both constitution amending and replacement. In such a conception, judging would be the task of judges. In order for these moves to be possible, another step was needed in the move from sovereignty to limited supremacy, namely the development of a notion of the people or the nation able to encompass societal plurality and division, beyond unitary embodiment. That would happen in the late nineteenth-century German *Staatslehre*, as well as early twentieth-century French public law. But its presupposition is the doctrine of the separation of powers.

IV *Separation of Powers*

The differentiation between constituent and constituted powers seemed to require the notion of popular sovereignty at least historically and arguably logically. As Egon Zweig's old and unfortunately nearly forgotten work has shown, logically the notion could also be derived from a Montesquieuian separation of powers.[88] And as more recent work by Julian Franklin has demonstrated, even in the English revolutions, the doctrine of mixed government, the antecedent of the separation of powers could play the key role in trying to formulate yet another fundamental power in the state.[89] That power could be given to the amorphous people, but it could be given to some existing bodies outside of central government or to a combination of these with one or another central organ. In short, all conceptions of power division among different agencies and institutions[90] were conducive to the development of yet another power that in extra-ordinary settings plays a constituent role, whether an entirely separate form or a combination where all or most of the existing state powers have to participate in its operation.

According to Julian Franklin, in England on the road leading to Lawson and Locke, the logically incompatible goals of maintaining the stability of the form of mixed, tripartite government and asserting the right of deposition of the king (first potential, than actual) played an important role. The power to depose could not be given to the chambers of parliament, to the estates of the realm as in Monarchomach theories, without undermining the balance among king, lords and commons in the English constitutional system. The solution was found in terms of asserting a fourth power, the constituent power that could alter and transform even the form of government, and certainly could depose a king deemed tyrannical. This step corresponds, of course, to the migration of the imputed notion of popular sovereignty from parliament to other bodies

---

[88] E. Zweig *Die Lehre von Pouvoir Constituant* (Tübingen: J. C. B. Mohr, 1909).

[89] Franklin, *John Locke and the Theory of Sovereignty*.

[90] Including mixed government and separation of powers, but also, as Dicey will note for the United States, the division of powers in federalism.

and agencies, as in Morgan's analysis. Thus, historically the argument cannot be entirely separated from notions of popular sovereignty. Yet logically, it may be prior to and can be differentiated from it. The argument anticipates an effort, whereby the branches of government are denied the power to change their own jurisdiction to the expense of other branches. As Sieyès for one noticed, the problem could be dealt with by checks and balances such as the royal veto.[91] This solution of course leads to a strongly conservative outcome, making not only usurpation but also significant constitutional change very difficult, and it is for this reason that Sieyès was to reject it. Another solution would imagine yet another power, exercised by another body in the state. If it were another governmental body however, the danger of usurpation would then arise on its behalf. This was one of the points for assigning the role to the people, and even Locke's reluctance in developing a concrete organizational form for it. An extra-ordinary power had to be kept extra-ordinary.

But there also could be extra-ordinary forms of organization, like the convention in its original meaning in America.[92] As we have seen already, much depends on the form of organization or mobilization imagined for the people that alone supposedly have the constituent power, and the postulates concerning the legitimate use and activation of that power. In Lawson, concrete organizational forms such as an expanded convention were imagined, along with relatively easy activation. In Locke, there was no organization, and the opportunity for constitutive action was reduced, inconsistently, only to extreme cases. But even then, Locke faced the problem how the people could assume this role and yet be deprived or deprive themselves of all other governmental roles. This is a problem that would be difficult to solve within the model of mixed government Franklin focused on, because in that model inherited from Rome all "branches" exercise all the governmental functions.

Part of the solution lay in the move from mixed government, to the separation of powers, a move anticipated by Locke but in a version no more followed than Rousseau's later one. It is the scheme of Montesquieu, one of relatively strict separation of institutions as well as functions that had the greatest influence, but this version neither stressed popular sovereignty, nor included a notion of the constituent power.[93] Yet when there are different powers, it remained important for each that none of the others have the power to unilaterally change the constitutional rules of their relationship,

---

[91] *"Dire sur la question du véto royale"* in *Écrits politiques*, op. cit.

[92] Morgan, op. cit; G. Wood *The Creation of the American Republic* (Chapel Hill: University of North Carolina Press, 1969).

[93] Vile, op. cit.

of the distribution of power.[94] Moreover, as Sieyès thought, it was exactly the version of Montesquieu that most required a separate notion of the constituent power, because in it the other powers were linked to the most rigid limitation to a single function.[95] Two of them, the "more dangerous branches" of the legislative and the executive (Hamilton), were, of course, capable of usurpation. We might also add that the third, the judicial, was historically too weak. Moreover, both the executive and the legislature could utilize the very powers traditionally used to inhibit usurpation by the other, impeachment or veto, to foster their own unconstitutional goals.

After Montesquieu, historically, two ideas could be used, sometimes separately and sometimes in combination, to protect the separation of powers from its own branches, namely the constituent power and review by the least dangerous branch. Assigning either of these forms only a very specific function, amendments needed to correct or inhibit, or judicial invalidation by an entirely new and more powerful type of court, would conceivably block usurpation attempts without empowering a new entity that too could usurp the powers of others. Yet we now know full well that the solution by the judiciary is itself very much open to the charge of usurping other powers, generally the legislative, the charge once called *"gouvernement des juges"* and now going under the name of "juristocracy".[96] That issue did not arise till relevant experience, toward the very end of the nineteenth century. Today, in the United States at least, few people would call the judiciary the least dangerous branch. The amending power was, of course, always in principle a corrective of the judicial one, and perhaps it is for this reason that they were initially combined as in the case of the Pennsylvania censors, and the constitutional jury of Sieyès. Yet the problem also arises in the case of the constituent and amending powers, in France under the heading of "convention government". If the power to correct or inhibit is understood through the function of constitution making, what is to stop the constitution maker from aggrandizing its own power thereby? What is to stop the amending power from attacking the basic structure of the constitution?

---

94 This is the dimension stressed by Franklin, op. cit. and will come back in interpretations of Sieyès stressing his debt to Montesquieu see Carré de Malberg, *Contribution à la générale Théorie de l Etat* (1920) (Paris: Dalloz, 2004).

95 Equally important, for the post sovereign conception, Montesquieu's separation of powers banned any embodiment of popular sovereignty in an operative political power. The same was true for Kant, who insisted on separation of powers even more than Montesquieu. See Gierke, op. cit., 52–153; 158.

96 É. Lambert, *Le gouvernement des juges* [1921 ed.] (Paris: Dalloz, 2005); R. Hirschl, *Towards Juristocracy* (Cambridge: Harvard University Press, 2004).

Within the separation of powers scheme, there were three possibilities of guarding against usurpation. One was the abovementioned scheme of checks and balances, which Vile has shown represented fusion with elements of the doctrine of mixed government.[97] Each branch would accordingly police its own integrity by being able to check the others' usurpatory actions, by partially assuming functions of another. This is the conservative option, advocated by *Federalist* 51 after criticizing the Pennsylvania censors, and the Jeffersonian theories of frequent constitutional amendments (Numbers 48–50.) The second was the one associated with Sieyès, and radicalized by Carl Schmitt. This approach postulates a fourth power, the constituent one, and puts it on an entirely other, deeper and more powerful level than governmental powers. Yet as Locke first realized, and periodically Sieyès too, it would be difficult to distinguish this power from popular sovereignty, and keep it from assuming all other powers in the state.

A third approach, contained within the Pennsylvania censor scheme as well as the Sieyès jury but best developed by Condorcet,[98] was to establish a fourth power – one partly side by side with the others, restricted to one or two fundamental functions, amendment and replacement, a power that could have a governmental as well as a popular participatory component. Some modern amendment rules incorporate this idea, one that in the case of Condorcet amounted to a domestication and legalization of the radical idea of the constituent power. It is this third possibility that points to the deep link between the separation of powers and the post sovereign model of constitution making, freed of the notion of the embodiment of an imaginary popular sovereign.

More than the constituent power is at stake. The model of the separation of powers allows a reformulation of the doctrine of popular sovereignty, which then could also point in the post-sovereign direction. Relying both on a trend within the thought of the American and French Revolutions, and the German *Staatslehre*, R. Carré de Malberg came up with a concept of national sovereignty that contested any claim of the embodiment of the people in any institution, or organ of the state, including even direct democratic practices.[99] It was the idea of the separation of powers that led him and his forerunners to contest the real presence of the people's will not only in any of the branches of government, but also all the other institutions and movements that have

---

[97] Vile, op. cit.

[98] "*Projet de constitution Française*" Title IX in *Oeuvres*, vol. XII (Stuttgart: Fromman Verlag, 1968). See my chapter 5, below for more details.

[99] Op. cit. *Contribution à la générale Théorie de l Etat* (1920) (Paris: Dalloz, 2004).

made similar claims. The new idea of the people or the nation that emerges from this conception is a negative principle of legitimacy, referring to a whole that cannot by definition be embodied in a part, and can be represented only through plurality and division, leaving the power of the king an empty place.[100]

V *Political Theology and Revolution*

The alternative that for a long time became dominant, intellectually and politically, involved filling that empty space. The best interpretations of this choice point in the direction of political theology, namely to the interpretation of the people as a secularized monotheistic divinity, with sovereign power, above all law, beyond or on a normatively deeper level than any possibility of the separation of powers.

We have seen in the preceding sections that contract, sovereignty, the people and the separation of powers could all be interpreted as leading to either the sovereign or the post-sovereign conception of the constituent power. Having differentiated state and constitution making, contract could imply constitution making without limits, in the state of nature, *or* under the fundamental norms established by the contract. Sovereignty could be interpreted as outside of law, *or* under it. The people could be embodied, *or* represented only by plurality, and even then imperfectly. And, finally, the separation of powers could entail an unlimited meta-power on a different level than the other powers of the state, *or* a constituent power confined to a specific tasks, under rules.

It is not mysterious why all these options survive, since each is associated with distinguished interpreters and important political traditions. What is nevertheless astonishing, is that in historical projects dedicated to liberation and the establishment of free institutions, namely revolutions, the sovereign alternative, with its logical and empirical links to dictatorship is almost always the dominant one. This is a question that deeply puzzled Hannah Arendt, but because she relied on American exceptionalism even she could not fully answer it. Most certainly, she could not make a proposal according to which the post-sovereign alternative could be formulated and reinforced. For that we had to wait for this alternative to become more universally important in the world of politics than the historically unique case of the United States.

Let us leave aside the question of causality, inevitably very complex, with the political process of revolutions having played a role in the emergence or modernization of the alternative ideas of contract, sovereignty, people and

---

[100] C. Lefort, *Democracy and Political Theory* [DPT] (Cambridge, MA: MIT Press, 1989).

powers, during which these very ideas helped to orient and channel revolutionary processes and the political options within them. For the moment, we should be satisfied with the notion that the search for an alternative form of legitimacy capable of competing with that of divine right led to a conceptualization of the people and its sovereignty in political theological terms. The very rupture of revolutions, with their gaping legitimacy problem, made this solution plausible, one that has been thematized as early as Sieyès' post-Thermidor address to the Convention,[101] and utilized since then by Tocqueville, Arendt, Lefort, Morgan, and Gauchet, among many others. The people were the new absolute power, put into the empty conceptual seat of the sacerdotal king, uniting authority and power. This was ultimately the place of the divinity, implying freedom from law, omnipotence, and the unity of all powers. What even Arendt did not understand, however, was that the sovereign idea was never uncontested in France, and the Americans also did not unambiguously banish sovereignty from the domain of constitution making.

VI *Rousseau as the Heir of both Hobbes and Locke*

Rousseau may have taken the most important intellectual steps to the sovereign theory, but even he did not yet go the full distance.[102] While clearly a political theologian, as Carl Schmitt noted,[103] he was also a republican thinker with a distinct stress on the rule of law, and the fear of tyranny. It is not only that he had a doctrine of the separation of powers. His two powers, legislative and governmental, were on entirely different levels. The sovereign legislature, the people, were prior to all law and not under it. Yet he utilized the figure of

---

[101] "*Opinion de Sieyes, sur plusieurs articles de titres IV et V du projet de constitution*" in *Oeuvres*, vol. III (Paris: EDHIS, n.d.).

[102] As Joel Colon-Rios seems to suggest, in "Rousseau, Theorist of the Constituent Power" (forthcoming in 2016 in the *Oxford Journal of Legal Studies*). I have read the ms. of this article, one with many interesting points in it after completing this book. I should, however, make clear that I do not agree with its claim that the Rousseau of the Social Contract differentiated constituent and legislative power. It is based on the notion, incorrect textually, in light of Rousseau's distinction among political, civil and criminal law, that he meant constitution every time he wrote law. It goes without saying that I reject the radical populism of Colon Rios (see chapter 6 of my *Post Sovereign Constitution Making*) that he wishes to reinforce through Rousseau's normative doctrine, which arguably anticipated elements of populism. Rousseau himself however, applied his own doctrine, in *The Government of Poland*, in a conservative-reformist manner. It is only in that work that we see a tendency to distinguish the constituent and the legislative, in an ingenious attempt to partially save the old institution of the *liberum veto*. Even his defense of the imperativ mandate in that text adopted an existing Polish institution, not for the needs of a direct democratic constituent power, but for a conception of federalism.

[103] *Political Theology*, vol. I (Chicago: University of Chicago Press, 1985), p. 46.

the *législateur* to indicate not only cognitive deficiency, at the time of original constitution making at least, but also a continued problem of authority.[104] He noted the importance of religious authorization, with Machiavelli, presumably because the self-authorization of the secular god, the people, was insufficient. Nevertheless, the concept of sovereignty in his work, traditional in spite of the popular turn he gave it, did not allow the differentiation of law making power. Relying on his particular doctrine of popular sovereignty, he could develop only a constituent power that absorbed the legislative. Evidently he combined several Hobbesian and Lockean moves in his theory, in a highly original way that superimposed them unto the already discussed republican foundation, using elements like the legislator and the dictator largely absent in liberal contract theory.[105] I would stress the following elements as important:

1. The first lines of chapter 1 of the Social Contract indicate the funda-
    mental interest in the problem of *legitimacy*. We should take extremely
    seriously Rousseau's only half serious declaration that he does not know
    the actual origin of political forms, and can only explore what can make
    (some of) them legitimate. This means that the contract will be hypo-
    thetical, as in Hobbes, and the principles deduced from the ideas of state
    of nature, contract and even constitutional law making are to be under-
    stood as norms or standards that can be imputed to some existing or
    possible political formations. This must be so even if the language of the
    treatise generally implies a fundamental political model, within which
    the classical three types of government appear as alternatives, less impor-
    tant than the model of sovereignty. Unless we make this assumption, the
    Rousseauian dimension in the thought of the French Revolution, and
    specifically Sieyès, cannot be made sense of, because whatever they were
    doing, they were not actualizing Rousseau's social contract scheme.[106]

---

[104] That Rousseau's understanding of the difference between power and authority was the most sophisticated in the history of classical political thought is indicated not only by his treatment of the figure of the law giver in the *Social Contract*, but even more his analysis of the form of kingship compatible with a republic in a large, federated polity in *The Government of Poland*, pp. 52–53.

[105] Hobbes mentions the dictatorship, but given the absolutist government flowing from his sovereignty doctrine does not need it in his scheme. The Lockean prerogative represents, in my view, an absolutist remnant that actually is more authoritarian than Machiavelli's theory of dictatorship. The lawgiver is replaced by the contract in theory, and alas, by force in practice in liberal conceptions that is to be made legitimate in ways discussed here, including result already discussed by Machiavelli.

[106] Or for that matter his more realistic alternative in *The Government of Poland*. Almost no one who mattered during the Revolution proposed any developed version of direct democracy or the imperative mandate for the legislatures. Federalism too was promoted only by the losers, some of the Gironde and their supporters in the provinces.

2. As against Locke, Rousseau completely recovers the Hobbesian concept of *sovereignty* as a single, unified center of ultimate power, capable of legislating on all matters, but itself outside and above all law.[107] The social contract here too produces a sovereign legislator. This agency, however, is identical to the body of the *people*, a point that seems to resemble the origin of the community = society = people in Locke, except that here it is called sovereign = state = people, a more modern triad. It could also be said, however, that of the three types of sovereignty understood as equally legitimate by Hobbes, Rousseau chooses only the popular "democratic" one. And it could be said that Rousseau's synthesis of sovereignty and people returns to the views of Lawson. But, and this is important, there is only one sovereign in Rousseau, both in general conception and in the powers that are assigned. He thinks it is fundamental that government or any of its parts should not become a second sovereign (III: 1), even though he has difficulty not assigning a corporate status to executive government.[108] Otherwise it is true that his notion of the popular sovereign resembles (indeed: radicalizes) that of Lawson's real sovereignty as the highest power of the state. Even more radically, it is here that all power returns not only when government is in crisis, but also whenever the sovereign assembly wishes without the need of justification, the opportunity being provided at regular intervals. In Rousseau, there is no need even for Lawson's "just and necessary cause" to activate the sovereign power in the constituent sense. In terms of the most traditional absolutist principle inherited from Roman law,[109] each sovereign assembly begins with two questions, one of which is: "Does it please the sovereign to preserve the present form government?" (Book III: 18).[110]

---

[107] "*Princeps legibus solutus est*" or: "the prince is not bound by the laws," according to Ulpian's maxim.

[108] See Gierke, who calls this "filling the void of representation." Op. cit., 130. In general, Gierke's reconstruction of Rousseau is very intelligent, even if the idea that the conception makes constitutionalism impossible because of the constituent power of the sovereign is perhaps an overreaction, even given its affinity with Carré de Malberg's critique of sovereign constitution making on which I rely below.

[109] Ulpian's second famous maxim: *Quod principi placuit legis habet vigorem* or: "What pleases the prince has the force of law."

[110] He retreats from this idea in *The Government of Poland*, where following one idea inherited from contract theory he distinguished between the unanimity (in Poland: the use of the liberum veto) legitimately required in constitution making and fundamental revision, and the majority principle to be used for ordinary legislation and administrative acts in order to avoid "anarchy." With this stress he took a step toward the differentiation of the constituent power, one that was in that form probably without influence at the time. The fact that the *Sejm* was a

3. In order to make his a true form of sovereignty moreover, Rousseau gives it a temporary coercive power (before the creation of government, and it seems by implication during the times the sovereign is (re)assembled). This is the insufficiently known but important idea of the sovereign organized as a provisional governing power, as a "democracy," before legislation creates or institutes a more permanent government (III: 17, also 14). The difficulty Rousseau wishes to solve is how there can be law without sanction, or as he says "an act of government before government exists." Since democracy is the form where the whole would take on executive functions (acting perhaps through temporary committees as he says in relation to the British parliament), the sovereign can solve this problem by provisionally becoming a democracy. The self-transformation is presumably only provisional because of the disadvantages of democracy as he defines it. But if that were nevertheless the form adopted, the provisional arrangement could be made into a permanent one (that is until the next session of the sovereign assembly). This argument anticipates the pattern of the 1793 *Convention Nationale*, and, more generally, the need for provisional governments during sovereign constitution making projects, to be sure, if we forget that these rarely had the democratic form Rousseau postulated.[111]

4. Against Hobbes, and with Locke, the popular sovereign is, strictly speaking, not government, or can be that only in a provisional form. Against Locke, it is a legislature, and the job of constitutional lawmaking is only to constitute the executive. Government means the executive only, and is the result of institution or legislation, not a contract, a point forgotten by many Rousseauians in the Revolution (III: 1; 16; 18).[112] State and constitution making are now fully differentiated. As the result of the contract, the people = state = sovereign makes laws, including constitutional laws that produce government. Moreover, like Locke but against Hobbes' counsel on mixed governments, Rousseau is able to develop a theory of the separation of powers. The sovereign is only a legislature, except in

representative body helped him make the distinction, anticipating the same reason playing a key role for Sieyès. Involving many levels of voting, between unanimity and simple majority, depending on the type of decision involved, Rousseau's conception was more subtle than that of Sieyès. On this issue of the multi-leveled constitution, see chapter 5 below.

[111] The French National Convention, elected through universal manhood suffrage, came closest, though it too was a representative body. Its executive committees, and, above all, the Committee of Public safety played the executive role Rousseau assigned for such a context, though he did not (unlike Schmitt later) understand its likely dictatorial form.

[112] On their conflicts, see Baker, *Invention*.

constitution making moments. Otherwise, Rousseau has similar doubts about "democracy" where the people exercise also executive power, as will Kant, namely that it makes separation of powers impossible (III: 4). But since unlike Locke, Rousseau famously banishes representation from the legislature (III:15), the most important power in his scheme is, in our terminology as well as by Greek precedents, directly democratic.

5. Thus, the sovereign people are understood here as a constituent power that produces all the laws, with the crucial difference that initially this happens on the recommendation of the expert legislator. That republican feature separates ever so slightly (and perhaps on a one-time basis only!) constitution making and legislation, but much more clearly authority and power, as already said, namely the classical Roman republican differentiation of *auctoritas* and *potestas*, whose absence Rousseau laments in the case of the decemviri. Again, that original restriction does not seem to bind future constituent acts of the popular sovereign that can remake (as in Hobbes) any laws, including all and any fundamental laws and transform the contract itself (III: 18) without apparently any need for lawgivers,[113] who are outside the state and have no office in it, though it is still unclear whether the sovereign has the right to (probably not) to abolish or replace popular sovereignty itself, the only legitimate form! (In Hobbes there was an option among three equally legitimate forms, among whom the choice is merely prudential.) The right and power to break and transform the social pact, while unclear in Rousseau, may then be taken to refer to the extensive structure of the state (territory and population), the parts of multitudes it may include or exclude at its foundation.

6. Thus, in Rousseau's presentation the constituent power is not based on a Lockean double differentiation from the legislative power. Indeed, as in Hobbes, but using a different device, the two powers are differentiated only to the extent that original constitution making is not identical to later lawmaking. As in Hobbes, this is a consequence of the strong theory

---

[113] Colon-Rios, op. cit. makes the interesting claim, based on a letter of Rousseau (*Letter to Beaumont*), that he meant to keep the legislator within a republican system. Whether this was generally true I cannot tell, but the idea in fact contradicts the claim that Rousseau discovered the popular constituent power of Sieyès and Schmitt. To translate the legislator as a constituent assembly, and not even an American type convention, wrongly assumes that the device of the referendum was always used by such bodies. More importantly, what happens to the imperative mandate, if the people are reconceived as the citizen body in a referendum? If the constituent assembly is supposed to play the role of Rousseau's legislator, its deliberations must be free.

of sovereignty. There is, however, a reversal in the Rousseau of the *Social Contract*. The constituent power is very broad, and it embraces and absorbs the legislative one. In Hobbes (as in the main line of the British tradition) the reverse was the case: a governmental power, whether the king's or an assembly's could encroach on constituent functions by altering fundamental laws, and even this, initially, more by implication than outright attribution as in later thought e.g. Blackstone's.

7.   What is nevertheless surprising is the absence of the type of differentiation, double in Locke, which we have ascribed to the postulate of the people distinguished from government. The *Social Contract* has that postulate, and yet does not fully differentiate constituent and legislative powers. The strong doctrine of sovereignty leads to a form of constituent power, one that also absorbs the legislative one. But why is it impossible to generate a legislative power that is forbidden to alter its own constitutional foundation, which in other words lacks constituent power? The reason is obvious (and will be reversed by both the Rousseau of the *Government of Poland*, and by Sieyès!): the absence of representation, and the affirmation of direct democracy that leaves no room for two legislative powers. We should recall that the decemviri were elected, and thus even the related problem of the differentiation of the authority and power seems to be most serious in Rousseau's eyes for an elected but not a directly democratic body.[114] Historically, the concept of representation was a necessary assumption of the development traced by Morgan, with the result that for someone like Lawson the concept of the people (implying "the whole people" [ch 4: 9]) could imply a difference between the constituent power and the power of representatives. However fictionally, the people were then understood as the real body of the whole against parliament, which was its merely symbolic body. By famously banishing representation from the legislature as a medieval form of heteronomy (correct in terms of history and British practice of the time), and by postulating a direct democratic sovereign, Rousseau surrenders the tension between two powers capable of legislating in the name of the people, directly and by representation, making fundamental and ordinary law. The representative organs he postulates, government or the magistrates, are only executive, in other words inferior, and must be in his scheme (quite unrealistically of course) deprived of all and any legislative power (III:1; 15). This is what leads to the re-absorption of

---

[114] In the case of an elected body, even when bound by the imperative mandate, he differentiates power (the legislature's) and authority (the king's). See *The Government of Poland*.

legislative powers in the constitutive power, and ends the possibility of double differentiation.

8. There is another expansion of the constituent power in Rousseau, and it involves the discovery of the amending power albeit in a form that does not distinguish it at all from the original *pouvoir constituant* (unless we assume the unmentioned absence of the legislator to be that distinction). This step beyond Locke, anticipating (and perhaps inspiring) one of Jefferson's schemes and more likely also Condorcet's 1793 constitutional proposal, opens up an option mentioned only by Locke: the people freely judging when there is need for constitutional revision or renovation. But in Locke there is nothing to activate or "justify" such judgment except forms of usurpation and injustice, and possibly when it is already too late. Since Rousseau's popular sovereign is also the legislative body, it meets regularly, and it automatically activates the amending power as its first order of possible (not necessary) business. It is true that technically the amending power is understood as a full exercise of the constituent power, deconstituting the old form, and creating a new one.[115] Of course Rousseau leaves the door open to the integration of new elements in the old form, one which would be formally renewed. The scheme is difficult to operationalize once representation is accepted, though Condorcet was to make a brilliant if futile attempt.[116]

As powerful as the Rousseauian synthesis was, containing also the important distinction between power and authority that he himself could not consistently maintain, the lack of institutional differentiation between constituent and constituted powers represented a step back from Locke.[117] Thus Rousseau helped to create the foundations of the sovereign conception, that despite the conscious efforts of Sieyès, the one who first fully elaborated it, indeed involved great difficulty in maintaining the double differentiation inherited from Locke. Admittedly some of Locke's weaknesses invited a cure by using the concept of sovereignty. This could at the time be understood only in terms of organ sovereignty and not the abstract state sovereignty concept under law that

---

[115] Cf. Beaud, op. cit., pp. 224 ff.

[116] "Projet de constitution Française," Title IX, op. cit.

[117] Again, there is no institutional differentiation even in *The Government of Poland*, only the distinction between voting by unanimity and by different types of majority in the elected national legislature. In South Africa during the controversies of the 1950s such a device was referred to by D.V. Cowen as having two legislatures. But in my context at least this argument seems artificial given the possibility that there indeed can be separate bodies making the respective decisions. See: I. Loveland, *By Due Process of Law? Racial Discrimination and the Right to Vote in South Africa, 1855–1960* (Oxford: Hart Publishing, 1999).

would have been compatible with the Lockean notion of double supremacy. For this reason, when Lockean representation was added back to the theory, the sovereign conception could not be used to make sense of a notion of the people that could, organizationally, retain its full constituent powers only in Rousseau's directly democratic scheme. In transferring sovereignty to the representative body that alone could exercise it, the way was opened to the development of the theory in a direction implying constitutional dictatorship on behalf of the people.

VII *The Constituent Power According to Sieyès, as Interpreted by Schmitt*[118]

The theory of sovereign constitution making was fully developed by E.J. Sieyès, through a version of his theory of the constituent power that would become the dominant and best-known one. It was further elaborated and system-atized by Carl Schmitt in two twentieth-century texts: *Die Diktatur* (1921) and *Verfassungslehre* (1928). In all these versions the theory's debt to Rousseau was enormous,[119] which is clearly admitted by Schmitt.[120] In one well-known con-struct Schmitt presents Sieyès' doctrine of the constituent power as involving a synthesis of Rousseau's concepts of dictatorship and lawgiver, as giving the *législateur* the powers of *le dictateur* (the dictator) or of *la dictature* (dictator-ship), producing a dictatorial lawgiver or a lawgiving dictator, and bringing the giver of laws into the state as a magistrate like the dictator, if an extra-ordinary one. Schmitt considers the move inevitable to break the circle he already dis-covers in Rousseau's concept of the people: the *législateur*'s recommendation does not become law without the affirmative vote (interpreted as a kind of referendum here) of the people, but the people are incapable of giving such a

---

[118] I interpret Sieyès as antinomic, implying the possibility of two very different interpretations of the main trajectory of his work. Again, here I focus on the best known, most influential version, which was propagated above all by Carl Schmitt, and became the foundation for the sovereign conception. The next chapter will explore both the other trajectory, and also the antinomy itself.

[119] Earlier versions of the concept, if not the theory, of the constituent power were generated in the English Revolution as well as authors influenced by it, Lawson, Locke and Harrington, as well as many of the thinkers and participants of the American Revolution, above all the authors of the *Federalist* and Jefferson. Along with the American practice, as well as Montesquieu, they were to influence Sieyès, in working out elements of a second, less dominant or even known conception that never came together as a theory either then or later. I will present this alternative below, when I treat the antinomic American variant of sovereign constitution making, and its influence.

[120] *Die Diktatur*, 7th printing of second ed. of 1921 original (Berlin: Duncker & Humblot, 1928) pp. 114ff.

vote when not under law, or already formed by law.[121] He considers the great soul of the lawgiver, his charisma, not to speak of religion, an unreliable and inconsistent means of breaking the circle: *"Was geschieht, wenn die Abstimmung gegen das weise Gesetz und die große Seele entscheidet?"* Only power will do as an answer, taking a step back toward Machiavelli's view of politics which he cites positively.[122] In other words, returning to the second of my questions raised in the introduction (of whether or not sovereign constitution making is possible) Schmitt, the author of *Die Diktatur*, answers no, or not in the version of Rousseau's popular sovereignty, because the people it is supposed to rely on is not produced by the contract and therefore cannot be found prior to the constitution. It is not even possible in the dualistic version of the theory of *Du contract social*, because despite the great soul of the legislator, and with all his authority, he has no power. Sovereign constitution making is however possible, but only in the form of *sovereign dictatorship*. The resulting new concept of the sovereign dictator, one fusing power and authority,[123] according to Schmitt was thus the commissioner not of a constituted power like the Roman type of dictator defended by Machiavelli and Rousseau, but of the new figure supposedly introduced by Sieyès, the *pouvoir constituant* of the people.[124]

Sieyès was indeed proud to have introduced the notion of constituent power, even though he was hardly the first to use it.[125] But to be sure he never spoke of dictatorship, which was instead left to his critics, like J.J. Mounier.[126] Moreover, he could have been aware of Rousseau's warnings about fusing sovereign power and constitution-making authority, and its tyrannical or despotic implications. While Schmitt too does not fully merge sovereignty as such and legislative

---

[121] This is a serious admission that he will more or less forget or suppress as he goes along. But see *Die Diktatur*, pp. 125–126. Schmitt interprets the circularity in the formation of the people in terms of the formation of a true general will, based on justice and enlightenment – characteristics Rousseau did not consider fundamental for generality. But Schmitt is right to notice the contradiction: according to Rousseau the sovereign cannot assemble, either regularly or in an extra-ordinary manner accept when lawfully assembled. Illegal assemblies and their results are said to be null and void (II. 13). This argument breaks down for the origins of law, since the social contract is not itself law. In that case the people should not be able to assemble at all without power and authority exercised by another entity. The paradox is well known, but not that Schmitt too has admitted it, and that he answered it with his theory of sovereign dictatorship that is an answer, but is based on state rather than popular sovereignty.

[122] Ibid., p. 126; cf. 6–9.

[123] Schmitt at times fuses and other times separates power and authority. In the case of the supposed constituent power of the people, as against the monarch, this tendency is unification in an identity. See Chapter 1 of my *Post Sovereign Constitution Making*.

[124] *Die Diktatur*, sixth ed., pp. 126; 134ff; 143.

[125] Post Thermidor address: *"Opinion de Sieyes"* op. cit.

[126] Noted by Carré de Malberg in *Contribution*, op. cit. See also R.R. Palmer, *The Age of the Democratic Revolution*, vol. I (Princeton: Princeton University Press, 1959), pp. 489–500.

authority,[127] the concept of sovereign dictatorship seems to involve at least an extra-ordinary, if temporary synthesis of all three concepts: sovereignty, authority and power. And admittedly it is based on a serious reading of the most famous Sieyès text, *Qu'est-ce que le Tiers État?* This can be best seen positively and negatively. The nation as the constituent power is treated by Sieyès as the only relevant actor with both power and, implicitly, authority. This actor is prior and superior to all constitutional law, as well as the separation of powers. It is repeatedly described as unlimited in law, and bound by no procedure, whether legal or even ethical. At the same time, Rousseau's concept of the *législateur* or any substitute never makes any kind of appearance in Sieyès, despite his own considerable role in making recommendations to the third estate of the *Estates General*, to the *Assemblée Constituante*, and later even the *Convention Nationale*. He even successfully opposed submitting the Constituent Assembly's product, as a mere recommendation, for the approval to the electorate in referendum. This resistance to a version of a dualism that already had important American precedents indicates a shift to a more consistent modern version of a theory of sovereign constitution making. It makes plausible an interpretation according to which Sieyès united the ultimate source of authority and power in the same entity.[128] It also opens the road to Schmitt's interpretation of Sieyès in terms of dictatorship, although this is not, as we will see in the following chapter, the only one possible.

Indeed Sieyès' own link to the problem of dictatorship exists on a deeper level than abandoning the Rousseauian dualism of power and authority, or suspending the separation of powers and legal limits. As is well known, he explicitly goes beyond Rousseau in accepting the concept of representation in the legislative power. This move, one that would otherwise only put him in the camp of liberal democracy, had devastating consequences given the fact that otherwise he adopted the implications of Rousseau's sovereignty doctrine for his notion of the constituent power. It is certain that he worked out his view concerning representation first.[129] After one of the very best critiques of direct democracy in a large country, and any project to link together direct democratic bodies through imperative mandates and repeated renewal of

---

[127] In his view the sovereign dictator is the commissioner of the true sovereign, the constituent power of the people. Note, however, that the adjective implies that the dictator is to act in a fully sovereign manner, even if the category of commissioner implies a limit, namely that the agent's commission could be revoked by its principal.

[128] Arendt, *On Revolution.*

[129] "Views of the Executive Means Available to the Representatives in France in 1789" was the first of three pamphlets written in 1788–1789. I refer to the English translation in Sonnenscher ed.'s Sieyès: *Political Writings* (Indianapolis: Hackett, 2003).

instructions, Sieyès made a serious attempt to try to link the Rousseauian doctrine of the general will of the sovereign people to the will generated in a representative assembly. This effort failed because it had to fail.[130] From a Rousseauian perspective, such an assembly's will cannot but be a partial or separate corporate will.

Having nevertheless produced a creditable argument for deliberative democracy and the modern representative principle, Sieyès had reason to think that he validated his notion of such an assembly producing a constitution for France. He returned to the concept of representation, which was a necessary condition for the original English distinction of the constituent and constituted powers. Now he too, unlike Rousseau, could make this differentiation. But his argument concerning the necessity of representation in a large country with the division of labor applied to both levels, a problem already noticed by Lawson who proposed therefore only a larger, more representative body on the constituent level (Politica ch. 4:8). But the concept of unitary sovereignty presupposed by Sieyès, inherited from Rousseau, was more radical than that of Lawson's dualistic concept. Thus, what remained to be shown was that the representative assembly making the constitution should and could nevertheless have the plenitude of powers. Sieyès indeed admitted that the French people omitted delegating a separate assembly for constituent purpose[131] (already showing his American sources[132]) and therefore the inevitability of the same body also undertaking normal legislative functions. But this did not yet justify the acquisition of all power, and the exclusion of all other powers from the work of the assembly, or the claim of complete freedom of action. It is only what is intellectually most problematic here that did so, the transference of both the general will, and the idea (Rousseau's) of a provisional governmental form absorbing temporarily all state powers from the people to the representative body. This will be clearly seen in *Qu'est-ce que le Tiers État?*

While the political recommendation of this justly famous work was quite ambivalent, and its preferred institutional option ("What should have been done") was, as we will see, closer to the American model recently generated in Massachusetts than to either of the dominant French Revolutionary ones that were to emerge under his own influence, it was its influential sovereignty based theory that founded the tradition Schmitt was to canonize. Just as the assemblies of the English revolution,[133] Sieyès was quite obviously concerned with fashioning a new, democratic principle of legitimation for a representative

---

[130] Ibid., pp. 11–13.   [131] Ibid., p. 34.   [132] See chapter 2 below.
[133] As described by Morgan, *The Invention*.

assembly that could rival and replace monarchical sovereignty.[134] The task was complicated by the fact, that even the part of this assembly that he considered more or less the image of the nation, the third estate was formed in elections for an ordinary estate general the he considered without competence in constitution making (141). The best prospect at the time of his writing was for an assembly where the three estates would vote together, and it was still possible that they would vote separately. Thus, Sieyès was initially concerned with simultaneously legitimating representative assemblies and establishing limits for them. This he did brilliantly in terms of the distinction of the two powers: constituent and constituted power, *pouvoir constitué* and *pouvoir constituant*. Here at least, whether consciously or not, he was thinking more in the path of Locke than that of Rousseau. The constituted power, though acting through representatives of the nation (135–136), must act through fixed forms, in other words under and bound by the constitution. But, and here is the decisive point derived from Rousseau, *the nation*, the *constituent power* is not bound by any forms at all:

> The nation is prior to everything. Its will is always legal It is the law itself. Prior to the nation and *above the nation there is only the natural law.* [my italics, to be compared to Schmitt] p. 136 . . . The nation is formed solely by natural law. Government . . . is solely the product of positive law . . . Not only is a nation not subject to a constitution . . . it *cannot* and *should* not be . . . Is there any antecedent authority able to have told a multitude of individuals "I have united you under this set of laws, and you will form a nation under conditions which I have laid down?" . . . Every nation on earth has to be taken as if it is like an isolated individual outside all social ties or, as it is said, in the state of nature. The exercise of their will is free and is independent of all civil forms. A nation never leaves the state of nature . . . it can never have enough possible ways of expressing its will . . . a nation is independent of all forms . . . it is enough for its will to be made known for all positive law to fall silent in its presence . . . (138)

It is these passages that are formative for Carl Schmitt, who recognizes the historical priority of some English forerunners of Sieyès (*Die Diktatur*, 128ff.). He leaves behind Sieyès' unclear reference to natural law, and emphatically repeats the normatively and legally unlimited nature of the pouvoir constituant. Moreover, twice violating Sieyès' actual text, he adds that this means also the impossibility of all self-limitation as well as the loss of relevance of the

---

[134] As he later noticed, without self criticism, in his Thermidor address, "*Opinion de Sieyes*" op. cit.

inalienable rights of man (*sind gegenstandlos*) (137).[135] With respect to rights at least, logic may be on the side of Schmitt, and with respect to self-limitation so is the text of the *Tiers État*, as against the more mature, later text of Sieyès, "*Préliminaire de la constitution.*"[136] According to Schmitt, even in its creativity, like its model the theological *natura naturans*, the *pouvoir constituant* is not tied to any form of action or outcome. It is not even tied to states of emergency; the *jura dominationis* of the nation can intervene in constitutional affairs at will, before, during or after a constitution (139–140). This is the meaning Schmitt assigns to the phrase of Sieyès concerning the nation being in the state of nature, a construct obviously no longer having its character of atomistic individualism. Referring to a fused collective, it is yet not a construction in the sense of international law. Instead of describing the relation of the nation to other nations, it indicates its relation "to its own constitutional forms, and above all to the functionaries acting in its name" (140). This relation is said to be totally one-sided, involving only rights and never duties.

But who or what exactly is the entity external to the constitution, with an entirely superior status to the constitution, and how is it to be found? Schmitt knows, of course, that these are the questions that were the most difficult to solve, especially since he at least never found convincing the abandonment of the imperative mandate in favor of the principle of representation (*Die Diktatur* 141; *Verfassungslehre*). Yet a representative and deliberative assembly was Sieyès' way of breaking the circle. Paradoxically, this way of constructing or identifying the nation became one of the best justifications for the depiction

---

[135] Sieyès dedicated a text to the necessity of the recognition of the rights of man by the pouvoir constituant, that also affirms the possibility of self-limitation of this power that is "*libre de toute contrainte, et de toute forme, autre que celle qu'il lui plait d'adopter*" "*Préliminaire de la constitution*" (often cited as *Exposition raissonée*) in *Ecrits Politiques*, p. 199: the two limits are connected, because the adherence to natural rights, as in the case of the absolute monarch can only be self limitation. The staunch positivist Schmitt interprets such a limitation as removable by the same self.

[136] In "What is the Third Estate" after asking whether "a nation that by its initial act is truly free of every form [could] undertake to will in the future only in a determined manner" Sieyès goes on to argue that self-limitation is both *impossible*, because the right to will by an absolute will cannot be alienated and a contract with one-self is not a genuine contract, and *undesirable*, because self-limitation could only be achieved by constitutional forms, and the nation must remain outside of these forms that involve the separation of powers to be able to guard them against violations in emergencies and by one of the branches of power. Both of these clever arguments were fallacious, as shown by several of his own definitions of the nation as under law and involving equality with respect to the possibility, and his later concept of the constitutional jury with respect to the desirability. But they do sustain both Schmitt's and (as we will see) Carré de Malberg's readings that do not take e.g., the self limitation involved in the renunciation of legislative power by the Sieyès version of the constituent power seriously.

of the model as a type of dictatorship, a logical relationship or elective affinity that Schmitt was to make famous, if on different grounds.[137]

The major questions facing France in 1789 necessarily involved changing the constitutional status of incumbents. In Sieyès' view, even if they were elected in a better way than the three estates, incumbent representatives would be incompetent to enact just such constitutional change of their own status. Again, this was the perspective of both Lawson and Locke. Accordingly, it is to the nation as the constituent power that the major legislative and constitutional questions facing France necessarily devolve. But how does one access a nation of 25 million or allow it to speak? In what sense does it already exist in a society of orders? To his credit, unlike Schmitt, who most of the time seemed satisfied with an abstract conceptual mythology, Sieyès did try to answer these questions. But the idea, as in the cited segment, that the nation is the product of natural law is even more unenlightening than Rousseau's use of the hypothetical social contract in this place.

In fact Sieyès turns to another mode of explanation, namely socio-economic function.[138] All those who play an active role in reproducing it through their activity are part of the nation. Then he identifies the relevant segment, the immense majority, as the third estate that Rousseau too already identified as "the public interest," as against the particular interests represented by the first two estates (III.15). Yet the third estate as it then stood was a juridical construct of the old regime, in its 1788 version of absolutist reform. It signified both social order and a political representative body. And indeed Sieyès too supplies a famous definition that seems inconsistent with both the socio-economic foundations of his argument, and his later insistent claim that the nation is in the state of nature: "What is a nation? It is a body of associates living under a common law, represented by the same legislature, etc." (97).[139] Thus,

---

[137] Granted, an additional element was needed, namely the incorporation of executive power too in the assembly in the pattern of Rousseau's provisional government. This could not be done in reference to the *Estates General* or the *Assemblée Constituant*, because the king retained (supposedly) executive powers. The adoption of the full sovereign dictatorship model could occur only under the republican *Convention Nationale*, four years later, with committees of the assembly assuming full executive powers.

[138] "What is the Third Estate" in: Sieyès, *Political Writings*, chapter one: "The third estate is the complete nation" P. 94ff.

[139] About the a year later a similar definition, seemingly inconsistent with the state of nature metaphor, and even the notion of absence of any legal limitation is offered: "*La nation est l'ensemble* des associés, tous gouvernés, tous soumis à la loi, ouvrage de leur volonté, tous égaux en droits, et libres dans leurs communication, et dans leurs engagements respectifs." "Préliminaire de la constitution" (often cited as Exposition raissonée) in *Écrits Politiques*, 198. Perhaps he had in mind a distinction between a *nation constituant* and a *nation constitué*, though that too is inconsistent with the idea of the nation remaining in the state of nature even during the life of the cosntitution.

the overall argument produces very mixed bases for identifying the nation: the socio-economic, with its nearly 25 million, and the political, involving a few hundreds of thousands or perhaps a bit more of the actually represented. As Marx was to point out in 1843, in an argument probably influenced by Sieyès' pamphlet, the way was being opened for one particular stratum to represent its interests as universal.[140]

Having identified the nation, however ambiguously, Sieyès still had to bridge the gap between social and political forms, or even between the political nation that elects and the body the acts on its behalf.[141] In light of his early argument this had to be done by representation, not however as a *constitué*. Thus, he postulates the possibility of an extra-ordinary representation of the *constituant*. But will not all representation be constituted, namely by laws determining the timing, the mode of election, the size, etc., of the legislative body? Without raising this question, he answers it by arguing that under extra-ordinary conditions a constituent assembly (he does not yet use the term) is a replacement or surrogate for the assembly of the whole nation à la Rousseau, and as such replaces the nation in its whole status: *"il remplace la nation dans son indépendance de toutes formes constitutionnelles... il leur suffit de vouloir comme veulent des individus dans l'état de nature... leur volonté commune vaudra celle dela nation elle-meme"*(164).

It is this view that became canonical for the tradition, whether treated positively by Schmitt or critically by Hannah Arendt, despite the fact that it was inconsistent with Sieyès' other postulate that the extra-ordinary assembly need not be given the plenitude of all national powers, and can be restricted to one, the constitution-making task, or even a time frame.[142] However, its

---

[140] Marx, "Introduction to a Critique of Hegel's Philosophy of Right" [1843] http://www.bopsecrets.org/CF/marx-hegel.htm.

[141] See Pasquale Pasquino's fine book *Sieyès et l'invention de la constitution en France* (Paris: Éditions Odile Jacob, 1998).

[142] How can an unlimited body be stopped from legislating and even abrogating other powers? This has been the lesson of constituent assemblies within the tradition as we will see. Of this obvious contradiction Sieyès was not aware, perhaps because of American experience (three to be exact: Massachusetts, New Hampshire, and the Federal Constitution)) to the contrary, and because he already stated in the earlier pamphlet ("Executive Means," op. cit.), that in France the uniting of all functions in the one assembly was unavoidable. He was in fact much more concerned about another practical problem, that made him descend from the ideal level of philosophy to the practical level of the administrator as the epigram of "What is the Third Estate?" (probably contrasting himself with Rousseau) implies. This had to do with the Estates General and even the third estate being ordinary assemblies, and yet the necessity of producing a constitution for France, without waiting for a proper procedure. This lead to his postulate of a possible second best: an interim or provisional constitution under which a proper, extra-ordinary assembly that, in principle, then could also have specialized in a single function could have been elected. On this see chapter 2, below.

deepest problems were explored by Raymond Carré de Malberg, according to whom adding representation to popular sovereignty is the fundamental problem with the model. Still, Carré de Malberg is not in all respects a hostile critic of Sieyès. He defends the "double differentiation" (the actual term is introduced as far as I know by Claude Klein[143]) inherent in the differentiation of constituent and constituted powers that he thinks derives from Montesquieu rather than Rousseau,[144] at least in its French rather than American version. The differentiation is double, because not only are the legislative power and the ordinary legislative procedure not allowed to assume the competence to make or alter the constitution, but the constituent power is also forbidden to take on legislative or any other power functions in the state.

As we will see below, Sieyès failed in his proposals to promote double differentiation, both for reasons inherent in his own antinomic theory, and also because of external circumstances. Carré de Malberg has no objection against the representative government that is the foundation for his own theory of *national* sovereignty, according to which all governmental powers, the powers of state organs should be mere delegations from an abstract state sovereignty that must never be embodied in an institution, a person or a group. According to him, *popular* sovereignty, even in Rousseau's sense, involves an attempt at such embodiment of the assembly of the whole in concrete persons. He considers it important even for the constituent power to be delegated to a plurality of organs rather than reserved to the people in the form of referenda, although he is willing to think of the referendum too as yet another state organ.[145] However, according to him what produces a really toxic mixture is when the model of embodied popular sovereignty is transposed to representatives.

---

[143] *Théorie et pratique du pouvoir constituant* (Paris: PUF, 1996).

[144] He rightly notes that Rousseau, who has identified the legislative power with sovereignty, could not make this distinction, thereby overlooking that the Social Constract drew a similar distinction elsewhere, between sovereign and governmental powers. *Contribution*, vol. II, p. 513ff. But the Montesquieuian derivation is also right, and Sieyès did make use of the constituent power to help stabilize the differentiation of the three constituted powers, none of which could be therefore constituent if the integrity of the other two were to be preserved. See "*Préliminaire de la constitution*" (often cited as *Exposition raissonée*) in *Écrits Politiques*; as well as "What is the Third Estate?"; and *Dire*, op. cit.

[145] *Contribution*, pp. 193–194. Contrary to Schmitt, for Carré de Malberg the constituent power is not identified with what he calls national sovereignty, Schmitt's *Subjekt* or *Träger*, but with the assemblies that actually make the constitution. Unlike Schmitt, he visualized this possibility only under law, and as we will see the amending power thus became the only version of the constituent power he deems worth discussing. This left the original moment of constitution making entirely outside of public law, in the world of fact or force. As he famously wrote: "*Il n'y a point place dans la science du droit publique pour un chapitre consacré à une théorie juridique des coups d'État ou des révolutions et leurs effets*" a well-stated claim that (fortunately for us) his whole treatment in the chapter on the constituent power repeatedly violates.

At least Rousseau's model was impossible to practice for a large centralized state such as France, with most revolutionaries and pre-eminently the greatest constitutional thinkers, such as Sieyès and Condorcet, rejecting all thoughts of a federal or confederal arrangement linking together the small democratic republics of the primary assemblies.[146] Sieyès' synthesis of legitimation by popular sovereignty and embodied representation was however very possible and practicable.

Carré de Malberg does notice the latter's attempts to restrict or constrict the constituent power, though he does not note all the relevant texts. Thus, his theoretical evaluation of Sieyès becomes more negative than it might have been.[147] More importantly, however, he thinks that given Sieyès' theory of popular sovereignty the concession is worthless; the model must fall back into the same structure given to it by Rousseau, but with representatives rather than the people as a whole having all the power (534). He supports the case with several key passages. How can a body be denied or deny itself any power in the state, he asks, when it is said "to replace the nation in its independence of all constitutional forms... for whom it is sufficient to will as individuals will in the state of nature" (528–529) meaning a will without conditions (534)? Assuming an attempt of such a body to bind itself, such a limitation would be then without value as in the case of the nation itself, and could be removed in a similar act as it was established in the first place (531). The same is true for the duration of the power. If the people's sovereignty is without time limit, so the sovereign legislature, once assembled has this power indefinitely irrespective of any prior limitation that has been enacted (534). Thus, according to Carré de Malberg, Sieyès winds up attributing the plenitude of the nation's

[146] Sieyès, "*Dire*," p.234; and, in more detail, Condorcet, "*Plan de constitution*" (presented to the Convention, February 15–16, 1793 in *Oeuvres*, XII, pp. 337–40 (*Selected Writings*, Indianapolis: Bobbs Merrill, n.d.) 145–146. See also M. Ozouf, "Federalism" in F. Furet and M. Ozouf eds. *Critical Dictionary of the French Revolution* (Cambridge, MA: Harvard University Press, 1989).

[147] He notes several times the relevant section of *Préliminaire*, p. 192 concerning the less than ideal character of the National Assembly (possibly because of its mode of election primarily), that certainly called for the election of a new one for the single and unique purpose (*pur cet unique objet*) of writing the final constitution. With respect to "What is the Third Estate?" he notes only the lines that there is no need to entrust the extra-ordinary assembly with the plenitude of powers (139), that is indeed somewhat weak, but not the long argument concerning "what should have been done" that outlines the problem of incumbent interest as the reason for not mixing the two powers, the problem of being interested in the powers of a body in which they might serve (143). This problem could be responded, however, to even for an assembly having all of the power, as can be seen from subsequent proposals that banned the members of the Constituent Assembly from being elected to the Legislative Assembly in 1791. But such a measure did not alter the other state of affairs: an assembly having too much power, disabling the separation of powers. Cf. Gauchet, *La revolution*.

sovereignty to one *organ* of the modern state, the constituent assembly, in the process fatally undermining the distinction between constituent and constituted powers (534).

Organ sovereignty with constituent powers is dictatorship to Carré de Malberg, though unlike Schmitt he has no full theoretical analysis to underwrite this claim that is directed, above all, against a favorite target of the republican authors of the Third Republic, namely "convention government" as practiced during the Reign of Terror.[148] Sieyès was no architect of that government, and Carré de Malberg on the whole admires the effort of the makers of the Constitution of 1791, among whom Sieyès was a leading protagonist. But that role is chalked up to his pragmatism. His theory, one which indeed not his alone during the debates of the Constituent Assembly, is represented as the anticipation of convention government – not simply through hindsight, but through the then contemporary warnings of Mounier, who already spoke of the supreme dictatorship of the assembly.[149] The historical logic seems convincing enough, even if during the period 1789–1791 France was not under a dictatorship in our later sense, and the theory of the National Convention represented, as we will see, in some essential respects a different form of Rousseauian theory than that of Sieyès and the one in the end settled on by the Constituent Assembly.[150] As to the completion of theoretical argument began by Carré de Malberg, I return to the work of Carl Schmitt.

Whether he noticed the relevant texts or not, Schmitt never mentions Sieyès' abstract preference of a doubly differentiated model. This may be because he considers the link of the constituent-constituted distinction to a separation of powers model spurious (*Verfassungslehre* 7th ed. p. 77). But more deeply, his theory of dictatorship, at least in its more radical version, considered attempts to limit the possessor of a dictatorial commission to be impossible.[151] Interestingly, he first derived the link of the sovereign model to dictatorship in a different, if complementary way than Carré de Malberg,

---

[148] And possibly against the Constituent Assembly of 1848? On its dictatorship, see Marx, *The Class Struggles in France 1848–1850* (New York: New World Paperbacks, n.d.). While devastatingly critical of the dictatorship of Cavaignac for its suppression of the June workers' insurrection, just before, Marx was also critical of the leaders of the Frankfurt Assembly for rejecting dictatorship against the reactionaries that sought to sabotage it. See his 1848 articles: In *Neue Rheinische Zeitung* https://www.marxists.org/archive/marx/works/subject/newspapers/neue-rheinische-zeitung.htm

[149] See Baker's outstanding reconstruction in *Invention*, pp. 275–8, and R.R. Palmer's *Age of the Democratic Revolution*.

[150] Ibid.

[151] *Die Diktatur* admittedly contradicted in "*Die Diktatur des Reichspräsidenten*" reproduced in the same volume, with respect to procedure, before the former view became his dominant perspective once again.

with representation playing only a subordinate role. This was I think because Schmitt considered representation to be an aristocratic form, and dictatorship (for him the contrary of liberalism, or "constitutionalism" not democracy) to be possible only on democratic foundations.[152] With this said, in spite of their fundamentally different attitudes to dictatorship, the conceptions of Carré de Malberg and Schmitt turn out to be consistent with one another, with the latter supplying important additional considerations that allows us to understand the strong link of the sovereign model to dictatorship not only ideally but also quite often in practice.

Most fundamentally for Schmitt, modern as against classical dictatorship lies in unlimited *iura dominationis* linked to the appearance of sovereignty as the constituent power of the people that gives older ideas such as representation and commission an entirely new content. (*Diktatur* 139–140). As he will later express it, the sovereign constituent power of the monarch (that may have been invented strictly speaking after the appearance of the popular version) can work without dictatorship. The problem for the people is double: first there is a rupture with all constituted authorities (the people are in the state of nature) and second the people in the state of nature is an entity not directly capable of action or even a will ("*Der Wille kann unklar sein. Er muß es sogar sein, wenn der pouvoir constituant wirklich unkonstituierbar ist*"; *Die Diktatur* 143). Or: the people as the constituent power has the great disadvantage that its will is "easy to misunderstand, misinterpret, or to falsify" (*Verfassungslehre* 83). Neither problem exists in the case of the monarch whose person represents dynastic legal continuity, and whose will is clear and therefore capable of giving concrete orders and instructions to commissioners (*Verfassungslehre* 82). This is where dictatorship comes in, and it cannot be the commissarial type used by the monarch. Its task is above all to constitute (Sieyès), or at the very least to clarify (Schmitt) the will of its supposed commissioning instance. As any authoritarian form, this dictatorship will suspend the previous separation of powers (and where relevant the division of powers too), but here assuming the legislative power instead of silencing it (thus: there is a full substitution of the dictator for the sovereign) (*Verfassungslehre* 59). But, and here is a difference between Schmitt and Carré de Malberg, as all dictatorships, this will still be a commission and not sovereignty itself, tied to the carrying out of a concrete task (the making of a constitution) and is revocable when and if the

---

[152] *Verfassungslehre*, p. 237; and before then more famously in the essay on parliamentarism. He is not entirely consistent, because he mentions the possibility of aristocratic and oligarchic dictatorships, in the modern world typified by the fascists and the Bolsheviks. But in the case of these latter he insists that they have not "definitively renounced consulting the will of the people, whose true and unfalsified expression the presuppositions must be first created." *Verfassungslehre*, p. 82.

commissioning instance is fully constituted or even before, if its will becomes clear (*Die Diktatur* 146) (*Verfassungslehre* 59–60).

But what happens when the task is completed and the will is still unclear, or said to be unclear, or if social pathologies make the completion of the task impossible? (*Die Diktatur*, 145ff; *Verfassungslehre* 82). Here Schmitt, coming close to Carré de Malberg's insights, is forced to establish a surreptitious link between his concepts of sovereign and commissarial dictatorships.[153] In the case of disorders, and until the re-establishment of order, the revolutionary power can establish a provisional charter that Schmitt means only in the sense of the rules of provisional government and not any kind of constitutional-ist interim constitution.[154] Speaking of the *vorläufige Verfassung* (*das Gesetz über vorläufige Staatsgewalt*) of the Weimar National Assembly, he says it is a mistake to treat such a thing, revocable by simple majority, as a genuine constitution (*Verfassungslehre* 58–59). At most one can speak of a "minimum constitution" that is always there when the constituent power is recognized, that is when sovereign dictatorship is active (*Die Diktatur* 145–146). Recognizing, therefore, that a representative body is indeed constituted, this is seen under the minimum constitution that should be thought of as "the only consti-tutional magistracy of the political entity" and "the only representative of the state" not yet otherwise constituted. In my view this means the recognition, already there in Rousseau (*Social Contract* III.17), that between the figure of the social contract, and the enactment of a constitution there must logically be a provisional government, one that cannot be anything else in terms of Schmitt's theory than a dictatorship, if a preparatory and transitional one. And, at least in the case of the German revolution of 1918, he recognizes this provisional government as the political form of the transition from the fall of the monarchy until the full enactment of the Weimar Constitution (*Verfas-sungslehre* 58–59). Without making the point entirely general as he should have, the Weimar constituent assembly's existence and functioning from the beginning to the end presupposed such a provisional government, that legally came to be rooted in the assembly, but politically, of course, much as its fore-runner, the Committee of Public Safety, had a lot of control over that body itself.[155]

---

[153] See my "Good-bye to Dictatorships?" in *Social Research*, Vol. 67, No. 4 (Winter 2000).

[154] I make this essential distinction against Olivier Beaud's otherwise excellent analysis, who does not make it, thereby bringing preconstitutions in the sovereign model, and interim constitutions in the post sovereign one too close together. *La puissance de l'état* (Paris: PUF, 1994).

[155] Böckenförde op. cit. who makes provisional government rather than constituent assembly the central dimension of sovereign dictatorship. This is an interesting contrast to Carré de

The point concerning provisional government does not appear in the theoretical sections of *Verfassungslehre*, which perhaps deliberately tries to deemphasize the concept of sovereign dictatorship.[156] But Schmitt was quite aware of the French revolutionary origins of the institution. According to *Die Diktatur*, it was a special feature of convention government 1793–1795, or especially the *"gouvernement révolutionnaire"* declared in 1793, that after the ratification of the Constitution of 1793 its own provisional status was continued, supposedly "until the peace," but in fact until the enactment of the next constitution by the Thermidorians. It was this precedent that Schmitt tried to explain with his conception of the unclear will and the hindered assembly. Well before Leninism and Fascism established "permanent" dictatorships, he saw the link between sovereign dictatorship and an open-ended one as not only historically, but also theoretically very possible if not inevitable.[157] Through a strange historical alchemy, the effort of finding a truly democratic beginning for constitutionalism has not only produced dictatorships in practice, but grounded this outcome theoretically. How likely and how avoidable we consider this outcome depends on our evaluation of the American case(s), and the possibility that they represent historical exceptions.

VIII *Sovereign Constitution Making as Ideology and as Reality*

To avoid all confusion, it is not possible for a sovereign people existing outside all constitutions, to be created by social contract (Carré de Malberg, op. cit., pp. 484–486) or to be fully formed in the state of nature, and thus to produce or even authorize a constitution. At the very least, the concept of sovereignty should imply either an agency or a set of agencies capable of domestic political supremacy,[158] or a legal order embodying a hierarchy of decision.[159] To be politically supreme or to be the ultimate center of decision an entity or an agent must first exist, and second be capable of action. Neither of

---

Malberg's assembly-centered model, but in reality the two institutions presuppose one another. A revolutionary government that does not establish a constituent process for a new regime represents little more than a permanent *coup d'état*, and a sovereign assembly cannot function without a provisional government.

[156] Making some interpreters wrongly conclude that he abandoned the theory of sovereign dictatorship in favor of a democratic theory of the constituent power. See A. Kalyvas, *Democracy and the Politics of the Extraordinary* (Cambridge: Cambridge University Press, 2009).

[157] Whether this analysis is to be taken as a critique of convention government, and more importantly of Leninism in 1921, is much disputed. In my view he admired these precedents, and sought to imitate them also on the right.

[158] As in the whole tradition from Bodin to the German Staatslehre, and Carré de Malberg.

[159] As in Kelsen's *General Theory*, pp. 189; 255; and 383ff.

these pre-conditions are fulfilled for a sovereign people before the constitution is made. While a legal concept, sovereignty requires minimum sociological translatability to be relevant, even legally. The monarch may never have the factual power ascribed to him or her by the classical theory of sovereignty, but the power of decision the monarch (or a small group around him or her) can exercise is real enough and significant enough to make the legal concept effective in practice. The same cannot be true of the people. "[T]he people – from whom the constitution claims its origin – comes to legal existence first through the constitution. It can therefore be only in a political, not in a juristic sense that the people is the source of the constitution." Kelsen is evidently right, and proceeds to take back the last concession immediately: "It is further obvious that those individuals who actually created the constitution represented only a minute part of the whole people – this even if one takes into consideration those who elected them."[160] And it is obvious that even Rousseau and Schmitt (in his case at least initially) concede that such a people or nation could not act in the manner required by the theory: enlightenment or dictatorship would be first needed. To avoid begging the fundamental question, Rousseau is forced to use the traditional *deus ex machina* of the legislator, who convinces through authority but without power, but this was no longer convincing in the age of enlightenment even to his followers. Sieyès uses the device of representation, with free representatives, both rejected by Rousseau. He thereby dramatically redefined the nation, making its will, very implausibly, identical with the will of its representatives who are themselves (as Marx in 1843 rightly maintained)[161] always a sociologically specific group, a part rather than the whole. And Schmitt finally broke the circle through his concept of sovereign dictatorship – that is, the concession of an element of the *constitué* in the *constituant* because the agencies that exercise dictatorship even in his view do so on the bases of a "minimal constitution." That minimal constitution belongs to an already formed state of some kind (sometimes only in the form of an army), otherwise dictatorship could not be exercised in France or Germany, any more than in ancient Rome. Thus, the theory is saved, but only by shifting the emphasis to state sovereignty, and to its bearer dictating to the unenlightened or hindered or endangered popular will that needs to respond through mere acclamation. The same is true in Sieyès turn to representation. What the representatives exercise is state rather than popular sovereignty. In both these theorists there is a shift from popular to state power. If that is avoided,

---

[160] Kelsen *General Theory*, p. 261. The insight is at least as old as J.J. Mounier in 1789: See Baker, op. cit., p. 276.
[161] Marx "Introduction to a Critique."

as in Rousseau, this makes his theory impotent in the eyes of the others: all authority but without power.

Admittedly, there seems to be a shift in Carl Schmitt's *Verfassungslehre* in the opposite direction, from sovereign dictatorship to popular sovereignty.[162] As R. Cristi has already proven, however, the shift is an illusion, in part explainable by the legal theoretical subject matter.[163] The theoretical sections on the popular constituent power do not speak of sovereign dictatorship directly, though here too one can see between the lines the fundamental notion that the popular will is unclear and is easy to falsify. More importantly, the concept of sovereign dictatorship does return in the discussion of the Weimar Assembly, although it could now be taken as a critique of constitution making through a representative assembly, without popular ratification. Such an interpretation of Schmitt, focusing on the people rather than the state, makes little sense, especially after Schmitt has developed his whole theory of the sovereign dictatorship in *Die Diktatur* for the Convention Nationale that inaugurated the assembly model with popular ratification in a referendum. It is simply more likely that Schmitt thought it either less relevant (than in a book on dictatorship) or less convenient to discuss the link to dictatorship in his theory of popular constitution making. He should not have been so reticent, having repeatedly linked dictatorship to democracy.[164]

In any case, *Verfassungslehre* has a new important element justifying my conception, namely the insistence on the absolute priority of the modern state to the modern theory and practice of the constituent power. A people will not be created by contract à la Rousseau, nor can it become a subject in the state of nature by the laws of nature a la Sieyès. Instead, the work of absolutist statemakers was first needed to create political community, coherent enough, homogeneous enough, capable of being organized for this purpose. It was their defenders and ideologists who postulated a doctrine of state sovereignty that made the state or its highest organ *legibus solutus*, even if they did not explicitly make this the source of the constitutional structure itself (*Verfassungslehre* 47–49). It is here, in the most realistic part of his argument that the role of conceptual mythology becomes the clearest. The absolutist state creates a political subject *in itself*, for possible self-transformation, but not yet a subject *for itself*. That can be the result only of self-formation and self-transformation. It is as if Schmitt just read or re-read Lukács' staunchly Hegelian *Geschichte*

---

[162] cf. Kalyvas, op. cit.

[163] R. Cristi, "Constituent Power and the Monarchical Principle," *Constellations*, 18(3).

[164] See *Crisis of Parliamentary Democracy* (Cambridge, MA: MIT Press, 1994), pp. 14–16; 28–32; also *Verfassungslehre*, pp. 236–237 on the dictatorship and democracy link.

und Klassenbewusstsein, and retraced the origins of that Marxist's attempt to reinterpret Leninist substitution of the party for the class (the logical equivalent of sovereign dictatorship) to the myth of the revolutionary class subject as in Rosa Luxemburg (paralleling the popular constituent power). A myth, however, cannot replace political facts, as Lukács was soon to find out. On a lower level of abstraction, the choice will be either using the state's institutions for state transformation, or positing a self-creative new subject that could transform all of them *ex nihilo.* The theory of sovereign dictatorship, as reintroduced through the institutions needed to carry out the constituant project indicates that it takes at least one state institution (and perhaps more than one), old or new, inherited or restructured to be the foothold of the shaping and ordering of the rest. The dictatorship that accomplishes that *in the name of* the people, must however also be *over* the people. Here the Leninist topos converges with Schmitt's rightist one.

We rightly call a form of legitimation that systematically confuses norm and reality an ideology. Popular sovereignty can be such an ideology of legitimation, especially in the context of constitution making efforts relying on internal state sovereignty. The state, or rather a given state organ like an assembly, a board, a junta or an executive person, can in this context simulate the imagined position of the popular sovereign in the state of nature by acts of illegality breaking off its previous constitutional limitations. This happens in the case of the Estates General on its way to becoming a National Constituent Assembly, in the case of the Napoleonic coups, and also in the case of the National Convention, whose election and ratification rules were ordained by the Legislative Assembly it supplanted, in violation of the Constitution of 1791.[165] Such mimicking the condition of the state of nature, mentioned by Sieyès, is at the very heart of the claim of powers directly derived from an imagined entity that was itself entirely unlimited. All the organizational and institutional forms that appeal to the sovereign theory make this claim, even when they (seem to) submit to self-limitation giving the problem of omnipotence one of its possible solutions.[166] Classical revolutionary constituent assemblies, ordinary parliaments claiming sovereign constitution-making powers, plebiscitary leaders offering a constitution to be ratified in referenda, and even American-type conventions that convert themselves to sovereign assemblies do make such a

---

[165] The amendment rule of the Constitution of 1791 was clearly violated. It could be argued, however, that the more general right of change contained in the same constitution allowed in principle this procedure that was nowhere mentioned in it of course. [Constitution of 1791 title VII] If that were true, the interpretation of the rights of the Convention implied that it would be as free of previous constraints as in the case of an illegal rupture.

[166] P. Suber, *The Paradox of Self-Amendment* (New York: Peter Lang, 1990).

claim. Each one of these "models" or their advocates however entail that the constitution making work is done by a sovereign organ and its agents. This is a power that transcends the separation of powers, and claims the right to do so by representing the sovereign people who either do not have to be consulted, or need to be consulted only in a minimal way, to give a global "Yes" or "No." The point of this consultation is more to guard the model against the tyrannical usurpation that is the danger of all dictatorships, than for the sake of genuine consultation. Sovereign constitution making is organ sovereign constitution making that (if we use the term carefully) earns the title of sovereign dictatorship in all its forms, with an elective affinity, if not a logically tautological link, to permanent dictatorship, that the ancients indeed called tyranny.

And yet, speaking historically, sovereign constitution making and modern political revolutions have had a very close relationship. They are linked together not only through a principle of legitimacy based on popular sovereignty, but equally through legal rupture, the necessity to establish regimes, and the role of elites in the process of liberation. While sovereign dictatorship is normatively difficult to defend, revolutions are often capable of justification. They are moreover empirically real even in our own epoch, one which many of us may have been too quick to depict as post-revolutionary. Thus, we have very good reason to ask whether the link between revolution and sovereign dictatorship is necessary or, despite empirical evidence, contingent. There is no better way to begin exploring this problem than via the path of Hannah Arendt, comparing the forms of self-understanding of the American and French Revolutions, both of which paid special attention to our problem of constitution making. That is the task of the next chapter.

2

The Antinomies of Constituent Power
in America and France

Whether or not the American model of constitution making, understood as the doubly differentiated form[1] that emerged in Massachusetts (1781) and New Hampshire (1784), and relied on by the Federal Convention, belongs to the paradigm and history of sovereign constitution making has been and should remain controversial. Carl Schmitt includes the federal convention type in his relevant typology, but considers it unclassical because state making and constitution making were not (yet) differentiated.[2] Böckenförde then proceeds to leave it out altogether, in spite of the resemblances to the making of the *Grundgesetz*.[3] The latter he then classifies, without much justification, but as German doctrine and the text seem to require, under the aegis of the popular constituent power.[4] On the other hand, Carré de Malberg, among the critics of the sovereign form, considered the making of the Federal Constitution a process that escaped his strictures against popular organ sovereign constitution

---

[1] To reiterate the previous chapter, by this I mean that both that the governmental powers receive at best a partial constituent role, while the main bodies involved in constitution making are deprived of governmental functions. As Carré de Malberg noticed, this form of the separation of powers is incompatible with organ sovereignty. Conversely, K. Loewenstein, in focusing on the making of French amendment rules, shows how difficult pure double differentiation is in practice, even when required by theory. *Volk und Parlament* [1922] (Munich: Scientia, 1967) Third Part, Fourth Section.

[2] The point applies in his view to the states, as well as the Federal Union. *Verfassungslehre* (Berlin: Duncker & Humblot, 1928) 8: ii 2 and iii 4, b and c [77–78; 85–86].

[3] E.-W. Böckenförde in *"Die verfassunggebende Gewalt des Volkes – Ein Grenzbegriff des Verfassungsrechts"* in *Staat, Verfassung, Demokratie* (Frankfurt: Suhrkamp, 1991). In my view, the Parliamentary Council that made the Grundgesetz, delegated by state legislatures, resembled the Federal Convention, though the ratifying role of the regular legislatures meant that the West German process was less popular, and less differentiated in the sense of fn.1.

[4] See also D. Murswiek *Die verfassunggebende Gewalt nach dem Grundgesetz für die Bundesrepublik Deutschland* (Berlin: Duncker & Humblot, 1978).

making.[5] More radically, Hannah Arendt is famous for her positive blanket judgment:

> ... the great and, in the long run, perhaps the greatest American innovation in politics as such was the consistent abolition of sovereignty within the body politic of the republic, the insight that in the realm of human affairs sovereignty and tyranny are the same."[6]

She has linked this idea, if not clearly enough, to an analysis of American constituent power that, according to her, was based on small, organized republics, rather than the state of nature a la Sieyès (OR 153–155); as well as to a theory of authority that was not reducible to power (OR Chapter 5).[7] I will return continually to these two themes.[8] As powerful and imaginative as her arguments were, at least textually they cannot be easily sustained,[9] and are contradicted by the very words of the famous Preamble that refer to the popular sovereign as author of the constitution, the *Federalist Papers*, many individual state constitutions,[10] as well as an important tradition of Court cases, from *Chisholm v. Georgia* to *McCulloch v. Maryland*.[11] The debates of the period of the founding, and the cases for a period of about thirty years were indeed not about the relevance or irrelevance of sovereignty, but where its locus should be found.[12] Even

---

[5] *Contribution à la générale Théorie de l Etat* (1920) (Paris: Dalloz, 2004), p. 546.

[6] *On Revolution* [OR144] (New York: Viking, 1963). Partially supporting her judgment, and speaking of sovereignty in a less monolithic, less doctrinaire, less threatening manner is W.P. Adams in *The First American Constitutions* (Lanham: Rowman & Littlefield, 2001). Unlike Arendt, however, Adams pays a great deal of attention to the presence of the sovereignty doctrine in the states.

[7] Arguably, the constituent power is not within the body politic, but before it and outside of it. However, the thrust of Arendt's analysis focuses on precisely the constituent power, and she leaves sovereignty intact only for external affairs of the state.

[8] For a reconstruction and critique of this conception see A. Arato and J. Cohen, "Banishing the Sovereign? Internal and External Sovereignty in Arendt." *Constellations* 16.2 (2009): 307–330.

[9] Carré de Malberg alone seemed to have noticed the contradiction in America, between the double differentiation of constituent and constituted and the positing of popular sovereignty, but he did not develop the implications. Op. cit., p. 546.

[10] Adams, *The First American Constitutions I*, chapter VI.

[11] In his very fine book, Stephen Griffin suggests only that the Americans, dividing and diffusing power, should have eliminated the concept of sovereignty, but unfortunately did not do so. Common to Griffin and Arendt is identification of sovereignty with Bodinian organ sovereignty, a position transcended already by Jellinek, Carré de Malberg, and Kelsen. See: *American Constitutionalism: From Theory to Politics* (Princeton, NJ: Princeton University Press, 1996), pp. 19ff. Griffin's alternative concept of political authority is however not an adequate substitute for sovereignty defined as a concept under law, pertaining to the whole of the state. His attempted separation of domestic from international sovereignty cannot work any better than Arendt's. Cf. Arato and Cohen, op. cit.

[12] Griffin, op. cit.

recently, though very much influenced by Arendt, Bruce Ackerman has made
the Preamble, interpreted in the sense of a unified, popular sovereignty, the
fundamental idea behind his theory of extralegal constitution making. If anyone has made a determined attempt to subsume the American model under
the European theory of sovereign constitution making, it is he, in spite of his
fear of permanent revolution and hostility to dictatorship.[13]

According to Ackerman, in *We the People* (WP I. 184ff.) the model of separation of powers that bans the full appropriation of the people's sovereignty
by one of the branches of power applies only to *normal* politics. Ordinarily,
each branch of power can only *represent* the people, and does so in an incomplete and partial manner. He claims for example that "There can be no hope
of capturing the living reality of popular sovereignty during normal politics"
and "No institution of normal politics can be allowed to transubstantiate itself
into the People of the United States" (WP I 182). Moreover, Ackerman interprets the *Federalist # 63*'s "total exclusion of the people in their collective
capacity from any share" in government in much the same spirit: not only
cannot the body of the people collectively claim sovereignty in the American
scheme of government, but it ought not be given governmental functions to
avoid the danger of such incorporation (WP I 182). The perspective is close to
that of Locke's original formulation, as he made a determined effort to keep
the role of the people, in its corporate capacity, outside of government and
constitution, restricted to constitution making itself. Nevertheless, according
to Ackerman and his reading of the *Federalist*, the banning of embodiment
that very much resembles Carré de Malberg's concept of national sovereignty,
as well as Claude Lefort's concept of democracy, does not apply in *constitutional* politics. In the dualistic American model, on extra-ordinary occasions,
mobilized movements, and political forces leading them supposedly *earn the
right to speak fully in the name of the popular sovereign*. According to Ackerman, the *Federalist* "treats constitutional conventions as if they were perfect
substitutes for *the people themselves*" (WP, I, 178).[14] These are echoes of some
of the best-known lines of Sieyès, and the dominant language of the Constituent Assembly. It is with such bifurcation of politics between normal and
constitutional, important in many respects, that Ackerman manages to satisfy
both the Arendtian demand of banishing sovereignty, and serving the letter

---

[13] See *We the People* (WP) I (Cambridge, MA: Harvard University Press, 1992).
[14] He does not notice the contradiction in his sentence, between the plural, conventions, and
     the singular, the people, that is repeated in his quotation, that has the people = nine states.
     The editions [e.g., Rossiter's] that omit the words "the people" from *Federalist* 40 here are a
     lot more logical than Ackerman. But the text in any case has many references to the same
     singular.

of texts such as the Preamble and *Federalist* 40 that seem emphatically to be speaking in the name of the popular sovereign. But there were other founding texts, and he too is eventually forced to proffer another interpretation.

THE THREE ANTINOMIES AND THE PROBLEM OF SOVEREIGNTY

My thesis is that the American process of constitution making as a whole, including the states as well as the federal union, originally as well as in its early court interpretations, and the procedures as well as the relevant intellectual justifications taken together allows for diametrically opposed interpretations. In my view, each of these have strong arguments supporting them, but they are together mutually exclusive. Thus, I claim that the tradition is deeply antinomic. Indeed, I believe that if we look at the American founding period in an extended sense, rather than selecting one favorite theory or one aspect of the constitution, we will run into three different but interlocking antinomies. Two of these are well known. The first involves the older tension, already discussed, present under all forms of representative government, assuming the modern sovereignty doctrine, between popular and governmental sovereignty.[15] This dualistic tension was already characteristic of the development of natural law theory broadly understood, where the contract implied direct participation of each citizen, and the making of the law (at least before and after Rousseau) was generally the function of representative organs.[16] I will pay attention to this particular antinomy, well presented by authors from Karl Loewenstein to today's advocates of popular constitutionalism, primarily to the extent that it exacerbated the other two, by adding the legitimating weight of "the people" to sovereign claims made by political bodies, conventions and legislatures, on the national as well as the state level.[17] Note that in America in the beginning even this antinomy worked itself out as a contest between organized bodies:

---

[15] See Griffin, *American Constitutionalism*.

[16] Still the best treatment is Otto von Gierke's *Natural Law and the Theory of Society*. Karl Loewenstein's extended treatment in *Volk und Parlament* is also very important.

[17] As a political factor, I consider participatory democracy and popular mobilization to belong first and foremost to the domain of civil society actions and initiatives, rather than that of formal constitutional institutions and politics that in the modern world involve mainly forms of representation, and only very partially direct participation. I accept this state of affairs, and whatever sociological and political importance they may have, do not consider anarchist or direct democratic dreams to be productive from the constitutional point of view. The point of view of social movements and civil society is another matter, and their possibility is certainly related to constitutional substance, not my topic here. The role of civil society and social movements will play a greater role in the second part of the book, dealing with comparative cases. See Andrew Arato and Jean Cohen *Civil Society and Political Theory* (Cambridge, MA: MIT Press; 1992).

state legislatures vs conventions or township assemblies.[18] But this institutional stress does not alter the difficulty that the idea of popular sovereignty, if it is to describe an actor at all, has a *pars pro toto* logic.[19] Whether a representative assembly or a popular form of mobilization, a part of society is supposedly authorized or authorizes itself to speak and act for the whole.

But which *part* was the legal and legitimate stand in or representative for the whole people? And were the *legal* and *legitimate* incarnations the same? The American idea of convention, once fully developed, was an ingenious attempt to solve this problem. It preserved representation through a legally elected or designated body. But it distinguished this extra-ordinary form of representation, from ordinary legislatures by its higher legitimacy. Thus, the convention was supposed to be a synthesis of mobilized participation and representation. Yet the problem thereby did not fully disappear. Aside from the legally authorized convention there were always in America extralegal congresses, conventions, assemblies, committees, movements and initiatives that retained direct democratic claims outside of representation.[20] In the nineteenth century with the increasing role of referenda, and the twentieth with its discovery of civil disobedience, notions of the people again assumed direct forms that politically mattered, but never losing the questionable *pars pro toto* or ultimately even a representative status.[21] Most certainly, the classical popular institution of the founding period, the monocameral convention was itself representation, if elected for extra-ordinary occasions and at times in a way that included broader suffrage and larger membership.

[18] There were to be sure insurrections, like the famous Shays rebellion, that presumed to speak in the name of "the people". By contrast, in France, the government of 1792 was brought down and replaced by such an insurrection, with the same thing partially happening also in 1793 when as a result the Gironde was expelled from the Convention. In America however no insurrection ever successfully identified itself with popular sovereignty. A convention like that of Pennsylvania in 1776 was a wholly different matter.

[19] M. Canovan, *The People* (London: Polity, 2005); Laclau, *On Populist Reason* (New York: Verso, 2005) and my critique: "Political Theology and Populism." *Social Research* 80.1 (2013). See also J. Frank in *Constituent Moments* (Durham, NC: Duke University Press, 2010) who starts with a critique of the idea of the people derived from Lefort and Rosanvallon, and winds up, like Canovan, in arguing for the myth as a kind of political performative, whose validity depends, on guess what: political success. When that happens we can according to him speak of constituent moments. Why deprive that label for the efforts of the two Bonapartes? Where is the distinction between moment and moment?

[20] G. Wood, *The Creation of the American Republic* (Chapel Hill: University of North Carolina Press, 1969); C. Fritz, *American Sovereigns* (Cambridge: Cambridge University Press, 2008).

[21] "We are the 99%," claimed Occupy Wall Street. But the agrarian movement called "populism" was much more successful in making such a *pars pro toto* claim. See Michael Kazin, *The Populist Persuasion: An American History* (New York: Basic Books, 1995).

The second antinomy was more specifically American, and much more
fateful. I have in mind two ways of locating sovereignty in American constitutional politics, whether "popular" or "governmental," that involved a deep
tension between national and state locations,[22] one that was not resolved by
the text, its amendment rule, or any one interpretation, from the founding
of the Union at least till the Civil War.[23] For some, it is alive even today.
This antinomy was only exacerbated by the theory of popular sovereignty, but
obviously was not the product of theory alone but also of the political constellation of separate states forming a federal union. It became, as I will argue, one
concerning the constituent power only via the sovereign theory of constitution
making, by way of two moves entailed by that theory as defined here: the identification of sovereignty as that of an organ, and the constituent power with
the work of the sovereign organ. Without the sovereign theory it is imaginable
that the federal antinomy concerning the location of sovereignty would not
have been as disruptive. It could have been accepted, that the constitution
(or secession from it) is (should be!) not the work of any sovereign, whether
located in the nation or the states, but rather a multiplicity of actors who made
agreements and who were willing and able to compromise.[24] Yet whichever
choice is made here, national or decentralized, a multiplicity of actors making
the constitution is thereby not avoided. As the difference between formal and
informal channels, ratification and amendment rules indicates the problem
of the one and the many, highly relevant in space, returns in time as well.
In the United States, the people of the Preamble, Article VII, Article V (that
has four possible options within the rule), of the various amendments, and of
the informal patterns of change at so-called constitutional moments are always
significantly and even structurally different.

This brings me to the third main antinomy, one that is much less obvious
and well known probably because of the ringing words of the Preamble. It is

[22] See Adams, *The First American Constitutions*, pp. 130–132.
[23] My order of analysis is different than Stephen Griffin's op. cit. He focuses on the problem
of the alternative loci of sovereignty, and presents popular sovereignty as the failed solution
attempt of this problem, what I call an antinomy. I follow those authors instead who consider
the antinomy of direct and representative forms as inherent in the natural law tradition, and
thus older than the American federalism problem. But logically it does not matter where one
begins; the antinomies lead to one another. As Griffin realizes, the claim of popular sovereignty
does not stop the re-emergence of the national-state dualism. In my view it is re-expressed in
the distinction between people and peoples.
[24] As to the consequences for a theory of secession not discussed here see Supreme Court of
Canada: Quebec Secession Reference. The best treatments remain Allen Buchanan's *Secession*
(Boulder, CO: Westview Press, 1991) and the edited volume *Secession and Self Determination*
(New York: NYU Press, 2003) especially Buchanan's essay in the latter.

between a version that refers to the popular sovereign embodied by a political actor as the author of the constitution, and another that, focusing on a multi-stage process that has not a single agent or author, allows sovereignty only in the body politic as a whole, assuming that no one organ, body, institution or person can legitimately claim full and exclusive authorship. In my view, as against Ackerman's, the two opposing positions of the antinomy cannot be neatly divided according to the schema normal and extra-ordinary, because it applies to the conceptions of constitution making itself. Throughout his major work in public law, Carré de Malberg called this antinomy one between popular and national sovereignty.[25] But that phrasing is misleading, given the common identification of "people" and "nation." Instead I prefer to stress the conflict between sovereign and post-(organ) sovereign conceptions. It is in terms of the latter that the double differentiation of the model and its multi-stage character, namely all that was really specific about the American form of constitution making after 1780 at least, will be here reconceived. But I must stress that the other version focusing on embodied popular sovereignty has been important down to our day, in theory and ideology in the USA,[26] and in practice elsewhere, when the American model was supposedly being followed.

THE PEOPLE OR ITS REPRESENTATIVES?

It is true that the institutional form of the extra-ordinary constitutional convention was a highly innovative solution to the problem of whether it was the people directly or its representatives who were to be the author(s) of the legitimate constitution. The *Federalist* even makes this idea the distinguishing mark of a constitution as against a treaty. This was to forget the history Jefferson already pointed out (in *Notes on Virginia*) for the case of Virginia – that many of the early state constitutions were the work of ordinary legislatures.[27] In fact, the term convention had many meanings by 1787, from extra-institutional popular bodies to legislatures deficient in the English sense, from extra-ordinary legislative bodies assuming all functions in a state to constitutional conventions differentiated from the legislature, restricted to the task of constitution making or drafting. The meanings of drafting and ratifying conventions were also significantly different, in the case of the making of the Federal

---

[25] *Contribution.*
[26] On this see the works of A. Amar, S. Levinson, even Ackerman, and more recently Fritz, op. cit. But see Griffin, op. cit in opposition to all of them.
[27] He focused specifically on Virginia, and perhaps for rhetorical reasons assumed that nine other states had extra-ordinary conventions. While true of the then recent case of Massachusetts, as well as the earlier one of Pennsylvania, the claim was false in general.

Constitution. Yet one element was in common for all the meanings: conventions were bodies of representatives rather than Rousseau's citizen bodies in assemblies, modeled on ancient and medieval city republics. Only the New England American townships resembled the latter – however, interestingly they were not called conventions. More importantly, their role in constitution making, though greater than of the federal ratifying conventions, was still a partial one. Yet, there was no doubt that the constitutional conventions themselves were supposed to represent the people.

The big question was, which people? The people of the first formulation of the preamble, namely "We the people of the States of New Hampshire, Massachusetts, Rhode-Island and Providence Plantation, etc."[28] or that of the second, and final one: "WE THE PEOPLE OF THE UNITED STATES, IN ORDER . . . " that seems to have been adopted without discussion, and could have meant, probably did mean different things to different framers.[29] Two distinctions were here involved: people (in the sense of a form of action considered more direct or popular) vs. government, and "the people" vs "peoples" (meaning institutions speaking in the name of whole populations). Neither was resolved by the ringing declaration of authorship or authority, whose authenticity could be supposedly tested in ratification. What concerns me is that even such a declaration could mean two things to the same person, in particular James Madison. What it did not mean to him, obviously, was that the people would be the direct source of the Constitution in their corporate capacity, whatever Ackerman implies.[30] Moreover, Madison's notion, like that of Sieyès, was that of free representation. Supported by James Wilson, he argued that the representatives at the Convention cannot or at least do not know the opinions of the people, and should decide on the bases of what *they themselves* think is right. (Madison's Notes [MN][31] June 12 p. 107; June 16 p. 125), As Wilson said, however, this involves no usurpation, because the Convention only recommends; it is "authorized to *conclude nothing*" (ibid.). Let me note the change here from the meaning of an extra-ordinary assembly

---

[28] MN: August 6: p. 385, supporting J. C. Calhoun's contention that in the eighteenth century people did not have a plural as it does today. The first preamble obviously meant people or peoples as a plural.

[29] The same issue came up for states like Massachusetts, during the drafting of the 1780 Constitution. Was "the people" the people of Massachusetts acting through its numerical majority, as the Preamble suggests, or the quasi-federal people of the townships of Abington, Acton, Adams, etc.? During the ratification of this Constitution, the issue came into the open, but was unresolved.

[30] See Arendt, *On Revolution*, p. 228.

[31] J. Madison (A. Koch ed.) *Notes of Debates at the Federal Convention* of 1787 [MN] (New York: Norton, 1987).

that fully represents the people, and can do everything the people themselves could do, to one that can only recommend and can conclude nothing. The argument is further radicalized then in *Federalist* 40, surprisingly less populist than in Ackerman's reading:

> Since it is impossible for the people spontaneously and universally to move towards their object; and it is therefore necessary that such changes be instituted by some *informal and unauthorized propositions*, made by some patriotic or respectable citizen or number of citizens . . . as the plan to be submitted to *the people themselves*, the disapprobation of this supreme authority would destroy it forever; its approbation blot out antecedent errors and irregularities. (#40 p. 249)

In passing it is worth pointing out some similarities and differences with the Schmittian model of constituent power derived from Sieyès. Clearly, there is the distinction here between *constituant* and *constitué*. The people are identified as the agent of constituent power, but they are pronounced as unable to act on their own. A group or one man ("respectable citizen or . . . "!) is needed to make them mobile, and this is done by acting in their stead, *instituting* changes, that, however, only have the status of recommendations to "the people," who in a ratification process make the final judgment. However, while Madison feels entirely no need to mention this fact obvious to all, the assembly making the recommendation does not have or claim to have any other power in the political community. It is not even an organ of the Confederation. It is certainly not an assembly that has all the power and lack of limitation of Sieyès' constituent assembly, and nor is it a sovereign dictator in any sense whatsoever. Curiously, instead, the model with its possibility of a single authoritative citizen, invokes a status that resembles Rousseau's *législateur*, which Sieyès, and, following him, Schmitt, were to expunge from the modern theory. Of course, the authors of the *Federalist* also broke with all traditional ideas of lawgivers. But something of the logical need for such a figure survives in their theory, and instead of uniting the concepts of legislator and dictator, following the practice of the Convention they found the solution in a differentiated, and implicitly multi-actor model where success in ratification would provide the necessary confirmation of the Preamble's language. Since the recommending agent is neither sovereign nor a dictator, this was also not the theory of the Jacobins who originally led the French *Convention Nationale,* and who also accepted ratification through referendum, but who demanded and achieved the plenitude of all power for their assembly. With this said, it is important that Madison is torn between an ideological appeal to *the* people, that has a singular spirit (but disguises the possibility of a plural reading) and a careful legal

(Ackerman says "legalistic") analysis of exactly what role people or peoples in the form of conventions play in the constitution making process.[32]

The case for the ideological appeal is eloquent enough. The Convention stood accused of usurpation, and illegal acts in producing an entirely new constitution instead of an amendment to the articles, and for altering the rule of amendment through a new ratification rule. Madison hopes to make these charges go away by admitting some of them,[33] but claiming that they have led only to recommendations to the true sovereign, *the* people. Radicalizing even the terms of the Declaration of Independence,[34] the popular sovereign, according to *Federalist* 40 has the "transcendent and precious right to abolish or alter [their] governments" depending on the needs of both (or either?) "their safety and happiness," to give itself an entirely new constitution without any reservation, or to keep the old one, if a project or recommendation of revision or replacement were turned down. This argument then again will be the basis of the classical introduction of judicial review in the American system by Hamilton in *Federalist* 78. According to him, a "fundamental principle of republican government" does give the right to the people themselves "to alter or abolish the established Constitution whenever they find it inconsistent with their happiness." The same power, however, is not given to their representatives, even when supported by a mere "majority of their constituents." And, until the people themselves have done so, "by some solemn and authoritative act," judges must enforce the constitution, as fundamental law, against statutes, against the people even, "collectively as well as individually."

The appeal was, however, not entirely ideological. It is true that, as Stephen Griffin argues, a sovereign body of the people as such cannot be identified within the American scheme of government, nor, especially, can the people resolve constitutional conflicts and crises as they arise.[35] Yet, at least in the

---

[32] That this allows him to play to two political perspectives simultaneously is not disguised at all, especially not in *Federalist* 39, the key text for one side of the argument, the legal side.

[33] That is so from the point of view of constitutional law. Elsewhere, from the point of view of international law, that relies on his legal rather than ideological argument for secession, he claims no illegality. See Notes 141; *Federalist* # 43. Yet the argument was at variance with some of his and especially Hamilton's remarks on treaties and the supposed right to break them. See: *Federalist* # 22 speaking of a "gross heresy" before warning about the reality of treaty breaking under a weak allaince.

[34] By adding "transcendent and precious" and excluding the italicized parts, all paraphrasing Locke: "*whenever any Form of Government becomes destructive of these ends*, it is the Right of the People to alter or to abolish it, and to institute new Government, laying its foundation on such principles and organizing its powers in such form, as to them shall seem most likely to effect their Safety and Happiness. *Prudence, indeed, will dictate that Governments long established should not be changed for light and transient causes.*"

[35] Op. cit., pp. 21 and 24.

beginning, some constitutional framers seem to have adopted a framework that resembled Rousseau's bifurcation of authority and power between the *législateur* and the assembly. The claim of sovereignty wandered from the drafters, who spoke, to the ratifiers in whose name the drafters spoke. It was the latter, the ratifiers, who were to supposedly make the final decision. The new American theory basically stated that legitimate constitution making requires a process of ratification by deliberative bodies recently assembled for that very purpose. It was this version of mixed representative and direct democratic government, pioneered in Massachusetts in 1780 that came closest to fulfilling the Rousseauian hopes concerning democratic constitution making.[36] The problem was that the application of the model to the making of the Federal Union[37] was fraught with difficulties. And it was the latter, with its thoroughly representative structure and ambivalence about the locus of sovereignty, which was to assume the character of the American model.

IDENTIFYING THE PEOPLE: THE ONE AND THE MANY IN SPACE

There is no question about the presence of popular sovereignty in the *Federalist*: it is perhaps the central idea. Even assuming the resolution of the dualism of representation, however, there are two fundamental problems with this presence. We are left in doubt concerning the sociological identity and even the geographical location of the popular sovereign of the founding.[38] And we do not know its temporal identity, in other words if this sovereign is the same, in Hamilton's statement, at the founding, as at subsequent moments. The term "by some solemn and authoritative act" does not either tell us whether the actor behind the act, the sovereign, is always the same, or even if the "solemn act" must be the same type. If it is always the same sovereign, as Schmitt too might have maintained, then there is a clear opening, paradoxically to the views of John C. Calhoun or, perhaps in a more modern form, William F. Harris.

---

[36] And even here the sovereignty claims of the townships were highly doubtful given the limited role the ratifying bodies had in actual constitution making, and the absence of any procedures that would allow their input through amendments. In my view, despite appearances and the rhetorics of the time, the new model of 1780 was multi-stage and post-sovereign.

[37] And also, as we will see, independent unitary states. This was also rehearsed in America, in Pennsylvania in 1776.

[38] Lefort "The Permanence of the Theologico-Political" DAPT 230 and P. Rosenvallon, *Le Peuple Introuvable* (Paris: Gallimard, 2002), Introduction and Part One. At the moment of its greatest authority and supposed power, the people become anonymous, or sociologically impossible to identify.

And this is why. Let me return to the point repeated by John Marshall (as late as *McCulloch*) that the Federal Convention only made a recommendation. The biggest problem with the argument is that if this recommendation was to the popular sovereign, as it had to be, the convention had the right to recommend only to the sovereign as it was, not to a sovereign of its own creation. If it were to the latter, a fundamentally creative act would negate or strongly relativize the necessarily posterior idea of a mere recommendation. While this problem is entirely papered over by the noun repeatedly used, *the people*, the sovereign(s) under the Articles were the 13 states, or the people of each of these states (Hamilton in # 15), but in any case acting unanimously, with each state having to have a majority for a decision. Now the Constitution seems to have determined either, what is less likely, that there is a national sovereignty, as in one reading of the Preamble, or, what is more likely given the method of voting proposed, that the people of nine states (or their majorities in conventions) are sufficient to represent the People of the United States.[39] But this would be a new people with respect to the old people of the Articles. Not only is the Federal Convention then making a recommendation to a sovereign, but it is also recommending to a sovereign of its own choice and construction. And while the convention indeed rejected the proposal of Gouverneur Morris to elect one ratificatory convention for the nation as a whole,[40] choosing 9 conventions out of 13 was a formula as arbitrary (though less clearly "national") as choosing one convention where the majority of delegates would decide according to some yet to be determined rule[41], probably more so.[42] Moreover, if it was one national sovereign acting through nine states, its decision ought to have had the power to bind and constrain one to three dissenting states.

---

[39] The same issue came up at the time of the making of the *Grundgesetz*, where to be sure, the ratification majority was binding also on a non-ratifying state like Bavaria that did not ratify, ever, but where the West German states were said to act for the German people as a whole, including the ones in the Russian occupied zone who could not participate, and where the *Grundgesetz* would not be law. Peter H. Merkl, *The Origin of the West German Republic* (New York: Oxford University Press, 1963).

[40] MN July 21 (353). The proposal was not even seconded.

[41] Morris did not suggest that the ratifying single convention should be chosen proportionally, or by equal representation of the states, or, more importantly, whether voting would by states and majority rule, by states by unanimity, or by head according to some majority. We can presume he implied that the new convention would choose its own rules, probably in line with the Philadelphia Convention, i.e., by state and simple majority. He probably was against any binding instructions to the delegates.

[42] Whatever counting rule Morris were to suggest, the people of the United States as it was under the Confederation would arguably be counted. The same is true of course under the unanimity rule of the articles. It is not true under the 9 out of 13 rule, which in principle constructs a new people even if all 13 can wind up ratifying.

We know that Art. 7 stated the contrary: "The Ratification of the Conventions of nine States, shall be sufficient for the Establishment of this Constitution between the States so ratifying the same."

Madison does not go into this difficulty, because he thinks his legal analysis has already dealt with the problem. But if it did so, then the task was accomplished by diminishing the distance between treaty and constitution. If the key text for Ackerman's initial reading was *Federalist* 40, the main text here is #39. When Ackerman finally came around to understand the significance of this text,[43] he too internalized the foundational antinomy. In #39 Madison discusses the levels on which the Constitution is national, "federal" (at that time the meaning was closer to confederal) and mixed. While I will return to the amendment rule later, and its supposedly mixed character, for the moment I am interested in the original foundation that Madison calls federal. In *Federalist* 40, in the midst of passages with references to an apparently unified popular sovereign, he states, in response to Anti-Federalist charges: "Do they require that in the establishment of the Constitution the states should be regarded as distinct and independent sovereigns? They are so regarded by the Constitution." But what could he mean, given the idea often attributed to him, and rightly so, that the constitution mixed federal and national powers? We find out the answer in the very *Federalist* 39 where the theory of the mixed constitution is propounded. While he still claims that the Constitution "is founded on the assent and ratification of the people of America" we are here told that this is not the people "as distinct and independent individuals as composing one entire nation, but as composing the distinct and independent States." To the possible objection that this is just a formula for counting the same people, a point that John Marshall and many others will later argue,[44] he energetically then explains the crucial difference:

> a positive outcome follows neither from the *majority* of the people of the Union, nor from that of the *majority* of the States. It must result from the *unanimous* assent of the several States ... Were the people regarded in this

43 In volume I of *We the People* he cites it (185), without realizing that the multiplication of perspectives being applied to the foundation itself is inconsistent with his idea, that foundations are trans-perspectival because they are based on the incorporation of sovereignty. He also does not seem to be bothered by a federal foundation (here in the meaning of "confederal" as opposed to national, which is inconsistent with the "We the People" slogan as commonly understood. The argument of volume II (Cambridge, MA: Harvard University Press, 1998), shifting to an international law perspective is completely different (pp. 34–35; 53; 64), but forces no re-examination of the earlier position.

44 *McCulloch v. Maryland*, where he entirely unconvincingly states that this is the only way, through state conventions, that the people in the singular could assemble (and we should ask, vote?)

transaction as forming one nation, the will of the majority of the whole people of the United States would bind the minority . . . the will of the majority must be determined either by a comparison of individual votes, or by considering the will of the majority of the States . . . Neither of these rules has been adopted. Each state in ratifying the Constitution, is considered a sovereign body independent of all others, and only to be bound by its own voluntary act. *Federalist # 39* (239–240)

What is described here is the making of a treaty, among many parties, requiring their unanimity. As to the distinction between constitution and treaty laboriously rooted in the popular factor, in this context its role can be re-evaluated too. Since Madison was acutely conscious that entry into the new Union required constitutional change in almost every state,[45] according to the already cited famous distinction between people and government, he did believe that only the people and not the legislatures of each state were empowered to make such a change, even under the cover of making a new treaty.[46] One motivation here was making the task of ratification easier in popular, mono-cameral assemblies, i.e., conventions. But the more important goal was to overcome illegality. To Americans who considered conventions as the functional equivalent of "the people," the demand for popular ratification in each state was easy to make legitimate even in states with specific amendment rules where the demand was illegal. Yet the popular demand converged with the status of a treaty, supposedly made by peoples rather than governments.

Of course, making a treaty, a type of contract or compact, is only one side of the story as the beginning of the passage, referring to the American people, implies. Madison was indeed deadly serious about wanting a United States constitution rather than a mere treaty, and therefore it was important to also conceive ratification by the people (if acting through peoples) and not only by peoples (acting on a deeper, constitutional level, for states). But that only makes the story two stories in one, rather than a fully unified narrative, and it was possible to separate the two. Justices like Wilson, Marshall and Story[47] could focus on the preamble and the popular character of the ratifying conventions,

---

[45] Ackerman, vol. II, p. 36ff.

[46] July 23 at the Federal Convention, [MN] p. 352; August 31, pp. 563–564. It was the second of these that will be relied on by Akil Amar, "Popular Sovereignty and Constitutional Amendment" in S. Levinson, *Responding to Imperfection* (Princeton: Princeton University Press, 1995), p. 97. The bill of rights in question was the Maryland bill of rights. How this was going to be transferred to the federal level is another question, difficult to answer. Maryland was a unitary state, where the first antinomy I have been treating did not and could not appear.

[47] The latter brilliantly in *Martin v. Hunter's Lessee* 1816, the *locus classicus* of the theory of national popular sovereignty along with Wilson's opinion in *Chisholm*, and Marshall's in *McCulloch*.

while their opponents in the main legal cases could fasten on a compact theory derived from Madison,[48] and the unanimity rule of Article VII. The narrative was easy to decompose, and difficult to hold together.

And the second, the compact or treaty story, has important implications. In his second volume Ackerman came to consider several of them, now from an internationalist rather than a constitutionalist point of view. The most important one (that should have disturbed him more than it apparently did) was that the 9 out of 13 in the formula clearly indicated, as he says, *secession* from the Articles of Confederation.[49] The 9 or even 12 potentially were invited to secede by Article VII of the Constitution, the one that *Federalist* 39 comments on, from the Union of the Articles, or: the majorities of the people of the 9+ (counted by states) were so invited, from the people of the 13, if they could not get the unanimous vote of all 13, or rather all their majorities.[50] 11 actually did secede before North Carolina and Rhode Island ratified the Constitution.

Was it an illegitimate secession? Had there been a national one person one vote, argued for by some at the convention and, most recently, Amar, perhaps the constitution would have lost. Was it an illegal secession? After confessing something very close to illegality from a constitutional point of view in # 40, Madison changes his mind in *Federalist* # 43, after a shift to the perspective of international law. Here he explains the right of the parties to a treaty to consider a treaty as a whole breached and potentially void upon the violation of one article, and the absolution of all others from their obligations under that treaty, their authorization to pronounce it "violated and void."[51] While this may not be good international law today under the Vienna Law of Treaties, and Hamilton already had doubts concerning it back then,[52] it

---

[48] For the role of a compact theory in Canada, see Peter Russell, *Constitutional Odyssey* (Toronto: University of Toronto Press, 2004).

[49] As A. Buchanan brilliantly argues this was already the second American secession. The first was the separation of the 13 from the British Empire, according to him "secession" rather than "revolution" since the government of the original whole remained the same, though in control over a seriously reduced geographical area. See *Secession* (Boulder, CO: Westview Press, 1991).

[50] Ackerman, vol. II, p. 34. It should have been more disturbing, because he is an advocate of following the model, rather than the text of the framers. If that model was secession, then the Southern secession of 1860–1861 followed the tradition of the framers, according to the Ackermanian formula, and indeed one could apply every one of his steps from signaling on to this "rebellion." I would bet that in this crowded field I am not the first to point this out.

[51] At the Federal Convention he has already made this argument, at the time for the ratification of the Constitution by the people to distinguish it from a Treaty that would be much easier to violate, either by a state responding to an assumed breach (June 5) or legislative derogation (July 23) (p. 70 and 352).

[52] At the Federal Convention: June 19, (MN) p. 153, where he explicitly says that he is not yet prepared to admit the doctrine that Madison was later to advocate. See also *Federalist* 22.

was probably a possible interpretation of *the law of nations* as it then stood.[53] In that case the question of illegality would have to be moved to the level of the states, where what would be at issue is the status of informal changes of state constitutions through treaty making that would by-pass and in some cases violate their amendment rules.[54] Again today, as, e.g., in the European Union, constitutional courts require formal amendments of national constitutions in most such cases, but that was not so obviously the requirement in the eighteenth century. But could a treaty under that international regime, and under American state law as it then stood, trump domestic constitutional law? Probably not. In any case, as it is clear from remarks of Madison at the Federal Convention, appeal to state popular sovereignty was to make such legal-constitutional issues moot, on the state level, cancelling out the illegality by popular legitimacy that was supposedly a higher legal principle in the states themselves. But: if successful, there was no illegality on the Union level[55] to balance or entirely neutralize by an appeal to the American popular sovereign, a central feature of the thesis of Ackerman.[56] And if, on the other hand, the illegality could not be neutralized on the state level by popular

---

Here seems to refer only to arbitrary revocation of a compact or treaty by a party, and not to a revocation after illegal violation, he also says that in any case the doctrine he seems to consider a "gross heresy" has respectable advocates., perhaps thinking of Madison, already at the Federal Convention.

[53] I am not the right person to decide, but this is Akil Amar's view, relying on the Madison texts and tracing them to Blackstone. He considers the treaty narrative before Ackerman, and comes out for a no illegality thesis, based also on popular sovereignty, but in the states! About that argument as a precedent for extra Article V change, I have more to say more below. I note in passing that Amar is wrong on Hamilton, who retained his doubts on the question of treaty violations even in the *Federalist*. See op.cit. "Popular Sovereignty and Constitutional Amendment" in S. Levinson, *Responding to Imperfection* (Princeton: Princeton University Press, 1995), pp. 93–95.

[54] Amar, op. cit., pp. 95–96; Ackerman, vol. II, p. 36f.

[55] There are other arguments for the absence of illegality like F. MacDonald's. He argues that since the 13 states all established conventions as proposed by the Federal Convention, and the Constitution's Article VII, they in effect implicitly amended the Articles of Confederation. "Introduction" to *Ratifying the Constitution* (Lawrence: University of Kansas Press, 1989). Here the interesting volume he introduces supplies the counter-evidence. The Rhode Island legislature and a referendum as well refused to establish a ratifying convention on at least four occasions, and such a convention was not established or called into session until 1790, 1½ years after the first meeting of the new Congress. The second North Carolinian Convention that ratified the Constitution was however established before then, in November 1789, six months after the meeting of the 1st Congress.

[56] For Akil Amar, such neutralization indeed occurs on the state level. The two differ in that for Ackerman legitimacy based on popular sovereignty makes up for deficient legality, while for Amar it is the bases of legality. There is nothing the popular sovereign could do that would be by definition illegal, an idea that corresponds to the judgment of the French *Conseil constiutionnel* in 1962 both abstractly, and concretely with regard to referenda.

legitimacy, then it also could not be cancelled out by "the American people" as a whole.

Much depends here on point of view, both politically and legally. The *Federalist* is acutely conscious of this, and hopes to get advocates of both states and national sovereignty on board by alternating between the perspectives of international and constitutional law. And to put it all together, there was the option of shifting to the powers of sovereignty, to competences, that indeed can be distributed and then combined or "mixed" among states and the Union. Generally this is the theory of sovereignty that one attributes to the *Federalist*, leading to latter conceptions of dual sovereignty along the lines of enumerated (Union) and reserve (states) powers. But it does not solve the question of the location of the supreme power in the political community, which in the sovereign paradigm is supposed to be the ultimate source of the constitution, on the symbolic level well illustrated by unresolved tension concerning the one and the many in the concept of *the people*.[57] This tension kept the field open to diametrically opposed procedural interpretations, as we will see. But since these turn around the problem of amendment, always a living issue, or most radically around the question of re-founding or "replacement," as against the historical one of the founding, I will turn to it first.

THE ONE AND THE MANY IN TIME, AND THE ANTINOMIC RECOURSE TO PROCEDURE

The amendment rule is a very important stake in the discussion concerning the people of the United States, because it is possible (given the paradoxes of omnipotence) to interpret even the original sovereigns to have created a treaty, or more properly a constitutional treaty, that fundamentally alienates the old governmental sovereignties to a new popular one. It is the latter that appears national and unified, illogically enough in the Preamble not as the result but as the author of the same constitution.[58] In that case the legal locus of sovereignty in the constitution would be, as Dicey claimed, the amendment rule.[59] The amendment rule of the new constitution seems to reflect the mixture theory rather than the unitary language of the Preamble, and indeed Madison describes Article V. "neither wholly national nor wholly federal" just as the fundamental law itself, "neither a national nor a federal Constitution, but a composition of both." Thus in this depiction it is the amendment rule, not

---

[57] This is one of the antinomies of the concept of the people treated by M. Canovan in *The People*; in my view the most important one.

[58] J. Derrida, "Declarations of Independence" *New Political Science*7.1 (1986): 7–15.

[59] *The Law of the Constitution*, 8th ed. (Indianapolis: Liberty Press, 1982), p. 82.

the ratification rule, that reflects the Constitution. Its active agent is defined by Carré de Malberg[60] in terms of a composite organ that excludes organ sovereignty and Dicey as a popular sovereign consisting of three-fourths of the states, which replaces for both the authors of the original constitution in constitution making and constitutional change. Accordingly, even if the Constitution was made as a treaty, the terms of that very treaty made it into a *constitution* where combined majorities (of two types, national and state majorities) admittedly qualified, now bound minorities. Further changes, as already the Bill of Rights made under Article V rules, were constitutional change and not changes by treaty as against, on the formal level at least, repeatedly in the European Community, later Union.

In the given context, Dicey did try to apply his distinction between legal and political sovereignty. While in the UK Parliament, the legal sovereign, could change any feature of the constitution, without limit, given the barest majority, it was in fact limited by the conventions of the constitution in this and other respects, conventions for Dicey expressing the political sovereignty of the British people or at least its electorate.[61] Political sovereignty in this context represented a significantly higher threshold of change, as Carl Schmitt pointed out (*Verfassungslehre*, 26). He may have interpreted the alternative as a revolution, but one also could maintain that there was and still is the convention that fundamental constitutional change in the UK cannot be based simply on the decision of one parliament, and that it required a mandate, achieved in a new election where the plan for constitutional revision was clearly articulated.[62] Given the difficulty of Article V change in the USA, here it can be historically and theoretically argued that political revision of the constitution could take place on a lower level of difficulty, as constitutional change as against alteration or replacement. (German terms: *Verfassungswandlung, Verfassungänderung*: Jellinek[63]) This claim has been fleshed out by the theorists of informal constitutional amendment such as Ackerman and Amar. Both maintain the non-exclusive nature of Article V, and Ackerman in particular, argues that at important constitutional moments like the Reconstruction and the New Deal other paths of change have in fact been followed. And while he attempts to provide a five-step common procedure (signaling, etc.) given its highly abstract, non-legal and, I think, truistic (every temporal process has a beginning, a middle and an end) character it is hard to avoid the conclusion that at each of his constitutional moments, starting with the Founding, the

---

[60] Op. cit.   [61] Dicey, op. cit., pp. 285–291.
[62] Jennings, *The Law and the Constitution* (Lonon: University of London, 1959), pp. 176–179.
[63] *Verfassungänderung u. Verfassungswandlung* (Berlin: Häring, 1906).

meaning of the people was significantly different with respect to what came before.

Thus, relying either on the amendment or revision power to identify the new constituent power in the United States, formally quite a sound argument, or on variously conceived informal methods of constitutional change, makes nonsense of the "one people" idea, not in space as before, unavoidably, but in time. Accordingly there was one "people" of the United States, defined at time one by the Articles of Confederation, a second people, potentially secessionist, at time two, defined by Article VII of the Constitution, a third by Article V (and a 3b, 3c, and 3d if we vary its rules) and a fourth and fifth people by the formally undemanding terms of Ackerman's informal constitutional amendments, and a sixth (as we will see) by the national referendum always possible under popular sovereignty, according to Akil Amar.

We could of course say that behind all of these many bodies of the people there is "we the people," whose precise institutional expression is impossible to predict or define to whom full access is guaranteed by a variety of very different forms, some codified some not, but in each case arbitrarily declared to be the privileged representation or embodiment among all such forms. According to Schmitt, "There cannot exist a regulated procedure through which the activity of the constituent power could be bound."[64] According to Ackerman, "Since the People expressed itself through revolutionary mobilization, it was impossible to predict the precise institutional route the next movement would take in exercising popular sovereignty."[65] Many uncomfortable questions follow. For example: who decides which of the several possible people is activated, and when? Certainly, the people cannot decide, without logical circularity. How do you account for the very possibility that the outcome would depend on that prior decision? And, most importantly, how do you avoid usurpation by a leader or an elite capable of mobilizing sufficient number, with populist slogans, to be able to claim to be the part that expresses the will of the whole? Thus, the perspective should not be a very satisfactory one, even for advocates of the sovereign theory criticized here.[66]

---

[64] *Verfassungslehre* (Berlin: Duncker & Humblot, 1928), 8 III 1: "*Ein geregeltes Verfahren, durch welches die Betätigung der verfassunggebenden Gewalt gebunden wäre, kann es nicht geben.*"

[65] *We the People*: I. 218. I think Colon-Rios and Kalyvas have the same position: J. Colon-Rios, *Weak Constitutionalism* (London: Routledge, 2012); A. Kalyvas, "Popular Sovereignty, Democracy and the Constituent Power" *Constellations* (2005) 12(2).

[66] If we say the opposite and say that none of representations are privileged or complete embodiments of the people, we are fairly close to Carré de Malberg's theory of national sovereignty, which has influenced my post-(organ) sovereign conception. That is incompatible with the Ackerman's claim, e.g., that in constitutional politics the limited form of representation through

That it is unsatisfactory is demonstrated by the search for procedures, expressing the substantial continuity of the sovereign constituent power through time. Accordingly, while the agents of less important constitutional change can vary within and outside of Article V, the agent of the most important types of change, of "the basic structure" of the constitution must be always the same. But how do we find this agent: Unlike in countries where there is an explicit difference between the rules of amendment and replacement, in the USA one must look outside the explicit text to find such an agent, to the original constituent power as against the derived one.[67] Unfortunately, when this search is undertaken at the procedural level, the spatial antinomy returns now in time, in terms of the alternatives of continuous peoples versus people.

Assuming the need to anchor even extra-textual arguments in either the text, or the history of the constitution, three procedural interpretations seem especially interesting. One, proposed by William Harris, is based directly on the text, on Article VII, which was never formally eliminated from the Constitution. Another, made famous by John C. Calhoun, also refers to Article VII, albeit less directly, focusing on its demand of unanimity and its secessionist potential. Finally a third, that of Akil Amar, relies on the supposed pattern of constitution making in (some) states, the proper historical precedent for the sovereign constituent power in a polity that has become national, supposedly through the constitution itself.

I proceed in order of the plausibility of textual foundations, rather than historically. The article VII-based thesis of William Harris represents the best possible and most consistent case for continuity. Given the assumptions of a theory that tends to assume that a creative agent will not and cannot be obliterated in or by its product,[68] it makes a great deal of sense to assume the continuous identity of the people at least from the making of the Federal

the separation of powers is overcome. I think these two perspectives of constitutional politics are confused by Ackerman in I. 181–186; 217–218.

[67] See Spain Part X: Arts. 167–168; Bulgaria Chapter 9: Arts. 153 to 163; Republic of South Africa Art. 74; Germany Arts. 79 and 146; Canada Arts. 38; 41–44; Colombia Art. 374–379; On all this see also chapter 5 below.

[68] *Verfassungslehre*: 8 I. 3 (8th ed., pp. 76–77). Yet Amar assumes exactly that the 13 sovereigns disappear as such with their final ratification of the constitution, recalling Hamilton's suggestion at the Convention, to abolish the states as states. Given the assumptions of the theory, Schmitt and Ackerman are on much firmer ground when they date the end of such original sovereignty, and the creation of a "national" one, to the Civil War, though Ackerman still wishes to say that it was not war and force that accomplished that change, but the act of We the People. But such national people is the result, not the agent. Ackerman himself shows how the authors of the 13th and 14th Amendments constructed their people in both the Congressional and the ratification part of the process, i.e., by exclusions of parts of the people, either as before, or as after.

Constitution on,[69] when the Preamble was ratified, in which case Article VII could be interpreted as the most important rule of change of the Constitution.[70]

Harris admittedly built on an earlier argument of Selden D. Bacon. The latter proposed an internal hierarchy of Article V with the version allowing both drafting and ratifying conventions put apparently in the highest position.[71] The problem was that because of Madison's obvious reluctance to give way to a demand by George Mason to include "the people," namely conventions, within the amendment rule, this highest form, never actually used, did not receive any procedural definition at all.[72] According to Mason, a national convention was required to draft a new or seriously revised constitution, because having only state ratifying conventions would not guarantee sufficient popular role, and, in particular, initiative.[73]

Harris now steps into the breach, and (not illogically) argues that Article VII presupposing a convention such as the one in Philadelphia, as well as the state ratifying bodies, was the clue to the missing procedure in Article V. Either the "incorporation" of Article VII in V or the interpretation of Article VII as a surviving higher rule, could thus lead to the election of a convention such as the one at Philadelphia. Such an extra-ordinary assembly, side by side with Congress, could then arguably recommend changes that would be adopted by a process of ratification through newly elected state conventions. Thus, in a quite imaginative synthesis, Harris argues that the

[69] As Eric Foner rightly reminded me, one could take the initial sovereignty to be a national one, dating back to the Declaration of Independence when the Continental Congress took over the prerogatives of the British Crown. This was Lincoln's position, and Justice Sutherland's in Curtis Wright. In that case, one would have to deny the sovereignty of states altogether, a position inconsistent with the regime of the Articles of Confederation that was after all a reality, mutually and internationally recognized. Justice Wilson's position in Chisholm only stated that Georgia was not sovereign under the Constitution. This assumed most likely that sovereignty could be voluntarily alienated in a compact. Note however that the Chisholm majority was overruled by the 11th Amendment.

[70] Here I will follow and criticize William F. Harris in his highly interesting *The Interpretable Constitution* (Baltimore: Johns Hopkins University Press, 1993).

[71] Followed by congressional-conventional, conventional-legislative and congressional-legislative in that order. To Bacon amendments touching basic structures like federalism, required assent by three-fourths of the state conventions. Cited in Harris, op. cit.

[72] MN: Sept. 8 (609) and Sept. 15 (649) for their interesting exchange. Only Hamilton seemed to have been conscious of the fact that they were fashioning too difficult a rule for necessary technical changes (609). But he was also for a purely Congressional formula of initiation, drafting, and submission that was proposed by Madison. The latter's poorly argued critiques of Jefferson and of the Pennsylvania scheme of amendments (*Federalist* # 49 and 50) indicate that he wished to keep the amending process in governmental hands.

[73] For the difference between popular initiative and ratification, see Karl Loewenstein, op. cit., pp. 315ff.

four rules within Article V can be hierarchized as gradual approximations of Article VII. Accordingly, Article VII itself, remaining alive in the Constitution after ratification, could then be seen as the fifth rule of formal change. The four of Article V are within the Constitution, and would be what the French would call *constitué* or *constituant derivée*. Article VII would refer to the popular sovereign before, above, and outside the Constitution, and would be the vehicle for the *constituant originaire*.

But three issues remain unclear. First when do the various procedures (and especially the highest one) kick in? As things stand today, the choice between two forms of ratification belongs to Congress, while the calling of a federal convention is the prerogative of two-thirds of the state legislatures. But when and how and by whom would the Article VII procedure be initiated, and what exactly would it consist of? And, secondly, does an Article VII amendment or constitutional replacement require the affirmative vote 9/13 (= 70 percent = (today) 35 states) or, alternately, all the states? Finally, third, if only a 9/13 qualified majority is required, as in 1787, does the affirmative vote bind the minority as under Article V? Or, alternately, if the 1787 precedent is followed, what happens to states that do not ratify amendments that do receive the required support, do they just nullify these at least when that is logically possible, or more drastically, are they thereby allowed and even forced to secede from the Union?[74]

The probable, if very partial answer to the first question, that I dealt with elsewhere,[75] is that procedurally the task of calling a convention is already assigned to Congress, and, substantively, the only "triggers" imaginable are issues having to do with the basic structure of the Constitution, preferably indicated by some constitutional text, and necessarily interpreted by something like an apex court that would have to invalidate an amendment made under a lower-level rule.[76] There is one such a text in the US Constitution, hardly

---

[74] Article VII says only: "The Ratification of the Conventions of nine States, shall be sufficient for the Establishment of this Constitution between the States so ratifying the Same." Obviously, this cannot mean nine states anymore, but the same proportion. That means 7/10, or 35 today. This is three fewer than what is required by Article V. Assuming that Article VII means a convention recommends to state conventions, as Harris and I both would, this formula is easier than the convention route of Article V unless it is given one of two interpretations that I will mention here. The inability to bind the minority, and hence passing the amendment by 35 and risking nullification or secession by or of the rest, or, as Harris is inclined to do, assume that this rule now and has always meant unanimity. Originally, however it was unanimity for perspective treaty members, i.e., nine at least, and now all current members, presently 50.

[75] See my "Multi-Track Constitutionalism Beyond Carl Schmitt," *Constellations* 18.3 (2011): 324–351.; and also chapter 5 below.

[76] Harris does not and cannot, of course, restrict himself in this way since the US text provides no guidance here, until perhaps the very highest level as we will see. Actually, as

exhaustive in this respect, having to do with the fundamental limitation on Article V, namely that the two-person representation of each state in the Senate cannot be changed without its consent. This logically means that Article V itself, or at least its relevant part, cannot be changed by its use, without making the original rule meaningless, if in a two step-procedure. While H. L. A. Hart has shown self-referring laws are indeed possible, Peter Suber has demonstrated that in such contexts we must assume implicit self-referential entrenchment.[77] So, as Harris himself claims, Article VII is the only rule that one could legitimately use to change (an implicitly self-entrenched) Article V. This has substantive as well as formal implications. One could, in other words, arguably extend the scope of such high level change (and the corresponding self-entrenchment of Article V) to include, e.g., reducing the competences of the Senate, or even weakening federalism in the system that the Senate is meant to express.[78] What can equal membership mean in a body of no importance, we might ask?

The second and third questions cannot be answered definitively, without any textual guidance. If we interpret the constitution as a treaty, as does John C. Calhoun, the answer would have to be either unanimity, or the 9/13 rule linked to secession. If we interpret it as a full-fledged constitution, then 9/13 could bind the minority. Note, however, that this last answer would be doubly

---

already indicated, he proposes a five-level structure based on the four possibilities of Article V (legislatures-legislatures, legislatures-conventions, convention-legislatures, and convention-conventions) adding Article VII the highest level. Unfortunately, there is no way, by the light of this particular US Constitution, to arrange permissible changes among the first four levels of Harris. He knows the courts have refused to regard the structure this way, in spite of the inherent plausibility of the convention formulas representing something higher than the legislature based ones. So he imagines he can give guidance to Congress, that has the choice of choosing amendment routes supposedly (incorrectly, since it is "on the Application of the Legislatures of two thirds of the several States" that Congress "shall call a Convention" having in that case ("shall") no choice in the matter, and it cannot otherwise order such a Convention!) pp. 199–200. But this enterprise is hopeless, even if the ideas are intelligent. There could be other, equally intelligent bases for classification, and Congress in the end will be stuck with some rationalization for the politically convenient formula of ratification (where it does indeed have the choice) at the time. In my view, the fifth level is another matter, because both textual support for it, namely the unchangeable provision in Article V, and also because whatever is highest in a constitution, or most basic, the amendment rule must logically be on the same level in order to avoid making the changes on this highest level more easy, through an indirect route.

77 P. Suber's *The Paradox of Self-Amendment* (New York: Peter Lang, 1990). The same is true for any other article that touches on amending powers. There are many in the Indian Constitution, and in the Turkish, Article 148 that deals with the Constitutional Court.

78 The attempt has indeed been made, unsuccessfully, when contesting the 18th Amendment. See W. Marbury's classic article: "Limitations Upon the Amending Power." *Harvard Law Review* 33 (1919): 223.

illogical. It would not maintain the same people as did Article VII, and that was the basic aspiration of the very turn to that Article. And it would be illogical to link a more fundamental change to a lower qualified majority of 70 percent of the states, when lower-level changes required 75 percent, ie. the three-fourths figure of Article V. I note that Harris opts for unanimity (p. 191), which would allow basic alteration without the threat of secession, but at the same time would, as in Canada after 1982, make change extremely unlikely.

This argument has an important place in the theory of sovereign constitution making, of which Harris is an unabashed adherent without ever referring to European theory. Interpreting Article V as a constituted power, or a derived constituent power, and Article VII as the expression of the original constituent power of the people à la Carl Schmitt, one not extinguished by the Constitution,[79] one could say that what is off-limits for V and its constituted people (Harris: "the constitutional people") is not off limits for VII and its constituent people (his "sovereign people" or "sovereign constitution making people").[80]

Nevertheless, there has never been a serious attempt to use Article VII (or for that matter the national convention formula within Article V) or even a context in which this use became highly likely. And this is so not only because of the general neglect of the convention formula usually linked to the fear of runaway conventions or the plausible view that Article VII *did* extinguish itself upon ratification. For a federation already in existence, one cannot strictly follow a ratification rule that brought it together in the first place. The idea thus leads to two bad choices. To expand the meaning of ratification to mean unanimity, with possible vetoes by even single states as Rhode Island in the past, would greatly reduce the significance of this conceptual innovation. It was, among other things, to avoid such vetoes by small minorities that the

---

[79] Op. cit., 201. "However it may be a necessary invention from the inside, that sovereign seems to hover outside the constitutional order capable of reasserting itself as the maker of an entirely new order." It is not clear whether it is only the people *within* the Constitution that Harris exempts from the judgment from Kelsen to Derrida, that it is created by the legal text itself, and its constitutional authority. But how did the sovereign *outside* the constitution emerge? If he thinks that it is also constructed, then by whom and through what text? If it is by the constitution, that imposes formal limits on all agents, including on those under Article VII, what puts it outside nevertheless, and what is the justification to treat its capacity to remake the whole thing as unlimited? The reference to "the whole people" as an actor is evidently mythological.

[80] Some constitutions, as I will show in part express this relation more clearly and deliberately in multi-track amendment rules, see fn. 64 above. There are constitutions, as in the case of India, without formal limits to amendment and Turkey, with such limits where issues of basic structure have been referred to by apex courts to as within the jurisdiction of original acts of constitution making only.

Constitution was created in the first place. But to use the ratifying formula, as it was written, one aping the original creation of the Union, had to mean inviting or allowing dissenting states to secede from the Union, since there is now a new constitution, the supreme law of the land with an altered basic structure, to which they may not agree.[81]

The deep relationship between the views of Harris and John C. Calhoun's is indicated by the insistence on Article VII in the one case, and the sovereignty of each state in the other.[82] In either case, the result is conservative with respect to the old treaty, whether the weapon will be the requirement of unanimity or the threat of secession. The dissenting state or states can achieve the same end, as with a secession threat of stopping a new type of federation from emerging by having a veto on all possible Article VII amendments.

As is well known, Calhoun was extremely insistent that the Constitution was to begin with and remained an international treaty that in no way extinguished the original sovereign powers of the states that gave it birth.[83] We the People of the United States must be understood as a plural (93f; 96) as in the original version of the text. (Why the original version was replaced in that case he does not tell us.) With this said, however, he very much linked the topics of original sovereignty, fundamental amendment and secession. As far as he was concerned, this implied that no new regulation coming from the Federal Government could impair the sovereignty, or diminish the jurisdiction of the sovereigns, whatever the federal courts may say in a given case. It is up to a sovereign state to protect its prerogatives, and this it does through nullification of the simple statutes in question, by not applying them in the state.[84] Above all, he denied the supremacy of federal laws vis-à-vis state laws. He was more careful with the constitution, that he had to accept as supreme for reasons of text, but adding the proviso that this was below the level of the sovereign powers that it did not extinguish. Moreover the supremacy did not transfer to ordinary legislative acts.

---

[81] It would seem furthermore, in the treaty narrative, that the burden of violation would be on the rest for adopting it without unanimity. That was Rhode Island's position in 1788 before it was forced to buckle under pressure

[82] The latter is not Harris' view: he regards the American popular sovereign as the whole people, which alone justifies the claim of unlimited power. This could be close to the Carré Malberg concept of national sovereignty, since the whole people can never appear or act, and so no one could be given the unlimited power to act and change. But identifying Article VII as the vehicle of the whole constituent people outside the constitution produces the same outcomes as insisting on individual state constitutive sovereignty.

[83] J.C. Calhoun, "A Discourse on the Constitution and Government of the United States"in *Union and Liberty: The Political Philosophy of John C. Calhoun* (Indianapolis: Liberty Fund, 1992).

[84] 198ff; "Speech on the Force Bill," 428–429; in *Union and Liberty*.

Calhoun did not go so far, however, as to argue that federal statutes could be definitively and irrevocably cancelled by state acts. Thus, in the case of a nullification of a federal statute (or: presidential order; or: court decision) a state act could be trumped by a Federal Article V amendment, by the voice of three-fourths of the states against the one.[85] All these imaginative ideas are simply made up; there is no textual foundation for them. What is behind it is the notion of constitutional supremacy that in his view can be exercised, but only by amendment and not through judicial interpretation. It is with this move that Calhoun recognized that the U.S. was more than an alliance or a limited form of a treaty organization, and that (qualified) majority voting of the whole polity had a higher status *within* it than the dissenting voice of any single member. It could, however, trump the legislative will of a member, but not its sovereignty. That member remained *both* an entity and an organ within (when it legislated), and a "constituent subject without," to use Harris' term (when sovereign).[86] Thus, it could decide whether it wished to remain in a polity that was being fundamentally modified in its estimation, and without its consent. Dangerous laws could be resisted by nullification. Even more important, fundamental amendments within the system, could be resisted by constituent sovereigns, standing outside the system, ultimately by secession (200f; 206; 212). To continue this train of thought, if such amendments were rightly understood as violations of the original treaty, secession would be legal. The banding together of seceding states in a new federation or confederation would be legal too. All this would mean applying the model of the framers, in its treaty narrative, based on the constituent sovereignty of the states that survives the constitution as in the theory of sovereign constitution making, to a new situation, to be sure in the most radical version.

As I argued, the temporal continuity thesis, remains vulnerable to the spatial antinomy of sovereignty. This is so because there are equally radical and

---

[85] Interestingly, Calhoun avoided the convention formula in Article V, or the precedent of the framers in this respect, not only for the abstract reason that they were more national than the two-chamber, qualified majority formulas of the same Article V. A national convention could have much more easily generated an anti-slave majority, than Congress where it would have to gain the two-thirds of each chamber to be relevant. And a runaway convention could again change the three-fourtha ratification rule, to the detriment of the slave interest in the South that could then always muster more than a fourth.

[86] We see similar doubling in the European Union today, where states appear as organs of the Union, and as "masters of the treaties," both inside and outside. It is an interesting question whether individual country Constitutional Courts can claim rights that would amount to nullification, in terms of state sovereignty. Even in Calhoun such acts could not be final. In Europe, where the ultimate amendment rules remain based on unanimity, Calhoun's option of the next stage would not work however.

consistent stories to tell, in the unitary narrative, assuming the sovereign theory of constitution making and constituent sovereignty. Let me just select
the most radical one[87] I can think of to balance Calhoun's now (hopefully)
obsolete claims.[88] To begin with, Akil Amar denies the claims of illegality of
the founding made recently and most emphatically by Ackerman.[89] Whatever
international lawyers now would think of the matter, Amar fully buys into
Madison's story about treaty violation, and legal secession. Fine. As to Ackerman's stress on the violations of state constitutions he tends to dismiss this
matter as well. Whether these had to do with amendment rules, governmental
like that of Maryland which he mentions,[90] or involving popular conventions
that he curiously neglects, these are all made good by a reference to a higher
legal principle, popular sovereignty, in the Declaration of Independence, in
some (not all, at least explicitly) state bill of rights and constitutional texts. The
reader suspects that Amar systematically confuses legality and legitimacy, by
considering what is legitimate in his eyes also to be legal. It goes without saying that for him the freely elected conventions recommended by Article VII
are expressions of popular sovereignty. Nevertheless it is not clear how the
decision of these bodies, could trump (and therefore extralegally amend) the
state constitutions, that in Massachusetts and New Hampshire were made by
freely elected conventions, and in addition were ratified by the townships.
Amar mentions one not entirely convincing reason: they involve time limits,
and the people can change their constitution *any time*.[91] He does not seem to

---

[87] Not, however, the most interesting one, namely Lincoln's and Justice Sutherland's in *Curtiss
Wright* v. *US*. They, however, did not concoct a purely national amendment rule, as did
Amar.

[88] It is because of greater radicalness that I chose Amar here, and not because of importance or
influence. That honor goes to Ackerman, who has tried to deal with American constitutional
history from the point of view of the sovereign theory, and did so relatively effectively. As to his
views of the founding, I think I have sufficiently articulated some its difficulties and antinomies
already, that reflect but do not resolve those of the Framers. Amar's conception is a simpler,
and more consistent case of lawyering, one might say, one that has absolutely no relation to
what may be done in future constitutional change in the USA. But whether he knows it or not,
the argument from simple, majoritarian popular sovereignty has had many followers in places
where unitary sovereignty was an easier claim to make, or where plebiscitary leaders added
their charismatic authority to the argument.

[89] Yet, especially after Ackerman's second volume that included a treaty-based narrative, there is
now less of a difference between what they are really saying about the process then they may
imagine.

[90] But even here the new election between two legislative acts, producing a new legislature,
counts to him as of lower democratic pedigree than the act of an elected convention, or worse
still, or mere representation as against embodiment of the people or its will.

[91] Op. cit., p. 101.

notice the different meaning of the people in each case, or simply discounts it, nor the problem that a more democratic and participatory process establishing the time limits was overruled by a less democratic one, not involving the townships in these two cases.

But what really matters for Amar is not the level of democratic participation, but the point stressed by Harris, except more clearly: to be outside the constitution. This move to the outside allows Amar to follow the Framers in constructing his own idea of who the people are, in each case, and in this he is no different than Ackerman. Both assume that the genuinely sovereign people exists outside the amendment rule and therefore outside of constitutions, and come thereby close to Harris' idea of two peoples, the constituent and constituted one, that is the staple of the sovereign theory of constitution making.[92] Moreover, they are all trying to imitate the model of the founding, but with the difference that while for Harris and Ackerman it is the Federal Founding that is central, for Amar it is the emergence of its components in the individual states. Only there can he find a constituent people, the unified popular sovereign that created the constitution.[93] Did this people also survive the making of the constitution? If so, Amar would fall into Calhoun's trap. Thus, what he maintains is that it did not, and the state sovereigns can be referred to only for the purposes of an analogy. Amar has a continuity thesis, but his continuous people begins with the federal union itself. Yet how can a people created by the federal constitution be outside it?

Here is where the problems begin for Amar, who wishes to transpose the model based on the manner the individual states have dealt with the claim of illegality during the founding of the Union. In this view the states simply cancelled out illegality having to do with the violation of their amendment rule, by a turn to a higher, if unwritten amendment rule, namely popular sovereignty, meaning assembling and voting in a newly elected convention. I note in passing that this is not the same as a state referendum, as Amar seems to think, nor ratification by direct democratic townships. In any case, it is this model of the states that should be followed, according to Amar, not the model of treaty breaking and secession. But on what bases? On the bases of two principles: the unitary state and pure majority rule.

---

[92] For Schmitt's interesting idea of three peoples (1. Before and above; 2. In; and 3. Next to the constitution that includes in addition the people of the public sphere). See *Verfassungslehre*, chapter 18.

[93] E.g., that the original popular sovereign, assembled in a convention, supposedly survived the making of the Maryland constitution with its two-phase amendment rule with a popular election (although it does not express the constituent people!) in between two legislative acts.

I do not want to spend too much time on the latter, which I consider unsuitable as anything but a partial decision rule for complex societies.[94] As a rule for constitution making and revising, majority decision should be rejected along with the makers of most of today's constitutions.[95] It is, of course, amendment rules such as theirs that Amar wishes to bypass through the argument of a non-exclusivity of these rules, and the eternal co-presence outside the constitution of a higher rule, based on popular sovereignty, in his case acting through majority rule. But who is that sovereign, and what should be the relevant higher rule? For the USA, since the full enactment of the Constitution, according to Amar, it is the whole people of the United States, acting through its majority, which would have to act through a majoritarian and populist referendum of the voters counted as individuals.[96]

Thus, Amar's postulate leaves Article VII as well as the convention of Article V well behind and points to a national referendum on amendments proposed by a majority of American voters, which would have to approved by a simple

---

[94] It is true that only unanimity and majority rule resemble non-arbitrary rules, but even they have an element of arbitrariness because one can always have unanimity or majority of all those eligible, or only those participating, and these numbers can be vastly different. Qualified majorities, or as their opponents like to call them, minority vetoes, may be more arbitrary, since the number can vary from 51 to 99 percent of either the whole or those present (Amar op.cit. 111). But their principle is not at all arbitrary. It is based on the value of consensus, that is, coming to agreement with minorities and devising formulas fair to both sides, rather than majority rule, which can mean intolerable imposition on small or large minorities. Consensus is different than the proto-consociational formula of Calhoun's concurrent majorities, applied in his nullification argument. Consensus always reflects a majority's will more than a minority's, but does not do so completely. It usually means that the majority must accept a second or third best, while a minority must live with the third or second worst. Or: it will mean that when there are many issues of disagreement, on a few issues the minority will prevail. Majority rule can mean that the minority will never prevail. The more divided a society, the more important the principle of consensus becomes. One may disagree with this principle, but it is certainly not more arbitrary than that of majority rule. One may wish to restrict it by a few fundamental principles that cannot be compromised, but this means that when such principles are not involved pragmatic compromise is morally acceptable. Now, when it comes to voting rules, and types of majority, the principle of consensus in general requires empirical consensus in each situation about the actual if arbitrary number. The principle here is not arbitrary, even if the eventual number may be.

[95] And along with the US framers, who quite consciously opted for a rule with two types of qualified majorities in it. See D. Dow, "The Plain Meaning of Article V." in Sanford Levinson, ed., *Responding to Imperfection: the Theory and Practice of Constitutional Amendment* (Princeton, NJ: Princeton University Press, 1995), pp. 125 and 139. Dow rightly says that our commitment to majoritarianism is at best partial

[96] Several arbitrary decisions are lurking in this proposal, but for now I only mention them: for majority vs unanimity, for relative vs absolute majority, for referendum v. electoral democracy, for atomized vs deliberative referenda or caucuses. On almost all points I would choose the opposite, except perhaps on unanimity, since I am no fan of the *liberum veto*.

majority of these voters. Absurd, this initiative of over 70 million registered voters, but this is what he says. More significantly, he commits himself to the theory, namely James Wilson's, that the Constitution established the sovereignty of the national people, and that "We the People" as well as the language of the 9th and 10th Amendments indicate a singular, a unitary national sovereignty. We should, according to him, think of a merger in which two previously independent entities, firms became one. It is strange, I note, that the USA did not accordingly become a unitary state in 1787, perhaps a decentralized one, or that Hamilton's suggestion that the states "as states" should be abolished was not even seriously entertained by the Convention. Nor was Morris' suggestion for a single ratifying convention. What was the point of these suggestions, if the constitution did the work of full unification without them? What Amar is seeking is a pure model based on popular sovereignty, and finds it only on the level of the states, in the process forgetting the procedures of the Federal Convention, that he is shrewd enough to recognize will not fit his abstract conception. Though the generation of alternative legality from popular sovereignty did not occur on the federal level, the example of the states in this respect could now be seen as the precedent for the Federal Union too. It was not the Federal Convention, not its Article VII, nor the process as a whole, and certainly not any part of its Article V that are to be the true precedents for future popular constitution making, but the acts of the popular sovereigns of those states that have all transformed their constitutions merely through voting affirmatively, sometimes by the slimmest majorities as he says.[97]

But Amar is right on one thing, technically. Divided sovereignty is a problem conceptually, and perhaps even a contradiction in terms, as the opposing sides in 1787 realized.[98] Yet the important argument against divided sovereignty notwithstanding, the dismissive treatment of Madison's thoughtful reflections in *Federalist* #39 on the mixed nature of the constitution they made is entirely unwarranted, especially since the sovereignty mix he had in mind, dealt with the powers of the sovereign that could indeed be distributed. Amending powers too of whatever sort can be combined.[99] Moreover, it seems especially

---

[97] p. 103. Never mind that these deliberative bodies were also not referenda! He considers this to be only a liability because of the bad communication conditions of the time. The lack of knowledge here about the history and problems of plebiscites and referenda is appalling.

[98] Though probably not because of their attachment of popular sovereignty understood in a majoritarian manner as Amar imagines (114), but because of the classical definition involving supremacy: no equal within the state, only equals internationally.

[99] Ackerman shows this for his informal amendments, which make use of various institutions and various majorities, but always a popular factor, eventually stressing, rightly, that of relevant elections.

questionable for Amar to pronounce the establishment of a unified national sovereignty an open and shut case in 1787, when the Jeffersonian revolution was yet to take place, and a Civil War was going to be fought over this very matter in less than four score years.[100] As David Dow suggests, this is just the view that Madison wrote *Federalist #39* against, based on the accusation of the anti-Federalists: "They ought with equal care to have preserved the *federal* form, which regards the Union as a *Confederacy* of sovereign states; instead of which they have framed a *national* government which regards the Union as a *Consolidation* of States."[101] Madison is, of course, obviously right in answering that neither perspective completely describes what they have done, and aside from the form of sovereignty, discussed only in the segment on ratification, the theory of a mixed form limited to the *powers* and not the ultimate locus of sovereignty is quite convincing. It is also right in the matter of sovereignty, that on the level of constitution making the states are said to be sovereign, while in the case of amending – there is no clue that Madison considering the amending power a lesser one – we get a mixture. But it is a mixture in which no part can act alone, no organ is sovereign. It is a mixture fully compatible with the concept of United States "state" sovereignty, if not understood as internally unitary, nor as Amar actually realizes, as the notion of popular sovereignty understood in terms of an organ.[102]

That is what Amar wants to replace with a new form of organ sovereignty, the body of the people in a referendum for which the constitution supplies not a clue, and if anyone imagined it possible, the document could never

[100] For an effective counter-argument see Dow op. cit., 140–141, with whom I do not agree on the narrow question of sovereignty (not in my view merely a matter of the residual sovereignty distributed to the states), but who does give a strong and correct defense of Madison's mixed model of the new state.

[101] p. 239.

[102] Again the eighteenth century, and indeed the correct critique of divided sovereignty, was on the level of state sovereignty, not with popular sovereignty as Amar hints at. If an amendment rule were to allow the states on their own initiative, and the institutions of the federal government, separately, to amend the constitution, on the same level, we would have a divided form of state sovereignty on the level of its constituent competence, to many the Kompetenz-Kompetenz. By *combining* acts of these levels Article V does not divide sovereignty, but forces different powers to cooperate in its exercise. It is true that such a mixed formula makes it difficult to say who expresses the will of the people in it, though someone like Dicey had a point insisting, in terms of the European tradition of ratification, that it is the ultimate instance that ratifies, namely three-fourths of the states. The other instance only recommends. But a ratification that cannot alter anything has to share the power with the drafting organ, which will force ratification through the design. So the people's power is shared, even if its authority, under the constitution, is practiced through the ratifying instance alone. But then the latter shares authority as well: with the Constitution itself. The pure popular sovereign as a body is nowhere to be found.

have been ratified in most of the states. In practice, the method of change he insists is not likely to be ever practiced in America – unlike France in 1962, when de Gaulle extraconstitutionally adopted a referendum formula close to Amar's.[103] But on the level of pure theory too, if one could interpret the unified We composed of individuals (Calhoun's "king numbers") of the Preamble as standing outside the constitution, and surviving outside it as its highest agency of change, one could do the same with the states of Article VII. In each case there will be a high level of arbitrariness regarding the alternative method of proceeding, well illustrated by both Amar's conjuring up a never-thought-of national, majoritarian referendum as his vehicle, and by Harris' structuring an imaginative five-stage amendment sequence without sufficient textual guidance. Sadly enough, it is Calhoun who has generated the most consistent and least arbitrary scheme based on his notion of the original sovereign constituent powers that survive the constitution, implying the possibility of secession. And yet, this proposal too is for the moment dead, even if we cannot say that it will never return.

Given all this textualism does not seem as unattractive as its critics wish to make it, even if Article V can today be rightly seen as a prison, one that has harmful consequences for constitutional politics. But in any case it just will not do to point to all the arbitrary features and well known liabilities of Article V to defend one's own "going out to sea," as does Amar.[104] The problems of such an overly difficult rule, with its nearly unamendable clause but only implicit self-reference, as well as the lack of institutional guidance for its convention formula are all real, but it is just as real what Dicey says that in this rule the framers have given a clear functional equivalent of the people in the form of elected bodies of ¾ of the states (admittedly leaving room for some congressional tinkering with the convention-legislature choice). That is

[103] The Gaullist turn from legality to popular sovereignty was imitated recently in Colombia and Venezuela, with quite different results in the two cases. Renata Segura and Ana María Bejarano. "¡Ni una asamblea más sin nosotros! Exclusion, Inclusion, and the Politics of Constitution-Making in the Andes." *Constellations* 11.2 (2004): 217–236; Nicolás Figueroa, "Counter-Hegemonic Constitutionalism: The Case of Colombia." *Constellations* 19.2 (2012): 235–247; Allan R. Brewer-Carías, *Dismantling Democracy in Venezuela: The Chávez Authoritarian Experiment* (Cambridge: Cambridge University Press, 2010). On these cases see chapter 4 below.

[104] "Going out to sea" even better describes S. Levinson's proposal, where he proposes starting out under Article V. by using a lot to choose the national convention. Its members would have to have a couple of years of legal instruction before they could deliberate, presumably by Levinson himself, but possibly by a representative collegium of jurists. And who chooses them? Sanford Levinson, *Framed: America's 51 Constitutions and the Crisis of Governance* (Oxford: Oxford University Press, USA, 2012); Andrew Arato, "Framed. America's 51 Constitutions and the Crisis of Governance" *Constellations* 20.3 (2013): 503–507.

not a model of mixed sovereignty, but a form of national legal sovereignty in which state legislatures and Congress, must act together, and neither alone nor even a specially elected convention can fully embody the American people. It is this latter embodiment model that the contrasting alternatives of Calhoun and Amar share. Yet neither version could be made sense of within the type of Union established in 1787, a Federation, or even the Federal State that emerged after 1865.

THE USA AS A FEDERATION AND THE PROCESS OF ITS CONSTITUTION MAKING

According to Carl Schmitt, beyond and between the dichotomous form of treaty organization, including alliance or perhaps confederation (Allianz, Bündnis), and unified state including the federal state (*Bundesstaat*), we should take cognizance of a third political form, the federation of states (*Staatenbund*) or federation (*Bund*).[105] While he analyzes mostly the abstract form, according to him the United States till the Civil War was an example of such a federation. Today (as he saw it, in the 1920s, i.e.) the USA is no longer a federation, but a federal state (*Verfassungslehre*, 189). Schmitt regarded federation in general, or constitution making by contract, and the US pattern in particular, I think wrongly, as inferior forms of the modern constituent power. Nevertheless, his theory of the federation is particularly useful, because it is almost free of the mythologizing and ideological elements of his theory of the unified constituent power under a state.[106] It may even be possible to derive important lessons from this conception for a theory of legitimate, post sovereign constitution making.

In Schmitt's depiction, a federation is formed when two or more states, each with its own independent constituent power, form a new unit, intended to last (ibid., pp. 62–63; 366–368), for the evidently Hobbesian purpose of the political self-preservation of each of the members, to guard against external war and to maintain the internal peace. Like a treaty, this involves a contractual

---

[105] Recent attempts to use his theory: Murray Forsyth, *Unions of States: The Theory and Practice of Confederation* (London: Burns & Oates, 1981); Olivier Beaud, *Théorie de la Fédération* (Paris: Presses Universitaires de France-PUF, 2007); Jean Cohen, *Globalization and Sovereignty* (Cambridge: Cambridge University Press, 2012).

[106] See *Verfassungslehre*, chapters 29 and 30. This is not to claim that the section of the book did not have a political purpose like all his texts: it was to show that a nonhomogeneous treaty organization of nations like the League of Nations (in German *Völkerbund* = Federation of Peoples) could not be a true federation. There is no polemic involved in the application to the United States, except perhaps the desire to show the priority of the French revolution's model, and its greater relevance to "states."

agreement, a "contract" made by organized entities with one another as against the individuals of natural law theory. In contrast to a treaty in international law (71), this agreement is a "status contract." The new unit has a constitution, or a constitutional treaty that essentially changes the status, the constitution of each member whether or not there are any formal changes made in the documentary constitutions (63; 366–368). While there is constitution making on two levels, then, the new unit, and the member states, this does not change the nature of the constituent power, which continues to inhere in the members. The new unit, according to Schmitt, has no constituent power as such. This is an error, and it can be construed, as I will show, in terms of the sovereign theory of the constituent power of the people, requiring the kind of unity characteristic of a state in acts of constitution making. It is on this level that Schmitt, even when apparently backing away from political theological discourse of the sovereign theory hoped to satisfy its requirements.[107]

The constitutional treaty of the federation, the *Statusvertrag*, is not a free contract (chapter 7: 67–68). This should mean, contrary to Madison's view in 1787, that the treaty cannot be voluntarily renounced by its members; the union is meant to be "eternal" or perpetual, even if Schmitt in the end cannot make this point consistently once he takes into account actors' perspectives he considers possibly valid. While his analysis is clearly informed by a variety of European, especially German experiments with the form of federation, when coming to the most serious problems of this form he seems to particularly focus on the American case. He thinks the form is unstable, and leads to antinomies, and while these antinomies are manageable through political or social homogeneity, he argues that the democratic form of homogenization leads to the abolition of the form itself. This too is wrong, or is based on an anti-liberal, anti-republican, even anti-institutional notion of democracy, namely plebiscitary leveling democracy.

Putting a complex analysis very simply,[108] according to Schmitt the federation is antinomic because it establishes a new political organization with a will that is capable of independent action, and yet maintains the old members in their ultimate independence (370–372). This leads not to a division of sovereignty, rejected in principle, but alternative sovereignty claims from both sides, each of which can be theoretically sustained until a final conflict can decide the issue. While one leads to the right of secession, the other

---

[107] Thus, the inclusion of the American Federal constitution making under the possible forms that satisfy his theory of the constituent power has to do with the constituent power of the individual states that ratify the constitution. 8 IV 3c. The singular of "We the people" is disregarded.

[108] For a more detailed account, see Cohen, op. cit.

equally resolutely denies it.[109] He illustrates for the USA only John C. Calhoun's side, one that he considers important, but as a theory (rather than the language of an actor) ultimately unacceptable because of its neglect of the opposing equally valid actors' perspective. (He would have to say the same on the other side about the James Wilson, Daniel Webster, Lincoln, the Justice Sutherland of *Curtiss Wright*, and now Akil Amar line as well, at least until the Civil War.) According to Schmitt, the supposed division of sovereignty, or rather of sovereign powers, as a compromise between these positions, works only as long as a fundamental conflict can be avoided (378–379). According to him, this too is not a division of sovereignty, but a suspension, a deferral of the conflict and the decision over sovereignty. But a fundamental conflict cannot be avoided when the units are as divided as the American states were over slavery and other issues like the tariff or the freedom of trade.

Thus the precondition of the longevity of the federation, or its dealing with its deep-seated antinomy, is homogeneity, social, or, as he says, citing Montesquieu's stress on a republican form, political (375–378). It is exactly the last solution, however, that did not work in America, where, at least initially, all states had similar forms of government but very different societies. So social homogeneity or democratic government representing all adult members is the answer, but it is a self-destructive one, according to Schmitt. A social form based on equality (Schmitt follows Tocqueville here) is tough to reconcile with the federation, which implies equality of states, but given their very likely different size not necessarily equality of citizens. The option of a republican or liberal democracy, one based on the equality of rights rather than substantive equality, and especially social homogeneity, is not even entertained. According to Schmitt, a democratic America thus moves away, after the defeat of the South, from the form of the federation, and it is only loyalty to the original constitution that preserves it as a federal state rather than a unitary one (388–389). The last point is historically and, in part, tautologically correct, even if the cause is misidentified. Only the assumption of a plebiscitary democracy based on leveling and massification leads to Schmitt's conclusion, and that picture never described American society and politics.[110]

---

[109] It is in this sense that the perpetual nation of the federation is understood. There is no right of secession from the external observer's point of view; while the participant's perspective is deeply antinomic concerning the same question.

[110] One finds the same outcome in the logic of American state formation as described recently by S. Skowronek, *Building a New American State* (Cambridge: Cambridge University Press, 1982) and R. Bensel, *Yankee Leviathan: the Origins of Central State Authority in America, 1859–1877* (New York: Cambridge University Press, 1990).

I am certainly not interested in debating here whether Schmitt has really succeeded in establishing a third type between treaty organization and federal state, or just an uneasy transition or "hybrid" between them,[111] and even less in whether the USA under the constitution of 1787 was always a federal state or, alternately, remains even now a federation, as before the Civil War. I note only that the most plausible historical stage models of American constitutional development support the Schmittian case about America,[112] and thus we do not merely have to take the word of an outsider about American constitutional history to seriously entertain its most basic shifts (namely: confederation to federation; federation to federal state). There are certainly other plausible ways to conceive this history. What is helpful about this model is that the central antinomy stressed by Schmitt converges with the alternative ways of seeing the constituent power in America from the founding to the present.

I note again that these attempts were all influenced by early versions of the same theory (both of participants and of theorists) of sovereign constitution making that Schmitt will bring to its culmination. Assuming the antinomies of the political form itself, and their source, namely the antinomy of state or "national" sovereignty, did these have to be reproduced in the corresponding theories of the constituent power? My answer is: only if we assume the theory of sovereign constitution making that fundamentally links popular sovereignty and the constituent power through an organ of the state. Then it is easy enough to take one more step that Schmitt admittedly did not take (perhaps under the influence of Calhoun, or because for him constituent power must always be unified) and say that it is equally arguable that the constituent power can be assigned to each of the alternative or antinomic conceptions of the sovereign in the federation. To see this we first have to convict Schmitt of a mistake: the suggestion that the federation has no constituent power that would parallel the opposite error of the blanket denial of the constituent power of the states outside the constitution. This error was of a theorist either caught up in one of the two possible actor or participant perspectives, namely Calhoun's, or of one with a highly unified conception of what it takes to have the constituent

---

[111] I agree with Jean Cohen that Kelsenian language of degrees of centralization, decentralization could be an equal description of the phenomena that Schmitt treats in terms of discrete ideal types. Op. cit.

[112] Most recently and impressively, Ackerman *We the People*, even if he was later forced to modify the three-part model as in *Failure of the Founding Fathers*, focusing on the Jeffersonian revolution. See also Robert G. McCloskey, *The American Supreme Court* (Chicago: University of Chicago Press, 2010), 14–15. McCloskey helpfully depicts the first stage as occupied with "the greatest of all questions left unsolved by the founders – the nation-state relationship . . . whether a nation or a league of sovereign states was created by the Constitution." 17, 13.

power. Most likely it was a case of both. From an external perspective that sees both antinomic sides, the theorist could have noted that participants on the two sides claim both sovereignty and constituent power as their own, and regard the untenable illusion of their combination as a matter of deferral.

However, Schmitt's mistake is instructive. It is his insistence on the sovereign theory of constitution making that leads to the inconsistency here. He is able to entertain sovereignty claims on behalf of the federation, but, inconsistently, constituent power claims only on behalf of the units. He implicitly moves from state to popular sovereignty in doing so. In other words, the move is a consequence of his theory of popular sovereignty, one that entails the identification of the constituent power with a unified actor, whether popular or an organ of the state, the latter speaking in the name of the former. He can claim the existence of such an organ of the unified popular will in the case of the states, but not for a federation held together by a status contract involving necessarily a plurality of agents or actors among whom there is no hierarchy. At the same time, since he has claimed sovereignty for both units and federation in terms of actor perspectives, the denial of constituent power to the federation violates his theory of sovereignty, which after the positivization of law must entail the constituent power. The conception here puts into doubt the claim that federation can be conceived of as an independent form.

The problem disappears, however, if the constitution-making claims are also processed in terms of the post-sovereign theory. That theory could and should still recognize the actors' perspective, which on both sides of the national divide presupposed popular sovereignty as the only legitimate basis of constitution making. Given the common assumption, the constituent power of the federation becomes as conceivable as those of the units. That would correspond to the antinomic conception of the constituent power in America till at least the Civil War, and in theoretical discussions till today. But from the external perspective, the post-sovereign theory can point to an alternative, mixed logic of constitution making that better characterizes the actual American process than either of the antinomic alternatives.

Schmitt himself provides a way out with his discussion of the possible amendment rules for a federation. According to Madison's *Federalist* #39, the federal amending power, with its convention formulas modeled on the process of the framing, is a rule that "mixes" federal and state powers. On the contrary Schmitt does seem to suggest that a treaty rule (obviously implying unanimity like that of the Articles of Confederation[113]) should be the default position for

---

[113] See Forsythe, op. cit., who groups the articles regime under the federation type. I would not, following also the Federalists, though admittedly there were many who in the 1780s insisted

a federation,[114] and a route containing a federal legislative dimension would mean moving away from the political form. That would be consistent with his mistaken idea the idea that a federation does not have constituent power, which seriously weakens his three-term framework, namely the distinction among confederation, federation and federal state (*Bündnis, Bund* and *Bundesstaat*). At the same time, he concedes (admittedly he says: "in a transitional stage" toward a federal state) that a rule that combines federal legislative action with ratification by simple or qualified majority of the member states would preserve the character of a federation (101–102). He is probably thinking of Article V – but this provision of the Constitution was however original, never transitional, for the American federation. If we have three types of polity linking state like entities together, namely Confederation, Federation and Federal State, then we should have three amendment rules. Thus, on the contrary, I tend to think that it is exactly Article V that is the classical type of rule for a federation, and what Schmitt thought of as the treaty like default rule represents the other side of the antinomy linked to the (deferred) conflict over sovereignty. Thus a pure treaty type of rule, as the US ratification rule would belong only to a proto-federation type,[115] or represent the actor's perspective of one of two antinomic sides under a federation.[116] On the other hand, as the USA became a federal state, Article V was no longer the right amendment rule, and it has indeed become a prison house of the constitution, helping to liberate an overactive judicial review that has no convincing trumps over it in the system.[117]

on the closeness of the two constitutional regimes, that the nomenclature also found hard to distinguish.

[114] Even given the sovereign theory of constitution making, the rule Schmitt suggests would be inconsistent with the conflict of sovereignties, or the lack of a decision concerning sovereignty that leads to the antinomy. When the rule he suggests did exist, under the Articles of Confederation, there was no such antinomy. Under that system few claimed that the Union was sovereign or that the states were not. At the convention James Wilson came close; And especially Rufus King, June 19, p. 152.

[115] I think, ideal typically, unanimity, of course, is the rule for a treaty organization. For a federal state Article V is most inappropriate, in my view, given the high veto potential of a small minority of the population. A German rule of two-thirds of each chamber, or perhaps a ratification rule having one more than half the states as in India, and South Africa would still appropriate. A multi-level rule, of course, as in Canada, would be best, where non federal technical issues do not become hostage to rights or federal issues. About that more in Chapter 5.

[116] The antinomy would be represented by Article VII and Article V in actual history, though a hypothetical rule like Amar's national referendum would represent the national side more purely. Historically this last position has no status in America.

[117] Thus, in my view, it should have been revised, along with the post-Civil War amendments. A genuine multi-levelled rule, as in the federal state of Canada after 1982 but without the level of unanimity, would have been preferable to the existing Article V.

Be that as it may, even for Schmitt Article V is still a federation rule. What he does not notice is the relevance of that rule to the American founding itself from which it historically emerged. This is so not only because of his focus primarily on the treaty narrative, but also because of the absolute distinction in his theory between constituent power and amending powers.[118] Without trying to obliterate the distinction altogether, or maintaining the obvious error that the Constitution was after all an Amendment of the articles (pointed out by Ackerman), I want to relativize that distance somewhat, as, e.g., George Mason might have wanted to (and, as we will see, Condorcet, even more so!) when he proposed to include national conventions under the amendment formula of Article V. This will help me try to extricate the American model from the sovereign theory, to which and to whose antinomies I have so far linked it. Schmitt too has ideal typically depicted this model under the sovereign forms, but he has missed the complexity, and mixed nature, of the actual process. Describing it as a form involving great difficulties, he had little to say about the relation of its various institutions, constitutional and ratifying conventions, to one another (86). His theory of the federation put the emphasis on the ratifying instances, where each individual state comes to sovereign agreement concerning a proposal, in the form of a contract or a treaty that produces a constitutional treaty. This follows Madison's view of the founding process (in distinction to the amendment rule) in *Federalist* #39, but to the neglect of #40. It sees the US Constitution as the product of what in Europe today would be called an Inter Governmental Conference, making it inexplicable, why in 2002, European constitution makers, thinking they were following the US pattern, resorted to the device of a general convention.

Above, I used Madison's treaty narrative, to construct an alternative to one based on the unitary "We the People" trope used by Ackerman. This is the antinomy, which cannot be avoided for a federation type as long as we stay within the classical theory of sovereignty. It transfers the inevitable antinomy about state sovereignty to the question of the constituent power, making the construction of a single narrative involving the American founding impossible. We have seen the antinomic narrative in Madison, echoed by Ackerman. Can a single, non-antinomic narrative be constructed? Yes, if we stop looking for the one sovereign people whose deed it all was. In that case admittedly there will still be the fundamental opposition between the theory and the practice,

---

[118] I will argue for this relativization in the next chapter, using the ideas of Carré de Malberg, but not quite in his sense, because I want to maintain a limit to the power to amend, as did his colleague M.Hauriou. That this move is possible for the USA is shown by Ackerman's theory of fundamental amendments that greatly reduces the distance between the work of the framers, and the radical reformers in subsequent constitutional revolutions.

or between two theories: one based on the search for the sovereign actor behind the process, and the other focusing on how the constitution was really made. That making *combined* the structure inherited from earlier processes of Massachusetts and New Hampshire with the ratification processes of a new treaty.[119]

The first step is to look again at the process itself, using the amendment rule as a clue. *The mixed formula of that rule allows us to see that the original process was itself mixed.*[120] Of course, the making of the American constitution has been looked at a countless number of times, but I think not from a point of view that tries to consciously think beyond the theory of popular sovereignty,[121] and certainly not from a comparative point of view guided by recent efforts at constitution making. As I see it, these are the key components of the American constitution making process, during the making of the Federal Constitution:

1 *Multi-Stage Character, and Multi-Actor Process*

Those comparing the Constitutional Convention with constituent assemblies, in particular the *Assemblée Constituant*, often imagine that both were *the* makers of constitutions in the same manner.[122] The Convention was, however, only one relevant actor, even if the most important stage and agent of the process. It is true that I too have some doubts concerning the idea that its work was merely to recommend in the manner of Rousseau's legislator. The recommendations were backed both by the sense of crisis, and even more the power of the strongest states behind it. Nevertheless, this body was certainly not sovereign. As its deliberations make clear, it had to act "in the shadow" of Congress, and of the ratifying instances, and, given its choice of the latter, elections for them. It could only pass, prudentially, what would be approved at least passively by Congress, what would get majorities in elections for the ratifying conventions, and gain support there. Important things happened in all

---

[119] If we treated ratification by townships as analogous to previously sovereign states, then the two forms would be even closer, with the exception that for the Federal convention the delegates were not elected.

[120] Again, contrary to Madison in *Federalist* #39, who called it "federal," i.e., confederal in today's language, or treaty-like.

[121] Hannah Arendt, who postulated a post-sovereign perspective, notably did not closely look at the process. Carré de Malberg, who regarded it as an example of how organ sovereignty could be transcended, focused only on one dimension: double differentiation, which was undoubtedly important. But he does not make clear why the ratifying instances should not be seen as themselves sovereign, a basic assumption of Schmitt's theory of the federation.

[122] Jon Elster, "Arguing and Bargaining in Two Constituent Assemblies," *U. Pa. J. Const. L.* 2 (1999): 345.

the stages, eventually modifying the outcome and its future interpretations.[123] This is true for Congress' short deliberations, without which the project would have been stillborn, the much longer public discussion without which we would not know what it meant, the election and ratification process that again were required to make it happen and that in the end influenced its changes, and finally the process in the first Congress and the states that produced the Bill of Rights on the wishes of the ratification conventions, but using its own power to actually design these first amendments.

2 Double Differentiation

The federal convention was a peculiar body. While it may go too far to say that it was juridically private,[124] at its sessions it was admitted that as a legal institution "This Convention is unknown to the Confederation."[125] In point of fact, the calling of the Convention, and the manner of appointing delegates to it has been enacted by Congress, which retained, in its own original view, the actual power to suggest amendments to the states. Madison refers to this in *Federalist* #40, but then shifts to "informal and unauthorized propositions, made by some patriotic and respectable citizen or number of citizens." As the phrase that follows makes clear, however, this is so because of "the irregular and assumed privilege" of recommending a whole constitution. It may also be that lack of representation of some states as mandated by Congress had a role in this assessment.[126] So the convention was transformed or transformed itself into an irregular body. As the phrase "unauthorized" indicates, it had no

---

[123] See Pauline Maier's interesting and informative *Ratification: The People Debate the Constitution 1787–1788* (New York: Simon and Schuster, 2010). Aside from the book's acceptance of the mythological language of "We the People," I agree with its argument that the "Take this or nothing" character of the Constitution submitted to Congress and the state conventions was difficult to defend. Maier does not, however, see the point that the Convention's deliberations and decisions were in the "shadow" of the next steps and therefore influenced by what was possible to ratify in separate states. She in any case shows, that in the end it was possible to amend, even if not in terms of a "second convention."

[124] Attempts to declare it a committee of Congress, or its second chamber adjourned *sine die* were stillborn, as Maier shows. *Ratification*, p. 55.

[125] Gouverneur Morris, July 23 (MN 351).

[126] Cf. Ackerman WP II. 35–36. This analysis is useful, though it goes too far to call the Convention "a secessionist body" or to say that it "was taking the law into its own hands." It is true that it recommended secession, but it itself did not secede from anything, nor violated law – it remained within a general legal and governmental structure entirely adhered to. A comparison to the secessionist conventions of 1860 would be instructive. They considered themselves competent to secede, not only disregarding the federal law of constitutional amendment, but the constitution as a whole.

legitimacy in doing so, and the result was indeed a legitimation crisis, even if it was subsequently managed. That is one reason why, unlike in the case of the French Constituent Assembly of 1789, what the Convention "institutes" is only a recommendation. But what is recommended is already, in a sense, instituted. This is the case because even if the Convention lacks legitimacy for what it has drafted, behind it was a lot of power (I will not try to explain the obvious political reasons why this was so.[127]) But it was not all the power. There is not a moment when anyone would imagine that this body could, like the Estates General, which became the National as well as the Constituent Assembly, could take over the government of the country. Double differentiation is central, not only because of the example of Massachusetts and New Hampshire, but also as a fact of life. Chosen in the manner as it was, without elections, the convention could not even imagine that it could be the sole repository of power of the people or the peoples. There was moreover no need: unlike in France, the government of the country was in the hands of republican institutions (mostly the states, but Congress too, continued to meet even in this period). It was never assumed finally that Congress could be entirely bypassed in making the constitutional recommendation: the only debate was whether its formal approbation was needed, or a passive referral to the states would be enough.[128] Finally, the ratification conventions, called for one single purpose, were also doubly differentiated from the legislative power. The state legislatures were deprived of the power to do anything but to assent to calling a convention (this, however, was a power, and was refused, repeatedly in Rhode Island); the conventions were given no other power but to participate in constitution making.

3 Attempts to Repair a Torn Legality: No State of Nature

Almost no framer saw the possible illegality of their actions as a virtue. They thought of it, to different extents, as a problem, perhaps unavoidable, but a problem nonetheless.[129] None of them saw their own body, the Convention

---

[127] See Maier, *Ratification*, which stresses this power and its sources (pp. 72–73).

[128] September 8, last day: 611–614. Alexander Hamilton and others offered intermediate proposals. On the meaning of all of these, see Ackerman, WP, II, 50–53; 54–55; Maier, *Ratification*, pp. 52–59.

[129] It is one of the peculiarities of Ackerman's argument that he often seems to see it as in itself positive, e.g., I, 175–177. On 178 he puts it this way for Publius: "Given his revolutionary background, how could the People be represented better than through an illegal, public spirited, deliberative body that..." Try as you might you will not find this phrasing, or this particular spirit, in a framer's text.

in the state of nature, legally unbound or unlimited.[130] The Convention continued to debate the problem of the illegality of calling for the affirmative vote of only 9 conventions, when 13 state legislatures were required, and, in the end, also the question of having Congress agree to the proposal. If this is to be called "legalism" by some modern lawyers, the framers, not being modern lawyers, were all more or less legalistic. Madison, who is said to be the most legalistic among the nationalists, took the matter of trying to make the process legal to Congress as well, and the very critics of his legalism admit that his success in getting that body to confirm the Convention's proposal for calling state conventions "was crucial, as events soon proved."[131] Given the North Carolina ratification, and that of Rhode Island especially, after secession *by* as well as elections *in* the 11, it is certainly also going too far to say that the whole process was legal because in effect the articles were amended by Congressional assent and eventual 13 state ratification. What is impressive rather is *the ongoing attempt to repair a torn and threatened legality*, evident at the convention and even more Madison's subsequent acts. At the Convention, the notion that the act was legal because of prior treaty breaking, advanced by Madison in *Federalist* 43 was not yet actually proposed.[132] When it was proposed it was part of a legal fiction that legality was never actually violated by the process. This was however, as always, a potent fiction, guarding the rest of the process from other illegalities. The all too frank admission of illegality, and worse, claiming some kind of normative advantage for it has an affinity to tyranny and usurpation, and in our context constitutional dictatorship.

4 *The Role of Elections, and Public Discussion*

The Federal Convention was not elected. This was understood as a lack, ultimately mistakenly,[133] and contributed to its authority or legitimacy problem.

---

[130] This is conceded by Ackerman, but in his second volume, where the stress comes to be reliance on existing institutions. That at the very least meant limiting illegalities to a minimum, and trying to legally redeem them at a maximum. Only the most extreme defenders of the Constitution put the convention in the state of nature. This required the preposterous claim that the Confederation has already dissolved (Maier, *Ratification*, pp. 61–62). It was preposterous, because Congress was still in session, and was the source of authorization of the convention. Moreover, the state governments were intact.

[131] Ackerman, pp. 50 (elsewhere he also calls Hamilton legalistic, however) and 53–55.

[132] This argument at that time was only applied by Madison to the need to make the future Constitution stronger than a treaty. Perhaps it would have entailed admitting that the new constitution, unlike those of the states, would still be made as a treaty, by seceding states. When the argument was finally used by Madison, it was also possibly part of a concession to the anti-Federalist side.

[133] See my chapter 3 of *Post Sovereign Constitution Making*.

The suggestion to have state conventions ratify was also a way of bringing in elections into the process, but midway through rather than in the beginning. This is the important legitimating dimension behind the political theological declarations in the name of "We the People," whether then or now. It is crucial that these elections, unlike those for the classical constituent assemblies, occurred when there was already a proposal being debated. The role of public discussion both before and after the elections for the ratifying conventions in America cannot be underestimated. It is also very important that the public discussion culminated in deliberative bodies, state conventions, and not atomized referenda. In fact, as illustrated by most collections of Anti-Federalist texts, it is very difficult to separate the extra-conventional publics from the political publics of the state conventions. The same people, the same arguments, the same debates, the same proposals appear in both.

5 Active Ratification and Open-Ended Process

And this is not all. The ratifying conventions were not as active as the townships in Massachusetts during the ratification of its 1780 constitution.[134] But they were certainly deliberative, and in the end not as passive as the Anti-Federalists feared and charged.[135] Given the element of truth in the charge, it is difficult to consider in anything but a very formal sense these conventions as the 13 sovereigns of the polity. It is true that formally they were restricted to a "Yes" or "No" vote, and this motivated calls for a second federal convention in the case of the failure of ratification where the suggestions made at these state conventions, elected unlike the Federal Convention itself, could be utilized.[136] This already shows, however, that the ratifying conventions were quite different in this respect than classical European referenda (whose shadow can also matter, admittedly). The state conventions were able debate, and pass amendments that were not binding, but nevertheless highly influential. They were even able to call for a "second convention" in their resolutions. And in the end part of what was aimed at with the second convention proposal was, in fact, achieved.

---

[134] Where they had a legal right to propose amendments, as well as to reject parts of the constitution proposed by the convention. In actual fact, this led to confusion, and charges of usurpation or manipulation, because there were no clear decision rules concerning how recommendations could be integrated. See R.R. Palmer, *Age of Democratic Revolutions*, vol. I, pp. 221–232; Wood, *Creation*, pp. 339–341; Maier, *Ratification*, chapters 6–7. Also: Jan Smolenski, "Semi Federalism: The Principles and Implications of the Making of the 1780 Constitution in Massachusetts" New School, unpublished seminar paper.

[135] See Maier, *Ratification*, op. cit.

[136] Maier stresses the failed proposal of Mason, Randolph and Gerry, and its subsequent influence, op. cit., 44–45.

The Bill of Rights that was initially rejected by the Federal Convention was the most important result. The closeness of connection, and the causality is indicated by the case of North Carolina where amendment proposals were passed, but ratification first failed.[137] It succeeded only the second time, *after the submission* for state ratification of the first ten (originally 12) amendments to the Federal Constitution, the Bill of Rights, which overlapped with these and many other state proposals. This was in fact the scheme first proposed by Jefferson: ratification, followed by amendments aiming to secure the support of the remaining non-ratifiers.[138] He was thinking of four possible holdouts, but one or two turned out to be enough given the agreement of several ratifying conventions concerning the substance. Thus the North Carolinian ratification process played a role in the incredibly quick enactment of the Bill of Rights. In other words, the ratification process, and indeed even the making of the Bill of Rights to which it was linked, could be considered from two different points of view. They were indeed the last acts of the making of the original constitution, the process of closing the process. Thus it was the moment when the secular religion of the constitution is said to date from, the completion of its process of legitimation.[139] They can also said to be, with equal justice, the first two steps of the subsequent constitutional history indicating the open-ended nature of having a democratic constitution. Also, this shows that Article V was originally meant to be used as part of the future constitution making, and was inhibited from this not because of its *legal* definition but only because of its own particular design, whose difficulties few recognized at the time.[140]

Let me conclude this argument. The 1787 process as a whole is ultimately impossible to capture within the theory of sovereign constitution making. None of the multiple actors can be said to be the privileged organ in which the people's sovereignty is re-posited. Not the Federal convention, the more national instance, that was not capable of definitively deciding anything, not Congress that could choose between a passive or a negative role, not the electors who could only choose representatives whom they could not bind,

---

[137] *Ratification*, chapter 14.
[138] See "Letter to Alexander Donald February 7, 1788"; Maier, 275–276.
[139] L. Levy, "Bill of Rights" ed by L. Levy, *Essays on the Making of the Constitution*, 2nd ed.
[140] Hamilton was one such a prescient critic at the Convention (September 10, p. 609); Patrick Henry was another, even noticing the somewhat higher, anomalous, ratification ratio of V (three-fourths) than of Article VII (7/10). His warnings were quickly and of course wrongly forgotten because of the enactment of the Bill of Rights. It is another matter that the numbers he feared were to protect states rights, something he missed because of his misreading of the Constitution. Hamilton was the one who saw more deeply, fearing the states blocking necessary amendments.

and not the ratifying conventions that could only say yes/no formally, and could only influence but not enforce the altering of the main text. We are, of course, free to say that each of these instances are *a* body of the people, or the people with a lower case p, or that each of them is an expression of the People, that can be defined negatively. Either way we get what Carré de Malberg called national as opposed to popular sovereignty, or the kind of non-embodied popular sovereignty that Ackerman too has admitted works only through the separation of powers. But Ackerman restricted this type of sovereignty to normal politics, whereas my point is that it ruled constitutional politics too, and was expressed in Article V.

We might say that this type of non-embodied state sovereignty worked through the division of powers. Neither the states acting through convention, nor the national polity, represented in the Federal Convention, could embody sovereignty given the claims of the other. In other words, the antinomy between state and union sovereignty led to a process where no sovereignty embodied in a single organ was possible. While the participants on both sides preferred the language of embodied popular sovereignty, our theoretical language should register the impossibility of such an embodiment in a setting where there are equal, opposing claims. Does this mean that an antinomic conflict over state sovereignty is a necessary condition for a practice beyond organ sovereignty, whatever the theories of the participants? Fortunately for my thesis, the pioneering use of the doubly differentiated multi-stage process in the unitary states of Massachusetts and New Hampshire already before 1787 tells us the contrary.[141] The fundamental presupposition here too would be a multi-actor model, but differentiated on other than central/federal lines. Indeed, all these instances, along with the Federal constitution making, underwent the "double differentiation" entailed in the constituent/constituted distinction: the constitution making instances have no other powers, and the normal legislatures have lost most of the control over the constituent power.

In an important analysis, Carré de Malberg has written of the tendencies of constituent assemblies (*les Constituants*) that assume the *highest* power in the state to try to assume *all* of the power. Given the evidence of French history, he considered this trend especially facilitated for assemblies under the aegis of the doctrine of popular sovereignty, implying the substitution of the people and its will by an organ of the state. As he defined it, *national* sovereignty, for him the true doctrine of the public law inherited from the French Revolution

---

[141] Arendt's treatment of the townships as small republics may be a way of creating an analogy between these two states and the federal process. My thesis, however, is that societal pluralism is in itself an adequate foundation as well as reason to avoid a single organ, acting through majority rule imposing a constitution.

as against the *popular* one, implied that a constituent assembly (whether set up for revision or by implication: the original constitution making that he declared off limits "for jurists") must have only one power, the constituent one. Taken in by the American rhetoric of popular sovereignty (confirmed by the theories analyzed here), and perhaps by the fact that it was an original process involving legal break that could not in his view be legally limited, Carré de Malberg did not consider American constitution making to be strictly an example of the national sovereignty type. But he is forced to admit that it had the two essential components that deprived the Convention of the possibility of being sovereign organ: double differentiation and ratification by popular bodies.[142] It is presumably the latter representing "popular" sovereignty in the scheme that misled its American interpreters. But the ratification conventions had less power by far than the Convention, they were also part of a scheme of double differentiation, and to identify them fully with the people follows only in disputable schemes as we have seen. Such scheme, whether it focuses on the state convention or on Article VII, would misrepresent how and by whom the constitution was actually made, and could not explain why, if the state conventions were *the* People, they had such limited constituent power, submitting even, arguably, to their self-abolition in favor of another "people," that of Article V, in reality a composite of several actors in all its formulations.

Thus, it makes sense to identify the American process as it actually was organized, in terms of the somewhat awkward older, French idea of national sovereignty, or my equally unusual but new, post-sovereign constitution making. I believe moreover that it makes better sense to see the origin of a political form of federation in terms of such a post-sovereign process than the contractual, ultimately sovereign process favored by Schmitt (in the footsteps of Madison in *Federalist* #39). The US Constitution was not made at an intergovernmental conference by high contracting parties. It was also not made, with any plausibility, by a single actor in the name of a single author, a national demos, whatever the Preamble told the world. It was made in a multi-stage process, by many actors, none of whom were sovereign, and only whose combined action could produce a constitution. Article VII describes only the ratification part of the making, and that correctly. It is Article V that comes closer to describing the rest of the process, not through any one of its formulas, but by it mixed character. But it is also true that different stages of the process emphasized different parts of the mixture. The Convention's deliberative form, made possible by the absence of imperative mandates for most delegations, was the most national part, and, of course, the process of ratification

---

[142] Carré de Malberg, *Contribution*, II, 536; 540–541; 550–551; 549 fn. 33.

was carried out by the states. To the extent that the model of the federation was going to be defined by the deferral of questions of state sovereignty, and the resulting antinomies, there were important elements of the process that would give support to the claims of each side. As long as we do not see the constituent power as having been lodged in either side during the making, however, there is no reason to consider it a latent reservation subsisting in one or the other contending sovereign forms during the life of the constitution. In other words, with all its problems, and internal non-hierarchical choices, Article V becomes the highest rule of change of the constitution, rather than Article VII, or a national referendum, or yet some other unwritten rule, or combination of rules that claims to embody the sovereign.

THE AMERICAN MODEL ABROAD: THE RETURN OF THE SOVEREIGN?

1 *The American "Model"*

I consider the multi-stage model of US constitution making, with two doubly differentiated stages, to be a forerunner of the post-sovereign model here presented and even argued for. I think this is makes sense despite the antinomies of this tradition, which reach into conceptions of the constituent power. The tradition remained in the end antinomic, in that it had oscillated between a sovereign self-understanding, and the post-sovereign practice. I have argued that the sovereign self-understanding was to begin with internally antinomic, divided between conceptions of direct popular action and representation. Both ideas have a *pars pro toto* logic, but there was and had to be a fundamental disagreement about which part has the right to stand for the whole. The American idea of convention seemed to solve this problem, with a specially elected "part", the convention being a synthesis of participation and representation.[143]

But even legally elected conventions could be challenged by "the people out of doors" as it was said, in other words, extra-ordinary forms of mobilization and participation.[144] In my view it was above all federalism that helped to manage the emerging open conflicts, or even defuse them pre-emptively. Federal crisis management played an important role in states like Pennsylvania and later Rhode Island;[145] and we can assume pre-emption through the production

---

[143] E. Zweig, *Die Lehre vom Pouvoir Constituant* (Tübingen: J.C. B. Mohr, 1909); Loewenstein, op. cit.; Wood, op. cit.; Morgan, op. cit.

[144] Wood, op. cit.; Fritz, *American Sovereigns*.

[145] On constitutional struggles in Pennsylvania and Rhode Island, see C. Fritz, *American Sovereigns: The People and America's Constitutional Tradition Before the Civil War* (Cambridge: Cambridge University Press, 2008).

of the Bill of Rights, solving the legitimation crisis of the federal framing that never became a system crisis.

But the same federalism, coupled with the sovereign conception, was itself deeply conflicted, with contradictions that appeared after the founding and rooted in the form of federation itself. This is true especially for the best-known antinomy concerning the location of sovereignty, most clearly exhibited by the issue of secession, the political Achilles' heel of this type of formation. The antinomy of the location of the constituent power was parallel, and almost as important. Without the theory of sovereign constitution making, the making of a federation could perhaps have been interpreted as what it really was, as a multi-stage process of agreement and compromise among different legitimate instances. I strongly believe that federation itself was not, as Carl Schmitt thought, the ultimate source of the problem. In my view the main source was commitment of the framers to a theory of unitary and potentially embodied popular sovereignty in the original process. Admittedly, conceptions of the new federal entity, given the setting, did generate an antinomy between the sovereignty of the whole and sovereignty of the units. But while this antinomy neither had to be transferred to the dimension of the constituent power, its highly contentious nature lay ultimately not in the conflict between two constituent powers, but in the fundamental social conflict that could not be mediated without deciding who had state sovereignty in the polity.

I am thus arguing the following complex proposition. As Hannah Arendt articulated in her theory of the small republics that did not exist in a state of nature, the federal context initially helped to tame the antinomy inherent in popular sovereignty, the contradiction between the people antecedent to the constitution being its producers, and the reliance on representative bodies or organs with state sovereignty to carry out the constituent task.[146] In the process of its domestication, however, the same antinomy was transformed it into a new one that on the level of identity-forming theories was to eventually contribute to the destruction of the original federation. Here even the obviously and undeniably "mixed" amendment rule could not do the job, since one side rejected its threshold three-fourths rule as too conservative, and the other feared that the same rule, given the inclusion of new members, was potentially revolutionary.

True, the convention formula of the amendment rule offered the example of the framers that could perhaps overcome the difficulty, if at the possible

---

[146] See Loewenstein, *Volk u. Parlament* for the fullest development of this antinomy; also Carré de Malberg, *Contribution*, vol. II, p. 489ff on the illogic or circular logic of representation as the form of the *constituant*.

cost of illegality. Yet the solution of the convention form could not help, because, given the absence of constitutional text on the subject, a new drafting convention could be elected according to quite different rules on the level of the Union, or that of the states. In 1860, given the substantive issues that divided the country, it was highly doubtful that the "recommendations" of a new federal convention could have been accepted or ratified, any more than the proposed Crittenden amendments.[147] In the end, instead of calling a national convention for purposes of mediation and compromise, it was secession conventions or congresses in the states that ended the old union, one that to its defenders never ended because it could not be dissolved by individual state action.

According to what has been argued here, the antinomy concerning the location of the constituent power in America, in the whole as against the units, was the result of the contending interpretations of a mixed process of federal constitution making, partly contractual and partly constitutional, through the sovereign theory as applied to a federation. This theory, as already shown, did not represent the founding process correctly. Had it really guided the founders in practice, the chances of success would have been in my view much diminished. Given the political divisions of the time, the antinomy between unitary and unit sovereignty could not be solved. Either ratification was to be national, or it was to be state-by-state. By designating state-by-state ratification as one by the unitary "We the People" the division and the potential conflict could be only papered over, or deferred. But the issue could be deferred because for the *actual* process of constitution making a method was adopted that was post-sovereign, even if it was theoretically unsupported at that time. With the Americans, as Karl Loewenstein was to succinctly claim, it was above all their practice that mattered, rather than abstract theory. But in the end, the theory mattered as well, for one thing because it has remained alive in the literature down to this day.

In my view the American prototype was and is still open to distortion, depending on context, under the impact of two vulnerabilities: not only the presence of the sovereign theory on which authors insisted on from Hamilton to Ackerman, but also the potentials of the Convention as the drafting model. Given the powerful symbolism of convention in America, and its common association with popular sovereignty, using this type of assembly for drafting comes dangerously close to the type of sovereign constituent assembly, and could easily turn into that form. This was best seen by French public lawyers like Carré de Malberg and Hauriou, both critics of convention government

[147] For the Crittenden Amendments, see Ackerman, *We the People*, vol. II, pp. 128–129.

in its French sense defined by the experience of 1793–1795.[148] But such was already the experience of Pennsylvania in 1776, before France, that was perhaps the first place where sovereign constitution making was ideologically hege-monic in practice, as well as theory. Although there was an attempt in that state to maintain double differentiation, this devolved quickly into a system of dual power, each side with its own legitimacy. In 1776, the more recently elected constitutional convention did not confine itself to making a constitution. It aimed at, and in the end took all the power from, the regular legislature.[149] The resulting legitimation crisis, and the struggles over sovereignty and the constituent power, lasting into the 1790s, anticipated aspects of French history. That even Pennsylvania's highly conflictual process did not lead to breakdown, as it did not in Rhode Island decades later, was most certainly due to the federal form, in these cases not as the presupposition of small republics, but rather as the overall container that had the power to stabilize through its command of military forces in the revolutionary war in the first case, and through the federal judiciary in the second. Until the Civil War at least, seemingly irresolvable conflicts on one level could be moderated and contained by the stability of power on other levels. The federal form also helped to contain or manage the potential legitimation crisis of the country-wide framing and ratification pro-cess. Here dual power between Convention and Congress could be avoided, because of the stability of state governments that actually governed Americans, and who (or: the social forces behind them) were willing to compromise to achieve a new union. Conversely, Pennsylvania's and Rhode Island's consti-tutional crises could be moderated and resolved because of the existence of the Federal frame. Even the conflicts between the Massachusetts convention of 1780 and the townships, which sought without success to revise at least part of the latter's work, were probably mediated by the same Federal container.

The ability of pre-existing forms to stabilize the constituent process is by no means assured, as we will see with respect to France. Had the dissatisfaction with confederal and federal forms, present at the Federal Convention among a few members like Hamilton, been so radical and so general that they could not serve as the framework of stabilization, the attempt to rely on them, in Arendt's sense as *pouvoirs constitués*, would have only become proof of unacceptable conservatism. The latter could then only have been overcome in a process

---

[148] See Hauriou's on the vulnerabilities of the form in *Précis de Droit Constitutionel*, 1st ed. (Paris: Sirey, 1923), pp. 294–295; also Carré de Malberg, op. cit.. 540–541; 548–549 where he thinks a different theory based on double differentiation -his own "anti-embodiment model of national sovereignty -can limit the dangers).

[149] On the highly important Pennsylvanian constituent process see Palmer, I. op. cit; Wood, *Creation*, op. cit.; Adams op. cit.

that used the Federal convention for a much more radical break than the actual one, emancipating itself from the shadows of reporting to Congress and ratification by states. Such proposals, truly revolutionary, were advanced at the Federal Convention, but without getting much support.

What I am arguing, in other words, is that the stabilization of the American form, even by federalism, the neutralization of its vulnerabilities, could not have occurred in a radical, unlimited revolutionary process that put the society into a "state of nature." This was already a point made by Hannah Arendt. But in her desire to defend revolution as a form of transformation, Arendt did not go far enough. If the vulnerabilities due to the antinomic theory, and the overly powerful convention form did not come to the fore, or could be stabilized by federalism, this was because the country was not undergoing a revolution[150] or even a counter-revolution in 1787,[151] and because a genuinely serious broadly supported revolutionary drive to clearly abolish the form of sovereignty based on the states, and to replace it with a national one did not emerge.[152] This was the source of the creation of the already discussed, new form of the federation, whether or not we ultimately regard it a deferral and an unstable compromise, or a form not ultimately successful because of the clash of the two different social systems in the Union.

But the initial stabilizing role of federal forms, their cancelling of vulnerabilities was only tacit, and, as Arendt was forced to admit, historically and exceptionally linked to the functioning of "small republics" with a lot of popular support. The vulnerabilities were not consciously seen as such, and could not be thematized until very recently, till a post-revolutionary ideology helped to overcome the sovereign theory.[153] Only then could the drafting assembly, denied any sovereign claims, no longer step in the place of previous rulers. Only then, in my view, could the modern institutionalization of the post-sovereign form be secure, one no longer exposed to the same vulnerabilities. That will be the theme of my succeeding chapters below. Here I want to show

---

[150]　Pace Ackerman's *We the People*, vol. I; changed in vol. II.

[151]　See again the interesting argument of Allen Buchanan, concerning the American Revolution as secession, rather than revolution. It converges with Arendt's argument on the role of small republics.

[152]　Even in Hannah Arendt, constitution was seen as the second phase of revolution. But this is not the same as a revolution against the Articles of Confederation regime, which Ackerman clearly has in mind. Moreover, Arendt's constitution occurs in the states between 1776 and 1781, and the Federal Constitution was that of a polity that did not require a new liberation, and was already constituted. The continual reference to the framers as revolutionaries, perhaps to battle the now largely irrelevant Beard thesis is rather strange.

[153]　Here too there were anticipations by theorists of public law in the Third Republic, specifically Hauriou and Carré de Malberg, critics of "convention government."

how the theoretical vulnerability of the American model in the context of the sovereign conception, and the convention model worked out in practice, when adopted *in a different setting* than the original one.

2 *The American Model in France*

The best proof of the strength of the thesis, concerning the great difficulties entailed in the export of the US American pattern elsewhere, especially in non-Federal settings, would undoubtedly come from a comparative survey of the Latin American constitution making experience.[154] Regarding Latin American cases, it would be my tentative hypothesis that efforts like that of Peron in 1949 and Chavez in 1999 are emblematic examples of most, if not all of the attempts to use initially the doubly differentiated convention form in polities more centralized than the United States. Accordingly, it would have been the revolutionary war setting of Pennsylvania in 1776, rather than the more stable federal one of Massachusetts (1780[155]) and New Hampshire (1784) that would be the important anticipation of the likely outcome. In the two instances of Argentina and Venezuela, what started out as an extra-ordinary assembly designed to deal solely with constitution making, side by side with the normal legislature continuing its other functions, first produced unstable regimes of dual power, with the constituent assembly or convention then transforming itself into a sovereign body with the plenitude of all powers leading to semi-authoritarian plebiscitary regimes.[156] This was not only a Latin American scenario. The same happened in Russia in 1993,[157] first involving dual power and second a sovereign constituent process here too under presidential leadership.[158]

[154] See the writings of David Landau, e.g., "Constitution-Making Gone Wrong." *Alabama Law Review* 923 (2013), and also the writings of Brewer-Carias, Nicolas Figureoa, R. Segura and A. Bejarano cited in chapters 4 and 5 below; as well as G. Negretto, *Making Constitutions: Presidents, Parties, and Institutional Choice in Latin America* (Cambridge: Cambridge University Press, 2013), et al.

[155] The revolutionary war was not yet over, when the new constituion of Massachusetts was drafted and ratified, but the state was not a military theater after 1778, and perhaps earlier.

[156] Negretto, op. cit., for Argentina; Brewer-Carias, op. cit., for Venezuela.

[157] William Partlett, "Separation of Powers without Checks and Balances: The Failure of Semi-Presidentialism and the Making of the Russian Constitutional System, 1991–1993." *The Legal Dimension in Cold War Interactions: Some Notes from the Field. Law in Eastern Europe Series* (Leiden: Brill, 2012).

[158] Ackerman in the *Future of the Liberal Revolution* (New Haven: Yale University Press, 1994) promoted this type of plebiscitary form, but has now abandoned it. See, e.g., his "To Save Egypt, Drop the Presidency" http://www.nytimes.com/2013/07/11/opinion/to-save-egypt-drop-the-presidency.html?_r=0 that rightly stresses the "perils of presidentialism" in a divided society.

Unfortunately, I have neither the space nor the extensive empirical knowledge required to explore this thesis, one that I will leave for others to further elaborate. Here I want to focus only on the first and most important historical case that is relevant, one highly influential also in Latin America as well as elsewhere, namely the case of revolutionary France. In that setting, I will argue, in 1789 and after, the influence of American examples was very significant. Yet in France, the fundamental antinomy of popular sovereignty became much more destructive than in America. Without the federal form to frame and mediate its consequences, and in a radical revolutionary setting, the *pars pro toto* logic of both representation and direct popular action or the insurrection, led to repeated clashes between and among agents claiming to stand for the whole.[159] While the American idea of the convention was indeed received and influential in France, the double differentiation pioneered in Massachusetts and New Hampshire between extra-ordinary and normal, between constituent and legislative, could not be achieved because of the nature of inherited "normal" institutions based on hierarchy and legal inequality. Others have made this point, of course.[160] But I go further. Double differentiation could have been achieved in theory when the Legislative Assembly in 1792 called for the election of a new constitutional convention. Had that happened, the development would have resembled the learning experience that took place between the American assemblies of the 1770s and the 1780s. But once again, in France the struggle between popular insurrection and representation continued through the period of the *Convention Nationale*, and even beyond. The Legislative Assembly was dissolved even before the making of a new constitution could be attempted. All projects like Condorcet's to legalize or constitutionalize or domesticate this very struggle failed. In the end, the conflict of insurrection and representation ended temporarily, only when both representation and popular participation were abolished, by the Napoleonic combination of raw power and plebiscite.

As R. R. Palmer has already shown, and before him Karl Loewenstein, the constitutional work of 11 American state conventions and legislatures, helping indeed to confuse the meaning of convention[161], was available in France before 1789. It was well known not only to Lafayette, who was most identified with American positions, but also to constitutional architects and politicians like Mounier, Sieyès and Condorcet. The latter, along with Brissot, was the first

[159] François Furet, *Interpreting the French Revolution* (Cambridge: Cambridge University Press, 1981); Claude Lefort, *Democracy and Political Theory* (Cambridge: Polity Press, 1988).

[160] Especially Palmer in *Age*, vol. II, op. cit.

[161] Palmer, *Age*, vol. II; Loewenstein, op. cit., pp. 83–88; 89–91. Only two were in the end the double differentiated type.

leader associated with the Gironde writing important essays on conventions.[162] From his once-famous essay of August 1791 to his remarkable constitutional proposal of 1793, Condorcet strongly came out for double differentiation, very much under the influence of American constitution making and amendment models[163] in Pennsylvania, Massachusetts and the Federal Convention along with its Article V.[164]

Thus, contrary to charges later made by Lafayette, and echoed by Laboulaye and even Carré de Malberg, at least the best of the French framers were aware of the American pattern of double differentiation, and this influenced their idea of the constituent power. And this is even true, in a highly instructive way of Sieyès, a friend of Condorcet, who has been specifically accused of getting the American theory all wrong.[165] Indeed, in the end, Sieyès went further than anyone in America, as far as I know, when specifically and dramatically warning about linking the concept of an unlimited sovereignty to that of the constituent power. Admittedly, he made that point after Thermidor, speaking to the Convention, during the debate of the post-terror constitutional proposal that was to establish the Directory.[166]

There have been interpretations of Sieyès largely based on this later turn, which aimed against Rousseau as well as the sovereign theory of the constituent power. In fact, as against the best-known readings based on popular sovereignty by Loewenstein, Schmitt and following them Arendt, there is also a liberal reading of Sieyès to my knowledge first proposed by Paul Bastid,[167]

---

[162] Condorcet, "Discours sur les conventions nationales" [August 7, 1791] in *Oeuvres* X (Stuttgart-Bad Cannstatt, 1968).

[163] He thought the middle way between supposedly eternal constitutions and perpetual flux has been discovered by the model of conventions, created in America. "Discours," 209–210. While primarily thinking of democratic amending process ("the, establishment by the constitution itself of assemblies charged with reviewing, perfecting, reforming the constitution") as far as he was concerned the convention form was used by the Americans also for original constitution making, under law. He was unsure if this aspect was applicable to France. Ibid., pp. 213–214 for difference between two types of transitions that he was the very first to see: from despotism to a free constitution, and from a free constitution to a more perfect one.

[164] See Constitutional Project Title IX art. II-III in *Oeuvres* XII: that was lost in the Constitution of 1793 [art.116] that assigned all powers to an amending *convention nationale*, mirroring its progenitor. That is the origin of the model of the convention as sovereign dictator. Also see *Discours*, 214f; 220f; Plan de constitution, *Oeuvres* XII.

[165] Carré de Malberg, *Contribution*, vol. II, pp. 512; 534–535 who did notice, however, that there was another side to Sieyès 502.

[166] "Opinion de Sieyes, sur plusieurs articles de titres IV et V du projet de constitution" in *Ouevres* III (Paris: Edhis, n.d.), p. 7. See K. Bakers articles in F. Furet and M.Ozouf eds. *Critical Dictionary of the French Revolution* (Cambridge, MA: Harvard University Press, 1989); "Sieyès," 322; and "Sovereignty," 857. See also Richet's entry: "Revolutionary assemblies" 537.

[167] Paul Bastid, *Sieyès et sa pensée* (Paris, 1939).

and renewed even more emphatically by Pasquale Pasquino.[168] In this read-ing, Sieyès is the heir of Locke and Montesquieu, though Bastid mentions also the influence of Rousseau. And it is true: the attitude of Sieyès concerning rights was closer to Locke than to Rousseau, and his views on the separation of powers resembled Montesquieu's rather than Rousseau's version.[169] The place where these interpretations go partially wrong is when they project the liber-alism of 1795 backwards, turning it into the main position Sieyès has always held. Pasquino, for example, notes that the concept of popular sovereignty attacked in 1795 was not anywhere present in Sieyès in his early revolutionary writings.[170] Yet the other side focused on by not only Schmitt and Arendt, but also Zweig and Loewenstein, and, in France, Lafayette, Laboulaye, Hauriou, and Carré de Malberg among many others (recently Lucien Jaume; F. Furet and Keith Baker) cannot be imagined away. Carré de Malberg, who did rec-ognize the influence of Montesquieu on Sieyès, had full textual justification nevertheless to even write: "the great theorist of the constituent sovereignty of the people has been . . . Sieyès" (487).[171] But neither should the liberal side be forgotten, suspicious of anyone holding the plenitude of powers and the possible threats not only to other branches, but also to rights.

Thus, the best way to see Sieyès is in terms of an antinomic duality of sovereign and post sovereign elements in his thought. We have seen in the Americans another version of this: popular sovereignty in theory and post-sovereign practice. The antinomy may be seen as the reverse one in Sieyès, in terms of post-sovereign theory and sovereign practice. In the case of the Americans, it was the sovereign theory that helped to make the conceptions of the constituent power antinomic in the context of federalism, even as this antinomy was contained by the safety valve of federalism that made any one sovereign impossible to identify. At the moment of 1860 secession crisis we might say that the antinomy finally penetrated the American practice as well.

Conversely, in the case of Sieyès, sovereigntist or monistic practice pen-etrated the theory too, in the form of his conception of an all-powerful extra-ordinary representation. This idea indicated a simultaneous departure from both Rousseau and Montesquieu, affirming representation through the

---

[168] Pasquale Pasquino, *Sieyes et l'invention de la constitution en France* (Paris: Odile Jacob, 1998).

[169] Carré de Malberg, op. cit., pp. 516, 520; Zweig, op. cit.; Cutting across these issues, he is also a follower of the physiocrats, and his notion of *pars pro toto* representation of the nation through its largest part comes from them and the absolutist critics of privilege.

[170] While I indeed was able to more or less confirm this by finding only one text to the contrary, the claim cannot be sustained in light of most of the passages on the nation and its representation in *What is the Third Estate?*

[171] The following are from Carré de Malberg, op. cit.

legislature on the one hand, and abandoning the separation of powers on the other. Thus, supposedly bereft of theory, the move has been even interpreted as political opportunism.[172] I don't buy this. A more charitable and fair interpretation could stress realism even in a revolution, and sensitivity to the historical givens in a country such as France. Moreover, the antinomy of theory and practice had roots in his thought itself, having to do with the significant influence of *both* Rousseau and Montesquieu. The same commentators who imply opportunism also note a synthesis of Rousseau and Montesquieu, with Sieyès taking the all-powerful embodied sovereign from the one, and representation from the other.

The result of that synthesis was, of course, the sovereign conception, rightly identified with an affinity for dictatorship by Carré de Malberg (535). Yet what Sieyès took from Montesquieu's separation of powers, reinforced by what he most likely learned from America, did not disappear but became a minor chord in his thinking. After seeing the devastating consequences of the practice of sovereign constitution making in two rounds, he was to opt for the post-sovereign conception during the third round, Thermidor. To do this, he only had to deploy the minor chord, by making institutional suggestions concerning the separation of powers in constitutional politics. This was the meaning of his famous jury of the constitution, or *jurie constitutionnaire*, anticipating a new type of constitutional review or jurisprudence, but without any chance of adoption in 1795. What is important here is that other suggestions, with the same goal, were made as early as the *Tiers état*, and in his subsequent major essays.[173] But, it was only the sovereign side of his conception that was ever influential, in the given circumstances whose factual power he was ready to concede.

Looking back in 1795, it is impossible to suppress the feeling that Sieyès is exercising self-critique, at a time when its humiliating Stalinist or Maoist form has not yet been invented. According to him, attributing omnipotence to the sovereign that encompasses the constituent power leads in the political direction that France just left, a *ré-totale* rather than a *républic*, in his unique but suggestive terminology of that time.[174] However, this was an attack on the very doctrine that first made him famous and whose consequences he often defended, with arguments against the imperative mandate, against two

---

[172] By Zweig, op. cit; Loewenstein, op. cit.

[173] I have in mind the idea of a provisional constitution, and the notion of the pouvoir constituant as a judge when controversies between the executive and the legislature arise (see "*Exposition raisonnée*"; "*Dire sur le veto royale*" *Écrits*).

[174] On this see Pasquale Pasquino, who has made this particular version of Sieyès the key to his interpretation. *Sieyès et l'invention de la constitution en France*.

chambers of the legislature, against the veto as an appeal to the people, against a role for the primary assemblies, and against popular ratification. Now he was ready to claim only the authorship of the separation of constituent and constituted powers, a historically untenable claim that has been often ridiculed.[175] Without going back to the solutions that remained discredited in his eyes, in the post-terror context, it was Sieyès who as the first of very many (from Constant to Arendt and Lefort via Tocqueville) to use the image of the king replacing the divinity, and the people replacing the king in the theory of absolute sovereignty that in his then view should, as all absolutisms, be rejected.[176] Noting his own supposed invention of the distinction between the constituent and constituted powers, he now implied not only that the concept of unlimited popular sovereignty endangers it, but also (more disputably) that he has never linked these notions, having derived the very differentiation more from the separation of powers. To insist on the Montesqueuian side of his thought was indeed plausible, as against the suppression of the other initially more dominant side that he, after the terror, had good reason to wish to suppress. Yet, it is not to be denied that his earlier idea of the nation in the state of nature was based on the concept of sovereignty, namely Rousseau's, and, as I have argued, made all the more dangerous, by the giving up of the (traditional) concept of the legislator, and the turn to (modern) representation.[177]

What partially saves Sieyès from the charge of pure opportunism during Thermidor is the post-sovereign side of his thought, almost from the beginning. Moreover, from almost the outset, he distinguished his attitude, stylized as that of an "administrator" who must be different from the philosopher, with whom he shares his goals, by the duty "to measure and adjust his step according to the nature of the difficulties." Yet, just as Weber many years later, Sieyès does not propose to abandon the philosophical end simply in favor of a pragmatic ethic of responsibility. A dialectic between the two ethics characterizes all his works. "The Executive Means" (written before *Tiers état*) also begins with a motto: "Projects should be tailored to the available means" (2). He is referring to the project to establish a new constitution for France by freeing the creativity of the constituent power. Fundamental for the constituent-constituted

---

[175] *Oeuvres*, vol. III, p. 11.

[176] *"la souveraineté du peuple Ce mot ne s'est présenté si colossal devant l'imagination, que parce que l'esprit des Francais encore plein des superstitions royales . . . la souveraineté du peuple n'est point illimitée"*; *Oeuvres*, vol. III, p. 7.

[177] So on this I disagree with Pasquino's learned and interesting presentation, in spite of the fact that he supplies a couple of texts on sovereignty, one from 1791 and one from 1795 (op. cit., p. 173 and p. 179) where a concept of limited sovereignty in representative assemblies is introduced. These have to do alas only with constituted powers.

Part I: History of the Idea

distinction he introduces here, were two notions: the existence of an ultimate
authority that can act only through an expressedly designated representation,
and the corresponding denial that a part of government, including a body of
ordinary representatives can legitimately alter its constitution or make a new
one (34). Even such an extra-ordinary representation he argued should be limited in time and substance (!), and should be revocable (12). But the problem
encountered immediately was that in France there was no institution such as
here implied, or rules under which it could be established, or even demands in
the famous Cahiers to establish either. Since in France therefore "the nation"
has not provided for an extra-ordinary assembly, but only an ordinary one (he
could have added "though under extra-ordinary circumstances") there was
no alternative but for the ordinary assembly assuming both legislative and
constituent powers (34). This move, under the pressure of circumstances, it
should be clear, surrendered even single differentiation, at least for the initial
constitution making process.[178]

The *Tiers état* represents some serious steps in reasserting the ideal, but
unfortunately Sieyès had two of these. Here the antinomic nature of his thought
comes fully in view, with two incompatible concepts of the nation already
noted, and with the already described transference to an assembly the powers
of the nation in the state of nature, bound by no constitution, no rules and no
procedures.[179] Note that suggesting the transformation of the Estates General
into a national assembly as his preferred road, he was now claiming unlimited
rights for an extra-ordinary representation. This implied single differentiation,
where only an extra-ordinary legislature would have all the power, but not
its predecessor, the ordinary Estate General or its successor, the Legislative
Assembly. He does not fear abuse of power, or postulate the need for safeguards,
because the extra-ordinary representation would have only such powers and
time limits that "the nation was pleased to give it" (*Écrits*, 164). What these
limits were and how they were to be to be enforced he did not say, and as he
did not it could be easily claimed that the nation delegated all the power.

However, Sieyès does not stop there, and it is at this point his second ideal
comes into play. Under the heading of what should have been done, he argues
that he would not have wanted to give the extra-ordinary assembly any powers
under which it could act as an ordinary one. The danger that he sees, rightly,
is the tendency of such a body to be then guided by the interests of the

---

[178] Defending the assumption of all powers by the assembly on non-pragmatic grounds, see
Arnaud Le Pillouer's excellent *Les pouvoirs non-constituants des assemblées constituantes* (Paris:
Dalloz, 2005).

[179] This was asserted even for an ordinary assembly, the Estates General by the earlier essay
('Executive Means," p. 34) "the only rules will be the ones . . . it made for itself."

legislative body they were about to form, in that case a body in all respects like themselves. The argument is made squarely in terms of Montesquieu's separation of powers. "In politics mixing up and conflating power is what makes it constantly impossible to establish social order" (*Political Writings*, 143; *Écrits*, 168). He does not even accept the objection that what is done is done and the past is the past (at least in the third 1789 edition of *Tiers état!*). Because even if all power has been de facto assumed by the Constituent Assembly, "knowledge of what should have been done can lead to a knowledge of what will be done" (*Political Writings*, 143).

Perhaps he was thinking of "safeguards," among which there was to be the unfortunate one, actually adopted, of not letting deputies of the Constituent Assembly run for the Legislative Assembly. This safeguard did not work as intended, and had negative unintended consequence of depriving the Legislative Assembly of the best potential members who stayed outside, and in part agitated against it. However, Sieyès was so intent at pursuing the theoretical point that he repeated it in two later contexts. It is not necessary for the members of society to individually exercise the constituent power; "they can give their confidence to representatives who assemble *only for that purpose, without the power to exercise any constituted powers*" (my italics: 20–21 July, 1789. "*Préliminaire de la constitution*" in *Écrits*, p. 99).

That coach has left by the time the lines were written; the constituent assembly was exercising most of the powers.[180] But his prediction was only partially right: while tempted by the vision of a future assembly government, the *Constituant* established a version of the separation of powers, with a fairly strong though certainly not absolute royal veto. As Karl Loewenstein argued in detail, the assembly's self-interested nature was manifested by blocking all channels of potential popular or local participation, and, in particular, a very rigid amendment rule, that was directed as much against future parliaments as popular actors.[181] Sieyès himself opposed this amendment rule, thus his strong stance against any form of royal veto in the constitution, as well as appeals to the people. This was the case also because he was initially very attached to

---

[180] Except for a narrow and weak executive power in the hands of the king, until the flight to Varennes.

[181] Constitution of 1791: amendment rule: Title VII, articles 1–9. The rule involved calling an assembly of revision, in effect a fourth legislature, after three successive regularly elected legislatures agreed to forward the exact same proposal to that assembly whose members could not have served in the previous regular legislature, and whose size was doubled by additional members. The assembly of revision had to declare its loyalty to the Constitution as a whole, and was limited to the amending task elected for. It was not permitted to legislate till the amending task was done, and the additional members were asked to resign. Needless to say this rule was not only never fully used, but no amendment process was even initiated.

the separation of powers in its "pure version" without balances and checks, not understanding that this version itself threatened the separation of powers by the assembly government he otherwise opposed.[182] Thus, he insisted that the full separation of powers should be maintained between constitution and legislation, between constituent and legislative powers. Constituent powers in the hands of a legislature would allow the usurpation of other powers in the state by the assembly. Speaking in front of the constituent assembly, he lamented that "imperious circumstances" and (now also) their "special mandates" obliged them to fulfill "simultaneously" or "successively" constituent and legislative functions, and added: "we recognize that this confusion cannot take place after this session." Quite contrary to the spirit of the amendment rule that was to be adopted, he insisted that if it will be necessary to review or reform a part of the new constitution, that should be done by a "convention" expressly delegated and limited to the task by the nation itself ("*Dire sur le veto royale*": in *Oeuvres* 239). While rejecting the British veto as the safeguard of the royal prerogative, in the case of conflicts between constituted powers, Sieyès suggested that these too could be adjudicated by calling a constituent convention for that purpose alone, and with no other powers (ibid. 240). He thus anticipated his later notion of the jury, that even more clearly made the constituent power simply one of the powers in a framework inherited from Montesquieu ("a veritable corps of representatives" *Oeuvres*, III, p. 11).

Granted, the idea of the jury could have been inherited more directly form the "censorship" of the 1776 Constitution of Pennsylvania, well known in France, and most likely influencing Condorcet, with whom Sieyès was associated. With respect to the need for separation of functions even with respect to the constituent power, they were in agreement, and also with respect to the imperious circumstances that did not allow in France the fulfillment of the desideratum. Condorcet was speaking for many of his radical contemporaries when he has made the very important distinction between the revolutionary transition from despotism to a free constitution such as the one occurring in France, from that in America, whether he meant 1787 or more likely 1776 or both, where the transition was from a free constitution to a more free one. The first, where people are recovering their rights against "despotic usurpation," cannot avoid revolutionary turmoil and cannot presumably follow the same forms as the second.[183] But in 1791 when others called for a second

---

[182] Vile, op. cit., on Sieyès, pp. 204–206; as well as pp. 216–218, where he traces the move post-Thermidor from pure separation of powers to the introduction of checks and balances, mainly in terms of the constitutional jury.

[183] "*Discours sur les conventions nationales*," pp. 213–214. This is one of the most important insights for this book, anticipating Arendt's thesis about the two type of constituent power. Below, I will

"convention"[184] again with the plenitude of all powers, he now maintained that it was time to instead separate the forms of power.[185] This is not what happened in 1792, however, when indeed a second convention was called. The fact is, double differentiation was abandoned not once but twice in France – in the very beginning[186] and the second time in 1792 with an elected Legislative Assembly in place. Then it was hard to argue that the conditions made it equally necessary, or that transition was again from despotism to a free constitution, to use Condorcet's important distinction.

3 *The Failure of Double Differentiation in France: 1792–1795*

It may be worthwhile to look, very briefly and summarily, at the specific historical givens in France, in 1789 in 1792, the two revolutionary or constituent moments. The first has been extensively discussed by the historians, and already at the *Assemblée Constituant.* Their character is not made particularly clear by the polemical concept of despotism, used at the time. A dynamic mix of absolutism and society of orders, with vestigial estate institutions, is a better description. Traditionally, France had aristocratically dominated estate assemblies, both for the country and for certain provinces, the pays d'états. The major one, the Estates General, has not been able to meet for 175 years, and it was primarily this development that allowed the replacement of the *Ständestaat* by royal absolutism. Thus in a revolutionary period that revived this body, it would have been difficult, if not impossible to rely on it in its original form to do the business of governing that was never its function. The famous *parlements* were only courts, ones that admittedly assumed at

---

have to make clear that there is a fundamental difference between a post sovereign model used in the transition from dictatorships and how, its principles can be re-applied in democratic states where there is a new constitution to be made. That will however not imply a full circle back to the American model itself.

[184] Condorcet carefully called the first only as *"la première assemblée constituante"* studiously avoiding calling it a convention. Not differentiated, and perhaps also because not offering its product as recommendation, it was thus not a true convention for him. Ibid., p. 219.

[185] Ibid., pp. 219–220. He does not identify the *"amis de la liberté"* whom he is criticizing here, and I cannot exclude that he had Sieyès in mind, with his explicit proposal of electing a new constituent power. While in my reconstruction, any consistent position for Sieyès would have involved a doubly differentiated form, the relevant texts are from 1789, and Condorcet here was making a criticism in 1791. It seems more likely that he had other "friends of liberty" in mind, perhaps radical members of the Jacobin Club then already gaining strength and support. In fact the original address was delivered to the Club, then called, *Société des amis de la constitution séants aux Jacobins à Paris.*

[186] And, of course, ever after until 1958. It was only the amendment rules that expressed it, usually, but these were rarely used for major change.

times a quasi-legislative function to very partially substitute for the Estates General.[187] France was secondly a society of orders, where instead of small republics stressed by Hannah Arendt in the path of Tocqueville all the constituted corporate powers were believed to be, and indeed were, suffused with privilege and injustice.[188] And, third, as M. Gauchet stresses in a brilliant analysis,[189] France had a powerful monarchy that the revolution first wished to keep, a kingship with traditional, and even theological legitimacy. Only a very powerful constituent body according to this argument could be seen as a sufficient counterweight to this power and this authority.

Very well. The conservative constitutionalists led by Mounier and, in a rather more traditionalist version by Burke,[190] did not think these three givens excluded building on the *pouvoirs constitués* even in 1791. The bulk of scholarly opinion now disagrees with them, in my view rightly. But the same three conditions in any case did not apply in 1792, during the second revolution that overthrew the monarchy. Aristocratic society and constituted bodies were already a matter of the past, abolished in 1789–90. The king too was under arrest, and the monarchy was to be replaced by a republic. The Legislative Assembly, was itself, however, a product of the revolution. It could have been preserved, until new elections under a new constitution would replace it. This did not happen. One could say perhaps that, despite the writings and speeches of Sieyès and Condorcet, the actual practice of 1789–1791 and the path it established mattered more than the precedents of the Americans, especially given the antinomic nature of both their theory and the way it was received. More importantly, in a non-federal setting, in a revolutionary process guided by the theory of popular sovereignty, it was probably difficult for the main actors to leave a key component of the constitutional monarchy like the Legislative Assembly, in place. No matter that the Legislative Assembly of 1792 was elected less than a year before by the voters of the population of the whole country, even if by a restricted suffrage. Now it decreed or rather was forced to decree by "the people," in other words the insurrectionary Commune of Paris, the election of a "convention" that was unknown to the Constitution of 1791. This patently *illegal act* created a constitutional break, one which was arguably necessary given the very high level of rigidity of that Constitution.

---

[187] Still an excellent source: Loewenstein, op. cit.   [188] Palmer, *Age*, vol. II, op. cit.
[189] *La revolution des pouvoirs* (Paris: Gallimard, 1995).
[190] Despite Burke's reliance on Mounier, they fundamentally disagreed on what was to be conserved, and what the new form was to look like. They relied, I think, on two different strands of Montesquieu: Burke on his defense of the society of orders and estates; Mounier on his proposal of a supposedly English type of separation of powers. It is probably true that Mounier thought the latter could be built on the foundations of the former, but this would have entailed more radical changes than Burke could have accepted.

But did its rigidity require the complete abrogation of the Constitution, and a *full legal rupture*, even before a new constitution, and a new assembly was put in place? Legally, there would have been alternatives. Assuming that parts of the Constitution implied the fundamental right of a people to change their government, any time, without limit (Title VII: Article 1 first half sentence, "the nation has the imprescriptible right to change its Constitution") this could be used to trump the detailed (and disastrously difficult) amendment rule (VII, Articles/2–5). The Legislative Assembly moreover was not compelled legally, even by this interpretation, to declare its own self-dissolution, once the new constituent body, the convention, was assembled.[191] But it did, and perhaps politically there was no way out of this with power temporarily in the hands of the Parisian revolutionary Commune.

The act of dissolution of the Legislative Assembly eerily foreshadowed that of the Constituent Assembly in Russia about 125 years later, and the dissolution of the Venezuelan Congress 80 years later still. It could be justified by a variety of (I think: ultimately untenable) arguments, ones that will reappear not only in Bolshevik texts but also in other radical democratic and revolutionary conceptions. From the beginning of the debates over the constitution, there was one stream of opinion that did not accept the notion of the identity of the nation's will with that of its representatives. In a liberal version, this position led to attempts to establish the royal veto as a form of appeal to the people, in the form of the primary assemblies; in a more democratic version to calls for popular ratification of the constitution.[192] Both efforts failed, and the suspensive veto given to the king established only an indirect form of appeal,[193] and was used for other purposes.[194] For radical democrats, there

[191] Furet's brilliant history, *Revolutionary France 1770–1880* (London: Blackwell, 1995) depicts the reappearance of the conflict between two versions of democracy, representative and direct, the latter taking an insurrectionary form that wipes way the representation (pp. 109–111).; also Richet "Revolutionary Assemblies" (p. 534). Richet describes a kind of dual power between the insurrection of August 10 and the first meeting of the Convention, between the revolutionary Commune and the (informally purged) Legislative Assembly, where the real power was in the hands of the Commune and the insurrection. Thus the last significant act of the Legislative Assembly was to decree the election of the Convention, and the need for a referendum ratifying its work (September 21, 1792). Even this decree can be surmised to have been at the instigation of the Paris Commune, which most likely did not wish to leave the last word to the Convention to be elected (by all of France). This was, of course, an issue debated since 1789.
[192] Loewenstein, op. cit., 225ff; Baker, "Fixing the French Constitution," op. cit.
[193] No immediate popular consultation was linked to the veto, though after two additional regular elections two successive parliaments could override. It could be argued then there were two popular consultations involved, though in the context of regular elections such a claim was weak.
[194] For Furet this veto changed nothing in the fundamental structure of sovereignty, supposedly delegated to the representative body (*Revolutionary France*, 77–78) while to Baker it represented a fundamental ambiguity in it, the concession that the general will did exist

was no formal way to stop representatives from usurping the sovereign will of the nation under the Constitution of 1791. Accordingly, it came to be strongly advocated, in theory and practice, that usurpation by representatives can only be stopped by direct democracy, in the form of the popular insurrection.[195] Once this became the leading idea of revolutionary Paris on the road to the general insurrection of August 10, 1792, it was easy to demand that the old representation of the French people, convicted of usurpation, not be left in place. The key point here was that representative democracy was either not democracy at all, or that it could be trumped by a higher form, namely direct democracy. In Paris "the insurrection" was seen as this higher form, while in Petrograd it was the soviets in whose name the "bourgeois democracy" of the All Russian Constituent Assembly was abolished. Unsurprisingly, in both cases dissolution of representation in the name of a particular mobilized part of society contributed to the civil war.[196]

But there were also other arguments. Anticipating Lenin and Trotsky in 1918, it was said that the earlier voice of the people does not count, because it is *no longer* their voice. In a revolution, supposedly, opinion changes quickly. The later voice of the people was to count as its true voice, especially since the Convention would be elected on the bases of universal manhood suffrage, rather than the property qualifications still in effect for the election of the Legislative Assembly.[197] Finally, it was argued that the constitutional monarchy was still monarchy, and therefore all the reasons still applied that disqualified despotic regimes from yielding elements of the new *pouvoir constituant*.

None of these arguments involved legal continuity, and nor was the stabilization of radical change through rule of law valued at all. Ultimately legality was entirely devalued, and herein lies the greatest difference with America – lost in Ackerman's account, as revolution became a model of change prized not only as a means but as an end. Revolution was no longer a reluctant

outside the assembly (853). Precisely this ambiguity was the source of the conflicts, which broke out openly in 1792, and are detailed by Furet himself (110–111).

[195] See Baker's "Sovereignty," 852–854.
[196] Oskar Anweiler, *The Soviets: The Russian Workers, Peasants, and Soldiers Councils, 1905–1921* (New York: Pantheon Books, 1974). See my Epilogue below.
[197] On this see the highly skeptical views of Richet, "Revolutionary Assemblies" (according to him, the passive citizens of the Constitution of 1791 either did not know they could vote, or were afraid to vote); and P. Gueniffey "Elections" in *Critical Dictionary*, pp 40–41, who shows that the elections of 1792 were a thoroughly controlled affair in Paris, leading to an *overwhelming* Jacobin victory, while in the provinces the Gironde could hold its own.

necessity as in Condorcet's theory,[198] but became almost a new Religion.[199] Thus it is not ultimately the institutions of the old regime that I would hold responsible for the consolidation of a French pattern, but the development of a radical revolutionary dynamic abolishing them that continued even against the new institutions generated by the revolution itself, such as the Constitution of 1791.[200] The institutions of the old regime, may have only overdetermined the initial pattern. Radical revolution was factor enough, even when these institutions were gone.

Once in place in this scenario, with the Legislative Assembly self-dissolved, American example and name aside, the National Convention had no other option but to take all the power. It had no established institutions (like the American state governments, or even the townships of Massachusetts) to share power with.[201] Not only the historical pattern started in 1789, and the revolutionary nature of the context seemed to predetermine this choice. The reigning theory of the day contributed as well. The clubs, which originally saw themselves as defenders of the Constitution of 1791, abandoned that posture soon after its promulgation. By 1791, along with Robespierre, they called for a new constituent assembly or national convention, understood not on the model of the American prototype, but previous French experience and the idea of sovereignty.[202] Could a different conception, one based on post-sovereign constitution making, along with the still potent American example,[203] have made a difference, if accepted widely enough and early enough? In principle, a

---

[198] Again, given "despotism." It is not revolution that he elevates to a principle, but rather the necessity of doing away with despotism.

[199] See from Tocqueville, *Old Regime and the French Revolution* to Ozouf's "Revolutionary Religion" in *Critical Dictionary*, op. cit.

[200] This point is stressed by Arendt in her critique of permanent revolution, followed by Ackerman. Keith Baker, in his article on Sovereignty, argues that it is the tension between popular sovereignty and representation that was the source of this dynamic. This resembles, but very much improves upon Arendt's critique of a sovereign constituent power in the state of nature that could not be the foundation for stable institutions. Elsewhere (Post Sovereign: chapter 2) I follow another stream of her argument, concerning the failure to found a new structure of authority. In any case, the failure would belong to the making of the Constitution of 1791. Most historians focus on its contents, which certainly contributed to the disaster: a veto that became absolute, an amendment rule that was completely rigid, and a way of structuring the executive that gave the king too much power to sabotage functioning. Furet, *Revolutionary France*, pp. 76–77.

[201] Of course, there was the insurrectionary Commune. But there was no mechanism to coordinate the two forms of power, representative and direct. Moreover, France was not only Paris, and relying on the Paris insurrection led to "federalist" risings elsewhere. With this said, there was something like a system of dual power till the Convention suppressed the Commune (fn.: Furet et al.).

[202] Furet, op. cit., p. 109.

[203] During the terror, the American reference became a sign of guilty conservatism.

legislative assembly would have been able to govern, while a republican constitution was being made. And if the constitution makers wished to replace the old assembly quickly, rapid, consensual constitution making and full enactment could have been the way to accomplish this goal. Neither happened. Indeed, Condorcet was still in the leadership of the Legislative Assembly that was unable to restrain or channel the popular rising. But he could not return to the theme of the right form of constitution making, until somewhat later, when, briefly as a leader of the constitutional project of the Convention, he did so obliquely in his suggestions for amendment rules for the future.[204] The sovereign status of the new Convention was not going to be challenged, at least not by any old established power. If anything, this was a period in which not only revolution, but the terms people and nation were becoming part of a cult, and it was simply not permissible to imagine its embodiment to have only limited power.[205]

In the end the old constitution was abandoned, and the Jacobins imposed the new process. The efforts of people like Condorcet, to "domesticate the revolution" were mostly, if not completely disregarded, and he himself was forced into suicide. In any case, in the midst of an insurrection even the new constitution drafted and ratified in 1793 could not be actually institutionalized. Less than a year after its ratification and suspension, its main architect, Hérault de Séchelles himself went to the guillotine. Emergency or revolutionary government remained the order of the day, and all efforts to domesticate the revolution, were without effect. Thus in the French pattern, the renewed revolutionary context and theory guided by the unitary symbolism of the people all converged.

---

[204] It is hard to know to what extent he blamed the makers of the Constitution of 1791 for not following his advice at that time, that consisted of the following options (Discours 212ff; 220):

1. an amendment rule involving both periodic conventions, and popular initiatives for calling extra-ordinary conventions, and
2. Popular ratification of the Constitution of 1791, or
3. Keeping its status interim, until a new convention ratifies it, or
4. Calling a convention of revision soon after enactment, and allowing it to work side-by-side with the legislative assembly in perfecting constitution.
5. Unclear whether he wanted popular ratification for these revisions, or left that up to the new convention.

For his expanded 1793 model of amendment, see Chapter 5 below.

[205] Furet is nevertheless right, the issue between the people themselves and their representatives, that destroyed the Legislative Assembly, was not resolved, and could not be resolved until the most radical force rose to power by insurrections and the Jacobin government came to destroy the insurrectionary potential. It could not be resolved in theory, because of the bifurcation of the heritage of Rousseau, and, in practice, because the quest to find the true embodiment of the people by either representative or direct democracy was as always futile.

With respect to the context, it is important to focus not only on the revolutionary conditions that vitiated the American model in France, but also on the absence of these that helped to stabilize it in its home setting. It is true, in revolutionary Pennsylvania, where Gordon Wood has traced the origins of the idea if not the practice of double differentiation, the assumption of all powers by the General Convention, and the expropriation of the regular legislature did take place.[206] On the other hand, double differentiation worked very well in Massachusetts and New Hampshire. Leaving aside all the possible internal differences among these states, and there were many crucial ones, I note only that 1776 and 1781 were extremely different times, and the United States was a very different place at these two times. At the moment of the revolutionary war, Pennsylvanians were in the midst of a grand political rupture, and the old legislature was suspected and accused of being close to the old, colonial regime or the proprietary interest that used to control the state.[207] The institutions of the whole country were in flux, and one could not speak of any viable federal arrangement. However, at the time of the final rounds of the Massachusetts and New Hampshire constitution making, the revolutionary war was more or less won, and a confederation was largely consolidated. There was neither the problem of weakening the state against an external enemy, nor the lack of some external guarantees if the conflict between old and new, legislature and convention became harsh. As a hypothesis then, war and a unitary system, as in France,[208] are not conducive to the stabilization of the American model, which easily descends into dual power and, with the victory of one side, to the sovereign pattern with a constituent assembly. And peace[209] and a federal system are conducive to its stabilization. Since the point is that normal government should be able to continue functioning on one level, while a constitution is being made on the other, the argument about federalism applies not only for member units, but the overarching one as well. The point is well illustrated by the history of the making of the Federal Constitution, a time of peace when normal government functioned in all the states as it did during the Confederation almost without interruption.

[206] Wood, op. cit; Palmer, *Age*, vol. I; Adams, op. cit.

[207] Wood, op. cit.; Palmer, *Age*, vol. I with the latter seeing the connection between the Pennsylvanian and French revolutionary models very well.

[208] France was at war since April 1792, and, of course, that played a crucial role in the renewal of the revolutionary dynamic stressed here.

[209] That point was made by Rousseau, who indeed saw the link between peace and federalism. See *The Government of Poland* (Indianapolis: Hackett, 1975), the *Social Contract*, book II, chapters 8 and 10, and especially *A Lasting Peace Through the Federation of Europe* http://oll .libertyfund.org/titles/rousseau-a-lasting-peace-through-the-federation-of-europe-and-the -state-of-war

The role of theory in the outcome remains still a question. Evidently, the theory of unitary organ sovereignty is incompatible with double differentiation. And this incompatibility was indeed played out in France. If the Legislative Assembly was sovereign there was no need for a constituent convention, and if the latter was sovereign the former had to be dissolved. Yet can the wrong theory bring down an experiment even when the conditions, peace and federalism are conducive to success?[210] Apparently not given the American example, though the wrong theory can contribute to the instability of the result. It is possible that the antinomy concerning the constituent power, a function of theory, has exacerbated the struggle over the location of sovereignty, by inflating that power whose locus could not be decided. Thus the (always disputed) power of secession became a veto power over constitutional amendments, in the work of Calhoun but not only there. There were nullification attempts and even secession plans before him, and not only in the South. Could, conversely, the right theory, compensate for the absence of one or both of the favorable contextual conditions?

It may not be possible to show the exact causal role of theory (or its absence) in the many deformations of the American model abroad, historically, given the inherent difficulties of stabilizing it in revolutionary contexts. But without an alternative theory, post-sovereign or democratic involving multiple levels of participation, it is not likely that under adverse conditions one would seek to save what was essential in this model. Even more, unless the conditions are extremely favorable, it is not likely such a pattern can develop without some theoretical guidance (Weber's ideal signposts) that, of course, do not have to take the form of a grand synthesis. But theory alone, even the most sophisticated, probably cannot lead to a post-sovereign pattern; it can become the young Marx's "material force" only under some favorable conditions, cultural or political.

There was available theory in France, but it surely did and could not become a material force. I return to Sieyès. Within an antinomic structure, he held on to the right theory even under adverse conditions, where the institutions and conditions that stabilized the model in America (namely federalism and

---

[210] This question too could be empirically explored by looking at the cases of Latin American history, where I think, without exception, the sovereign theory was dominant. But the political conditions relevant to making of new conditions were probably sufficiently variable to be able to test the proposition better than using the single case of the USA, where there was constitutional stability, but also a process leading to civil war not unrelated to the possibility of constitutional change. The main fear of the Southern elites in the struggle over the territories concerned arguably the possible change in the numerical relationship of free and slave states that would make Article V amendments abolishing slavery possible.

peace) were neither present nor desired, and what was present, namely a revolutionary rupture with aristocratic constituted powers, worked against its adoption. His theory, however, was internally conflictual or antinomic in its relationship to sovereignty, implying both an unlimited constituent power, and the separation of powers implying that all power, including the constituent, should be limited and therefore under law. Moreover he was also suspended between "ought" and "is," the power of norms and that of factual constraints. The power of factual constraints at first reinforced the sovereigntist dimension of his antinomy, before factual disaster reinforced the other side, the separation of powers. While continually running up against the adverse conditions (necessity, as he called it, in a discussion more with himself than anyone else), he did not abandon *either* the perspective of "what ought to have been done" or would have been desirable (new elections of a doubly differentiated convention) *or* that of the possible and necessary, the turning of the imperfectly elected Estates General into the all-powerful national assembly. While Sieyès is often seen as the champion of this necessity as the new desirable, this interpretation is wrong.

4 *The Idea of the Interim Constitution*

Not only did Sieyès not ever abandon the norm of separation, but he even proposed an entirely original and originally disregarded scheme of realizing it. When he gave up on double differentiation, for one time only, he came to be concerned about a constitution adopted by an assembly with the plenitude of powers. Thus, he was thinking of revision even before the thing was adopted, in part under his influence. He was to lose the battle concerning a well-designed amendment rule, unsurprising given his qualms about an all-powerful drafting assembly that would have the inclination to deeply entrench its product, much too deeply as it turned out.[211] When this happened, or was about to happen, in two texts he went even further, in the direction of immediate revision. Let us treat, he proposed, the work of the Constituent Assembly, the Constitution of 1791, in effect as provisional, something that would have to be confirmed as definitive, by a new assembly or convention, properly elected *only for that purpose*.[212] Since the Constituent Assembly did not rigorously conform to a

---

[211] See Loewenstein's excellent discussion of the amendment rule; op. cit., pp. 289ff.; 317ff.; 365–372.

[212] "*Reconnoissance et exposition raisonée*" in *Écrits politiques*, p. 192; in "What is the Third Estate," where the case for double differentiation was repeatedly argued (139; 143) the idea of electing a new, extra-ordinary assembly seemed to have been just one of two alternatives. He accepted the transformation of the Estates General into a Constituent assembly as the other

representation required by that form of power, we should treat its product as provisional until confirmed by a new properly elected extra-ordinary body properly commissioned and limited. ("*Extraordinairement convoqué pour cet unique objet*") He nowhere implies that the new body would have the power only to say yes or no, and he definitely does not mean a referendum by either the primary assemblies or by the atomized population.[213] His friend Condorcet recorded his partial assent. It would be useful, he argued, to consider the constitution in the making (that of 1791) to be provisional, until a new convention, after discussion, would ratify it. If a ratificatory referendum, he otherwise considered justified, would not take place, Condorcet thought a second convention would be all the more important, one doubly differentiated, being able to combine popular participation with serious deliberation, existing side by side with the legislative assembly, under the provisional constitution it was meant to review and revise.[214]

In a sense the call for a new convention as Condorcet called it anticipated the republican demand made in 1792 that led to the election of the Convention Nationale. But we should be clear that Sieyès at least had a different purpose than the ending of the constitutional monarchy that he defended famously against Tom Paine (*Political Writings* 163ff.), namely the rightful conclusion of the constituent process that began in 1789. That process had two legitimation gaps in his mind, its mode of election and the plenitude of powers assumed by the Constituent Assembly. Certainly, the double differentiated model he had in mind for the second convention, supported by Condorcet, was significantly

---

possibility. The two ideas were not yet combined as in the later essay. Ibid., 151–152 Carré de Malberg, op. cit., 502;

[213] I think L. Jaume's otherwise interesting interpretation, reproducing (twice) the key text, is wrong on this point (in "Constituent Power in France" in M. Loughlin and N. Walker eds., *Paradox of Constitutionalism* (Oxford: Oxford University Press, 2007) pp. 69–70). Sieyès indeed spoke of a new constituent power to be elected. His deliberative idea of representation, of the formation of the general will, did not permit a passive role for such a body. Moreover he was against any doubling of the will, and thus ratifications in referenda, by what was then debated, the "small republics," namely the primary assemblies. See "What is the Third Estate" in *Political Writings*, p. 152 ("they do not need to consult those who mandated them about a disagreement that does not exist"). A single assembly like that proposed by Gouverneur Morris at the Federal Convention would have been a different matter, or Edmund Randolph and George Mason's second convention that was explicitly proposed to have an active role in taking the expressed views of the people into account. (MN: August 31 and September 15; pp. 567 and 651). But where would be the justification of treating this body as a lesser instance than the imperfect National Assembly, unable to debate and amend?

[214] *Discours*, 220. Unlike Sieyès, Condorcet was for popular ratification of the constitution, by the primary assemblies. Why and how he thought this could be done, without endangering unity and the formation of a general will become clearer in the 1793 Plan. *Oeuvres*, vol. XII, pp. 342–349

different than the unitary model that emerged with the premature dissolution of the legislative assembly that was incompatible with their proposal. While not stated clearly, it was evidently assumed by Sieyès that the new process would occur, at least initially under the Constitution of 1791.

This is the first time the important idea of the provisional or interim constitution made its appearance in constitutional thought. Confronted with the problem of inevitably imperfect beginnings, this idea was to have an important carrier from Sieyès to our century, first in France in 1946, followed by Germany and Japan, and then from Spain to South Africa and beyond. It is a different idea than that of the pre-constitution to which a sovereign constituent power submits itself voluntarily.[215] Here the interim constitution is not self-imposed by the constituent body, it is external to this second assembly, and binds it as well as all other actors until the enactment of the second constitution. All this follows clearly from Condorcet's notion of convention as ultimately a type of amendment procedure, however total it may be. For him the subjection of even the popular sovereign to law was central, and that is what allowed the full separation of a constituent function.[216] Admittedly, Sieyès did not say as much, and perhaps his antinomic conception did not allow him to do so. But it follows from one of the two things he wished to achieve, along with Condorcet, through the two-stage model: (aside from proper elections), namely double differentiation. Given the imperfect beginnings unavoidable in France, double differentiation was possible only if enforced under the prior, interim constitution.

New elections, of course, very much mattered to Sieyès. If forced to create a constitution by a body with less than full "democratic" or electoral credentials, its work has to be taken seriously, but it must be open to full revision if it is to become legitimate. On this point, as on so much else, he was anticipated

[215] Olivier Beaud is one of the very few authors who caught the significance of the interim constitutions, starting with the French little constitution of 1946, and continuing in the new or renewed democracies from Greece to Spain. I think he assimilates this form a little too much to the pre-constitutional decisions that, in some cases, do not significantly limit the provisional government or the constitutional assembly. But he sees the main theoretical point, certainly, the purpose of limiting all the constituent instances, and denying omnipotent sovereign power in constitution making. In this he follows Carré de Malberg (if not in all else, and even on this point not consistently). He also sees, at least implicitly, that genuine interim arrangements emerge from bargain and compromise as in the case of the making of the Vth Republic that he puts under this heading as well, probably because of the pioneering role of constitutional principles. *La puissance*, pp. 272–276.

[216] Only being rigorously under law would guarantee even that the forms of assembly of the empirical people preserve the equality and universality required by the abstract concept of the people. Condorcet, *"Plan de constitution,"* 347.

by some Americans as he may not have known.[217] At the Federal Convention first Edmund Randolph and then George Mason followed by Elbridge Gerry expressed their willingness to sign the constitution only if it were not final, and explicitly involved calling a second convention.[218] They were disturbed by the fact that the ratifying conventions had only a passive role, being able to say yes or no, thus leaving the real drafting work to an unelected body, the Federal Convention itself. "A second Convention will know more of the sense of the people, and be able to provide a system more consonant to it. It was improper to say to the people, take this or nothing." Randolph here focused on the fatal flaw of all referenda, and even passive grass roots bodies linked to ratification. But the idea of a second convention corresponded to the proposal of Sieyès. Given his link to Jefferson, the friend of these Virginians, it is possible that their concept influenced the thinking of Condorcet.[219] What really tied the latter to an American like Mason was the idea of active participation by different bodies, one that unfortunately neither ever thought to be in opposition to the sovereign theory.

But in America, as I showed, the idea of double differentiation was easier to practice because of federalism. And while Condorcet tried to be as American as he could, neither he nor Sieyès could or even wished to propose federalism for France.[220] Moreover, giving real power to the ratifying conventions to propose amendments, and to a second convention that could make them, a body yet again more national in character, was to re-emphasize the multiple agents that were required to establish the constitution, under a legal order. In other words, even without Federalism one could have a multi-actor, post-organ sovereign model producing their constitution, that was after all possible in Massachusetts and New Hampshire that were unitary states, if small ones. Thus Condorcet's idea was probably guided by eighteenth-century American practice, if not by

[217] He could not have known the records of the Federal Convention, of course, but may have known something of the relevant works of the Anti-Federalists or the opinions of Jefferson.

[218] See Maier, op. cit., pp. 45–49. Four state-ratifying conventions wound up calling for a second convention.

[219] Jefferson's view, which was at least initially different from Mason's. He proposed ratification by nine states to guarantee the benefits of the constitution to Americans, and the last four holding out for amendments before they ratified. See "Letter to Alexander Donald February 7, 1788." Jefferson here focused on the need for a bill of rights, and relied in fact on the formal Article V process rather than a second convention. The difference was that a second convention, with the same status as the first, could change everything, as against a more focused and partial Article V process.

[220] Sieyès, "*Dire*" p. 234; in more detail, Condorcet "*Plan de constitution*" (presented to the Convention 15–16 February 1793 in *Oeuvres*, vol. XII pp. 337–340 (*Selected Writings*, Indianapolis: Bobbs Merril, n.d.), pp. 145–146. See also M. Ozouf, "Federalism" in F. Furet and M. Ozouf eds. *Critical Dictionary of the French Revolution* (Cambridge: Harvard University Press, 1989).

the statements of Randolph, Mason or Gerry either at the Convention or in the press.[221] In their case, the passing of the Bill of Rights, represented a partial realization of the demand for second convention, even if in a different sequence and under a different legal form but certainly without a new legal rupture or even illegality. Most importantly, the ordinary amendment structure of the Constitution, used for the first time, was able to take into account the amending proposals emerging from the ratification conventions of the states. Condorcet had to be aware of this development, namely the passing of the Bill of Rights, which was so important to Jefferson, who originally suggested the use of the new amendment rule for this purpose. Whether or not Condorcet was aware of Jefferson's positions on this subject, in his own case, however, unfortunately, a similar way of thinking led only to an elegant constitutional proposal that went nowhere.

The same was indeed true of the idea of a provisional constitution first articulated by Sieyès. Paradoxically, it was easy to lose the real power of his proposal, because of his legitimate focus on elections. It would be possible to say, and this is what the tradition strongly implies, that he only made it because the Constituent Assembly was not properly elected, and in the future that would have to be one of the keys to the improvement of the same form. What I argued, however, is that it was equally the failure to achieve double differentiation due to the historical circumstances that may have motivated Sieyès. The second constituent assembly or convention could have been doubly differentiated, and this is indeed what he literally proposed, with Condorcet echoing exactly this proposal in his constitutional draft.[222]

Even the need to have new elections points to more differentiation, and the relativization of the sovereign status of any one assembly. It could be claimed, of course, that the rightly elected assembly, say the Convention, that was linked to a ratificatory referendum would not require double differentiation or

---

[221] See op. cit. P. Maier's interesting reconstruction of these.

[222] Projet, Title IX *"Des conventions nationales."* The proposal called for both periodic conventions, and extra-ordinary ones initiated either by the legislature or from below, the primary assemblies. The separation of the legislature and the convention was to be complete in space, and through membership. The convention has to concentrate only on the constitution making tasks it is established for, and all existing powers would continue in their legal activities till a new constitution was fully enacted; a critique, implicitly of what happened in 1792–1793. The new constitution would be ratified according to the rules of the old one. No convention could function for longer than a year; if its work was rejected, in the first two months, the convention could resubmit the parts that have a chance to be approved. Otherwise, if there is not time, the legislature would begin a new process of possibly electing a new convention. These last provisions sound ironic in light of the coming usurpation of power by the National Convention to which the plan was submitted.

interim constitutional arrangements. Sieyès, as already said, following either Montesquieu or the Americans or both, believed that having all the power in the case of a constituent assembly could lead to the wrong kind of government. But elections present another kind of problem, one more general than even Sieyès might have realized. Free elections do not happen by themselves. While this is supposedly less of a dilemma in places where there are constitutions and electoral systems already in place, elsewhere it is provisional governments that hold the key to and can structure the form of elections. In these settings, former dictatorships or semi-authoritarian systems, the Sieyès formula concerning interim constitution has special relevance. In order to have elections one needs a (minimal) constitution. But such a constitution would be the work of unelected instances. If a provisional government answers this problem by simply enacting one, it will tend to be an undemocratic one, serving its own purposes. If it does not, it will inevitably handle the road to the constituent assembly even more arbitrarily, and will try to structure the elections and most likely control the assembly as well.[223]

Sieyès' answer is to have a genuine constitution-making process, to make a constitutionalist constitution, but an interim one. (He does not solve the general political problem of how this is to be possible, and how one is not just moving the same problem one step back. He did not have to, since the making of the constitution of 1791 qualified because of the structure of the three estates represented both old and new in France). And this answer is relevant even where there is no previous dictatorship or authoritarian system. It is easy to charge, as did the followers of Chavez recently, that the rules in place favor the old oligarchic constitutional regime, and no democratic constitution can be made under these rules. The impulse to break the rules, and to turn at one point to embodied sovereignty as the substitute for law becomes obvious. Here too the idea of beginning democracy democratically has become a problem, and the sovereign conception seems to supply the missing answer. There may not be democracy or the right kind of democracy, but the people always exist, supposedly. And whoever can represent their will can begin the process. In that case, of course, there seems to be also no reason for that instance to share power with anyone else. This is the road to sovereign dictatorship, whether an assembly is its main form, or a plebiscite takes pride of place, or even the two are combined.

---

[223] These lines were first written in 2008, and have been dramatically confirmed, unfortunately enough, by the Egyptian Revolution of 2011. On that see chapter 4 below, as well as A. Arato and E. Tombuş, "Learning from Success, Learning from Failure: South Africa, Hungary, Turkey and Egypt," *Philosophy & Social Criticism* (2013).

There is an alternative to the answer of cutting through the vicious circle[224] by the concentrated power of sovereignty, represented also by the better-known side of Sieyès. Both his and Condorcet's disregarded suggestions in France, as well as the more influential[225] proposals of Randolph and Mason in America echoed by other "Anti-Federalists," those suggesting a genuinely two-stage drafting process, were important clues about how this could be done, even without the stabilizing conditions of America itself.[226] Yet there had to be not only other institutional innovations, but also a fundamentally transformed attitude to the modality of change, namely revolution, for this conception of a multiplicity of stages, provisionality, and, implicitly, the desirability of having a set of different actors, none of them sovereign, to reappear in new guises. With respect to Sieyès, it was ultimately not only the dogma of sovereignty, interpreted in terms of organs, but the spirit of revolution that dictated which side of his antinomic theory would be influential, not only in the midst of a revolution, but in the subsequent nearly 200 years with the undiminished prestige of revolutionary change. All else, namely his shifting preferences or his antinomies, could be chalked up to his pragmatism, opportunism, or worse still: anti-popular liberalism. Even in America, in part under the impact of an admittedly weaker ethos of revolution, the theory of sovereign constitution making, at variance with the original practice, has played a role historically and has certainly not disappeared. It took a revolt against the spirit of revolution, for the post-sovereign conception to really come into its own.[227]

---

[224] Arendt, *On Revolution*, p. 152.

[225] Again: more influential because of the adoption of the Bill of Rights in the process that continued under Article V. For this history, see Maier, *Ratification*.

[226] How those conditions worked is again illustrated with the history of the Bill of Rights, which was in effect the main issue raised at the state conventions whose full participatory rights Randolph and Mason, and after them many anti-Federalists, defended. Jefferson too was a supporter, of course, and had some relevant schemes concerning how state ratification processes could be used to get a bill of rights. See Leonard W. Levy's "Bill of Rights" in L.W. Levy ed., *Essays on the Making of the Constitution* (New York: Oxford University Press, 1969).

    The ratification process of North Carolina directly effected the passing of the Bill of Rights, if not by a second Convention, the Congress doing to an extent what the Randolph and Mason proposal (implicitly supported by Jefferson) implied: taking into account the wishes of the elected representatives expressed in the conventions.

[227] Ackerman's two volumes reflect this shift, although unnoticed by him. The emphasis in the first is on revolution, though short of the extreme of the permanent one. The second volume shifts to revolutionary reforms, based on an unconventional relationship to inherited institutions. I think this reflects the new pattern that is the theme of this book, especially the third part, even if Ackerman never did clearly see the difference between presidentially led self-coups and post-sovereign regime change. See my essays from the 1990s, collected in *Civil Society, Constitution and Legitimacy* (Lanham, MD: Rowman & Littlefield, 2000).

PART II

POST-SOVEREIGNTY AND THE RETURN OF REVOLUTION

3

The Evolution of the Post-Revolutionary Paradigm

From Spain to South Africa

Quel que soit celui qu'on adoptera l'on ne doit pas oublier ce que j'ai dit dans le Contrat Social de l'état de foiblesse & d'anarchie où se trouve une nation tandis qu'elle établit ou réforme sa constitution. Dans ce moment de désordre & d'effervescence elle est hors d'état de faire aucune résistance & le moindre choc est capable de tout renverser. Il importe donc de se ménager à tout prix un intervalle de tranquillité durant lequel on puisse sans risque agir sur soi-même & rajeunir sa constitution.[1]

J.-J. Rousseau, *Considérations sur le gouvernement de Pologne* (1772)

Written before the great revolution he influenced, one that was to confirm his fears, Rousseau's lines anticipated the modus operandi of American constitution makers from 1780 in Massachusetts to the Federal Convention of 1787. They succeeded in founding new regimes, while avoiding total ruptures of law and power. Yet when applied elsewhere, the American model of constitution making, presupposing political stability at home, most often led to forms of highly conflictual dual power and revolutionary usurpation, anticipated by the French Revolution.[2] It was not until the 1970s in Spain, and even later in

---

[1] No matter what plan is adopted, you should not forget what I have said in the *Social Contract* [Book II; chapters 8 and 10] regarding the state of weakness and anarchy in which a nation finds itself while it is establishing or reforming its constitution. In this moment of disorder and effervescence, it is incapable of putting up any sort of resistance, and the slightest shock is capable of upsetting everything. It is important, therefore, to arrange at all costs for an interval of tranquility, during which you may be able without risk to work upon yourselves and rejuvenate your constitution. http://www.constitution.org/jjr/poland.htm (accessed 11/25/2015) XV: Conclusion.

[2] Two major exceptions, where something relatively close to this ideal type worked were Australia in the late 1890s and Germany after World War II. It is not coincidental that these were successful attempts to unite provinces in new federations. The more complex and dramatically incomplete case of Canada in the 1860s should not be counted here, because of the fundamentally governmental top down process in the United Province of Canada, which was then brought together with the maritime provinces. I would also not count the making of the Union

Central Europe followed by South Africa, that a paradigm was generated capable of guaranteeing if not exactly an "interval of tranquility," then its functional equivalent, the continuity of state structure, for the democratic framing and consolidation of a radically new constitution.

As an ideal type the new paradigm was linked to an underlying idea as well as several crucial elements. That fundamental idea, within an overall democratic method, was to apply constitutionalism not only to result but also to the process of constitution making. The method turns on the following essential elements: 1. A two- (or multi-)stage process and the making of two constitutions, where the making of the first, interim constitution regulates and limits the making of the second. 2. Round table negotiations that lead to the making of the first constitution. Here the important thing is not the name (for instance, in South Africa, CODESA and the Multi Party Negotiating Forum), but the relative inclusiveness of these bodies. 3. An emphasis on legal continuity throughout the transition, even if in some of the cases it is violated. Central to this continuity is the formal role (indeed strictly formal role) of parliamentary institutions of an old regime in ratifying the initial changes, including the interim constitution, according to an old amendment rule. 4. The central role of a new, democratically elected assembly in drafting the second and final constitution. This assembly is different from the classical European type of constituent assembly, given the limitations of the interim constitution to which it is bound, but also different from the merely ratifying role of the American state conventions of 1787–1788. 5. The significant role of constitutional courts, generally created by interim constitutions, in policing the procedural (in South Africa also substantive) limitations stipulated by first or interim constitutions. The initial refusal of the South African Constitutional Court to certify (thereby invalidating in effect) the final constitution was extraordinary in this regard, but in line with the basic logic of the method.

This ideal type is an intellectual construction. Nevertheless, it represents a normatively motivated interpretation of several actual cases that confirm its relevance. The South African pattern comes closest, but many of its features were anticipated, from Spain in the 1970s to Poland, Hungary, and Bulgaria

---

of South Africa 1908 to 1910, with its dramatically exclusionary character, where the outcome was a unified state. Technically, Canada, Australia, and South Africa were under the constituent and legislative authority of Westminster until 1931. On Canada, see P. Russell, *Constitutional Odyssey* 3rd ed. (Toronto: University of Toronto Press, 2004); on South Africa see L.M. Thompson, *The Unification of South Africa* (Oxford: Clarendon Press, 1960); on Australia, John La Nauze, *The Making of the Australian Constitution* (Melbourne: Melbourne University Press, 1972) and on West Germany, Peter Merkl, *The Origin of the West German Republic* (New York: Oxford University Press, 1963). These cases will be discussed in detail in a forthcoming work together with Julian Arato.

in the late 1980s and early 1990s. Thus, the paradigm was less a product of design than the result of evolution at times relying on conscious learning. That learning was sometimes direct and at other times was mediated by the international public discussion, leading to the search for a new alternative to revolutionary ruptures. Retroactively, it is possible to reconstruct a rational developmental pattern among the cases, but with two caveats. First, within that empirical pattern there were also cases that failed, almost always having to do with the destruction and replacement of an inherited state structure. And second, negative learning or unlearning has also taken place, as demonstrated by the eventual fate of the paradigm in countries as diverse as Iraq, Hungary, and Nepal. Thus, the teleological nature of the development should be seen normatively, rather than empirically. The existence of a new paradigm of constitution making in itself never did nor will guarantee a happy ending in any individual country.

Accordingly, it is important not only to reconstruct the development of the paradigm, the primary task of this chapter, but also to explain failures of application or of learning to whatever extent possible. This chapter has both of these goals.

FROM SPAIN TO POLAND

The desirability of learning from Spain has been clearly expressed by actors in the first two Central European dominoes[3] to fall within the Soviet imperium, in 1989–1990.[4] And there is no question that important lessons were learned. But this learning took the form of both adopting Spanish solutions, as well as breaking with some of them. The most important positive lesson, followed by all the Central European countries, was the need to combine processes of what were called *reforma* and *ruptura*, which could be done through the middle term used in Spain, namely *pactada*. The combination of *reforma pactada/ruptura pactada* represented the transcending of the

---

3 See photo on the cover and p. 76 of M. Bernhard and J. Kubik, *Twenty Years After Communism: The Politics of Memory and Commemoration* (Oxford: Oxford University Press, 2014).

4 Leaders of the democratic oppositions like Adam Michnik and Janos Kis were particularly interested in the lessons of the democratic transition that has most conspicuously succeeded by the mid 1980s. Kis, who was a faculty colleague at the New School in New York in 1988 while he continued to lead the Hungarian democratic opposition, repeatedly asked Jose Casanova and myself to explain the Moncloa Pact, which at that time he assumed was the central agreement between government and opposition producing the transition scenario. See A. Michnik, *Letters From Prison* (Berkeley: University of California Press, 1985); Jose Casanova, "A spanyolországi demokratikus átalakulás tanulságai" A. Bozóki et al. eds *A rendszerváltás forgatókönyve*, vol. VII (Budapest: CEU Press, 2000), p. 682.

revolution/reform dichotomy in a new model of change involving both legal continuity and regime replacement.[5] Nevertheless, it was implicitly recognized that the specific way that Spanish political actors achieved this new synthesis, could not and did not need to be imitated in all its steps.

Here I can only concentrate on the formal elements of the Spanish transition, leaving aside most of the very important historical specificities that in any case never could have been imitated elsewhere. One such specificity that I will mention, however, was having a monarchical head of state, whose initial appointment as such by the former dictator was to say the least unusual, and whose personal commitment to liberal democracy, repeatedly demonstrated, was equally unique. Juan Carlos was important, because he began the process by securing the appointment of A. Suarez as head of government, an official he clearly put in charge of initiating a transition to democracy. The formal point here, however, is that the Spanish transition, though responding to crisis and to popular protest, was initiated and initially steered from above.[6] Thus, legally it was a reform, following earlier reluctant and partial reforms,[7] but one that became a rupture within a reasonable time frame primarily because of the democratic commitment of two individual actors. As the results of the referendum ratifying the *Ley para la Reforma Politica* indicate, these actors could have gotten away, at least in the short term, with merely reforming the Francoist political regime. This is not, however, what they chose to do either from the outset, or midstream when they were still in charge. As a result, the time of transition was extended with respect to a possible but hardly likely revolutionary rupture, but was reduced when compared to a completely open ended reform.[8]

The *Ley para la Reforma Politica* of 1976 was the central instrument of initiating the process, approved by the last authoritarian *Cortes*, and was overwhelmingly ratified by the electorate in the referendum of that year. Its two

---

[5] As it already should be obvious, I was never, even for one moment, convinced that Spain represented a miracle whose results could not be reproduced elsewhere. See A. Przeworski, *Democracy and Market Political and Economic Reforms in Eastern Europe and Latin America* (Cambridge: Cambridge University Press, 1991) and my critique in Chapter 1 of *Civil Society, Constitution and Legitimacy* (Lanham: Rowman & Littlefield, 2000) as well as Casanova's in "A spanyolországi demokratikus átalakulás tanulságai," 683.

[6] J. M. Maraval and J. Santamaria "Political Change in Spain and the Prospects of Democracy" in G. O'Donnell and P. Schmitter v. iii *Transitions from Authoritarian Rule* (Baltimore: Johns Hopkins University Press, 1986); Casanova "A spanyolországi demokratikus átalakulás tanulságai" 690.

[7] A. Bonime-Blanc *Spain's Transiton to democracy* (Boulder, CO: Westview Press, 1987); in a recent article she calls it *autoruptura:* "Constitution Making and Democratization. The Spanish Paradigm" in *Framing The State* (Washington: USIP, 2010), p. 420.

[8] See G. di Palma on this important issue of time, *To Craft Democracies: An Essay on Democratic Transitions* (Berkeley: University of California Press, 1990).

brief pages hardly amount to a constitution, even an interim one though it was to play that role.[9] Instead of clearly outlining a process of transition and its legal regulation, the document worked through a series of deliberate ambiguities.[10] While new, freely elected legislative institutions were established, many of the old ones of the dictatorship were preserved. The new legislature was to be bicameral, with one-fifth of the Senate appointed by the king.[11] Both of these provisions were inconsistent with the idea of a freely elected constituent assembly, assumed as the proper democratic constitution-making body by most European legal opinion, and demanded by all major democratic oppositional forces also in Spain. Since the project of constitutional reform was explicitly stated by the law, and no limits of reform were postulated, it was possible to interpret the planned new assembly as a constituent Cortes irrespective of its form.[12] But it was also very possible to interpret the same assembly as an ordinary one, allowed to amend but not to replace.[13] That is certainly how the document was interpreted by the leaderships of the main left-wing parties, the PSOE and PCE, as they rather unsuccessfully called for popular abstention from the referendum on the law.

In retrospect, the ambiguities of the law are easy to understand. Since it was enacted mainly from above, the incumbent government had to worry above all about hardline forces within the regime that tried to block not only negotiations with the democratic parties, but initially even their legalization. Thus, the law had to achieve two things. It had to confirm the democratic intentions of the king expressed in several important addresses. Only thus could Suarez hope for an overwhelming victory in the referendum. In order to get to a referendum at all, however, and to gain the assent of an authoritarian

---

[9] Technically, it was the eighth and last of the series of Fundamental Laws that dealt with the public law structure of the dictatorship. See F. Rubio Llorente, "The Writing of the Constitution of Spain" in R. Goldwin and A. Kaufman, *Constitution Makers on Constitution Making* (Washington: AEI, 1988) whom I here follow.

[10] Bonime Blanc, *Spain's Transiton to Democracy* (Boulder, CO: Westview Press, 1987); Rubio Llorente, op. cit.

[11] *Ley para la Reforma Politica, Articulo Segundo*, 3 (Art. 2:3); Bonime Blanc 25. In the Constitution of 1978, art. 69, the Senate became entirely elected. But the partially appointed Senate did have to approve the Constitution, first separately by absolute majority, and if not in a joint meeting of the two chambers, again with absolute majority. Article 3:2. I thank Emmanuel Guerisoli for translating this important document. J. Casanova tells me that the King appointed more liberal members than the ones chosen by the electorate. In that case the point of the undemocratic provision was democratic, reminiscent of the packing of the House of Lords before the Reform Bill of 1911.

[12] Rubio Llorente, "The Writing of the Constitution of Spain."

[13] J.M. Maraval and J. Santamaria, "Political Change in Spain and the Prospects for Democracy." According to Maraval and Santamaria, only the 1977 elections and their pluralistic outcome decided this question, in favor of a constituent Cortes.

Cortes and its social supporters, the law had to also confirm, or appear to confirm, their aspiration of merely reforming the existing system. For the same reason, if prior informal negotiations were to be held, they could involve only hard line forces linked to the government.[14]

We do not know if these negotiations altered some of the contents of the law. In any case what was important was its structure of calculated ambiguity. Since no negotiations with the most important parties of the democratic opposition took place before its enactment, we can safely regard the *Ley para la Reforma Politica* as a form of top-down imposition, in spite of its popular acceptance.[15] Those who consider the Spanish case to represent a paradigmatic form of pacted transition, tend to discount, if not entirely disregard this important fact.[16] Only after soundly defeating the democratic oppositions was Suarez ready to negotiate with these actors, and then legalize them.[17] By then the scenario of transition was largely in place and this scenario had important effects on the outcome. This sequence is particularly significant, if we are to understand the innovation that took place in Central Europe with the invention of the round table.

In any case, serious negotiations did eventually take place in Spain, characterizing all subsequent phases of the transition. Of these, negotiations with the Franquist hard right may have been the most important, and it has been strongly argued that the electoral law offered "correctives" to the original project of proportional representation postulated in the *Ley para la Reforma Politica*.[18] Yet the turn of the democratic opposition did also come. There was no question who the partners of the government and its new party formation, the UCD, should be, since the PSOE (the Socialist Party of Spain) and the

---

[14] Bonime-Blanc mentions discussions in general, without saying with whom, how serious these were and what issues were discussed or compromised. "Constitution Making and Democratization. The Spanish Paradigm" in *Framing the State* (Washington, DC: USIP, 2010), p. 420. Linz and Stepan mention these consultations, but also two private, informal, and, it seems, secret meetings of Suarez with Felipe Gonzalez, the leader of the PSOE. Op. cit. In any case, most agree that there were neither formal nor serious negotiations with the opposition before the referendum. See Casanova, op. cit., 691.

[15] As so often, the voters were asked to decide between affirming the law, or keeping the old regime in place. Thus, the overwhelming positive vote was to be expected.

[16] Juan Linz and Alfred Stepan, who do consider the Spanish process as the "paradigmatic case for the study of pacted democratic transition," also call it a "regime-initiated transition": *Problems of Democratic Transition and Consolidation* (Baltimore: Johns Hopkins University Press, 1996), chapter 6, pp. 87–88.

[17] Jose Casanova, op. cit., 691; Linz and Stepan omit altogether the attempted, but failed boycott of the referendum by the main democratic parties, as does Bonime-Blanc in the cited article.

[18] See R. Gunther et al., *Spain After Franco* (Berkeley: University of California Press, 1988), p. 44.

PCE (the Spanish Communist Party) each had a political umbrella organization of their own now united in a single one (*Coordinacion Democratica*), and then initiated the formation of a Committee of Nine that further included liberal and more conservative partners.[19] This pattern of wide inclusion anticipated the pluralistic structure of later negotiated transitions in Hungary, GDR, and Bulgaria. Having been defeated in the referendum, however, even this combined democratic opposition was much weaker than the government.[20] Thus, the negotiations were neither formal, nor was there any formal agreement that came out of them, in distinction to the round tables to come.[21] The final formulation of the all-important electoral law that could be said to have been influenced by these informal negotiations illustrates this relative weakness.[22]

At issue was the concretization of the provisions of the *Ley para la Reforma Politica* that called for proportional representation, making the 50-odd provinces the electoral districts, thereby implying many small districts. The new law arrived at a minimum district representation size of two.[23] Smaller parties (including the CPE) evidently objected during the negotiations concerning the disproportional consequences of this law that would most likely advantage the Union of the Democratic Center (UCD), the new governmental party, but in vain. However, a deal subsequently emerged between the UCD and the PSOE, to their mutual advantage, making the law of 1977 even less proportional, involving a d'Hondt system of conversion, keeping the small minimum district size and adding a 3 percent cut-off.[24] Moreover, the elected part of the Senate was made, in terms of population, severely disproportional, with each of 50 rather unequally sized provinces receiving 4 representatives.[25] This arrangement very much favored smaller and more conservative provinces over those in which large cities were found.[26] And this was only one of the many issues where the democratic opposition was forced to make important concessions, for example, they also had to give up the idea of a power-sharing transitional

---

[19] Maraval and Santamaria, pp. 82–85.   [20] Ibid., p. 83.

[21] Gunther, in *Spain After Franco*, p. 44.

[22] REAL DECRETO·LEY 20/1977, de 18 de marzo, sobre normas electorales. For a precise analyis demonstrating the sources of disproportionality in the D'Hondt method combined with the existence of many small districts, see *Spain After Franco*, pp. 45–53.

[23] On the disproportional consequences of small district size under PR, see Tagapeera and Shugart. *Seats and Votes: The Effects and Determinants of Electoral Systems* (New Haven: Yale University Press, 1989) as well as *Spain After Franco*, op. cit.

[24] Rubio Llorente, 246–247.

[25] The plan for appointed senators was now replaced by an entirely electoral, if still malproportioned body.

[26] Bonime-Blanc *Spain's Transition to Democracy*, p. 76.

government supervising the elections. All that they were able to secure in return for their concessions and compliance was legalization and amnesty for some of their members, which the government, in any case, was not opposed to.[27] Thus, if the rules of transition are to be considered negotiated at all, we must add that the second pre-election stage of the process, marked by its initially top-down character, involved asymmetrical negotiations among unequal parties.

Yet, as we will see in the case of Poland, elections can have unpredictable consequences. In spite of the seriously disproportional electoral rule, which, as predicted, converted 35 percent of the votes for the UCD to 47 percent of the seats, with the PSOE also receiving a small bonus. Counting the PCE and a small breakaway socialist party, the end result was a situation of relative equality for the Right and the Left. Even if the UCD could have created a majority with the hard right AP (People's Alliance) of Fraga, this could have compromised all that Suarez and the king achieved up to that point. Yet only the rejected option of a government of the Right alone could have converted the Cortes into a classical sovereign constituent assembly, acting through majority rule and calling the result the will of the people. Neither the government nor the opposition liked that scenario, albeit for partially different reasons. The shadow of a bad past of failed constitutional experiments and the civil war loomed over the whole process. It is true that the opposition very much favored the sovereign constituent assembly formula, but their hopes of possibly controlling such a body were dashed by the elections. Thus, the government and the opposition came together to choose a fundamentally consensual methodology of reiterated[28] comprehensive pacts,[29] relying ultimately on background agreements between the UCD and the PSOE,[30] the classical reformist-moderate combination.[31] The result was a new constitution and a new regime, a *ruptura* achieved through the method of *reforma*, now *pactada*, as opposed to the beginning of the process.

There is no need here to detail the many excellent qualities of the consensually made Spanish Constitution. Many of the new institutions, parliamentary government strengthened by the constructive no confidence vote, a strong table of rights, the strong constitutional review, and the many leveled

[27] Maraval and Santamaria, op. cit.
[28] See G. Di Palma, op. cit. on the importance of reiterated pacts, which gradually change the identities and the interests of the participants.
[29] There were three such pacts: the Pact of Moncloa between the parties and the government on economic matters, a Pact on proto federal organization of the state with restored regional autonomies, as well as a Pact on the text of the Constitution itself. See Maravall and Santamaria op. cit., Casanova op. cit.
[30] Rubio Llorente, op. cit.   [31] Przeworski, op. cit.

amendment rule were important achievements even if influenced by provisions elsewhere. Less successful was the resolution of the conflict between center and regions, though here too the changes made represented progress.[32] Illustrating the theory of freezing, the negotiated electoral system was almost the same as the rules of 1977 provided for, though somewhat greater proportionality was achieved in the actual 1979 elections.[33] Admittedly, there were no longer to be appointed members of the new Senate. But what is crucial for me here is that the overall pattern of the Spanish transition, as well as most of its constitutional results, together yielded the beginning of a new paradigm that could be imitated as well as improved elsewhere. Perhaps curiously, this took place in Central Europe rather than Southern Europe or Latin America, during the end of dictatorships that were completely different than the Spanish authoritarian regime. Especially in Poland, the paradigm was adopted under inauspicious circumstances, and the likelihood that Central European activists would improve upon the Spanish process was small. Yet improve on it they did.

The possibility of such improvement becomes clear if we focus on the main weakness of the Spanish process, the top-down, imposed character of its initial stage. In some very revealing speeches, the prime minister, Suarez, claimed that he did not negotiate at the very beginning, because there was no one with whom he could negotiate legitimately. Only free elections supposedly could produce legitimate partners. Juan Linz (with Alfred Stepan) takes these passages at face value, perhaps because he admired Suarez a great deal, admiration that the PM richly deserved.[34] Nevertheless, we have good reason to also notice the self-serving character of these very remarks, that at very best tried to justify what was perhaps necessary under conditions already alluded to, but nevertheless was not justifiable in terms of democratic arguments: neither the government nor the opposition had democratic legitimacy. Yet initially one side got a chance to impose, while the other was denied the chance to negotiate. Further, the advantages the method provided to incumbents remained important beyond even the first free elections. Moreover, with whom the government ought to have negotiated was perfectly obvious whatever Suarez

[32] On this see the detailed presentation by Linz and Stepan op. cit, pp. 98–107; Bonime-Blanc *Spain's Transiton to Democracy*, p. 81ff.

[33] The index of disproportionality D was 17 percent in 1977, and hovered around 10 percent in all subsequent elections under more or less the same rules. That is still quite pernicious from the point of view of constitutional politics, but the bad potential effects are warded off by the moderately difficult multi-tiered amendment rule and the strong Constitutional Court.

[34] *Problems of Democratic Transition*, pp. 94–95. Linz, as we are told, was present at the Cortes during the vote on the *Ley para la Reforma Politica*, 95 note 15.

claimed: the main parties and blocs of the democratic opposition as well as the labor unions were well known, organized and led. They even had addresses in Spain and abroad. Indeed, the very Suarez who had made this statement did seriously negotiate with these actors after his victorious referendum, but before the democratic elections in which they gained a new type of legitimacy.[35] It is true, however, that democratic elections had the results, contingent and unexpected as these were, of equalizing the partners in new negotiations.

At issue nevertheless is something important: the desirability of negotiations before the initial rules of the new democratic game are enacted. Only if we understand such initial negotiations to be highly desirable, normatively and for the sake of the subsequent process, will we seek ways in which we can accomplish them despite inhospitable circumstances. That is what the main Polish, Hungarian, Bulgarian, East German, and South African actors on both sides were to do over a decade later. Whereas Suarez either implied that one can begin democracy democratically, or, if not, then an imposed beginning is a reluctant necessity, the new paradigm of transformation came fully into its own when actors elsewhere realized that there is also the possibility of legitimate beginnings that must come *before* rather than *after* the first free elections.

Let me note here that the democratic success of Spanish transition and its outcome depended heavily on the democratic commitments of the king and Suarez at the very least at three important junctions: the beginning of the process when democratic norms were indeed introduced even if ambiguously, during the initial negotiations when Suarez could have used his great win in the referendum to deny the democratic opposition any concessions whatsoever including even legalization, and after the free elections when the UDC could have legally made a coalition on the right, with the AP and Fraga. In all these cases, democratic commitments, often disregarded by social scientists, did push the process in the normatively democratic direction. But elsewhere and in general, such commitments cannot and should not be assumed. Guarantees are needed,[36] and these can only be achieved by negotiations at all-important stages of the process, and especially at the very beginning. That is what the Polish opposition was the first to achieve.

Today the Polish Round Table has become an extremely controversial subject.[37] Different interpretations are linked to competing contemporary

---

[35] As Linz and Stepan admit (p. 96) without realizing the inconsistency.

[36] Di Palma calls this *"garantismo."* Op. cit., 44, 47, 50–61. I have distinguished between guarantees and forms of conversion in *Post Sovereign Constitution Making*, chapter 3, and even earlier "The Roundtables, Democratic Institutions and the Problem of Justice" in Bozoki ed., *The Roundtable of 1989.*

[37] See M. Bernhard and J. Kubik "Roundtable Discord." In *Twenty Years After Communism: The Politics of Memory and Commemoration* (Oxford: Oxford University Press, 2014).

political positions, and all the important ones contain an element of truth. The Round Table did initiate an accelerating process of transition from Communist rule. It also made important concessions to the Communist government, which seemed to be unparalleled in the history of democratic transitions. What is undeniable, however, is that it brought the model of *ruptura-reforma pactada* to Central Europe.[38]

Given Soviet occupation and the previous repression of democratic movements in Central Europe in 1956, 1968, and 1981, the Polish democratic opposition in 1989 was, on the face of it, in a weak position to commence a Spanish-type regime change, which would be, unlike in Spain, comprehensively negotiated from the very beginning. Yet it was to accomplish this very result and it could do so because the regime was equally weak.[39] Certainly, the failure of previous reform attempts from above, and the deep economic and financial crisis in the country played a great role in making such a process possible. But the democratic opposition, very likely aware of the Spanish precedent, aimed at achieving a historical pact with the Communist government from the days of the first Solidarity. As is well known, in August 1980 that movement was legalized after extended bilateral negotiations in Gdansk. Throughout its life, both legal and illegal, Solidarity sought an even more extensive agreement with the regime, conceived on the line of the New Evolutionism (Michnik) or self-limiting revolution (Kuron) that aimed at a full democratization of social life in the context of a more partial reform of the political sphere narrowly understood.[40] In 1987, it was the Hungarian opposition, led by Janos Kis, and deeply influenced by the Polish KOR, that worked out a detailed scenario of such dualistic change in its pamphlet, strikingly titled "Social Contract."[41] In that scheme, beyond the legalization of free publics and associational life, the political sphere was to be reconstructed by creating a democratically elected lower chamber, and an upper chamber based on

---

[38] It is a serious mistake, however, to interpret the Polish case as *"reforma"* as against the Czechoslovak scenario of *"ruptura."* Cf. J.K. Glenn, *Framing Democracy* (Stanford: Stanford University Press, 2001), p. 21, who on this very important point misunderstands Linz and Stepan whom he nevertheless cites. In their view, as well as mine, both the Spanish and Polish transitions combined the form of reform with the result of rupture. Thus, they represent *ruptura reforma pactada*. The error is based on Glenn's inexplicable treatment of "pact" and "from above" as the same type of transition (see, e.g., pp 21 and 29), and thus the Polish pacted transition becomes one initiated from above. His own more or less correct retelling of the story (e.g., 5–6; and chapter 3 passim) through his book makes this interpretation (or semantics) impossible.

[39] E. Matynia, *'a demokrácia századvégi berendezkedáse, avagy a lengyel kerekasztal in A. Bozóki et al eds A rendszerváltás forgatókönyve'* (Budapest: CEU, 2000), vol. VII, citing Michnik.

[40] See one of my first articles on Poland, Arato "Civil Society Against the State: Poland 1980–81," *Telos* 47 (1981): 23–47. now in *From Western Marxism to Democratic Theory* (Armonk, NY: M.E. Sharpe, 1993).

[41] *"Társadalmi szerződés,"* *Beszélő*, Special issue, (1987/2) vol. 1, # 21.

the old Communist central committee. This mixed scheme resembled to an extent the institutional dualism of the Spanish *Ley para la Reforma Política*, and undoubtedly it was meant as a proposal that, as in Spain, would have led to democratic acceleration if adopted. The Polish process was to resemble just such a self-accelerating mixed scheme.

But what was special about the Polish case was the emergence of the institution of the round table at the very beginning of the process that was to replace the Communist regime. It is easy to overlook the significance of this step because of the initially mixed institutional result, which, as we now can be certain, was more a function of the untested and obvious geopolitical constraints of the time than of the method itself. In actual fact, as I will show, at the Round Table, the democratic forces gained much more than they initially could have hoped for, when they sought only a second legalization of the Solidarity union.

The form of the round table was no one's conscious creation, and the name itself has been used before.[42] It was not created from above nor simply from below,[43] but took place after a series of informal "talks about talks" between regime and opposition figures, under the mediation of the Catholic Church.[44] It emerged, of course in a very special context, during the reform period in the Soviet Union associated with Mikhail Gorbachev's leadership, as a result of the failure of top-down political and especially economic reforms of the Polish post-martial government of the 1980s. The last step in that failed reform from above, one that was meant to resemble the successful top-down beginning of the Spanish process, was the attempt to enact authorization for rather unclear political change, along with a much more obvious economic reform plan (in essence, austerity) by way of a popular referendum in 1987. Under the government's own rules, the positive answers to two questions, one on the authorization of economic reform, the other similarly on political

[42] Most significantly in London, during three rounds of negotiations with and among leaders of nationalist movements and groups in India. See J. Keay, *India: A History. Revised and Updated* (New York: Grove/Atlantic, 2011).

[43] This view of Glenn (op. cit.) overlooks both the continual pressure of the democratic opposition from 1980 on for comprehensive negotiations, that was continued and resumed at the end of the 1980s, as well as the many two- (and with Catholic groups and bishops: three-)sided "talks about talks" as they were called in South Africa, needed to set up the negotiations. Similarly, in *Problems* (op. cit., p. 265) Linz and Stepan treat the Polish Round Table as initiated from above, even as their main source, W. Osiatinsky, showed the contrary. See the latter's "The Roundtable Talks in Poland" in J.Elster ed. *The Roundtable Talks and the Breakdown of Communism* (Chicago: University of Chicago Press, 1996), pp. 24, 26–27, 28.

[44] Osiatynski, op. cit., pp. 26; 28–29; and 37. Also see: Elżbieta Matynia, *Performative Democracy* (Boulder: Paradigm Publishers, 2009).

"democratization," both failed because they represented only minorities of the registered voters. The underlying cause was an insufficient level of participation that was at least in part caused by the call of the underground Solidarity organization for abstention.[45]

It took two more strike waves, and a great many suggestions by many actors, to replace the strategy from above with a fundamentally negotiated alternative that was itself the result of informal negotiations. Of course, the government hoped to use a round table, as they were first to call it, to enact its own alternative, which was not sustained in the previous referendum. In particular, the government of Pres. W. Jaruzelski, PM. M. Rakowski and, the strong man, interior minister W. Kiszczak, hoped not only to dampen the expanding strike movement, but also to obtain a significant partner for the next round of economic reforms, inevitably involving more austerity that otherwise could have led to even more strikes. That could be achieved by somehow incorporating Solidarity in the governing structure, but, of course, without giving the organization any significant power. It was certainly calculated that the cost of a deal would be the restoration of the legal status of Solidarity, which was always also a social movement as well as a union.[46] It was with exactly that aim in mind, following a successful televised debate with the leader of the official unions, and a secret meeting with Kiszczak, that Lech Walesa, on the advice of the intellectual group then closest to him (Michnik, Kuron, Mazoviecki and Geremek), accepted to attend a round table, a suggestion the government finally picked up from Solidarity, the Church, as well as independent intellectuals who previously called for negotiating an "anti-crisis pact."[47]

Had Walesa and his advisors been revolutionaries the offer would not have been accepted, and indeed the partisans of revolution like the KPN (Confederation of Independent Poland) and Fighting Solidarity rejected negotiations

---

[45] Glenn's reconstruction of what happened is correct, but cannot explain why the results were not falsified (most likely a significant split in the ruling elite was either *the* or *a* cause) nor does he notice that this was the last attempt at top-down reform, significantly different than the move toward the round table based on negotiations before the formal negotiations themselves. Op. cit., 42. A better explanation for the outcome of the referendum is offered by D. Ost, *Solidarity* (Philadelphia: Temple, 1990), pp. 170–172, whom Glenn otherwise follows.

[46] See A. Touraine et al., *Solidarity: the Analysis of a Social Movement: Poland, 1980–1981* (Cambridge: Cambridge University Press, 1983).

[47] Osiatynski, 27; Glenn, 72ff.; Ost, 179ff. I do not, however, buy Ost's idea that the pact to be made pointed to a neo-corporatist arrangement. While a pact could be a one-time extra-ordinary form of crisis management, neo-corporatism requires the institutionalization of pacting. There was no question of the latter in Poland, even with the legalization of unions and associations. Even if I myself, as Ost indicates (op. cit. 119), spoke of a possible societal corporatist option in 1981, I never applied that concept to the Round Table agreements.

from the beginning.[48] Later on as well, the partisans of a second revolution
and a "fourth republic" were to denounce the Round Table not only for the
deal that was made, but for it having taken place at all.[49] Yet it is certain
that the more proximate goal of Walesa and his advisors was to return to a
potentially accelerated process of change that from the mid-1970s till the 1981
martial law declaration was interpreted under concepts like "new evolutionism" (Michnik), "self-limiting revolution" (Kuron), as well as "the reconstruction of civil society."[50] The results realized, and indeed greatly surpassed, this
expectation.

And this can be even said for the deal itself, however deficient.[51] Certainly
it was a compromise between relatively (but only relatively!) moderate opposi-
tionists and government reformers.[52] Yet it would be incorrect to see it merely
as a compromise among pre-existing positions. As G. di Palma rightly noted,
viable agreements and pacts of this type work only if the participants, their
interests and aspirations, change in the process.[53] The Solidarity participants
understood that, aside from specific policy goals, the Communist side sought
to relegitimate the government itself in the midst of a serious crisis of legitimacy. The Gorbachev reform in the Soviet Union shook the ground under
the negative legitimacy[54] of especially Polish and Hungarian governments,
according to which their rule could be justified not in terms of their positive
normative qualities or its results, but rather by the more negative examples

[48] Glenn, op. cit., pp. 72 and 81. Some of their members, however, chose to contest elections for
the competitive seats, uniformly without success.

[49] Bernhard and Kubik, op. cit.

[50] See my essay "Civil Society Against the State: Poland 1980–81," *Telos* 1981.47 (1981): 23–47.
Glenn criticizes my expectation concerning the power of the self-limiting strategy (op. cit.,
p. 25) but then repeatedly has to call attention to the successes of that very strategy (e.g., p. 124).
His idea that we (Arato and Cohen) should have understood "civil society" as a framing strategy
rather than referring to "real" institutions and initiatives is to insist on a truism. Concepts are
never "real," nor are they copies of reality. Above all as my book *Civil Society, Constitution and
Legitimacy* (Lanham: Rowman & Littlefield, 2000) demonstrates, I do not think that political
transitions are achieved only by civil society initiatives and movements, from below.

[51] Thus it is an error to overly stress the undemocratic features of the deal, as do Linz and Stepan
(op. cit., pp. 268–269), who, after making the mistake of assimilating the Polish context to that
of Chile and Brazil, go on to stress the greater concessions to the old regime in Poland. Given
the geopolitical context, the achievements were greater, the concessions were understandable,
and their stability was far weaker.

[52] Przeworski, op. cit.

[53] Di Palma, op. cit., p. 49; Osiatynski depicts this change as from a confrontational to a concilia-
tory posture by the government, and the reverse for Solidarity (op. cit., pp. 41–42). I buy the first
depiction, but not the second. The idea of self-limitation remained characteristic for Solidarity
through the parliamentary elections, and even the election of Jaruzelski as president.

[54] J. Kis, "Between Reform and Revolution" (Spring 1998) 12 *East European Politics &
Societies* 2.

of other Central and East European dictatorships, and the limits of Soviet tolerance. The Solidarity negotiators were, of course, quick to inform the government that only political pluralism could produce new political legitimacy. This point only seemed to correspond to what was already planned by the Communist side. In Poland, there was a tradition to provide a very small representation to Catholic deputies, in particular members of the Znak grouping. Why not, then, involve Solidarity itself in a similar structure, and give it some pre-arranged seats in an entirely non-competitive election?[55] It is with this plan in mind that the government began to discuss at a separate negotiating table matters well beyond union legalization, accepted by both sides. Solidarity did the same with the goal and perhaps the expectation that the seats they would gain could be redesigned as a fully competitive part of the over-all elections. After all, just a few months before, a constitutional amendment in the USSR provided for one-third of the competitive seats for the next Supreme Soviet elections, and, earlier still, in Hungary in 1985, there were two candidates allowed for individual seats, even if with a small number of significant exceptions both were nominated by the official Patriotic People's Front.

When the principle of some competitive elections was conceded also in Poland, at issue was not only how many deputies would be freely elected,[56] but rather how much power could they have in relation to significant forms of decision like constitutional amendments,[57] and what would be the power reserve of the Communists, after subsequent elections that, as Solidarity absolutely demanded, may be completely free. Out of these discussions came institutional solutions no-one probably imagined before January 1989 when the negotiations started: 35 percent of the deputies would indeed be freely and competitively elected, with potentially some real power because two-thirds of the votes would be needed to achieve constitutional amendments. In addition, however, the Communists wanted a new presidency with new powers including a strong veto, as well as war, foreign policy, parliamentary dissolution and emergency powers.[58] This type of presidency was especially hard for Solidarity to accept, especially in exchange for a partially free election that everyone

---

[55] Glenn, op. cit., pp. 92–94 for a good explanation of the difference from the point of view of Solidarity between 35 percent guaranteed, and 35 percent fully competitive seats. On this point I follow Glenn and his several relevant citations rather than Osiatynski, who states that competitive elections for a portion of the Sejm were accepted by the government before the Round Table in a negotiation with the Church. Op.cit. p.37.

[56] It would be the same 35 percent, who were supposed to be put in a joint slate in unfree elections.

[57] Osiatynski, op. cit, 45–46.   [58] Ibid., 56–57.

assumed would still guarantee that the old ruling party would control the new government. Thus, given the reluctance of Solidarity to accept the new presidency, and, even less, an appointed Senate also suggested by the Communists, a new concession by the government to the opposition was needed. This was based on an idea of the later president Kwasniewski, then a new but still junior member of the Communist delegation, who proposed a second entirely freely elected chamber of parliament with some power to block legislation.[59] Among other things, the Senate would take part in the election of the new president, in a joint assembly, with an absolute majority required for the winning candidate. Moreover, it would take an improbable two-thirds of the Sejm to override a Senate veto. The government also accepted the proposition that the subsequent regular elections would be entirely free for both chambers.[60] This was finally an offer that Solidarity could not possibly refuse.

It is interesting to compare the Spanish and Polish beginnings of democratization.[61] In Spain, the government managed to secure support for its reform program in a referendum, while in Poland it did not. In Spain, actors within the government, the king and his PM, sought democratic elections from the beginning. In Poland, the government leaders at best sought to gain partners in making unpopular economic policy, and, as in the USSR previously, to pluralize a small part of parliamentary "representation". In Spain, a plan for the change could be and was instituted by the government in place. In Poland even or especially for such a relatively small change, partners were needed and comprehensive negotiations were began with the main democratic opposition, consistent with their mutual but different aspirations. In Spain, when negotiations did take place before free elections, very little was conceded to the opposition, and the government's admittedly ambiguous reform program in essence remained in place. In Poland, very important concessions were made to the opposition, well beyond what it first hoped to achieve. Thus, it would be misleading to merely compare the rules leading to free elections in Spain, and the ones in Poland, clearly inferior, leading only to partially free electoral competition. This is to forget not only what was gained in each case in negotiations, but also the environments in which the two changes took place: Spain was in Western Europe on the edge of the European Community that the elites of the country were anxious to join, while Poland was perhaps

---

[59] Osiatynski op. cit. 53–54. We do not know, of course, with whom Kwasniewski consulted before making his suggestion; it could have been Kiszczak or Geremek, or both, or neither. The smoothness of acceptance seems to suggest some kind of prior consultation.

[60] Glenn op. cit., 94–95.

[61] In 1990 David Ost has hazarded such a comparison, but using the standards of the last years of Francoist reform, rather than the ruptura-reforma pactada. Op. cit., 197ff.

the most important country of the Soviet imperium, and was at the time still partially occupied. While it was true that some reforms were welcomed by the Gorbachev government, it was hardly clear in early 1989 where the limits of this tolerance lay, especially since the Soviet Politburo and military leadership had many influential hard line elements opposed to the First Secretary.[62]

Finally, elections in both countries were to change everything, in Poland in light of the compromises of the Round Table much more radically. I will not review the nature of the electoral victory of Solidarity, which consisted of winning almost every contested seat for both chambers with the exception of one in the one-hundred-member new Senate. In Spain, by contrast, the government, helped by the electoral rule it designed, won the elections. Thus, PM Suarez remained in power, even as he had to accept a fully consensual process of constitution making. In Poland, the slogan "Your president, Our prime minster" of Michnik (launched just after the elections) came into its own, with the appointment of T. Mazowiecki as prime minister, after the unpredicted, but understandable defection of hitherto obedient bloc party allies of the Communists. Even Jaruzelski could be elected as president, as implicitly agreed upon, only with the support of some Solidarity deputies arranged by Walesa.[63] After this turn of events, it should have become clear, except perhaps in the unique case of East Germany, that the Soviet Union constituted no limit to political democratization in Central Europe. It is only in a context facilitated by its own actions that the compromise of the Round Table in Poland could appear deficient, and to its most violent opponents, even corrupt. The truth is that these very compromises were followed by the June 1989 election results, which would not have been possible without them. Together, the Round Table and elections opened the floodgates for democratization in Central Europe and beyond.

I do not wish to de-emphasize the problematic aspects of the results of the Polish Round Table. The new presidency was a huge burden, that opened

[62] Unlike Glenn, I put my emphasis on Soviet willingness to violently repress, rather than domestic repressive capacities. Those of us who lived through 1956 and 1968 know that whatever leaders may have said, their apparent confidence in using domestic forces was misplaced, and the idea of a Tiananmen-type repression some dreamed of was impossible without Soviet backup. Thus, Polish martial law could be sold to the military command, and especially to the lower officer corps and enlisted men only with the argument that the national army was protecting the country from something worse, namely Soviet intervention. Relying on the comparative results of Western social science is highly misleading in the case of occupied countries like Poland, GDR, Czechoslovakia, and Hungary. In Romania, finally, there was a test of the two theses, Glenn's and mine, with only the Securitate rallying to the regime, as against the regular armed forces that defeated it.

[63] Glenn, op. cit., 126.

the way not only to Walesa's "war at the top" leading to the withdrawal of Pres. Jaruzelski and the defeat of T. Mazowiecki, but also to Walesa's own very presidential presidency that threatened to undermine the new parliamentary system. The difficulty was fully removed only with the new constitution, during Kwasniewski's presidency in 1997.

As the eight-year gap demonstrates, constitution making itself was heavily burdened by the Round Table compromise. It is worth noting how the latter were legalized. With the Communist dominated old monocameral Sejm still in place, the government at the Round Table guaranteed that the agreements would be passed. Though some features required constitutional amendments, these too had not the slightest difficulty of being enacted (the April Amendments).[64] Such was the last important lesson in the meaning of Communist parliamentary government and constitutionalism to those who still needed it after more than sixty years. Thus, the Round Table agreements amounted to a contract between two strongly opposed sides, which moreover scrupulously observed its terms. As a result, the new legislature after June was itself based on a contract, the more powerful lower house being called the "contractual Sejm." The agreements, moreover, though serving as an interim document for the political transition hardly represented more of a constitution than Spain's sketchy Ley para la Reforma Politica.

Thus, as in Spain a new constitution, replacing that of the dictatorship, was desperately needed. This was done in Spain after the first entirely free elections. The contractual Sejm, however, did not have the legitimacy to play the role of a constituent or constitutional assembly. The Senate, which arguably did, lacked the legal authority. Each chamber in fact tried to generate a constitutional draft, each using also Western or Western-educated advisers, Prof. A. Rapaczynski, and Prof. Z. Pelczynski for the Sejm, and Prof. W. Osiatynski for the Senate. Neither draft was terrible, but they could not be reconciled.[65] At best, some limited amendments were generated, in particular the so-called December amendments of 1989, which managed to remove some of the most objectionable features of the inherited Communist constitution still largely in place, introducing rule of law provisions.[66]

The next election of 1991, probably because of a new, totally passive electoral rule, representing an overreaction to the previous contractual procedure,

---

[64] Lech Garlicki and Z. A. Garlicka, "Constitution Making, Peace Building, and National Reconciliation: The Experience of Poland," *Framing the State in Times of Transition: Case Studies in Constitution Making* (2010): 350–390.

[65] W. Osiatinsky, "Poland's Constitutional Ordeal" (1994) *Eastern European Constitutional Review*, 3, 29. Osiatinsky was constitutional advisor to the Senate.

[66] Garlicki and Garlicka, "Constitution Making, Peace Building, and National Reconciliation" 393.

produced an extremely fragmented parliament with 29 parties. Especially with a strong president, now Walesa, such a fragmented parliament should have had difficulty in governing at all, but, remarkably enough, a still partial constitutional product was generated in a compromise with Walesa anxious to preserve his prerogatives that the government wished to greatly reduce. The result was the Small or Little Constitution of October 1992.[67] It served as Poland's interim basic law, about two years after Hungary has adopted such a document. From being the leader in the process, Poland retreated to being a follower.

But being a follower had advantages in terms of learning. Even before the enactment of the Polish Little Constitution, in early 1992 a Constitutional Law was adopted on the procedures of producing a permanent constitution. Thus, the Polish temporary constitutional arrangements, in contrast to the earlier Hungarian interim constitution, incorporated detailed rules for constitution drafting, enactment and ratification.[68] This advantage was not initially apparent, however. Even after the 1993 elections, which enabled the formation of a strong government by the reconstituted Left, battles between the parliamentary majority, its constitutional committee and Walesa, who claimed to represent those excluded by a new, and this time highly disproportional electoral rule, made the enactment of a new constitution very difficult. But in stark contrast to Hungary, the constituent process was completed in 1997, though it took not only pre-existing rules, but also a disproportional parliamentary election, a new presidency and a referendum to achieve this result.[69]

That result was technically a very acceptable liberal democratic constitution. But its origins, the multi-stage, fragmented nature of its creation, referred to as an "ordeal" by a major participant, as well as the conflicts between 1993 and 1997 associated with its final enactment in which the reconstituted post-Communist party played a major role, did not produce a high level of legitimacy for the new regime, the Third Republic.[70] Thus, down to this day there is a challenge calling for a fourth one,[71] a "republic" that in its ideology at least would correspond to the FIDESZ regime in Hungary established after 2010. The fact, however, that the making of a permanent constitution was completed in Poland, may have played a role in reducing the appeal of, and hopefully even blocking, that alternative.

---

[67] Ibid. W. Osiatinsky, "Poland's Constitutional Ordeal."

[68] Garlicki and Garlicka, op. cit., 394–6.

[69] Arato, *Civil Society, Constitution, Legitimacy*, chapter 6; Garlicki and Garlicka, op. cit., 399–401.

[70] For a more optimistic picture, that nevertheless notes the problems with such a long, fragmented process see Garlicki and Garlicka, op. cit. 408–410.

[71] Bernhard and Kubik, op. cit.

FROM POLAND TO HUNGARY

The failure of the completion of liberal democratic constitution making in Hungary,[72] and the success, hopefully temporary, of a more authoritarian alternative, does not mean that there was no learning from Poland, nor that there were not important innovations made during this process. As to lessons, three major things were learned from the Polish pattern. First, it was the form of the round table itself,[73] which was partially anticipated by the part of the Hungarian democratic opposition influenced by KOR and Solidarity.[74] By the summer of 1989 it seemed almost natural that Hungary would also have a Polish-style round table, even though here there was no vast mass strike movement capable of pushing in that direction. Previously, there had been attempts on the part of various regime reformers to try to negotiate with one or other less radical sector of an opposition that was not only much weaker but also far more divided than its Polish contemporaries. To their credit, all important parties eventually rebuffed these attempts, which came to an end when the more radical democratic forces, with the help of the Independent Forum of Jurists, organized the Oppositional Round Table (EKA), as the umbrella groups of eight parties and associations. Whether the similar Spanish pattern of creating umbrella groups in 1976 played the role of an example here I cannot tell, but in any case the innovation was momentous.[75] The parties and associations of the EKA agreed to engage in negotiations only if all their members were included.[76]

---

[72] For a more detailed presentation of the Hungarian case, see my *Post Sovereign Constitution Making* (Oxford: Oxford University Press, 2016), chapter 4.

[73] In Poland the opposition argued for a two sided rectangular table. The government however did not concede this, and successfully pushed through a round shaped table to accommodate the official trade unions. In Hungary, the opposition then proceeded to ask for a Polish style table, that the government also did not concede, and managed to hold out for a three sided or triangular table. While considered important at the time, the shape of the table in the end made no difference at all, and the name used in both countries remained "round table" as in the Hungarian NKA, or Nemzeti Kerekasztal.

[74] In particular, Kis, and the circle of the samizdat journal Beszélő, that published the pamphlet *Social Contract* in 1987 ("*Társadalmi szerződés*" cited in n. 40).

[75] See A. Bozóki et al. eds, *A rendszerváltás forgatókönyve* (Budapest: CEU Press, 2000) documents and analyses in seven volumes. The seventh volume has a collection of essays by different authors on which I have greatly relied. There is also a shorter English version of volume VII: Bozoki ed., *The Roundtable Talks of 1989: The Genesis of Hungarian Democracy* (Budapest: CEU, 2002).

[76] In Spain at issue was the inclusion of the CPE, indeed its legalization, eventually conceded by Suarez. In Poland, there were unsuccessful attempts of the government to exclude A. Michnik and J. Kuron, and a possible agreement of government and Solidarity to exclude radical nationalists. On Spain see Linz and Stepan, op. cit., p. 96ff; on Poland see Glenn, op. cit., pp. 72–73 and 81. Even in Hungary there was a case of exclusion of a very small left party

Second, it was clearly understood after the outcome of the Polish elections of June 1989, that the Soviet Union would not interfere with the replacement of Communist government by a liberal democratic one. Thus, there was no reason to accept unfree or even partially free elections, or any other form of direct undemocratic conversion of power. The earlier model of the *Social Contract* was now obsolete for its own authors. With the help of the Polish outcome, a Hungarian Round Table would be able to work for mutual guarantees, rather than forms of conversion for the old regime.[77] This point was understood by the leaders of the ruling party as well as the opposition, even if some hardliners were unconvinced. While these leaders still hoped for a Polish-style strong presidency, to guarantee some of their power, the major opposition parties were not willing to go along with this, though their majority was willing to concede the popular election of a president with moderate powers. The Communist Party (MSZMP) was forced to compromise on the electoral rule, accept the model of the strong constitutional court preferred by the opposition, and concede, in spite of its intentions, an all-important slower time frame for free elections.[78] The point, however, is hardly that the Hungarian opposition was more courageous than its Polish counterparts, but rather that they were able to fully benefit from the lessons of the latter.

Third, and this gain was more ambivalent, observing the hardly modified constitution of Poland during partially free elections, the idea of creating an enforceable interim constitution was born. Initially, the Hungarian opposition also wished to generate only the minimal rules for democratic elections. It was the reformers of the ruling party who were thinking of producing a new constitution, in their case from above, and some of the more radical party reformers as well as external allies were even thinking of a constituent assembly whose early election they could control, as Lenin had feared in 1905.[79] The democratic opposition here read its Lenin text carefully, and was not willing to fall into either version of the same trap. But the project of producing a detailed set of constitutional rules at the National Round Table (NKA as against the EKA) seemed more convincing. Gradually, the opposition came around to the idea that even minimal guarantees have further legal preconditions, which, if

not in the EKA, the Hungarian October Party. The attempt of the government to exclude FIDESZ was resisted and it failed.

[77] See A. Arato and Z. Miklosi, "Constitution Making and Transitional Politics in Hungary" in *Framing the State in Times of Transition: Case Studies in Constitution Making* (Washington: USIP, 2010), pp. 350–90; also my chapter 4, *Post Sovereign Constitution Making* on the difference between "conversion" and "guarantee".

[78] Ibid., as well as Schiemann's *The Politics of Pact-making: Hungary's Negotiated Transition to Democracy in Comparative Perspective* (London: Palgrave Macmillan, 2005).

[79] "Two Tactics of Russian Social Democracy" in *Selected Works*, vol. I, op. cit.

extensively interpreted, would amount to a new constitution, even if enacted by the amendment rules of the old one. Once accepting this idea, the opposition came to also accept its corollary, namely that such a constitutional document, even if an interim one would be "worthy of defense," or, in other words, should be fully enforceable. It was assumed by all sides that only a constitutional court could provide the necessary enforcement. Such a court was part of the government's reform plans, but in a self-contradictory form that allowed it to appoint the members, and at the same time posited a parliamentary override clause. The opposition was willing to go along only when their insistence on a more balanced form of appointment based on each side proposing candidates was conceded, along with the elimination of the possibility of parliamentary override. Note that genuine compromise was involved in generating this all-important form of guarantee. The ruling party did get a chance to nominate almost half the first justices. Moreover, the constitutional amendment rule that was only slightly more difficult (two-thirds of the body as a whole vs two-thirds of those present) than the proposed and surrendered over-ride clause was kept in place.

Even if partially compromised, the making of an interim constitution, along with strong constitutional review, were momentous innovations, with both positive and negative implications. On the positive side, for the first time, a process of radical system change from an authoritarian regime was put under constitutionalist rules. On the negative side, which was hardly noticed at the time, it became possible that both institutions, the interim constitution and the new court, would be seen as substitutes for a process of democratic constitution making, namely for the necessary second stage of the process that could secure the full legitimacy of the results. This dangerous interpretation was facilitated by the fact that, while the Hungarian interim document did declare its own status provisional, in contrast to both the Polish Little Constitution and the South African Interim Constitution, it contained no rules or procedures whatsoever for the second stage, the making of a permanent constitution.

The Hungarian transition had, however, other innovative dimensions. I have mentioned already the attempt to introduce a directly elected presidency into the parliamentary system in the making. Here a creative use of both consensual and direct democracy played a role in blocking the initiative of the regime, and its candidate for the presidency, Imre Pozsgay. Eventually, four out of eight EKA players opposed the initiative. The creative use of consensus involved going along with the bare majority of the nine-member EKA in agreeing to the package as whole, desisting from the use of agreed-upon vetoes, in order to save its mainly valuable elements. The use of direct democracy had to do with the organization of a popular referendum, under a recently enacted law, to defeat the provision for an even one-time free election of the president that might have decisively influenced the subsequent parliamentary elections as well.

Unfortunately, the Hungarian process, in spite of its combination of learning and innovation, was itself hardly perfect. And there were at least three major errors of commission, the first of which occurred in 1989. Unlike in Poland, the Hungarian opposition accepted right from the beginning the demand of the Communists that only the few plenary sessions would be open to the public, as against the middle- and lower-level meetings. Thus, the opposition deprived its own leaders and positions of the possibility of becoming better known. More importantly, public fora and civil society initiatives were deprived of the ability to make inputs on a fully informed basis.[80]

The second major error dates to 1990. It is customary to interpret the Hungarian process of constitution making as being as fragmentary and multi-stage as the one in Poland. In the country to the north, this was unavoidable, whereas in Hungary it was not. The first parliament elected in Hungary in 1990 was neither contractual, as in Poland in 1989, nor fragmented by a large number of parties, as in Poland in 1991.

There was no necessity in Hungary to initiate a form of gradual, open-ended process of constitution making through the use of the amendment rule. Even less was there a compulsion to add additional elite-driven pacts to the earlier historically necessary pact. Yet this is exactly what the two leading governmental and opposition parties did in 1990, each freezing out its own allies from the main dimension of creating a comprehensive amendment package. There was again no reason not to have extended public discussion of the proposals, and yet this too was excluded as supposedly reminiscent of the social consultations during the very end of Communist rule. While in content the amendments made were mostly reasonable, the process was rightly viewed by all the excluded as exclusionary, and also by some members of the Constitutional Court, as comical. Moreover, with these changes, Hungary now had a highly efficient, more or less complete liberal democratic constitution (except for its always preserved amendment rule) and this led to the third major error by apparently diminishing the interest of many participants completing the process.

This is where there was an attempt to make up for the previous false moves, one that unfortunately led to the third important error, in 1996. A new coalition government came to power in 1994, of the ex-Communist MSZP and the

---

[80] For a detailed discussion, see M. Vásárhelyi, "A tárgyalások nyilvánossága, a nyilvánosság tárgyalása" in A. Bozóki et. al. eds, *A rendszerváltás forgatókönyve*, vol. VII.

liberal SZDSZ, the party of the earlier democratic oppositions. One of the motivations of the latter in joining this coalition was to complete the process of constitution making.[81] By this time in Hungary as well as in Poland, in the face of various denunciations of pacts, the need to create a final democratic constitution by a freely elected assembly became clear, at least for the moment. The problem in 1994 was that, in Hungary as well as in Poland, the disproportional results of elections implied that socialist and liberal forces, could make a constitution all alone under the inherited amendment rule that required only the consent of two-thirds of parliament. In Hungary, as opposed to Poland under the Little Constitution, even a ratificatory referendum was not required. Undoubtedly conscious of the ringing denunciations of a potential "constitutional dictatorship" led by Walesa in Poland and the parties of the right in Hungary, the coalition parties, on the advice of their intellectual supporters,[82] and with the support of FIDESZ outside, generated highly consensual rules for constitution making. These rules were fully in the spirit of the earlier the round tables (EKA and NKA). They required four-fifths of parliament to adopt a set of rules for constitution making, and then, under these new rules, the creation of a parliamentary drafting committee of all six parties, requiring the consent of five to any article of the draft. In line with what Kis called conservative constitution making, where 5 out of 6 would not agree to a provision, the corresponding article of the interim constitution would be preserved. This last move was also there to guard against the dangers of the high consensus requirement. Finally, the coalition voluntarily agreed on a moratorium on ordinary amendments using the two-thirds rule, as long as the constitution-making process lasted. These rules were sophisticated, as well as innovative, but they did involve the grievous and hardly explicable provision of coupling the new rules with a sunset provision tied to the life of that particular parliament.

I have repeatedly described the fatal outcome of this process.[83] The problem was not that the consensus requirements were too high, since the drafting committee successfully agreed to a consensual proposal. Only one right-wing

---

[81] At that time, I supported the making of this coalition, primarily for that reason. In retrospect, given what happened to the project of a new constitution, this may have been a mistake.

[82] Janos Kis wrote an important article in *Népszabadság* proposing consensual constitution making, ("A rendszerváltást lezáró alkotmány," *Népszabadság*, 1994. August 19) and I did the same in *Magyar Hírlap* "A magyar közjogi rendszer két súlyos fogyatékossága," 1994, May 30, as well as in Kritika, "Választás, koalició és alkotmány Magyarországon" 1994 no. 12. Both essays are in *Civil társadalom forradalom és alkotmány* (Budapest: Új mandátum, 1999).

[83] First, in chapter 6 of *Civil Society, Constitution and Legitimacy*, and, most recently, in chapter 4 of *Post Sovereign Constitution Making*.

party objected, but it was with that actor that MSZP ministers of the coalition government, along with a minority of their party, conspired to vote down the consensual draft to which their representatives have already agreed. Undoubtedly, in 1996 the socialist ministers could bring down the new project in good conscience, not only because it did not entirely correspond to their own preferences, but also because the fallback position of a fully functioning constitution already existed. Thus they could repeat the meaningless claim that there in any case was no "compulsion to make a constitution" [*alkotmányozási kényszer*].

Here lay the foundation of the third and most fundamental error of the Hungarian process, and it was made not only by the socialist ministers of the second freely elected government. Following the failure, the liberal SZDSZ could also relieve its conscience in not leaving the coalition by maintaining that there was no compulsion to make a constitution. Most importantly, perhaps, that very view represented the mistaken position of the president and the majority of the Constitutional Court. At least Justice Sólyom, if not all the judges on his Court, considered their own work of to be the proper completion of the rule of law revolution of 1989, as he calls it. This was a very serious mistake even if repeated by some Western commentators.[84] In the often-declared view of J. Sólyom, the interim constitution was a permanent one even if it did have one serious weakness, the overly flexible purely parliamentary two-thirds amendment rule, that FIDESZ now made as famous as it should have been before. According to him, this rule could be used simply to amend itself, to establish a new rule and a more entrenched constitution. He disregarded the legitimation problems of such "revision of the revision," well known from British and French constitutional history, as well as a great deal of legal theory, along with the lack of interest of parties to so bind themselves in case they themselves achieved a constitution-making two-thirds majority in the future.[85] Only in the context of a new, consensually made constitution would such a revision of the revision be more likely, as well as more legitimate, and I note that FIDESZ also ultimately omitted this step in the making of their

---

[84] Most recently: K. Scheppele "Unconstitutional Constituent Power" in R. Smith and R. Beeman (eds.), *Constitution Making* (Philadelphia, PA: University of Pennsylvania Press, 2015). Also see the earlier article: K. Scheppele, "Constitutional Negotiations. Political Contexts of Judicial Activism in Post-Soviet Europe" in S.A. Arjomand (ed.), *Constitutionalism and Political Reconstruction* (Leiden: Brill 2007).

[85] L. Sólyom, "The Role of Constitutional Courts in the Transition to Democracy. With Special Reference to Hungary" in S. Arjomand (ed.), *Constitutionalism and Political Reconstruction* (Leiden: Brill, 2007); and L. Sólyom, "A jogállami forradalomtól az EU csatakozásig. Az alkotmányfejlődés keretei" in L. Majtényi and Z. Miklósi (eds.), *És mi lesz az alkotmánnyal* (Budapest: Eötvös Károly Intézet, 2004), pp. 15–16.

Fundamental Law in 2011.[86] In any case it was the making of the FIDESZ constitution that was the most important outcome of the mistakes and failures of the Hungarian process. Many of these failures could however be avoided, as the South African process was to show.

BULGARIA, GDR, CZECHOSLOVAKIA: THREE DEVIANT CASES

In my previous writings I have focused initially on two prerequisites for effective, and, at least in part, legitimate round table agreements, a history of civil society self-organization,[87] and a relative balance of forces on the sides of government and civil society, real or at least imagined. Without the first, under conditions of authoritarian state socialism, there would be no actors capable of negotiating with the government. Without the second, the obviously stronger side would have no motivation to negotiate. In my Iraq book I then added a third criterion derived from Linz and Stepan, namely "stateness." If the state structure is uncertain, unstable, or falling apart, negotiations are either not possible or at the very least must first focus on reconstituting "a state." The absence of the third desideratum does not make round tables impossible, but changes their primary task from the organization of free elections to reconstructing the structure of the state. But what if it is impossible to fully reconstruct the state at a round table? Must the process led by that body fail?

The three cases I depict as deviant each lacked two of the three criteria. After the Polish and Hungarian forerunners, the German Democratic Republic (GDR), Czechoslovakia, and Bulgaria all had a round table, the institution that by this time counted as the very symbol of the break with Communism.[88] These took place in Czechoslovakia between November 26, 1989 and January 11, 1990, in the GDR between December 7, 1989 and March 12, 1990, and in Bulgaria between January and May 1990. Their historical sequence is significant, but not all-determining. There is no doubt concerning the influence of the Polish and Hungarian round tables on each, though their importance for one another is less obvious.[89] At the same time, in comparison to Central

---

[86] I describe that process in Chapter 4 of *Post Sovereign Constitution Making*. It was no longer part of the round table paradigm, and thus I can omit its discussion here.

[87] Or as Glenn prefers: history of self-organization framed by various concepts of civil society. See my *Civil Society*, Chapter 1.

[88] W. Templin, *"Die Diskussion über the Verfassungsentwurf des Runden Tisches"* in B. Guggenberger and T. Stein, *Die Verfassungsdiskussion im Jahr der deutschen Einheit* (München: Hanser, 1991) p. 350.

[89] See the articles by R. Kolarova, and D. Dimitrov, "The Roundtable Talks in Bulgaria" in J. Elster ed., *The Roundtable Talks and the Breakdown of Communism*, pp.: 178–212; and by R. Peeva, *"A bolgár kerekasztal tárgyalások összehasonlító szempontból"* in A. Bozóki et al. eds, *A rendszerváltás forgatókönyve*, vol. VII.

Europe, Bulgaria had a stable and undisputed territorial state structure, but had only a weak and short experience with civil society self-organization. Thus, the government was overwhelmingly stronger in 1989 than the opposition, both in terms of support and ability to act. This was expressed, above all, by the organization of elections a mere two months after the end of the Round Table, a deeply disadvantageous timing for the weak opposition.[90] Yet strong mass mobilization did emerge, if mainly after the elections of 1990. Compared to Bulgaria as well as Poland and Hungary, the territorial status and organization of the GDR and Czechoslovakia, for different and even opposite reasons was uncertain and insecure. Yet one of these round tables, the one in Czechoslovakia, did not make state reconstruction a priority, while the other, that in the GDR, tried but failed. Moreover, in these two relatively late dominoes, with Polish and Hungarian round table results as well as their Soviet tolerance clearly visible, wide mass mobilization, in part based on earlier civic activity, developed very rapidly late in 1989, making the opposition potentially[91] (GDR) or actually (Czechoslovakia) stronger than the governments. The differences of these three countries from Poland and Hungary were to effect the deliberations of the round tables, the legitimacy of their results (Bulgaria), or their stability (GDR and Czechoslovakia).

Thus, as significant as the historical sequence was for ending Communist regimes in Central and East Europe, the way in which the constitution-making process developed (or failed) was a function of significant national givens among which the level of previous self-organization, and territorial structure were the most important. I start with the first of the three cases, Czechoslovakia, which admittedly was influenced not only by Polish and Hungarian events, but also by the fall of the Berlin Wall on November 9, 1989. Nevertheless, the Czechoslovak Round Table negotiations, which began as well as ended before the GDR *Runden Tisch* had some of their most important sessions early on. Yet the Czechoslovak Round Table and, in particular, especially its most important first segment (out of 10) involved also the shortest overall period by far of any of the round tables, signifying that they were the scene of the least actual negotiation. Where all the other round tables produced constitutional rules for political transition, if not necessarily interim constitutions, the Czechoslovak Round Table focused almost exclusively on the removal and replacement of the government, state president and even many parliamentary deputies in power, and also the establishment of an interim government, the Government of National Understanding, in the place

[90] Kolarova, and Dimitrov, op. cit.
[91] As the Round Table progressed, the potential became actual. See U. Preuss, "The Round Table Talks in the GDR" in J. Elster ed., *The Roundtable Talks and the Breakdown of Communism*.

of the previous Communist monopoly. Aside from the adoption of the round table form itself, there was little learning here from Poland and Hungary, the previous cases. While primarily non-violent ("velvet"), among the round table countries the Czechoslovak process came closest to a revolutionary scenario involving the rapid seizing of power by a new elite, using the form of a negotiated process and legal continuity for what was, in effect, dictation[92] by agents representing social movements.[93] This way of proceeding, generally seen in terms of the advantage of more rapidly ending Communist rule, also had its significant liabilities, among which was arguably a causal relationship to the break-up of the country, against the will of majorities of its populations.

Three interrelated earlier givens played a role in making the Czechoslovak Round Table unique. The most important of these was the highly repressive and largely unreformed nature of the Communist regime in 1989, on the eve its collapse. This was linked both to the weakness and the unpreparedness of independent social initiatives,[94] that were nevertheless better established as a "moral presence" (see Linz and Stepan 321) than counterparts in the GDR and Bulgaria, and to the weakness of reformist elements within the Communist Party, weaker even than in the other two countries because of the purges of the "normalization" period after 1968. Second, and partially independently, was the explicitly anti-political nature of the civil society concept as it was developed and used in Czechoslovakia by Charta 77 and the groups close to Havel.[95] The third was the availability of large, educated popular sectors (students and artists) for mobilization under the impact of both external and internal events, but the total absence of any organizational or political experience for these strata.

The repression that contributed to these other factors had to break in 1989 given developments in the Soviet Union, Poland and Hungary that could not be hidden, even in Czechoslovakia.[96] Once it was believed no longer possible

---

[92] The Communist PM Adamec accused Havel of issuing ultimatums, and at one point Havel conceded this. M. Calda "The Roundtable Talks in Czechoslovakia" in Elster ed., *The Roundtable Talks and the Breakdown of Communism*, p. 139.

[93] Linz and Stepan thus rightly contrast "collapse" as in Czechoslovakia, with "revolution" as in Romania, and negotiated transition as in Poland and Hungary. Op. cit., 322.

[94] Calda, op. cit., 161.

[95] On these points, see Linz and Stepan, op. cit., 321ff.

[96] I think the idea of Glenn, op. cit., that the forces of repression were intact and capable of action on the eve of the collapse is quite unbelievable, given previous experiences in Eastern Europe and subsequent experience in Romania where the armed forces played a major role in destroying the regime. Once open repression is no longer believable to mobilized sectors, as it was not in Czechoslovakia by November at the very latest, it remains possible only if the authorities in place believe their orders to kill a lot of people will be obeyed by the armed

to violently repress mass demonstrations, as in the GDR, these became very large and increasingly radical. The success of the initially intellectual and cultural movement in penetrating and mobilizing industrial and clerical workers implied a power that could hardly be resisted under the circumstances, even as it was oriented to radical, but hardly specific or consistent goals. In part, formal negotiations were conceded by the authorities to help control the mobilization and its radicalism, but instead their logic very quickly penetrated the Round Table itself. This was moreover made even more likely by the anti-political self-understanding of the recently formed (only on November 9, 1989) Civil Forum (OF), which understood itself to be the expression of a united societal public, or civil society. Thus, even if the demands of OF leaders like Havel were initially remarkably modest and restrained, they were quickly forced to give way to the more radical demands from below that could be satisfied only by the visible replacement of governing personale.[97] Thus, instead of negotiating they tended to convey ultimatums demanding the resignations of the government and the president, which were, remarkably enough, satisfied very quickly by a collapsing regime suddenly without external support. When that happened, and both government and president were replaced, the latter by Havel, the next step was demanding the resignation of a certain number of parliamentary deputies and their replacement by co-optation of OF (and VpN, Public Against Violence, the Slovak counterpart) activists.[98] This too was done. There is, of course, little to object to such governmental replacement,[99] but it should also be stressed at the same time that in comparison to Poland, and Hungary before, as well as in East Germany soon thereafter, what was not done was at least of equal significance.

Leaving the constrained conditions of Poland to the side, in Hungary as we have seen a complete interim constitution was negotiated at the Round Table, and in the GDR too a complete constitutional document intended to be a final one emerged from the negotiating process. In Czechoslovakia, such a result would have been much more needed than in Hungary, because of the unworkability of the inherited document, disguised by the fact that the actually operative material constitution was based on domination by the Communist Party. In late 1989, when at the very least a few constitutional amendments were needed, everyone seriously in politics had to notice that the amendment rule of the constitution of the CSFSR had potentially fatal federalist vetoes, in

forces. The point is discussed by Linz and Stepan on the bases of data from the GDR and documents from Czechoslovakia (pp. 324–327).

[97] On all this see Glenn, and Calda, op. cit.   [98] See Calda, pp. 164–165.

[99] But see Preuss, op. cit.

what in effect was a three chamber legislature with two of them established on national lines.[100] Yet we must wonder whether the actors of OF able to push through their all too few demands for amendment really took the problem seriously. Under the Communist regime one must assume that the Slovak veto was never used, since the ruling party could co-ordinate all the votes. Then the constitution was "workable" in the highly repressive context. Only after the death of that regime did this constitution come alive and show what it really meant if taken seriously. Quite exactly, it was during the effort of "packing" the old parliament in February of 1990 that, probably for the first time, over two-fifths of Slovak deputies in the House of Nations resisted their own packing by constitutional amendment.[101] This was sign of bad things to come. One solution of the problem could have come previously, namely to negotiate a constitution at the RT when the OF was still dominant, preferably an interim one, with a new more flexible amendment rule. However, since constitution making was neglected at that forum, the old unworkable structure survived into the freely elected next parliament, when it was to do its disastrous work.

There were several possible reasons for the neglect.[102] First there was the old European democratic theory which implied that only freely elected

---

[100] In short 2/5 + 1 of either the Slovak or the Czech chamber of the House of Nations could veto constitutional amendments. See Elster, "Transition, constitution-making and separation in Czechoslovakia." *European Journal of Sociology* 36.01 (1995): 105–134.

[101] This episode is misinterpreted by those who imply (Glenn, op. cit., 207–208) that it was indirect proof that the new electoral rule enabled sabotage by the forces of the old regime. But, first, it was in the old non-competitively elected parliament that this form of "sabotage" took place. Second, the PR electoral law did not enhance the possibility of Communists to veto constitutional provisions on their own, and indeed they received a great deal less than 2/5 of either the votes or the seats (a little more than 1/6 in each) for each of the two chambers of the House of Nations. Third, a first-past-the-post rule was eschewed by OF, rightly or wrongly, among other reasons because it could have created a two block parliaments, where in the two chambers of the House of Peoples, the second placed party would have gotten closer to the 2/5 veto power). See: P. Jehlicka et.al. "Czechoslovak Parliamentary Elections 1990" in J. O'Loughlin et.al. eds. *The New Political Geography of Eastern Europe* (London: Belhaven Press, 1993). It is, of course, true that more cautious representatives of the old regime may have welcomed PR as a guarantee against elections like that of the Polish Senate.

[102] Elster, Offe and Preuss state that it was weakness on both sides that caused the neglect of institutional reconstruction. *Institutional Design in Post-communist Societies: Rebuilding the Ship at Sea* (Cambridge: Cambridge University Press, 1998), p. 55. This is unclear as well as implausible. The antipolitical perspective stressed by Stepan and Linz, op. cit., p. 331 is more plausible, but this too is a partial explanation only. The claim of Calda, op. cit., that it was ultimately the insistence on legality and legal continuity by OF that made the enactment of a new constitution impossible is more serious. As the resistance of the Slovak deputies to the packing of parliament indicated, they were now able and willing to use their veto power to stop constitutional change they did not favor. See "The Roundtable Talks in Czechoslovakia," pp. 162, 163, 166 and 164.

constituent assemblies had the right to make a country's constitution. To make sense of this argument, however, one needed to establish a classical constituent assembly not bound by the highly constrained amendment rule. That was not done, nor even really contemplated. Unfortunately, secondly, the same rather incoherent perspective was reinforced by the antipolitical posture of the leaders of OF, who wanted to negotiate as a particular party with a perspective and with interests as little as possible. They were confident that controlling a provisional government was sufficient for the democratic forces to be able to secure free and competitive elections, forgetting the task that would come after. Finally, it was perhaps already noticed that there were fundamental disagreements with Slovaks, both old regime actors and new ones, concerning the nature of the new state whether it should be centralized, federal or confederal.[103] And, without the agreement of the deputies of both nationalities, the constitution could not be changed at least through the method of legal continuity using the inherited amendment rule. But if this was the case they were only delaying a problem to a time when it could very well get worse. Thus the moment of the greatest strength of the OF, facing a parliament with weak legitmacy, with a large popular movement behind it, would have been as good a time as any to try to push through a new constitution or at least interim.[104] Facing freely elected deputies in the future, under the same amendment rule, would only make the problem worse. Abstractly speaking, round table negotiations logically imply a two-stage transition process, and the structure of the state at the very least must be dealt with in the first stage if there is to be a second stage at all. But given legal continuity, in Czechoslovakia at least this was the hardest issue of all to deal with.[105]

Nevertheless the often-criticized electoral rule arrived at after the RT in February of 1990 showed that the OF was capable of enacting important quasi-constitutional change. It was then used in the election of 1990, after new negotiations that were more inclusive than the before.[106] The new law was enacted by the parliament already transformed through the recall of old and

---

[103] See "The Roundtable Talks in Czechoslovakia," p. 154; Elster, "Transition, Constitution-making and Separation in Czechoslovakia."

[104] Indeed, during the second reading of the bill adding new deputies, the initially recalcitrant Slovak deputies seemed to have backed down.

[105] Calda implies both that "in the midst of a revolution" it was in the regime's interest to insist on legal continuity, and that it was this assumption that made the making of a new constitution at the Round Table impossible ("The Roundtable Talks in Czechoslovakia," 162, 165–166). Since he rightly links the break-up to this failure, he seems to wish that the line to a revolution in the legal sense would have been crossed. But, the post-revolutionary idea was even deeper in the political culture of the dissidents like Havel than their anti-political posture.

[106] Jehlicka, "Czechoslovak Parliamentary Elections 1990."

the appointment of 120 new, mostly non-Communist deputies. It is agreed that it was Havel and OF that made the choice, and it is often said that there were no rational reasons for choosing PR.[107] There were, however, several good reasons, traditional, normative and even strategic to do this very thing. As to the least important, tradition, the interwar republic as well as the restored one of 1946, had PR, and it was the Communists who after their coup introduced the majoritarian system, not that it ever mattered in single slate elections. More importantly, it was rightly believed that only PR is a fair system of representation when the issue is not so much governability, but the making of a new constitution in which all relevant political opinion ought to participate. It was also rightly thought that it was not fair, at a time when different political forces have not crystallized, that the one organization already formed should impose a rule to its own advantage. Finally, it was thought undesirable to adopt a majoritarian system that could have easily led to a two-block parliament, in which the leaders thought, rightly or wrongly, the communists would be the second largest block capable of constitutional sabotage.[108]

PR was obviously not going to make the sabotage of constitution making impossible, as long as parties could coalesce around a negative project, which the Slovak parties did indeed manage to do. The making of the electoral rule, with its 5 percent threshold, should have alerted its makers to the fact that they must do more to avoid the possible deadlock of the freely elected parliament than simply enact this one rule. Had they tried to enact a new amendment rule, they might have found compromise possible here as well, as long as they negotiated a larger constitutional framework allowing multiple trade-offs. If there had been many significant actors on the opposition side of the Round Table as in Hungary,[109] if the one important actor, OF, had understood itself as political as in Poland, if its leaders had allowed the negotiations to consider many more topics during a significantly longer process, it may have been possible to do much more on the constitutional level. We will now never know. Given, however, the high mobilization of a radical popular movement, and the ability of only one political force to negotiate on its behalf, given a main actor that did not understand itself as political at all, but had dramatic success in one highly visible area, the composition of government, the failure of constitution making then and after was more or less preordained. And in

---

[107] Elster-Offe-Preuss, *Institutional Design*, p. 57.

[108] "Czechoslovak Parliamentary Elections 1990."

[109] Formally, their number gradually expanded as the Slovakian Public Against Violence, the counter-part of the OF was brought in, followed by smaller parties as well as the bloc party allies of the Communists. "The Roundtable Talks in Czechoslovakia" 149 and 154. But the main force making the key choices remained the CF throughout.

Czechoslovakia failure of constitution making meant the dissolution of the inherited state.[110]

The movement of the GDR was as large and mobilized as that in Czechoslovakia, but fortunately at the round table here – in German: *den Runden Tisch* – there were a plurality of actors ready to speak in the name of different segments of opinion. It may be that in retrospect the survival of this then sovereign state (recognized as such by the Basic Treaty or *Grundlagenvertrag* of 1972) was even less likely then that of a unified or federal Czechoslovakia. Nevertheless, one must note that a more serious effort was made here to insure that survival, or at least the greater independence of the GDR, through a new and attractive constitutional synthesis. On the other hand, admittedly, the very strong trend toward German unification, which eventually separated the Round Table from the popular movement to which it has owed its existence and influence, may have also made the constitutional product irrelevant.[111]

There are many similarities between the GDR and Czechoslovak round tables. Both emerged as a result of popular movements that in the given new geopolitical context caused the collapse of the regimes. In both cases, oppositional forces were dominant, and in neither did really serious bargaining occur between regime and opposition. In both the oppositional actors exhibited a strong anti-political bias, though only in the Czechoslovak case was this linked to a lack of interest in institutional design. Yet in both cases oppositions in the end accepted roles in transitional or provisional governments, in Czechoslovakia sooner, and in the GDR later. Nevertheless, the oppositional actors of both were post-revolutionary in their self-understanding and deeply attached to the legal continuity that the governments in place understandably also espoused. Thus, all participants accepted action under the old constitutions, until it was legally replaced. And, most importantly, all actors of both round tables were attached to the existing state structure, Federal Czechoslovakia or independent GDR, that they considered revising in most likely converging directions of new federal or confederal arrangements.

But there are two important differences as well, with an uncertain causal relation between these. While the Czechoslovak Round Table was dominated

---

[110] That story is told by Linz and Stepan, op. cit. For a full treatment of the breakup of Czechoslovakia, that astonishingly does not discuss the negotiations of 1989, nor their failures, see E. Stein *Czecho/Slovakia: Ethnic Conflict, Constitutional Fissure, Negotiated Breakup* (Ann Arbor, MI: University of Michigan Press, 1999).

[111] By far the best treatment is by Ulrich Preuss, who has written an important theoretical essay even as he described the work and the logic of the *Runden Tisch*. I follow his treatment, but will indicate reservations on a few issues. See "The Roundtable Talks in the German Democratic Republic" in *The Roundtable Talks*.

by one force, Civic Forum, there was a large plurality of important civic organizations, proto-parties at the *Runden Tisch*, negotiating with the parties of
the old regime led by the SED. Thus, while the interaction in Prague often
took the form of ultimatums issued by OF and reluctantly accepted by the
government, in the GDR the role of Diktat was rare, if equally effective. In
general, Ulrich Preuss has no difficulty in representing the GDR Round Table
in terms drawn from Habermas and Koselleck, as a process of dialogic interaction where the opposition relied on its moral rather than political authority to
exert power backed up by the pressure of a mobilized public that was involved
in the open, mostly televised process of interaction.[112] And from the outset,
though accepting the temporary validity of the Constitution of the GDR, the
Runder Tisch insisted on the making of a new constitution for the GDR (!)
as one of its main tasks, establishing a constitution-making subcommittee on
day one.[113] It is hard not to assume that this priority had something to do with
the threatened identity of the state, in the context of a collapsing regime.[114] Of
course, such an identity was also under threat in Czechoslovakia as it is now
obvious. Yet at the time of the Round Table in Prague the threat was perhaps
not yet perceived clearly, and, paradoxically, its institutional causes inhibited
the prospects of constitution making at that venue. In the GDR, there was no
such institutional limit, given the amendment rule of a centralized state with
monocameral legislature,[115] whether the one already in place or the one to be
elected in the first genuine, competitive elections.

We can assume, though hardly prove the influence of other round tables on
the *Runden Tisch*. They had in front of them a substantively almost entirely
new Hungarian constitution, pronounced as interim, as well as the neglect of

---

[112] Ibid.

[113] Preuss himself was an expert advisor for this committee: "The Roundtable Talks in the German
Democratic Republic," pp. 112 and 120.

[114] Bernhardt Schlink, a second important Western advisor at the *Runden Tisch*, explicitly notes
the double intention of producing a constitution that would be a model of order for a shorter
or longer transitional period, and a determination of the position of the GDR (DDR) in the
negotiations with the Federal Republic (BRD) on the future shape of Germany. "*Deutsch-
deutsche Verfassungentwicklungen im Jahre 1990*" in *Die Verfassungsdiskussion im Jahr der
deutschen Einheit*, p. 21.

[115] The Constitution of the GDR in 1949 originally had a simple two-thirds absolute majority
amendment rule, Article 83, but it allowed though did not require either ratification in
referendum or passing amendments by referenda. Amendments could be temporarily vetoed
by the then existing upper chamber of the "Länder," but they could be repassed by the initial
majority. In 1952 the Länder and in 1968 the upper chamber were abolished. Article 63:2 of
the new Constitution of 1968 (unchanged in 1974) changed the amendment rule to two-thirds
of all the deputies of the monocameral parliament. Until 1989 at least, it made no difference
obviously whether two-thirds or 50 percent + 1 were required.

constitution making in Czechoslovakia. Given their problems, they could have understood the superiority of the Hungarian choice, though because of the obvious legitimation problems involved they departed from it by submitting their product to the freely elected rather than the last Communist-dominated legislature. Thus, on the question whether a constitution or elections should come first, they decided to write a constitution *before*, and have it submitted to a legislature *after* elections. This normatively quite understandable choice was, however, also the riskier one as we will see, because the *Runder Tisch* had power only over the old *Volkskammer*. This power was based on both greater legitimacy, and on the traditional role of the Communist government in enforcing parliamentary compliance. The new *Volkskammer* would, however, have democratic legitimacy based on elections, and could also generate its own government, a different and responsible type. Moreover, the *Runder Tisch* was supposed to go out of existence even before the free elections, and thus its constitutional product would have had to rely on pure persuasion, rather than any institutional power. Even in a different context, not marked by a drive to German unification, such a purely moral influence was not likely to be enough.

During its existence, the East German *Runder Tisch*, in fact, came to exercise more power than any other round table.[116] This was paradoxical, given the self-understanding of most of the groups. In the context of a collapse, however, with the very survival of the state at a razor's edge, the government in place was quite willing to concede not only constituent, but also legislative and in the end also some executive power to the opposition groups. The first of these powers was used in producing a constitution, and, separately, a series of constitutional amendments. Only the use of the amending power was to have important results. As to the legislative power, it took the form of making implicitly binding recommendations to the old *Volkskammer*. As far as I can tell, this power, along with the amending power, and the exercise of quasi-parliamentary control functions, was used effectively to move the GDR to democratic elections that were going to be free and fair.[117] It is true that the *Runder Tisch* in the end allowed these elections to take place too early for most of the civic groups to properly organize, campaign, and become known. Here this was more on the wishes of the new Eastern social

---

[116] See the detailed discussion of the power question in Preuss, op. cit.

[117] Thus, it is actually incorrect to depict the results of the GDR Round Table as simply "non-decisive" or as not having played "a significant role in the transition process"–Bozóki, "Introduction: The Significance of the Roundtable Talks" in *The Roundtable Talks of 1989*, p. xx. That role, moving the country to free elections but not really beyond, was no less but also no more significant than that in Czechoslovakia.

democratic party, the SPD and the former bloc parties that had West German sponsors, rather than the weak SED.[118] Time was as important in the GDR as everywhere else, and the round table lost control over it under the pressure for unification.[119]

Finally, it was the assumption of executive power that was most problematic and damaging for some of the opposition groups at the *Runden Tisch*.[120] This was certainly agreed to on January 28, 1990 in light of the previous Czechoslovak case, where Havel and CF decided to include some of their important members in the Government of National Understanding formed on December 11, 1989. In Czechoslovakia, however, the move involved the coming to power of a new PM, was in full conformity with demands from the street, and was balanced in favor of Civic Forum when Havel soon after, on December 29, was elected to the presidency. In the GDR, it was to the existing Modrow cabinet (renamed as the *Regierung der Nationalen Verantwortung*) that the new civic members were co-opted. Thus, it appeared as a move shoring up the old government, as well as an independent GDR that by then the majority and especially its mobilized sections did not want. The damage became even greater when some parties of the Round Table were strongly critical of participation before they wound up joining anyway.[121] Several interpreters trace the decline of the influence of both the negotiating forum and the civil movements within it to this historical mistake, even if it was not based on their seeking power for themselves.[122]

That decline clearly affected the fate of the Constitution drawn up at the *Runden Tisch*.[123] Despite its hasty process of drafting, the document itself was sophisticated and forward-looking, far more interesting than any other constitutional draft then enacted or even proposed in East or Central Europe.[124] It

---

[118] See C.S. Maier, *Dissolution* (Princeton: Princeton University Press, 1997), pp. 198–199 for a good discussion of this process, as well as its electoral consequences.

[119] B. Hohmann, "*Etappen des verfassungsrechtlichen Diskurses*" in *Die Verfassungsdiskussion im Jahr der deutschen Einheit*, pp. 98–99.

[120] Ibid.

[121] Preuss, op. cit.; Maier, *Dissolution*, p. 180; D. Childs, *The Fall of the GDR* (London: Longman, 2001), pp. 112–113.

[122] See, e.g., Preuss, op. cit.

[123] For a commentary and depiction of the context, see the detailed article Peter E. Quint, "The Constitutional Law of German Unification," 50 *Maryland Law Review* 475 (1991). Available at: http://digitalcommons.law.umaryland.edu/mlr/vol50/iss3/3.

[124] Of course it was attacked on this very ground, by G. Roellecke, "Dritter Weg zum Zweiten Fall" in *Die Verfassungsdiskussion im Jahr der deutschen Einheit* who claims that this result, incorporating many progressive decisions of the Western Bundesverfassungsgericht, BvG, but going even beyond them was achieved by the Western advisors of the *Runden Tisch* who came from the ranks of the then oppositional SPD and Greens (p. 397). Roellecke incoherently

contained an expanded set of rights, including the postulate of rights against "third persons" (namely private powers), ecological and feminist concerns,[125] political rights of participation for civil society organizations, a restored system of decentralization based on renewed Länder and once again a two chamber legislature,[126] as well as a plausible scenario for an equitable and democratic form of German unification which will be discussed below. Yet, leaving aside the question of the qualities of this legal document[127], its political relevance even to a new constitutional discussion at the newly elected *Volkskammer* depended on the makeup of that body. Obviously, that makeup itself depended on the election, its timing and, potentially, the electoral system. As to the latter, a highly equitable proportional rule without a cutoff (as against the 5 percent in the BRD) was negotiated at the round table.[128] Nevertheless, the alliance around the former bloc party CDU won an overwhelming victory with nearly half the seats of the new *Volkskammer*.[129] In a coalition with the social democrats, the new government now had constitution-amending majority on its own. With the *Runden Tisch* in part discredited, and with interest shifting from loose civil movements to well-financed and Western-influenced political parties, there were few elected to the new body who would take up the case of a new constitution in general, and even fewer the round table version in particular. Given the overwhelming triumph of parties affiliated with West German partners, the very ground under any new constitution for the GDR was finally removed, by constitutional amendments first, followed by the state treaty of May and the unification treaty of late August.

In the face of what happened in Czechoslovakia and the GDR, it would be easy enough to say now that no constituent activity at the two round tables could have saved the day, and thus the only function of these bodies was to move the two countries to free elections. That would mean that when in doubt the structure of the state could not be renegotiated, nor even rules for its renegotiation could be produced. Here the two cases are different.

claims that incorporating the constitutional draft in any way would have led to the end of the state, without saying which state, and to a kind of Leninism led by the civil rights activists.
[125] B. Schlink, "*Deutsch-deutsche Verfassungentwicklungen im Jahre 1990.*"
[126] "The Constitutional Law of German Unification."
[127] Indeed, these very qualities provided targets for the attack of commentators from the right who did not wish for any East German input in the state and constitution making process, or any significant changes in the *Grundgesetz* as it then stood.
[128] Childs, *The Fall of the GDR*, p. 126.
[129] This result was achieved through a massive personal presence of Chancellor Kohl during the elections promising a currency unification, based on the 1:1 conversion of the much less valuable Eastern Mark into Deutschmark See Habermas, "Der DM Nationalismus" in http://www.zeit.de/1990/14/der-dm-nationalismus."

In Czechoslovakia what stood in the way of such renegotiation was only an unusable institutional framework with its inherited amendment rule. There was never, not even during the very break itself, a mass movement or even popular support in either republic to destroy the federal state. In the end it was the politicians, whose second-best outcome was separation, who were able to exploit the institutional framework to eliminate the possibility of a federal state, preferred by the Czech government, and of a loose confederation, the Slovak preference. These two preferences, however, could have been compromised at the Round Table, if there was a constitution-making effort at that venue. It no longer matters whether such compromise could have been achieved within legal continuity, or only with a legal break bypassing the inherited amendment rule in some kind of democratic process.[130]

The GDR round table shared many of the features of its recent predecessor in Czechoslovakia. The negotiations were enabled and propelled in both by a great popular movement, and the representatives of the opposition in both saw themselves in anti-political terms. Nevertheless, as the GDR case shows, constitution making was thought necessary in such a setting, and, as the production of amendments shows, was actually possible. What was not predetermined in the GDR, however, were the deeply related problems of the type of constitution that was to be made and to whom it should be submitted. The protagonists of the GDR *Runden Tisch* did not believe that a permanent new constitution could have been passed by the old *Volkskammer*, because of its obvious legitimation problems. But the protagonists and their advisors made two fundamental mistakes, both understandable, but nevertheless fatal. First, they thought that a mere draft of a constitution that they produced, that was intended to survive as long as the GDR survived, could be meaningfully submitted to a new, freely elected *Volkskammer*. The answer would have been to adopt the Hungarian option of a more or less complete constitution, perhaps more modest in content, but explicitly interim in its form,[131] and pass it through the old rather than the new *Volkskammer*. Only in the purely formal sense would this have been the work of the old legislature,[132] and there was

---

[130] That such a careful use of a legal break can be made legitimate is demonstrated by the case of Colombia, dealt with in the next chapter.

[131] In one passage, hard to even notice, the GDR draft speaks of itself as a *"vorläufiges Grundgesetz"* Article 135. Here the term *Grundgesetz* rather than *Verfassung* as elsewhere seems to refer to a relationship to a future *Grundgesetz* for all of Germany. In Hungary in 1989 and in Poland's little constitution in 1992, the provisional status was indicated from the very beginning. The South African constitution of 1994 was called an interim constitution.

[132] Of course the representativeness of the *Runden Tisch* was much debated both outside and within. See Preuss' detailed discussion op. cit.; Grimm, *"Das Risiko Demokratie" Die Verfassungsdiskussion im Jahr der deutschen Einheit* and Hohmann, op. cit. But while democratic

at least a chance that the creation of such a constitution, especially if ratified in a referendum, would have been supported and helped the later (or especially: simultaneous!) election chances of the civic groups. More importantly, if given the appropriate formulation, it could have improved the bargaining position of the GDR government in the coming negotiations. If there was enough legitimacy to pass an all-important electoral rule through constitutional amendment, the same was true for passing rules for other transitional arrangements.

Of course, it was undeniable that there was a need for interim constitutional arrangements, and this led to the second mistake, either by commission or by omission. The civic groups at the *Runden Tisch* agreed to, and even demanded, the rapid passing of a few constitutional amendments that would indicate the break with the existing system, such as the elimination of the leading role of the SED and "the working class," the pluralization of forms of property, the electoral law, the status of military service and of unions. This implied a double strategy of simultaneously making amendments and producing a new constitution, one that is in itself problematic.[133] Unfortunately, as should have been foreseen, the first strategic path subverted the second. A need for an interim new constitution seemed to be lessened by the amendments that could be passed faster, and with less controversy. This was the mistake by commission, complemented by an equally serious omission. The amendments passed by the old *Volkskammer* under the influence of the *Runden Tisch* did not contain any requirements for the negotiation of unity with the BRD. This allowed the new *Volkskammer* to pass the relevant amendments enabling unification to proceed under an increasing time pressure. After some hopeless discussion of passing an interim constitution different than the round table draft, yet new amendments were produced. The final one of these clearly recognized the transitional or interim character of the so amended GDR Constitution, but, under the influence of the new majority, contained no conditions that would have strengthened the hand of the GDR negotiators.[134]

What the GDR case proves, in spite of the failure of the *Runden Tisch* in the constitutional domain, is that the existence of a social movement causing

---

representation as such was absent, the Round Table in fact represented all the forces of East German society, including the eventual winners of the March elections, the remade CDU and its allies. Moreover, under the guidance of the Round Table (neglected by Quint) the old *Volkskammer* did pass some important amendments to the Constitution of 1968/74. If the level of representation was sufficient for that purpose, it was also sufficient to enact an explicitly interim constitution, which the amendment themselves in the end amounted to.

[133] B. Hohmann, "Etappen des verfassungrechtlichen Diskurses," 91; 92–95.

[134] Hohmann, op. cit., 98–99; Schlink, op. cit., 27–28.

an imbalance in the negotiating forum in favor of the opposition and inter-est in institutional design were not logically incompatible, as we might have thought given only the single case of Czechoslovakia. Of course not only the existence of a great mass movement, but also its character mattered. As against Czechoslovakia, in the GDR where the slogan at demonstrations switched from "*Wir sind das Volk*" to "*Wir sind ein Volk*," there was indeed strong popular sentiment for abolishing the existing state, and this was very much exploited by the parties that won the election. So it is clear that unification or reunification could not have been averted, as long as the major relevant powers, the United States, France, the UK and eventually the Soviet Union agreed to it. Nevertheless, there were two questions that could have been kept open, and an interim constitution designed by the Round Table and passed by the old *Volkskammer* could have kept them open through both its mere existence, and some of its provisions. First, if there was to be unification, what form should it take? A sovereign country with a new democratic constitution could have held out for its own terms, whether the majority wanted a federal state for Germany as the Bundesrepublik or some other type of federal or confederal arrangement. Second, even if alternatives to the old federal state had little support, a *Volkskammer* under a new constitution, before agreeing to a unification treaty could have held out for the making of a new constitution for Germany as a whole. Having a new, valid, consensual interim constitution probably would not have ultimately changed the general outcome of a new, unified state, but it might have improved the bargaining position of the citizens of the former GDR and their representatives, and hence their genuine partic-ipation in the finalization of the shape of that new state. Had that happened, a new all German constitution made under Article 146 could have represented the last and final stage of the East German self-limiting revolution.[135]

    To see what might have possible, or at least not impossible, it is still worth-while examining the constitutional draft of the *Runden Tisch* that paid a great deal of attention to the negotiating position of the East in the pro-cess of unification.[136] Admittedly, the protagonists were originally themselves

[135] Of course, it is possible and even likely that no constitution in itself could have slowed down the dive to unity, accelerated by the proposed currency union that involved, at least initially, a huge economic redistribution from West to East. On this logic see Maier, *Dissolution*, p. 228ff.; and the baleful remarks by Habermas, op. cit.

[136] The relevant provisions are entirely left out by Quint in his detailed treatment of the draft. See op. cit., 493ff. Bernhardt Schlink notes this aspect (op. cit., p. 26), but seems to think that the ultimate choice indicated by the draft, which he worked on, was between using Article 146 or Article 23 for unification. He seems to focus here merely on the choice offered in Article 136 of the draft. I read the text differently, because Article 132 to which 136 refers as one of the two choices (see its point 3), insists on an all German constituent process even if the

committed to an independent East Germany, possibly within a new all-German confederation that even chancellor Helmut Kohl advocated for a brief time.[137] By the time their draft was finalized, however, they understood the new public mood in the East. Thus, they expressed their own commitment to a united Germany (Articles 41–2[138]), and concerned themselves only with the constitutional process leading to unity as well as its contents. They postulated two possible ways of replacing their constitution, by the creation of a new constitution through a new, all-German constituent assembly (Article 136) or by the entry of the East into the Federal Republic under the latter's *Grundgesetz* (Articles 131–2). These were the two roads available under the *Grundgesetz* itself, as indicated by that constitution's Articles 146 as against 23. As is well known, it was Article 23 that was eventually followed, in a process (correctly, if highly polemically) described by many as an *Anschluss* or annexation. But to avoid that outcome and that interpretation, the constitutional draft of the Round Table set demanding conditions for the treaty that was to open the road to an Article 23-type process. First, the treaty was to be approved by two-thirds of the Volkskammer and ratified by an East German referendum (Articles 132–2). Two, the treaty had to contain a provision for the election of an all-German constituent assembly, as a necessary guarantee of the right of participation and self-determination of the public of the GDR (Articles 132–3). This step would have meant a combination of using first Article 23 and second Article 146 procedures. Third, the treaty was to require the constitutional entrenchment of rights in the draft that were not then part of the *Grundgesetz*, in particular the rights of individuals against third parties. Fourth, and more problematically, the drafters wished to exempt the East German reconstituted Länder from Article 31 of the *Grundgesetz*: "*Bundesrecht bricht Landesrecht.*" This was a remnant of the confederal principle in the draft. Finally, the constitution that contained these provisions could itself be changed only by the absolute two-thirds majority of the Volkskammer, ratified in a referendum (Article 100–1).[139]

GDR enters the BRD, presumably by Article 23. Thus the choice was between the method of Article 146 (an all German constituent process), and a combination of 23 and 146 (accession followed by an all German constituent process). Either way, the draft would have bound the GDR authorities to require the making of a formally new German constitution, either before or after the act of unification.

[137] See M.E. Sarotte, *1989: The Struggle to Create a Post-War Europe* (Princeton: Princeton University Press, 2009), pp. 72–73 and 81–87; also see Quint, op. cit. for further references to advocates.

[138] "*Die Deutsche Demokratische Republik bekennt sich zu dem Ziel der Herstellung der Einheit der beiden deutschen Staaten.*"

[139] Following the *Grundgesetz*, Articles 100–2 of the Draft then postulated a series of eternity clauses that would not have been threatened under old or new *Grundgesetz*.

Returning to a version closer to the earlier amendment rule of 1949 (Article 83: 2 and 3), leaving behind those of the 1968 and 1974 Constitutions that did not require or even contain a referendum as an option (Article 63–2), the drafters were making sure that within legal continuity at least, its restricting provisions for the future inter-state treaty could not be easily evaded. To be consistent, they tied the ratification of their own draft to the same two-thirds-plus refer-endum rule (Article 135). This last provision painfully illustrates my point that the draft had a chance only within the old rather homogeneous rather than the new much more complex Volkskammer.[140]

Of course, I stress again that constitutional provisions in themselves could not have halted the acceleration toward unity on purely West German terms. The constitutional draft, even if approved by a *Volkskammer*, old or new, could have been voted down in the referendum that text itself proposed (Article 135). The new constitution could have been later amended, on the wishes of the Federal government, if supported by a referendum, to eliminate the conditions requiring the use of GG Article 146 (Article 100). At the same time, I should add, that the use of Article 146 was supported by many also in West Germany. Indeed, in what was a great all-German discussion, the question of using Article 146 as against 23 was hotly debated during the beginning of the 1990s.[141] Relying on the very promise of 146, and the well-known provisional status of the *Grundgesetz*, lawyers on the Left and Center Left argued either for an Article 146 process or a combination of one based on Articles 23 and 146. These indeed were the two options contained in the draft of the Round Table as its two alternatives.[142] But now the side insisting one way or the other on an all-German constituent process no longer had any means of pressuring the politicians who, with few exceptions in the dominant parties, wished to avoid the supposed democratic turmoil and the possible innovations of a new constituent assembly, even if the latter could have remained under the control of the (German Federal Constitutional Court (BvG)).[143] In this debate the constraints of a new GDR constitution were entirely absent, even as the right repeatedly used the round table draft to warn what terrible things could happen

---

[140] There was nothing wrong, however, with requiring a referendum to enact the draft, thereby lending it greater authority.

[141] See Quint, op. cit.; see especially the essays of *Die Verfassungsdiskussion im Jahr der deutschen Einheit*.

[142] E.g., by D. Grimm's "Das Risiko Demokratie" in *Die Verfassungsdiskussion im Jahr der deutschen Einheit*.

[143] More recently the BvG asserted its jurisdiction even over Article 146 that in an altered form remains in the *Grundgesetz*: See: BVerfG, Judgment of the Second Senate of 30 June 2009–2 BvE 2/08 – paras. (1–421).

if autonomous forces from the GDR could make an input into an all-German constitution. Thus, as laudable as the effort to make a round table constitution was, it ended in complete failure.[144] But this does not mean that the failure was inevitable, even in an inhospitable context of the collapse of the state, along with the regime that established it and maintained its existence.

Bulgaria is historically the last of the three cases of round tables I consider deviant, however for the opposite reason of Czechoslovakia and the GDR. Here, even after the fall of all the other dominoes of Central and East Europe, it is commonly accepted that the regime remained strong and the opposition weak during the transition process, and the making of the new constitution. The relative strength of this regime and corresponding weakness of the opposition located the country, despite the influence of earlier experience, logically, in an "earlier" East European temporality.[145] In other words, the regime fell in Bulgaria because it was part of the overall geopolitical context and sequence, but the Communist Party and its successor, the BSP, remained strong because of the historically unique context of the country itself. Nevertheless, the fact that there were serious negotiations, and that in the end a viable liberal democratic constitution emerged in a two stage process[146] indicates that the difficulties of national context when not linked to an uncertain and disputed state structure, which can be at least partially balanced by the organization of the process itself, especially if relevant adjustments are made. This adjustment in Bulgaria took the form of serious round table-type negotiations both before and during the constitutional assembly itself.

The undisputed initial strength of the regime should not be confused with an authoritarian, or manipulated or Communist-dominated process.[147] That

---

[144] Thus, the last hopes of Ulrich Preuss a key participant, that the draft would enrich constitutional reality in a unified federal Republic, were not fulfilled. Op. cit. However, some of the provisions dealing with rights and ecological desiderata found their way in amendments made by the new Volkskammer before and after the first state treaty, and, more importantly and lastingly, in the constitution of the one state Brandenburg, with a center left government after unification. See Quint, "The Constitutional Law of German Unification."

[145] What I am saying is that there is a sense in which all the East European cases were in the same developmental "time," hence the importance of sequence and mutual influence, and there is a sense in which they were in different "times," determined by national givens and resulting in different outcomes within the general collapse of Communism in the region. The role of time for the cases is often emphasized (see Peeva op.cit.) but generally only in the first sense, in terms of a developmental sequence. Linz and Stepan use a typology ("Early Post Totalitarianism") that indicates that Bulgaria's later transition was in a different, earlier time than the countries to the West, at the time of the beginning of their transitions. Op. cit., 337.

[146] Peeva, op. cit., 744–745 and passim.

[147] This confusion appears in many Western treatments. E.g. Elster et al., 54–55; elsewhere they concede that the negotiations were real 69; Linz and Stepan op. cit.: "initiated and never lost

dominance in the end manifested itself only in one factor, the control over time, specifically the acceleration of the road to elections at a time when the opposition was hardly organized or known. On most other issues, as we will see, the opposition's positions dominated, or a genuine compromise had to be accepted by the government for the sake of gaining time. This particular imbalance reveals a stronger government side, one that expected to become weaker as time passed. Here the earlier regional sequence, including the revolutionary collapse of the Romanian regime, played a major role in the structuring of expectations.

In many respects, the Bulgarian regime was part of the complex further to the East. For long term historical reasons there was little nationalist opposition here to Soviet domination, and there were no serious reform attempts initiated by the regime before the break itself. Bulgaria in a way resembled some of the national republics within the Soviet Union, and indeed it was the only East European country where joining that union was raised as a possibility after World War II. Nevertheless, one thing was missing in Bulgaria precisely because of its formal independence, namely the existence of a subordinate republican organization around which resistance to the old regime and an electoral path to change (in particular: secession) could be organized. This was possible even in the imperial center, namely Russia itself, where the republican government eventually led the opposition to the Soviet framework. In Bulgaria, the government represented the old regime, and it had no formal imperial framework to secede from. Nevertheless, this government was as strong sociologically as the republican governments to the east, in the Soviet Union. It remained strong even after the very late palace coup in November, involving the removal of the increasingly unpopular T. Zhivkov. As everyone agrees, the opposition in Bulgaria was weak, fragmented, as well divided by the antagonism of the Bulgarian majority and Turkish minority, and attempts to unify it came very late with the formation of the Union of Democratic Forces (UDF) and was only partially successful.[148]

It seems clear that the experts of the ruling party knew that the economic condition of the country resembled all the unreformed Soviet-style economies, and feared a complete collapse, probably sooner rather than later. Thus, the party's new leaders did not think they could avoid significant economic reforms

---

control of the transition" 333. But see Arato, *Civil Society, Constitution, Legitimacy*, p. 162f. All interpreters rely on basically one treatment, by Kolarova and Dimitov along with their concept of preemption, though even that fine study reveals that negotiations were genuine and had significant results. I was fortunate to also have the New School PhD dissertation by Ralitsa Peeva, whose thesis is partially available in a Hungarian version in op. cit.

[148] Kolarova and Dimirov, op. cit.; Peeva, op. cit.

involving austerity, and therefore the type of relegitimation of their rule that only a competitive electoral process could provide. Here it is undisputed that the positive examples of Poland and Hungary, as well as the negative one of Romania, played a significant role in their calculations.[149] It is disputed, however, who first suggested adopting a Polish- and Hungarian-style round table, whether elements of the regime, intellectuals close to the government, the opposition, the new independent trade union Podkrepa, or even the Turkish movement. It is also disputed whether there were genuine preparatory negotiations before the RT, i.e., "talks about talks."[150] What is obvious, however, is that the government in Bulgaria did not imagine, as did the leaders of many Soviet republics, that free elections could be organized purely from above if they were to serve their legitimation function. Thus, its leaders jumped at the chance of having a round table, especially when they perceived that the opposition was weak.

In retrospect, the strategy of the government in these negotiations appears clear. It seems that they were ready to sacrifice many of their own preferences for the sake of quick negotiations, and an equally quick move to elections that they expected to win. Successful elections were conceived as their strategy of converting one form of power into another. Thus the government's very concessions and compromises have been seen as themselves being a negotiating tactic.[151] It is not certain, however, if this intention was fully clear to the BCP negotiators from the beginning. Two factors could have influenced their move away from a more maximal program structured around issues like the creation of a freely elected presidency as well as first past the post elections and a long session for the first freely elected parliament, to a more minimal program involving compromise on all these issues. First, the international context was becoming less and less hospitable for any attempt at Communist imposition. Second, and probably more important, was the unwillingness of the weak opposition, and surprisingly the regime's hitherto obedient agrarian partner (BANU), to agree to the propositions insisted on by their much stronger opponent. As to the opposition, in a logic well described by Janos Kis,[152] its very weakness could not allow making agreements that could be portrayed as mere submission, and absence of independence. Weakness in negotiation could lead to total loss of their already weak public support. As for BANU, they too obviously recognized, as did the bloc parties of the East

---

[149] Peeva, op. cit.   [150] See Peeva, op. cit., 747 vs. Stepan and Linz, op. cit., p. 338.

[151] Kolarova; Peeva, 194–195.

[152] Stressing what the weaker Hungarian opposition could not accept in distinction to their much stronger Polish forerunners in Kis, op. cit.

German SED, that their electoral success would depend on independence, even if newfound. Thus neither the opposition nor BANU accepted to be included in the government during the round table negotiations, unlike the much stronger Czechoslovak and East German oppositions.

As to the government, or the BCP (from April the BSP: Bulgarian Socialist Party), when it became clear that they could not simply impose their own preferences and give these the mere form of negotiated settlement, they began to concentrate on the essential. Though certainly receiving more support than the HS(W)P or the PUWP, the fate of these parties in Hungary and Poland in the first free elections indicated the danger, even if less serious than the one in Romania (whether we see the latter process of change as the result of a revolution, or an internal civil war within the regime). The first free elections had to be won at all costs, and they might not be won if too much time was wasted at the round table. Thus, the concessions, first on the form of the negotiation (two sided rather than "circular" that would have given regime satellite organizations an equal voice), as well as the acceptance of wide publicity for the proceedings,[153] were followed by another on the electoral rule providing a mixed structure of ½ PR and ½ FPTP, and finally the most important one on the presidency, that provided for a relatively weak president, who would be elected by the old national assembly. Even though that president was likely to be a leader of the BCP, P. Mladenov, his power would be weak and his legitimacy limited by this form of election. On these issues the Bulgarian opposition not only surpassed the achievements of their forerunner in Poland, but also at least equaled and arguably improved upon those in Hungary before the latter were corrected in a referendum.[154] Moreover, unlike in Hungary and Poland, it was made clear that the first free elections would produce an assembly whose main task would be the making of a constitution. The opposition achieved this through its insistence that this assembly would be a Grand National Assembly (GNA), rather than the ordinary four-year one advocated by the BCP. While allowing only a shorter term for a body in which the Communist deputies were initially expected to have close to a majority could have been the main motive here, nevertheless the creation of a constitutional assembly was the main by-product.[155] I call this constitutional, rather than constituent, because with both sides under the veil of ignorance, there was no attempt to establish the GNA as sovereign. Not only was the old

---

[153] Kolarova and Dimitrov, op. cit., 187–188; 199.

[154] Jaruzelski was elected by a new parliament, and had far greater powers. Pozsgay would have been elected directly, before parliamentary elections, until the 4 Yes referendum reversed these initial agreements.

[155] Peeva, op. cit., 759.

two-thirds constitutional amendment rule not challenged, but the GNA was further bound to limits concerning, e.g., the structure of the new presidency, the main constitutional result of the negotiations.[156]

But the price for these victories was UDF acceptance of the BCP's timetable providing for elections, in June 1990 a mere month before the end of the Round Table talks.[157] Here BANU too played a crucial role.[158] Having earned its independence by supporting the opposition on several issues, on the most important issue of all it was free to follow the BCP or its own self-interest as an already well organized entity, or both at the same time. Given the outcome, that indeed provided BCP (after April, BSP) the parliamentary majority it sought, it was this victory on the question of time and the resulting Communist or ex-Communist ability to form a government that is the main evidence behind the claim, made in Bulgaria and in the West, that the Bulgarian Round Table was a front for an imposed solution. It would be wrong, however, to argue that the BCP alone took advantage of the factor of time. The opposition, buoyed by democratic victories in other countries, and having clearly recognized the interest of the BCP in accelerating the process, used that knowledge to gain more concessions as the discussions continued.[159]

Moreover, it should be also stressed that what the BCP or BSP achieved in the end, by having to accept a more proportional electoral rule than intended, was well under a constitution-making two-thirds majority. Equally important, the UDF alone obtained well over one-third of the seats. Thus, while the inherited amendment rule was the institutional blockage on constitution making in Czechoslovakia, in Bulgaria that rule became the reason why the making of the constitution would be consensual. Using it, Bulgarians were to produce a very well developed liberal democratic constitution, notable for its multi-leveled democratic amendment rule.[160]

---

[156] Peeva, op. cit., 762–763 v. Kolarova and Dimitrov, op. cit., p. 200, although they are not addressing the same issues. Peeva is clearly right on there being limits, since the absence of a two-thirds majority for the BSP played an important role in the outcome.

[157] Kolarova and Dimitrov, op. cit., 90; 193; 200; thus, it seems incorrect to ascribe that date merely to the action of the Communist parliament that would have involved going around the RT by the BCP. Linz and Stepan, op. cit., 339. Kolarova and Dimitrov affirm the supremacy of the RT.

[158] Peeva, op. cit.

[159] Ralitsa Peeva's depiction of this two-sided dynamic is especially cogent (pp. 754–756).

[160] Thus, Linz and Stepan come to the conclusion that Bulgaria "overperformed" in terms of democracy, given its regime type, op. cit., 342. Actually, this paradox can be reduced if we understand the Round Table as having involved genuine negotiations, with many results corresponding to the goals of an admittedly sociologically weak opposition, as for example the fairly proportional electoral rule mentioned by Linz and Stepan. The popular movement emerging after the elections, reinforced these positive results, and helped to remove the concession of the presidency to the Communists.

That did not happen without a political struggle. To the Bulgarian opposition, or at least a large part of the UDF, the concession of even a weak presidency, the rush to elections and the formation of a BSP government put the legitimacy of the result in great question. It turned out, moreover, that the Bulgarian government was right: time was on their side only in the short run. Having used it to their benefit during that time, they endangered their power and influence in the longer run. Led by the UDF, the popular mobilization that took place before the round tables in Poland, the GDR and Czechoslovakia, occurred in Bulgaria after the elections.[161] As their direct result, Pres. Mladenov was removed even before the first meeting of the GNA, and was replaced by that body with the leader of the opposition UDF, Z. Zhelev. Soon thereafter, the one-party BSP government was also brought down by continued street protests, and a general strike led by the new, independent union, Podkrepa.[162] Both the formation of a government led by non-party experts, and the constitution-making process could proceed only after new negotiations were organized by President Zhelev, which in turn resembled the earlier Round Table.[163] Even though a hardline group of 29 within the UDF boycotted these talks and the drafting as well as the vote on the Constitution, the document was enacted, if not necessarily designed, in a consensual manner that involved the cooperation of the majority of the UDF (115 out of 144) deputies, with the BSP and the Turkish-led Movement for Rights and Freedoms.[164]

The Bulgarian case shows that it is not necessarily fatal for a round table-type process that initially the government side is stronger, at least under some conditions. First, and most obviously, the government and its legitimacy cannot be so strong that it need not concede a round table process at all, or concede it as nothing more than fig leaf for imposition. Second, the opposition must recognize that in its weakness lies a certain strength, and therefore it should not

[161] Kolarova and Dimitrov, op. cit., 200–201; Linz and Stepan, op. cit., p. 340.
[162] R.R. Ludwikowski, *Constitution-Making in the Region of Former Soviet Dominance* (Durham, NC: Duke University Press, 1996) 112.
[163] Kolarova and Dimitrov, op. cit.
[164] Thus, I find unconvincing the claim by Kolarova and Dimitrov, op. cit., 202 that the BSP simply pushed through the new constitution through its majority in the GNA. First, it did not have constituent majority. Second, only 29 UDF deputies did not vote for the document. Third, the document itself does not sustain the idea that the BSP simply pushed through its preferences. It may be correct, as they say, that the BSP continued its strategy at the RT. But in both cases this involved concession and compromise on the part of the BSP, rather than imposition. Note that Kolarova and Dimitrov admit that now it was more in the interest of the BSP to delay elections. This however would have meant a significant shift in strategy, and it failed in any case since new elections were held on October 13, 1991, exactly three months after the adoption of the new constitution, and 15 months after the election of the GNA. That too was in line with the intentions of the opposition, both in 1990 and 1991!

accept the imposition of terms considered obviously unacceptable. Third, the international context can help to equalize otherwise unequal sides. Fourth, when part of an international trend of change, as in East and Central Europe, but also previously in Southern Europe and Latin America, time is likely to be on the side of those that wish to make a more radical break with an authoritarian system. And fifth, since time in such a case is on the side of the opposition, the regime, as in Bulgaria, will be in a great hurry to get to elections it can dominate. Thus the opposition playing for time can achieve important concessions not imaginable previously.

Of course, unbalanced forces may lead to an unbalanced election, and the partial conversion of power into a new democratically legitimated form. Here the Bulgarian process shows that correctives were possible. Even out of the standard sequence, popular mobilization and protest, as well as new negotiations are ways of correcting the earlier outcome. It is important that these two correctives repeated the logic of many of the round tables elsewhere, with popular mobilization playing the role of equalizing two forces, only one of whom, the government, possessed the means of violence.

THE PARADIGMATIC CASE: SOUTH AFRICA

The constitution-making process of the Republic of South Africa has been rightly considered a paradigmatic or archetypical version of a negotiated transition from one regime to another, through legal continuity. From a developmental perspective, I have long argued that it represents the highest level of realization so far of a paradigm pioneered in Spain, and continued in Central Europe.[165] Admittedly, the type of social formation and societal divisions involved were completely different in South Africa than in either Southern or Eastern Europe. Thus, there is good reason to compare the South African transition to other African cases instead, especially Namibia and Zimbabwe, which had their own experience with apartheid-type structures of exclusion as well as ethnic division. While there has indeed been positive as well as negative learning from these cases in South Africa that I will discuss, the differences of their constitutional processes seem even more significant. In both Zimbabwe and Namibia, the role of a colonial power remained important, the United Kingdom in Rhodesia-Zimbabwe, and the South African mandatory power

---

[165] From a broader internationalist perspective, H. Klug sees the South African process as part of a massive trend that culminated "in the collapse of state socialism in 1989." These views are compatible, though I see South African constitution making as itself the culmination. See: *Constituting Democracy. Law, Globalism and South Africa's Political Reconstruction* (Cambridge: Cambridge University Press, 2000), p. 1.

in South West Africa-Namibia.[166] In South Africa itself there has not been such an active colonial power since the early part of the twentieth century.[167] Moreover, the role of other international actors was fundamental for Namibia, played a role in Zimbabwe, but was negligible in South Africa at least at the formal level.[168] Finally, foreign design expertise played a great role in Zimbabwe,[169] a striking, if less important one in Namibia,[170] but almost none in South Africa[171] in spite of the availability of important books by outsiders.[172]

[166] On Namibia see M. Wiechers, "Namibia's Long Walk to Freedom: the Role of Constitution Making in the Creation of an Independent Namibia"; on Zimbabwe, see M. Ndulo, "Zimbabwe's Unfulfilled Struggle for a Legitimate Constitutional Order" both in L. Miller ed. *Framing the State in times of Transition. Case Studies in Constitution Making* (Washington: USIP, 2010). On Zimbabwe, see also J. Mtisi et al. "war in Rhodesia 1965–1980" in B. Raftopoulos and A. Mlambo, *Becoming Zimbabwe* (Harare: Weaver Press, 2009) and J. Macumbe, "Electoral Processes and Procedures in Zimbabwe" in O. Sichone, *The State and Constitutionalism* (Harare: Sapes Books, 1998).

[167] When there was, the constitution of the four South African white colonies had to be formally enacted by the British parliament. Materially, however, these colonies followed a method of constitution making using a special convention that resembled the US American type, and had an equal debt to the Canadian "compact" model of the 1850s and 60s as well as similarities to the Australian process. This is the case even as they negotiated a unitary state of the Westminster type, against all these forerunners as well as the proclivities of the British colonial office. The enactment of the South Africa Act by the House of Commons, as against the Canadian and Australian constitutions, was not without serious problems because of the issue of racial disenfranchisement. See: L.M. Thompson *The Unification of South Africa* (Oxford: Clarendon Press, 1960). This historical precedent, with its intrinsic feature of black exclusion, had at best a negative influence on the developments of the 1990s. This time the actors not only generated a new type of entirely independent, and fully inclusive process, but broke both with the Westminster model, and the unitary state.

[168] In *Constituting Democracy*, pp. 94–95, Klug rightly stresses the difference between the processes of Zimbabwe under colonial and of Namibia under international guidance, but overly assimilates the South African process to the one in Namibia. While the intellectual influence of international trends in South Africa was probably as considerable as he argues, the level of outside participation and involvement was low. Nevertheless, elsewhere he does argue that the ANC wished to avoid any form of external imposition, even an international one, op. cit., 78.

[169] See J. Macumbe, "Electoral Processes and Procedures in Zimbabwe," p. 65, emphasizing design by British government experts.

[170] Wiechers, "Namibia's Long Walk to Freedom," 88–89 on the choice of experts, including himself.

[171] On the signal failure of an attempt to introduce international mediation, see D. Kotze, "The New South African Constitution" in M. Faure and J.-E. Lane, *South Africa: Designing New Political Institutions* (London: Sage, 1996), pp. 46–55. The desire to avoid external involvement went so far as to do without significant foreign participation in the electoral process, with the exception of allowing international monitors to observe the process. See Claire Robertson, "Contesting the Contest. Negotiating the Election Machinery" in S. Friedman and D. Atkinson eds., *The Small Miracle* (Johannesburg: Ravan, 1994).

[172] See A. Lijphart, *Power-Sharing in South Africa* (Berkeley: IIS, 1985); D.L. Horowitz, *A Democratic South Africa?* (Berkeley: University of California Press, 1991).

Thus, whatever the contextual differences, the constitution-making process in South Africa, like the ones in Central Europe was an internal process without outside negotiators, mediators, or even experts allowed to play a significant role.

The South African process of constitution making, especially the first stage of negotiating an interim constitution, took place only slightly later than the round tables of Central and East Europe. It would be foolish to deny that it was part of a historical sequence, especially since the collapse of the Soviet system of states played a major role here as well. Moreover, there were important formal similarities to Central European forerunners. First and most obviously radical transformation occurred through the legal continuity. This was clearly shared with the Spanish and Central European transitions. As in the latter, formal reliance on inherited undemocratic institutions was compensated for by the invention or adoption of the all-important, extra-constitutional institution of negotiating forums, called round tables in East Europe.[173] The South African negotiating venues, Codesa and the MPNF were as inclusive as any of their Central European forerunners. Second, as in Poland and, in terms of the initial intention, Hungary, the process involved two stages and the making of two constitutions. This allowed not only significant learning between the two stages, but also the compromise between strategies insisted on by old regime actors, with the preferred options of radical oppositions. As in these countries as well as Bulgaria, the rules for free elections were negotiated rather than imposed, with elections taking place after the first and before the next stage in constitution making. Third, as in Bulgaria and Poland, the final drafting assembly was explicitly understood as under limitations, therefore as a version of what I call non-, or post sovereign. Finally, similarly to Hungary, but even more explicitly and radically, a strong constitutional court was set up to enforce the interim constitution.

Admittedly, in terms of actor biographies it is more difficult to document any explicit South African learning or borrowing from Europe rather than from African countries. Many ANC members spent time in African countries, and, as the name tells us, the famous Harare declaration of 1989 was published in Zimbabwe. Experts of both the ANC like Arthur Chaskalson, and the NP like Marinus Wiechers played an important advisory role in

---

[173] The term itself was avoided in South Africa, both for the CODESA or the MPNF. That the idea was relevant is also indicated by a very Central European debate about the shape of the table, that here too remained round, rather than the two sided one demanded by some participants like the Inkatha Freedom Party. See: Kotze, "The New South African Constitution," 50–51.

Namibia.[174] There are repeated positive references in the South African literature to the Namibian constitutional principles, considered as anticipations of
the South African device, as well as primarily negative references to the Lan-
caster House process that produced Zimbabwe's first postcolonial constitution.
At the same time, explicit references of South Africans to Central Europe, as
in the death penalty case's citing a prior Hungarian case, were very few.[175] I
believe the understandable reason for this should not distract us. It seems quite
likely that the reference to the dissolution of Communism would have been
embarrassing for the two most important parties. For the ANC it was a matter
of the disastrous performance and decline of many of their erstwhile allies
and supporters. For the NP the problem was different, namely their playing
the role of the party of the old regime, similar to the Communist parties they
hated for both ideological and political reasons.[176] Nevertheless, all actors in
South Africa were acutely conscious of the fact that the collapse of the USSR
and its satellites had a dramatic effect on their situation, even if they did not
wish to see themselves in similar roles as Central Europeans on either side.[177]
Undoubtedly, however, it was easier for both major sides to see themselves in
more usual African roles: as representatives of a new, primarily Black African
majority, or as defenders of a threatened minority, the previously privileged
white part of the population. The example of Namibia was therefore especially
important, since it seemed to show that both of these demographic groupings
could win.[178]

---

[174] The former, Chaskalson, close to the ANC, along with Francois Venter, close to the NP,
was to draw up the South African 34 constitutional principles. R. Meyer, "From Parliamentary Sovereignty to Constitutionality: the Democratization of South Africa 1990–1994" in
P. Andrews and S. Ellman eds., *Post Apartheid Constitutions* (Athens: Ohio University Press,
2001), p. 66.

[175] See Klug *Constituting Democracy*, p. 164. However, I myself had the pleasure at the Central
European University of meeting in 1994 a delegation of SA constitutional justices and their
advisors on a study trip to Hungary and to its already functioning Constitutional Court.

[176] Thus, an important exception to the disregard of Central Europe was Alex Boraine, the
initiator of the truth and reconciliation process, whose party and civil society links tied him
neither to the NP nor the ANC. See *A Country Unmasked*, op. cit.

[177] The ANC lost a very important source of support for its armed struggle, and the NP, the
implicit support of the United States for its resistance to Communism. This is documented by
the ANC National Executive Committee, as the geopolitical source for a negotiated solution.
See "Negotiations: a Strategic Perspective" (Document 28) point 1.3 in H. Ebrahim, *The Soul
of a Nation: Constitution Making in South Africa* (Capetown: Oxford University Press, 1998),
p. 596.

[178] That was not the lesson of the Zimbabwe process, where arrangements produced under
strong UK pressure had a zero-sum quality. First, the settlers won through guaranteed representation absolutely entrenched (ten years), and high-level of property protection. Then the
African population supposedly "won" (actually both lost) when the entrenchment and property

Here too there were formal analogies that could and should be mentioned. There is no question that Namibia had serious and repeated negotiations.[179] There was also an interim constitution enacted in 1978. And the making of the final constitution was by an assembly under limits, even if called a constituent assembly. But these similarities with South Africa hide more important differences. The making of the interim Turnhalle Constitution, negotiated under external, South African tutelage, involved the exclusion of the most important liberation movement, SWAPO. The document was considered illegal and illegitimate by all institutions of the UN and by most countries. It did not play the role of constitutionalizing the rest of the process. Thus if that process was organized and legalized, this was done by UNSC Resolution 435 of 1978, and the constitutional principles negotiated among the countries of an external contact group of five, implicitly linked to that resolution in 1982. That was the first stage of the Namibia process, and it was entirely external in its organization.[180] It was the constitutional principles that helped to organize and limit the constituent assembly, though it should be made clear that they did so only in a very abstract and narrow manner.[181] The eight Namibian principles amounted to nothing like a full interim constitution, whether in Hungary, Poland, or South Africa. Moreover, neither the unrecognized interim constitution nor the constitutional principles had provided for any internal enforcement, which was, in the former case, left in the hands of the South African government, and its Administrator, and in the latter one left without serious and effective enforcement.[182] If South Africans, including the NP experts who participated in the Namibian process, learned anything from it, they learned not merely the form of constitutional principles, but even more that the international level should be "patriated" and that strong domestic enforcement was needed if agreements in negotiations were to be adhered to.[183]

protection could be removed or modified. See M. Ndulo, "Zimbabwe's Unfulfilled Struggle for a Legitimate Constitutional Order"; and Horowitz, *A Democratic South Africa*, pp. 134–136.

[179] In this section I follow Wiechers' reliable summary: "Namibia's Long Walk to Freedom."

[180] D. Kotze, "The New South African Constitution" in *South Africa: Designing New Institutions* (London: Sage, 1996), pp. 37–38.

[181] Principles Concerning the Constituent Assembly and the Constitution of an Independent Namibia (1982) UN Department of Political Affairs http://peacemaker.un.org/ sites/peacemaker.un.org/files/NA_820712_Principles%20ConstituentAssemblyConstitution IndependentNamibia.pdf.

[182] With respect to the principles, the point is made by Ebrahim, *Soul of a Nation*, p. 178.

[183] The fear of external involvement is striking in the ANC's "Negotiations: a Strategic Perspective" 1.2; and, remarkably, the ANC and NP were united in rejecting external mediation called for by Inkatha. C. Ramaphosa, "Negotiating a New Nation: Reflections on the Development of South Africa's Constitution" in *Post Apartheid Constitutions*, p. 81. For a different view of a more important international role see Chris Landsberg "Directing From the

To sum up: if South Africans learned from Namibia's process, this involved both avoiding negative lessons of an exclusionary and partially imposed interim constitution, and even the overly high level of external involvement, as well and improving on the forms of positive ones like the adoption of constitutional principles. The same can be said for learning from Central and East European cases, even if in this case the direct influence on process (as against constitutional provisions) is more difficult to document. Here I will not attempt such a documentation and will focus only on the significant improvements the South African process generated when compared to all its forerunners.

To begin with, the improvements involved do not lead to a classification of the South African transition as a revolution or a reform for that matter, in contrast to the Central European cases of "regime change," or the earlier Spanish *reforma pactada-ruptura pactada*. As for reform, certainly the NP has attempted top down innovation as consistently as the Spanish government. But so did several Central European regimes, before consenting to negotiations. It is true that the use of referendum by President de Klerk in 1992 resembled the top-down initiation of the Spanish transition, which also involved a referendum. But in South Africa this was a whites-only referendum, which only helped to weaken opposition on the government's own side, and did not effect the position and strength of the ANC or its immense popular support. In Spain, the referendum aimed also at the population at large, and its successful result weakened the negotiating position of the democratic opposition. In South Africa, moreover, the transition proper began with the various "talks about talks" between the government and the ANC, prior to the referendum rather than with a top down constitutional initiative.[184] Thus the South African transition had the character of mere reform even less than the Spanish *reforma/ruptura pactada*.

As to revolution, there were indeed revolutionaries in South Africa, and especially the ANC. But, as moderates on both sides of the divide rightly stressed, the advocates of revolution who resisted negotiations were marginalized in the given context, and by the process that was most appropriate for

---

Stalls? The International Community and the South African Negotiating Forum" in *Small Miracle* (Johannesburg: Raven Press, 1994). Yet Landsberg too is forced to conclude after describing a failed mediation or arbitration attempt by Kissinger and Lord Carrington, that international influences (or rather active interventions!) were "supplementary rather than primary." He is right to mention the traditional interest of weaker liberation movements in foreign participation, but as Claire Robertson points out, by the time of CODESA the ANC felt sufficiently strong to do without such support: "Contesting the Contest" in *Small Miracle* 50.

[184] See Ebrahim, op. cit.

transforming it.[185] South Africa's transformation was as strictly within legal continuity as the Spanish, Polish, Hungarian, and Bulgarian constitutional processes.[186] Here too amendment rules of an old regime were used till legally replaced. At the same time the transformation involved was as comprehensive and radical as in Central Europe, even if it did not involve replacement of one type of economy by another. The replacement of the apartheid political order with its links to the Westminster model of parliamentary sovereignty, by a non-racial political order linked to constitutionalism was at least as radical as the establishment of constitutional democracies in Central Europe. Moreover, since apartheid penetrated every social structure and relationship, the social transformation involved in South Africa was as significant as the economic one in the Communist countries. While there were continuities between old and new regimes in both contexts, this, as we know since Tocqueville, is also a characteristic of revolutions. Thus in South Africa too we should be speaking about "regime change" rather than reform or revolution, or at best use the now famous Spanish formula combining these terms. As in Central Europe, but not quite in Spain previously, the main agency that allowed the combination of *reforma* and *rupture* was the new institution of the round table.

The new institution was not called a round table in South Africa, and, more significantly, there were two of them, CODESA (*Convention for a Democratic South Africa*: 1991–1992), and what was unofficially and confusingly called the Multi Party Negotiating Forum or Process (MPNF, MPNP: 1993). Admittedly, two venues are not in themselves an improvement over one. CODESA is commonly said to have failed, because the main parties over-estimated their own strength and under-estimated that of their opponent.[187] Thus, one side, the ANC, held out for a constitution made by a constituent assembly, while the other insisted on a negotiated constitution approved by a referendum, or at the very least a constituent assembly having to decide by a very high 75 percent qualified majority. In spite of this fundamental disagreement, it is also clear, however, that many of the formulas and institutional possibilities generated at the first venue, CODESA, were used and improved upon in the second, the MPNF, and during the informal and formal agreements in between them. Thus, South African political actors learned that failure is not necessarily complete failure, and that it is worthwhile to stick with the

---

[185] See Meyer, op. cit., p. 49 and Ramaposa, op. cit., p. 72.
[186] See "Record of Understanding" in *The Soul of a Nation*, 589.
[187] Friedman, *The Long Journey* (Pretoria: Ravan Press, 1992); D. Atkinson, "Brokering a Miracle? The Multi Party Negotiating Forum" in *The Small Miracle*, p. 13.

negotiating process even when it seems to be completely deadlocked. As the main actors convincingly tell us,[188] failure even at CODESA was not inevitable, and many (if not yet all) formulas that could and should have allowed the process to continue without apparent disruption were already available. With these considerations in mind, there is strong justification to regard CODESA and MPNF as parts of a single stage, and South Africa's process as fundamentally a two-stage process.[189] It is the actors themselves who insist on this structure,[190] and, more importantly, it is they who established it when they agreed on an issue that previously divided them, namely that two constitutions would be made, one before and the other after free elections, in the form of the duality of interim and final document.

The logic of making two constitutions in two great stages was implied by the previous cases, but was never completely conscious and nor was it fully realized before South Africa. The *Ley para la Reforma Politica* did not amount to a full interim constitution, and nor did the results of the Bulgarian Round Table. The failed constitutional product of the GDR *Runder Tisch* never clarified its own interim nature. Only the Hungarian Round Table produced a complete liberal democratic interim constitution, but the actual agreements did not call their product provisional. This status was indicated only by a formulation in the Preamble that emerged from the last undemocratic parliament needed to legalize the results. In South Africa as in Hungary, the democratic forces originally maintained that only a freely elected assembly has the right to produce a new constitution. Thus, at the negotiating forum initially they wanted to generate only a minimal document needed to move to free elections.[191] As in Hungary, this proved impossible, and not only because of the interrelations of all parts of a liberal democratic constitution, and especially the framework of rights with the political process. In South Africa even more than in Hungary, compromise between the two sides, the ANC and the NP required two constitutions because of the very different guarantees desired by both sides, in the one case the requirements of genuinely free elections, and

---

[188] Rolf Meyer, who was willing to compromise around the majority needed to pass a constitution. Op. cit., pp. 54–55.

[189] Rather than a three- or multi-stage one. The latter could be argued on the bases of the important "talks about talks" at several venues before CODESA, and the meetings and agreements between the two main negotiating setting in particular "Peace Accord" of September 1991, and the important "Record of Understanding" of September 1992. See: H. Ebrahim for a history as well as a partial documentation in *The Soul of a Nation*.

[190] See Meyer, op. cit., 57–58; 65; Sachs, "The Politics of Accommodation: Constitution-Making in South Africa" NDI occasional paper # 3, July 1998, p. 18; Klug, "Participating in the Design: Constitution-making in South Africa" in *Post Apartheid Constitutions*, pp. 140–141.

[191] Klug, op. cit., 108; Ramaposa, op. cit., 76; Meyer, op. cit., 52.

in the other the protection of minority interests in a process that will lead to majority rule. This was the origin of the interim constitution.[192]

It is an impressive fact, however, that in the end the adoption of a two-stage or two-phase process was seen by each as the triumph of their own alternatives, by both the NP and the ANC.[193] From the observer's point of view, it is fairly certain that each side initially aimed at two different single-phase processes, and that both underwent a change in perspectives through the very logic of negotiations. They were thus able to modify "their opening gambits" to reach a "mutual second best solution."[194] When this happened both sides came to fully identify with the result. What is also crucial here is that South African actors on both sides, and even those of the minor parties, were able to fully understand and draw out the implications of the model they have adopted.

Below, a comparison with Hungary and Poland (as well as Germany) will be used to demonstrate the importance of South African actors having become fully conscious and self-reflective concerning the two-stage process they had to construct to be able to compromise their differences. As a result, time became a resource that the actors could deal with in an economic way, avoiding both dangerous acceleration and a purely open-ended process. Next, I will use a broader comparison with Czechoslovakia and the German Democratic Republic as well as Hungary and Poland to show that conscious understanding of their action in terms of stages in finite time allowed South Africans to solve the problems of forming a transitional government as well as confidence-building power sharing in a way superior to their forerunners elsewhere.

If there are to be two stages, how can actors make sure that the second stage can and will happen within a reasonable time? And how do they make sure that the two stages are fundamentally connected, yet leave significant room for the autonomy and creativity of the second stage? As to the seriousness of the first of these questions, the case of Hungary shows that a temporary or interim constitution always has the tendency to become quasi-permanent. Once there is a liberal democratic constitution, it becomes a fallback position

---

[192] Formally: Constitution of The Republic of South Africa, Act 200 of 1993. The origin of the idea is disputed, even if it was a necessary consequence of having to compromise two alternatives: a constitution drawn up in negotiations and one enacted by a democratic assembly. See Meyer, op. cit. and Record of Understanding, p. 589 that still fudges the distinction between a (more minimal) "constitutional framework" and a "transitional constitution."

[193] That it was so regarded by the ANC, and especially Ramaposa, see I. Sarakinsky "Rehearsing Joint Rule. The Transitional Executive Council" in *The Small Miracle*, pp. 70; 72–73. For the corresponding view of the NP moderates, see Meyer, op. cit., pp. 56, 58 and 65.

[194] Sarakinsky op.cit. 70. See also Atkinson "Brokering a Miracle?"; D. Kotze, "The New South African Constitution" in *South Africa. Designing New Institutions* (London: Sage, 1996), p. 96, though Kotze is wrong about a Zimbabwean precedent in this context

for many actors some of whom even believe that any possible new constitution is likely to be normatively inferior, or will less correspond to their interests and constitutional ideas than the supposedly interim one. Many actors will thus deny, whatever the interim constitution itself seems to promise, that there is a "compulsion to make a constitution." The absence of constitutional crisis will further validate this conservative perspective, even if staying with an interim constitution that was not created in a democratic process implies serious legitimation problems. We have seen this logic play out in Germany in 1990–1991 the year of unity, with respect to the supposedly provisional *Grundgesetz*, and in Hungary in 1996 to 1997 when the project to make a new constitution failed.

Note, however, that neither the *Grundgesetz* Article 146, nor the Hungarian interim constitution of 1989–1990 contained any rules or procedures for the making of a new constitution. Nor did the constitutional amendments that emerged from the Polish Round Table, thereby opening the way to contradictory projects in the two chambers, one of which, the Sejm, had the legal jurisdiction, while the other, the Senate, democratic legitimacy. Polish constitutional legislation by the first freely elected legislature improved on this state of affairs by producing detailed rules in 1992, implicitly incorporated in the somewhat later interim Little Constitution, but without serious deadlock breaking devices. Thus even the next legislature of 1993–7 managed to enact a permanent constitution only at the very end of its long tenure.

The South African interim constitution represented great improvement over the work of these predecessors. Its negotiators made sure that the first democratically elected legislature would see constitution making as its primary task. Following a French model from the nineteenth century, and similarly to interim Polish constitutional legislation, the joint meeting of the two chambers of parliament, titled "Constitutional Assembly" (in Poland: "National Assembly"), was given the task of constitutional drafting and enactment.[195] A new constitution was supposed to be enacted within two years by a two-thirds absolute majority of the Assembly. (Article 73: 1–2). If this failed, a series of deadlock-breaking mechanisms, initially insisted on by the ANC would be put into effect.[196] The first of these mechanisms involved an appeal by the parliamentary majority to a board of independent experts chosen by two-thirds

---

[195] Interim Constitution: chapter 5, 68 (1–2). A reliable description of the whole framework is in Klug, op. cit., 108–109.

[196] Letter of Mandela to De Klerk in July of 1992 (Document 26) in *The Soul of a Nation*, p. 580. This was agreed upon in the Record of Understanding of September 1992. See op. cit., p. 589, balancing the constitutional principles and interim constitution also agreed upon in that document.

of the assembly or by the larger parties having at least 40 seats. If this board failed to make a unanimous recommendation, or if such recommendation was not approved by two-thirds of the assembly, that latter could pass by a 50 + 1 percent absolute majority a draft to be ratified in a referendum that needed 60% majority of the votes cast (Article 72:2–3; 73:3–8). That was the second deadlock-breaking device, and there was also a third. If the referendum failed, a new constituent assembly had to be elected, that would have been given only year, and could enact a constitution by 60 percent absolute majority (Article 73: 9–11). All the deadlock breaking devices, including a possible referendum, would apply also to the second constitutional assembly. (Article 73:12).

Was this complicated scheme necessary, given that it turned out to be possible to generate a two-thirds majority before any of the deadlock breaking devices kicked in? The logic of the mechanisms was to incentivize high-level consensus, through more majoritarian fallback possibilities. Thus, we cannot know whether the devices were unnecessary or were actually effective in helping to achieve consensus. If the latter, would that mean that the consensus was a sham? In fact, the uncertainties involved in extending the process applied to all sides, and therefore there was a common incentive for all to come to a compromise agreement. Neither of the main parties had an interest in pushing matters to a referendum, thus they needed to compromise on many issues.[197] Moreover, even consensus around a draft did not end the options of determined minorities to resist: they could still appeal to the Constitutional Court. Thus, as Christina Murray cogently argues, the appeal to the Court was in effect yet another deadlock breaking device, perhaps the most important one. Parties could vote for the draft constitution, in the hope that the Court would eliminate or force the alteration of some provisions they objected to.[198] Before the full enactment of the constitution by any of the possible means, the Constitutional Court was required to certify the draft as consistent with the constitutional principles, and the parties and even individuals could formally present their objections (Article 71: 1–4; 73: 6 and, by implication, 12).[199]

---

[197] See Ramaposa, op. cit., 82–83; C. Murray, "Negotiating Beyond Dead-lock: From the Constitutional Assembly to the Court" in *Post-Apartheid Constitutions*, pp. 118–119.

[198] Murray, op. cit., pp. 118–119; Carmel Rickard makes the same important point: "The Certification of the Constitution of South Africa" in *Post Apartheid Constitutions*, p. 229. Here the logic was the same as at the Hungarian Round Table, already mentioned, where parties could accept the agreements, but appeal to the voters in referendum on a few disputed points.

[199] The provision of certification by the Court is not formally mentioned in the case of enactment by a second constitutional assembly, but it is very strongly implied in Article 73:12. The Court also received the right to give a consultative opinion concerning parts of the constitution and their consistency with the principles (71:4).

This allows a return to my second question. The answer to the linkage of the two stages and the two constitutions lay not only the process rules imposed by the first on the second, but also by substantive limitations implied by the constitutional principles, explicitly to be enforced by the Constitutional Court. It is here especially that the status of the Constitutional Assembly in South Africa becomes fully clear. It was not sovereign in at least two senses, having to adhere to both formal and substantive limitations, and having to answer to a higher authority whose decision was final, from which there was no appeal, not even by constitutional amendment, since the relevant parts of the interim constitution were not open to any amendment whatsoever (Articles 71:3 and 74:1(b)ii).[200]

Such a role for constitutional principles and for a Court enforcing them was new and unique in the history of constitution making. A relatively few constitutional principles have been used in Namibia, and before then in France during the making of the 5th Republic,[201] but in both cases without the possibility of enforcement. The 34 South African Constitutional principles involved an entirely new level of detail, as well as opportunity for the Court to enter into the process. Moreover, they also applied to the makers of provincial constitutions whose products needed to be certified by the Constitutional Court (art. 160: 3a and 4). Having judiciable principles binding a democratically elected constitution making body was of course a great concession to the NP by the ANC that initially sought a sovereign constituent assembly without limitations. It is not the case however that the actual principles drafted by A. Chaskalson of the ANC and F. Venter of the NP implied the same kind of concession, since most of them corresponded to long time demands of the ANC itself. Thus most principles were consensual, and many of them implied a direct reversal of arrangements under and leading to apartheid, in particular parliamentary sovereignty exercised by a racially exclusive legislature.[202] If there were previous disagreements having to do with the liberal and democratic principles of the new South African polity, these were now gone. The ANC and the NP no longer represented fundamentally distinct positions on universal

---

[200] The ANC still insisted on a sovereign constitution-making body or Constituent Assembly even when conceding constitutional principles that would limit it. See the letter of Mandela to De Klerk, 579 and 581. This was possible because of different meanings of sovereignty that could be appealed to. However, the role of the Contitutional Court in certification made any claim of sovereignty for parliament very problematic.

[201] In Namibia only nine principles bound the Constituent Assembly; in France there were even fewer, namely 5 principles. See O. Beaud, *La puissance de l'état* (Paris: PUF, 1994), pp. 275–276; See also J. Foyer, "The Drafting of the French Constitution of 1958" in *Constitution Makers on Constitution Making*, pp. 17–18.

[202] See Klug, op. cit., chapter 2.

suffrage, constitutional supremacy, entrenched and judiciable fundamental rights, the separation of powers, the independence of the judiciary, etc.[203] These principles, fundamentally entrenched or otherwise, in any case would not have been vulnerable to the new majority of the Constitutional Assembly that was to be elected.

Such vulnerability did exist regarding the concessions the ANC had to make with respect to the provisions entrenching federalism, or, as South Africans tend to prefer, a relatively high level of regional self-government.[204] While the interest of Inkatha and even the NP played a crucial role in entrenching these principles, they were defensible on democratic grounds.[205] A large and complex country like South Africa, with all its divisions, deserved the federal structure long denied under apartheid.[206] Moreover, the constitutional principles dealing with regional self-government (especially principle XXI[207]) left ample room for the national decision making, and in case of conflict concerning concurrent powers gave precedence to the national government (principle XXIII). The overall arrangement structurally resembled the Canadian federalism enacted in 1867, one that has been called quasi-federalism.[208] It should be recalled that exactly this type of federalism was explicitly rejected by the whites-only Convention of 1908 that created the Union of South Africa, creating a Westminster type unitary state that with the subversion of a limited form of constitutional entrenchment greatly facilitated first the abolition of limited black and colored voting rights (in the former Cape Colony) and then the introduction of *legal* apartheid.[209]

---

[203] For the full list, see Schedule 4 of the Interim Constitution (Constitution Act 200 of 1993); for a discussion see J.J. van Tonder, "The Salient Features of the Interim Constitution" and D. Kotze, "The New South African Constitution" both in *South Africa. Designing New Political Institutions*.

[204] See Kotze, "The New South African Constitution," pp. 40–42.

[205] That cannot be said for the principle (XIII) establishing or preserving indigenous law, under "traditional leadership," though this provision was made a little more palatable, by subordination to the fundamental rights of the Constitution.

[206] Horowitz, op. cit.

[207] For all the 34 principles, see Constitution of the Republic of South Africa, 1993/Schedule 4.

[208] K.C. Wheare, *Federal Government*, 4th ed. (London: Oxford University Press, 1963), pp. 18–20, whose last word on Canadian federalism was "quasi-federal in law . . . federal in practice"; see P. Russell, *Constitutional Odyssey*, 3rd ed. (Toronto: University of Toronto Press, 2004), chapters 3 and 4 for how this hybrid came about.

[209] L.M. Thompson, *The Unification of South Africa*, pp. 97ff; 102; 106–107. On the connection between the rejection of federalism, the subversion of limited entrenchment, and the resulting battle of the nationalist government with the Appeals Division see: I. Loveland, *By Due Process of Law? Racial Discrimination and the Right to Vote in South Africa 1855–1960* (Oxford: Hart, 1999).

Thus not only federalism, but the related issue of entrenchment of the constitution, the establishment of a two-track structure was highly salient in South Africa given the history of apartheid. Here too the constitutional principles marked a great transformation, but without controversy. By the time the agreement was concluded, no one seemed to defend a Westminster-type parliamentary sovereignty. On the question of amendments and entrenchment in the new, final constitution, a constitutional principle established the requirements of "special procedures" and "special majorities." (principle XV). These principles were already active in the interim constitution itself, which came into force on April 27, 1994 with the election of the two chambers of parliament. Amendments of the interim constitution required two-thirds absolute majority of the Constitutional Assembly,[210] or the two chambers meeting together, but excluded both the constitutional principles and their enforcement by the Court (74: 1 and 2) that were not amendable.[211] The same was the case for the power sharing arrangements, but with a time limit, until April 30, 1999 (principle XXXII). These limitations *implicitly* established the power of the Constitutional Court to police amendments, by implication to any part of the interim constitution, which could not derogate from the constitutional principles. More importantly, in relationship to the final constitution, and its adherence to the principles, this form of very powerful jurisdiction was *formally* provided for. This too fundamentally reversed the earlier victory of the apartheid state over the Appellate Division of the Supreme Court.[212] It was now up to the Constitutional Court to decide the level of entrenchment that would satisfy the constitutional principle.[213]

The development, even with its unique South African background, was entirely new in the history of constitutional review.[214] Now not only statutes, or even amendments, but also a whole constitutional draft could be (and as it

---

[210] Although not provided for in the interim constitution, the document was twice amended by the old tricameral parliament even before coming into force, as a result of a last minute deal that allowed Inkatha to participate in the elections. Subsequent amendments to the interim constitution, 8 in all, were by the constitutional assembly.

[211] Theoretically, this meant that parts of the complex constitution making procedures of chapter 5 of the interim constitution could be amended by two-thirds. But this was the same threshold for passing the new constitution, and thus there was no reason for amending the rules by the same two-thirds that could just pass a new constitution instead.

[212] See Loveland, *By Due Process of Law?*; as well as D. Davis and M. le Roux, *Precedent and Possibility. The (Ab)use of Law in South Africa* (Capetown: Double Storey Books, 2009).

[213] Indeed, in the first Certification Decision the Court judged the level provided for, with respect to the Bill of Rights, inadequate and forced its alteration. See Rickard, op. cit.

[214] Of the unprecedented nature of the enterprise, the Court itself was fully aware, and noted it in its first Certification judgment. See Rickard, op. cit., 263–264.

turned out, was) pronounced "unconstitutional."[215] Even with the basic structure doctrine, the Indian Supreme Court established review powers only over amendments, not the making of a new constitution or the use of the original constituent power as it is now often called. Arguably at least, the German Constitutional Court's implicit power to enforce the eternity clauses was limited to amendments under art. 79, rather than the making of a new constitution under art. 146.[216] The powerful Hungarian Constitutional Court after 1989, South Africa's closest forerunner and occasional reference point, even deprived itself of amendment review in a series of decisions, until very recently.[217] Nevertheless, the power of the South African Court to participate in the constituent power followed from the logic of the two-stage process. Linked together by new constitution making procedures and the constitutional principles, both missing in Hungary, the two stages required guarantees and enforcement for this very linkage. Aside from purely political forms of enforcement that would have continually renewed explosive confrontations between the sides, only an independent body like the Constitutional Court could accomplish this task. While the guarantees sought by the NP were at the basis of this mechanism, the ANC also benefited through the higher legitimacy that would be guaranteed for a final document certified by the Constitutional Court. Through this requirement, the ANC leadership was also protected from the radical revolutionary demands of some of its own militants. Indeed, the new role of the Constitutional Court was possible only under the conditions of an emerging alliance of the moderates of both sides. The advantage in legitimacy became fully clear when the Court refused to certify the first draft of the new Constitution, passed by 80 percent of the votes. It was from this moment that the Court was considered an institution for all of South Africa, and its subsequent certification of the second draft helped to lend prestige to the new Constitution.[218]

Did the combination of principles and Court deprive the constitutional assembly not only of its sovereignty, but also of the freedom of action long sought by the ANC? At least ANC moderates see the matter in terms of a middle road involving both guarantees and a freedom of action.[219] What was not included under the principles indicates the correctness of this interpretation. Above all the structure of national government, whether parliamentary or presidential or some combination of the two was left for the constitutional

[215] Murray, op. cit., 105.
[216] Recently, but well after the South African process, the BvG tried to extend this power, in principle, to article 146 as well. See: BVerfG, op. cit.
[217] See my Chapter 4 in *Post Sovereign Constitution Making*.
[218] Rickard, 287–9; Klug, 178–179.   [219] Ebrahim, op. cit., 178.

assembly to decide. While the need for constitutional entrenchment was indicated, its level and type were not. Nor was the jurisdiction of the Constitutional Court defined, aside from the role in the constituent process. Moreover, while the principles were absolutely entrenched for the transitional period, it is not formally stated that they also would bind a future amending power or could be objects for enforcement under the new Constitution. All limitations of the amending power would be up to the Constitutional Assembly to decide anew, if still desired. No property arrangement was entrenched by the constitutional principles, allowing the Constitutional Assembly to re-regulate the property clause. Finally, the structure of government established for the period of transition was not entrenched by principles beyond a relatively short period. The Constitutional Assembly was thus free to legislate that structure in the longer term.

In the last area lies the second major dimension of innovation of the South African constitution makers, the design of the transitional executive power. In South Africa, there were to be two phases of this design, before and immediately after free elections. Under classical revolutionary scenarios these two phases were united, with the elite actor successful in the task of liberation from old regime establishing its own provisional government until the enactment of a new constitution. It is this actor that convokes a constituent assembly, establishes the electoral rules for it, and may be able to exercise executive power for its duration. In South Africa too, revolutionaries in the ANC and outside of it called for a provisional government of this type. But there was no revolutionary taking of power in South Africa, as both sides realized. The problem did not thereby disappear, because, as Lenin already and rightly warned in 1905, an old government controlling the period of constitution making would likely deform the process, and turn it to its own advantage.[220] Nevertheless, as already argued, in Central Europe some democratic oppositions, like those of Hungary and Poland, refused to accept governmental responsibility in the period, thereby depriving themselves of reliable guarantees that the road to elections would be free and fair. The Czechoslovak and East German democratic oppositions chose the opposite course of participation, but as we have seen in the latter case, at least thereby endangering its own legitimacy.

The first phase of the South African process, before free elections, represented an original and viable solution of the dilemma.[221] Already at CODESA, the ANC, abandoning its demand for a classical provisional government, more

---

Lenin "Two Tactics," op. cit. On this, see the Epilogue below.
For the best discussion of this whole problem and its South African solution, see I. Sarakinsky "Rehearsing Joint Rule."

or less agreed that the given government would stay in place till the elections. But it had no interest in designating ministers to serve in that government. While the NP certainly did not wish to cede its dominant governmental position, it did, however, agree at a CODESA working group to set up one or more multi-party councils supervising different aspects of the governmental process, including electoral procedures and the media. There was no agreement yet on the powers of these councils, especially the main co-ordinating one, which was to be the Transitional Executive Council (TEC). But the ANC now was on the verge of having the alternative that most suited it, since it would or could not itself assume (revolutionary) transitional power. It did not have to participate in the old government, yet stood to gain powers that could potentially "level the playing field" on the road to free and fair elections. All that was required was to give the new councils significant powers as well as funding.

To an extent this is what happened at the MPNF. Here contentious issues were more or less ironed out or submerged in ambiguity, including the composition of the TEC, the degree of consensus required by its voting rules, whether its decisions were binding on the government, who controlled states of emergency, whether the mandate of the TEC extended beyond guaranteeing free and fair elections, and if not what that phrase required.[222] According to the best expert, the very real power of the TEC though certainly not without limits, was shaped not as much by the statute that set it up before the interim constitution, as the increasing power of the ANC in society.[223] I would add however that it seems to me that the existence of this institutional device gave the various forces in society outside the government the ability to exert power without always resorting to mass mobilization and even violence.

After free elections, the table turned, and now it was the new minority parties, namely the National Party and Inkatha, that required guarantees against the utilization of incumbent advantage on the level of the executive. The formula of the first phase, implying lack of trust and the need for monitoring and supervision, could no longer be applied to a freely elected government.[224] The answer in this new phase, agreed to during the making of the interim constitution, lay in power sharing, long advocated by some external observers,[225] as well as demanded by the National Party. But to the ANC consociational power sharing maintained an element of the old racial classification and separation, and was understood as undemocratic even by liberal leaders of the

---

[222] Sarakinsky, 80–83.   [223] Ibid., 85–87.
[224] Thus, the TEC went out of business after four months of existence and activity, after the elections of April 1994.
[225] Lijphart, op. cit.

NP itself. The answer to the dilemma lay in sunset clauses first advocated in South Africa by Joe Slovo, a leader of the SACP allied with the ANC.[226] There would be governmental power sharing for five years, in the Government of National Unity, implying the option that parties with 80 seats (or, alternately, the first two parties) were to be guaranteed a deputy president, and, those with at least 20 seats, participation in the cabinet in proportion to their number of seats (Interim Constitution 84:1–2; 88–2). According to a constitutional principle (No. XXXII[227]), this arrangement could not be altered by even a parliamentary super-majority during the tenure of the Constitutional Assembly, though the idea of an option for minorities did mean that they could decline to participate.

It is not my task to evaluate the success and the problems of the successive arrangements to organize transitional executive power. The first phase, dominated by the TEC and related bodies especially the Independent Electoral Commission[228] (but also the Independent Media Commission, and the Independent Broadcasting Authority) and its own sub-councils, certainly managed to get South Africa to free elections, and helped to contain, if not eliminate the violence that this process involved. The second phase, temporary power sharing, probably helped to promote the largely cooperative attitude present at the Constitutional Assembly, at least until de Klerk's resignation after the constitution was drafted, but not yet certified. In neither case can we, of course, forget the personal role of Nelson Mandela in helping to reduce the level of violence, and to promote a spirit of a common enterprise. We also do not know what would have happened if these two safeguards were not used in a country where many actors had the potential to use means of violence. Speaking more abstractly, the institutional devices contributed to the development of the two-stage paradigm in a significant way, by helping to solve the always difficult transition from one governmental form to another by introducing two mediating steps in that process.

That each of these steps represented an advance is shown by admittedly comparisons to a different country in each case. When compared to the East

---

[226] Klug, "Participating in the Design: Constitution-making in South Africa," 140–141; Ramaposa, op. cit., p. 78.

[227] The constitution according to this principle was to provide for this but only till April 1999, the projected date of new elections, but it is unclear which constitution was to do so. The interim could not do so after the coming into force of the new one in 1997. But, the new constitution, did not so provide in its section on the executive, yet apparently this was not challenged under principle XXXII. By then the issue was moot, as the NP immediately after the final vote on the Constitution voluntarily withdrew from the Government of National Unity.

[228] Claire Robertson, "Contesting the Contest. Negotiating the Election Machinery" in *The Small Miracle.*

German co-optation of members of the opposition to a Communist-led government, the use of a transitional council the TEC promised to be, and indeed was
at least as effective in guaranteeing equal political competition, but without
the negative consequences for legitimacy. Indeed it helped in the later respect,
in that the National Party insisted to the end, wrongly in reality, that the TEC
was only consultative, without binding governmental power.[229] With respect
to the second device, namely power sharing, the closest analogy in Central
Europe was the creation in Hungary of a large number of laws that could be
enacted or altered only with a two-thirds majority. This quasi-consociational
device potentially implied just as much participation for minority parties as
power sharing in South Africa. But the restriction in the case of each relevant legal area could be removed only by a constitutional amendment. South
Africa's power sharing device on the contrary would automatically disappear
in five years under the sunset clause. While the transition from consociationalism to constitutionalism is facilitated by the two-stage process, the difficulty
of getting a minority to agree to surrender its guaranteed governmental role
persists even in this model of change. The restrictions are difficult to remove
because of the phenomenon of "freezing." In other words, they require a
consociational agreement to remove consociational safeguards. In the Hungarian case, accomplishing the elimination of a large number of two-thirds
laws required yet another pact of the two major parties, after free elections, out
of sequence, and therefore difficult to legitimate. In South Africa, as opposed
to Hungary, the transition was guaranteed by coupling power sharing with a
sunset provision.

   So far, I have argued that the South African negotiated transition was superior to its forerunners by pointing mainly to the elements of *cognitive* learning
involved. There was, however, also *normative* learning, with respect to two
important desiderata: democratic participation and justice. As to the first, compared to all the Central European cases, public participation in the process
was not only permitted but greatly facilitated by both organizing education
and a media campaign about constitutions and constitutionalism, and the
organization of grass roots inputs into the process. The scope and seriousness
of this effort has been well described by others,[230] and I am not the right
person to evaluate its concrete results, or, more importantly, its consequences
for the legitimacy of the outcome. I have no doubt, however, that even in

---

[229] Sarakinsky, op. cit.
[230] See: Ebrahim, *Soul of a Nation*, chapter 13; H. Klug, "Participating in the Design:
   Constitution-Making in South Africa" in *Post-Apartheid Constitutions*, pp. 141ff and 148ff;
   Murray, "Negotiating Beyond Deadlock," 106ff.

and of themselves, public openness and participation are high values, and it is admirable that these values were seriously pursued in South Africa. This required creative means[231] in a country where the level of education and even literacy were low because of the workings of the apartheid system, and where previous experience with constitutional government was non-existent for most of the population.

What I would like to stress here is the relationship of participation to the logic of the two-stage process. As many opponent of the process charged, the first stage was inevitably elite-driven and involved the participation of leaders and groups who recognized and selected one another. I have no doubt about the representative character of this stage, in South Africa involving about 16 to 21 party and civil society participants, even if a different meaning of representation than the electoral one was involved. While a high level of inclusion, and public visibility (and audibility!) of many of the sessions reduced the legitimation problems involved, from a democratic point of view these could not be entirely eliminated. Had the NP's and Inkatha's plans for the making of a final constitution at the negotiating forum been conceded, even if ratified in a referendum, the democratic origins of the constitution would have remained in grave doubt. Thus, free elections for the assembly producing the final constitution were essential. But these could not help but reproduce the power position of the major parties that negotiated the interim constitution. Not only were they already legitimate representatives of main sections of South African society, but they also further consolidated this status through the successful negotiations. The participatory dimension was thus greatly needed in order that popular strata, groups, interests and forms of life could come to understand the process and the outcome as their common possession with the important parties. Lawyers of a skeptical perspective could surely point out that participation made only a marginal deference in the outcome. I have no doubt this could be demonstrated, and yet the attitude is wrong. The same view was successfully represented in Hungary, where I was one of the very few promoting South African-style participation and public education during the process of 1994–1996. I still believe that the lack of such participation most likely contributed to the failure at that time to enact a liberal democratic final constitution. It is also probably true that the lack of public attachment to the supposedly interim constitution of 1989–1990 contributed to the ability of a new elite in 2011 to replace it by a much more authoritarian variant.

---

[231] I have in mind the travel of members of the Constitutional Assembly to local meetings all over the country, the publication of different forms of popular literature, and the organization of TV programs around the constitutional process.

As to the problem of justice, along with all the democratic transitions from Spain, to Latin America and to Central Europe, South Africa faced a fundamental dilemma, one that was linked to the antinomy of revolution and reform. Historically, revolutions had availed themselves of the option of trying and punishing a potentially wide circle of leaders of old regimes responsible for acts of extreme violence, as well as the perpetrators engaged in such acts. Generally disinterested in legal forms, victorious revolutionary actors have tended to establish political tribunals bound by few rules of procedure or even by the ban against retroactive laws. Reform processes do not involve regime change, and they generally do not revisit crimes of a recent past. If they do, in rule of law states at least existing legality represents a narrow limit to the possible criminal prosecutions. A form of change beyond the antinomy of reform and revolution, seeking to establish the rule of law, the negotiated regime transition, has both strategic as well as, I believe, normative reasons to seek a "third way" here as in other areas.[232] The strategic reasons have to do with the surviving power of the rulers of the past during the transition. The normative reasons are linked to the contractual arrangements made with these rulers, the "solemn promise" (South African Constitutional Court) the actors give to one another that was binding, even when the forces of violence have changed hands. Moreover, even if many violations under old regimes could be prosecuted under inherited law, their sheer number in most places makes such effort unviable or unfair, since only a small number of the guilty – not necessarily the figures most responsible – could be prosecuted. And, yet the obligation to do justice cannot allow the crimes of the past to be unaddressed, and the responsibility of the perpetrators left in the dark.

Fortunately a model for proceeding was available in South Africa, this time originating in Latin America (initially Argentina and Chile) that could be adopted and very much improved: the truth commission.[233] In South Africa it was called Truth and Reconciliation Commission (TRC). Even if, strictly speaking, the interim constitution included reference to amnesty and reconciliation only as an afterthought, in its "postamble," the idea of establishing a unique process followed from the negotiated process itself. The participants were former enemies, who, transformed through the process, became political opponents ready to be joint citizens of a new South Africa.[234] As in the case

---

[232] Paul van Zyl, "Dilemmas of Transitional Justice: the Case of South Africa's Truth and Reconciliation Commission," *Journal of International Affairs* (Spring 1999), 52(2).

[233] R. Teitel, *Transitional Justice* (Oxford: Oxford University Press, 2002) who not only describes this general approach, but makes a strong legal and normative case for it.

[234] A. Boraine, *A Country Unmasked: Inside South Africa's Truth and Reconciliation Commission* (Oxford: Oxford University Press, 2000), pp. 7; 13 and 264.

of constitution making, however, this reconciliation initially took place only between political elites, not within the wider population, and especially not between victims and perpetrators. The postamble, and the National Unity and Reconciliation Act of 1995 which drew out its implications, aimed at just such a wider reconciliation.

Amnesty had to be part of the truth and reconciliation, and it was a promise incorporated in the interim constitution. The reasons were initially strategic. There had to be a promise of amnesty, if the agreements were to be made, and free elections were to be held. And yet the justification became normative as the process successfully concluded. Once part of "the solemn promise," amnesty had to be actually made available.[235] In this context, it was an important innovation in South Africa that under the Act amnesty would be partial, rather than general.[236] More precisely, amnesty would be given for "truth," meaning that those who chose not to participate in the process remained targets of prosecution under laws that already existed in the previous system. Thus, both sides had to surrender something important. The winning side had to renounce most criminal prosecution that the crimes deserved on behalf of the victims. The rulers of the past had to accept that they only had the choice of voluntarily making damaging revelations or remaining open to prosecution. It is true, amnesty allowed them and their servants to escape criminal responsibility. But the cost was accepting political and moral responsibility in front of their country, and even the international public.[237] Unlike the earlier truth commissions in Latin America, the TRC publically presented all its findings, and the name of those it found responsible, directly or politically. Thus, the TRC represented a model of justice, albeit not perfect justice, but the justice attainable under the circumstances. It is another matter, a political one, that the subsequent ANC government only occasionally and inconsistently followed the demand of the TRC, that there should be prosecution of perpetrators who did not avail themselves of the exchange of truth for amnesty.[238]

The South African transition has its staunch critics but the process itself has responded to some of the criticisms. The objection to the negotiated

---

[235] Boraine, *A Country Unmasked*, pp. 363–4 rightly refers to Hannah Arendt's concept of the promise, thereby interpreting the phrase used by the Constitutional Court in the certification judgment.

[236] Ibid., chapter 8.

[237] For a thoughtful article explaining the difference between these forms of responsibility see Antje duBois-Pedain's "Communicating Criminal and Political Responsibility in the TRC Process" in Du Bois and Du Bois Pedan eds., *Justice and Reconciliation in Post Apartheid South Africa* (Cambridge: Cambridge University Press, 2008).

[238] Cf. F. Du Bois in *Justice and Reconciliation in Post Apartheid South Africa*.

character of the first stage, and its partially power-sharing outcome,[239] was dealt with by the second stage based on democratic elections that ended consociationalism and replaced it with constitutionalism. There are, however, still critiques of the second stage, or the process as a whole. It is hard to suppress the impression that many of them continue to lament the absence of revolution, and link it to the survival of many of the inequalities inherited from the past. It is important to notice, however, that the negotiated transition is compared not to actual revolutions and their results, especially but not exclusively in Africa, but to an imaginary one. This type of comparison is behind the many critiques of the truth and reconciliation process as well. Undoubtedly the critics have a point. To use a recent typology introduced by Mahmoud Mamdani, South Africa achieved political justice, at the (partial!) expense of criminal and social justice.[240] As he has previously explained, the TRC focused on crimes under apartheid, rather than the crime of apartheid. It unmasked violent perpetrators, leaving both the creators of the system itself and its white beneficiaries untouched. It compensated a few of the victims of direct violence, and did nothing for the victims of the social system.[241] These points are not without justification. Yet whether Mamdani so intends or not, we are implicitly given the illusion that there could have been a revolution in South Africa that satisfied all these claims of justice. The continuities of all revolutions with the past are disregarded, along with the new forms of injustice they have always tended to generate. Leaving aside a sober assessment of what demands of justice have been satisfied also in the social-economic domain, we should note not only the obvious fact that there was no classical revolution in South Africa. Had it been launched in the 1990s, in very high probability it would have led to disaster whether it failed or even in the highly unlikely case that it succeeded. We know this from the experience of both failed and successful revolutions all over the world. South Africans learned a lot from that experience and this learning took place on both sides of the struggle. Thus, they have provided us with the admirable example of revolutionaries capable of learning from the history of revolutions, an unusual phenomenon in that history. Fortunately, they had positive experiences, in Namibia, Spain, Central Europe as well as Latin America that they could learn from, build

---

[239] See C. Jung and I. Shapiro. "South Africa's Negotiated Transition: Democracy, Opposition, and the New Constitutional Order," *Politics & Society* 23.3 (1995): 269–308.

[240] Lecture, New School for Social Research, October 26, 2015.

[241] See E. Christodoulidis and S. Veitch, "Reconciliation as Surrender: Configurations of Responsibility and Memory" in *Justice and Reconciliation in Post Apartheid South Africa*; and M. Mamdani's "Amnesty or Impunity? A Preliminary Critique of the Report of the Truth and Reconciliation Commission of South Africa (TRC)," *Diacritics* 32, no. 3 (2005): 33–59.

upon, and improve. It is thus that they generated a post-revolutionary model of transformation that should be an important source for future actors engaged in the tasks of democratic constitution making especially in deeply divided societies and polities.[242]

---

[242] See E. Said, *From Oslo to Iraq and the Road Map. Essays* (New York: Vintage, 2004), pp. 48–50; 186–187. What Said grasped is the dimension of black–white alliance and cooperation, but not the negotiated dimension of a two-stage process. The potential model character of the South African transition for Israel/Palestine should in any case be taken very seriously, as the control system over the territory of the old mandate as a whole increasingly resembles apartheid, in spite of some key differences, such as the Palestinian franchise west of the Green Line.

4

The Time of Revolutions

After a period of thirty years dormancy, revolutions have made a dramatic return, this time in the Arab world. Whether the outcome in each setting is a liberal democratic constitution, a new dictatorship, or civil war and the decomposition of states, this state of affairs forces us to return to the problems of the revolutionary constitution. Suspending my normative doubts about revolutionary processes of change, I feel compelled to ask under what condition these can be legitimated and made effective. My thesis is that the new paradigm developed in this book offers some important clues and correctives even in the case of revolutions. In particular, I will stress two dimensions that are relevant: the pluralistic and temporal features of the post-sovereign process.

I will proceed in the following steps. First, I will investigate the criteria according to which we can speak of revolutions today in light of those of the 1990s. If the "revolutions" of East and Central Europe had indeed been revolutions, along with the South African abolition of and replacement of apartheid, it would make no sense to speak of a return. In that case, revolutions would have never left the modern world scene for very long. Thus, I will make yet another attempt to explain and define what I mean by revolutions in both the hermeneutic and logical senses. Second, I will consider and affirm the possibility that revolutions so understood could be *externally* imposed or facilitated phenomena, and I will compare the possible consequences of such an external role in comparison to indigenous revolutions. With the cases of Iraq and Nepal in mind, I will explore the possibility of, and the relevant reasons for, the grafting of the post-sovereign model of constitution making within an initially revolutionary process. Third, I will explore whether the revolutionary sovereign paradigm of constitution making could exist independently of revolutions in my interpretation and definition. I will use the cases of India, Colombia, and Venezuela to affirm this possibility, rooted in both the dominance of the revolutionary imaginary in theories of constitution making, and the interests of particular political actors. In these three cases, I will seek to understand the conditions under which revolutionary constitution making can after all "go right." Fourth, after applying the re-interpreted and re-defined concept of revolution to several recent cases in the Arab world, I will explore the alternative scenarios of change that have emerged there, that have to do both with attempted state restructuring, and constitution making. Thus, using the parallel pairs of examples of Colombia and Venezuela, on the one hand, and Egypt and Tunisia, on the other, I will explore the possibility and the consequences of the presence of the principles of post-sovereign constitution making, if not the entire method within revolutionary forms. Throughout this chapter, I will compare the time dimensions of revolution, reform, and post-revolutionary regime change, to be able to argue that the legitimacy and success of even revolutionary constitution making depends on adopting the form of temporality of the post-sovereign form. It is in this context that the two concepts that I have often used, self-limiting revolution and post-sovereign constitution making, will converge.

1 THE MEANING AND DEFINITION OF REVOLUTION

If all constitutions that have been *made* emerged from a revolutionary process, we would have many more revolutions that historians have managed to keep track of. In that case all the constitutions that were made in the 1990s, a large number indeed would have been the products of revolutions. Undoubtedly, the reader will reply that no one has, or could have, taken this position, but they would be wrong. In a sophisticated and much needed work on the European Union, John Erik Fossum and Augustin Jose Menendez[1] have distinguished revolutionary processes, the only source of made or designed constitutions, from evolutionary constitutionalism as in supposedly a large number of countries beyond the United Kingdom. And they are not alone, since they seem to be following the distinction of Peter Russell between "Lockean" revolutionary and "Burkean" evolutionary constitution making.[2] That clearly Anglophone distinction to my mind would exclude the French Revolution itself (let us call it: "Rousseauian") that is certainly not the point of Fossum and Menendes even if they do not seem to stress – or even note – the crucial distinction between American-type conventions, and French constituent assemblies. Moreover, after making their own binary differentiation, they hardly manage to remain consistent: constitutions

---

[1] J.E. Fossum and A.J. Menendez, *The Constitution's Gift* (Lanham, MD: Rowman & Littlefield, 2011).

[2] P. Russell, *Constitutional Odyssey*, 3rd ed. (Toronto: University of Toronto Press, 2011).

made by treaties, imposed (*octroyé*) constitutions, constitutions produced by reiterated reforms all make an appearance in their work. They try to avoid inconsistency, by suggesting that for non-revolutionary constitutions, "transformative constitutionalization" (constitution revision through formal or informal amendments, from Jellinek's *Verfassungsänderung*[3]) and "simple constitution-alization" (revision through statute, executive or court action, from Jellinek's *Verfassungswandlung*) have played an important role in development. That is certainly true, but the very same forms have played a major role for revolutionary constitutions, as even the reading of Ackerman, on whom they rely, should have made clear.

So let me restate my own position. Constitutions can be, in some places, the result of evolutionary development, and the so-called un-written and non-legal ones were such in the pre-modern world. In modernity, however, they are generally made, by revolutionary assemblies, non-revolutionary conventions, contracts among independent polities, forums of negotiation recently in two- or multiple-stage processes, but also by organs of government whether the executive or the normal legislature in what could be regarded as reform.[4] Of course, constitutions are only partially made or designed, since the role of informal development through various means is as important today, as when Jellinek first thematized this issue in 1906. The relevant distinctions among forms of constitution making, if not all of them, are to be found not only in my work, but already in C. Schmitt's *Verfassungslehre*, those influenced him like E.-W. Böckenförde, as well as the works of Arendt and Ackerman on which the authors rely.[5]

Undoubtedly, the fact that they offer no definition of revolution at all helps Rossum and Menendez vastly inflate the concept. Recently Ackerman, operating with a three- (four-)part distinction between revolutionary, evolutionary, (imposed) and elite negotiated constitutions does offer something along these lines.[6] He distinguishes between revolutionary, evolutionary, and elite-negotiated forms of change, identifying revolutions in terms of the mass mobilization of revolutionary outsiders, their taking of power whether violently

---

3 G. Jellinek, *Verfassungsänderung und Verfassungswandlung* (Berlin: O. Häring, 1906).

4 A. Arato, *Civil Society, Constitution and Legitimacy* (Lanham, MD: Rowman & Littlefield, 2000) last chapter; A. Arato, *Post Sovereign Constitution Making* (Oxford: Oxford University Press, 2016), chapter 3.

5 E.W. Böckenförde in "Die verfassunggebende Gewalt des Volkes" in *Staat, Verfassung, Demokratie* (Frankfurt: Suhrkamp, 1991); H. Arendt, *On Revolution* (New York: Viking, 1965); B. Ackerman, *The Future of the Liberal Revolution* (New Haven: Yale University Press, 1992).

6 MS. 4–5; 13ff. I thank Ackerman for sharing this not yet complete ms. with me, before a long and productive discussion at Yale, during the Spring of 2016. For an early version of these the distinctions, see his article B. Ackerman, "The Rise of World Constitutionalism," *Virginia Law Review* (1997): 771–797.

or peacefully, and the enactment of a new constitution in the name of the people. What he used to call revolutionary reform, but now rechristened as "revolution on the human scale," is a revolution that seeks to change only some spheres of society, thus relying or preserving some inherited institutions.[7] "Elitist constitutionalism," on the contrary, is defined by the absence of popular mobilization, when a power vacuum allows new elites to dominate a regime the transition and the constitution-making process.

I leave aside for now the implicit de-emphasis of a legal orientation in a jurist trying to define revolutions, and note only that Ackerman's new categorization is still too limited. Neither the type of mere elite negotiation nor revolution would adequately characterize the Spanish, Namibian, Polish, Bulgarian, South African, Iraqi, or Nepali constitution making, which, with their two- or multi-stage character, united some of the very dimensions stressed by Ackerman in a single, but extended process, achieving revolutionary-type results through negotiation and (in some of these cases) legal continuity as well as democratic elections. Thus, here too we can notice an inflation of the concept of revolution, which Ackerman seemed to have already been aware of when, in the second volume of *We the People*, he has (rightly) redefined the making of the Federal Constitution as "revolutionary reform," and even flirting with the Madisonian idea that it involved legal secession from The Articles of Confederation – in other words, an international rather than a constitutional law event.[8]

---

[7] A partially analogous distinction between constitutionalist and Bolshevik-type revolutions, is offered by Nader Sohrabi in his highly interesting and important work *Revolutions and Constitutionalism in the Ottoman Empire and Iran* (Cambridge: Cambridge University Press, 2011) I find the idea of the French Revolution as constitutionalist as against the pattern of the Bolshevik revolution (pp. 4–6) unconvincing, even as Sohrabi makes a plausible point about legislative versus executive centered revolutionary transitions. I think Trotsky is more right in seeing the parallel between the French, the Russian and all great revolutions in terms of the logic of dual power whose almost inevitably authoritarian outcome is hostile to constitutionalism and separation of powers. *The Russian Revolution*, trans. by M. Eastman (New York: Simon and Schuster, 1936), chapter 11. A parallel point is made by Hannah Arendt as she compares the logic of permanent revolution with constitutions as the desirable second stage of revolutions. *On Revolution* (New York: Viking, 1962). She has rightly stressed both that all revolutions aim at constituting new regimes, but also that very few (for her only the American Revolution) have succeeded in doing so in the form of constitutionalism. The so-called "constitutional revolutions" in Iran and Turkey no more established constitutionalism than either the French or the Russian that they resembled in many ways, in spite of their self-description that Sohrabi focuses on, even as he documents the authoritarian outcomes. It is moreover wrong to define constitutionalism merely by the existence of a written constitution or even the establishment of a separated legislature.

[8] B. Ackerman, *We the People*, vol. II (Cambridge, MA: Harvard University Press, 1998); A. Buchanan, *Secession* (Boulder, CO: Westview Press, 1991).

Let me therefore again try to outline my own understanding of the concept of revolution.[9] Initially, when mainly concerned with how actors and analysts use the term, I have isolated cognitive-structural, experiential, hermeneutic, and legal dimensions. The first dealt with changes of systems and subsystems, and would understand revolution as the fundamental alteration of the principle of identity or organizational principle of a subsystem or subsystems of society of which the political must be one.[10] In order to distinguish this concept from long-term changes, it was important to add to the sociologist's system analysis the historian's category of event.[11] The second, experiential one, derived from Hannah Arendt and Walter Benjamin, focused on the public experience of the relevant actors, their dramatically contracted or accelerated sense of time, as well as their special rhetorics and discourses. The third, derived from Marx, recorded the role of the revolutionary tradition in the self-interpretation of actors such as Rosa Luxemburg, Lenin and Trotsky who, contrary to the prediction in the 18th Brumaire[12], depicted themselves and their action in terms of categories derived from the French Revolution, such as Jacobinism, Thermidor, and Bonapartism. Many of their successors would do the same in terms of the Russian Revolution. I derived the fourth, the purely legal meaning, from Kelsen according to whom "a revolution . . . occurs whenever the legal order of a community is nullified and replaced by a new order in an illegitimate way, which is in a way not prescribed by the first order itself."[13] The second and third of these concepts relied on hermeneutic methods of interrogating the language of actors from participant's perspectives; while the first and the fourth required the empirical analysis of institutions and laws.

As I noted in my book published in 2000, none of these conceptions are sufficient on their own to establish the undeniable presence of revolution, and at the same time, their overall combination may demand too much from interpreters. They are insufficient on their own because each contains some fundamental difficulty. The structural concept suffers from the absence of

---

[9] For previous attempts: See my chapter2 of *Civil Society, Constitution*; chapter 3 of *Post sovereign*; and http://www.resetdoc.org/story/00000022167.

[10] T. Skocpol rightly distinguishes between social and political revolutions, and indicates that political transformation is always part of even social revolutions that she interprets in terms of the class structure. *States and Modern Revolutions* (Cambridge: Cambridge University Press, 1979), p. 4.

[11] See the forthcoming book of Robin Wagner Pacifici, who has already written great monographs on several events.

[12] See K. Marx, *The 18th Brumaire of Louis Bonaparte* on poetry from the past.

[13] H. Kelsen, *General Theory of Law and State* (Cambridge, MA: Harvard University Press, 1945), p. 117.

being able to establish clear thresholds of alteration. The experience referred to under the second concept may be misleading given the propensity of organized and mobilized people to live in imagined, alternative realities, whether religious or secular. The reference to the tradition of revolution was necessarily missing in America and France, and could be blocked in societies such as Hungary in 1956, where a revolution was against a revolutionary government without being the counter-revolution denounced by the regime in place. Finally, the legal meaning Kelsen developed is unable to distinguish between coups, and palace revolutions involving little structural change, from processes where the magnitude of such a change is obvious.

With that said, the presence of the concept of revolution in four and perhaps more alternative discourses indicates the condition of possibility of the inflation of the concept. Changes will be identified as revolutions or revolutionary according to each of these criteria, with the result that there will be many more revolutions indicated than would be possible with any more rigorous usage. What such more precise usage or definition will consist of is itself open to interpretation. My attempt here will be motivated by the legal and political theoretical interests of this study. This means that emphasis will have to be on the legal and structural rather than phenomenological and hermeneutic perspectives. Following Janos Kis, however, I will expand the legal conception. According to Kis, it was Kelsen's identification of legality and legitimacy, which was responsible for his own form of inflation of the concept of revolution. Thus, if they were differentiated, we would gain a more adequate legal definition of revolution, and the parallel identification of other modes of change, reform, and regime change, as well as Ackerman's revolutionary reform. Revolution would be identified not only by the changing of a regime outside its own rules of change, that remains its necessary, though no longer sufficient condition, but also with the crisis and rupture of legitimacy. Continuity in both domains would yield reform, while a break in legitimacy but continuous legality would allow us to identify the type of transition that occurred in the 1990s in Central Europe and South Africa. Finally, a break in legality in the context of continuous legitimacy, a box left open by Kis, allowed me to identify the American model of constitutional alteration in 1787, at least from the point of view of constitutional law, along with other changes, especially in Latin America, that would later mimic its pattern.[14]

---

[14] As an international law event, as already mentioned, this case could be dealt with as the combination of legal secession and legal re-federation.

As I always suspected,[15] this powerful legal definition, though a vast improvement on Kelsen's, could nevertheless be accused of "legalism." One could easily charge that especially legal continuity in many cases is based on fictions and hides serious legal breaks. Thus, there would have to be more revolutions than the concept would allow. Similarly, the continuity of legitimacy could be depicted as itself hiding legitimation ruptures, thus giving us even more cases of revolutionary change. Once so criticized, the definition would not be a secure guarantee against the inflation of the concept of revolution.

Thus, within the tradition of a two-sided legal-political approach,[16] I would like to add a political definition to the legal, derived again from a classic, Leon Trotsky, and our contemporary, Charles Tilly, who followed him. According to Trotsky, the revolutionary dynamic is based on *dual power* or, more exactly, *dual sovereignty* (*dvoevlastie*).[17] All revolutions thus are said to involve one or more, but generally temporary, extra constitutional doublings of state power. At such moments, the legality and legitimacy of the old state has broken down, even if its forces continue to battle to restore these. This was Trotsky's translation of the Marxist concept of revolutionary struggle, according to which the old rulers are no longer, and the potential new ones are not yet able to rule. Thus understood, the two or more sovereign claimants are seen as classes or their political vanguards, and generally domestic or indigenous actors. Trotsky considered revolutionary double sovereignty, by the very meaning of the concept implying the breakdown of the state monopoly over violence, and therefore fundamentally unstable for both internal and external reasons, a mark of crisis that can culminate in open civil war when the contenders establish their sovereignty limited to territorial parts of the old state. But the revolutionary crisis can and usually does end as in Trotsky's examples of seventeenth-century England, eighteenth-century France, or twentieth-century Russia with the

---

[15]   See my remarks on Schmitt's views in *Civil Society, Constitution*, chapter 3. The objection was directed against Kelsen's concept, which, however, remains a necessary if no longer sufficient component of the new legal definition of Kis that I subsequently followed.

[16]   The *Zweiseitenlehre* of G. Jellinek's *Allgemeine Staatslehre* 3rd ed. (Berlin: Springer, 1920) that was made better known by Max Weber in *Economy and Society* (Berkeley: University of California Press, 1978), vol. I, pp. 311ff. It was rediscovered, probably via Weber, by H.L.A. Hart in *The Concept of Law* (Oxford: Oxford University Press, 1962).

[17]   *The Russian Revolution* pp. 206ff. Many others have used this conception, in a creative manner. Here it will be enough to mention H. Arendt's theory of revolutions in *On Revolution*, pp. 231–233; Also see S. Arjomand's productive application of the concept to the more recent Islamic Revolution in Iran. See *The Turban for the Crown* (Oxford: Oxford University Press, 1988), chapter 7; as well as its implicit use by N. Sohrabi for the 1906 "constitutional revolution" in the same country in *Revolution and Constitutionalism in the Ottoman Empire and Iran*.

complete triumph of one sovereignty over the other that must however take the form of dictatorship,[18] given the necessity to subdue the contending force or forces. Thus, a revolution is successful, when a new force, in Trotsky's view a new class, establishes its sovereignty in the form of dictatorship, and unsuccessful when it is the old force that is capable of re-establishing its rule.[19]

Charles Tilly, though unfortunately less forthright about dictatorship, assumes Trotsky's conception and further generalizes it. Thus, a revolutionary situation exists when one or more collective actors convincingly battle for state sovereignty, and are potentially in the position to defend or conquer it. A revolutionary outcome is achieved when one of the new forces, or several in combination, succeeds or succeed in establishing a new sovereignty.[20] The revolutionary process consists of the strategies, the making of alliances and the mobilized events that make such a transfer of sovereignty possible.[21] A revolutionary outcome is one where a new political regime is established and institutionalized. This view is consistent with Hannah Arendt's very important, though more normative conception,[22] according to which a revolution, having the two moments of liberation and constitution, is completed only when a new institutional framework is established. Admittedly, Arendt left open whether "constitution" as the completion of revolution should be understood in normative terms as the institutionalization of freedom, or merely in terms of the material constitution of a new regime establishing a new form of sovereignty whose legitimacy would be only empirical. Thus, with her help, we get two concepts of revolution, in line with the two concepts of legitimacy used here, an empirical one and another that is normatively legitimate. The latter, of course, depends on the political philosophy we adhere to.

It should be noted that the political conception thus presupposes or partially converges with the legal conception, especially in Trotsky's version insisting on

---

[18] See especially Trotsky's *Terrorism and Communism* (Ann Arbor, MI: University of Michigan Press, 1961).

[19] Admittedly, this was not his only view. See also *The Russian Revolution*, "Preface" p. xvii; where he speaks of the "direct influence of masses" on historical events, and the realm of rulership. To my mind, and to modern scholarship in general, this attempted definition applies to all the great social struggles of history, on the one hand, and mystifies the role of leaderships and elites whose work Trotsky understood particularly well.

[20] *From Mobilization to Revolution* (Reading, MA: Addison Wesley, 1978), pp. 190–196.

[21] Here I disregard Tilly's inclusion of coups (revolutionary situation, not a full revolutionary outcome) and silent revolutions (revolutionary outcome, without revolutionary situation) that is his own attempt at an unfortunate inflation of the concept. Here Theda Skocpol's conception, which restricts revolutions to the great revolutions of Tilly (revolutionary situation cum revolutionary outcome) is much more convincing. See *States and Modern Revolutions*, op. cit.

[22] Arendt, *On Revolution*.

the collapse of the legality and legitimacy of the old state. But it adds another important element to it, namely the open struggle of political forces, some with popular and possibly international support, each of which is capable of controlling forces of violence whether the struggle is particularly violent or not.[23] Thus we can bring together the legal and political definitions, by postulating that *we can speak of revolution when legitimacy is in crisis, legality is ruptured, and there is open struggle of two or (generally) more political forces to establish a new sovereignty, in other words a new foundation for both legality and legitimacy.* Alone, as already stated, the legal definition is incomplete, because continuities of formal legality and legitimacy can hide their implicit collapse or rupture. But so is the political definition, because a struggle of political forces for mastery can occur under the legal conditions of a constitutional regime, even a democracy. Trotsky denied the category of revolutionary dual power to such struggles, but he could do so only by assuming the ruptures of legality and legitimacy as necessary conditions of revolution. Finally, Trotsky rightly emphasized the element of the acceleration of time in revolutions, corresponding to the experience of revolutionary action, even if the time of revolutions can be vastly extended by civil wars that can pre-date, or post-date the transference of sovereignty. The "the forcible over-turn" he speaks of, which often includes the making of the constitution, is indeed "accomplished in a brief time" if civil war can be prevented or pre-empted, or when its attendant military conflict is resolved.[24] To this problem of time, I will repeatedly return.

Establishing a definition in social science can only mean gaining an ideal type that will apply variously to specific historical cases. My definition, having been tailored to the history of the Great Revolutions, the English, American, French, Russian, Mexican, Algerian, Cuban, Chinese and Iranian cases, works well for them, of course, and for processes resembling them, including the recent series in the Arab world. There will be other cases, however, that will fit partially, and I do not begrudge others applying the concept to those where one or another element is missing. What we should recognize, however, is

---

[23] I have not made large-scale violence either a necessary or a sufficient criterion of revolution. Some revolutions can be relatively bloodless or peaceful, whereas some cases of legal transition can involve a lot of violence. Nevertheless, historically the struggle over sovereignty generally does involve not only multiple sides controlling means of violence, in their view legitimately, but also a good deal of actual violence. Conversely, forms of negotiated regime change generally involve one-sided control over the means, and little open violence. The actions of the "popular" side most often involve civil disobedience.

[24] *The Russian Revolution*, p. 207. Postulating a time frame, as Tilly once attempted to do, is however always a mistake.

that adding terms like "legal," "self-limiting" as I have done in the past, or "negotiated," or "peaceful" to revolution, or as now Ackerman does contrasting "on a human scale" with "total," means the introduction of a new concept. What is involved in all these supposed redefinitions is the desire to establish or describe a model of radical change without the dictatorial logic of classical revolutions. That project is admirable, but it is better accomplished in my view by using a term like "regime change" or even the inelegant "coordinated transition" however less attractive than "revolution." This is all the more important, because the revolutions with the adjectives just mentioned historically involved federal pacts (the USA), round table negotiations (Poland, Hungary, and South Africa) or non-sovereign constitutional assemblies (Bulgaria, and again South Africa) in contradistinction to the emphatically preferred model of great revolutions in history, namely the sovereign constituent assembly.

Note, however, that here I wish only to speak of an elective affinity, and indeed did not include a specific constitution-making process in my attempted definition of revolutions. As will be made clear below, I consider revolution and sovereign constituent assembly as separable in spite of the elective affinity. Contrary to Hannah Arendt's making the link to constitution almost definitional for revolution, in distinction to rebellions that involve only acts of liberation, by my definition, derived here from Trotsky, a revolution that establishes a new sovereignty may not establish a new *formal* constitution. In the material sense, too, many revolutionary regimes, with or without façade constitutions, may imply permanent revolutions, or a permanent emergency regimes or dictatorships. While most revolutions will call a constituent assembly, many of these should not be described as sovereign or even constitutional. As it obviously turned out in the Russian case, sovereign dictatorship was not exercised by the brief, elected and immediately dissolved constituent assembly, but by the Bolshevik provisional government.[25] In this work I will not focus on the "permanent" revolutionary regimes emerging from some revolutions, despite their great historical importance.

I am, however, very interested in two types of cases violating the elective affinity just insisted on, revolutions that have utilized alternative democratic forms of constitution making, and conversely, cases where a sovereign constituent assembly emerges from an arguably legal and I believe non-revolutionary process. It is to these two types of cases that I will turn, before discussing another set where the link between revolution and sovereign constituent assembly was re-established.

---

[25] See Epilogue below.

2 REVOLUTIONS WITH POST-SOVEREIGN CONSTITUENT PROCESS: IRAQ AND NEPAL

There is no question that Iraq and Nepal have formally adopted the two-stage, post-sovereign method of constitution making. This should not lead us therefore to tautologically deny their political transformation the character of revolutions. If that categorization should be contested, it would be better to do so on the bases of the role of external actors in both, and a supposed legal continuity in the case of Nepal. I believe however, that an external role or even agency need not violate either the definition of revolution offered here, or the predominant historical meaning and references of the term. Moreover, I also believe that the argument for legal continuity in Nepal is ultimately unconvincing. I will first make these two arguments, before turning to the cases individually.

In almost every revolution there is an external role, and indeed in her influential book Theda Skocpol has insisted on a causal role for this factor.[26] All depends on the kind and degree of intervention. In terms of my definition, what is significant is that there be a deep crisis or collapse of the old legitimacy, a legal break, and a contest over sovereignty leading to a new sovereign actor replacing the old. Getting the support, and assistance, of a foreign power, or international actors to achieve this goal, whether that support takes the form of diplomatic pressure, sanctions, military assistance or even intervention all belong to the possible strategies within a revolutionary process. Of course, such an intervention can go so far as the replace an indigenous form of sovereignty by a foreign one, that of an occupying power. In such a case, of which Japan after World War II supplies a good example, the constituent process itself can be expropriated by the occupying power, under the thinnest veneer of the legality of a constitutional reform. Yet even the presence of occupying forces need not mean the establishment of a foreign sovereignty. There were American and British troops in Italy (and France) during most of its post-World War II constituent process of 1946–47,[27] yet the Italian and French constitutions were the work of indigenous political forces that in the main emerged from the resistance.[28]

At issue in terms of my definition is, first, whether there was an internal contestation over sovereignty, before the external intervention, and, second, whether an indigenous force or forces were established as the new sovereign.

---

[26] Theda Skocpol following Otto Hintze, in *States and Social Revolutions*.
[27] The constituent assembly was elected in June of 1946, the Peace treaty with the allies was signed on in February of 1947, and the constitution was enacted in December of 1947.
[28] These cases will be discussed in Ackerman's forthcoming book on world constitutionalism

One mark of the former is the internal political military struggle, while the mark of the latter is the autonomy of constitution making. The marginal German case shows the importance of both. Here there was no such internal struggle, the new actors after the war were said to have been in "internal" or external exile during the Third Reich, and interestingly they rejected the demand of the allied commanders to organize a constituent assembly, produce a constitution and ratify it in a referendum as in France and Italy.[29] Hence the names *Grundgesetz* for the document and *Parlamentarische Rat* for an assembly that was, in effect, an American-type convention, based on the *Laender* governments. To my knowledge, no one ever referred to the making of the Federal Republic as a revolution.

There is also the matter of the degree, the manner, and area of interference by outside powers. In Japan admittedly the constitution-making process produced an entirely new regime. Yet American intervention in this process was extremely high, direct, and dealt with the whole constitution even as the American framers were strongly influenced by Japanese drafts and proposals.[30] In Germany it was low, indirect, and dealt with the federal structure of the state that impinged on the external interests of Germany's neighbors.[31] In France and Italy, external influence was limited to the composition of governments after the making of the constitution. Of course, the cultural influence of American texts, institutions, and disputes played a role in all these countries, but to my knowledge at least American constitutional experts made no attempt to influence any of these projects, except, of course, the one in Japan where they could influence the American framers directly.

From this partial integration of the external factor[32] it follows that if the processes of the creation of the French and Italian new regimes in 1946 qualify

---

[29] P. Merkl, *The Origin of the West German Republic* (Oxford: Oxford University Press, 1963). The formal reason of the governments of the *Länder*, plausibly enough, was the occupation and the division of the country, but it seems also likely that they did not yet trust the population to ratify a liberal democratic constitution. This is repeatedly described by authors as the fear of the people, by the makers of the *Grundgesetz*. See e.g. Christoph Möllers, "We Are (Afraid of) the People: Constituent Power in German Constitutionalism" in M. Loughlin and N. Walker, *The Paradox of Constitutionalism* (Oxford: Oxford University Press, 2007).

[30] Koseki Shoichi *The Birth of Japan's Post War Constitution* (Boulder, CO: Westview Press, 1997).

[31] Merkl, op. cit.

[32] I could have, of course, included the post-World War II East and Central European cases in the examination of the external role. I chose not to, because the identity of the outcomes as constitutions in other than the narrow formal sense remained in doubt, and because the question of to whom the sovereignty was transferred remained in doubt as well, the choice being the external power or its local agents. Only if the latter were the case, as eventually in Romania, do these processes qualify as revolutions. The revolutionary ideology of the new

as revolutions, and they do, so does the Iraqi "externally imposed revolution."[33] It is true that this "revolution" would not have happened at least at that time had it not been for the external invasion and occupation, but the same is true for the Italian and French processes. The internal Iraqi contest for sovereignty, taking into account the Shi'ite revolts of 1991, and the existence of a de facto Kurdish-controlled territory since that time, was as significant as the existence and struggles of the French and Italian resistance movements. In Iraq moreover the legal break involved was more explicit than in Italy and France. In the former, it was the monarch in place through the whole dictatorship who legally dismissed Mussolini, and formally authorized a liberation government, and it was his son who, following the abdication, ordained the referendum on the monarchy and the election of the constituent assembly. In France, the liberation government at least offered the possible restoration of the 3rd Republic to the electorate in referendum, an offer that, had it not been refused, would have partially hidden the legal rupture involved. In Iraq, no established power played any role, and the break with the past was in no way hidden. It is on this point that Nepal represents a boundary case of revolution.

There is no question that also in Nepal external actors, particularly India but also the USA, the UN, the EU, and even China, played a role, if without any direct military intervention. After 2002 some but not all of these powers (the UN, and the EU, but not India or the USA[34]) denounced the king's assumption of direct powers with the dismissal of parliament and under an emergency regime. When this move took on the character of a self-coup in 2005, leading to a situation of open dictatorship, all the powers resolutely turned against it, and even threatened sanctions. Thus, external actors contributed greatly to the collapse of legitimacy of the royal dictatorship.[35] India went so far as to sponsor the making of the key initial agreement in November 2005 between the seven main parliamentary parties and the insurgents of the CPN (Maoist), and remained its monitoring and guaranteeing actor.[36] Subsequently, many of the same governments and international agencies repeatedly offered suggestions concerning the resolution of military and constitutional conflicts, and the

Communist regimes is however without any doubt, and so is the process of revolutionary type justice they have instituted. At the same time, the Chinese, North Korean (result of Soviet occupation), Vietnamese, and Cuban revolutions, all supported externally to one degree or another, fully qualify as revolutions as defined here.

[33] See my *Constitution Making under Occupation* (New York: Columbia University Press, 2009).
[34] ICG Nepal: Obstacles to Peace ICG Asia Report No. 57, June 17, 2003, p. 4.
[35] "Nepal's Royal Coup: Making a Bad Situation Worse," ICG Asia Report No. 91,February 9, 2005, p. 11ff.
[36] A. Adhikari, *The Bullet and the Ballot Box: The Story of Nepal's Maoist Revolution* (London: Verso, 2014).

UNSC established a key intermediary agency, the UN Mission in Nepal (UNMIN), to facilitate the peace-making process and the integration of the Maoist militia in the Nepali Army. It is with the help of UNMIN, and especially Ian Martin, its director, that a 21-point Comprehensive Peace Accord was negotiated on November 22, 2006. The issues that most concerned the external actors had to do with state making, initially involving only the re-establishment of peace and a monopoly of violence in a country torn apart by civil war. But external NGOs like the International Crisis Group,[37] as well as several embassies, played important roles in "democracy promotion" and thus in the active the transmission of new constitutional ideas to Nepal.[38] The shape the constitution-making process took would have been unthinkable without such forms of soft intervention.

Nepal's status as a national revolution is certainly not threatened by the level or kind of external interventions that played a role. From 1996 onward, the struggle for sovereignty took the form of a violent Maoist insurgency and a civil war, one that was renewed in 2001. It became a three-way struggle with the emergence after 2002 of a vast movement mobilized by the parties of the dissolved parliament that in the end forced the king in 2006 to yield to their demand to "restore" that body.[39] It was especially the last movement, the so-called Jana Andolan II, more than the insurgency, which on the domestic level produced the collapse of legitimacy, anticipating, complementing, and indeed probably causing the international delegitimation.[40]

---

[37] See e.g. ICG "Towards a Lasting Peace in Nepal: The Constitutional Issues," Asia Report No. 99 – June 15, 2005.

[38] In the case of the Crisis Group this took the form of excellent reports, full with historical examples and advice for the Nepali actors. I will rely on many of these reports in my evaluation of the Nepali case. Nevertheless, I myself participated in making recommendations, before, during and after my September 2–9, 2006 visit to Katmandu, where I had a chance to talk to civil society activists, lawyers, diplomats of the US Embassy including a very gracious Ambassador Moriarty, and politicians of all parties except the Maoists. I was to meet and have a really interesting discussion with PM Prachanda, Chairman of the CPN (Maoist) in New York. http://lists.csbs.utah.edu/pipermail/marxism/2008-September/180189.html.

 In all these discussions I stressed the importance of party agreements, interim constitution and democratic second-stage process, as I now see in full agreement with the proposals of the Crisis Group.

[39] See Adhikari, *The Bullet and the Ballot Box*.

[40] I emphasized this fact in two public sessions with PM Prachanda in 2008, and PM Bhattarai in 2011, both in New York. At that time, admittedly, I insisted that that Nepal's transition was not a revolution but a peaceful, negotiated regime change. This was not incorrect in terms of the method of constitution making that evolved, but was not right in relation to the act of liberation that preceded it, that satisfied the characteristics of a revolutionary break as outlined here. For the two discussions: with Prachanda 2008, https://vimeo.com/1843688. With Bhattarai 2011, https://www.youtube.com/watch?v=OYw32a7gMkU.

At issue, however, is the question of legality. In the previous chapter, discussing the regime change in Czechoslovakia, recognizing the existence of great popular mobilization and the replacement of one sovereignty by another, I nevertheless insisted on that country representing a post-revolutionary form of change. I did so because of the presence of the important element of legal continuity that was to have serious consequences for the outcome. Thus, I depicted Czechoslovakia as a marginal case of post-revolutionary regime change, closer to revolution than all the other cases from Spain to South Africa. Perhaps surprisingly, Nepal's process partially resembled that of Czechoslovakia, with huge mobilized population sectors,[41] with the quick collapse of the old government under challenge, and, most interestingly, with the use of the device of parliament packing to establish a workable and relegitimated transitional legislature. Nevertheless, Nepal differed from Czechoslovakia in two essential respects which may initially appear inconsistent with one another. While there were genuine and repeated negotiations here, between the Maoists and the parliamentary parties, extrication from the dictatorship occurred through popular pressure and ultimatums, rather than negotiations with the king's government. In Czechoslovakia, while the legitimacy of the last Communist government became increasingly weak, it was nevertheless necessary to negotiate with it the precise mode of extrication that involved mainly the construction of a new government. As we have seen, in Czechoslovakia no constitution emerged from the Round Table, and this was to have very negative consequences for the survival of the state.

In Nepal, too, secondly, the survival or reconstruction of the state was a serious challenge. In contrast to Czechoslovakia, here the transition process involved the negotiation, again among new forces, of an interim constitution. How this combination of forced extrication and interim constitution was possible in Nepal, I will consider in detail below. What I wish to stress is that Nepal, in contrast to Czechoslovakia, was a country involving genuine legal breaks with the Constitution of 1990. The first of these breaks was arguably, if not definitively, the use of emergency government and Article 127 of the 1990 constitution by the then Prime Minister Deuba and the king to displace in 2002 parliamentary, responsible government by a discretionary one.[42] The dissolution and the imposition of an emergency by executive fiat were arguably legal, but the election of a new parliament in six months would have been

---

[41] *The Bullet and the Ballot Box*, chapter 8: "Uprising."

[42] Constitution of the Kingdom of Nepal VS 2047 (1990). Article 127 Power to Remove Difficulties: If any difficulty arises in connection with the implementation of this Constitution, His Majesty may issue necessary Orders to remove such difficulty and such Orders shall be laid before Parliament.

also required. This did not take place and executive government, established under an extremely vague Article 127 of the 1990 Constitution, followed.[43] Admittedly, it could be the case – as was argued at the time – that only a "legal revolution" took place, similar to the questionable use of this very concept at the end of the Weimar Republic. Unfortunately, the highest courts of Nepal, which were packed with royal appointees, sustained such a use of Article 127.[44] However, no one could or ever did sustain the king's self-coup in February 2005, when Article 127 as well as Article 115 (1) on states of emergency were interpreted as rules entirely outside of constitutional limits.[45] That it was a coup, politically, is indicated by the arrest of party leaders, as well as the suspension of many fundamental rights of the Constitution.

It is in this historical context that the illegality of the so-called restoration of the 1999 parliament, by the eight parties, under the impact of the popular movement, must be considered.[46] Elected in May 1999, the five-year terms of deputies were in any case over by May 2004.[47] Moreover, parliament was dissolved by the king, and this dissolution, however questionable, was upheld in Court. The deputies elected in 1999 thus had no public law status. They were moreover recalled not in an advisory capacity, like the parties to a round table, but to make sovereign decisions directly. Thus Nepal missed the double structure, what I call "double differentiation," of the first stage of most of the countries of radical transformation through legal continuity, formed by the old parliament legally in place and a new institution, the round table controlling its agenda and decisions. While the old parliamentary parties, especially the Nepali Congress, demanded the *restoration* of parliament as an alternative to the round table demanded, surprisingly enough, by the Maoists, in the given context this was merely a choice between two revolutionary alternatives, based on two different types of revolutionary assembly with potentially very different composition. It was the first, the restorationist option that was followed,

---

43 See Whelpton's reliable and interesting discussion in *A History of Nepal* (Cambridge: Cambridge University Press, 2005), pp. 219–221. I have relied on this history on several points. Unfortunately it stops with 2004, before the crucial beginning of the transition.

44 Even the very permissive wording of the article requires that the king's orders "be laid before Parliament". If there is no parliament this provision cannot be satisfied. SEE: International Crisis Group [ICG] "Nepal's Royal Coup: Making a Bad Situation Worse," Asia Report No. 91 – February 9, 2005, fn. 8.

45 This interpretation is even less plausible in the case of Article 115 (1) requiring parliamentary endorsement. On the double illegality involved, see ICG, "Towards a Lasting Peace in Nepal: The Constitutional Issues" Asia Report No. 99 – 15 June 2005 pp. 7–8.

46 For a less skeptical treatment than mine, see ICG, "Towards a Lasting Peace in Nepal: The Constitutional Issues" Asia Report No. 99 – 15 June 2005, a report that tries to be even handed among the various party proposals.

47 Constitution of the Kingdom of Nepal VS 2047 (1990) Article 45 (3).

eventually made more palatable to the Maoists by the eventual packing of the restored parliament with their militants. That act was even more important in Nepal than in Czechoslovakia, where new OF deputies were to play the analogous role, and it represented, in effect, a compromise between the restorationist and revolutionary demands. This compromise was unstable, exclusionary and led to serious difficulties – an important matter to which I will return.

I am not arguing that the formal façade of political, if not exactly legal continuity in Nepal was unimportant. It may have played a role in decelerating revolutionary time, and allowing the legitimate binding of the constituent assembly, thus the grafting of a post-revolutionary constitution-making process into what was legally a revolution. But I would also maintain that the revolutionary status of the transition, here as in Iraq, was to transform the post-sovereign process adopted in very important ways. I will consider how this was so by a separate treatment of the two very different countries, with their different relations to the external factor.

Iraq

I need not retell here the history of the Iraqi constitution-making process.[48] Given the unlikely combination of revolution and post-sovereign form, I wish to discuss and address primarily two questions. First, how was it possible in Iraq for a revolutionary process to be complemented by this version of a constitution-making project? And, second, what were the consequences of the grafting, for the revolution, and, equally importantly, for the future, for our understanding of constitution making.

I have documented elsewhere the basic empirical claim made here that Iraq, in spite of a revolutionary rupture of legality and legitimacy, wound up, at least formally, with a post-sovereign constitution-making scenario close to my ideal type derived from Central Europe and South Africa.[49] Here it will be sufficient to list the main characteristics that justify this claim, as well as the deviations involved from the ideal type. The key element that I stress is the production of an interim constitution, the TAL, in 2004, and the organization of the rest of

---

[48] See *Constitution Making Under Occupation*. Most likely, and admirably enough given what I said about the US role therein, it was because of my authorship of several articles later included in that volume, and my insistence on the importance of a South African-type process, that the State Department sponsored me a Democracy lecturer first in Nepal, and later in Zimbabwe. In between I refused to go to Thailand and was refused eventually by US embassies in Sri Lanka, Malagasy Republic and Swaziland. Given my views, I try to stay clear of imposed processes. In Zimbabwe in 2009 I still had the hope of contributing to a pluralistic, consensual process. http://harare.usembassy.gov/andrew_arato.html.

[49] Ibid., chapter 2 and throughout.

the constituent process under it. This was part of a two-stage process involving free elections in 2005, and the convening of a constituent assembly, which remained under the rules of procedure and ratification of the TAL, and hence was not a classical sovereign body. In the end, a new constitution was ratified by referenda, in 2005, with Iraq joining Poland as only the second country completing the process in this manner. In South Africa, a referendum would have been required if the necessary qualified majority had not been attained.

The deviations from the ideal type of the post-sovereign process were nevertheless important. Following the American destruction of its government, Iraq had no longer any kind of inherited legislature as even Japan did in 1945. The attempt of the Coalition Provisional Authority (CPA) to construct one by co-option failed decisively and embarrassingly. The constituent assembly elected in 2005 was therefore the first post-Saddam parliament in Iraq, and the interim executive before then was not under any legislative supervision.[50] Even more importantly, the negotiations that produced the TAL were seriously weak on the inclusion of important internal forces (excluding both Sunni nationalists, and the most radical Shi'ite movements) and too strong on the inclusion of foreign experts who did most of the drafting. As I have shown, the real negotiations that occurred were mostly between the US occupation agency CPA and the Kurdistan Regional government, with very definite and, I think, negative consequences for the transition that was to follow.[51] Next, after direct elections took place under rules unfavorable to producing any Sunni presence in parliament, there was, on American insistence, an attempt to engineer such participation by co-option, in the form of open and arbitrary packing of the key parliamentary committee that could not have sufficient legitimacy or political effect by that particular time. Finally, and very unusually, the Iraqi constitutional assembly was not asked or allowed to vote on the constitutional draft before it was submitted to the referenda, as required by the TAL.

The deviations were serious, but not sufficient to fully reclassify the process as externally imposed, as in the case of Japanese constitution making. Above all, its origins indicate much more Iraqi political autonomy. As in all places where the two-stage process emerged, it was the product and synthesis of two earlier projects. One of these was indeed a project of top-down American imposition. Impressed by MacArthur's actions in Japan, CPA chief Paul Bremer did initially plan a US-made constitution. Not having an Iraqi legislature to enact it, he and his advisors cooked up the idea of passing their own product

---

[50] The legal supervision was also negligible, with the Supreme Court of the TAL constituted playing no role.

[51] *Constitution Making Under Occupation.*

in a referendum, the typically Bonapartist device of military rulers. As I repeatedly described it,[52] this project was met head-on by the Grand Ayatollah Sistani's several fatwas, who, in the style of Thomas Paine as well as earlier Iranian and Iraqi precedents, demanded that the new constitution be produced by a freely elected constituent assembly. In the end the classic compromise of two constitutions, made in two different procedures, emerged. Of course, this did not simply happen as a spontaneous synthesis. UN missions, led first by Sergio Di Mello and later by Lakhdar Brahimi, included a great deal of expertise regarding recent efforts at constitution making, ranging from Europe to Africa and Afghanistan. Their role on the outcome was significant, even if not ultimately decisive. They could influence the type of process adopted, and could help diminish Shi'ite opposition to it, but they could not eliminate the elements of distortion caused by the American occupation, and also the arbitrary spirit of the CPA. Thus, in spite of their efforts, the making of the TAL was characterized by weak representation, exclusionary negotiations, and indeed ultimately under the sign of American imposition. Yet a model did emerge and it was a compromise one. While the Ayatollah Sistani never accepted the compromise, because of the absence of an electoral legitimation of the provisional executive, it was grudgingly recognized by the two main Shi'ite groups in the Interim Governing Council that had formally enacted the TAL.

If the problem of exclusion and the external role were the main defects in the making of the interim constitution, the main problem in drawing up the final constitution had to do with time and sequence. The attempt to introduce significant Sunni representation would have been possible during the first stage of the process, when all the members of the IGC owed their role through co-option. After free elections, however, additional representation based on American choice was very difficult to legitimate. By this time the explicit American role in the negotiations was greatly reduced, and rightly so. Still, one aspect survived, namely the insistence on the speed of the process because of the political needs of the US government to produce relatively quick results. Under these conditions, Sunni participation was interpreted as an unnecessary roadblock, as was the genuine participation of the Constituent Assembly itself. To make sure that Sunni provinces would nevertheless vote for the draft, in referenda initially tailored to enable Kurdish vetoes if necessary, concessions were offered to one Sunni Party, the Iraqi Islamic Party (a branch of the Muslim Brotherhood), that were supposed to be enacted *after* the constitution was ratified. That bargain was never honored, however. The new constitution

[52] Ibid; as well as earlier in *Constellations*.

was thus born with legitimation problems it has never overcome.[53] In my view, these problems were to make a significant contribution to the subsequent chaos, and renewed civil war in Iraq, all the way down to significant Sunni support for Al Qaida in Iraq, and its morphing into ISIS, an organization that was capable of holding Iraqi territory.

The question relevant to this chapter is whether the grafting of the post-sovereign process to a revolutionary break in Iraq inevitably had to fail. My answer is no, it was not inevitable. But first, I should note the radicality of the Iraqi externally imposed revolution, which involved not only the replacement of one regime by another, but the destruction of the inherited Iraqi state. Revolutions most of the time destroy regimes, but allow the preservation or at least the rapid rebuilding of sovereign statehood. An externally imposed revolution unfortunately had the ability to go further on the bases of a military occupation that helped destroy the state, and had the ability to inhibit its rapid reconstruction as well. Already, during the beginning of the US-led intervention, the Iraqi state no longer controlled a significant part of its internationally recognized territory, the Kurdistan region. Given the relatively small size of the occupation forces, with the destruction of a large part of the Iraqi army, and the subsequent dissolution of the rest by Ambassador Paul Bremer, the ability to control much of the rest of the territory was lost, with decentralized militias and tribal associations stepping into the breach. Many members of the IGC controlled their own militia such as the Badr organization in the case of the Supreme Council of the Islamic Revolution (SCIRI). The answer to these fundamental problems was state reconstruction, which under the circumstances could only take the form of a new, federal Iraq. But what form would this federalism take, who was to create it, and when? The TAL expressed that aspiration in terms of a double structure of geographic provinces, and possible ethnic regions modeled on Kurdistan, with a complex delineation of the powers of the center, provinces, and regions. Such an arrangement could only be based on the agreement – or at least consent – of all the supposed partners to a future federation, and the exclusionary form of the negotiations took made that impossible. The TAL, as it turns out the relatively fairer arrangement of the two constitutions, was rejected by Sunni actors because of its imposed character, and because of their exclusion from the process. The final constitution, tilted more in the direction of Shi'ite interests, was even less

53 See two books: Zaid al Ali (*The Struggle for Iraq's Future: How Corruption, Incompetence and Sectarianism Have Undermined Democracy* (New Haven: Yale University Press, 2014) and H. Hamoudi (*Negotiating in Civil Conflict: Constitutional Construction and Imperfect Bargaining in Iraq* (Chicago: University of Chicago Press, 2013)) as well as my review in *ICON* (214) vol. 12.

acceptable, especially since in that process Sunni inclusion turned out to be a sham.

The radicality of the revolution certainly made any constituent process afterwards more difficult. But the two-stage sovereign process had greater promise in this regard, than a pure American imposition, or for that matter a revolutionary imposition by the Shi'ite majority in a sovereign process would have had. Ideally, the structure of the state could and should have been agreed upon during the first stage by all the relevant political forces, under international supervision. Thus, speaking abstractly, the choice of constitution-making methods was promising, but it should have been practiced more consistently with its normative as well as structural assumptions: international rather than merely American monitoring, pluralistic inclusion, fair deliberation and keeping to both the proper sequence and the extended time implied by the logic of a two-stage process. The case, therefore, and its failure were not a test of the constitution-making method under revolutionary circumstances, but only of a version deformed by an external agent that unfortunately had the power an influence both to exclude relevant participants, and to overly accelerate the time frame of the process.

Nepal

After a revolutionary break, brought on by a vast movement of civil disobedience that for the moment absorbed the Maoist insurrection, Nepal's main political actors embarked on a process of two- or multi-stage, post-sovereign constitution making. The main marks of this process were the negotiation of an interim constitution in November 2006,[54] its full enactment in January 2007, the negotiation of a comprehensive peace agreement (CPA) on November 21,[55] the election of a non-sovereign constitutional ("constituent") assembly,[56] and the enactment of a constitution by the second such assembly in 2015. By restoring the legislature elected in 1999 and dissolved in 2002, under the title "legislature-parliament," Nepal, whose process was largely indigenous, came closer to the ideal type of post-sovereign constitution making than Iraq, whose

---

[54] Decisions of the Summit Meeting of the Seven-Party Alliance and the Communist Party of Nepal (Maoist), November 8, 2006. The bulk of the draft was produced by an Interim Constitution Drafting Committee formed in June 2006, working on the bases of the 1990 Constitution. All controversial issues, including the adding of additional members to parliament, had to be politically negotiated by the eight parties. The Interim Constitution of Nepal (as amended) (Nepal: UNDP, 2007), p. 8.

[55] Text of Comprehensive Peace Agreement (CPA) http://www.usip.org/sites/default/files/file/resources/collections/peace_agreements/nepal_cpa_20061121_en.pdf.

[56] Interim Constitution of Nepal part 7; Article 59.

own revolutionary break made the creation of a transitional parliament impossible. It is true that, like Iraq, Nepal, in spite of a relevant Maoist demand, did not have a formal round table. But a series of ad hoc negotiations between the seven parliamentary parties and the Maoists played the same role, first for launching the combined campaign from below, and then negotiating the interim constitution that was subsequently approved by the restored parliament, before it was expanded by new, mostly Maoist members under that new constitution. Thus Nepal had, at least informally, the double differentiated structure of constitution making in its first stage, characteristic of the round table countries, with a legislature playing the central role, at least formally.

Nevertheless, the revolutionary context was to seriously affect the ideal-typical elegance of the Nepali process. First, the interim constitution had to be significantly amended at least three times before even the election of the constituent assembly, first under the pressure of newly mobilized, mainly Madhesi movements from the Tarai, to include a federal redefinition of the state (1st Amendment) and then under Maoist pressure to declare a republic conditioned on ratification by the constituent assembly (3rd Amendment). The interim legislature-parliament was repeatedly obstructed during this process. It is fair to assume that the dignity of the all-important interim constitution was devalued by these controversial efforts.[57] Second, the first constituent assembly was a signal and disappointing failure that failed to produce a constitution, in spite of two extensions of its terms, both of them legally questionable.

As in the case of Iraq, the following questions are important in the Nepali context. How was it possible to graft a post-sovereign process into a revolutionary dynamic, and in a country where there was no external power imposing such a procedural framework, as was done arguably even in Iraq? And, second, did the revolutionary context play a major and possibly unavoidable role in the difficulties of making the graft viable?

In Nepal, as elsewhere, the post-sovereign two-stage framework was adopted as both a strategic compromise between actors with alternative plans of change, and a legitimate democratic framework in light of recent historical precedents insisted on by international actors. As was repeatedly detailed by the Crisis Group, one of the main international actors,[58] there were at least three plans

---

[57] I have repeatedly argued for the importance of the interim constitution in the Nepali press, on three grounds: the protection of the country from transitional dictatorship; the subjection of the process of transition to constitutionalism; and the enabling of learning processes. It could be argued that the amendments in question were the result of learning, but the damage to constitutionalism was also significant. See especially my article in *Nepal News*, September 29, 2007.

[58] ICG papers, op. cit.

to deal with Nepal's political and constitutional crisis produced by the insurrection, and even more the massive non-violent popular movement. The king and his government were willing to form a government based on the seven old parliamentary parties, and to entertain some amendments of the 1990 Constitution. This was a purely reformist option under the existing formal system, and it was offered in the King's first proclamation of April 21, 2006, gaining the support of most foreign powers. The seven parties that did not accept this version held out for the revolutionary restoration of the parliament elected in 1999. Though some of these parties, especially the Nepali Congress, were inclined to accept the reformist strategy of amendments, under the 12-point agreement with the Maoists during the previous year they were committed to electing a constituent assembly. The Maoists themselves rejected the recall of the old parliament, and proposed a classical revolutionary formula of a provisional government and a constituent assembly that was to create an entirely new constitution. With a concession to the spirit of the times, however, or because they could not hope to alone dominate the process, they also advocated a round table of all the parties to set up the provisional government and the procedures of election.

Note that between the reformist proposal of the king, and the revolutionary one of the Maoists, the proposal of the SPA (the seven-party alliance) represented not only a compromise, but also the two-stage solution close already to the post-sovereign model. Instead of choosing between parliament and constituent assembly, between top-down amendments and new constitution, this proposal chose both of the options. This resembled the resolution of similar conflicts in the round table countries, albeit without the institution of the round table itself. It is important to also note that neither the seven parties nor the Maoist proposals violated their earlier agreement, since the 12 Points contained both restored parliament and round table as possible solutions that still had to be negotiated. That negotiation never took place, or reached a conclusion. Actually, it was the king's second declaration of April 24, 2006 that tipped the scale toward the version preferred by the seven parties, the project of restoration that had to seem at the time as more compatible with the preservation of a constitutional or at least ceremonial monarchy. After expressing their disappointment, the Maoists accepted the formula, implicitly conceding that it was mainly the popular movement led by the parties that was for the moment in command.[59] That movement could not be disappointed without grave future consequences for the Maoists themselves. While undoubtedly what they initially had in mind was a vague desire for an

[59] Adhikari, op. cit.

all-powerful sovereign constituent assembly, their acceptance of the transitional formula implied, whether they initially noticed or not, that many of the key decisions would be taken before free elections, and the constituent assembly would be limited by prior rules. When they did notice, however, they began to pay a lot of attention to the interim constitution, a device that never had a role previously in Leftist folklore.

Nevertheless, the restoration parliament of 1999 was composed of members of the seven parties, principally from the centrist Congress and the reformist UML (United Marxists Leninists) and did seem to exclude the Maoists from the new, transitional structure. Given that there was no new institution like the round table representing the new constellation of forces, the Maoist demand to include by co-optation their own members in the "legislature-parliament" was impossible to resist. Thus, the transitional formula had to include this feature, variants of which we have already seen in Czechoslovakia and Iraq. Unfortunately, however, under the pressure of the Maoists and the earlier agreement, primarily that party was given seats in the restored legislature, diminishing but not eliminating its exclusionary character that was to be challenged by new actors. Moreover, the interim constitution, which included not only the restoration of government responsible to parliament, as against the presidentialist preference of the Maoists, but other issues insisted on by the latter regarding the future structure of the state (more inclusive, more sensitive to ethnic aspirations) and especially the electoral machinery. The latter became more proportional than the previous FPTP rules, but not sufficiently proportional to allow new parties to enter in sufficient force and numbers. While on the whole, initially at least, a spirit of compromise seemed to rule over the first stage of the process, it could be still interpreted as an exclusionary one. Had the round table formula of the Maoists been adopted instead of parliamentary restoration, a more inclusive model of participation could have been generated. This choice was to have decisive and negative consequences.

My second question had to do with the effects of the revolutionary context on the viability of the post-sovereign constitution-making method. The process certainly turned out to be a troubled one. As in Iraq, and elsewhere, the difficulties were multiplied by the confluence of tasks of state reconstruction and regime design. Moreover, both of these tasks were made much more difficult by the return of Nepali normal politics within the constitution-making process. Here, a partial failure of institutional design rather than the revolutionary context deserves to take at least part of the blame.

Undoubtedly, revolutionary context did create problems for the transition model. In a revolution, whether violent (as in the Maoist insurrection) or peaceful (as in the vast mobilization promoted by the seven parties), the actors have little doubt about their legitimacy. Yet the revolutionary dynamic regularly includes the challenge of older revolutionary actors by new ones that emerged through – rather than before – the process. This tendency creates great problems for the central legitimation principle of the first stage of the post-sovereign paradigm, namely inclusion. To the actors accomplishing the task of liberation, in this case two sets of actors, their own inclusion in the process seems fully sufficient and fully legitimate. The seven parties could claim to be legitimate representatives of the Nepali people through elections, and the vote of middle strata, the Maoists through the liberation struggle and the support of many of the poor and the excluded. It is in this spirit that the Delhi 12-point agreement, the CPA, and the agreement regarding the Interim Constitution were made. Contrary to many of the participants of the round tables, the actors in Nepal initially did not perceive a problem of legitimation.

They were wrong. The struggles they launched, both the insurgency and the peaceful mobilization, brought new strata and new leaders into politics. Especially the Maoist stress on the discrimination against and political exclusion of many of Nepal's subaltern ethnic and cast groups had a powerful effect. Once the Maoists made their deals with the old parties, these groups, initially the Madhesi from the Tarai, felt betrayed. For them even the Maoist's largely upper-caste leadership could not claim genuine representative status. New parties and groups were formed, and they believed they were not yet represented in the agreements made by the old parties. This was the origin of the famous Madhes Andolan (Madhes Movement), a grassroots movement that emerged exactly at the time of the enactment of the interim constitution. The new groups wished to be included in the renegotiation of the document and were willing to undertake active civil disobedience, including parliamentary obstruction, to achieve their goals. On the level of constitutional contents, they demanded a much more explicit recognition of the future federal form of the state, preferably with units based on ethnicity, an electoral rule favoring small parties, and a parliamentary composition that would guarantee them seats as the Maoists were granted at that very moment.

There is no question that the Madhes Andolan, whatever its substantive justification, disrupted the attempt to regulate the process of new regime creation under a constitutionalist umbrella, the main virtue of an interim constitution. Fortunately, in this case, another virtue of the interim constitution supplied the corrective, its in-built learning mechanism. After negotiations with the representatives of the newly mobilized, the government of the eight parties agreed to amend the interim constitution. In the first amendment, the state was explicitly defined as federal. The electoral law was also modified by adding more proportional seats and also reserved seats for minorities. Unfortunately, the nature of that federalism – the number of states, their boundaries, their powers, their naming, etc. – was left for the future, as a function of the outcome of elections for the constituent assembly. It perhaps would have been easier to negotiate a structure still under the veil of ignorance, possibly with international mediation,[60] but the traditional parties may have, mistakenly, hoped for a huge victory in the elections that would have allowed them to limit the concessions to federalism, especially to one ethnically motivated and defined.

The best time to fully negotiate a deal was also missed with respect another important matter regarding the structure of the state, this time having to do not with the organization of the territory, but the nature of its military force. At the time of the beginning of negotiations, there were two armed forces, the Royal Nepal Army and the Maoist militia. As important as the November 21, 2006 CPA (comprehensive peace agreement) was, it amounted to only a temporary disengagement and restriction of forces, and not their eventual demobilization or integration. As in the case of the geographical structure of the state, it was left ultimately to the Constituent Assembly to sort out this matter as well, which was extremely hazardous given the violence of the previous civil war, and the memories associated with it. Thus, the Constituent Assembly was supposed to be not only the agent designing the new regime, but also the creator of a new state structure. Yet the design of this body, and the outcome of the elections for it, were to make it particularly difficult to reach agreement around both questions having to do with state structure.

At issue is what I called here "double differentiation," meaning the institutional separation of legislative and constitution-making assemblies. Such differentiation was absent in the classical form of the constituent assembly pioneered during the French Revolution. Its classical paradigm was based on the American institution of the (federal) convention, and it has been successfully practiced mostly in states forming federations, whose local assemblies could retain all legislative tasks during constitution making. The making of the US Federal Constitution was the model, and it was successfully followed in a few places like Australia, post-World War II Germany, and arguably (if not formally) under the so-called compact model Canada. Double differentiation was used during the making of the old Union of South Africa, though there

---

[60] India's interest in this matter turned out to be very serious, as we recently found out. But in general, the territorial structure of states concerns all neighboring countries, as well as the international community. See my "International Role in State-Making in Ukraine: The Promise of a Two-Stage Constituent Process," *German Law Journal* 16 (2015).

the result was a unitary state made up of earlier autonomous entities. As we have seen in Chapter 2, double differentiation was long considered attractive in France, but entered into only rarely used amendment rules. Similarly, in Latin America, in many important cases, what began as double differentiation culminated in the constituent chamber asserting its dominance and sovereignty. This even happened in Russia, in 1992, where double differentiation turned into a form of dual power characteristic of revolutions, in that case a top-down version. Finally, the model almost never worked in unitary states, unless they were already parts of federations, like Massachusetts and New Hampshire originally, and other American states throughout their constitutional history.

Obviously, Nepal was a unitary state at the time of the election of the Constituent Assembly, whose members were elected on the bases of nationally delineated districts and electoral lists. Moreover, its sitting parliament was a recalled as well as partially co-opted body that could not match the legitimacy of a freely and newly elected constituent assembly. Thus, as in Iraq, the constituent assembly was to be also the legislative assembly, designated by the Nepali interim constitution as having the functions of the unicameral "legislative-parliament" previously exercised by the restored-coopted assembly (*Interim Constitution*: art. 45 and 59; art 63). Obviously in this setting classical American-type double differentiation was impracticable. But there were other options that I would like to refer to as "partial" or "incomplete" double differentiation, and these could have accomplished the purpose of separating two tracks of politics from one another, and, above all, protecting constitution making from the tensions and narrow deals of ordinary political conflicts and alliances. Several such options were known to Nepali experts and their contacts from abroad. The first, the South African (and Polish) option, based on French precedents from the beginning of the Third Republic, involved the election of a two-chamber parliament, who would meet together as a constitutional or national assembly. The two (or rather three) bodies would meet separately and concentrated on entirely different issues. Neither was sovereign in the sense of being unlimited, or having the plenitude of all powers. Both remained under the jurisdiction of the Constitutional Court, although in different ways and according to different rules. Only the constitutional assembly and its committees and subcommittees concerned themselves with constitutional drafting and debate. Although obviously known, this particular option became closed to Nepali constitution makers when the decision for a single-chamber parliament was made on Maoist insistence, expressing traditional Communist antagonism to checks and balances that dated back to Marx (*Civil Wars in France*) and realized in all Soviet-type constitutions. In Nepal, however, the establishment of a second chamber ran into other difficulties. Assuming a federal reconstruction of the state, there would have to be a federal upper chamber. But as there was no attempt yet to establish the number or the territory of these units, no election could be based upon the federal principle. The old method, which for the constitution of 1990 still involved a significant number of royal appointees, was no longer acceptable (Constitution of 1990, Art. 46).

Thus, only a second option was available, the even more well-known Indian solution.[61] According to this model, once the three-chamber model of the defunct British Cabinet Mission plan became irrelevant due to the departure of the Muslim deputies whose districts became parts of Pakistan, the Indian Constituent Assembly was reunited as a single chamber with equal membership. That body, according to its own decision, then began to meet as a constituent assembly under one set of procedural rules, and as a legislative parliament under another, different set. How well this worked for legislation it is hard to decide, but certainly the assembly as a constituent one completed its work, after vigorous debates, in a timely fashion, with an impressive, if hardly perfect constitution. Undoubtedly, domination of both assemblies by one party, Congress, helped to generate this outcome, although that one party had many internal divisions that had to be and indeed were successfully negotiated.[62]

The Nepali makers of the interim constitution made no provision to follow the Indian example, and partially differentiate the constituent and legislative tasks of the new assembly. Indeed, they simply enacted that the Constituent Assembly would practice all the functions of the interim legislature-parliament (Articles 45–4, 59, 83). Once assembled, the Constituent Assembly itself still had one more option left to separate the tasks of constitution making and ordinary politics, namely the establishment of a strong, relatively independent constitutional committee allowed to produce a draft on its own before presenting it to the assembly as a whole. The members of such a committee could have been selected according to their relevant expertise. The thematic subcommittees, that were indeed established, demonstrated that it was possible to forge relatively consensual outcomes even regarding disputed questions;

---

[61] I recommended it in my September article, op. cit. See section on India below, in this chapter.

[62] G. Austin, *The Indian Constitution* (Delhi: Oxford University Press, 1999). Pakistan's constituent assembly too was dominated at that time by one party, the Muslim League, and there the results were distinctly inferior both in terms of the time taken, the constitutional outcome and its weak legitimacy. Did the lack of differentiation of two assemblies within one play a role? See Christophe Jaffrelot, ed., *A History of Pakistan and its Origins* (London: Anthem Press, 2004).

to make the relevant forms of compromise, and even vote if necessary.[63] But no expert parliamentary committee with sufficient autonomy was ever established. Thus, the relatively non-political subcommittees could either present their work to the highly politicized assembly as a whole, where all solutions ran into violent and obstructionist opposition, or to (two) committees composed of top party leaders who were publically committed to incompatible options. As to the first option, the highly divisive and obstructed debates in the assembly at large showed from the beginning that no consensus, absolute or even relative, would emerge through that route. As to the second, the example of Iraq shows the difficulties involved.[64] There an expert-based, relatively strong Constitutional Committee (as expanded by Sunni participants: Constitutional Commission) was established and was well in the process of producing a viable, and relatively consensual, draft. When, however, because of the American enforced acceleration of time, the negotiations were moved from the Constitutional Commission, and transferred to the top political leaders of the dominant parliamentary parties, "the Kitchen" that again proceeded to exclude Sunni representation, the chances of a compromise draft collapsed. In Iraq, too, the nature of federalism was at issue, and the top political leaders publically committed to rigid positions on this question were not able to deviate from their party lines. In Nepal, where there was no expert constitutional committee, where the differences on the question of federalism were as sharp and even more complex than in Iraq, and where party leaders had to face external, identity based mobilizations, the top party leaders were even more confined, at least until repeated failures taught them important lessons.

As we now see after the second Constituent Assembly, agreement or at least compromise on many of the divisive issues like federalism, (presidential or parliamentary) structure of government, electoral rule (first past the post or proportional representation or their combination) was possible. This was also indicated by the early, nearly unanimous first Constituent Assembly vote definitively abolishing the monarchy and establishing a republic. During that earlier time, however, such agreements were not possible on deeply contested issues, except on the level of subcommittees, because the highly divisive party politics of the 1990s returned in the Constituent Assembly. These conflicts immediately penetrated and deformed the process of constitution making.

---

[63] According to members, cited by A. Snellinger: "The Production of Possibility through an Impossible Ideal Consensus as a Political Value in Nepal's Constituent Assembly" *Constellations* (June 2015) 22(2): 233–245. It was in these subcommittees that the members could feel and act as citizens of Nepal with a particular expertise, rather than merely representatives of parties.

[64] See my reconstruction in *Constitution Making Under Occupation*, pp. 220ff; 226ff.

The antagonism among the parties was greatly exacerbated by the results of the 2008 elections for the Constituent Assembly. Contrary to all expectations, and with the help of the FPTP component of the electoral rule they themselves opposed, the CPN (Maoists) gained a distinct plurality in the number of votes (29 percent), and an even greater one in the number of seats (38 percent). Along with two other parties, the UML and the new Madhesi Jana Adhikar Forum, the Maoists were able to form a government with their leader Prachanda as prime minister. Even together, these parties were short of a constitution-making two-thirds majority. Moreover, the constitutional ideas of the Maoists and the UML greatly differed. Thus, the need to produce relatively consensual solutions was built into the parliamentary arithmetic.[65] Even if there were moments when a two-thirds majority could have been cobbled together to push through a constitution, these were not productively utilized. Even Prachanda was to later describe foregoing decision by voting a serious mistake. Yet anything less than a solution supported by all the main actors was continually exposed to violent protests both within and outside of parliament.[66] Even relatively consensual solutions were difficult to attain as the parties engaged in extreme and even violent confrontations.

The main issue that parties fought over was not even the constitution, but the state structure in its most basic dimension of control over forces of violence, an issue that was unfortunately never resolved before the meeting of the constituent assembly. The festering problem confirms the theory, supported by Iraqi experience, that a constitution can be successfully made only where the state structure is previously agreed upon and resolved. At a time when the other main parties, and the Maoists themselves, were not yet entirely clear about that party's commitment in the longer term the liberal, competitive democracy, the possession of an armed force by the former insurgents presented a problem that the party's actions in power managed to exacerbate.[67] While the charge

---

[65] Unfortunately, in her fine article on the Constituent Assembly, Amanda Snellinger fails to distinguish between relative and absolute consensus, and follows many Nepali actors in thinking that consensus mentioned in the Interim Constitution and in political discourse must mean the latter. In fact, the two-thirds majority rule already imposes relative consensus on the actors, at least in the context of a genuinely multi-party parliament. There is no reason to assume that the Interim Constitution aimed at a higher-level support. A. Snellinger, "The Production of Possibility."

[66] Snellinger, "The Production of Possibility," 233ff. Snellinger describes the constraints, but tries to derive the need for consensus from Nepali traditions, rather than the parliamentary arithmetic and the constitution-making rule.

[67] Adhikari's sympathetic treatment lists the following points: Partial purge and packing of the bureaucracy; partial attempted purge of the judiciary; maintaining their military apparatus or integrating them into the armed forces on fully equal terms (pp. 211–213). One could also the refusal to elect the leader of Congress, Koirala as president, and the premature move

that they were trying to organize a type of takeover characteristic of Eastern Europe in the 1940s was less than fully plausible, it was impossible to fully overcome as long as the question of the Maoist militia was not fully dealt with one way or another.

According to the Comprehensive Peace Accord of 2006, mediated by the UN, the Maoist armed forces (of about 18, 000 combatants) were to be confined in seven main and several sub "cantons," with their arms securely locked up, under UNMIN supervision. The UNMIN was to similarly supervise the confinement to barracks of the Royal Nepal Army (80–90,000 soldiers), and the enclosure of an equal number of their armaments. The two sides agreed not to carry out any acts of aggression whatsoever against each other, and to forego any recruiting of new combatants.[68] What was omitted, however, was any formula of either disarming the Maoist militia or integrating it into a reconstructed army. It is not my task to enumerate or judge the violations of these agreements, though there were indeed many violations on both sides. To counter them, one side, led by Congress party leaders, the Nepal Army command itself, as well as Indian actors behind the scenes, sought to definitively disarm and disband at least most of the Maoist forces. The other side, the Maoists in government, tried to integrate the largest possible number of their fighters in the Nepal Army on "an equal basis," and to establish full civilian control over its command. Neither side succeeded until the "Seven Point Agreement" of November 2011, which showed that a genuine compromise between the positions would have been possible all along. But by that time, the first Maoist government fell in 2008 over this issue, when PM Prachanda was unsuccessful in replacing the Commander in Chief of the Nepal Army. Subsequently, the Constituent Assembly found it very hard to generate stable coalition governments given the relative weakness of the other major parties and the fragmentation of much of the assembly. The Maoists made things even more difficult, by temporarily turning from parliamentary politics to radical forms of extra-parliamentary protest, as well as the obstruction of the Assembly.[69] That failed, but only when the Maoist-led coalition returned to power under a new PM, in

---

against the command of the army. These two acts were later recognized by Prachanda himself as among his party's two main mistakes. A. Snellinger, "The Production of Possibility," 242, note 2.

[68] Comprehensive Peace Accord November 22, 2006 http://www.constitutionnet.org/files/comprehensive_peace_accord_between_gon_and_the_cpn-m.pdf; Adhikari, 227–8 who attributes the change not to parliamentary success, but to a reconciliation of the Maoists with the Nepali Army, based on their joint opposition to prosecutions for earlier human rights violations.

[69] Adhikari, 213–218; 223.

August 2011 were negotiations successful concerning the military issue. By that time, however, the May 2010 deadline of the Constituent Assembly's allotted time has passed.

A fundamental feature of the post sovereign two-stage process is legal continuity. Even after a legal break as in Nepal, it was important to maintain the legality of the rest of the process. Facing the problem of a deadline, the Constituent Assembly proceeded to violate the interim constitution, which allowed only a one-time extension for six months, under a state of emergency. There was no state of emergency in May 2010, and the assembly extended its own tenure for a year rather than only six months. This was then followed by another year's extension, something that even more clearly illegal.[70] The time gained was mostly used for government formation, however, and the admittedly important negotiation of the agreement over military matters. When the latter was accomplished in November 2011, about six months were left to focus on all the rest, because in the same month Nepal's Supreme Court finally ruled that no further extensions of the tenure of the Constituent Assembly could be legal under the interim constitution. Nepal was headed for parliamentary dissolution and new elections.[71]

It was not unprecedented that, after a legal break, it would take two constituent assemblies to produce a new constitution. France, for example, went through a similar process in 1946. In Nepal, as in France, the electoral arithmetic changed significantly in the two elections. The Maoists, having just experienced a split with their own fundamentalists, and who were widely, if not entirely fairly blamed for the failure of the first Constituent Assembly now suffered a significant defeat (18 percent of the votes; 13 percent of the seats) and the two older parties, Congress and UML, winning the bulk of individual races, made significant gains (32.6, 29 percent of the seats respectively). A government led by Congress was formed, and after initial protests that failed the Maoists agreed with the two other major parties to create a new High Level Political Committee (HLPC) integrating the tasks of constitution making that would be now concentrated on.[72] This was predictably followed by a new parliamentary obstruction by the other parties, who were finally included in a

---

[70] Ibid., 237; See also D. Williams, "Nepali Constitution-Making After the Revolution," *Constellations* (June 2015) 22(2), 250.

[71] The motives of PM Bhattarai in moving to new elections have been questioned, even though this was clearly the legal alternative. It may be that he imagined that his party would do well, or even better, under the circumstances. I had a chance to explain to both Prachanda (2008) and Bhattarai (2011) in public meetings that this expectation was most likely illusory. See https://vimeo.com/1843688; and https://www.youtube.com/watch?v=OYw32a7gMkU.

[72] "Major Parties Agree to Form HLPC," *Republica*, March 25, 2014.

new version of the same plan of integration.[73] Equally predictably, the HLPC could not agree on a federal formula, and the main parties were deeply divided on whether or not a constitution including a solution should be approved by the Constituent Assembly according to a two-thirds-majority vote, or only a consensus of all the parties (meaning at least 10, and possibly 30). There were 6, 7, 8, 11 and 14 state or province models floated around already from the first Constituent Assembly onward, and it was also disputed whether the provinces should or should not have ethnic names, and even (at least originally) special rights for the majority ethnicity. All the formulas involved clashes not only among the parties, between Kathmandu and the peripheries, but also among the imagined regions or provinces themselves. When finally, after the devastating earthquake of April 2015, the main parties (Congress, UML, and the Maoists) realized that only voting, i.e., relative consensus can produce a constitution, and indeed came up with a plan around which they at least could agree,[74] they were widely accused of elitism not only in Nepal but even more vehemently by the Indian Press that took the side of the small Madhes and Tauru ethnic parties, supposedly discriminated against in the plan.[75] Note that four parties representing 90 percent of the seats in the Constituent Assembly originally adopted this plan![76] In the assembly itself, it was enacted by a vote of 507 to 25, in other words by 84 percent of the members, even counting abstentions and boycotts as negative. It is hard to find another constitution that had greater support in a constituent assembly.

Yet it did not seem to work, with the battle moving on to violent extra-parliamentary mobilization in the Tarai.[77] Given intense and illegal Indian participation in the form of a devastating transportation boycott, it is very possible that new negotiations and another compromise would follow, using the amendment rule of the new constitution. The situation currently resembles the open-ended constituent process in Iraq, after the enactment of the

---

[73] "Nepal Parliament Resumes Following All-party Deal," *Hindu*, June 11, 2014.

[74] "1st Draft of Nepal Constitution to be Presented in Parliament," *Economic Times*, June 29, 2015. "Fast Track to Nowhere," *The Kathmandu Post*, July 16, 2015.

[75] "It's Time to Drop the Arrogance," *Hindustan Times*, August 25, 2015.

[76] It did not help matters, however, that the same four parties first agreed on an eight-province scheme in a 16-point agreement, then went on to a six-province version, before adding a seventh one prompting the withdrawal of the smallest participant, one of the Madhes parties from the deal. Nor was it a good idea to leave the exact territorial demarcation and names of the provinces for later determination, a procedure that was deemed unconstitutional by the Supreme Court that had no way of enforcing such a decision. While the solution clearly opened the way to further violent confrontations, so would have any definite territorial demarcation and naming. http://www.satp.org/satporgtp/countries/nepal/document/papers/16-point_Agreement.htm

[77] "Handle With Care," *Kathmandu Post*, October 30, 2015; "Nepal Crisis Deepens as Madhes Movement Marks 100 Days," *Hindustan Times*, November 23, 2015.

supposedly permanent constitution. Indeed, the Nepali constitution-making process seems, at the moment at least, to be no more successful than Iraq's imposed revolution. Thus, I return to the question of whether it is possible to successfully graft the post-sovereign two stage constitution-making paradigm unto a process with a revolutionary break, and, in Nepal at least, given the powerful presence of a party with a revolutionary self-understanding to which many of its militants remained attached.

It is impossible to offer a definitive answer to the question. On the one hand, the successive mobilization of large population sectors, from the early 2000s to the present, which is a characteristic of most revolutionary experiments, has made it very difficult to stabilize the stages of the process, and to bring it to an end. This was already the case with the making of the interim constitution, and its challenge in the so-called Madhes Andolan. During the first constituent assembly popular mobilization was relied on mostly by the Maoists, but the possibility that ever-new actors could be mobilized was one reason why coming to a consensus was difficult, and why coalitions were afraid to rely on even qualified majorities to enact a constitution. Repeated parliamentary obstruction, too, was a constant threat hanging over the assembly and dramatically slowing down its work. The same happened under the second Constituent Assembly. When responding to various challenges, including the electoral results, and the natural disaster, that assembly – or the parties that dominated it – tried to finish their work, or rather, after they did so, new popular challenge made all the results achieved tenuous.

Before we give a negative answer to the question at hand, however, we should recall and summarize the grave mistakes made by the parties in designing the process. It was a mistake to recall a parliament elected in 1999, notorious for its failures and without much legitimacy, when a new inclusive process was called for in the very beginning. Adding Maoist members only made obvious the exclusionary character of an assembly so designed. The Maoist proposal of a new round table, though coming from a strange source, would have had the potential of a fully inclusive negotiation of the interim constitution. It was also a mistake, which the Maoists opposed but initially benefited from, to design an electoral rule as disproportional as it initially turned out to be. This too contributed to the mobilization of those representing the many small parties who thought they would be further excluded by such a rule. As already argued, it was a mistake to design a constituent assembly not in the least differentiated from a legislative one, thus allowing constitution to become hostage to a traditionally highly divisive normal political process. As Prachanda realized only too late, it was a mistake not to aim at relative consensus expressed by the constitution-making qualified majority rule, and to try to achieve the consensus of every party. Not only was the latter not possible, but the practice of seeking complete consensus, still insisted on by the Maoists and the Madhes parties during the beginning of the second constituent assembly, accustomed public opinion to regard voting – even by very high majorities – as somehow illegitimate. Finally, it was a failure, if not a mistake, not to settle state-making questions, both the type of federalism and the control over means of violence during the first stage of the process, the period of the making of the interim constitution. Of course, had that stage been fully inclusive, a solution fairer to minority actors could have been found than the one eventually settled on which relied on the legitimacy of electoral results. That legitimacy turned out to be both insufficient and contestable.

Let me conclude. The revolutionary context did indeed make a consistent and successful adoption of the post-sovereign model very difficult. Given the mistakes just enumerated, however, we cannot say that such adoption had to fail. We can certainly say that revolutionary constitution making, with its logic of majority imposition, would have released most of the same conflicts, and possibly much worse, perhaps even involving massive repression, in a deeply divided society. Adopting the post-sovereign alternative, without the mistakes in design, at the very least would have had a chance to generate more participation as well as results based on fair compromise. It is not yet excluded that Nepal's experiment in the end will yield such an outcome as the result of the learning process the admittedly chaotic constitution-making practice inevitably involved. The parties already learned the importance of the vote based on electoral results. Yet the losers in elections and parliamentary decision making also have to learn the democratic art of self-limitation. Unfortunately, of this they currently show no sign.

5 REVOLUTIONARY CONSTITUENT PROCESS WITHOUT REVOLUTION

Different interpreters can use different concepts of revolution. Used in the broadest sense of regime replacement, as in the phrase "the revolutions of 1989," no constitution-making method would be assignable to revolutionary change even in terms of an elective affinity. While the French Revolution did indeed pioneer two forms of the constituent assembly, the American Revolution on the level of the states used constituent assemblies (Pennsylvania), ordinary assemblies (Virginia) as well as doubly differentiated conventions (Massachusetts and New Hampshire Conventions, Federal Convention). Napoleon's coup of 1798 relied on executive constitution making. And the so-called revolutions of 1989 in Central Europe relied on round tables and a multi-stage process.

If, however, we define revolutions as I did here, legally in terms of breaks in legitimacy and legality, and politically in terms of the duality of sovereign power, the form of organization around sovereign constituent assemblies can be said to be the classical form. In the case of revolutions in this demanding sense, which applies to all the "great revolutions" of modern history,[78] we can understand the logic of this affinity. While the legal break eliminates the use of old rules (used in the case of reform), the break in legitimacy does the same for reliance on old institutions (used in the case of "revolutionary reform") at least if they do not reinvent themselves as did the Estates General in 1789, in an entirely new form. The struggle of sovereignties finally implies that the victorious force in a revolution needs to assert its sovereignty prior to any rules, in the state of nature, according to the famous phrase of Sieyès. This combined logic leads to what Carl Schmitt called "sovereign dictatorship" at least in the transitional period of constitution making.[79] Of all the democratic constitution-making forms we know, it is the sovereign constituent assembly that comes closest to a sovereign dictatorship.[80] Admittedly, a military coup like the famous 18th Brumaire of Napoleon Bonaparte, relying on constrained plebiscite as in his famous quip *"je suis le pouvoir constituant" or "le pouvoir constituant, c'est moi"*), is clearly a dictatorship. But that form, while revolutionary, falls outside of the domain of democratic politics. For revolutionary democracy, then, whether in the French or, initially, the Russian Revolution, the constituent assembly is the classical form.[81]

---

[78] The American is only a partial exception. It has been argued by Allen Buchanan (*Secession,* op. cit.) that it was a case merely of secession rather than a revolution. He argues this on the bases of the persistence of colony/state-level institutions through the process. It would be more convenient though to treat the case as both secession, and revolution. Note: unlike Ackerman in volume I of *We the People* (Cambridge, MA: Harvard University Press, 1992) I do not consider the making of the US Constitution a revolution, but only as a case of revolutionary reform, as he does in volume II of the same work six years later. In such a case, relying on continuity of legitimacy, the legal break is almost always debatable. The revolutionary reform in America was linked to a constitution-making form based on non-sovereign convention, first in Massachusetts and then on the Federal level. The earlier secession–revolution phase, however, involved a variety of constitution-making methods, with Pennsylvania at least pioneering the revolutionary constituent assembly still under the name convention, with other states coming closer to the reformist–secessionist paradigm Buchanan has in mind, relying on the inherited ordinary legislatures renamed as conventions.

[79] Marxist writers like Marx, Lenin and Trotsky openly admit the link of revolution to dictatorship, and given their idea of an extended transitional period the Leninists at least maintain the necessity of a quasi-permanent rather than a temporary sovereign dictatorship. See Trotsky, *Terrorism and Communism* (1920) (Ann Arbor: University of Michigan Press, 1961).

[80] Admittedly, even here there is a fictional element to the extent that an old institution like the Estates General transformed itself, when an old voting rule was relied upon.

[81] On the disastrous Russian story of the constituent assembly see Oskar Anweiler, *The Soviets: The Russian Workers, Peasants, and Soldiers Councils, 1905–1921* (New York: Pantheon Books, 1975); as well as my Epilogue below.

I have argued here and elsewhere[82] that there is an elective affinity also between negotiated regime change and round tables, and between reform and constitution making through regular legislatures, as well as, following a category of Ackerman, between revolutionary reform and doubly differentiated conventions of the US type. To repeat, making such a claim I have relied on ideal-typical "logical" connections, or "elective affinities," rather than unavoidable "empirical" linkages and relationships. At the same time, I did not claim a one-to-one relationship between a type of change and any constitution-making paradigm. Indeed, I have argued that a constitution-making process can begin in one form, and change into another, whether for reasons of internal blockages, political interests, or ideological assumptions – in particular, a strong concept of popular sovereignty. Finally, I should add that, whatever my own reservations, the rhetorical prestige of democratic constituent assemblies has historically outweighed the status of the other forms, though it is still too early to be sure in case of the round tables.[83] Thus, we can easily demonstrate the appearance of this type under other than revolutionary forms of change.

Yet the prestige of the democratic constituent assembly is such in modern history that the term can be used for assemblies that are not intended to be fully sovereign either in the sense of concentrating all the powers of the state, or that of the absence of any limitation. For example, in Latin America *"asemblea constituyente"* or just *"constituyente"* does not automatically signify a sovereign assembly, as many of the historical examples indeed were, but could also mean a doubly differentiated convention in the US American sense. Only occasionally are the actors conscious of the difference, as in Colombia, where the negotiators replaced *"asemblea constituyente"* by *"asemblea constitucional,"* denying its sovereign and unlimited status, before the Supreme Court (astonishingly) reversed on this all-important question.[84] Yet even when a sovereign status or the "original constituent power" is asserted, as variously

---

[82] See especially chapter 3 of my *Post Sovereign Constitution Making*.

[83] Since the South African negotiations, there has been, as we have seen, only two processes arguably of the round table type, Iraq and Nepal, while there have been bodies called constituent assemblies in Venezuela, Ecuador, Bolivia, Egypt, Tunisia, Libya and Yemen as well as several African countries.

[84] Colon-Rios, *Weak Constitutionalism* (London: Routledge, 2012), pp. 292–294. *Constitutional* he implies means under a constitution, while *constituent* means a source of the constitution in "the state of nature." In South Africa the framers of the interim constitution, chose constitutional rather than constituent, and undoubtedly they knew what this meant, given their 34 principles and the role they assigned to the new Constitutional Court. The limits proposed in Colombia were admittedly more modest. Re South Africa, see the Constitution of 1993: "Art. 68 Constitution-making Body[:] (1) The National Assembly and the Senate, sitting jointly for the purposes of this Chapter, shall be the Constitutional Assembly. (2) The Constitutional Assembly shall draft and constitutional text in accordance with this Chapter."

in India, Colombia, and Venezuela, we cannot speak of revolution in the full sense defined here. India, with its great ideological diversity, is a special case, but in Colombia at least the actors did not speak of revolution, although in Venezuela they did (with the "Bolivarian Revolution"). More important, however, is the fact that in all three countries there was at least a strong argument for legal continuity in spite of the form of constitution making used. Admittedly, one can find a legal break if one looks hard enough, as have clever legal analysts in each of the three cases. But what they cannot find is a complete collapse of the legitimacy of inherited institutions, whether provincial assemblies as in India, or the presidency in Colombia and Venezuela. Thus, rather than simple reform, the three cases seem to belong to "revolutionary reform" as I have defined it,[85] and indeed this is indicated by the element of double differentiation I will locate in India, and the initial use of the US-type convention form in Colombia and Venezuela, belying the terminology adopted. Yet the terminology does not completely lie, fundamentally because of the assumption of the theory of sovereign constitution making behind it. The three cases, each in their own way, testify to the instability of the doubly differentiated US-type convention, and its tendency to produce a sovereign constituent assembly not only in name but also in practice. This instability is manifested in two ways: the weakening of double differentiation manifest in both Colombia and Venezuela, and the transition from an US republican type of revolutionary reform to its plebiscitary variant, as in Venezuela alone.

Below I will examine the three cases in their historical sequence, first considering how they were possible without full revolutionary breaks; second, the reasons why double differentiation, or at least the republican model of the convention was maintained in India and partially in Colombia, with both collapsing in Venezuela; and third, to what extent and why the first two cases remained compatible with constitutionalist outcomes, and the third did not. I will proceed to argue that for each setting it was the collapse or blockage of a previous modality or modalities of constitution making that led to the adoption of the type of assembly best known from revolutions. I will then make a case that for legally sovereign assemblies, elements of double differentiation in the American sense and attempted interventions by constitutional courts were less able to guarantee "constitutionalist" procedure and outcome, than the incorporation of fundamental elements of the post-sovereign logic, like negotiation and pluralistic inclusion. I will argue it was inclusion and pluralism in India that protected the important elements of double differentiation,

---

[85] See especially chapter 3 of *Post Sovereign Constitution Making*.

which also had a positive effect on the outcome. In Colombia, where double differentiation was indeed endangered, it was the consensual element of what has been called "the pre-assembly moment" that wound up limiting in fact, if not in law, the supposedly sovereign assembly. That type of assembly showed its revolutionary face only in Venezuela with results incompatible with constitutional democracy. I will conclude the section by countering the objection that external limits on assemblies like prior agreements, and internal limits, like constitutional courts, cannot succeed against constituent assemblies. The objection, still presupposing sovereign assemblies, disregards the importance of combining the external and the internal forms of limitation.

Revolutionary Reform in India

India's 1950 Constitution was made by a constituent assembly, clearly so named. This was a case that, in many respects, came close to a revolutionary process according to my definition, not only in the legal sense as in Venezuela, but also in the political one. Yet I will treat it here as a case of revolutionary reform, one that was successfully stabilized. That treatment is confirmed not only by the outcome of an undeniably constitutionalist constitution that in its now 65 years of existence, whatever problems it may have encountered, and there have been many, has provided several important lessons in the practice of constitutional democracy. It is even more justified by the Indian constitution-making process on which I will here focus.

Let me note first that India did not unambiguously satisfy the "legal" conditions of revolution I insisted on. Thus, it may be more plausibly treated as a case of "revolutionary reform," with its almost always attendant ambiguity concerning a legal break.[86] Admittedly, there was indeed a "political" battle over sovereignty between two or rather three sides, even if it was to a significant extent non-violent. Yet while the legitimacy of the colonial system has indeed collapsed some of the institutions colonialism helped to establish did not, and especially the provincial legislatures of the 1935 Government of India Act. There was moreover a strong, though not uncontestable, argument for the legal continuity through the process, and from the point of view of the previous colonial legality there was arguably no legal break at all.[87] It should be clear that this is no irrelevant formal matter. From the point of view

---

[86] It makes a great deal of sense to treat India's decolonization as a case of revolutionary reform, like the making of the US Constitution in 1787, rather than a revolution, the first anti-colonial case of 1776.

[87] This very ambiguity, present also in 1787 in the USA, seems to be a characteristic of "revolutionary reform."

of the inherited legality, it could be said that the validity of India's constitution (similarly to Australia earlier and Canada, technically later) was established by an Act of Parliament at Westminster, the Indian Independence Act of July 1947. It was one in a series of at least five Government of India Acts, dating back to 1833, of which the most important one was the 1935 Act, regulating provincial and central legislatures and (unsuccessfully) providing for a federal system.[88] It was according to this last act that the mode of election for the constituent assembly was organized by the Cabinet Mission Plan of 1946, which was, in turn, instituted by the incumbent viceroy, Lord Wavell. India remained under this Act until 1950, and, again, this was not merely a formal matter. The provincial legislatures as well as the Central Legislative Assembly were elected under the 1935 Act. The former not only remained in office till 1950, but also elected the members of the Constituent Assembly. Even the latter, the Central Legislative Assembly, remained in office till August 1947, at least formally, when however it was the Indian Independence Act that established the Constituent Assembly as, temporarily, the legislature of "the Dominion."[89] It was with and by the Act that the Central Legislative Assembly was disbanded and immediately replaced. I note already the presence of double differentiation in the arrangement, reminiscent of the US Federal constitution-making process, but even more so of the Canadian and Australian processes. I will try to show that the Constituent Assembly took this double differentiation seriously even in its own internal arrangements.

Admittedly, the claim of legal continuity was certainly not unchallenged during the process and after. It was debated among the Indian participants themselves, and with the British. The issue was raised in terms of ultimate sovereignty. To British spokesmen, sovereignty remained at Westminster until at least 1947, and possibly 1950, though only a few diehards of an incoherent notion of parliamentary sovereignty would have said that it persisted thereafter. What was conceded from at least 1940 (the so-called "August Offer") and 1942 ("The Cripps Proposal") was not only a Dominion status, but, more importantly, that Indians and their representatives would make their constitution themselves, unlike in the case of the previous Government of India Acts. But this concession drew on previous efforts in Canada, South Africa, and Australia, which already had dominion status, where the substantive process was indigenized, but where the ultimate authority to enact constitutions remained at Westminster. In other words, what was conceded was a process

---

[88] J. Keay, *India: A History. Revised and Updated* (New York: Grove/Atlantic, Inc., 2011).

[89] "Indian Independence Act" point 8 in Jennings ed., *Constitutional Laws of the Commonwealth* (Oxford: Clarendon Press, 1957).

substantively indigenous, but not fully autochthonous and, most importantly, not yet sovereign.[90] In other words, the wartime proposals conceded constitution making by Indian representatives in India in an assembly of Indians alone, but not a sovereign constituent assembly.[91]

An interesting exchange of notes of a newly formed by Congress Working Committee and Lord Pethick-Lawrence, the Secretary of State for India and the leader of the Cabinet Mission in May 1946 expressed this fundamental disagreement. The Working Committee demanded full sovereignty for the body of the constituent assembly, while the Secretary of State conceded only an Indian-based process requiring ultimate British agreement to the constitutional result.[92] It is not merely of historical interest that even some of the leaders of Congress, who had indeed been demanding a constituent assembly since 1934,[93] disagreed on the question of sovereignty, with Gandhi stating as late as July 1946 "that it is no use considering someone else's creation a sovereign body."[94] Was he only concerned with an apparently formal matter, concerning whose authority the constituent assembly was ultimately or at least originally able to draw upon? Steeped in English jurisprudence as much as Nehru, and almost as much as Jinnah, it is very unlikely that the Mahatma did not understand the full meaning of a sovereign constituent assembly, which entailed, among other things, the plenitude of all power, and, even more

[90] For the difference between autonomy and autochthony, see Wheare *Constitutional Structure of the Commonwealth* (Oxford: Oxford University Press, 1960), pp. 58ff; 89ff.

[91] Thus, "the August Offer" (http://www.houseofdavid.ca/in_a_off.htm; accessed February 5, 2016): "There has been very strong insistence that the framing of that scheme should be primarily the responsibility of Indians themselves, and should originate from Indian conceptions of the social, economic and political structure of Indian life. His Majesty's Government are in sympathy with that desire, and wish to see it given the fullest practical expression subject to the due fulfillment of the obligations which Great Britain's long connection with India has imposed upon her and for which His Majesty's Government cannot divest themselves of responsibility. It is clear that a moment when the Commonwealth is engaged in a struggle for existence is not one in which fundamental constitutional issues can be decisively resolved. But His Majesty's Government authorize me to declare that they will most readily assent to the setting up after the conclusion of the war with the least possible delay of a body representative of the principal elements in India's national life in order to devise the framework of the new Constitution and they will lend every aid in their power to hasten decisions on all relevant matters to the utmost degree."

[92] Presented by Wheare, *Constitutional Structure of the Commonwealth*.

[93] Austin, *The Indian Constitution*.

[94] Cited by Austin, op. cit., p. 7. Did Gandhi have other concerns than just the formal one? One such a concern could have been the implications of sovereign claims, as interpreted through the Westminster model, for the Hindu–Muslim conflict, and its negative results for the unity of India. Admittedly, however, he was hostile to the idea of groups in Plan, even if he did not think that the feature could be removed by the fiat of sovereign claims. https://sites.google.com/site/cabinetmissionplan/Behind-the-scenes-Gandhi. Accessed February 7, 2016.

importantly, the absence of legal limitations whereby the assembly not only could cut all links with its convener, but could divest itself of all limitation regarding the rules of the convener. And indeed, at the very time Gandhi gave the interview, namely July 22, 1946, Congress leaders were not only demanding the sovereignty of the assembly, but also interpreted it in terms of its complete freedom of action to transform its structure, including the concessions of the Cabinet Mission Plan made to the idea of Pakistan within an Indian Federation. Nehru's famous Press Conference on July 10 of the same year asserted this very conception of sovereignty, and it is hard not to think that Gandhi, who had his own problems with the Plan, was answering Nehru on this most fundamental point while rejecting the idea of a sovereign constituent assembly.

Yet, after replacing the three- (or rather four-)assembly scheme of the Cabinet Mission Plan, the reconstructed Constituent Assembly did declare that whatever its origins, it was now meeting on the authority of the People of India and could be dissolved only by its own (two-thirds) vote, rather than by British authorities, whether the viceroy or the Westminster Parliament. Expressing the point of view of the leaders of Congress, specifically Nehru, this was both a claim of complete autochthony as well as a revolutionary declaration of sovereignty. We will also meet similar declarations in originally non-sovereign assemblies in Colombia and Venezuela. But in India, since the British never contested the claim, and in the Indian Independence Act that wound up denying the right (of the even the Judicial Committee of the Privy Council, by implication) to declare anything the Constituent Assembly enacted as repugnant to British law,[95] one can say that the perspective of Nehru concerning sovereignty had not only fully triumphed, but was also legalized by the previous sovereign. One could argue, of course, that the end of British sovereignty, though not in the form of Indian sovereignty, was anticipated already from the moment in 1946 when the UK Government declared its intention to leave India.[96] It was not yet clear, however, whose sovereignty the new one would be, whether there would be one or two new sovereigns, and whether sovereignty

---

[95] Indian Independence Act 6(2) also conceding the right of the Indian (and Pakistani) Parliament to repeal this very act. That repeal occurred in both cases, along with the Act of 1935, in India by the new constitution.

[96] Keay op. cit. Y. Khan, *The Great Partition: The Making of India and Pakistan* (New Haven: Yale University Press, 2007); R. Guha, *India after Gandhi: The History of the World's Largest Democracy* (Delhi: Pan, 2007). What that declaration meant was that whatever the status British constitutional law in India was purported to be, it would not be enforced by the military and police still under British control.

would be embodied in a constituent assembly, indeed in one or two constituent assemblies.

These questions were resolved during the road to partition. The Union Constituent Assembly never met in the form designed by the Cabinet Mission. It is almost beyond doubt that Congress' demands for its sovereignty, among other lesser contentious issues, played a huge role in the League's boycott. Sovereignty was successfully asserted in the rump Indian successor Constituent Assembly, and conceded in the India Independence Act of 1947, to the benefit of both India's and Pakistan's residual assemblies.

Remarkably, it remains debatable whether the transfer of sovereignty, eventually to two sovereigns, India and Pakistan, was a revolutionary or a reformist act. According to a still interesting analysis of Kenneth Wheare,[97] concerning the question of rupture and continuity, two equally coherent stories could be told regarding this choice. One could argue (as I did) that the sovereignty of the Constituent Assembly (or: two constituent assemblies), whatever earlier claims to the contrary, was established by the Indian Independence Act enacted by another sovereign, the Parliament at Westminster. This is the continuity thesis, illustrating that even the conflict of two claimants of sovereignty may not mean revolutionary change. According to Wheare, however, it could also be argued that the assertion of sovereignty by the Constituent Assembly involved a legal rupture. He bases this not on the plausible *political* argument stressed by Granville Austin that the Indian Constituent Assembly convincingly declared that it could not be dissolved by the British, but rather on the equally plausible *legal* one, namely the Assembly's refusal to submit or allow the assent of the Governor General (till 1950: Mountbatten) to its constitution-making acts, during a time when ordinary legislative acts of the same body, meeting in another form and under a different title and rules, were so submitted and assented to. Based on Supreme Court decisions in Pakistan if not India, Wheare is therefore inclined to postulate an element at least of constitutional rupture.[98] The argument is based on the assumption that the Independence

---

[97] Wheare, op. cit., 95–100.
[98] Ivor Jennings, however, seemed to have been inclined to the continuity view, by which there was a legal transfer of sovereignty from the UK to India. He was most concerned to deny one remotely possible implication of this, namely that another British parliament could undo what the parliament has done, in other words could repeal the India Independence Act, and recover its sovereignty. See *The Law and the Constitution*, 5th ed. (London: University of London Press, 1959), pp. 166–168. Even if it were theoretically possible such repeal and reversal according to him would be meaningless, and without consequence. He uses the example to deny Dicey's influential idea that no parliament can be bound by a previous one.

of India Act required the assent of the Governor General to all acts of the Constituent Assembly, and not only the ordinary legislative acts for which the requirement was honored.[99] Since the constitution was not so submitted, its authority could not rest on the Act that supposedly required such assent and had to rest either on a new, if fictional entity, the people of India, or the body that de facto became sovereign, the Constituent Assembly.

According to this argument, one postulating rupture and a new constituent subject, the British view of retaining ultimate authority during constitution making in the two Indian dominions would be seen as a fiction,[100] but so should the claim that the Constituent Assembly was the people of India as stated by the Preamble of the 1950 Constitution.[101] Behind both fictions lay the power of Indian actors, who were unfortunately disunited till the partition on all the fundamental questions, and who achieved their sovereignty in fact only with the partition itself. Thus, the argument implies not only that the British government's sovereignty became fictional once the Independence of India Act was enacted, but also that the battle of competing sovereignties was lost by the British, by the time the constituent assembly was elected. In other words, before British sovereignty became purely fictional, and was then formally transferred, it was already reduced to a purely formal matter indicating very little power to do anything except to leave.

This loss of British government's power, despite the sovereignty claims still made, was expressed by its dramatic, if noble failure to keep India united in some fundamental sense. The federalist and confederalist plans of both the 1935 Act and the 1946 Cabinet Mission Plan, failed, and failed dramatically. The failure of the second of these efforts was indicated through the collapse of the assembly form the plan established. The Plan presupposed the results of the elections of 1946, when Indians voting in three separate religiously differentiated electorates, established Congress as the dominant force for Hindu majority provinces, while, more surprisingly, the Muslim League became dominant for voters of its own religious group. Thus, it was these two parties,

---

99 Unfortunately, the Act itself seems to both assert and deny the requirement under 6(3) and again denying it for the provinces under 8 (2c and d) yielding the conclusion that assent was needed, but veto was not possible; op. cit., pp. 178–180. This provision establishes as law what was mere convention in the UK as well as many dominions. Since however assent was not asked for, there was arguably formal rupture in India. Curiously, Wheare does not discuss the text of the Act, but instead turns to Pakistani Court decisions to resolve the issue. The combination of assent and without the possibility of veto has been the conventional rule for the monarch in the UK, who has last exercised a veto of an act of parliament in 1707. Vetoes by governor generals, or the monarch himself, remained however possible in the colonies and dominions, if increasingly rarely used.

100 Wheare, op. cit.; Jennings, op. cit.   101 Constitution; Wheare, op. cit.

whose views had to be negotiated and reconciled if a constituent process for India as a whole was to have a chance at all. During seemingly endless negotiations before the Plan,[102] it was obvious that the Muslim League's demand for two constituent assemblies, one for "Hindustan" and the other for "Pakistan" were irreconcilable with the demand of Congress for one constituent assembly for what was British India (including the Princely States) based on a new form of suffrage linking one person to one vote. Negotiations hardly brought the two sides nearer together on this essential subject.[103] Nevertheless, various British proposals and above all the 1946 Plan that the Cabinet Mission decided to impose[104] sought a compromise the actors themselves were unable to generate.[105] According to its terms, one constituent assembly would be elected by the provincial assemblies themselves, namely bodies that were the product of the old restricted rules. This one assembly would have a two or three tier structure.[106] The assembly as a whole, in a "preliminary meeting" in the beginning [19(iv)] and reassembling in the end [19(vi)] corresponded to the demands of Congress. The three groups, one composed of Hindu majority provinces (of the 1935 Act), a second composed of Muslim majority provinces of the West, and a third with relatively equal number of Muslims and Hindus from a mixed group of provinces in the East (primarily Bengal and Assam) seemed to express part of the League's demand for Pakistan, by keeping Muslim majority Punjab and Bengal united. Yet this was only a part of what the League fought for, because the two Muslim majority groups were kept separate.[107] Finally, the individual provinces that would eventually include the Princely States, would be given a constitution by each of the groups in which they were included. Paradoxically, a constitution for each group was

---

[102] See especially Khan, op. cit.

[103] Khan, op. cit. It is true that rupture between occurred around two limited questions, namely whether provinces could easily secede from their groups, and whether Congress could name also Muslims to the provisional government. Jinnah bitterly opposed these two options, but at issue was the irreconcilability of their macro perspectives on India.

[104] Austin, op. cit.; Khan, op. cit.

[105] For the details I rely on Austin; as well "The Cabinet Mission Plan" https://sites.google.com/ site/cabinetmissionplan/Cabinet-Mission-Plan-May16 [accessed February 16, 2016).

[106] Khan speaks of a three-tier one, but the deliberative bodies were meant to be the groups and the whole only. There was no provision for the provinces to meet separately for constitution making or secession, though, of course, their provincial assemblies were free to meet and pass resolutins. The groups would produce their constitutions. The compromise reflected Congress and League positions primarily, and less the position of the provinces, that in some cases represented alternative views on the organization of the state.

[107] Thus drawing the objection that Pakistan was thereby divided into two. Statement by Mr. M. A. Jinnah on the Cabinet Mission Plan, 22 May 1946. https://sites.google.com/site/ cabinetmissionplan/jinnahmlresponsetocmp.

only a possibility, not a requirement, reflecting probably competing Congress and League views on the subject. While not given the option to produce their own constitutions, the provinces could challenge their membership in a given group under difficult procedures immediately as the constitution was enacted, involving votes of their legislatures, while the constitution as a whole could be reconsidered on provincial initiative only after a ten year waiting period [19(viii)] vs. 15(6)].[108]

Under this overall scheme the first constitutions would be produced by each of the groups, with the Assembly as a whole (the Union Constituent Assembly) getting its turn only afterwards [19v–vii]. Deliberating last, the large body would or could establish a constitution for India that would entail "Federal" responsibility only in the areas of defense, foreign affairs, and communications, along with the financing necessary for these functions. The decisions of both the Union Constituent Assembly, and the projected Union Legislature, in areas touching on "major communal issues" would require the consent of each of the two major groups, defined apparently as General and Muslim. [15 (1) and (2); 19(vii)]. Note that the constituent assembly under this plan was not only formally structured in a way that implied significant procedural constraints and limitations, but, moreover, its substantive options were also greatly limited. This was to be hardly a sovereign constituent assembly, and much more a forum for competing state actors to come to contractual agreements concerning a confederation or federation. That many actors, such as the Sikh community, felt excluded was a function of the elections of 1946 that established Congress and the League as the only serious actors in the eyes of the British.[109]

Clearly, the Plan was a compromise construct, but equally clearly it was one quite remote from the stated positions of the two main actors. It tended to create a kind of confederation with very weak central government, a position hitherto entirely unacceptable to Congress. Yet it explicitly banned partition, and the creation of an independent state of Pakistan (for at least ten years!), rightly pointing to the obvious problems of India's complexity, that would only reappear in new states formed on communal or religious lines.[110] Nevertheless, amazingly enough, for one brief moment both sides accepted the Plan. As we now see it, the leaders of the League – and especially Jinnah – saw it as a

---

[108] Cf. A.G. Noorani, "The Collapse of the Cabinet Mission's Plan," *Economic and Political Weekly*, Vol. 14, Issue No. 47, 24 November 1979.

[109] Khan, op. cit.

[110] Drawing the immediate objection of Jinnah: Statement by Mr. M.A. Jinnah on the Cabinet Mission Plan, 22 May 1946. https://sites.google.com/site/cabinetmissionplan/ jinnahmlresponsetocmp.

foundation for further moves toward Pakistan, with intact Punjab and Bengal as two of its parts.[111] At the same time, Congress and Nehru saw it as a chance to declare popular sovereignty, and thus the right of the Assembly to redefine itself under the principle.[112] In particular, Congress sought to eliminate the three groups altogether, or at the very least sought to allow provinces like Assam and the North West Frontier province to be able to leave the Muslim majority groups to which they were assigned.[113] Thus we can see why Jinnah, who knew the Westminster system and interpreted majority rule in its spirit, feared a sovereign assembly even more than did the British, at least for the whole of India, since he strenuously, if inconsistently fought for pure majority rule in the mixed states of Punjab and Bengal. According to his deepest fears, if the assembly of the whole met it could vote by majority to be no longer be bound by the original rules, and could then establish itself as a sovereign constituent assembly that could decide all questions by the same majority dominated by Congress.[114]

---

[111] See Keay, op. cit., p. 500 who says that for a moment Jinnah may have backed away from a completely separate Pakistan.

[112] Ibid., 501. See "Jawaharlal Nehru's 10 July 1946 Press Conference on the Cabinet Mission Plan": "What we do there [in the Constituent Assembly], we are entirely and absolutely free to determine ... When the Congress had stated that the Constituent Assembly was a sovereign body,' Pandit Nehru said, 'Cabinet Mission's reply was more or less "yes", subject to two considerations. Firstly, proper arrangement for Minorities, and the other, a treaty between India and England ... ' Referring to grouping, Pandit Nehru said, 'The big probability is that, from any approach to the question, there will be no grouping. Obviously, Section A will decide against grouping. Speaking in betting language, there was 4 to 1 chance of the North-West Frontier Province deciding against grouping. The Group B collapses. It is highly likely that Assam will decide against grouping with Bengal, although I would not like to say what the initial decision may be, since it is evenly balanced.' Nehru then went on to interpret the plan for an all Union government in a highly expansive manner. Jinnah used this interview to back out of the plan, and subsequently, Nehru was roundly criticized by his own comrades. But perhaps he only made the mistake of openly saying what Congress intended." https://sites .google.com/site/cabinetmissionplan/nehrupressconference10july1946. Accessed February 6, 2016. Incidentally, Assam's legislature voted out of its group with Bengal seven days after Nehru spoke, even if this could not yet have any legal consequences. Cf. Noorani, op. cit.

[113] Mr Gandhi's article in *Harijan* 26 May 1946 https://sites.google.com/site/cabinetmissionplan/ congressopptogrouping, accessed on February 6, 2016.

[114] Text of two Resolutions passed by the All-India Muslim League Council at Bombay on July 29, 1946https://sites.google.com/site/cabinetmissionplan/Behind-the-Scenes-Jinnah accessed on February 6, 2016.

"The Congress have not accepted it [the Cabinet Mission Plan] because their acceptance is conditional and subject to their own interpretation which is contrary to the authoritative statements of the Delegation and the Viceroy issued on the 16th and the 25th of May. The Congress have made it clear that they do not accept any of the terms or the fundamentals of the scheme but that they have agreed only to go into the Constituent Assembly and to nothing else; and that the Constituent Assembly is a sovereign body and can take such decisions as

Many Congress statements gave ground to these fears, and by 1946 there was also no hope that the British, who were used to the idea of parliamentary sovereignty, could enforce the previously agreed upon rules.[115] Thus Jinnah chose not to allow the assembly, as it was originally conceived, to ever meet, and he could accomplish that goal by instructing League representatives for the second and third groupings never to attend. Extreme communal violence followed, one that need not be detailed here. The Plan failed, and along with it the last unambiguously reform project of state and constitution making. From a legal point of view at least, the Partition, with all its horrors, even though explicitly and convincingly rejected by the Cabinet Mission, became unavoidable. Under the partition plan and the Independence of India Act, the rump constituent assembly and the absent Muslim delegates from the second and third groups became two constituent assemblies, as originally demanded by Jinnah.[116]

Here I focus only on the Constituent Assembly for India. In this context, the failure of one type of assembly to function led to the successful work of another. While legal continuity could be claimed between the pre- and post-partition assemblies, and indeed the members who actually did meet before and after were in their greater part almost exactly the same,[117] in reality, the structure of the assembly did not resemble the plan of its original conveners. The three groups were never formed. There was an overwhelming majority for one party, Congress (82 percent), even as League representatives from Hindu-majority

it may think proper in total disregard of the terms and basis on which it was proposed to be set up . . . The attitude of the Congress clearly shows that these conditions precedent for the successful working of the constitution-making body do not exist. This fact . . . leaves no doubt that in these circumstances the participation of the Muslims in the proposed constitution-making machinery is fraught with danger and the Council, therefore, hereby withdraws its acceptance of the Cabinet Mission's proposals . . . "

[115] In January 1947, before Muslim League withdrawal from the Constituent Assembly, in the face of British insistence on the groups, Congress "climbed down" from its perspective of a sovereign assembly, and its intention to abandon or reorganize the Groups of the Plan. See "Text of Resolution passed by the All-India Congress Committee on 6 January 1947." Subsequently, and more clearly in a discussion with Bengal deputies, "Mr. Patel said that the Constituent Assembly was not a sovereign body as it had many limitations and it must work through the limited scope of the Cabinet delegation's statement of May 16th. It is only to give the people of India some confidence in themselves that the Congress is giving out that it is a sovereign body." https://sites.google.com/site/cabinetmissionplan/congress-climbdown-and-jinnah-s-rejection (accessed February 7, 2016). By then, it was too late.

[116] Yet he lost parts of Punjab and Bengal, and got a "moth eaten Pakistan," while Nehru gained the possibility of a unified, though much smaller India. As everyone well knows, the cost to millions was unimaginably great.

[117] The addition of delegates from the Princely States, a key dimension of Indian state formation, proceeded slowly through the period.

provinces and the delegates of the Princely States, along with a few others, took their seats.[118] The Assembly formally declared that it would continue to meet on its own authority, and the substantive limitations of the Cabinet Mission Plan for the powers of the Federal government to be were never mentioned again, as far as I can tell from Granville Austin's great study. There was to be federalism, but centralized and flexible.[119] The transformation of the assembly thus uncannily resembled that of the three-chamber Estates General in 1789 into the single-chamber sovereign assembly. The refusal to be dissolved by the convening authority also resembled the famous Tennis Court Oath (*Serment de Jeu de Paume*). And the denial of a British veto, whether by the Governor General under the 1935 Act, or by the Westminster Parliament as in the case of South Africa in 1910, similarly, resembled the denial of the royal veto (over the constitution, but not other decrees!) in France by the *Assemblée nationale constituante*.

And yet the Indian Constituent Assembly was different in structure and outcome than the famous French forerunner – despite similar claims to sovereignty by the two bodies. These differences, some legal, others empirical, indicate the reasons why constitution making by a legally sovereign constituent assembly in India case did not amount to sovereign dictatorship, and, equally important, managed to produce a constitutionalist constitution.

First, in spite of the collapse of the Cabinet Mission Plan, elections to the constituent assembly took place under the Government of India Act of 1935. This procedure was rightly criticized subsequently because of the limited franchise involved in electing the provincial assemblies in 1945, which in turn elected the members of the Constituent Assembly according to provincial quotas pre-assigned by the Plan. More important here is that though the rump assembly after the Partition had an 82 percent Congress majority, the actual members were delegates of the provinces. These too, almost without exception, had Congress majorities of congressmen from the provinces, and subsequently from the princely states, yet represented a wide variety of local, religious and political views. It is well documented, if unusual, that the National Congress itself made determined effort to get religious and ethnic minorities

[118] Austin, op. cit., 9–10. That figure would have been 69 percent only if the original assembly met. Thus Jinnah's fears would not have been allayed even by a two-thirds decision rule, though of course he could have attended if a demand for a 75 or 80 percent rule were accepted. Being very British in his political experience, qualified majorities did nevertheless enter his calculations. See Statement by Mr. M.A. Jinnah on the Cabinet Mission Plan, 22 May 1946.

[119] Cf. B.R. Ambedkar, "Basic Features of the Indian Constitution" in V. Rodrigues ed., *The Essential Writings of B.R. Ambedkar* (New Delhi: Oxford, 2002); Austin, op. cit.

and even women elected by the provincial legislatures.[120] There were at least
50 members of provincial legislatures elected, and these, of course, represented
the various local interests of their provinces.[121] I will return to this fact, one
which has been stressed by many.[122]

What has been less insisted on, probably because of the label "constituent
assembly" and the adjective "sovereign" added to it, was that the assembly,
until its own new constitution was enacted, remained under law, the 1935 Act.
Even the rupture thesis has to admit legal continuity regarding all but the
question of ultimate authority or autochthony. Moreover the legal continuity
involved the survival of fundamental institutions whose relation to the constituent assembly remained regulated by the 1935 Act. This entailed genuine
powers for the provinces, and even the ability of provincial legislatures to act
on the constituent assembly through their representatives therein. It is true, the
Indian Independence Act derogated from the 1919 and 1935 Government of
India Acts by transferring the powers of the Central Legislative Assembly to the
Constituent Assembly. That older body was then dutifully dissolved on August
14, right after the declaration of both Pakistani and Indian independence.[123]

That would have been the end of a second dimension of double differentiation, represented in America by the Confederation Congress-Constitutional
Convention duality of 1787. Very remarkably, however, the Constituent Assembly on its own moved to restore it, at least in part.[124] This was the origin of the
insufficiently known important differentiation of the Constituent Assembly,
into constitutional and legislative dimensions. The two bodies, the Constituent
Assembly and the Constituent Assembly (legislative), admittedly with the same
members, met at two different times under two different sets of rules, and with
somewhat different leaderships. Under the 1935 Act, e.g., the Legislative body
recognized the need, until 1950, to get the governor general's assent to its
decisions for the sake of their validity.[125] As already seen, the Constituent body
simply disregarded the requirement. More importantly, while Congress was

---

[120] Austin, op. cit.   [121] Austin, op. cit., p. 11.   [122] Austin, op. cit.; Guha, op. cit.

[123] Austin, fn. 32, p. 8. Most likely, the Central Legislative Assembly was dormant from the
time of the elections of 1946, with all (failed) attempts of Viceroy Wavell to form an interim
government rooted in the new Constituent Assembly.

[124] The dimensions of double differentiation in India are badly missed by Elster's "Legislatures
as Constituent Assemblies" in R. Bauman and T. Kahana eds, *The Least Examined Branch:
The Role of Legislatures in the Constitutional State* (London: Cambridge, 2006) because of
his almost entirely non-legal orientation. Thus he does not see how the double structure
of the Constituent Assembly, well explored by Austin op. cit., vitiated in part the negative
consequences of the non-differentiation of normal and constitutional politics that Elster
rightly criticizes in theory at least.

[125] Wheare, op. cit.

more of a united bloc as the "legislative" body, it could afford to be a genuine deliberative and debating body as the constituent.[126] In my view, this was possible not only because the venue of extra-ordinary politics was separated from that of the ordinary one, but even more so because of the dramatic extension of time that could be utilized for the discussion and debate of purely constitutional issues. Indeed, one mark of the deliberative character of a constitution-making body, and its willingness to take all views into account and make the necessary forms of compromise, is the time utilized for its deliberations. Up till 1947 the French *Assemblée Constituante*, itself a highly diverse body given its foundations of the three-chamber Estates General, held the record: namely two years. The Indian Constituent Assembly continued to deliberate on the constitution for nearly three years, extending its life in 1950 for another year.[127]

The partial internal differentiation of the Assembly, along with the dramatic extension of time, meant that constitutional issues could be handled more or less without the political and time pressures of day-to-day political concerns and conflicts as well as compromise. From the result it is clear that the Nehru government did not dominate the constitutional venue to the same degree that it certainly controlled parliament through its majority. On the constitutional level the government could lose votes without endangering its confidence. The possibility made the same deputies more independent at one venue than the other, more able to compromise with forms of minority opinion that were present but powerless in the legislative venue. The famous spirit of accommodation, stressed by G. Austin and demonstrated in terms of important compromises on rights, judicial review, property, religion, federalism, language, and the very important amendment clause, the famous concessions made by Nehru to Ambedkar, were all facilitated by the partially differentiated structure of the Constituent Assembly.[128]

Admittedly, and I here turn to the empirical level, formal differentiation between provincial and central assemblies, and within the Constituent Assembly itself, as important as it was, would have been of little help if the 80 percent + majority of Congress would have been coupled with homogeneity or tight party discipline. As we will see from the Venezuelan case, where the dominant

---

[126] See Austin, op. cit., p. 22ff. Elster, "Legislatures as Constituent Assemblies" op. cit. on this point more generally.

[127] That type of extension is common for sovereign assemblies, and is a problematic consequence of having also the normal political powers. In India, it could be justified by the immense problems of organizing election based on universal suffrage for the first time in such an enormous and poor country.

[128] Fully documented by Austin, op. cit.

majority was even larger in terms of seats than in India, formal differentiation can be easily overcome by a unified majority with sovereign claims. Fortunately, Congress was politically united around only two issues, both moot after the partition, namely the liberation and the unity of India. As to the rest, partially through design and intervention in the provincial legislatures as we have seen, the party at the Constituent Assembly contained members of all India's religions, as well as advocates of everything from free market ideology to classical socialists.[129] Even within the leadership the pluralism of views and perspectives was impressive. Among them were decentralizing Gandhian socialists, as well as law and order types like Sardar Patel. There were strong political centralizers as well as convinced federalists among the ranks, the latter representing many of the provinces and their interests. There were at least some women along with the men, and on their issues they played a significant role. The party had many Muslims, such as Maulana Azad, even in its top leadership, but also orthodox Hindus, like Rajendra Prasad, who was to become India's first president. There were even members who also belonged to nationalist organizations like the Hindu Mahasaba and the RSS ("National Volunteer Organization"), as well as various Communist factions. Unfortunately, the inclusion of the small socialist party turned out to be impossible, but the issue was interesting: the party demanded new universal suffrage-based elections for a new constituent assembly, which in that case would have become a truly revolutionary sovereign body. In the actual one, there were indeed mostly upper-caste members, but efforts were also made to represent lower castes, and especially Dalits, whose most important figure, B.R. Ambedkar, was arranged a new seat when his old one was lost with Eastern Bengal. He was even made the chair of the all-important drafting committee, in spite of his many criticisms of Congress.[130] Thus, there were staunch secularists, staunch opponents of the caste order and its degradation of women, as well as defenders of Hindu orthodoxy all present. There were advocates of a Westminster style of parliamentary government like Nehru himself, whose mistakes demanding a sovereign constituent assembly followed from that conviction, as well as his desire to initiate and carry out a social revolution. He was supported by B.N. Rau, the Assembly's constitutional adviser, who was instructed among others by F. Frankfurter concerning the dangers of entrenchment and judicial power. But the American-educated Ambedkar represented the opposite perspective of strong rights, entrenchment and strong courts, and Nehru in the

[129] Austin, op. cit., 10–15; Guha, op. cit., 116–117.
[130] For his own outstanding summary of the contents of the Constitution, see Ambedkar, "Basic Features of the Indian Constitution."

end compromised with him. Here the differences with other liberation leaders like Ben Gurion, Nkrumah, and Nyerere were significant, though Nelson Mandela was to follow the Indian example. In both settings, in South Africa as well as India, the prior commitment of the liberation party to fundamental rights allowed outvoted minorities to successfully appeal to the principles and standards of the majority.

Does the Indian outcome, a principled document for a new constitutional democracy, rehabilitate sovereign constitution making by an assembly, as a viable or even preferable democratic form? I do not think so. First, as we have seen, in its first appearance the sovereign conception repeatedly stressed by Congress participants in the debates with British and Muslim interlocutors played a fundamental role in wrecking the last chance for Indian unity. We cannot tell if Jinnah would have withdrawn the League from the process in any case, or that the three group assembly designed by the Cabinet Mission could have conceivably worked. But he had to withdraw on the dominant Congress theory of the assembly, or what he called, rightly or wrongly, the insincere acceptance of the Cabinet Mission Plan. Whether his own acceptance of the Plan was itself sincere is, of course, open to question. Second, the Indian assembly operated in a context of overall legal continuity. If there was a legal break at all, it was much more technical and much less significant than the illegalities of the American Federal Convention, for example. Thus, third, in spite of the terminology, as I have shown, the Indian Constituent Assembly preserved two aspects of the double differentiation characteristic of the American convention, but almost never sovereign assemblies. Partially similar to the American case, the element of double differentiation was sustained by the continuity of federalism, which was reformed but not abandoned. As with the round table model decades later, but in a different form, the Indian assembly was a synthesis of a French-type constituent assembly and an American-style convention.[131] Finally, the constitution-making process and the outcome did not resemble the sovereign dictatorship model, rightly ascribed to some constituent assemblies. This was not only the result of a fortunate plurality within the one dominant party, though that was important, but of a pluralism that was in part planned. While Congress was arguably, if controversially, a protagonist of a revolution, its leaders were not revolutionaries and did not have a revolutionary ideology. Whether Gandhi or Nehru or Ambedkar, they were different types of democrats who all valued rights and democracy, and valued – and even promoted – the pluralism of their movement. Gaining most of the parliamentary seats admittedly was not based on prior negotiations, but

---

[131] See my Chapter 3 in *Post Sovereign Constitution Making*.

Congress promoted a framework of multiple negotiations within the life of the assembly.

To conclude, India had a constituent assembly, which claimed and eventually achieved sovereignty. Yet India had a strongly constitutionalist outcome. What we cannot easily select is the most decisive one among three possible causes, which in this case interacted and reinforced one another. Was it the element of double differentiation, based in part on a precarious legal continuity, as expressed by the continuation in office of the state legislatures? Was it the functional replacement of double differentiation in terms of the dual structure the Constituent Assembly adopted for itself? Or was it the fact that Congress was a highly plural organization, more a national front for liberation than a disciplined, hierarchical, revolutionary political party? If these three explanatory candidates interacted, and reinforced one another, was one of them of greater importance than the rest? The next two examples of Colombia and Venezuela will help us consider this choice, pointing to the plurality of the constituent assembly as the decisive variable, even when double differentiation is abandoned.

Between Revolutionary Reform and Revolution: Colombia and Venezuela

Colombia's constitutional process in the early 1990s was organized around a constituent assembly that was eventually declared to be fully sovereign. It has been noticed that in Latin America at least, the convening of a constituent assembly without a prior political rupture, whether state collapse, revolution or at least *coup d'état*, yet outside the rules of constitutional revision, represented a fundamental innovation. The innovator of this model was indeed the Republic of Colombia.[132] Other states were to follow this model: Venezuela, Ecuador, and, in a failed attempt, Honduras. In Colombia at least, what happened was not clearly the reversal of the normal revolutionary sequence, involving a sovereign constituent process first, and a rupture second. Such a reversal could have been argued for in the case of Venezuela nine years later. There is a widespread, if not unanimous, agreement among the sources, reflecting the terminology of the actors, that what occurred in Colombia was at most structural reform with the goals of increasing inclusion, participation, and state strengthening. While it is true that the constituent assembly was established outside the given rule of change (Article 218 Constitution of Colombia 1886), it could be argued that by relying on the notion of

---

[132] A.R. Brewer-Carias, *Dismantling Democracy in Venezuela* (Cambridge: Cambridge University Press, 2010).

popular sovereignty the Supreme Court of Colombia managed to "legalize" the process. Such a role was itself innovative, appropriate for the epoch of what has been called "the new constitutionalism," but inconsistent with the rather Schmittian legal theory that the Supreme Court itself chose to adopt, according to which a Court is a mere *constitué* that should have no role in *pouvoir constituant*. In Colombia from the legal point of view, the Supreme Court did help to constitute the constituant, indeed in an unlimited, sovereign version.

Depending on our legal theory, we could interpret the ambivalent Colombian constitution-making process either in terms of a continuity of legality, or, equally likely, admitting a legal break, by stressing the continuity of legitimacy focusing on the role of the presidency.[133] Not only had two duly elected presidents, Virgilio Barco and César Gaviria, stayed in power through the entire process, but they played indispensable, if extra-ordinary roles facilitating it under legally declared states of emergency that, however, did not seem to formally enable them to change the constitution. Here too the role of another legitimate institution, the Supreme Court, was indispensable in making the acts involved marginally legal. Whether we stress the ambiguous continuity of legality or merely legitimacy either way, according to my definition of revolution in this chapter, Colombia's constitutional process was not a revolution, but at most, again using Ackerman's terminology, revolutionary reform.[134] Moreover, while there was a mobilized movement for change that Ackerman would stress according to his own concept of revolution, this mobilization was neither a plausible claimant of sovereignty, nor was it a dominant force after initiating the process.[135] There were to be sure many revolutionaries in Colombia in 1990, but they either stayed outside the whole constitution making process (the FARC), or entered it as born-again reformists (M19). On the contrary, the mobilized students did not see themselves as revolutionaries, and indeed called for the creation of a constitutional (*Asamblea Constitucional*) rather than [sovereign] constituent assembly – in other words, a body with limitations.[136]

---

[133] This is exactly the type of ambiguity that is characteristic of revolutionary reform.

[134] Here I disagree with N. Figueroa in his doctoral dissertation who relies on the legal meaning alone. Otherwise, I very much follow his analysis. Nicolás Figueroa, A Critique of Populist Jurisprudence: Courts, Democracy, and Constitutional Change in Colombia and Venezuela. *New School Doctoral Dissertation*. May 2016.

[135] N. Figueroa, "Counter-Hegemonic Constitutionalism: The Case of Colombia," *Constellations* 19.2 (2012): 235–247.

[136] Figueroa "From Democratic Openness to Political Irrelevance," Part II of *A Critique of Populist Jurisprudence*, p. 16, fn 21 According to him, President Barco followed this terminology, and so did Gaviria.

Since there was no revolution we might be tempted to redefine the constituent assembly in the center of the process. The frequent confusion in
Latin American terminology between the categories of *constituent assembly*
(*constituyente*) and *convention* might lead to the conclusion that what Colombia had was a US American type of convention appropriate to revolutionary
reform, rather than a revolution.[137] Unfortunately for this interpretation, however Colombian *Constituyente* began, it did become a sovereign constituent
assembly, and for three reasons. First, because the Supreme Court of Colombia declared it possessing "the original constituent power" and removed all
prior limitations previously agreed upon.[138] This was no mere formal matter,
since the Constituent Assembly proceeded to act on this assumption after
formally declaring itself "sovereign." Indeed, second, after repeated conflicts
with the Congress in place, the Constituent Assembly eventually did dissolve
the elected legislature, and for a transitional period, after the enactment of the
Constitution put a body chosen from itself, the little Congress (*Congresillo*) in
its own place. Third, while a classical convention of the U.S. type recommends
to ratifying instance or instances, the Colombian *Constituyente* enacted the
new constitution on its own, without further ratification, as did some sovereign
constituent assemblies since the French prototype of 1789, theorized by Sieyès.

And yet the constitutional product was strongly "constitutionalist," accomplishing a major reform of the Colombian regime. There was no regime
change even to the extent of India before, and, more clearly, Venezuela after.
How was such an outcome realized? How did what some regard as legally a
revolution[139] become a reform? Why did that reform, upon the declaration
of sovereignty by the Constituent Assembly, not become a revolution? How
did the unstable reform lead to constitutionalist outcome? The burden of this
section is to try to provide answers, first through outlining the Colombian
scenario, and then by comparing it to its Venezuelan counterpart.[140]

[137] Chapter 3 of my *Post Sovereign Constitution Making*.
[138] Nicolas Figueroa "Authoritarian Affinities and Democratic Potentials" Part I of *A Critique of Populist Jurisprudence* May 2016.
[139] Ibid.
[140] I do not claim originality here, given the convincing and sophisticated literature I relied on: Fox et al. "Lessons of the Colombian Constitutional Reform of 1991" in L. Miller, *Framing the State in times of Transition* (Washington: USIP 2010); R. Segura and A.M. Bejarano, "¡Ni una asamblea más sin nosotros! Exclusion, Inclusion, and the Politics of Constitution-Making in the Andes," *Constellations* 11.2 (2004): 217–236; Segura and Bejarano, "The Difference a Constituent Assembly Makes: Explaining Divergent Constitutional Outcomes in Colombia and Venezuela," ms.; G. Negretto, *Making Constitutions* (Cambridge: Cambridge University Press, 2013); as well as N. Figueroa, *A Critique of Populist Jurisprudence: Courts, Democracy, and Constitutional Change in Colombia and Venezuela*.

One plausible answer to my questions is based on the magnitude of the Colombian state crisis, the extreme level of uncontrolled violence in the country, the frequency of emergency rule, and the economic hardships caused by weak state capacity.[141] Under such conditions, it could be argued that political actors seeking stability would be more inclined to follow public-regarding rather than party political motivations. I accept the great general importance of these contextual factors, but am forced to note that in international comparison crisis or even state failure in themselves do not lead to any particular outcome. Equally important was the failure of repeated previous reform attempts, by presidents or Congressional majorities, who were blocked either by the inherited constitution's amendment rule, or by the Supreme Court.[142] It is uncontestable that an organized mass movement, starting already in 1980 and greatly intensified by the student movement of 1989–1990, initiated the process, eventually with the creative device of the extra-legal 7th ballot, unofficially supported by up to three million voters in the elections of 1990, calling for the election of a *constituyente* outside the existing rules of revision.[143] Given strong Congressional opposition, even this call would not have led to either a new assembly or to a new constitution had two presidents not used their emergency powers under states of siege to counterpose popular sovereignty to formal legality, in the form of organizing referenda and executive orders. The combination of all these factors then helps explain how Colombia was able to elect a constituent assembly in charge of making a new constitution.

But we have not yet explained the result of a "constitutionalist constitution." That such was not the only possible outcome is shown by the contrast with Venezuela, where, as we will see, a president was also enabled by previous deadlock and Supreme Court decisions to convene a constituent assembly outside the formal rules of revision. (Indeed, the Venezuelan Court, as we will show, tried to be less permissive concerning the nature of the constituent power than its Colombian forerunner.) Undoubtedly, Presidents Gaviria and Chávez were very different personalities, and yet I would not seek the explanation in personal psychology. I would rather follow Renata Segura and Ana Maria Bejarano in stressing what they call the pre-assembly moment, often neglected by students of constituent assemblies.[144] In my view that moment, and how it is organized, is even more important than the actual process within an assembly.

[141] Negretto, *Making Constitutions*.
[142] Figueroa, "Counter Hegemonic Constitutionalism."
[143] Fox, "Lessons of the Colombian Constitutional Reform of 1991."
[144] Segura and Bejarano, "Exclusion, Inclusion . . ."; see Elster, "Legislatures as Constituent Assemblies," op. cit.; and Negretto, op. cit., who follows him.

It is, of course, noted by many others that the new electoral rule for the constituent assembly in Colombia, in stark contrast to Venezuela, produced a highly plural assembly where power sharing and repeated compromise were essential if a constitution was to be produced.[145] But this electoral rule did not come from nowhere or even simply from President Gaviria's preferences. Yes, abstractly it is true that highly proportional electoral rules are normatively more appropriate for constitution-making bodies, than more majoritarian rules, adopted for the sake of governability. Elster is right: a constitutional convention (in my terminology "doubly differentiated") is more likely to be associated with this normative desideratum than a constituent assembly that is in charge of legislation or a legislature that assumes the task of constitution making.[146] Initially at least, Colombia's assembly was doubly differentiated, although in the beginning Venezuela also started out with a convention, whatever they called it. Yet the rule that arranged for its election was extremely disproportional, and, as I will show, predictably so. Thus, one cannot derive the nature of the electoral rule, from the type of assembly that is to be elected, without committing a functionalist fallacy. As we know from the round table countries, negotiated transitions produce relatively proportional electoral rules, especially if new or small parties participate in the negotiations as equal partners. This is the basis of the insurance model, itself normatively linked to the veil of ignorance.[147]

The key therefore to the Colombian outcome is the process of pre-assembly negotiations organized by President Gaviria, which were to produce the rules and limits of the constituent assembly along with the all-important highly proportional electoral rule for that body. Yet instead of the likely pluralistic sensibility of Gaviria as compared to the populist identity of Chávez, I would seek the main reason for this choice in the need of bringing in former guerrillas, i.e., revolutionaries (the M19 and, it was originally hoped, even the FARC) into the negotiating process in which the parties of the government too would remain important participants. The new parties had no incentive to participate under what they regarded as a rigged system, i.e., an oligarchic two-party system. They were brought in to the process in order to limit the violence in the country, and it is very unfortunate that similar attempts to do the same with the FARC failed. Once, however, such an actor, the M19, was present in the negotiations, and with the support of other small parties, as well as external political actors, it demanded a much more open electoral system for

---

[145] See the already cited works of Fox, Negretto, Segura and Bejarano; as well as Figueroa.
[146] Elster, op. cit.
[147] See my chapter 3 *Post Sovereign Constitution Making*; as well as chapter 5 below.

a differentiated constituent assembly. This demand, obviously made just for a constitution making assembly and not primarily concerned with governability, was accepted by the other participants.

I do not wish to fully assimilate the Colombian case to my round table countries with their post-sovereign logic. Indeed, as a testimony to the corrosive effects of bad theory, the important pre-assembly deal almost collapsed. President Gaviria did formally enact the results of the negotiations, under the relatively questionable instrument of his emergency powers, as *Decreto* #1926. This decree entailed not only the electoral rule, but also a number of crucial limitations on the constituent assembly.[148] The most important of these was the requirement that the Assembly could not change the mandate of the existing legislature, thus abolish double differentiation. Another limit was the requirement of a review of the product of the Assembly by the Supreme Court itself, to test its consistency with the original mandate the people gave in the referendum. To the president himself, these limits were important precisely to avoid a sovereign or run-away assembly that could undermine the separation of powers. Congress, on the other hand, feared the uncontrolled use of the president's emergency powers. Everyone expected the Court to agree, but to great surprise and inconsistent with its previous decision that had allowed the referendum in the first place,[149] the Supreme Court not only proceeded to fully abrogate the existing constitution's amendment rule, but also to declare all limits on the constituent assembly to be unconstitutional.[150] While the electorate was asked subsequently to approve in another referendum the details of the constitution-making project, its agreement to limits on the constituent assembly was declared irrelevant in advance, by the very unfortunate decision of the Supreme Court. Here, even on the theoretical level, the decision of the Court regarding *Decreto* 1926 was incoherent, and inconsistent even with the classical theory of the constituent power, as Nicolas Figueroa demonstrates.

---

[148] Fox, op. cit., 471.

[149] This seemed to call for the process within the established constitution, implying that the new assembly would not be sovereign, and thus could be limited. The decision moreover seemed to imply that the amendment rule of the inherited constitution could not be fully bypassed. Figueroa, part II, 20ff

[150] *Corte Suprema de Justicia de Colombia, Sentencia No. 138 del 9 de Octubre de 1990.* As Figueroa goes on to argue (pp. 24f), in line with the two basic tenets of populist jurisprudence, the court declared unconstitutional the limitations included in the executive's emergency decree regarding the topics that the assembly could discuss once convened. They considered the assembly to be the representative of the people in their condition as subjects of the constituent power; for this reason, no restrictions of any kind could be imposed on the actions of the assembly. From this moment on, the implementation of the political agreement consigned in the text of the emergency decree could not be enforced by legal means.

Since the Court interpreted the referendum as an act of popular sovereignty that could not be constrained by the amendment rule in place, it was entirely unclear why "the people" could not bind their delegate, the constituent assembly, as occurred, for example, in France in 1945–46.

The danger of this decision could be seen only later in Venezuela, where the Supreme Court tried in vain to resist the implications. But even in Colombia the decision could have been disastrous for the process. Not only the Court's own powers but also those of Congress and the president, all "constituted powers" were now in principle challengeable by the now-sovereign constituent assembly. Fortunately, however, the electoral rule could not be challenged, first because the Court left it alone, and, second, because the Assembly's own existence and make-up depended on it. Thus, the attempt to restrain the assembly through "external" rules and institutions, failed, but a similar result was achieved by the means of a politically divided, pluralistic assembly, an "internal" limit.[151] While the delegates, following the Court decision to this effect, "could not resist the temptation to declare the sovereign character of the assembly" there was no unitary party, no individual person who could claim to embody that sovereignty. And yet the assembly was serious about this matter, as Figueroa shows (29), first by excluding a role for the administrative courts, next by refusing any judicial review of their acts, and finally, and most importantly, in the end by revoking the mandate of the Congress. To achieve the last goal politically, an unfortunate trade-off was required: on the wishes of the dominant parties of Congress the new parties agreed that no member of the constituent assembly could run in the next legislative elections. This was a repeat of the famous self-denying ordinance sponsored by Robespierre,[152] and with adverse results for the project of change, and especially for the nontraditional parties who proceeded to do poorly under the restored, old electoral rule, whose restoration too was part of the price paid for the ability to dissolve Congress.

Admittedly, *El Congresillo* that served a few months in place of the old dissolved legislature did not seem to do any harm, as far as most interpreters are concerned.[153] More importantly, unlike later in Venezuela, the Supreme

---

[151] Figueroa, part II, 26; on the two types of limits see D. Landau, "Constitution-Making Gone Wrong." *Alabama Law Review* 923 (2013).

[152] I very much doubt Elster's guess that Robespierre knew or already planned the effect of this rule, namely Jacobin subversion of the Legislative Assembly. Op. cit. In Colombia it is more likely that the main older parties knew what they were doing. Of course there is always a veil of ignorance type justification for such a measure, to avoid self-dealing by would-be legislators.

[153] See Figueroa part II, who considers it a very dangerous precedent with harmful, unintended consequences for the new parties, including M 19, that initiated it.

Court was not abolished nor packed during either the constitution-making or the short transitional process, and in principle it remained an institution within the separation of powers. If there was an implicit temporary reduction of the power of the courts during the making of the Constitution, including the Supreme Court, this was compensated in the document itself by the establishment of a strong framework of independent judiciary, along with a new Constitutional Court with a wide and differentiated jurisdiction. Where the problem in the past was often oscillation between forms of hyperpresidentialism and congressional oligarchy, which continually weakened state power and capacities, the Constitution also established a more balanced relationship between the powers of the presidency and Congress.[154] The paradox that to me at least needs to be explained is that these reformist results were achieved by a sovereign constituent assembly that even declared its complete sovereignty, which could, in turn, be interpreted in the terms of revolutionary credentials or aspirations.[155]

Certainly after the Supreme Court's decisions, the results were not achieved by the separation of powers, or even the initial double differentiation. The Supreme Court, itself a potential part of the separation of powers, in effect neutralized itself in the process, and its decision on sovereignty exposed Congress to similar neutralization. Thus, the negotiated pre-assembly moment with its one result that withstood invalidation, namely the electoral rule, is the only way we can explain the outcome. The contrast with Venezuela, where the Court eventually did try to limit the Constituent Assembly, supplies further proofs of this thesis.

Venezuela was the first country to consciously and deliberately follow Colombia's innovation in constitution making. Here too, in 1997, there was no rupture of the political regime before the constituent process began. Here too constitution making by a constituent assembly, initially a convention, was convened for the purpose of constitution making, outside the inherited amendment rule (Arts. 245 and 246 Constitution of 1961) which, in contrast to Colombia, even contained something like a rule for total revision (called "general reform").[156] Here too a duly elected new president of the republic played an initiating role, one even more active than in Colombia. Here too the apex court, the Supreme Court of Venezuela, legalized a process that otherwise would have amounted to a legal break without any ambiguity. Here too

---

[154] Negretto, op. cit.   [155] On this, see Negretto, op. cit.; Figueroa, part II.

[156] Ordinary amendments required the support of the two chambers of Congress and two-thirds of state legislatures; total revision, however, required two-thirds of Congress meeting in a joint session, and ratification in a referendum.

there was an early sovereignty declaration by the *Constituyente*, and attempts to abrogate or reduce other powers of the state.

But, inevitably perhaps, there were also crucial differences between the two countries, some of them playing a causal role. On the one side, at least as Segura and Bejarano claim, the political crisis and the loss of legitimacy of the state were not as severe in Venezuela as in Colombia. As the same interpreters indicated, there have been some successful, and, I think, important amendments to the Venezuelan Constitution, prior to the new process.[157] More importantly, they argue that in contrast to the Colombian movement from below for constitutional change, to which two presidents responded positively, in Venezuela the project was a presidential one from the outset, and a Chavista one even before, during his failed coup attempt, for which support was mobilized, in the populist manner, from above. Thus, attempts to limit the Constituent Assembly in Venezuela came not from the presidents as in Colombia, but from the Supreme Court, which first played an enabling role, even if both of these efforts were equally unsuccessful in the two countries. The failure in Venezuela had much more important consequences: the suspension, and eventually dissolution, of the rival legislative body and the packing and weakening of the judicial branches of power during the last, transitional stage of the constituent process. Finally, and most importantly of all differences, the Venezuelan process produced a constitution that was formally much more presidentialist, with fewer safeguards for constitutionalism, much weaker courts and constitutional review, and in terms of its actual functioning, materially, a populist semi authoritarian constitution whose forms were violated from the outset.

Considering the result, Venezuela had already undergone regime change during the constituent process, whereas Colombia did not. Indeed, the main protagonists in Venezuela saw themselves as revolutionary actors. If this too was an example of "revolutionary reform" it came much closer to revolution, or even stepped over the threshold to it, involving a *coup d'état*. This hidden coup came not before the process, but from somewhere within it.[158]

Here I can make an attempt only to explain two of the differences, one in the process that turned Venezuela's assembly into a sovereign dictatorship, and the other, the deeply related, semi-authoritarian result. Again the overall

---

[157] "The Difference a Constituent Assembly Makes" op. cit.

[158] Such an internal coup within a legal regime change is difficult to identify. For example, in the very different case of the transition from the Weimar Republic to the Nazi Regime, it could have been the Enabling Act voted in by a purged Reichstag, or the subsequent elimination of the presidency, by decree, that was forbidden by the enabling act. See K.D. Bracher, *The German Dictatorship*, trans. by Jean Steinberg (New York: Praeger, 1970).

contextual difference cannot explain these: a less serious crisis of the state and its legitimacy could have had the opposite result of mere reform, rather than regime change. The populist movement mobilized from above was certainly a necessary condition, as was the fully populist self-understanding of the leading presidential figure. But even a genuine revolution with a charismatic leader cannot guarantee a pliant elected constituent assembly, as Lenin was to find out in 1918 before he decided to dissolve the assembly. Perhaps the Bolshevik leader had too much faith in his own doctrine of the dictatorship latent in representative democracy. Chávez and his circle, however, managed to significantly improve on Lenin's formula by controlling the electoral outcome in an unprecedented, but admittedly imaginative way.

Here too the contrast with Colombia was enormous, stressing "the pre-assembly moment." In Venezuela, unlike Colombia, there were no pre-assembly negotiations involving the major parties. The electoral rule, designed by two handpicked presidential commissions, was the product of pure imposition. It mandated individual candidacies, rather than party lists, organized in terms of 24 regional districts (104 members) and one national one (24 representatives), plus three "indigenous" representatives, 131 in all. Surprise, surprise: in the end 123 out of 131 candidates supported by the president were elected, converting 66 percent of the votes to 94 percent of the seats, a result unprecedented for any "democratically" elected constituent assembly.[159] To what extent the result was achieved by the admitted popularity of Chávez at that time (that could not account, in any case, for the disproportionality), or the mistake of the major parties of not matching the *chuletas* of Chávez with lists of their own, or the rules themselves, or their combination, cannot be fully determined. What is certain is that such a result could not be achieved in a divided country[160] without imposition and manipulation.

There was to be sure one attempt to limit the manipulation of the election through the construction of arbitrary rules. After an initial decision, which enabled a consultative referendum on having a constituent assembly outside the rules, the same Supreme Court, in two decisions did indeed try to limit the powers thus created. In its second major decision on the constituent assembly, the Court rejected the wording of the referendum that would have allowed the president himself to generate the rules for electing the constituent

---

[159] See L. Neuman and J. McCoy, "Observing Political Change in Venezuela: The Bolivarian Constitution and 2000 Elections." Carter Center 2001; Segura, "The Difference a Constituent Assembly Makes"; Brewer-Carias, *Dismantling Democracy in Venezuela*.

[160] In the presidential elections earlier the same year, Chávez received only 56 percent of the vote. It is highly unlikely that even this result could have been duplicated for an assembly, in a multiparty country, if the rules were fair.

assembly. After having justified this by the claim that it is the right of the people in a referendum to generate such a rule, however, the door was opened to the president to offer the rules his commission devised for a yes or no vote by the electorate. The Court was demanding the impossible: the people in a referendum cannot generate a complex instrument like an electoral rule. Already having been influenced by Colombian precedents, the legal body could have demanded instead a negotiated proposal that could have been also voted on in the referendum, instead of a presidential proposal. Not having done this, the Court opened the road to the same imposition it sought to block. Given this failure a third decision contradicting the language of the very first could have no effect. It was now in vain that the Court proceeded to postulate that the Constituent Assembly had only derived, but not the original constituent power, and thus had to stay within the limits of the inherited constitution, along with its separation of powers. Such a restriction could work only where an assembly reflected the pluralism of society itself, as it did in Colombia, where such limits were respected even after the Court postulated sovereign powers for the Assembly.

Given the enormous governmental majority in the Venezuelan Constituent Assembly, here the declaration of sovereign status had very different consequences than in Colombia.[161] Since the Colombian declaration re-affirmed the prior Court decision, where in Venezuela the contrary decision was explicitly violated, it seems formally correct to speak of a quasi-revolutionary break, or a *coup d'état* in Venezuela, though not in Colombia. The form did not remain mere form, as immediately demonstrated by President Chávez who formally resigned his office, before the Assembly almost unanimously reconfirmed it.[162] This was a sign of the coming destruction of the other independent branches. It was initially the turn of Congress, with many opponents of Chávez in the body. First it lost some of its jurisdiction, then its meetings were curtailed, and many of its functions were taken over, before it was finally dissolved and replaced by a *Congresillo*, named after its Colombian forerunner.[163] But whereas in

---

[161] See the cited texts of Segura and Bejarano, Figueroa, and Brewer-Carias.

[162] Landau, op. cit.

[163] Brewer-Carias, op. cit. The presentation of Brewer seems to be contradictory. He first indicates the dissolution of Congress early in the tenure of the Constituent Assembly, and then indicates this dissolution only for the transitional period. Cf. pages 58 vs. 73. I am not able to remove the contradiction. According to Nicolas Figueroa: the decree of August 1999 did not dissolve Congress. It did take away most of its power, prohibited its members from holding ordinary sessions, and claimed that in case congress refused to fulfill the tasks that were now assigned to it then the constituent assembly would do them. The actual dissolution was during the transition, after the constitution was already in place, when the *Congresillo* was created (December 1999)." Personal communication.

Colombia what has been called the "revocation of Congress" occurred only for the transitional period after the Constitution was enacted (after 16 months of coexistence during the constituent process), in Venezuela Congress was emasculated, if not formally dissolved, one month after the election of the Constituent Assembly and five months before the Constitution was finalized. The now thoroughly cowed Supreme Court proceeded to affirm the relevant decision (on the August 1999 Decree), inconsistent with its previous one on the lack of original constituent power and, as all main interpreters point out, thereby committed suicide.[164] Eventually, at the time of the dissolution of Congress, the Supreme Court was prematurely dissolved by the Constituent Assembly, its members were disbanded, and the jurisdiction of the replacement body was drastically curtailed, though it was fully packed with new members appointed without the restrictions required by the new Constitution or the old one for that matter.[165]

I do not propose to debate the contents of the so-called Bolivarian Constitution. Undoubtedly, speaking formally, it had some excellent elements, and equally likely some highly unfortunate ones. This is probably true of all revolutionary constitutions, whose biggest problem is that many of their emancipatory or progressive elements are never enforced or applied. My interest here is only in the process. One clue to the strength or weakness of a process is the element of time. Another is the constituent assembly's establishing a rapid, legal transference of power from itself to a newly elected legislative body. Let me take these two aspects in turn, using the historical experience of French revolutionary constitution making as a comparative guide, justified because the Venezuelan process and even the Colombian from the ideological point of view belonged to the world inaugurated in France from 1789 until Bonaparte's coup ten years later.

A coup or a revolution can produce a new constitution extremely rapidly. The *Convention nationale*, after the purging of the body, produced a Constitution in 1793 in a matter of 22 days during June 1793, and had it popularly ratified within two months. Napoleon Bonaparte, to give another example, carried out his coup of the 18the Brumaire on November 9, 1979, and had "the Constitution of the Year VIII," which named him First Consul, ratified, in a likely fraudulent plebiscite, less than two months later, on December 24

---

[164] Brewer-Carias, op. cit; Figueroa, Part I; Landau, op. cit.

[165] Brewer-Carias, op. cit., 79; 81; 230–231. To make matters clear, the Constituent assembly's transitional arrangements replaced the Supreme Court (SC) by the Supreme Tribunal of Justice (STJ); appointed all the new members, some of whom would have been ineligible, for terms of well beyond the time when the Constitution came into effect. The Constitutionality of all this was examined not by the SC but by the new STJ, on its own behalf.

of the same year. Between the two dates, the two commissions, appointed by Bonaparte from previous legislators and led by Sieyès, worked on the text for a few weeks at most before Bonaparte himself entirely restructured it in what has been called "a coup within the coup." While these cases are perhaps the most extreme ones, they do indicate the possible acceleration of constitution making time involved in revolutions when an executive power of one man or a vanguard is in charge. Admittedly, the French Revolution also offers other, contrary examples. The Constitution of 1791 was drafted and enacted by the *Assemblée constituante* in a period of over two years, the body that drafted it was the transmutation of the Estates General, plurally constituted. There were many staunch and moderate royalists present, as well as radical republicans, and many in between. The process also involved negotiations with the king, who was still in place. But even the already mentioned Constitution of 1793 took a total of nine months to make after the initial assembling of the *Convention nationale*, because of substantial divisions within the assembly until it was purged. Moreover, the process was interrupted by the large matters of the trial of the king[166] at the Convention, a new Parisian insurrection and the subsequent expulsion of the Gironde, meaning the radical purging of the representatives of the people elected by universal suffrage.[167] Only after the latter event in June 1793, leading to the abandonment of the famous Condorcet draft, was the new text of the Committee of Public Safety drafted (or finalized) and passed with extreme rapidity, before submitted to the plebiscite.[168] Finally, the Constitution of 1795, which obviously involved more deliberation and debate than its predecessor, took 13 months of work in the Convention, after the coup of the 9th of Thermidor against Robespierre and the Committee. In each of these cases the delays in the work of revolutionary assemblies[169] were due to serious internal conflicts within the body, and, equally importantly, conflicts of the drafting assembly with insurrectionary "publics."[170] Thus, revolutions,

---

[166] The convention's constitutional committee, though created on September 29, 1792 did not begin its work until the execution of the king, on January 21, 1793. The trial itself took place at the Convention, and obviously took up its energies. J. Godechot, *Les Constitutions de la France depuis 1789* (Paris: Flammarion, 1995), p. 70.

[167] F. Furet *Revolutionary France 1770–1880* (London: Wiley-Blackwell, 1995), p. 128.

[168] Furet, "Revolutionary Government" in F. Furet and M. Ozouf, *A Critical Dictionary of the French Revolution* (Cambridge, MA: Harvard University Press, 1989), p. 548; *Revolutionary France*, p. 129; R.R. Palmer, *The Age of the Democratic Revolutions*, vol. II (Princeton: Princeton University Press, 1964), p. 110. In spite of the purge of the Gironde, and the death of Condorcet, many aspects of his great draft were preserved, if in a watered down form.

[169] See D. Richet, "Revolutionary Assemblies" in *A Critical Dictionary of the French Revolution*.

[170] This factor explains the difference between relatively shorter time involved in the making of the US Constitution of 1787, and the longer one of the French process of 1789–1791. Elster has rightly stressed the exclusion of the public in the US case, even if such an exclusion is

which are said to generally accelerate time,[171] can do so in the domain of constitution making only if or after political power is sufficiently unified. As we have seen in the Indian case of revolutionary reform, a highly plural assembly, even in the hands of one party, will decelerate the time of constitution making.

Conversely, however, the dramatic acceleration of the time of constitution making implies if not a revolutionary process automatically, then at the very least the ability of a unified actor to impose its constitutional conception. Here lies a clue to the fundamental difference between two processes that may have been formally similar. In Colombia, the Constituent Assembly was elected on December 9, 1990, first assembled in February 5 1991, and enacted the Constitution on July 4, 1991, following six months of deliberations. In Venezuela, by contrast, these three relevant dates were July 1999, August 1999, and November 17, 1999 with a plebiscite at the end of December 1999. This formally involved three months of actual work, half the time for Colombia. But we must also take into account the observation by Brewer-Carias that the struggles with the established branches lasted until October 14, 1999, with the Court's ratification of the defeat of Congress as well as its own, along with the full and exclusive sovereignty of the Constituent Assembly. Thus, the political leadership at least had other matters to focus on than drafting. Given these constraints of time and politics, we have every reason to accept the view of Brewer-Carias, himself a participant, that the drafting process was characterized not only by exclusion, but also by extreme haste and brevity.[172]

Given this haste, the result could also create problems for a new regime, lacunae that a new freely elected legislature would have had to fill in ways that could not securely predicted. Here Colombia supplied an unfortunate precedent, as we have seen, of creating a transitional legislative authority *El Congresito*, the little congress, displacing (legally unnecessarily) the elected Congress, and being in charge of the transition between constitution making, and the new electoral regime. In Colombia, the negative effects of this had to do primarily with the trade-off required in a pluralistic framework, namely the prohibition of members of the Constituent Assembly to run for election for the new legislature. The members of the dissolved Congress seemed not to have been similarly restricted, and along with their parties they were in

---

not normatively desirable, even if functional. See, e.g., J. Elster, "Arguing and Bargaining in Two Constituent Assemblies," *U. Pa. J. Const. L.* 2 (1999): 345.

[171] (Koselleck; Walter Benjamin)

[172] Op. cit., pp. 60–61. He very plausibly claims presidential pressure, to finish the job quickly, for the sake of the legitimation of the new regime, one that a completely dominated assembly could be easily satisfied.

great numbers re-elected.[173] Thus, in Colombia *El Congresito* had ultimately a conservative rather than a revolutionary outcome.

It was otherwise with what was called *Congresillo* in Venezuela. Here the Colombian device was combined with an old pattern inherited from the *Convention nationale* of the French Revolution, for the maker of the Constitution to stay in power beyond the enactment of the Constitution, and to undertake measures inconsistent with it.

Let me first explore the examples of the French *Convention nationale*, to show that the comparison to Venezuela is not a far-fetched one. As all serious historians of the French Revolution have stressed, during June of 1793, in its radical phase, the leading protagonists organized into the Committee of Public Safety, a committee of the *Convention nationale*, drafted, and enacted what appeared to be a dramatically democratic new constitution, the so-called *Constitution of the Year I* [of the Republic].[174] After the plebiscite in August that ratified the document, for the Constitution to be put in effect would have required the dissolution of the Convention, and of its committees that exercised executive power. That would have been followed by free elections on the local level by universal manhood suffrage in a country where the dominant revolutionaries of Paris were in a minority. Whether because of the circumstances of war and counter-revolution, or because of the self-interest of the Convention that "envisage[d] its own indefinite continuation,"[175] or both,[176] the document was instead suspended by the Convention before it was ever applied, and was placed in an Arc to be preserved till the re-establishment of peace when it could supposedly be recovered and instituted. Along with the suspension, a supposedly provisional Revolutionary Government was declared, which was simply an institutionalization of the de facto dictatorship of the Committee of Public Safety of the Convention already exercised since the

---

[173] Negretto, op. cit.
[174] Many have long considered this text as the model for democratic constitutionalism, while others refer to it as "slapdash text" (Furet op. cit.) "drawn up in incredible haste" and "thrown together in a few days" (Palmer, *Age*, vol. II, p. 110). The interesting direct democratic features of this text were derived from the earlier much more carefully drawn-up draft of Condorcet, which was abandoned with the defeat and purge of his faction, the Gironde, just before the short formal work on the new and inferior text. The ambiguous reception is in part due to this historical state of affairs.
[175] Palmer, *Age*, vol. II, p. 110; Furet in both cited texts.
[176] It was argued that the weak executive power of the new Constitution would not allow the successful pursuit of the war and the civil war by the republic. That may have been plausible even if not true, but previously the victorious Jacobins argued against Condorcet's draft, incorrectly, that it created an overly strong executive (Godechot, op. cit.). What that draft did do was to seek to domesticate insurrections through the establishment of different democratic channels.

purge of the Gironde. Aside from other possible causes for the suspension of the Constitution, the interest of the Convention in staying in power is not merely the result of retroactive imputation of motives. Interestingly, such an interest was once again confirmed by the Convention's remaining (and partially restored) members after the body ended the Jacobin Dictatorship. After enacting the Constitution of the Year III (1795) that was again duly ratified in a plebiscite, the Convention decreed in special legislation, that two-thirds of the members of the two new legislative bodies would initially have to be elected from among its own members.[177]

Acknowledging partial historical repetition, Marx immediately sought to qualify the idea in the very famous lines of the 18th Brumaire: *"das eine Mal als große Tragödie, das andre Mal als lumpige Farce"* ["first time as [great] tragedy, the second time as [crude] farce"]. Of course, the farce could not produce an exact repetition of the events of the tragedy. What he had in mind was not merely the names of the protagonists, the two Bonapartes or the party labels, but the repeat of a specific logic. A similar logical tendency of a power without limits to perpetuate itself represents the link between the two self-perpetuating acts of the great French forerunner, the National Convention, in 1793 and 1795, and its Venezuelan epigon, the *Constituyente* of 1999. In the description of Brewer-Carias, just five days *after* the popular ratification of the Constitution the Venezuelan Constituent Assembly decided to extend its tenure to January 2000. There was no vacuum of public power that could justify the action until the Assembly proceeded to produce one. This then happened merely two days later, when it proceeded to pass a series of new transitional provisions never approved in a referendum or plebiscite, even though the new Constitution already its own transitional provisions. These provided for the final dissolution of the two chambers of the old Congress, whose members were merely displaced and disempowered previously, temporarily replaced by the *Congresillo*, the dissolution of all the state (i.e., provincial) legislatures, as well as the dissolution of the old Supreme Court still in office. Instead of the latter, a new Constitutional Tribunal was established with the appointment of all its members assigned to the handpicked *Congresillo*. That latter body was to establish and appoint several other bodies, including a new

---

[177] Palmer, *Age*, vol. II, p. 215; and the wonderful discussion of the "Law of Two Thirds" in Furet's *Revolutionary France*, pp. 165–167, which shows the conscious reversal of Robespierre's successful proposal self-denying ordinance of 1791. According to the relevant decree, "All members presently active in the Convention are re-eligible. Election assemblies may not take fewer than two-thirds of them to form the legislative body." As Furet explains, if the number fell under two-thirds, those so elected could and did co-opt a sufficient number of old members (about 100) to correct the proportion.

judicial control commission given many of the functions of the Constitutional Tribunal as provided for in the new Constitution, and the key institution of a new Electoral Commission in charge of administering the newly enacted rules for legislative and presidential elections. To complete the picture, the charge of unconstitutionality of this very act was to be considered by the new and packed Constitutional Tribunal, which unsurprisingly voted in favor of the Constituent Assembly having so extended its powers.[178]

Unlike in France, where the first extension of incumbent power was indefinite in length and the second was to last for two years, in Venezuela its different forms lasted for variously long periods, depending on the institution, on function and on terms of appointment involved.[179] The justification was different in each case: the vigorous pursuit of war by the revolutionary government in France, and the supposed facilitation of the democratic transition in Venezuela. But one purpose, if not the justification seemed to have been similar: to allow incumbents, whether the *Convention nationale* or the Chávez government, to control the process of change and to stay thereby in power. In France this meant that first in 1793 elections would be delayed indefinitely by a political dictatorship, till the end of a war that was nowhere in sight. In 1795 the meaning of the Two Thirds Law was that elections would take place, but that the results would be the return of mostly incumbents. In Venezuela, too, elections would take place, but they would be now controlled by the executive power through its new agencies. It does not matter that some members of the Convention in 1795, or the Chávez government in 1999, could perhaps have won entirely free elections at that time. The transitional measures meant that neither sets of incumbents were taking any chances, any more than the incumbents of 1793 and 1795 who would have most likely lost their election, if ever held, if not in Paris then certainly in the rest of France. Interestingly, all three efforts culminated in coup attempts. Thermidor in France is the most famous of these, but the two failed revolts against the Thermidorians, following the Law of Two Thirds, are equally interesting.[180] There was, of course, a nearly successful failed coup against Chávez in 2002.[181]

---

[178] Brewer, op. cit.; Figueroa, part II, op. cit.

[179] The *Congresillo* was replaced within a year; and new provincial legislatures were elected. But the new members of judicial bodies and electoral commission were to serve well beyond the free elections. See Brewer-Carias, op. cit. for the details.

[180] Furet *Revolutionary France*, p. 166; Palmer, *Age*, vol. II, pp. 215 and 232ff. These were the failed royalist coup of 1795, and the even more unsuccessful insurrectionary attempt, the Conspiracy of Equals of 1796.

[181] *The Silence and the Scorpion: The Coup Against Chávez and the Making of Modern Venezuela* by Brian A. Nelson, Nation Books, 2009, as well as the critical review by Gregory Wilpert https://nacla.org/article/venezuelan-coup-revisited-silencing-evidence.

In my view, for all these coups and coup attempts, the governments that controlled and abused the constituent power were at least partially responsible.

But there was no attempted coup against the Colombian Constitution of 1991, in a country that has known such attempts, some of them successful like the last in 1953. This could be explained perhaps by the unintended effect of the final agreements in that country, which allowed a measure of political restoration in the first free elections under the new Constitution.[182] But that would only explain the absence of an attempted coup on the Right, and not that of an insurrection of the disappointed Left. A deeper explanation in my view would return to the pre-assembly moment, which explains the consensual nature of the constitution itself as well as the absence of an attempt of a divided *Constituyente*, however sovereign in principle, to perpetuate itself. Indeed, the last agreement produced a self-denying ordinance that could have been harmful from a political point of view, but also could have increased the legitimacy of the assembly's work, and even the political outcome that implied the return of a nearly revolutionary process to the path of reform. It is an alternate story, one stressed by Nicolas Figueroa, which, instead of representing hegemonic preservation, the Constitution was a product of counterhegemonic constitutionalism, based on a powerful new Constitutional Court that would be a main agent of resisting future oligarchic and hyperpresidentialist efforts.[183] That too was possible only on the bases of a consensual process in the Assembly, itself based on the pre-assembly moment of negotiating the metarules of the game.[184]

In Search of an Explanation

With the three cases of India, Colombia, and Venezuela in mind we are ready to propose some hypotheses[185] concerning the chances of the "domestication" of constituent assemblies, to try to indicate under what conditions dictatorship can be avoided using this dangerous instrument, with constitutional

---

[182] Negretto, op. cit.; Figueroa, Part II, op. cit.

[183] Figueroa "Counter Hegemonic Constitutionalism"; see also chapter 5 below.

[184] Figueroa (Part II) seems to argue that such activity by the Constitutional Court was facilitated by the sovereign claims made for the prior constituent process. That may be the case for Colombia, though as he stresses, similar claims in Venezuela brought no such outcome. Thus, I would rather stress the high level of democratic legitimacy that is compatible certainly with an assembly under some limits.

[185] That could be tested by large N studies, as well as by examining its logic, and of course in practice. The next section on Egypt and Tunisia will attempt the latter, in openly revolutionary contexts.

democracy as the result. I have so far stressed three relevant mechanisms: double differentiation, judicial control, and pre-assembly negotiated agreements that can be plausibly interpreted as forms of such domestication. I would now like to evaluate the relative strengths and weaknesses of the three forms, as well as add the importance of the right theoretical self-understanding for each of them.

I start with double differentiation. Within my conception it is paradoxical to even mention it, since I have identified it as a characteristic of the "convention" paradigm, and thus belonging to another pattern of constitution making than classical constituent assemblies. However, most actors and interpreters do not make this distinction,[186] and in practice the form of the convention can easily turn into that of the constituent assembly. Yet even when this happens, some elements of double differentiation can survive and play a role, as I have tried to show in the Indian case. Arguably, double differentiation is a mechanism that keeps even constituent assemblies on the path of revolutionary reform. But, and this is my point, as we have seen in the case of Colombia and Venezuela, it is a weak mechanism, one especially vulnerable to revolutionary populist ideas of popular sovereignty. When that idea is present, double differentiation can devolve into the dual power of two assemblies, a destructive political competition between them, with the advantage going to the constituent assembly, because of an implicit hierarchy between the bodies and their tasks, and because the convention or constituent assembly is almost always elected later than the normal legislature.

I have argued in earlier chapters that, assuming the presence of the doctrine of popular sovereignty, genuine federalism is a form that is required to maintain the functioning of ordinary assemblies during constitution making. Federalism can play its stabilizing role in the case of units like Massachusetts (1781) or New Hampshire (1784)[187] or, more likely, the case of a union, as in the case of the 1787 process. The case of India supports the hypothesis. It is true that, in contrast to the case of the US Confederation Congress, in India the weak Central Legislature was disbanded when the remodeled (and in its own self-understanding, sovereign) constituent assembly began its work after the Partition. But the provincial assemblies remained in place, continued to govern and played a role through their delegates in the Constituent Assembly

---

[186] But see Schmitt, *Verfassungslehre*; Böckenförde, *"Die verfassunggebende Gewalt des Volkes"*; vs Elster, op. cit.

[187] It broke down in Pennsylvania, the first such a case, in 1776, when one could hardly speak of a federal union.

itself, as did the state legislatures during the making of the federal Constitution. Where federalism was weak as in Venezuela, or absent as in Colombia, this support for double differentiation was not there, and to two different degrees the mechanism proved vulnerable to sovereign claims. In India, however, it was almost as unlikely for the Constituent Assembly to exercise dictatorship over the provinces as in the case of the Federal Convention, and any attempt to impose a constitution not satisfying their federalist aspirations to an important degree at least would have failed. With this said, the conclusion must be that with the exception of federal settings, double differentiation based on a convention or a limited constituent assembly will likely fail. Even a quasi-contractual agreement as in Colombia is vulnerable to a constituent assembly's sovereign claims, because in distinction to a federal contract or treaty such agreements are not based on territorially differentiated and therefore viable forms of power with their own control over forms of violence. Thus any attempt to offer a US-based model of the doubly differentiated convention as a solution for the problems of constituent assemblies will probably fail most of the time.

Will judges do the job, they who have played an admittedly important role, not only for round table countries as Hungary and South Africa, but also in Colombia, Venezuela, Turkey, and Egypt? As Nicolas Figueroa convincingly argues for Colombia and Venezuela, not if they operate with the wrong theory in mind based on a strong notion of embodied popular sovereignty. Unfortunately, whether or not because of the influence of Sieyès interpreted through Carl Schmitt, they almost always seem to have the wrong theory. South Africa is the only possible exception, where it was during a formally two-stage process where the role of the Court was agreed upon in a "solemn promise" the parties made to one another.

Admittedly, as Figueroa also shows for Colombia, the very same wrong theory turns out to be important for courts seeking to limit constitutional usurpation by the constituted powers under the constitution. The same has been precisely the case in India in the 1970s, and Turkey during the first decade of this millennium. The basic structure doctrine (or the [non-]replacement doctrine) as generally formulated is based on this theory, and judges seeking to be active in the constituent process seem to think there is no alternative theory to rely on, other than mere legalism.[188] That alternative, insisting on the use of only the inherited amendment rule for constitutional change, will not help much in the case of extremely flexible rules as recently occurred

---

[188] I have tried to show, and will again in the last chapter, that there is an alternative theory.

in Hungary. And where the rules are or seem be very rigid, even when they provide a separate track of total revision, judges will find it difficult to resist a form of extraconstitutional or unconstitutional constitutional change when initiated by a charismatic populist executive, as in Venezuela.[189] This has been so since the effort of Charles de Gaulle to introduce a direct election of the presidency in 1962 under the Constitution of the 5th Republic that did not have such an amendment track, in Turkey during the (arguably unconstitutional constitutional) amendments of 2010,[190] and in Venezuela as treated here.[191] Even where the popular mobilization demands a "constitutional assembly" under limits, as in Colombia, a Court that relies on the sovereign theory may itself posit an unlimited constituent assembly, in line with the projects of populist leaders elsewhere.

The two cases of Venezuela and Colombia show how the sovereign doctrine introduced by apex courts helps to vitiate attempts at double differentiation, or other forms of limitation for constituent assemblies including by the same courts themselves. In the Colombian case, this meant the formal removal of limits agreed upon during the pre-Assembly moment, which had some negative consequences, but could not entirely vitiate the aims of the original negotiators. Undoubtedly, the loyalty of a popular, though not populist president to the agreements played a role in the mixed result. The Venezuelan case is more typical, though more tragic. Here, in a series of ambiguous and even contradictory decisions, the Court attempted to both admit the extraconstitutional road by referendum (though there was already a constitutional option for total revision), and to try to limit the constituent assembly by denying it the "original constituent power" – in other words, sovereignty in the sense of the complete absence of limitation. That last attempt failed dramatically, though it took the combined efforts of the new president and the assembly elected under his rules to defeat it. In the end the Court completely submitted to the logic it sought to oppose. Thus, we are forced to conclude that courts cannot on their own resist the emergence of sovereign dictatorship in constituent assemblies, even if they had at least limited success

---

[189] Even in Honduras, where the Supreme Court did so, it took an illegal military intervention to settle the case against the president.

[190] See my *Post Sovereign Constitution Making*, chapter 5.

[191] While seemingly resembling the theory of Ackerman, it was Akil Amar who literally introduced this theory of the always availability of amendment in a referendum, based on unitary popular sovereignty, through the very unlikely example of the United States. A. Amar, "Popular Sovereignty and Constitutional Amendment," *Responding to Imperfection: The Theory and Practice of Constitutional Amendment* (1995), pp. 89–115.

in opposing authoritarian projects of executives operating through ordinary legislatures.

This pessimistic conclusion regarding courts resembles the one argued for by David Landau, who agrees with my critique of the sovereign model,[192] and strongly implies that it is very difficult to devise a secure alternative. Not focusing on double differentiation,[193] he defines the possible limits of constituent assemblies in terms of the dual categories of internal and external. This useful distinction attempt is unfortunately not completely clear. Courts are seen as external, along with interim constitutions, while prior negotiations and electoral rules seem to be treated as internal. The party divisions within an assembly are called internal, and are rightly ascribed to electoral rules and the timing of elections, without seeing the role of prior, and in my view "external," processes in producing these. Here, I will focus on his treatment of courts, that I think is partially misleading, and that of electoral rules and assembly pluralism, where the treatment is only incomplete.

The skepticism regarding the power of courts to enforce limits on assemblies is not entirely unwarranted in light of cases like Venezuela, Turkey, and Hungary, but it goes too far. This is illustrated by the case of Colombia, where Landau actually argues that attempts by the Supreme Court to allow a constituent assembly while simultaneously imposing loose constraints on it proved ineffective (965). The statement is right for Venezuela, but the reverse was true in the most important decision of the Colombian Court that actually declared limits established in negotiations, and insisted on by President Gaviria, to be unconstitutional.[194] The question that remains open is therefore whether an apex court can play a useful role in enforcing limits established by another legitimate instance. The South African case, as I repeatedly argued, suggests that it can, that an instrument like a legitimately produced interim constitution can empower a court to play a countermajoritarian role even vis-à-vis a constitution-making assembly. Indeed, in South Africa, the pluralistically negotiated PR electoral rule was itself no help, because, in spite of it, the ANC

---

[192] Landau argues that I and others did not consider the question of what would make constraints on constituent assemblies possibly work. Actually, all my work on legitimacy and path dependence indicated my interest in the social and political conditions of possibility of the paradigm I describe, and admittedly, advocate. Landau, "Constitution Making Gone Wrong."

[193] Or even seeing the distinction between doubly differentiated conventions, and extra-ordinary constituent assemblies. As a result, he does not perceive the limitation possible in federalist arrangements, stabilizing the limits involved in double differentiation.

[194] Figueroa, Part I, op. cit.

obtained almost two-thirds of the seats, and thus it was in position to declare the assembly (and itself) sovereign, and abrogate the limitations previously agreed upon. Landau calls this a mixed case of combined external and internal controls, and proceeds to throw doubt on the effectiveness of courts only by considering an unmixed case of Venezuela and a misconstrued one of Colombia. In my view, the South African Constitutional Court could be very effective in enforcing constraints because of the absence of the sovereign theory, and the strong alternative legitimacy produced by what it called "the solemn promise" of the parties to one another at the conclusion of inclusive and pluralistic negotiations.

Yet Venezuela does prove something, namely that a court alone cannot enforce constraints against an assembly inspired by the sovereign theory of constitution making, especially when it shares that theory, as argued by Figueroa. With that I agree. The next obvious question then is whether electoral constraints, and delaying elections can constrain assemblies "internally" without court enforcement, or even in spite of it. The Colombian case seems to imply an affirmative answer. But I would add "in a highly precarious manner," as shown by this very case. In that country, as I tried to show, after the Court's declaration of the assembly's full sovereignty and its repetition by the Constituent Assembly, the previously established limits of the earlier constitution, and, in particular, the independence of other governmental branches were in jeopardy. In spite of the pluralism of the Assembly, some court review powers were indeed limited, and for the transitional period Congress was dissolved and replaced. These were important precedents, and they turned out to be disastrous for Venezuela where the attacks on the separation of powers went much further.

With that said, the constraints of the electoral rule, and the resulting party political structures of the two assemblies turned out to be very important, and the key to the difference with Venezuela, however precarious. Indeed, the difference between a largely proportional rule, and a dramatically disproportional one is the intermediate variable responsible for a genuinely negotiated constitution in the one case and an imposed one in the other.[195] But these electoral rules did not come from nowhere, were not simply the function of clever vs insidious "design", though their origins were obviously prior and

[195] Segura and Bejarano "The Difference a Constituent Assembly Makes" op. cit.: See also L. Neuman and J. McCoy "Observing Political Change in Venezuela". The combination of the "atypical plurinominal electoral system" and the use of "*las chuletas de Chávez*", or "Chávez' cheat sheets" together achieved the remarkably disproportional result. Segura and Bejarano deal effectively deal with the Chavista apologists of this process.

external to the two constituent assemblies. They were the products of Segura and Bejarano's pre-assembly moment. Landau stresses a pact made *within* the assembly, as against imposition, but somewhat neglects the prior agreements required to allow a process of compromise to happen. What Colombia had in common not only with South Africa, but with all the round table countries, was its negotiated pre-assembly moment, which produced not only an electoral rule conducive of pluralism, but also a level of political legitimacy for it.[196]

Let me sum up my last argument, and conclusion. Double differentiation is an expression of limits on a constituent assembly, but it is precarious without a strong federalist background. Courts are important enforcers of limits, but cannot do so entirely on their own. Prior agreements during a pre-constituent moment are the most important available constraints on assemblies, if such agreements yield also a pluralistic electoral rule. Yet an assembly elected under majoritarian rules, can still potentially challenge and endanger prior agreements, especially regarding substantive limits. This is the case, in particular, if its leaders are animated by the sovereign theory of constitution making. Finally, such agreements can be very much strengthened by an active pre-existing apex court, or one created by the agreements themselves, but only if the Court itself is liberated from the sovereign theory of constitution making.[197]

Thus, in ascending order of effectiveness, constituent assemblies can be limited, and kept in a framework conducive to constitutional democracy:

1. if they retain a dimension of double differentiation (as in India).
2. if there is an apex court still in existence and willing to assert jurisdiction also in constitution amending processes (as in Colombia and Venezuela).
3. if the rule electing the assembly is strongly proportional (as in Colombia).

---

[196] Even Segura and Bejarano (in "Exclusion, Inclusion . . . ") initially made a mistake in treating the electoral rules in three countries as expressing only various constellations of party interest. This was corrected in Segura and Bejarano ("The Difference a Constituent Assembly Makes") where the greater legitimacy of the Colombian rule is strongly implied.

[197] The case of Honduras seems to show what happens when the assembly is motivated by the sovereign theory, and the apex court by constitutionalism. Between two such sides, in that case, pure force decided the question. See: D. Landau, D., N. Feldman., B. Sheppard, and L.R. Suazo, 2011. Report to the Commission on Truth and Reconciliation of Honduras: Constitutional Issues. *FSU College of Law, Public Law Research Paper*, (536).

4. if limitations are agreed upon during a pre constituent moment in inclusive negotiations (as in South Africa, and initially in Colombia).
5. if there is agreement also on the enforcement of these limits by a relevant institution, most likely an apex court (as in South Africa, and initially in Colombia).

Finally, any of these five limits would work best if the populist theory of sovereign constitution making were absent or at least abandoned by the crucial actors, especially the apex courts.

The Return of Revolution and the Alternatives in the Arab World

Do these hypotheses concerning limitation derived from borderline cases of revolutions have any relevance where constituent assemblies emerge in genuine and unquestionable revolutionary breaks, involving contests over sovereignty and ruptures of legality as well as legitimacy? We now have important recent cases to help us consider this question. They have the added advantage that the revolutions took place after the relatively broad dissemination of the new paradigm of constitution making, as well as the "New Constitutionalism" with a significantly enhanced role of constitutional courts. Thus, I do not have to introduce my concepts merely from the outside.

There is little doubt concerning the return of revolutionary process in several Arab countries in and after 2011. The spectrum of outcomes too resembles previous revolutionary epochs, with restored old regimes, failed states and civil war among the consequences. Out of six relevant countries (Tunisia, Egypt, Yemen, Libya, Bahrain and Syria) with serious political contestation over sovereignty, Arendt's "liberation" from old regimes occurred only in four, while her "constitution" of a new or even restored regime succeeded at best in two, and possibly only in one, depending on whether we understand the category in normatively positive terms as "constitutional democracy."

It may be possible to extend my analysis to understanding the failure of revolution so far in Bahrain, Libya, Yemen, and Syria. Here I will attempt something less ambitious, if also hopefully significant, namely to use the post-sovereign conception as a diagnostic tool to understand the very significant differences between the two cases where new constitutions "framing the state"[198] did emerge, namely in Tunisia and Egypt. Only in the former,

---

[198] See L. Miller and L. Aucoin, eds., *Framing the State in Times of Transition: Case Studies in Constitution Making* (Washington: USIP, 2010).

Tunisia, can we speak of a constitutional democracy today, even if it is not yet "consolidated."

To anticipate this, I would like to argue that Tunisian success can be explained to a significant extent by the institutionalization within a revolution of elements of the post-sovereign paradigm, during the preconstituent moment.[199] Of course, the adoption of the relevant procedures was possible in Tunisia for a host of historical reasons that I will be able to barely mention. I will argue, however, that even the totality of these reasons removed only impediments or presented opportunities, and it took many conscious decisions by the main actors to adopt a negotiated, consensual procedure open to popular inputs that led to the constitutional result. In Egypt, as I will readily admit, the preconditions were far less favorable. Nevertheless, I will argue in some detail that the concepts derived from the post-sovereign model were present in Egypt as well, most likely because of the influence not only of Tunisia but also of international discussions and debates. Thus, several of the main actors had repeated chances to adopt a procedure resembling that of Tunisia, and even of some of the earlier round table countries. When they refused or omitted doing so, the very same concepts contributed only to the delegitimation and destabilization of the forms of imposed process these actors strongly preferred.

It is hard to contest the revolutionary character of the regime changes in Tunisia and Egypt.[200] What is decisive for me is not, however, large-scale popular mobilization resulting in the replacement of the holder of the executive power.[201] That occurred elsewhere under forms of regime change involving legal continuity, notably in the German Democratic Republic,

---

[199] See the Carter Center's "The Constitution Making Process in Tunisia. Final Report" (2014) for a description. Unfortunately the Center, as other human rights organizations, neglects to stress this dimension in its recommendations.

[200] Though not impossible. In the Egyptian case such an argument would point out the role of a military coup in two stages of the events. In the case of Tunisia, conversely, the supposed element of continuity is stressed. Neither of these instances exclude revolution. Most revolutions which involve a change in sovereignty include a coup by a contestant for power, and they always have dimensions of continuity pointed out by Tocqueville long ago. But see M. Ottaway "Democratic Transitions and the Problem of Power" Wilson Center Occasional Papers Spring 2014, p. 1 who assumes, along with others, that revolution equals social revolution, and contests the revolutionary character of changes in both countries because of elite continuity. Going a step further, C. Tugal denies even successful political revolution in the two countries, using Gramsci's concept of the passive revolution, but then continues to speak of revolution in any case. See C. Tugal, *The Fall of the Turkish Model* (London: Verso, 2016), pp. 159, 163.

[201] For how separate events and initiatives converged in this mobilization, see P. Baduel, "Le temps insurrectionnel comme "moment politique". Tunisie 2011," *Revue internationale de politique comparée* 2/2013 (Vol. 20), pp. 33–61.

Czechoslovakia, and Bulgaria. Legal continuity, however, was clearly broken in Tunisia and Egypt. In both, provisional governments announced the abrogation or, what amounts to the same thing, the indefinite suspension[202] of the inherited constitutions, and dissolved a good part (if not all) of the institutions under them. Both acts were extralegal, without foundations in the inherited constitutions. Admittedly, in both countries the governments that emerged with the fall of the presidents made efforts to maintain legal continuity.[203] In Tunisia this involved first the legal declaration by the Constitutional Council of the replacement of Ben Ali by the president of the legislature, with the incumbent prime minister remaining in place, and, second, the setting up by the government of a Committee of Political Reform (CPR or Political Reform Commission[204]), supposedly in charge of the legal transition.[205] The effort failed, with the new president in Decree-Law 14 suspending the Constitution of 1959, dissolving the chambers and the Constitutional Council[206] and, immediately thereafter creating an entirely new authority to oversee the process of electing a constituent assembly unforeseen by the constitution, the Haute Instance or High Authority.[207] In Egypt, too, there was a partially analogous effort by the provisional government of the Supreme Command of the Armed Forces (SCAF) to only suspend, and then merely amend, the

[202] There is a view that the suspension in Tunisia was initially, in March 2011 only partial, with the promulgation of Decree Law 14, and became complete only with Article 27 of the Little Constitution or OPPP (Organisation Provisoire des Pouvoirs Publics) in December 2011. See: Constituent Law No. 6–2011 of December 16, 2011 http://www.legislation.tn/sites/default/files/constitution/Pdf/loi2011_6fr1.pdf.
   See Carter Center, "The Constitution Making Process in Tunisia. Final Report" (2014) However, the call for a constituent assembly in the Decree Law with original constituent powers, along with the dissolution of the Chambers as well as the Constitutional Council had the same implication as that of the OPPP. See: S. Zemni, "The Extraordinary Politics of the Tunisian Revolution: The Process of Constitution Making," *Mediterranean Politics* 20:1, who says that Decree Law 14 replaced the Constitution of 1959. It was replaced, in turn, by the OPPP, which claimed it as one of its sources of authorization. The view of statement "Public Governance in Tunisia" (p. 5) by the Association Tunisienne de Gouvernance (2013) confirms the replacement of the Constitution of 1959 by Decree Law 14. http://pomed.orgwp-content/uploads/2013/11/Public-Governance-in-Tunisia-English.pdf.
[203] For Tunisia, see S. Zemni, "The Extraordinary Politics of the Tunisian Revolution"; for Egypt, I. Awad, "Breaking out of Authoritarianism: 18 Months of Political Transition in Egypt" in *Constellations* (June 2013) 20(2).
[204] M. Ottaway refers to it as the Higher Commission for Political Reform in "Democratic Transitions and the Problem of Power" p. 5.
[205] See Crisis Group, p. 14.
[206] Decree law no. 2011: 14 dated March 23, 2011, relating to the provisional organization of the public authorities. http://www.wipo.int/edocs/lexdocs/laws/en/tn/tn052en.pdf.
[207] Zemni, "The Extraordinary Politics," p. 6.

inherited Constitution of 1971, and to keep the last government of Mubarak in place. These attempts failed as well, and were followed by Constitutional Declarations decreeing rupture, and electing a constituent assembly.

Nevertheless, the extralegal election of constituent assemblies satisfies the meaning of revolution only from the legal point of view. I have illustrated such a scenario in the cases of Colombia and Venezuela, which were not revolutions in the political sense, and also where acts of rupture were legalized, as I have shown, by fundamental Supreme Court decisions. In Tunisia and Egypt, there were no attempts at such legalization, and the actors began to openly speak of revolution even before, and especially after, the fall of the two presidents.[208] More importantly, the provisional governments in both countries found themselves in the classical situation of dual power, that, following Trotsky and Tilly, I have indicated as the political dimension of revolution. In Tunisia, the government and its new Committee of Political Reform (CPR) found itself strongly opposed by the National Council for the Protection of the Revolution (CNPR), which assembled the trade unions (led by the umbrella organization, the UGTT, or *Union Générale Tunisienne du Travail*), the bar association, human rights organizations, the Islamists of Ennahda as well as the organization of civil society militants active in the streets (assembled by the Front of January 14).[209] It was the pressure of the CNPR that led to the legal break, and the calling for the election of a constituent assembly. In Egypt, where the provisional government was based on the armed forces, intense independent pressure was nevertheless organized by the street occupation, backed by labor union action, and, however inconsistently, by the powerful organization of the Muslim Brotherhood. When that last organization achieved formal political incumbency, however, it itself could not overcome the duality of power with the armed forces, temporarily backed by the alliance of civil groups and the street.

According to the classical conception, dual power is fundamentally unstable, and must be resolved for a revolution to be completed. While the logic of dual power propelled both of the two revolutions forward, the two different ways in which it was resolved played key roles in the diverging outcomes. In Tunisia after Decree Law 14 suspended the Constitution a new institution was created, the High Authority.[210] As the full name reveals, this body, also called

---

[208] In Tunisia, both Decree Law 14 and the OPPP did so.

[209] According to the Crisis Group the UGTT and the Bar were the strongest forces behind this organization. Op. cit., p. 13.

[210] or: *Haute instance pour la réalisation des objectifs de la révolution, de la réforme politique et de la transition démocratique.*

the Ben Achour Commission after its chair,[211] united the reformist CPR[212] and the revolutionary CPNR with the agreement, enthusiastic or reluctant, of most, if not all, of the latter's member organizations.[213] Dual power was resolved in Tunisia[214] by the creation of a body in some respects resembling the round tables of the post-sovereign paradigm, even if, as we will see, the formally revolutionary character of the transition was not eliminated.[215] In Egypt, on the contrary, dual power ended only when the SCAF suppressed first the MB, and then the popular mobilization that was its own temporary ally. In Tunisia, it became correct to say that "not one party, group or institution was able to speak solely in the name of the people."[216] In Egypt, by contrast, two instances, the SCAF and the MB, sought and in succession seemed to succeed occupying "the empty place" of the sovereign.

How to explain the divergence? Along with others, I would stress both the different structural features of the two countries, as well as the tradition of consensus building that emerged in Tunisia well before the revolutions of 2011. Here I can only hint at the main elements of the former. Tunisia was a much smaller, much wealthier, and, yes, much more modern country than Egypt. Among other things this meant that it had much lower poverty rates, an uncommonly strong and well-organized form of unionism,[217] a large, very influential and often-independent legal profession,[218] and, perhaps most

---

[211] A. Stepan (2012). Tunisia's transition and the twin tolerations. *Journal of Democracy*, 23(2), 89–103; Zemni "The Extraordinary Politics," 6–11; Crisis Group Report 106: Popular Protests in North Africa and the Middle East (IV): Tunisia's Way" 19ff.

[212] According to the Carter Center, this was the original commission headed by Ben Achour op.cit. p.22. Also see Crisis Group op. cit., p. 14. Thus it may be better to refer to the new committee as the Haute Instance or High Authority (Carter Center: "High Commission").

[213] See Crisis Group Report 106, p. 19: The Crisis Group rightly stresses the combination of reform and revolution, but it does not seem correct to depict the High Authority as the governmental CPR under a new name.

[214] "The situation of de facto dual legitimacy – that of the National Council for the Protection of the Revolution on the one hand and the government on the other – was no longer really appropriate" Crisis Group Report 106, p. 20.

[215] The High Authority rejected the idea of a "republican pact" demanded by its "secular, progressive and leftists members" in which fundamental liberties as well as the CSP would be entrenched against constitutional change. Zemni, op. cit., pp. 8–9. Thus, the High Authority affirmed the sovereignty of the constituent assembly to be elected, even as the electoral rule it produced made majoritarian functioning of that body impossible.

[216] Zemni, op. cit., p. 11.

[217] Many interpreters rightly stress the major role of the UGTT both in initiating Ben Ali's downfall, and in the negotiations that followed. See especially M. Omri "No Ordinary Union: UGTT and the Tunisian Path to Revolution and Transition" as well as 7ff; Zemni, "From socio-economic protest to national revolt: The labor origins of the Tunisian revolution." In *The Making of the Tunisian Revolution* pp 127–146, and Ottaway, op. cit., 4ff.

[218] Gobe, E. and Salaymeh, L., "Tunisia's "Revolutionary" Lawyers: From Professional Autonomy to Political Mobilization. *Law & Social Inquiry*" (Spring 2016) Volume 41, Issue 2, 331.

importantly, significantly reformed gender relations. The latter was symbolized by the Personal Status Code (PSC) enacted under Habib Bourguiba in 1957, the first full year of independence.[219] While radical Islam was hardly absent, it was significantly weaker than in Egypt, or for that matter Algeria.[220] At the same time, the offshoot of the Egyptian Muslim Brothers, Ennahda, was initially a much weaker organization than its parent, and both its weakness and its eventually moderate leadership inclined it more to pragmatic political conduct.[221] Perhaps as significant as any of these factors, geopolitically Tunisia was much less important than Egypt, the most powerful and largest Arab state. Tunisia was never in the front line of the Arab–Israeli conflict. As a result, its military was relatively small, did not have to be compensated with economic power after peace with Israel (that was never made), and did not generate the leadership elite of authoritarian regimes. It was also not in position to replace Ben Ali's regime when the latter collapsed.[222]

One might thus rightly claim that the different outcomes in Tunisia and Egypt where pre-programmed, or "overdetermined." That however would leave out the very important role of organizational agency. In Tunisia, the key political agents, seeking to unite secular and Islamic opposition to the dictatorship generated a consensual modus operandi relatively early, well before the events of 2011. Already during the beginning of the tenure of Ben Ali, who initially sought to reform Bourguiba's system, the National Pact of 1988 that the new president sponsored sought to bring together secular and Islamic politicians behind the government. It was then that the latter, the MTI (Islamic Tendency Movement, the later Ennahda) had to accept the new PSC

---

[219] F. Khokhosvar, *New Arab Revolutions That Shook the World* (London: Routledge, 2016).

[220] On the Salafis, see F. Merone and F. Cavatorta "The Rise of Salafism and the Future of Democratization" in N. Gana, ed. *The Making of the Tunisian Revolution: Contexts, Architects, Prospects*. (Edinburgh: Edinburgh University Press, 2013); on their relative weakness, see Tugal, *The Fall of the Turkish Model*.

[221] For the difficult relationship of the parent organization to democratic pluralism, see M. Tadros, *The Muslim Brotherhood in Contemporary Egypt: Democracy Redefined or Confined?* (London: Routledge, 2012) who indicates the differences with Ennahda as well, that leaders such as Ghannouchi tried to theologically justify. What even Tadros does not emphasize is that in Tunisia unlike in Egypt Ennahda had a powerful secular competitor for mass influence, the UGTT. In my view that is a precondition of what has been often promoted as the "Christian democratization" of Islamist parties.

[222] See, e.g., The Carter Center, "Constitution-Making Process in Tunisia" (2014) p. 22; S. Arjomand "The Islam and Democracy Debate After 2011" in *Constellations* (June 2013) v.20 No 2. 302–3; Ottaway, op. cit., p. 4; Crisis Group 106 p.11ff. It is thus erroneous to talk of parallel military coups in both of the two countries. M. Bishara, *The Invisible Arab: The Promise and Peril of the Arab Revolutions* (New York: Nation Books, 2013), p. 117. While the Tunisian military did not try to crush the uprising, and allowed Ben Ali to fall, it never seemed to have either the desire or the ability to take power on its own behalf.

that they initially wished to abrogate in favor of Islamic family law.[223] "The 18 October Coalition for Rights and Freedoms in Tunisia" of 2005 that united in a single project four main parties including members of Ennahda, along with smaller formations, was much more important. No longer in the shadow of the established power, it sought to bring down the undemocratic regime. Nevertheless, this document, signed by important members of Ennahda's, if not exactly its formal representatives, explicitly endorsed the PSC, thereby representing a watershed in the history of the main Islamic party. The Personal Status Code was now, for the first time, backed by free agreement of all the main parties, since the left-wing parties that refused to join the coalition were even stronger defenders of the Code and of women's rights.[224]

It is thus a mistake to characterize the secularist epoch between 1956 and 2011 as "The Lost Decades," as Alfred Stepan does.[225] This was the period that saw the consolidation of Tunisian unionism around the UGTT, and the lawyers' profession around the bar. Without these organizations and their activists, the culture of negotiation and compromise stressed by Stepan may never have emerged.[226] Quite obviously, it was in this authoritarian period that the comparatively very progressive Personal Status Code was enacted, as he notes.[227] It was less obviously, then, that the law established a level of acceptance and support that became almost impossible to reverse. The achievement was in significant part due to women's organizations formed, that would not have been possible without government support, as well as the beneficial effects of the Code itself.[228] Thus, Ennahda's pragmatic acceptance of the PSC from 1988[229] on was a fundamental precondition of the possibility

[223] K. Perkins, "Playing the Islamic Card: The Use and Abuse of Religion in Tunisian Politics" in N. Gana ed. *The Making of the Tunisian Tevolution*, pp. 67ff.; 69ff.

[224] L. Hajji, "The 18 October Coalition for Rights and Freedoms in Tunisia,"*Arab Reform Initiative, February* (2007).

[225] Stepan, op. cit., 99ff; see Mednicoff "Tale of Three Constitutions: Common Drives and Diverse Outcomes in Post-2010 Arab Legal Politics," *Temp. Int'l & Comp. LJ*, (2014) 28, 223ff.

[226] See Omri, "No Ordinary Union"; and Gobe, and Salaymeh, "Tunisia's 'Revolutionary' Lawyers."

[227] Stepan, op. cit., 100.

[228] See M. Marks "Women's Rights Before and After the Revolution" in Gana ed., *The Making of the Tunisian Revolution*, pp. 231–232. The evidence does not support her contention that today the Code is regarded by women merely as the product of benign despotism. All successful agreements between Ennahda and secular parties presupposed the Code, obviously regarded as fundamentally important by the latter, and unassailable by the former.

[229] There was nothing resembling that acceptance in Egypt, by the MB. On the contrary, partial attempts on the part of the secular regime to reform the family code, and attempts to apply international conventions on women and children in Egypt, were resolutely opposed by the MB, and indeed by its male led adjunct women's organization, the Muslim Sisters, that was in effect an anti-emancipation women's movement. See: chapter 7, Tadros, *The Muslim*

of important agreements with secular parties.[230] The most important outcome of these agreements was the formation of the CNPR in 2011 around its initial core of youth militants in the Front of January 14, which brought together the representatives of the street, civil society organizations, and union activists. It was the CNPR, expanded around the UGTT, human rights organizations, the Tunisian Bar Association (TBA),[231] and Ennahda[232] that was able to force the government to abandon its originally purely reformist scenario.[233] There were two reasons for the effectiveness of this organization: the prior, if partial resolution of worldview conflicts between Islamist and secular forces, and the apparent willingness of the youth-based mobilization to accept the leadership of a new umbrella political organization, thus the leadership of "political society."[234] Both of these preconditions, recognizable from East and Central European cases,[235] were to be absent in Egypt – with very negative results.

Thus earlier agreement on issues having to do with a worldview on terms fully acceptable to most secular parties played a key role in allowing the functioning of "the pre-assembly moment" in Tunisia. Actually, making the High Authority work seemed to have been a more difficult project than assumed by some interpreters.[236] First, uniting both revolutionary and reformist views of

Brotherhood in Contemporary Egypt. And also N. Bernard-Maugiron, "Personal Status Law in Egypt" *Promotion of Women's Rights, Egypt* (2010). As the latter shows, Egypt, like Tunisia, did however abolish Sharia courts litigating the personal law in 1955, placed the jurisdiction in secular courts in 1956, and established secular family courts in 2000 in conjunction with arbitration boards.

[230] It seems to me at least, that in the Tunisian context at least Ennahda and Ghanoucci had only the choice between acceptance of the Code and self-marginalization. The same thing was to occur in relation to the inclusion of Sharia, and other Islamist inspired provisions in the constitution of 2013 originally supported by Ennahda. See Marks op.cit.; M. Zeghal "Competing Ways of Life: Islamism, Secularism, and Public Order in the Tunisian Transition." *Constellations,* 20 (2), 254–274. and N. Marzouki, "From Resistance to Governance" in Gana, op. cit.

[231] Gobe, E. and Salaymeh, L., "Tunisia's "Revolutionary" Lawyers" 331. The authors depict the important role of lawyers in the uprising, which led to tensions with and within the TBA, as well as the tradition of the Bar's relative independence under the dictatorship.

[232] According to Ottaway, Ennahda was supportive but only on the periphery of the CNPR, op. cit., p. 5.

[233] Zemni, op. cit., 4–5.

[234] Stepan, op. cit. Again the mediating role of the unions and the lawyers seemed to have been central. Their activists were present and highly visible in the demonstrations, and tat the same time they had organizations capable of effectively negotiating on their behalf.

[235] The prior unification of the opposition before the establishment of the Round Table happened in Hungary in 1989, with the formation of the EKA that lead to the negotiating forum of the NKA. Reconciliation between rival worldviews, liberal and religious, was more characteristic of Poland, the only central European country with serious worldview cleavage within the opposition.

[236] Compare the analyses of Zemni, and the Crisis Group with that of Stepan, all op. cit.

the transition may have been attractive, but has led to some defections by revolutionary organizations. Second, as in the case of any co-opted body (as e.g. in Nepal) there were problems of exclusion and inclusion, which were eventually solved by the dramatic doubling of the number of members of the High Authority. Third, as in the case of South Africa's TEC (Transitional Executive Council), the relationship of the High Authority to the government, and the question who had the ultimate decision making power was never and could never be fully clarified. The formal legislative power according to Decree Law 14 remained in the hands of the provisional government, but the High Authority's proposals regularly became the decree laws of the executive. Thus as in the case of the round tables, the high authority had quasi-legislative powers.[237] Fourth, and most importantly, the conflict between adherents of a revolutionary logic and majority rule with others in the High Authority who considered the logic of negotiation and consensus building important was renewed in place of the earlier revolutionary vs reformist contention. Advocates of consensus insisted on "a republican pact" to be agreed to by the members of the High Authority, which would bind the constituent assembly regarding some important matters, such as the preservation of the PSC under the new constitution.[238] This was the debate concerning supraconstitutional principles, used first in Namibia and South Africa, a debate that was also to take place in Egypt. Unlike in the case of South Africa, but similar to the situation in Egypt, in Tunisia the fight was won by Ennahda, which insisted on the revolutionary principle of an unlimited, sovereign constituent assembly.[239] This resembled the removal of limitations on the *constituyente* we have seen in Colombia and Venezuela.

The High Authority moreover was constrained to agree that the assembly elected would be both constituent and legislative, a common feature of revolutionary constitution making that was achieved more gradually in Colombia and Venezuela. As a partial compensation, however, the secular side and smaller parties won the battle over the electoral rule. It seems that Ennahda's preference – or at least advantage – would have involved a majoritarian rule that would have indeed created an assembly that the Islamic Party could fully control. The highly, though not maximally proportional rule[240] that emerged

---

[237] Zemni, op. cit.   [238] Ibid.

[239] Thus, Said Arjomand op. cit. pp. 303–304 is not wrong in finding the pattern of a classical revolutionary constituent assembly in spite of the role of the High Authority that he mentions, without stressing its formative role.

[240] PR organized in terms of districts is less proportional than one national district would have been. But the huge actual disproportionality in Tunisia, not characteristic of the rules chosen, was the result of a very large number of parties receiving something like 30 percent of nationally

from the deliberations was, however, a typical product of negotiated forms of transition.[241] It was the most important achievement of the High Authority, even if precarious because, as we have seen in other cases, even PR can produce huge number of seats for a winning side.[242] In Tunisia, combined with historical givens like the relative weakness of the Salafists, the electoral rule produced a constituent assembly, where coalition building and consensual decision-making became the only options, whatever the difficulties involved in reaching a consensus.

It is important to stress both the differences of the High Authority with the round tables as well as the similarities between them. In Tunisia, the High Authority produced laws, but not an interim constitution. If there were interim constitutional rules, these were in the Decree Law 14 enacted by the government on March 23, 2011[243], and then more fully in the Little Constitution or OPPP (*La loi sur l'organisation provisoire des pouvoirs publics*) established by the Constituent Assembly.[244] The important point is that neither were entrenched on a higher level than ordinary legislation. The first did not constrain the Constituent Assembly in any way, while the second was a form of self-constraint that could be revoked or revised at any time, especially given the fact that the OPPP had included no amendment rule at all. Moreover, in Tunisia, when compared to especially Hungary and South Africa there was no

dispersed votes while obtaining no seats at all in any districts. The D benefited not only the leading party, but others as well.

[241] The rule has been treated as an extreme version of PR, because of its conversion rule and the large number of districts, but even the relevant interpreter admits that it may have been beneficial for a constitution-making body, avoiding the chances of majoritarian imposition. J.M. Carey, Electoral Formula and the Tunisian Constituent Assembly http://sites.dartmouth.edu/ jcarey/files/2013/02/Tunisia-Electoral-Formula-Carey-May-2013-reduced.pdf. Carey maintains that under different PR rules, Ehnnahda would have received 69 percent of the seats for about 37 percent of the votes. Why this level of disproportionality would be desirable for a future legislative assembly, as he implies, he does not say. I have my doubts, especially in light of the constitution amendment rule adopted in Tunisia.

[242] South Africa (66 percent for the ANC) and Egypt (almost 70 percent for Islamic parties). In Tunisia several factors however re-inforced the consensual logic of the electoral rule. These were, among others, the existence of a strong secular force, UGTT, whose leaders backed non-Islamic parties, attachment to the old "secular" order symbolized by the PSC that was felt by many under threat in case of an Islamic victory, whatever the formal positions of Ennahda, and the corresponding weakness of the Salafis.

[243] The fusion of two organizations in the High Authority on March 13, 2015 was prior to this Decree Law, and the new body may have already influenced its contents.

[244] Constituent Law No. 6–2011 of December 16, 2011 http://www.legislation.tn/sites/default/files/ constitution/Pdf/loi2011_6fr1.pdf. For an analysis see: "Public Governance in Tunisia" Association Tunisienne de Gouvernance (2013). http://pomed.org/wp-content/uploads/2013/11/ Public-Governance-in-Tunisia-English.pdf.

judicial authority that could enforce any interim constitutional rules.[245] The Constitutional Council was abolished by Decree Law 14, and the old Administrative Tribunal, though kept in place,[246] had only limited jurisdiction, and none regarding matters of constitutional content.[247]

Nevertheless, the electoral rule produced by the High Authority, undoubtedly because of its own pluralistic and inclusive composition resembled the rules produced by round tables, corresponding to the insurance model of constitutional change.[248] While PR was no guarantee against an assembly being dominated by one party, in Tunisia a pluralistic and inclusive constituent assembly did emerge from the way the rule functioned in the given social and political environment. In this manner the logic of the High Authority, requiring negotiation and compromise, was transferred to the Constituent Assembly. Thus, the Assembly, though not limited in advance, chose to limit itself in the OPPP or little constitution, which required absolute majority to approve any article of the constitution, and a two-thirds majority to enact the document as a whole. If that was impossible in two attempts, a document whose individual articles were approved could be enacted in a referendum.[249]

If due only to how the negotiated electoral rule functioned in Tunisia, these safeguards were certainly not foolproof. The little constitution arguably could have been withdrawn or replaced by the majority at any time. While Ennahda did not have the necessary majority, the ruling coalition that it led, the Troika of three parties, did. Since the latter had less than a constitution-making majority of two-thirds, it had the incentive to change the Little Constitution if the three parties (or even just Ennahda and the CPR of President Marzouki alone) could agree among themselves. Perhaps their agreement on this fundamental question was no more likely than consensus within the very contentious assembly as a whole. Had the party structure been stable with no force having the majority there would have been little danger of any force becoming the majority and establish a majoritarian process. But the parties were not stable, with a good deal of movement of deputies between them, who were not prohibited from changing parties.[250] Moreover, there was also the opposite danger, especially since no time constraints were established by the little constitution.[251]

[245] See especially Carter Center.
[246] By both Decree Law 14: Art. 3 and OPPP: Articles 22–23.
[247] Carter Center p. unclear role of Court of Appeal, also left in place by Decree Law 14: Art. 17. Decision regarding survival of rights of the Constitution of 1959.
[248] See Ginsburg; and my *Post Sovereign Constitution Making*, chapter 3.
[249] Zemni, op. cit., 14–15; D. Pickard, *Lessons from Constitution-making in Tunisia* (New York: Atlantic Council of the United States, 2012).
[250] Carter Center, p. 46ff.   [251] "Public Governance in Tunisia," p. 8.

The assembly could become deadlocked among its many parties. This indeed happened over deeply divisive issues like the place of Islam in the constitution, and the type of government to be established, presidential or parliamentary. As a result, there were attempts both within and outside the Assembly to bypass the rules established by Decree Law 14 and the Little Constitution.[252] Indeed, the Assembly's sessions were temporarily suspended, before a new compromise set was achieved among the main parties, mediated by an external organization of civil society organizations, the Quartet, that brought together the unions, the Bar, and the main human rights organization.[253]

Though certainly not without intense conflicts, under the negotiated rules the constituent assembly finally did succeed in making fair compromises over most contested positions, establishing in particular a semi presidential form of government, that in the given context seemed to indicate power-sharing[254], affirming Islam as Tunisia's religion but without any type of Sharia clause, and, under the impact of women's mobilization, eliminating the objectionable idea of the complementarity of women to men.[255] The parity of women in elected bodies was reaffirmed. Probably under the influence of human rights organizations,[256] the so-called limiting clauses regarding rights, concentrated in one article of the Constitution, were themselves limited by the phrase "without compromising their essence." To strengthen the modern table of rights provided for and the rule of law, judicial independence

---

[252] Carter Center, p. 28, referring to demands by a newly formed NSF (national salvation front, with the new party Nida Tounes as its main force) for the dissolution of the Assembly and the establishment of a new expert commission to finalize the constitution; Ottaway, op. cit., 7. While the latter claims that the rules were indeed fundamentally transgressed by the so-called Quartet that eventually forced through compromise solutions in the Assembly, this seems debatable at the very least. The Carter Center (p. 29) treats the Quartet as the facilitator of compromise between the NSF and the "legitimacy" camp in the assembly, mainly Ennahda and the CPR.

[253] The UGTT, along with the Tunisian Union, for Industry, Trade, and Handicraft (UTICA); the Tunisian League for Human Rights (Ligue Tunisienne des Droits de l'Homme or LTDH); and the Tunisian Bar Association. For its important efforts, the Quartet was awarded the Nobel Peace Prize for 2015.

[254] This was because it was (wrongly) assumed that Ennahda would continue to dominate parliamentary elections, and (correctly) that the fragmented secular parties could together elect a president. Choudhry, S., & Stacey, R. (2013). "Semi-presidentialism as a form of government: Lessons for Tunisia." *Center for Constitutional Transitions*.

[255] Marks, op. cit., 237–238; Marzouki, op. cit., 218–220; M. Zeghal, "Competing Ways of Life: Islamism, Secularism and Public Order in the Tunisian Transition," *Constellations* (2013) v 20, No 2; D. Johnson, "Beyond Constituent Assemblies and Referenda: Assessing the Legitimacy of the Arab Spring Constitutions in Egypt and Tunisia," *Wake Forest L. Rev.* (2015), 50, 1007. 1032.

[256] Carter Center, op. cit., 75–78.

was reinforced, and a strong Constitutional Court with a wide jurisdiction, unusual in Francophone countries, was created, with an appointment structure designed to block dependence on merely one branch of power. (Articles 118–124).[257] A many-leveled amendment rule was produced including Article 49: "No amendment may undermine the human rights and freedoms guaranteed in this Constitution", that added to the non-amendability of Articles 1 and 2 that provided for Islam as the religion of Tunisia, a republican and representative form of government and the rule of law. The distinction between ordinary legislation and organic laws, the latter changeable only through an absolute majority, added another layer still (Article 64). All amendment proposals therefore had to be submitted to the Constitutional Court, for the control their compatibility with the non-amendable articles (Article 120 point 2; and 144).

The negotiations took longer time than was perhaps necessary. The length of the Tunisian process, whether so designed or not, allowed a rather elaborate and extensive process of consultation with organizations of civil society as well as different groupings of citizens.[258] Yet, while allowing for contending parties to come to multiple agreements, the open-ended character of the time involved serious dangers as well. Parties were never under pressure to come to agreement at any predefined moment of time, and, paradoxically, this led some of them to demand the disruption and replacement the process. The many delays have been ascribed to a variety of factors: the existence of no time limits, the high level of absenteeism, as well as the dual role of the Constituent Assembly, having also absorbed the functions of a normal legislature on which government was based.[259] And, as we have seen, it took the extralegal, if not illegal intervention of an alliance of civil society organizations, the Quartet, capable of serious political pressure through its member unions, to bring the constitution-making process to an end. Thus, it may be said that

---

[257] T. Ginsburg, "The Tunisian Judicial Sector: Analysis and Recommendations" Center for Constitutional Transitons working Paper 5 June 2013.

[258] For a detailed description see The Carter Center op. cit. 58 to 72. While the Center is critical of the level of public participation, and the resulting feelings of "exclusion" they in fact demonstrate not only that public involvement was extensive, but alos that it was in many respects effective. This was due not only to the provisions and procedures of the Constituent assembly, but the organization of independent civl society inputs, like that of the the monitoring group Al Bawsala.

[259] Pickard, "Lessons," pp. 4–5. It is not clear, however, how under the circumstances of revolutionary rupture the differentiation of constituent and legislative assemblies could have been attained. Perhaps an Indian-type differentiation of two types of sessions with separate functions would have been possible. Something like that was tried in Egypt, with parliament electing a "constituent assembly" that could directly offer its draft to a referendum, but the project failed because of the conflicts over the body's composition.

the very partial adoption of institutions and practices resembling the round table negotiations remained highly vulnerable, given the absence of fully negotiated constitutional procedures and principles binding the constituent assembly, and the establishment of a judicial body capable of enforcing these. Fortunately, the parliamentary arithmetic as well as external civil pressure produced the repeated renegotiation of the constitution-making rules, rather than the subversion of the process, by either an internal majority or an external force.

Nothing resembling a negotiated and consensual process occurred under the two versions of a so-called constituent assembly established in Egypt,[260] nor in the commission organized by the SCAF (Supreme Council of the Armed Forces) after the coup against President Morsi. Here too the key lies in the pre-assembly moment or moments. As against Tunisia, in Egypt these involved a series of top-down, unilateral impositions, constitutional declarations, first by the SCAF, then briefly by Morsi on behalf of the MB (Muslim Brotherhood[261]), and then again by the SCAF. Perhaps it was unavoidable that the fall of President Mubarak was introduced in one such a declaration, which suspended but did not abrogate the Constitution of 1971. According to its own interests, in this respect similar to the first post-Ben Ali government in Tunisia, the SCAF initially sought only to reform the inherited Constitution.[262] Accordingly, a narrowly constructed and exclusionary constitutional reform commission was established whose task was merely to offer amendments. It included one member of the MB, a presiding jurist close to the MB,[263] as well as three members of the Supreme Constitutional Court.[264] The amendments this body proposed were then ratified in a Bonapartist-style referendum. A yes vote was strongly supported by the MB, the only oppositional force present in the commission, while various secular and liberal Muslim organizations that

---

[260] I rely on the excellent articles of T. Moustafa ("Drafting Egypt's Constitution. Can a New Legal Framework Revive a Flawed Transition" Brookings Doha Center paper series (March 2012) # 1) and Ibrahim Awad, op. cit. as well as the International Commission of Jurists "Egypt's New Constitution: A flawed process; uncertain outcomes" 2012. For Tunisia–Egypt comparisons, see Stepan, op. cit.; Jonson, op. cit.; as well as the European Parliament's Directorate B: "Comparative Analysis Between the Constitutional Process in Egypt and Tunisia" (2014).

[261] For a study of this organization, see M. Tadros (2012). *The Muslim Brotherhood in Contemporary Egypt*; M. Tadros (2011) "The Muslim Brotherhood's Gender Agenda: Reformed or Reframed?," *IDS Bulletin*, 42(1), 88–98.

[262] Awad, op. cit., pp. 275; 280.

[263] Arjomand, op. cit., 304; "Final Report of the Carter Center Mission to Witness the 2011–2012 Parliamentary Elections in Egypt," p. 9.

[264] For a study of the earlier history of this court, see T. Moustafa, *The Struggle for Constitutional Power: Law, Politics, and Economic Development in Egypt* (Cambridge: Cambridge University Press, 2007).

wished to abrogate the Constitution asked for a no. Leaders of the Copts and most likely their constituencies also voted no, because of their objection to the re-appearance of the Sharia clause of the amended 1971 Constitution.[265] Yet another SCAF Declaration, a few days later, sometimes referred to as the Interim Constitution, while preserving much of the contents of the amendments, did abrogate the Constitution itself, and established the executive and legislative powers of the SCAF for the interim. The document called for free elections to a parliament that, unusually, would itself choose a "constituent assembly" according to rules not yet specified, but permitting, whether by design or omission, dominance by the parliamentary majority.[266] Moreover, the SCAF established a very short six-month-long timetable for the constituent assembly to finish its work, and this was certainly unsuitable for either genuine negotiations or for a process open to public and civil society monitoring and inputs, as in Tunisia.[267]

The electoral rules too were imposed primarily from above,[268] although they had to be twice altered under small party, civil society and street pressure all demanding pure PR. Initially, the SCAF (and it was claimed by its critics, the MB) preferred more majoritarian, individual rather than proportional seats, and the final outcome of one-third FPTP and two-thirds PR was still less proportional in theory at least than the Tunisian rule.[269] More importantly, shortly before the elections, the SCAF tried but failed to impose

---

[265] Tadros, op. cit., p. 84.

[266] http://www.constitutionnet.org/files/promoting_consensus.pdf.

[267] Z. Al-Ali, "The New Egyptian Constitution: an Initial Assessment of its Merits and Flaws," *Open Democracy* December 26, 2012.

[268] Decree Law 120/2011. Nathan Brown claims they were negotiated, but without providing any detail as to when this happened, and who took part. See N. Brown (2014). Egypt: A Constitutional Court in an Unconstitutional Setting. *Political and Constitutional Transitions in North Africa: Actors and Factors*, 7, 33. p. 7. For one available study see D. Tavana, "Electoral System Choice in Revolutionary Egypt" who mentions negotiations with several unnamed parties. The Carter Center too, op. cit. p. 25, speaks of negotiations without providing the details. In my reconstruction, the SCAF tried at first to impose a rule involving one-third PR seats only, but was forced to retreat conceding first 50–50, and then 2/3 proportional seats in Decree Law 120 (cited by Tavana op.cit. appendix 1).

[269] It is difficult to measure and compare the actual disproportionality of the two elections, because of the large number of parties in Tunisia that received votes but no seats. What can be said is that in Egypt disproportionality favored only the largest party, the MB's Freedom and Justice, while in Tunisia it was distributed more across the board, among all the five main parties. Ennahda went from 37 percent of the votes to 41 percent of the seats, while MB 37.5 percent to 45 percent, with double the gain. Here the source of disproportionality lay in the one-third individual seats. The distribution of these seats benefitted Islamist candidates, who won over 80 percent, as well as individual candidates some of whom were linked to the old regime. On that see Tavani, op. cit., p. 10. The huge difference between the two countries was of course the success of the Salafi Al Nour in Egypt to gain 25 percent of the seats (with

supra-constitutional principles on the "constituent assembly" that would have tightly regulated the composition of that body. These were the so-called Selmi principles, to which I will return, defeated by the renewed mobilization of a very temporary alliance of the MB and the civil society based movements, the former opposed to limits as such and the latter only to the specific ones that sought to institutionalize military enclaves of power. Still this alliance was a sign of the strength of the MB, which indeed won both the upcoming parliamentary and presidential elections of 2012. In power, the MB-dominated parliament lost several battles against courts close to either the military or to some secular movements, or to both, that dissolved first one constituent assembly and then parliament itself. A second constituent assembly, as majoritarian and as objectionable from the secular point of view as its forerunner, nevertheless managed to escape dissolution by either the Supreme Administrative Court, that transferred its competence, or the Supreme Constitutional Court (SCC) that managed to come to a final negative judgment concerning the body only *after* its constitution was ratified in another Bonapartist referendum with little participation.[270] In fact, it was the newly elected MB president, Mohamed Morsi, who temporarily defeated the courts, with and following his own top-down constitutional declaration that removed his decisions and the authority and proceedings of the new constituent assembly from any possibility of judicial or constitutional review.[271] Supported by demonstrations organized by the MB, it was this move that enabled the second constituent assembly to enact its constitution without much support from non-Islamic forces.

In contrast to the Tunisian Constitution, the Constitution pushed through by Morsi and the MB with their pliant constituent assembly had included religion clauses that went considerably further than anything in previous Egyptian constitutions. It is true that the Sharia clause (Article 2) was taken over verbatim from the amended constitution of 1971, which replaced the word "a" in "a source of legislation" with "the." But many objected to that clause in the first place, understanding it as a concession of President Sadat to Islamist opinion to balance and constrain secular politicians and initiatives. Moreover, now, in Article 4, the 2012 Constitution required that in matters of Sharia interpretation the highest religious institution, the traditionalist Al Azhar, had

---

27.8 percent of the votes), but this was not the outcome of the electoral system. In Tunisia no Salafi party competed in the first free elections.

[270] Brown, "Egypt: A Constitutional Court in an Unconstitutional Setting," *Political and Constitutional Transitions in North Africa: Actors and Factors* 7 (2014).

[271] Morsi's Constitutional Declaration; I. Awad, "Postscript," in *Constellations* (June, 2013) vol. 20 # 2.

to be consulted.[272] Previously, the interpretation of the clause belonged exclusively to the jurisdiction of the Supreme Constitutional Court.[273] Moreover, Article 219, for the first time, went beyond the original clause by specifying that "[T]he principles of Islamic Sharia include general evidence, foundational rules, rules of jurisprudence, and credible sources accepted in Sunni doctrines and by the larger community." What the two or rather three clauses would have meant together is difficult to say,[274] though there are some interpretations to guide us.[275] While their actual wording may reflect the uneasy compromises among traditionalist, fundamentalist, and modernist forces in Islam, the clauses together certainly reflect the great dominance of Islamist forces in the constituent assembly.

It seems, however, that the MB's interest was not so much in these clauses as in completing the process within its unfortunate deadlines, and in keeping the government it dominated powerful within a constitution that had to reduce the powers of the previous authoritarian presidency.[276] Both goals succeeded. The previous powers of the presidency were reduced, in particular regarding the establishment of states of emergency (art. 148) as well as enacting very difficult conditions for the dissolution of parliament (art. 127), and the open-ended tenure of the president was altered by a limitation to 2 terms (art 133). But the presidency was kept very strong, especially in the domains of foreign and military affairs (articles 145–146), appointment powers that included one-tenth of the Shura Council members (art.128), as well as policy areas through the ability to preside over government sessions at will (art 143), and to call referenda on any issue chosen (art. 150). While it is impossible to judge exactly how strong a presidency was created, we can certainly say that as long as the same party elected the president and the majority of the chambers, the office was to be the center of power in Egypt.

At the same time, it should be noted that the version of semi-presidentialism imposed by the MB was not significantly different than the negotiated version

[272] For the filtering function implied in such a provision see Tadros, op. cit., p. 56ff.
[273] That Court seemed to have disregarded the Al Azhar requirement in one of its very few decisions under the 2012 Constitution, which it in any case opposed. See N. Brown, "Egypt: A Constitutional Court in an Unconstitutional Setting," p. 33.
[274] See Arjomand, who debates with an interpretation that compares the projected role of Al Azhar to Iran's "mandate of the jurists" exercised by the Council of Guardians. In his view, it resembles rather the arrangement of the 1906–7 Iranian Constitution, and thus still compatible with "constitutionalism". See op. cit., 308–9.
[275] C. Lombardi and N. Brown, "Islam in Egypt's New Constitution," *Foreign Policy* December 13, 2012; Z. Al-Ali, "The New Egyptian Constitution: an Initial Assessment of its Merits and Flaws," *Open Democracy*, December 26, 2012.
[276] Z. Al-Ali, "The New Egyptian Constitution: an Initial Assessment of its Merits and Flaws," *Open Democracy*, 26 December 2012.

that emerged in Tunisia. This was perhaps because in Tunisia, after the results of its first elections, semi-presidentialism could appear to be a power-sharing mechanism, while in Egypt, after its own first parliamentary election results, the same solution could be seen as enhancing the power of the party that hoped to win both future parliamentary and presidential elections. Yet the MB's Constitution did not express undivided optimism about the future strength of its makers. The document sought to placate the military that has previously expressed its desires when it forced several favored provisions into the defunct Al Selmi constitutional principles.[277] The possibility of military trial of civilians re-appeared in the document (art. 198). While the military did not directly receive control over its budget, as it did in the Al Selmi document, it did so indirectly through the provision for a potentially powerful National Defense Council whose majority would consist of high military officers, a body that would have a key role in determining that budget (art. 197).

And yet, as everyone knows, even the concessions to the military did not end the constitution-making story. It would be difficult to believe that it was the text of the Constitution that led to its downfall, and the mobilization of an immense mass movement led by the new organization Tamarod against the Morsi presidency. The concessions to Islam were few, and uncertain in outcome, the semi-presidentialism resembled Tunisian and indeed French versions, and, while the Constitution's extensive table of rights incorporated a deeply conservative vision, and forms of potential limitations of individual freedom, it could not be described as "Islamist" in orientation.[278]

If the document was erroneously denounced as Islamist and authoritarian, as Nathan Brown and Zaid al Ali claim, this could be due only to the process through which it has emerged.[279] While its accelerated character could be chalked up to the initial Constitutional Declaration of the SCAF, its majoritarian features were due to the MB parliamentarians originally, and subsequently to President Morsi. Under these rules Parliament would have been free to set up an inclusive constituent assembly that decided by relative consensus, even if it was not obliged to do so as subsequent Administrative Court and SCC decisions maintained. Even after the dissolution of the first constituent assembly, that was a serious warning whatever the merits of the decision, Parliament chose to elect another majority-dominated body. Moreover, President Morsi would have been able to replace the majoritarian assembly when he took

---

[277] Ibid.   [278] Ibid.

[279] Few clearly realize this. But see M. Revkin (2013) "Egypt's Constitution in Question," *Middle East Law and Governance*, 5(3), 343: "The legitimacy of the 2012 constitution, which survived a mere six months, was undermined not so much by controversy over its content, but by outrage over the exclusionary and opaque process through which it was drafted."

office.[280] Instead, in his Constitutional Declaration he shielded the acts of the constituent assembly as well as his own decisions from all subsequent judicial review. It was especially this last move, described even by relatively sympathetic outside observers as an *autogolpe*,[281] that gave the mobilization of the movement against him its energy and justification. While Morsi succeeded in pushing through a constitution, his and the MB's acts of omission and commission deprived the document of legitimacy, in spite of its ratification in a referendum with a very low level of participation. While undoubtedly the leaders of secular forces like the new NSF (National Salvation Front, grouping together liberal and left organizations) were also guilty of avoiding serious negotiations, it was certainly Morsi and the MB who appeared least able and willing to compromise with secular forces. And it was the process of majoritarian constitution making, rather than its result, that supplied the main evidence, a cautionary note to those who believe that method of constitution making does not matter.[282] It does, at the very least in the short run, and Morsi's constitution was to have only a very short run of six months.

In the end, led by the new organization Tamarod, the mobilization against Morsi, included almost all organizations and actors outside the MB, including Al Azhar and even some Salafis.[283] In an eerie repetition of the overthrow of Mubarak, popular mobilization was followed by another coup by the SCAF, a new Constitutional Declaration[284] suspending the Constitution of 2012, and another constitution-making project, this time openly authoritarian in form.[285]

---

[280] And indeed the whole constitution-making methodology instituted by the SCAF. Awad, "Postscript," 294; Zaid al Ali, op. cit.

[281] Brown, "Egypt: A Constitutional Court" pp. 8ff. Others describe the shielding of executive acts from judicial review as an unprecedented Awad "PostScript."

[282] A point repeated by N. Brown after a process, the MB led one (that very much mattered!) in "Egypt's Daring Constitutional Gang of 50" Foreign Policy September 20, 2013, http://foreignpolicy.com/2013/09/20/egypts-daring-constitutional-gang-of-50/?wp_login_redirect=0. I tried but failed to dissuade him on this point.

[283] For the details of the vast, pluralistic participation see Sharif Abdel Kouddous "What Happened to Egypt's Liberals After the coup?" in *The Nation*, October 1, 2013, an article hardly sympathetic to Tamarod and the overthrow of Morsi.

[284] http://www.constitutionnet.org/files/2013_07_08_-_constitutional_declaration_idea_english .pdf.

[285] For the details see N. Brown's three articles "Mrs. Lincoln's Egyptian Constitution," *Foreign Policy*, August 20, 2013 http://foreignpolicy.com/2013/08/20/mrs-lincolns-egyptian -constitution/;

"Egypt's Daring Constitutional Gang of 50" and (with Michele Dunne) "Egypt's Draft Constitution Rewards Military and Judiciary," December 4 in Carnegie Endowment for International Peace; http://carnegieendowment.org/2013/12/04/egypt-s-draft-constitution-rewards -military-and-judiciary; as well as Zaid al Ali, "Egypt's third constitution in three years: A critical analysis," Constitutionnet, December 20, 2013 and Johnson, op. cit.

After the production of a draft by 10 jurists (the 10C) chosen from above, a fifty-person body (the 50C) was chosen, also from above, to rewrite the document that was then passed in another Bonapartist referendum, with only slightly better participation than in 2012. The document expressed the views of the main forces of the unstable coalition that overthrew Morsi,[286] establishing a slightly improved and strengthened table of rights, eliminating the two new Sharia-related articles (4 and 219) to which secular forces mainly objected, strengthening the jurisdiction and autonomy of the courts, and in particular the SCC, but above all strongly re-enforcing the autonomy of the military as an institution and its jurisdiction, in case of conflict, over civilians.

Thus, clearly of the two main forces[287] struggling for mastery in the revolution, the military has succeeded, while the other, the MB, was repressed. The great puzzle in all this is the ultimately weak, or merely subsidiary, role of the movements whose forms of consciousness, and actions were initially justly celebrated by many of the interpreters of the Egyptian Revolution.[288] It is true that some of these interpreters[289] call attention to the anti-political consciousness many of the groups of civil society active in the streets, their inability to unite behind leaders or political organizations. I would add that this attitude, along with the greater salience of the religious–secular division made the creation of an umbrella organization like the CPRN in Tunisia, backed by unions as well as parties and civil society organizations, more or less impossible. The attempts in that direction in Egypt helped to bring down two governments, but were unable to produce an organization capable of negotiating the terms of change in a round table-type setting such as Tunisia's High Authority. But in addition, and this is what I would like to stress here, there was a failure to agree on constitution-making ideas on the side of secular and liberal Muslim organizations that made it impossible to oppose SCAF imposition and MB

---

[286] Here the Salafists who supported the Coup lost, but it seems Al Azhar did not object to the changes that eliminated its filtering role.

[287] I follow interpreters who treat the struggle as a three way one between the SCAF, the MB, and the liberal and left elements of the movement that overthrew Mubarak. Undoubtedly, neither the Islamic oriented groups, nor the more secular ones, and probably not even the SCAF can for all purposes be treated as a single force. See the already cited works of Awad, and Tugal for example, as well as J. Cole. "Egypt's New Left Versus the Military Junta," *Social Research*, 79.2 (2012): 487–510, that makes a clear deistinction between "the left" and "the liberals."

[288] See the articles by B. Challand, M. Bamyeh, C. Trip and A. Salvatore in *Constellations*, vol. 20 no 1; and, even more emphatically, H. Dabashi, who implausibly claims what his title advertises:*The Arab Spring: The End of Post Colonialism* (London: Zed Books, 2012).

[289] In particular, and most convincingly, Tugal, *The Fall of the Turkish Model: How the Arab Uprisings Brought Down Islamic Liberalism* (London: Verso Books, 2016), pp. 198, 214–215; see also L. Khatib (2012) "Political Participation and Democratic Transition in the Arab World," *U. Pa. J. Int'l L.*, 34, 336–339,

majoritarianism by adopting any genuinely persuasive competing model concerning the making of a legitimate constitution. That such ideas were available is shown by the pamphlets and submissions of many external NGOs and civil society organizations.[290]

To be clear, elements of a competing negotiation-based model were hardly absent from the discourse and aspirations of the politically active in Egypt, due to what I believe the international dissemination of post-sovereign ideas[291] like inclusion, consensus, negotiation, limitations on all actors, and the proper use of the dimension of time (and sequence). Almost from the outset, when the SCAF established a top down constitutional reform committee, the absence of fair inclusion became a key issue. Only one MB member, and possibly the Islamist chair, represented forces other than experts of the government in place. When an indirectly elected "constituent assembly" that was in reality a parliamentary commission[292] was put on the agenda, there were attempts to guarantee its inclusive and non-majoritarian character,[293] and the most important of these was the Selmi report that failed to gather significant support outside of the SCAF. Yet, when the courts proceeded to dissolve one such body, one of the issues was indeed its composition reflecting nothing but the parliamentary Islamist majority. The debate about the electoral rule too was concerning the issue of inclusion.

The issue of inclusion was closely related to, but was not the same as, consensual decision making. Admittedly, a body fully including the main social forces as in Tunisia had little choice but to decide contested matters consensually. But even a body with a distinct majority, as existed in Egypt, could have imposed on itself consensual decision rules, by high qualified majorities. When this was rejected by the MB and Salafi majority, it was over this issue that many liberal representatives, and even Al Azhar, were to leave the assembly. As to negotiations, these may have taken place during Egyptian constitution making, but if so, they would have been mainly between the SCAF and the MB, as during the early amendments to the old constitution when the Muslim Brothers were the only oppositional force represented in the drafting commission. Certainly, the MB alone among all oppositional forces supported the SCAF in the referendum concerning the amendments.

---

[290] See e.g. the already cited http://www.constitutionnet.org/files/promoting_consensus.pdf.

[291] See H. Klug, *Constituting Democracy: Law, Globalism and South Africa's Political Reconstruction* (Cambridge: Cambridge University Press, 2000).

[292] Although it was initially unclear whether the "constituent assembly" would have to make its recommendation to parliament, or, as it turned out, could submit its product directly to a referendum.

[293] On why a majoritarian constituent assembly was deemed inappropriate by Egyptian liberals, see Awad "Breaking out of Authoritarianism," p. 286.

The same possibility of collusion should be noted, when several guarantees demanded by the SCAF wound up being included in Morsi's constitution of 2012. There is no definitive judgment concerning the actual vs. the merely tacit co-operation of the MB and the SCAF.[294] What is obvious, however, is that the idea of negotiation and compromise were present in the Egyptian constitution-making process, but without diminishing the overall exclusion or mitigating the imposed character. Sources of potential legitimation thus turned out to have a delegitimating role.

The all-important issue of time and sequence too may have been resolved by exclusionary negotiations, though it is equally possible that here the interests of the SCAF, seeking to have its decisions confirmed in early elections, and that of the MB with its high level of organization converged merely spontaneously. As elsewhere, the issues of time and sequence were intimately linked. Given the authoritarian background, no organization, group or party, outside the SCAF with its old regime background, and the MB with the support of the mosques as well as previous electoral experience, was prepared for early elections.[295] This led to the raising of two interrelated issues: the delay of elections, and the enactment of a constitution before them. Abstractly considered, there were strong arguments on both sides.[296] As to delay, those against it argued that the old regime, or its successor the SCAF, would be in power until there were free elections. Therefore elections should be held as soon as possible, in order to establish civilian control. Those supporting delay argued, however, that elections could be fair as well as free only if all major forces were sufficiently organized to be able to compete. While cogent, the latter argument was somewhat undercut by the anti-political hostility of many of civil society and street activists to organization and representation. Similarly, those who claimed a constitution should come second pointed out that only freely elected assembly had the right and legitimacy to give Egypt a constitution. But those who wanted a constitution first rightly claimed that free and fair elections could be held only under sufficient constitutional protection that

---

[294] On the one hand, Tugal in *The Fall of the Turkish Model* (pp. 165ff; 168ff.) makes a case, with some evidence, of formal collusion between the SCAF and the MB. On the other side, Nathan Brown "Contention in Religion and State" (p. 544) denies that there is any such "serious evidence." In between them, I. Awad denies that formal collusion can be proved, but maintains that there was a "tacit" agreement: "Breaking Out of Authoritarianism" (p. 279). Also see M. Tadros, *The Muslim Brotherhood in Contemporary Egypt* (London: Routledge, 2012) who documents "collusion" in the early months of the transition.

[295] See, e.g., Awad, "Breaking Out of Authoritarianism," 283; see also T. Assad, "Fear and the Ruptured State: Reflections on Egypt after Mubarak," *Social Research*, 79.2 (2012): 275–276.

[296] See, e.g., the excellent documentary "The Square" in which militants argue for each of the positions.

neither the amended inherited constitution nor the SCAF Declarations could provide. In several round table countries (Hungary, South Africa, and Nepal), the solution to exactly this problem was a thoroughly negotiated interim constitution. In Egypt, however, that label was already taken, for an imposed rather than a negotiated set of rules, namely the SCAF's March 2011 Declaration that incorporated the previous amendments confirmed in the referendum. Thus, the problem of sequence could be raised, but without a mediating option like a normatively acceptable interim constitution no satisfactory solution could be found.

Assuming the decisions concerning time and sequence that favored the MB, the danger of majoritarianism had to be openly confronted.[297] Thus, exactly as in Tunisia, the key idea of post-sovereign constitution making, and namely the limitation of the ultimate constitution-drafting assembly was seriously raised, and ultimately defeated. This was the debate about supraconstitutional principles resembling the South African pattern, undoubtedly launched by secular politicians and their experts fearing the domination of the constituent assembly by Islamic parties.[298] The author of the eventual draft or at least of its main part, the vice-prime minister Ali el Selmi, was a member of the liberal Wafd party that has occasionally cooperated with the authoritarian regime. Initially at least, a consultative committee was appointed to help draft these principles, but given the refusal of many actors to participate its activity seems to have been discontinued.[299] Thus, the effort in the end became a top-down project of the SCAF, and this relationship very much affected the substance of the document, which would have become a second interim constitution if adopted. The document had three components. The first involved a restatement of rights and powers that were present in all constitutional documents of the period, sometimes slightly altered as in the case of the Sharia clause that here did not refer merely to "principles" as liberals might have wished if such a clause was to be present at all. Though broadly favorable to the interests of liberals, this was perhaps the least controversial aspect of the document. It was the last part, however, Section 3, seeking to bring majoritarianism under limits, that was presumably the most objectionable to the MB who sought a sovereign parliament, ruling through its majority.[300] This section outlined the necessary

[297] On the religious basis of the strong majoritarianism of the MB, see Tadros, pp. 96–97. Even when conceding pluralism, this implied only toleration of the people of the book, and not atheists or secular political tendencies.
[298] See "Draft Declaration of the Fundamental Principles for the New Egyptian State" http://www.constitutionnet.org/files/2011.11_-_constitutional_principles_document_english.pdf.
[299] Awad, "Breaking out of Authoritarianism," p. 285.
[300] In peculiar twist, Islamists who believed that assembly majorities had to be limited, and constrained by, higher – namely religious – law, were unable to accept such a limitation of a

composition of the constituent assembly, involving a great deal of representation for forms of expertise and even more for civil society organizations and unions, and only 20 out of 100 seats for parliamentary parties according to their proportion of the seats.[301] The same section also provided for the SCAF (as the holder of presidential powers) the right to appeal to the binding decision of the Constitutional Court, if any part of a new draft violated what were vaguely identified as principles of the state and of earlier constitutional history, including the interim constitution previously imposed by the SCAF. In the absence of genuine negotiations, the obviously intended resemblance of this last provision to the certification process of the South African Constitutional Court was only that of a caricature to a person portrayed.[302] Yet there was strong justification for including principles such as these, whose function was to point to consensual solutions and to block usurpation of the "people's" will and voice by merely a segment.

Had the Selmi principles contained no further objectionable features the constituent process could have been positively affected. Unfortunately, on its own initiative, and it seems contrary to the protest of Selmi himself,[303] the SCAF included a third part, two articles in the middle of the text that were entirely unacceptable to many liberals and secularists who might have otherwise supported the project, including those who demanded principles restricting the constituent assembly in the first place. The military used the opportunity of supraconstitutional principles to try to establish its full control over its budget as well as legislation effecting its interests (section 1: 9) and to try to create a National Defense Council, that, similarly to such bodies after coups elsewhere, would represent the military interest and rationale in executive decision making, next to the government. (1: 10). Previous to this affair, the MB was often regarded as an ally of the military, one that

---

parliament or a constituent assembly by manmade rules. It was, of course, to their advantage, that the latter in Egypt would have been again imposed, rather than thoroughly negotiated. On the relationship of divine law and majorities in the political doctrine of the MB, see Tadros, op. cit., 59.

[301] It is entirely erroneous to describe this section as giving the SCAF control over four-fifths of the constituent assembly. Cole, "Egypt's New Left Versus the Military Junta" (p. 495). Even the deformed published version of the principles did not deprive parliament of choosing members under the various categories.

[302] See Brown, "Egypt: A Constitutional Court," p. 8, who lists the differences of the certification process in South Africa with the intended role of the SCC in reviewing the Egyptian Draft. The constitutional principles in South Africa were explicitly codified, and were comprehensively negotiated. Moreover, as against the Selmi draft, the task in South Africa was given to a new court, created by the negotiated interim constitution. It should be added, that the right to appeal to the Constitutional Court in South Africa was broadly dispersed among citizens and parties, as against the monopolization of the power in the presidency.

[303] Awad, op. cit., fn. 21; p. 291.

supported e.g., the latter's constitutional declarations. Instead of providing new security for secular forces, the supraconstitutional principles helped to cement a temporary alliance between the MB and civil society organizations, very much legitimating the democratic claims of the former in the coming elections. However, what should be stressed is that the military was not the only loser in this affair; the secular forces that sought constitutional principles were greater losers still.[304]

Constitutional principles, of course, could have been negotiated among the main forces, and it is absurd to regard anti-majoritarian limitations of constitution making assemblies and especially parliaments to be undemocratic per se.[305] Along with interim constitutions, principles can play a democracy-enabling role, as long as they satisfy important legitimating desiderata, as in South Africa. Not only did the SCAF's supraconstitutional principles become in the end vehicles of attempted illegitimate imposition, but they carried that mark within their contents. As with the earlier interim constitution, the SCAF turned democracy-enabling instruments into undemocratic constraints. In each case, devices that could have legitimated the constitution-making effort as a consensual one instead helped to delegitimate it and indeed to destabilize it.

Finally, the active role of apex courts in the constitution-making process was also inherited from recent post-sovereign cases like South Africa, but also from struggles over constitutional amendments in countries such as India and Turkey.[306] The Selmi principles, as we have seen, attempted but failed to formalize Constitutional Court intervention in the final process, allowing this body to declare parts of a new draft unconstitutional. That Court already existed, surviving from the old regime and was confirmed in its function of controlling the constitutionality legislation by Article 49 the March Constitutional declaration, the interim constitution. Similarly, Article 48 confirmed the continuity of the Council of State, whose main body was the Supreme Administrative Court that had jurisdiction over the constitutionality of administrative acts, including, quite unusually, some of the internal procedures of Parliament. In spite of the failure of supraconstitutional principles, these two courts nevertheless intervened in constitution making if not with respect to substance, then with respect to process. At issue specifically was the composition of, first, the constituent assembly, and then of parliament, whose committee or commission that assembly actually was. Not only was the constituent

---

[304] Only Awad seems to grasp this point. Op. cit., 286.   [305] M. Lynch, p. 153.
[306] Such a role for constitutional court judges should no longer be considered paradoxical. See Brown "Egypt: a Constitutional Court."

assembly heavily (two-thirds) Islamist in its composition but, as already argued, it also established decisional rules that made minority opposition to drafts or their components irrelevant. This invited a series of minority defections and boycotts that were fatal to the legitimacy of the assembly. It was at that juncture, applying part of the Selmi model that was never enacted, and the rather vague language of the interim constitution[307] that the Supreme Administrative Court declared the composition of the constituent assembly exclusively from members of parliament to be unconstitutional, and the assembly itself dissolved. Shortly thereafter, parliament appointed another constituent assembly of similar composition.[308] In response, this time (June 2012) the Supreme Constitutional Court disbanded parliament as a whole, because supposedly its conditions of election were violated by the parties running members in individual districts that were said to be reserved for independents. In a new Constitutional Declaration, then, the SCAF not only temporarily recovered the legislative power, but proceeded to re-enact the provision of the Selmi draft allowing constitutional review of the draft of the constituent assembly.

The combination of the last two steps indicates that in the context of court actions too it was a question of using devices taken over from post-sovereign patterns, but for authoritarian purposes and in a degraded form. After the excellent work of Tamir Moustafa,[309] we need not assume that the apex courts of Egypt were simply agents of the deep state. Surely, however, they sympathized with secular criticisms of the majoritarian aspirations of the MB. Whatever the reasons, however, while they were responding to legitimation problems, court interventions in Egypt wound up producing new ones. It was perhaps not decisive that the decisions themselves were flimsy, based on next to nothing (or on a text that was never enacted) in the case of the Supreme Administrative Court against the Constituent Assembly, and on rather irrelevant Mubarak-era precedents in the case of the Supreme Constitutional Court against parliament.[310] More importantly, their authority, based on top-down constitutional declarations rather than a negotiated interim constitution as in South Africa was insufficient, in terms of legitimacy as against legality in the most narrow sense, to trump the decisions of the electorate under fair rules, and of parliament under a majority rule that was permitted under even these declarations. This

---

[307] The 2011 Egyptian Constitutional Declaration (of March 30, 2011) Art. 60: "to elect...100 members"! Whose members, it was not clear. Source: Carnegie Endowment for International Peace http://egyptelections.carnegieendowment.org/2011/04/01/supremecouncilofthearmedforcesconstitutional announcement.

[308] Awad, op. cit., 287. [309] Op. cit.

[310] Awad, "Breaking Out of Authoritarianism," 287.

illegitimacy was probably presumed by another Constitutional Declaration, this time by President Morsi in November 2012, which deprived the same courts of any jurisdiction in matters of constitution making, including the one awarded to the Supreme Constitutional Court by the SCAF in the previous June. Yet two wrongs in this instance certainly did not amount to one right. As a subsequent SCC decision seemed to indicate, a legally elected president arguably did not even have the right to issue constitutional declarations like the SCAF, a formally revolutionary body.[311]

Thus we can surmise what that court would have done with Morsi's Constitutional Declaration even before the voting on the Constitution, if allowed to consider it by the crowds that made its sessions impossible. What we can again say is that the very form of court interventions that helped to legitimate and stabilize consensual and negotiated constitution making in South Africa, wound up destabilizing and delegitimating the majoritarian process without being able to put a better one in its place. What this proves is not that devices of inclusion, negotiation, consensus, pre-assembly binding, and court interventions are all equally ineffective in controlling what has been recently called "abusive constitutionalism." Rather, as already argued in the case of Colombia and Venezuela, it seems to be true that only in combination can several of these safeguards do their proper work reliably. Neither negotiation without inclusion, nor inclusion without consensus, nor court interventions without prior agreement on constitutional principles, can do the job that various combinations of these elements would have been capable of doing.[312] In order however for such combinations emerge, the actors or at least the main ones, need to see their connections. They did not in Egypt, and thus the destabilizing role of the factors treated here.

Thus, it is the actors that failed in Egypt, ultimately. I return to the Tunisian comparison. With respect to the most important actor in Egypt, all we can say is that the Tunisian military was perhaps too weak to intervene, while the SCAF was too strong to stop itself from continually trying to steer the process. Yet the inconsistency of SCAF interventions is striking, and it is hard to believe that the turmoil of three years served its interests better than early and fair agreements with all the civilian actors concerned would have done. Perhaps the greatest chance of the SCAF to facilitate genuine democratization

---

[311] See Brown, "Egypt: a Constitutional Court." Op. cit.

[312] Again, the Colombian and Tunisian cases seem to show that negotiations leading to a fair electoral rule seem to be alone capable of constraining assemblies, that in the two countries the Supreme Court and the High authority considered, but refused. This optimistic assessment is based on the premise that a fair electoral rule will not lead to one-party domination of an assembly. Unfortunately, the premise is not true in general.

came after its removal of President Morsi in a military coup.[313] While there are exceptions, such a scenario is rarely conducive to democratic change.[314] Yet in June of 2013 the SCAF, whatever its real motives, acted on behalf of a massive anti-authoritarian mobilization, and for the moment regained a popularity that it had during the overthrow of Mubarak. Had it been able to learn from earlier grave errors, this would have been the time for the SCAF to facilitate comprehensive negotiations, and a process of legitimate constitution making. Many external voices called for such a scenario.[315] Unfortunately the SCAF, either unable to learn or driven by its innate conservatism together with its economic interests, chose a fully imposed process of constitutional change, more unilateral than before, and using civilian expertise only as a political fig leaf for military command.

As to the Muslim Brotherhood, it ought to be now clear to all, including their leaders in exile or underground, that types of fair agreement as pursued by Ennahda around both issues of worldview and transition rules would have benefitted the movement better than its authoritarian aspirations legitimated by a simple majoritarian ideology. Whether or not the MB directly coordinated with the SCAF at any point, only insistence on inclusive negotiations could have removed the appearance of collusion between these two conservative forces. That appearance was an important factor in the emergence of a vast social mobilization, led by Tamarod against Morsi's presidency. The last moment when comprehensive negotiations could have been attempted came during that presidency. Probably both the MB and secular parties, very belatedly "united" in the so-called National Salvation Front, were responsible for the fact that this process could not even properly begin: Morsi because he continued to fully rely on the supposedly plebiscitary legitimacy of a freely elected president that in his eyes allowed no equality with potential negotiating partners, and the leaders of the NSF because they would not moderate their

---

[313] Also plausible is Awad's contention, op. cit., 286 that the best chance for the SCAF establishing inclusive negotiations came right after the fall of Mubarak. Yet, after the fall of Morsi, there was also the possibility of learning from the previous experience. Aside from the SCAF's authoritarian inclinations, it was the insistence of the MB on full restoration of Morsi that was a roadblock at the second occasion. There were however compromise proposals available, even on that issue. Crisis Group Policy Briefing 35: "Marching in Circles: Egypt's Dangerous Second Transition", August 7, 2013.

[314] In general, in spite of the exceptions he relies on, I disagree with O. Varol concerning the overall likelihood of a democratic transition initiated by military protagonists. O. Varol, "Military as the Guardian of Constitutional Democracy, The," *Colum. J. Transnat'l L.* 51 (2012): 547. There are many more cases with authoritarian outcomes, with any type of military intervention. But it is true, the type of role Varol suggests is, in principle, available.

[315] See the Crisis Group, "Marching in Circles: Egypt's Dangerous Second Transition."

complete distrust of the leadership of the MB, and because they as it turned out mistakenly believed that they had another choice, General Sissi and the SCAF.

Finally, it is very likely true that in Tunisia too there was a great deal of anti-political sentiment on the street and among civil society organizations, and not only in Egypt. Nevertheless, in Tunisia the leading role of umbrella organizations of parties, unions and other civil society groups seemed to have been much more easily accepted. Whether this was due to the greater wisdom and moderation of parties, including Ennahda, than of social movements like the MB is hard to say. After a year or two of celebration of the grassroots by the literature it would be important to discover why and how the partial transition from civil to political society was managed so much more effectively in Tunisia than in Egypt. What we do know, however, is that it is this transition that is required for negotiated, relatively consensual, legitimate constitution making. Tunisia's example shows that *even in a revolution*, such a transition to organized political society is possible without a single political organization, or two in succession, monopolizing constituent power and authority. The case of Egypt, however, does show that the internal transition to a post-sovereign model in a revolution remains extremely difficult.

PART III

CONSTITUTIONAL CHANGE UNDER CONSTITUTIONAL REGIMES

5

Post-Sovereign Constitutionalism

The Domestication of Revolution?

The argument of this book has so far concentrated on procedures and processes of constitution making. Here and elsewhere[1] I have argued against imputation of the process from the result. Nevertheless, it goes without saying that the result matters a great deal. It is time to ask the question then: what kind of constitutions are likely to emerge from the post-sovereign process, and the more revolutionary forms that have incorporated its main element of comprehensive and inclusive negotiations in the pre-assembly phase. In light of the procedural stress of this book and its predecessor, I want to consider this question in terms of the procedures established in constitutions, primarily the two interrelated dimensions of amendment procedures and forms of constitutional review and control. My hypothesis[2] is that the post-sovereign process is likely to produce *constitutionalist* outcomes, and second, I would argue on logical-normative grounds, with some empirical evidence to support it, that this constitution making paradigm has at least an elective affinity with *democratic* constitutionalism.[3]

I will develop the thesis in terms both of two theories, as well as the relevant empirical cases of the round table countries supplemented by the two more revolutionary cases of Colombia and Tunisia where important features of multi-stage post-sovereign constitution making have been adopted.[4] I treat

---

[1] *Post Sovereign Constitution Making: Learning and Legitimacy* (Oxford: Oxford University Press, 2016), introduction and chapter 1.

[2] I am taking a friendly warning by Julian Arato to heart that I should not confuse my ultimately politically based judgment with an overly strong causal argument, that I at least do not have the skills to sustain.

[3] On that concept, see my *Civil Society, Constitution and Legitimacy* (Lanham: Rowman & Littlefield, 2000), chapter 4.

[4] I include Spain, which had no comprehensive negotiations in the very beginning, but had a multi-stage process with later negotiations, and Hungary where the completion of a multi-stage

Spain as full-fledged post-sovereign case, even though in that country comprehensive negotiations followed rather than preceded the initial enactment of interim rules. I will first examine the case for the relatively strong empirical *and* normative link between insurance, constitutionalism, and post-sovereign constitution making, and then the admittedly weaker logical as well as normative one[5] between the multi-stage process and a strongly democratic version of constitutionalism.

INSURANCE AND CONSTITUTIONALISM

First proposed by Adam Przeworski,[6] and then generalized by Tom Ginsburg, the insurance thesis suggests that in a constitution-making setting if "there are no parties that will be confident in their ability to win, all parties will prefer to limit the majority, and therefore will value minoritarian institutions like judicial review."[7] More precisely, the thesis implies pessimism or radical uncertainty on the part of parties whose consent is essential for agreement on a constitution. The aim of insurance is to guard against majoritarianism

process was not in the spirit of the post-sovereign paradigm. I will at the same time omit the two round table countries whose state collapsed during the process, Czechoslovakia and the GDR. (Actually, adding the constitutional results in Slovakia, the Czech Republic, and Germany would have increased the co-relation I found between insurance and negotiated phase! Of course, adding zeros for both the Czechoslovakia and GDR final stages would have decreased it. Given the arbitrariness of the choice, I chose to exclude these cases.) Thus I will focus on eight countries where constitutions were made for territorially and organizationally intact states: Spain, Poland, Hungary, Bulgaria, Nepal, South Africa, Colombia, and Tunisia. I will also add Iraq, in spite of the fact that the nature of its state structure, supposedly resolved by the Constitution of 2005, remains in a great deal of doubt. Admittedly, Colombia and Tunisia had more revolutionary processes, but as argued in the previous chapter, comprehensive negotiations and compromise friendly electoral rules made these cases resemble the logic of the round table model. Thus I have nine cases in all, to be compared to nine contemporary examples of reform and revolutionary imposition. Undoubtedly, for those wedded to mainstream social science methodologies, the thesis could be fully demonstrated only by using a large N sample, compared to a contemporary set of the same size as the selected cases, of either reformist or revolutionary imposition. The first set does not exist, however. In my defense, the argument throughout will rest not only on the empirical evidence of obviously too few cases, but also the elective affinities, logical as well as normative between process and outcome.

[5] I call it an elective affinity, following Max Weber's *Wahlverwandschaft*, because the link is logical, and because, while there seems to be covariance empirically, the apparent causal links are hard to demonstrate, and could be the result of other causes acting. This was the nature of the Protestant ethic-spirit of capitalism affinity in Weber's famous book.

[6] A. Przeworski, *Democracy and the Market* (Cambridge: Cambridge University Press, 1991).

[7] T. Ginsburg, *Judicial Review in New Democracies* (Cambridge: Cambridge University Press, 2003).

at the very least and even more fundamentally "abusive constitutionalism" where constitutional devices are used to establish dominance by one party or group or leader.[8] The contrast on the level of constitution making is with a single political force dominating the process, one that is optimistic about its future electoral chances, and therefore imposing a constitution in which its future majorities will not be restricted or limited by constitutional restraints, implied by judicial review and difficult amendment rules.[9] Certainly, even a party dominant at the time of constitution making can be pessimistic about its future chances, as in Ran Hirschl's hegemonic preservation thesis,[10] which in such a case may represent a special version of the desire for insurance. But as I have argued elsewhere, such parties will generally prefer particular institutional advantages, namely forms of power *conversion* benefitting them alone unless strong ideological commitments, internal divisions or outside pressures will force them to settle for more universalistic *guarantees* that will potentially benefit all future minorities including ones not yet on the scene.[11]

The insurance thesis solves many puzzles, including those proposed by Jon Elster quite a while ago[12] according to which "self-binding," or rather the binding of the "other," is both necessary for the protection of minorities (169) and yet unlikely to take place. This is supposed to be the case either because pre-commitment is (often) not desirable when feasible or (often) will not be feasible when desirable or will not (often) hold even when both feasible and desirable (157ff.). Thus, Elster evocatively proposes that pre-commitment implies that framers must make the bad choice of making "suicide pacts" (when they do pre-commit) or failing to "prevent suicides" (when they refuse to do so). Here his initial error, that he only partially and inconsistently corrected, of treating constitution makers as a single agent to be "self" bound, comes back to haunt the analysis.[13] As he himself recognizes for specific cases, such

---

[8] D. Landau (2013) "Abusive Constitutionalism," *UCDL Rev.*, 47, 189.

[9] For a model of this option, see G. Negretto, *Making Constitutions: Presidents, Parties, and Institutional Choice in Latin America* (Cambridge: Cambridge University Press, 2013).

[10] R. Hirschl *Towards Juristocracy: the Origins and Consequences of the New Constitutionalism* (Cambridge, MA: Harvard University Press, 2009).

[11] Arato, *Post Sovereign*, chapter 3.

[12] J. Elster, *Ulysses Unbound: Studies in Rationality, Precommitment, and Constraints* (Cambridge: Cambridge University Press, 2000) (revising earlier book of 1979).

[13] Two selves, the binder and the one that is bound, are not much more accurate sociologically than one. Even Ulysses as two persons, before and after, is in an entirely different situation than constitutional politicians.

as the origins of constitutional review in Hungary (171–2),[14] the maker of the constitution can be a plurality, whose members can gain insurance (as he explicitly says) by persuading their partners as well as themselves to pre-commit. That is what the thesis of insurance states, and, as Elster well knows, after World War II, especially but not exclusively in Europe, experience more often sustain the insurance thesis rather than his extreme paradox.

The insurance thesis was formulated in relation to judicial or constitutional review, but it is obvious that insurance can be attained through other institutions as well. Ginsburg, following the analysis of pre-commitment by Elster, rightly mentions constitutional entrenchment through amendment rules, bicameralism, and proportional electoral rules.[15] I do not agree, however, that judicial review will be preferred to these other devices because of its lower cost.[16] Instead, I would maintain that constitutional review by either a special tribunal or by other apex courts is necessary for insurance purposes even where the other devices are adopted. Whatever the mode of the two elections involved, bicameralism and even federalism, (as Tocqueville noted) could still produce the government by the same political force. Even PR is no guarantee against one-party dominance, especially in liberation settings as recently in South Africa.[17] Most importantly, entrenchment is not self-enforcing, thus the differentiation between legislation and amendment needs to be "externally" enforced, if the legislature is to be stopped from implicitly derogating from the constitution through ordinary statutes. It is true, conversely, that judicial review presupposes procedural entrenchment differentiating between the constitution, and ordinary laws, if the constitutional judges are to invalidate statutes enacted through the ordinary legislative process. Thus, while judicial review complements proportional representation and

---

[14] Even here another error is repeated, this time an empirical one, supposedly after John Schiemann, that it was the Hungarian Communists who initially sought a strong constitutional court. They wanted a court, but a weak one, open to override. It was the ideologies and insurance needs of other actors that led to the very strong court, though after some electoral warnings the MSZP was quite ready to go along. See chapter 4 in *Post Sovereign*.

[15] *Judicial Review*, p. 25. Presidentialism of the US type too could have been mentioned, but I agree with its omission because in most of today's settings the implication is a strong majoritarian executive.

[16] Frankly, I have never seen that issue of cost ever come up in any negotiated setting. It is a fiction, based merely on "law and economics" assumptions.

[17] Of course, given some structures of appointment, a court too can be of the same political complexion as other branches. Thus Ginsburg rightly considers independent forms of appointment to be a crucial dimension of insurance through a court.

bicameralism, it is logically presupposed by, as well as presupposes constitutional entrenchment.[18] In various empirical combinations, the institutions
together characterize constitutionalist constitutions.

The insurance thesis presupposes a setting of inclusive bargaining and
negotiation,[19] thus it is hardly surprising that Ginsburg, proposing it,
considered one or two round table processes to represent "text-book"
examples.[20] Nevertheless the link is not absolute. Constitutionalism has also
emerged in other settings, and not all round tables managed to produce strong
versions of constitutionalism implied by the category of insurance. As I just
claimed, following Hirschl, a hegemonic constitution maker may under some
conditions opt for an insurance model. An even more likely source of insurance is the making of a federal union by previously independent units, who will
almost always opt for bicameralism and strong entrenchment of the division
and distribution of powers, and, more recently at least, constitutional review.
Undoubtedly, these departures from the linkage can be explained. In the case
of hegemonic establishment of insurance, one can stress either the pessimism
of the hegemon, as did Hirschl, or the presence of plurality, either in the
form of outside civil society pressure (as, e.g., in Slovenia) or internal divisions
within the hegemonic party (as in India) that seek insurance also against one
another. With respect to federalism, it is easy to point to the plurality of the
main actors, and contractual nature of their agreement,[21] both resembling
the round table-type process. Finally, the round tables that failed did so in the
domain of state preservation, as in Czechoslovakia and the GDR, and constitution making was not therefore a realistic possibility for these previously
existing states.[22] Yet even with these explanations, nevertheless, the relevance

---

[18] Kelsen may have been the first in *General Theory of Law and the State* (Cambridge, MA:
Harvard University Press, 1945) to postulate this logic, even as he considered many earlier
constitutions to be "illogical."

[19] Unfortunately Ginsburg and his co-authors went on in *Endurance of National Constitutions*
(Cambridge: Cambridge University Press, 2009) to argue that all constitution making is through
negotiation (66ff.). Yes, even Bonaparte in 1798 did negotiate with his supporters, Sieyès and
a few others! But the authors rightly admit that negotiations can be more or less inclusive.
That is the point I repeatedly made for the round tables. Unfortunately, Ginsburg and his
colleagues first conflate inclusion with the equally important value of publicity, and then the
democratic devices of elections (upstream) and referenda (downstream). The conception thus
abandons the essence of the insurance theory namely inclusive negotiations between strong
poltical agents, who decide by relative consensus. (Ibid., p. 78ff; 97ff).

[20] *Judicial Review*: on Hungary, pp. 99–100; on South Africa, p. 55.

[21] C. Schmitt *Verfassungslehre* (Berlin: Duncker & Humblot, 1928), chapters 7 and 29.

[22] See chapter 3 above.

of the insurance model to the cases of successful constitution making under the post sovereign paradigm needs further demonstration.[23]

Yet another difficulty is the presence of constitutional review, most likely under the influence of international norms, in almost all constitutions made in the contemporary epoch. The same is true for tables of fundamental rights, that precisely for this reason I have left out from the list of "guarantees" relevant to insurance. Of course, it is true that rights represent potentially important guarantees for minorities, but only when capable of enforcement. In the case of constitutional courts, however, Ginsburg rightly argues[24] that the *strength* of this institution is not a product of international norms, which are rather agnostic with respect the specific nature of the review established, but rather of the desire of internal actors for insurance. For the insurance model, in part following his analysis, issues of (broad) standing or access, (strong) actual powers, and (consensual or professional) appointment structure of courts are especially relevant.[25] Analogously, in order to assess the working of the insurance model, for amendment rules, one should consider the strength of entrenchment, for PR, the degree of proportionality, and for bi-cameralism, the difference between the forms and timing of election for the two chambers. Admittedly, international influence and transmission of ideas can affect also the strength of insurance forms. Nevertheless, it is my tough to fully prove hypothesis that round table-led post-sovereign models tend to produce relatively stronger proportionality, bicameralism, amendment rules and judicial review than reformist and especially revolutionary forms in the same historical period, with the same tacit international norms at work in all constitution making efforts.

Below, I will, in an admittedly preliminary manner, consider the appearance and strength of these variables for the post-sovereign cases, of Poland, Hungary, Bulgaria, South Africa, and Nepal, supplemented by the borderline reformist case of Spain, the more revolutionary cases of Colombia and Tunisia, and the externally imposed revolution of Iraq.[26] The argument relating to

---

[23] This is especially the case, because when introducing the model, Ginsburg paid no special attention to forms of constitution making, and based his argument on post-election party pluralism, which could not be the source of the institutions of insurance unless we wrongly postulate that parties knew the electoral outcomes in advance. For the round tables moreover it is simply not true that we cannot consider party pluralism before the first free elections. Op. cit., pp. 60–61.

[24] Op. cit., p. 35ff.

[25] I am less sure about length of tenure of judges, and the size of courts. If someone wishes to include these for my nine cases, I will have no objection.

[26] On the classification of these, see chapters 3 and 4 above.

many of these cases has been so far based on historical reconstruction,[27] what others slightly dismissively call "anecdotal evidence."[28] However tentatively, the anecdotal evidence can be supported by a slightly more systematic effort at comparison. These results amount only to hypotheses, either because of the limited nature of my methodological skills, or because empirical comparative work cannot, in principle, do much more. I will in any case propose the hypothesis, which others can further test if they wish, namely that the round table countries and other cases of inclusively negotiated constitutions seem to represent strong examples of insurance. I will further propose, that many of these, the ones with interim constitutions, internalize the project of insurance or rather constitutionalism within the constitution making project itself. In one or two cases, most notably in South Africa, this internalization allows less reliance on insurance in the final constitution making assemblies.

With one partial exception, namely Poland, the round table countries had pluralistic, and inclusive forms of participation of important political forces.[29] In addition, there were inclusive negotiations in Spain, Colombia, Nepal, and Tunisia, and apparently inclusive but in part exclusionary coming to agreement in Iraq. Poland was the partial exception, because of the high uncertainty of being able to produce a negotiated agreement at all, and because the country had a very large social movement with high political legitimacy, Solidarity, incorporating a diversity of political forces. Yet, interestingly, as the first case among the Communist countries, initially the ruling party could still impose forms of conversion on its then weaker antagonist, such as partially unfree elections, and a presidency tailor-made for General Jaruzelski. By their very nature, all these examples, even Poland, relied on consensual decision-making, thus the agreement of weaker parties uncertain about their electoral chances. At the same time, the ruling parties, having many initial advantages in future elections, with the exception of Poland initially, were willing under strong pressure to surrender actually attempted forms of conversion of power

---

[27] See chapters 3 and 4 above, as well as chapters 4 and 5 of *Post Sovereign Constitution Making*.
[28] Ginsburg, op. cit., 49ff. When engaged in anecdotal reconstruction, Ginsburg's analysis is mostly convincing, though I do not buy the making of the Fifth Republic as a case of insurance. More importantly, I am not convinced of his own large N results in this context that suffer from obvious flaws: 1. Deriving the need for insurance from the results of the first elections, rather than the state of forces prior to it. 2. Not distinguishing the round table cases, where it would have indeed possible to determine the prior political strength in negotiations, and 3. Not being able to distinguish between the causal role of international influence, cross-country learning and the logic of insurance.
[29] See chapter 3 above.

in favor of more universalistic guarantees. This was especially possible in two- or multi-stage processes, where "guarantees" (i.e. forms of conversion) favoring the ruling parties such as a strong presidency (Poland, initially in Hungary) or mandated forms of power sharing (Hungary, South Africa) could be abandoned in the second or later stages.

Hungary represents a second exceptional case that I will include in my attempted comparison. There was in this country a genuinely negotiated first stage, which produced many of the forms (not all!) associated with insurance, and many of the actors were fully conscious of the uncertainty that required constitutionalist guarantees. Yet, the second stage of the post-sovereign model either failed to be realized in Hungary (in 1994–8), or in an alternative inter- pretation, was realized in a fully majoritarian form of imposition (in 2010–2011) that broke with the logic of insurance. Yet even here, some survivals from the interim constitution, like initially a weaker but still strong constitutional court, indicate the partial presence of the initial logic. Something similar can be said about the Czech and Slovak cases that I will not include because of the lim- ited results of the round table, and because new states were formally involved. Yet even here the much more proportional electoral logic coming out of the round table allowed elements of insurance to survive.[30]

I would like to distinguish between *political* forms of insurance, like pro- portional electoral rule and bicameralism, and *constitutional* forms such as entrenching amendment rules and judicial review. While focusing on the lat- ter, I begin with the former, the electoral rules for the chambers, two possible rules if there is bicameralism. I also distinguish between the rules of interim elections, from the final ones.[31]

1. Following others[32] I consider a single-country district PR as the most proportional system (3 points), a PR with many districts as less propor- tional (2 points), mixed systems as even less proportional, depending on the distribution between PR and majoritarian seats (1 to 1.5 points), first past the post outcomes whether one or 2 rounds as strongly dispro- portional (0 points). I subtract .5 for a significant threshold rule in PR races. I am forced to neglect the numerical conversion rules from votes

---

[30] According to my coding, the Czech constitution would receive (2, 2, 1.5, 2.5 = 8.5), and the Slovakian one (2, 1, 1, 2 = 6). If included under the round tables, they would very slightly lower the average, under the control cases they would raise it slightly.

[31] For the nine cases, I rely on interim and final constitutions readily available in websites such as: *Constitution Finder* http://confinder.richmond.edu/. The same for the nine control cases below, as well as the cases excluded, the Czech Republic and Slovakia.

[32] R. Taagepera and M. Shugart. *Seats and Votes* (New Haven: Yale University Press, 1989).

to seats, because their very real affect on the degree of proportionality is weaker than of electoral thresholds, and especially district size.

2. For the upper chamber, I stress difference with the lower chamber rule, as a minority-protecting provision, along with proportionality (1 point for proportionality; +1 point if different rules), but subtract .5 for asymmetrical bicameralism with a weak upper chamber, either because of weak powers, or the ability of the lower chamber to override the higher one.

Political Insurance: Electoral Rules for Two Chambers

Country	Lower chamber interim rule (s)	Lower chamber final rule	Upper chamber-interim	Upper chamber-final
Spain	2	2	.5[33]	1 (0+1)
Poland	[= 0[34]]/3/2.5	2.5	1	1
Hungary	1.5	1 (Fidesz 2011)	none	none
Bulgaria	1.5	2	none	none
Colombia	3	2	none	2
South Africa	3	3	2	2
Iraq	3	2	none	Mandated
Nepal	1.5	1.5	none	2
Tunisia	2	2	none	none

I proceed to constitutional forms, to be able to examine the whole structure of insurance. Again, I distinguish between interim forms, and final ones:

3. For Amendment Rule: 1 points for each:[35]
   a. qualified majority (-.5 if low % or -.5 if linked to a very disproportional electoral rule)
   b. participation of more than one lawmaking assembly
   c. ratification by states or provinces
   d. ratification in a referendum

---

[33] -.5: because 41 senators appointed by monarch, for one Senate only.

[34] First elections were only partially free.

[35] This list is close to Elster's in *Ulysses Unbound*, p. 101; except that I don't consider the size of quorums required generally very significant. Unlike he, I put approval by two parliaments, one a freshly elected one, as an amendment difficulty, rather than merely a time delaying device. The latter category that I consider less important applies strictly only to the same parliament voting more than once on the same amendment. It would provide very little insurance to those who needed it.

  e. eternity clause or high threshold or a separate, more demanding process for replacement. (These two options will be examined separately below, as competing alternatives from the democratic point of view.[36])

4. For the strength of judicial or constitutional review,[37] 1 point each for:
   a. broad standing
   b. strong powers including relative finality of invalidation (-.5 for override)
   c. consensual or professional appointment
   d. amendment review (only .5 if implicit in amendment rule only)

Constitutional Insurance

Country	Amendment or replacement rule		Strength of judicial review	
	Interim	Final	Interim	Final
Spain	.5	.5, 1, 1, 1 = 3.5	none	1, 1, 1, .5 = 3.5
Poland Interim: Small Constitution	Amend: 1 Replace: 2	1, 1 = 2	(1-.5) .5	1, 1, .5 = 2.5
Hungary Final: Fidesz Basic Law	.5	.5	1, 1, 1 = 3	1, 1, .5 = 2.5
Bulgaria	None	1, 1 = 2	none	1, 1, 1, .5 = 3.5
South Africa	1, 1, 1, .5 = 3.5	1, 1, 1 = 3	1, 1, 1, 1 = 4	1, 1, 1, 1 = 4
Colombia	None (formally sovereign con. assembly)	1, 1, 1 = 3 (4 with replacement doctrine of Con. Court)	None (according to decision of Supreme Court!)	.5; 1, 1, 1 = 3.5 (only procedural review of amendments?)
Iraq	1, 1 = 2	1, 1, 1, 1 = 4	1, 1, 1 = 3	.5, .5, .5
Nepal	1,1 = 2,	1, 1	1, 1, 1 = 3	1, 1, 1 = 3
Tunisia (Interim OPP by con. Ass.	Replace: 1, 1 = 2	1, 1, 1 = 3	Constitutional Council suspended	1, 1, 1, 1 = 4

---

[36] In this section, from the point of view of insurance thesis, I am interested in the general level of difficulty of amendment rules. In the next two sections, I will discuss the relationship of amendment rules to democracy, and there the type of insurance used will turn out to make an important difference.

[37] Again, I do not follow Ginsburg in making either size of the court, or the length and renewability of appointments, a mark of strength.

Combining the two tables:

Level of Insurance Score, Final Constitutions. Maximum: 14 points

Spain	(interim[38]: 3)	10
Poland	(interim: 6)	6.5
Hungary	(interim: 5)	4
Bulgaria	(interim: 1.5[39])	7.5
Colombia	(interim: 5[40])	10.5
South Africa	(interim: 12.5)	12
Iraq	(interim: 8)	7.5
Nepal	(interim: 6.5)	8.5
Tunisia	(interim: 4)	9

This yields an average of 8.26 for the round table or inclusively negotiated cases, even counting Hungary, the outlier, where the final stage broke with round table insurance logic. Without Hungary, the average would have been 8.6. I note already, that the level of insurance tends to rise with respect to interim arrangements, except for the cases of Hungary, where the process turned majoritarian in its second stage, and South Africa where the final constitution does not re-enact the unchangeable principles or contain eternity clause. To that issue I will return below.

Control Cases

Country	Electoral rule	Bicameralism	Amendment rule	Constitutional review	Level of insurance
Greece 75	1	None	3	1.5	5.5
Portugal 76	2	None	2	2.5	7
Romania 91	1.5	1	3	1.5	7
Russia 93	1.5	2	4.5	2	9
Serbia[41] 92	2	None	2	.5	4.5
Croatia 90	0 = 2 round majoritarian	2	1.5	1.5	6
Slovenia 91	1.5	2	2	2	7.5
Albania[42]	1	None	2	2	5
Venezuela 99	1/60% fptp	None	4	1.5	6[43]

[38] "rule": Ley para de la reforma politica, enacted from above, and approved in referendum, that the future opposition parties opposed.
[39] No interim constitution, relatively few rules.
[40] Supreme Court invalidates interim rules!   [41] And Montenegro.
[42] 1998. Albania had an interim constitution, in 1992, and by that criterion it could have been counted with the post-sovereign cases. The process itself does not justify that, and the differences between the interim and final constitutions are not significant for this comparison.
[43] Whether a feature of the constitution does, in practice, provide strong insurance, needs to be explored in detail for each case. There is a special reason to mention the purely paper or

Clearly, even such a roughly coded data can be exposed to the control of non-round table countries, where reformist or revolutionary constitution-making assemblies were not created through inclusive negotiations. Selecting famous historical cases from the USA, France, Latin America and Weimar Germany, before the worldwide spread of constitutional courts and judicial review, and in many cases before the advent of proportional representation, would make the task of demonstration skewed in favor of the round table countries. Given the obvious role of the international dissemination of constitutional ideas in the present period, I chose a set of cases from the same period more or less as the round table set. In each case, I chose the initial constitution, and neglected comprehensive amendment packages subsequently, and, even more importantly, the difference between the formal constitution and the constitution as actually enforced. The average level of insurance in the non-round table cases = 6.37. The Russian Federation is an outlier, and that can be explained by the federalist process organized by Yeltsin to counter the parallel effort by a conservative parliament, elected in only a partially free election. Without Russia, the average would be = 5.9. If the second stage of Hungary, involving clearly majoritarian imposition, were added here, the average would be 5.7.

Let me draw some conclusions, or rather hypotheses, from the admittedly rough data, that could be tested by those more adept at statistical analysis. The round table countries, and more generally where inclusive negotiations preceded constitution making have realized the insurance model of producing constitutionalism significantly more often, and on a higher level, than other contemporary cases. Of course, the relatively high level in both sets could and should be attributed to international influences, but, as Ginsburg argued for judicial review, the difference between them cannot be so explained. I believe the same result would follow if we used pairs of cases similar in geography and political culture, as Spain vs Portugal (10 vs 7); Bulgaria vs Romania (7.5 vs 7); Colombia vs Venezuela (10.5 vs 6; even with the latter's misleadingly high insurance formal rules). Moreover, the unique case of South Africa, which I have repeatedly claimed to be the most advanced realization of the post-sovereign model, has the highest insurance score among the 18 countries surveyed (= 12). Among the non-round table countries, interestingly, the highest score at least with respect to the formal constitution, has been attained by the Russian Federation (= 9; however compromised in practice),

formal character of Venezuelan insurance, that is formally high, but has been compromised by populist and plebiscitary practice from the outset. See: my chapter 4 above, and Brewer-Carias, Landau and Figureoa cited in that chapter.

suggesting the partial convergence between the two contractual models of round tables and federally based assemblies.[44]

Finally, the key institution of the interim constitution applied constitutionalism or insurance to the process of constitution making itself. It seems, however, that this did not necessarily mean the increase of the level of insurance, from the interim to the final, as three cases – Hungary, South Africa and Iraq – testify. The deviant end of the Hungarian process, which turned majoritarian and led to a decline of constitutionalism, is thus easily explained. Yet even before, during the 1990 constitutional pact, elements of consociationalism were removed from the constitution. This anticipated the more famous move from consociationalism to constitutionalism in South Africa's final constitution, and the removal of the three province interim veto over constitutional change in Iraq's. In general, it seems to be true, that where interim insurance is on a relatively low level in the absence of interim constitutions, as in Spain, Colombia, Bulgaria, and Tunisia, the final level is likely to rise. By contrast, where it is initially very high, as in South Africa, it may be reduced. While empirically it cannot be shown that this reduction of overly high level of insurance is motivated by the norms of democratic constitutionalism, logically at least a strong case can be made for the thesis. To this normative-logical relation I will now turn.

INSTITUTIONALIZING "RADICAL DEMOCRACY" AND DEMOCRATIC CONSTITUTIONALISM

On a normative level, constitutionalism, as a form of insurance against tyranny, is not the only value of liberal democratic orders. Democratic legitimacy[45] is equally important, even if its link to the endurance of constitutions is not easy

---

[44] Even if Yeltsin and his supporters controlled the Constitutional Conference of the regions, and pushed through a very strong presidency, they obviously had to make many concessions to federalist opinion to succeed. Many of these were subsequently eviscerated, under President Putin.

[45] As historians of the democratic revolutions, as well as recent transitions to democracy, could readily attest, this normative desideratum arises both from the international dissemination of constitutional ideas, and the form of experience of the main actors. Compare the text of the declaration of independence, and the *Federalist* (No. 78: referring to the "fundamental principle of republican government, which admits the right of the people to alter or abolish the established Constitution, whenever they find it inconsistent with their happiness") with Title IX of the Constitutions of 1791 (fn. 50) and 1793 (Declaration of Rights, Article 28) in France. See also the texts of Jefferson and Condorcet as cited in notes 52, 54 and 55 below. For the international context of South African attempts to reconcile constitutionalist and democratic values see H. Klug, *Constituting Democracy* (Cambridge: Cambridge University Press, 2000), chapter 5.

to demonstrate.[46] If constitutions should not be suicide pacts[47], they should also not be prisons of democratic participation in constitutional change.[48] This means that insurance can go too far, by creating rules of change that in effect make constitutions unchangeable. Such was the bitter experience of the first French written constitution of 1791, which had an amendment rule that was nearly impossible to use, and was overthrown in a second revolution after less than two years of existence.[49] But the rigidity of the US Article V, while bypassed through a long tradition of informal change centering on active constitutional review, has not been able to avoid serious legitimation problems focusing on the Supreme Court's quasi-constituent power. *Pace* Hannah Arendt, Woodrow Wilson's depiction of the Supreme Court as "a kind of Constitutional Assembly in permanent session" was, in the Lochner epoch, hardly meant as a compliment.

Indeed Hannah Arendt herself, famously, criticized the US Constitution, for succeeding according to her in establishing constitutionalism, but failing to institutionalize the possibility of the revolutionary experience that was its own source.[50] The argument goes back to Jefferson, who, along with his call for elements of institutionalized direct democracy (the so-called "wards"), repeatedly argued that each generation should have the opportunity to exercise the same constituent power as the founders. Jefferson's argued primarily in

---

[46] See Elkins et al., *Endurance of National Constitutions*; T. Ginsburg, Z. Elkins, Z., and J. Blount (2009) "Does the Process of Constitution-making Matter?," *Annual Review of Law and Social Sciences*, 5(5).

[47] Elster in *Ulysses*, p. 174; his slightly different contrast is between suicide pact, and enabling of suicide; that pertains to my idea that insurance should not go too far. But it is true, radical democracy in the sense of Colon Rios (*Weak Constitutionalism* (London: Routledge, 2012)) could lead to the subversion of democracy.

[48] Colon-Rios *Weak Constitutionalism*, 20 and 67 and elsewhere.

[49] "TITLE VII OF THE REVISION OF CONSTITUTIONAL DECREES: 1. The National Constituent Assembly declares that the nation has the imprescriptible right to change its Constitution; nevertheless, considering that it is more in conformity with the national interest to use only the right of reforming, by the means provided in the Constitution itself, those articles which experience has proven unsatisfactory . . . " Proceeding to the requirement that four successive legislatures, the last an "assembly of revision," would have to approve each change. See: http://www.historywiz.com/primarysources/const1791text.html. The same contradiction was there in the Constitution of 1793, between the Declaration's art. 28, and articles 115–117 of the main text. It is wrong to say that this constitution "refused to entrench itself," or that it was "silent on revision": Cf. *Endurance* pp. 13 and 169; with J. Godechot ed. *Les Constitutions de la France* (Paris: Flammarion, 1979), p. 191.

[50] *On Revolution* (New York: Viking, 1962), chapter 6, pp. 224ff. However, Arendt recognized that those establishing new foundations do have legitimate concerns regarding the stability of their work, if not its permanence. She did not clearly recognize that the solution of the problem, at least, in part, lies in the construction of suitable amendment rules as explored here. For the other part, see my Epilogue below.

the name of self-government and political autonomy, but he also stressed constitutional learning over time and in any given context. In his own case, learning involved moving from the untenable anarchic proposal of 1787 of a sunset clause of 19 years for each constitution, to the more famous later idea of a new constitutional convention every 19 or 20 years initiated from and by organized bodies, "the wards" from below.[51]

The "Jeffersonian" argument was partially anticipated already at the Constitutional Convention, by George Mason[52] and found its way in through the never used convention formula of Article V. But no one has made a more determined effort to institutionalize revolutionary constituent activity, to "domesticate" revolution, than Jefferson's friend Condorcet both in his introduction to his 1993 draft for France, as well as the draft itself, whose parts re-appeared in the never used Jacobin Constitution later in that year.[53]

Condorcet's effort was a conscious effort to replace insurrection or extralegal resistance as a means of political transformation by legally enacted and observed rules of revision.[54] Based ultimately on the same three ideas as many of Jefferson's letters, the problem of democratic self-government, that of the generations, and that of the imperfection of human products, he proposed three rules for the new constitution. One involved initiative from below, at any time, proposing revision (Title IX, art. II, V. and VI). A second proposed automatic revision every twenty years (art. IV). A third allowed the national legislature to commence the process, as long as supported by a majority of the electorate (Article VII).[55] In each case the body drawing up the constitution would be a newly elected national convention, which, unlike the then current one, would be doubly differentiated from the legislature. The latter would remain in place along with the old constitution until a new one was ratified by the electorate (Articles III, VII, and X) This move avoided the difficulties of a sunset clause as originally proposed by Jefferson, namely the periodic creation

[51] Letter to J. Madison, September 6, 1789; Letter to S. Kercheval, July 12, 1816; discussed in *Endurance*, 1–2; 112ff. Previously to these letters, Jefferson, along with his many criticisms of the 1787 proposal, seemed to support the idea of a second convention advocated by fellow Virginians E. Randolph and George Mason. See Letter to Madison, December 20, 1787.

[52] G. Mason on September 15, 1787 in M. Farrand *the Records of the Federal Convention of 1787* volume 2 (New Haven: Yale University Press, 1911), pp. 629–30.

[53] "Projet de Constitution Française," Title IX, *Oeuvres*, vol. XII (Stuttgart-Bad Cannstatt: Fromman Verlag, 1968). The Jacobin Constitution of 1793 kept one of Condorcet's three rules only, in articles 115–117 using popular initiative.

[54] "On Principles of the Constitutional Plan Presented to the National Convention" (presented to the Convention on February 15–16, 1793) in K. Baker ed. *Condorcet: Selected Writings* (Indianapolis: LLA, 1976), pp. 152–154. Insurrection could only be legitimate of the national legislature were to refuse a constitutional initiative of the majority from below.

[55] Projet 476–477.

of a constitutional vacuum along with potentially dramatic legal uncertainty. Yet the cost was not popular participation. Popular initiative, elections as well as ratification, though unclearly distinguished, would proceed from individual citizens in primary assemblies,[56] to each department, and then to the electorate as a whole, each time requiring a majority of those voting for passage. Rejection would first lead to a second draft, and then potentially to a new convention that, as its predecessor, could meet for no longer than a year (Articles III, XI–XIII). That last requirement was very much unlike, as it turned out the *Convention Nationale*, to which the proposal was made, and in whose name the gouvernement revolutionaire issued Condorcet's arrest warrant.

Note that Condorcet did not distinguish between the parts of the constitution accessible to each of his three amendment routes.[57] Since he insisted on a concept of total revision, it was left somewhat unclear if in principle any and every change could be made through using any of the rules, or whether each would be somehow bound to respect the original fundamental structure of combining representative and direct democratic forms.[58] Article V of the US Constitution, with its four rules, also did not distinguish between levels of their applicability, though an argument has been often made that these rules had a hierarchical implication, as Mason's distinction between government and the people made at the Convention indicated.[59] It is my contention that multi-track rules that do make such a distinction, such as the amendment rules of Spain, Bulgaria, South Africa, and Iraq, have an elective affinity with the post-sovereign multi-stage negotiated model.[60] Moreover, as the replacement doctrine of the Colombian Constitutional Court shows, when there is a strong apex court, even multi-track rules that do not explicitly assign each rule to a

---

[56] There is a slight ambiguity in the two texts concerning their continued existence, and on the level of ratification at least the preliminary text seems to suggest national referenda. See op. cit., 171. But Title III details their importance, and Title VIII on censure presupposes them, and this is taken over by Title IX, art. V.

[57] R. Albert uses two terms: comprehensive multi-track and restrictive multi track. Both the US Constitution's Art. V. and Condorcet's draft can be described as comprehensive, in that either track could deal with the whole constitution (in the USA with the exception of one quasi-eternity clause, the equal representation of states in the Senate). For the important distinction, see "The Structure of Constitutional Amendment Rules." *Wake Forest Law Review* (2014).

[58] "On Principles of the Constitutional Plan" op. cit., 154 vs 178–9. The actual draft does not seem to have an eternity clause.

[59] But cf. W. Harris, *The Interpretable Constitution* (Baltimore: Johns Hopkins University Press, 1993), and my critique in chapter 2 above. While the argument for an internal hierarchy can be defended, Harris' attempt to put Article VII on the highest level (implicitly as a revolution substitute) is an indefensible return to the idea of Calhoun that the Constitution remains ultimately a treaty.

[60] A. Arato. "Multi-Track Constitutionalism Beyond Carl Schmitt."*Constellations* 18.3 (2011): 324–351.

level of change, can be recast through judicial interpretation as distinguishing implicitly between the rule of amendment and rule of replacement.[61]

Recently, interpreters such as Bruce Ackerman and Joel Colon-Rios revived Arendt's argument.[62] I agree with their intentions, but not their specific solutions. I do not think that informal pattern such as the one proposed by Ackerman for the USA can be treated as a form of institutionalization, one that in his own depiction, reminiscent of Schmitt, takes radically different forms each time around. And I reject the idea of "weak constitutionalism" proposed by Colon-Rios, which seems to suggest that in the modern world democratic action and participation can be institutionalized without constitutionalism, i.e., strong insurance. As I will show, while the amendment rule adopted in Colombia seems to support his contention, actual practice as well as legislative safeguards in Colombia oppose it. And, the even more differentiated, hierarchical scheme of Venezuela, where constitutionalism was not securely institutionalized, shows the great problem with the populist conception. Nevertheless, these two countries, along with Spain, Bulgaria, and South Africa, indicate that replacement can be legally institutionalized as Condorcet once dreamed, but Carl Schmitt made it his business to fundamentally deny.[63]

---

[61] C. Bernal-Pulido. "Unconstitutional constitutional amendments in the case study of Colombia: An analysis of the justification and meaning of the constitutional replacement doctrine" *International Journal of Constitutional Law* (2013) 11(2), 339–357; N. Figureoa *A Critique of Populist Jurisprudence. Courts, Democracy, and Constitutional Change in Colombia and Venezuela.* New School for Social Research Dissertation, 2016

[62] *We the People*, vol. I (Cambridge, MA: Harvard University Press, 1991) pp. 204–212; though the analysis winds up with a view closer to Schmitt than to Arendt see. p. 218, e.g.; *Weak Constitutionalism*, op. cit., pp. 110, 112. In a soon to be completed Yale Law School dissertation Joshua Braver is going to further extend the Arendtian argument, primarily in the domain of new constitution making. It is called "We, the Mediated People: Revolution, Inclusion, and Unconventional Adaptation in the Creation of Post-Cold War S. American Constitutions". I have benefited from Braver's analysis of the Venezuelan case, as well as from his general theoretical considerations.

[63] Thus, today at least the idea of Elkins et al. in *Endurance* (p. 55ff.) that amendment is legal, and replacement is necessarily illegal or extralegal, should be rejected. Elkins and his co-authors already put the claim in some doubt, when they speak, rightly, of "the Sometimes Fuzzy Line between Amendment and Replacement". A similar ambivalence is in Negretto's book *Making Constitutions*, pp. 19–20. Where he first defines replacement as "disruption of constitutional legality", and then goes on to say on the next page that replacement is the "legal abrogation" of the existing constitution. There is a need obviously to distinguish, as I will below, between legal and revolutionary replacement. On the idea of revolutionary replacement, see G. Jacobsohn, *Constitutional Identity* (Cambridge, MA: Harvard University Press, 2010), pp. 49–50. But even he does not distinguish between revolution and legal replacement. Following Ulrich Preuss, he claims that "no constitution can contain rules which allow its abolishment altogether". Ibid., fn. 35.

The idea that a constitution should institutionalize its own formative process, or rather its spirit, takes on special meaning in the case of multi stage negotiated paradigm.[64] Unlike in the case of revolutionary sovereign constitution making, there is no need here to solve the insoluble problem of how to institutionalize or legalize revolution, which is, by definition, an extralegal affair. Generally, the post-sovereign paradigm operates through legal continuity. There is also no need to domesticate the political energies that produced the constitution, as in Condorcet's brilliant but failed project, because here these energies were already kept within limits during the original process. Nor is there a need, as in Carl Schmitt's conception logically enough, to confine legitimate replacement of the whole or its supposedly essential parts to a revolutionary break in legality resembling the origins. At the same time, there is also an in-built normative bias, against allowing an easily used amendment rule, as in reformist patterns, to replace the constitution as if that was merely a feature of parliamentary sovereignty.

Admittedly, when institutionalizing the post-sovereign paradigm as a model of revision, there is also no reason to imitate all the features of negotiated models. Where there are democratic elections already, there is no requirement to use the method of co-opting participants, except perhaps in the cases where the electoral rules are highly exclusionary.[65] Where there is already a constitutionalist constitution, there is no reason to enact an interim one. With this said, however, the normative principles of inclusion, public openness, and legality remain fully applicable. While the multi-stage character of the original process can be mirrored by the multi-leveled structure of the amendment rule, it is, as I will show, on the highest level rule of a tiered or graduated set of rules of change that the post sovereign spirit can be fully captured.

---

[64] It is with this move that I try to respond to the argument of David Landau ("Abusive Constitutionalism," p. 43. fn. 202) that I apply the post-sovereign conception that he seems to support only to the transition from authoritarian rule to democracy, and not to democratic constitutions. In the effort, I utilize his and R. Dixon's ("Constraining Constitutional Change," 2015, *Wake Forest L. Rev.*, 50, 859.) attempts to limit replacement, that they, however, do not link to constitution making where if anywhere such limits would have to be established. Given the Hungarian experience with the EU, I do not think that international constraints can do the job, in part because of the now well known Frankenstein argument that I first proposed.

On this, see R. Dixon and D. Landau, "Transnational Constitutionalism and a Limited Doctrine of Unconstitutional Constitutional Amendment," *International Journal of Constitutional Law*, (2015). 13(3), 606–638.

[65] A. Arato, "Democratic Constitution-Making and Unfreezing the Turkish Process (2010). *Philosophy & Social Criticism*, Vol. 36, Nos. 3–4, 2010." Available at SSRN: http://ssrn.com/abstract=2352307.

On an abstract level, the first stage of the post-sovereign model provides important clues to the first level of a complex rule of change. In all the round table countries the first formal agent of change had to be (and was) the inherited parliament of an old regime. This function was rightly preserved in the constitutions that emerged, in the lowest level of amendment rules in Spain (section 167), Bulgaria (articles 154–5), South Africa (art 74, 3a), Colombia (though without assignment of only limited topics: art. 375), and Iraq (though with a referendum: Art. 126). Admittedly, under constitutionalist constitutions, this function does not have to extend to "temporary replacement" in order to enable free elections to take place.

More importantly, the parliamentary amending power of the first stage was not unlimited in the round table countries, having been bound by prior agreements of a consensual character. Under the resulting final constitutions this limitation was expressed by both the qualified majority needed to enact, implying at least relative consensus, and (with the exception of Colombia) the explicit confinement of the most important matters along with full replacement to a higher rule, or to a rule between the lowest and the highest. The analogy becomes even more complete, if we notice that the interim constitutions achieved through negotiations in Hungary, South Africa, Iraq, and Nepal contained amendment rules, and in the latter three separate rules for new and more permanent constitution making. In Hungary, rules for new constitution making did emerge, between 1994 and 1996, but the effort to establish a four-fifths consensual rule was misconceived as to duration, and failed when FIDESZ revoking it by two-thirds was not successfully challenged.[66] Thus, in that country the amendment rule of the interim constitution remained or was restored as the final constitution-making rule. It implied no limitation, and coupled with a highly disproportional electoral rule led to with disastrous consequences during the making of the FIDESZ basic law.[67] Where there were rules for final constitution making, however, the interim amending power to be exercised by the first freely elected parliament was under limits as well as rules. These were, explicitly or implicitly, enforceable by the apex courts created in the same document as in South Africa (Interim Constitution, chapter 4 art. 62, and chapter 5 art. 74), Iraq (TAL articles 60–61) and Nepal (interim constitution: art. 148).

---

[66] See my "Post-Sovereign Constitution-Making in Hungary: After Success, Partial Failure, Now What?" (2010). *South African Journal on Human Rights*, Vol. 26, Part I, 2010. Available at SSRN: http://ssrn.com/abstract=2353856.

[67] *Post Sovereign*, chapter 4.

Even more importantly, where the interim constitution had detailed rules for final constitution making, as in South Africa (interim constitution, chapter 5 arts. 71 and 73) the logical implication was that there should be procedural limits even on the freely elected constitutional assembly.[68] Logically, and actually in South Africa, these limits too had to be enforceable through a new constitutional court, if such was established.[69] While this feature, and especially the postulate of substantive limitations by constitutional principles, was unique to South Africa, implicit limits were established by the strongly federalist nature of the possible three province veto of the new constitution in Iraq (TAL art. 61 c). In Colombia, too, there was an attempt to limit the constituent assembly at least procedurally by the previous negotiations, and subject it to the authority of the Supreme Court, an effort that failed unusually enough because of that Court's rejection of such limits on the "original" constituent power.[70] In Nepal procedural limits on the constituent assembly were established in the interim constitution (interim constitution, Articles 64 and 70), and implicitly (in the end actually) the constituent assembly was placed under the jurisdiction of the constitutional court (Articles 102 and 118). In Poland procedural limits were established on the final constitution making assembly.[71] And explicit procedural limits were self-imposed by the constituent assembly in Tunisia (Little Constitution or OPPP art. 3).[72]

Finally, in order to avoid the appearance that the final constitution is itself merely an interim one, in other words in order to tentatively close the

---

[68] Contrary to Elster, *Ulysses*, p. 101, I think it is not or at least no longer supportable that constituent assemblies (he calls the makers of the final constitutions thus) vote by majority, with the exception of South Africa. All round table countries, with the exception of Iraq, had supermajority rules for assembly approval. Elster vitiates his own claim when he notes (105ff.) that convening authorities do try to limit the constitution making assemblies. He generally, on the model of the US and French revolutions considers such attempts as hopeless. Yet for the round table countries, the limitations held without exception. It is also the case that many conventions and constituent assemblies, in principle, unlimited establish high qualitative thresholds for themselves, as did for example the Parliamentary Council in Germany (80 percent) and the Tunisian constituent assembly (two-thirds). Even these examples of "self binding" contradict the claim that constitutions usually "are adopted by simple majority."

[69] See, e.g., Klug, op. cit.

[70] See chapter 4 above; Figureoa, *Critique of Populist Jurisprudence.*

[71] See L. Garlicky and Z. Garlicka "Constitution Making, Peace Building and National Reconciliation: The Experience of Poland," in L. Miller and L. Aucoin, eds. *Framing the State in Times of Transition: Case Studies in Constitution Making* (Washington, DC: US Institute of Peace Press, 2010).

[72] This followed from the negotiated electoral rule that produced a parliament without a single party majority).

post-sovereign constitution-making process, it is important to enhance the democratic legitimacy of the final document. In the case of the interim constitutions of Poland, South Africa, Iraq, and Nepal this was done by interposing new elections between the body producing the interim document, and the final constitution-making assembly. Even in Hungary, new elections followed the round table, and preceded both the failed effort of 1994–8, and the making of the FIDESZ final constitution. The same was true in countries with provisional rules more limited than a full interim constitution. In Spain, Bulgaria, Colombia, and Tunisia, new and free elections preceded the constitution-making effort. Finally, in two countries, Poland and South Africa, the enhanced procedure of uniting the two chambers in one assembly (called constitutional or national) also differentiated and enhanced the legitimacy of the final constitution-making project. In two countries at least (Poland and Iraq), ratificatory referenda were used in part for the same purpose.

To sum up the empirical pattern emerging from the post-sovereign cases, relevant to final amendment rules, the following features seem important:

1. Parliamentary model of initial change.
2. Limitations on the interim amending power.
3. Limitations on the final constitution-making power.
4. Enforcement of limits by a constitutional court.
5. New elections enhancing the legitimacy of final process.
6. Symbolic procedural enhancement of the final stage, by uniting two chambers and/or using referenda.

As we have seen, not all of these desiderata were realized in all the round table countries. In Spain and Hungary only 1 and 5 were (though in Hungary the failed effort of 1994–1998 would have added 2, 4 and 6!) and in Bulgaria only 5 and 6. In Poland, eventually, 1, 2, 3 as well as 5 and 6 were made actual. In South Africa and Nepal, all 6. In Iraq, in the absence of a legislature, only 2–6. Even in the two quasi-revolutionary cases with constituent assemblies, Colombia and Tunisia, 5–6 were adhered to.[73] Assuming learning from case to case, we can clearly observe increased adherence among the genuine multi stage cases, partially reversed in the more revolutionary cases. What this means can be seen by looking at the amendment rules of the relevant cases, more carefully than before. Here the relevant categories are self-explanatory:

[73] See chapter 4 above.

Amendment Rules and Their Levels

country	Multiple rules	Multiple restricted rules	New elections for highest level	Symbolically enhanced highest level	Eternity rules	Enforcement through apex court
Spain	yes	yes	Yes	Yes	No	Implicit
Poland	no	Partial. Possible referendum	No	Yes. Possible referendum	No	No
Hungary	no	no	Not required	No	No	No. After 2011 procedural review possible
Bulgaria	yes	yes	Yes	Yes	No[74]	Implicit
South Africa	yes	yes	No	No	No	Explicit
Iraq	yes	yes	Yes	Yes	Yes (consent needed)	Implicit
Nepal	yes	yes	No	No	Weak (consent needed)	No
Colombia	yes	No (later corrected by Court)	Yes	Yes	No	Explicit
Tunisia	no	No	No	Yes. Possible referendum	Yes	Explicit

The table is illustrative of the logical relation, or better still elective affinity, between the post-sovereign paradigm and multi-track, enforceable amendment structures. To begin with, Spain, Bulgaria, Colombia, South Africa, Iraq, and Nepal, have multi-track amendment rules, representing six out of nine of my post-sovereign cases. Of these, only Colombia did not originally assign specific constitutional domains to each amendment rule, and it is interesting that only in Colombia was the final constitution making assembly announced as sovereign.[75] At the same time, graduated, multi-leveled amendment rules are present in only two of my nine control cases, federalist Russia (Articles 134–136) and populist Venezuela (Articles 340–349) both of which require

74   As Elster noticed (*Ulysses* 102), Article 57 of the Bulgarian Constitution states that "Citizens' fundamental rights shall be inalienable" or in other texts: irrevocable. But he is right, article 158 sets no limits to revision (not exactly to "amendment"). What should be stressed is article 158 is a rule for replacement, for the making of a new constituion. The restriction of 57 thus arguably applies to amendments under articles 153 to 156.

75   Interestingly, restriction to levels of change was assigned in Colombia by the Constitutional Court, still using the sovereign constituent power as an argument. For this paradox see Figueroa *Critique*.

the convening or calling (neither speaks of "elections"!) of a constitutional or a national constituent assembly for some matters in the case of Russia, and for replacement in the case of Venezuela whose assembly is explicitly said to be unlimited (art 349). While three of my post sovereign cases explicitly assign a procedural amendment review power to apex courts, this form judicial power is at best implicit in the cases of Russia and Venezuela. Admittedly the same implicit status is characteristic of three of my post-sovereign cases, and I note for the moment that implicit powers of this type depend on the strength and independence of apex courts, as in Spain and Bulgaria, but not in Iraq, Russia, and Venezuela. Unlike the Colombian case, graduated amendment rules were, in practice, disempowered by the dramatic weakening of previously stronger apex courts in both Russia and Venezuela.[76]

The lowest level of change, in each case, is a parliamentary amendment rule under limits that requires some consensus by a qualified majority between three-fifths and two-thirds, resembling the first stage of the original process. The highest level of change requires new elections in four out of the nine cases, but, of course, here, unlike in the case of the first stage of round tables, all constitution-making bodies are freely elected. Moreover, in six out of nine cases, the type of assembly in charge of replacement is symbolically enhanced either by the status of a constituent/constitutional assembly or by the use of ratificatory referenda. Most importantly, the highest level of change is procedurally constrained in seven out of the nine cases by the amendment rule, while in the eighth, in Colombia, there were such constraints established in part on the statutory level, and even in the constitution by the ability of the Constitutional Court to supervise referenda (art. 241f).[77] Finally, constitutional courts are explicitly designed or implicitly enabled in six out of nine cases to control and police the differentiation among the levels of revision. Up to this point, the elective affinity I have in mind is clear. Admittedly, however, there are only three cases that establish substantive limitations on the sovereignty of the assembly operating on the highest level of change. These are the three countries of Tunisia, Iraq, and Nepal, with eternity rules or their functional equivalent in the latter two as federal states, the consent of provinces to the diminution of their power or territory. Thus, the choice between eternity

---

[76] W. Partlett, "Separation of Powers without Checks and Balances: The Failure of Semi-Presidentialism and the Making of the Russian Constitutional System, 1991–1993" in *The Legal Dimension in Cold-War Interactions: Some Notes from the Field* (Leiden: Brill, 2012), pp. 105–140; L. Epstein, J. Knight, and O. Shvetsova, "The Role of Constitutional Courts in the Establishment and Maintenance of Democratic Systems of Government," *Law and Society Review*, (2001) 117–164.

[77] Figueroa "Critique of Populist Jurisprudence."

rules, what R. Albert calls "indefinite entrenchment" and his "heightened entrenchment" is not empirically ascertainable by the examination of the various versions of the post-sovereign paradigm.[78]

To anticipate, where the choice should be normatively is indicated by the South African case, if in preliminary fashion. For the round table countries, only the case of South Africa involved on the interim level substantive limits on the constituent power, in the form of constitutional principles. Yet South Africa ultimately produced a highest level of amendment rule (3/4 + over half of the provinces) that is ultimately without substantive limits on the amending power. While the related questions of the survival of the constitutional principles under the final constitution and the adoption of an Indian-style basic structure doctrine have indeed been raised, usually by dissenting justices, the dominant judicial view has up till now rejected both options.

To sum up, the case for an internal relationship of multi-track constitutionalism and the post-sovereign paradigm is relatively strong, even if many constitutions with codified or judicially established multi-track structures did not emerge in post-sovereign process. The elective affinity between the multi-track conception and post-sovereign origins has several dimensions: 1. Each relies on a multiplicity of amendment rules; 2. among which a simple legislative level is the first step for the post sovereign paradigm, and lowest level for the multi-track constitution; in both 3. all levels are limited at least procedurally, thus none are sovereign;[79] 4. new democratic elections for the last stage or highest level; and, perhaps most importantly;[80] 5. the multi-stage and multi-level character each allow many of the same legitimating principles to come into play: pluralism and inclusion (though in the case of the multi-leveled constitution this requires not only the right amendment rule but also suitable i.e., proportional electoral rules), publicity and public participation, The link to apex courts in each is also at the very least implicit, because 6.

---

[78] Albert, R. (2010). "Constitutional Handcuffs," *Ariz. St. LJ*, 42, 663. 671–672. Unfortunately, Albert's terminology in the article confuses the question whether entrenchment as such or only eternity rules (absolute entrenchment) are undemocratic. His earlier article Albert, R. (2009). "Nonconstitutional Amendments," *The Canadian Journal of Law and Jurisprudence*, 22(01), 5–47.

    Pp. 34–35 seems to have so convicted amendment review, along with eternity rules. Yet amendment review is also entailed by what he later called and supported as "heightened entrenchment." Actually, his useful but misleadingly named model of the "entrenchment simulator" in the later piece is a model of entrenchment, and a version of the multi-track conception, since even adding the dimension of time primarily adds the requirement of a new election into the highest amendment rule.

[79] See Hart on this step beyond sovereignty in UK in *Concept of Law* (Oxford: Oxford University Press, 1962).

[80] See Arato, "Multi-track."

such courts remain the most likely candidate in enforcing these limitations, at least logically if not always based on codified amendment review jurisdiction.

Multi-Level Amendment Rule and Judicial Review

Thus, I wish to argue that multi track amendment rules, and constitutional review have a deep internal relationship. Yet they have been rarely discussed and linked together.[81] Even the topic of amendment review, extensively elaborated in the recent literature[82] has only rarely brought the two issues closer, and then mostly implicitly without a strong argument. And this is understandable for American scholars at least, since the USA has indeed had four possible tracks in Article V,[83] without this ever being connected to amendment review in the practice of the courts. Even India, with its originally three-level rule did not raise the issue of amendment review until 15 years into the new constitution. In Spain and Canada, with their respectively two- and four-level structures of revision, the issue was never raised to my knowledge, though in the latter procedures of original constitution making (that could be regarded as amendments of the British North America Act of 1867) were reviewed in two references.[84] Finally, the most important theorist of the limits of amendment even without the benefit of text in the Weimar Republic, who in effect postulated an internal hierarchy in constitutions between essential, identity forming and unessential provisions, namely Carl Schmitt, has explicitly rejected the role of a court enforcing the differentiation of these levels,

---

[81] See, e.g., Albert's two articles cited in the previous fn. 76, each dealing with one of the two topics separately, as well as Landau in "Abusive" who considers the two issues separately, without seeing or at least stressing their intimate connection. Thus he sees the relative weakness of each alone, but not their relative strength together. But see: Arato, "Multi-Track Constitutionalism Beyond Carl Schmitt." *Constellations* 18.3 (2011): 324–351. Landau and Dixon, in their recent "Constraining Constitutional Change," treat amendment review and eternity clauses as well as a multi-track structure as options. Tiered constitutional amendments and amendment review are however linked in Landau, on the level of concrete analysis, in "Term Limits Manipulation Across Latin America" in Constitution Net, July 2015 http://www.constitutionnet.org/cn_front.

[82] Jacobsohn, op. cit; G. Halmai "Unconstitutional Constitutional Amendments: Constitutional Courts as Guardians of the Constitution?" *Constellations*, 19(2) (2012), 182–203; Y. Roznai, "Unconstitutional Constitutional Amendments – The Migration and Success of a Constitutional Idea." *American Journal of Comparative Law*, (2013) 61(3), 657–719.

[83] Comprehensive multi-track in Albert's terminology, as against the restrictive tracks of India, Canada and South Africa, where each level of amendment is relevant to a different class of constitutional topics. See his article: Richard Albert, "The Structure of Constitutional Amendment Rules" (March 1, 2014). 49 *Wake Forest Law Review* 913 (2014); Boston College Law School Legal Studies Research Paper No. 326.

[84] Patriation Reference and Quebec Veto Reference. See P. Russell, *Constitutional Odyssey: Can Canadians Become a Sovereign People?* (Toronto: University of Toronto Press, 2004).

as indeed he rejected constitutional review of legislation. Unfortunately, as I will show below, Schmitt never developed any clear criteria about what was essential, nor did he propose any way of enforcing the difference beyond either militant democracy as it was later called or a diffuse appeal to people when an amendment openly began to imply regime change. As far as he was concerned, only a revolutionary activation of the constituent power could replace one constitutional identity by another.[85]

Nevertheless, given the interests of most legal scholars in courts, it is highly likely that the issue of a many leveled, internally hierarchical constitution along with the possibility of an "unconstitutional constitution" has gained its new importance today by actions of courts in the domain of amendment review. The German Federal Constitutional Court (BVfG) led the way, affirming such a role in principle if not yet in an actual decision, and was able, unlike Schmitt in the Weimar Republic, to refer to text, the so-called *Ewigkeitsklauseln* (Eternity Clause: Article 79–3) of the *Grundgesetz* that did not have a provision, however, for any amendment review. Since the *Grundgesetz* had a replacement rule, Article 146 (distinguished from Article 79, the amendment rule), the decisions of the Court concerning its amendment jurisdiction (that did not actually invalidate amendments) implicitly established a three- or four-track constitution, depending on whether the eternity clause was to be interpreted as limiting even Article 146. Justly more famous are later decisions of the Indian and Colombian Constitutional Courts. In the Indian case, the basic structure doctrine affirmed in Kesavananda in 1973, and consolidated in Minerva Mills, in 1980, added a new level of limitation to the already three-level rule, forbidding amendments that would change the identity of the constitution. By implication, only a new constituent process, resembling that in 1948–1950, would be able to produce a new constitution. The Colombian Constitutional Court, unlike the one in India, found only a multi-path amendment structure where three different options were not assigned specific constitutional domains, and where there was a radically democratic path provided for that involved the calling of a new constituent assembly. This combination resembled the US Article V with its convention(s) formula. But where in the USA only a strand of scholarly opinion tried to establish an internal hierarchy of the four possible forms (or five, counting Article 7[86]), in Colombia the Constitutional Court was to accomplish exactly this task at least with respect to the

---

[85] Interestingly, he considered the Enabling Act of 1933 to have satisfied this requirement, even though inconsistently with his doctrine. Article 76 of the Weimar Constitution was used for the purpose in an already purged Reichstag.

[86] See Harris, op. cit.; and my chapter 2 above.

highest level of change, namely constitutional replacement.[87] Thus, instead of invalidating an amendment, interpreted as hidden replacement, by establishing in the manner of the India Court an implicit eternity doctrine, the Colombian Court assigned the type of change sought to the jurisdiction of a newly elected constituent assembly (Article 376).

Note that the Colombian Constitution, in contrast to the German or the Indian, explicitly provided for constitutional review of amendments on all tracks, but only according to violations of procedural criteria (Articles 379 and 241–2). The same was the case in Turkey's constitution of 1982. (Article 148). In articulating the "replacement doctrine," the Colombian Court, between 2003 and 2005, managed to show that in order to discover a violation of the relevant procedure, the substance that is amended must itself be examined. Thus, a procedural test was turned into an epistemological test.[88] With the help of eternity clauses, the Turkish Constitutional Court was to do the same, in its 2008 headscarf decisions. Unlike the Colombian Court, however, and more openly than the Indian Court, the Turkish Constitutional Court openly suggested that only a new revolution (or a coup like those of 1960 and 1980) could change or modify or replace the four permanent articles of the Constitution.[89] Given the nature of the process of constitution making in 1980–1982, the argument was logical, however lamentable the implicit reference to the making of the 1982 Constitution.

The strong role of courts in enforcing or establishing multi-track constitutions raises several important questions, especially because of the frequent reference to eternity rules or "indefinite entrenchment". First, could a multi-track structure operate without amendment review? If not, second, how can amendment review be justified, in light of the reappearance of the countermajoritarian dilemma, and the charge of juristocracy? Can a multi-track structure play a role in such justification? Third, should the highest level of change be an eternity rule, unanimity, or simply a very high qualified majority?[90] Related to this, fourth, is the question of what the highest level of change should require, a revolution or a legally established rule, and whether a constitutional court can have a role in either of these scenarios. Is the possibility of calling a new constituent or constitutional assembly the best option, and, if so, should it be limited substantively or only procedurally? And, finally, is there a doctrine of the constituent power, beyond Sieyès and Schmitt who still dominate the

---

[87] see: Carlos Bernal-Pulido, op. cit.; Figueroa *Critique of Populist Jurisprudence.*

[88] On substance as procedure cf. Colon-Rios, op. cit.; Bernal-Pulido, op.cit..

[89] Arato, "Democratic Constitution-Making and Unfreezing the Turkish Process" (2010). *Philosophy & Social Criticism*, Vol. 36, Nos. 3–4, 2010.

[90] See Richard Albert, "Constitutional Handcuffs." *Arizona State Law Journal* 42, (2010).

discussion, linking the post sovereign conception to the multi-track, internally hierarchical constitution? It is to these questions I now turn.

MULTI-TRACK STRUCTURE WITHOUT AMENDMENT REVIEW?

I would like to demonstrate my doubts on this score by comparing attempts to radically change the constitution in Colombia and Venezuela at roughly the same time, between 2007 and 2010, and over the same issue: the re-election of the president in office. Both Colombian and Venezuela have multi-track amendment rules in their new constitutions. Formally at least, Colombia has three rules (parliamentary, referendum and constituent assembly) without any specification as to substantive topics or levels of the constitution, each without any formal limits. The Constitution of Venezuela, by contrast, not only distinguishes between the three levels of amendment, reform and replacement, but assigns a specific procedure to each of these levels. On the other hand, only Colombia has a provision for amendment review, even if it was said to be restricted to the procedural form. As "anecdotal" as my analysis of only a pair of cases maybe, I maintain that the Venezuelan amendment rule, by assigning levels to rules,[91] was not only better designed, but taken abstractly implied both a higher-level insurance (4 in my earlier coding), *and* also, therefore, in principle at least, a greater likelihood of opening the terrain for renewed democratic constitution making.[92] Nevertheless, as this very similar pair of controversial cases shows, the Colombian rules were better able to protect the integrity of the more democratic rules, than the Venezuelan rules. And this clearly had to do with the nature of constitutional review in the two constitutions. Not only was the Colombian Court explicitly given the task of amendment review, but its appointment structure also guaranteed a more pluralistic and more independent court than the Venezuelan rules. While the story of the Colombian Court is one of independence of the political authorities, the Venezuelan Court was, from the outset, exposed to efforts of repeated packing and even intimidation, including arrests of judges.[93]

---

[91] See Albert ibid. who does not make a normative choice here; Landau who does in "Term Limits Manipulation across Latin America," July 21, 2015 IDEA Constitutionnet.

[92] Such as Colon-Rios argues for; op. cit. Undoubtedly, however, the makers of the Venezuelan constitution were more committed to such a radical democratic revival of the constituent power. Yet they subverted it, by amending essential matters on lower levels.

[93] A. Brewer-Carias, *Dismantling Democracy in Venezuela: The Chávez Authoritarian Experiment* (Cambridge University Press, 2010) on the role of transitional arrangements affecting court composition; Gregory Wilpert/Carlos Escarra "The Venezuelan Judicial System always was the Cinderella of the state Powers" May 17, 2004 venezuealalysis.com; Human Rights Watch "World Report 2012: Venezuela" www.hrw.org/world-report/2012/country-chapters/venezuela;

At issue in both countries was the project of populist chief executives to establish the possibility of presidential re-election, banned by the two constitutions, which originally restricted the president to one term in Colombia, and two terms in Venezuela. In Colombia, after successfully amending the constitution (on the lowest level of change) in 2005 to allow election for a second term, President Uribe sought in 2010 a new amendment allowing a third term as well.[94] In Venezuela, President Chavez sought, twice rather than once, in 2007 and 2010 to establish the possibility of elections to an unrestricted number of terms. The projects of the presidents were similar; it was the response of the apex courts, the Constitutional Court of Colombia and the Supreme Tribunal of Justice of Venezuela that was fundamentally different.

One implicit purpose of multi-track rules is to prohibit the main branches of power to amend the rules in their favor, in a self-aggrandizing manner. Yet it is always an open question to decide when an intended rule change seriously transcends the limits of change on a given level. Note that the first relevant decision in each country allowed an amendment to be made. In Colombia, that decision was preceded by a series of other ones, starting in 2003(C-551–03), when the Constitutional Court decided that it could review amendments that violated the identity of the constitution, thus replacing it or substituting for it.[95] In this series of decisions the Court made several important moves. First, it moved beyond the narrow limit in the Constitution to procedural amendment review, and rightly claimed that without considering the relevant substance it could not be decided if the right procedure was followed.[96] And second,

Gicherman, Jessica, "The judicial system in Venezuela & the lack of checks and balances" (2012). HIM 1990–2015. Paper 1269. Throughout this section, I rely on the New School PhD dissertation of N. Figureoa "A Critique of Populist Jurisprudence. Courts, Democracy and Constitutional Cahnge in Colombia and Venezuela."

[94] C. Bernal-Pulido "Unconstitutional constitutional amendments in the case study of Colombia: An analysis of the justification and meaning of the constitutional replacement doctrine." *International Journal of Constitutional Law* 11.2 (2013): 339–357.

[95] Colon-Rios, *Weak Constitutionalism*, pp. 133–138; Bernal op. cit. who indicates that there were several decisions involved, rather than just one: op.cit 341ff. See also Landau "Abusive," who considers this case to be one of the exceptional ones where abusive constitutionalism has been stopped. But how about all the post sovereign countries with multi-track rules: Spain, Bulgaria, South Africa, where abusive constitutionalism has not even been tried?? With Poland still undecided, Hungary, which he treats, speaks for the vulnerability of an unfinished process and single track amendment rules.

[96] The point regarding the relation of substance and procedure is entirely missed for the Turkish case, in this respect similar to the Colombian one, by Y. Roznai and S. Yolcu (2012) "An Unconstitutional Constitutional Amendment – The Turkish Perspective: A Comment on the Turkish Constitutional Court's Headscarf Decision," *International Journal of Constitutional Law*, 10(1), 175–207. I have argued this point even before the Turkish Constitutional Court's headscarf decisions they analyze, already in interviews in

the Court identified the level of change indicated by Article 376, calling a constituent assembly, as the one best corresponding to the re-activation of the (original) constituent power.[97] Note that the Court in 2003, Marbury-like, did not invalidate any amendments but only established its right to do so, following exactly the German BVfG.[98] Even in 2005, when the issue came back via the bid for presidential re-election, the Court decided that the possibility of one re-election could be enacted on the level of change controlled by Congress, not stressing the issue of whether each of the three rules should be assigned to a given level of change.[99] Nevertheless, even at that time, the Colombian Court reasserted its authority to review constitutional amendments, under the replacement doctrine. Thus, when the then popular Uribe tried to do the same thing again in 2010, for the sake of the possibility of a *third* term (a second re-election), the Court in C-141/2010 claimed that three terms would affect the whole constitution, especially the independence of many of its institutions, and thus change its identity. Undoubtedly, Uribe's actual attempts to co-opt the main institutions of society,[100] played the main role in this interpretation, rather than the perhaps weak distinction between two and three terms. In a third decision, it was clearly stressed that such changes of identity can be accomplished and enacted only through a new constituent assembly, as in Article 367.[101]

In Venezuela, interestingly, (but after two of the three relevant Colombian Court decisions!) the Chavez government in 2007 chose to enact its constitution-changing project of eventually 69 articles, in two packages, of which the first was more presidential, containing the re-election of the

---

Milliyet, in 2008, (http://www.milliyet.com.tr/Siyaset/HaberDetay.aspx?aType=HaberDetay& Kategori=siyaset&ArticleID=982363&Date=25.08.2008&b=AKP accessed December 3, 2015.) and after in "Democratic Constitution-Making and Unfreezing the Turkish Process" (2010). *Philosophy & Social Criticism*, Vol. 36, Nos. 3–4, 2010. Available at SSRN: http://ssrn.com/abstract=2352307. On the distinction between amendment review based on procedure and on substance, see Landau and Dixon, *Constraining Constitutional Change*, who concede that a sharp distinction is a difficult one to make in the relevant cases (pp. 6–9). See also Colon-Rios, *Weak Constitutionalism*, pp. 134–135: "in the context of constitutional reform, procedure and substance overlap." Yes, if there is a higher rule of change than the one used, or an eternity clause. The idea that the level of replacement can be substantively limited osee Dixon and Landau op.cit. is problematic, in spite of the interim (!) example of South Africa.

97 In Colon-Rios' presentation these moves were all part of the 2003 decision, C-551, whereas Bernal presents them as having emerged as the court specified its replacement doctrine in a series of decisions, including two on presidential re-eligibility.

98 Figueroa, op. cit., 184.

99 At that time, and later in 2007, the Court already declared parts of amendments as illegitmate replacement. See Bernal, 345.

100 Figueroa, 194–5. These attempts did not, however, succeed in co-opting the Constitutional Court.

101 Bernal, 346; Figueroa, 200ff.

president without limit. This was done under the constitution's second level revision rule, Article 343 providing for "reform" (as against amendment, and replacement) of the constitution, with a two-thirds vote of the National Assembly followed by a successful referendum. Arguably, the extensive set of changes that openly sought a new constitutional identity should have been enacted under Articles 347–348, involving calling a constituent assembly.[102] The Supreme Tribunal of Justice considered this objection, and took it no more seriously than other procedural complaints. The amendment referendum project was sustained on shallow technical grounds.

The rule actually used (Articles 343–344) required a two-thirds vote in the National Assembly, and then ratification in a referendum. In the actual case, the latter was to involve a single yes or no vote on each of the two packages, and, as has been widely reported, both proposals lost by a slim majority. The Constitution of 1999 Article 345 stated, however, that "[A] revised constitutional reform initiative may not be submitted during the same constitutional term of office of the National Assembly." This would have meant the Chavez government had to wait for the parliament to be elected in 2010 to re-enact the reform by a two-thirds majority, an uncertain prospect given his movement's gradual decline of support.[103] The government decided to evade the difficulty by introducing only a small part of the 2007 reform, containing presidential re-eligibility, and this time on the lowest level of change, as an "amendment" rather than "reform." The former method of change required only the majority of the National Assembly already in place plus ratification in a referendum.[104] But this time the proposal was challenged in Court far more seriously than previously. While the line between partial reform and complete replacement could be seen as unclear, that between amendment and the other two rules was fairly obvious. Moreover, the recent Colombian precedent of a judgment of unconstitutionality on the same issue had to be well known to jurists.

Note that the case of the litigants against Chavez was considerably stronger than the one against Uribe. Indefinite re-eligibility of all executive officers, as in the new amendment, changes the constitution more radically than the possibility of a third term for a president. Venezuela moreover had an apparent eternity clause in its constitution regarding the alternation of power, though it was not entirely clear how the text related to presidential re-eligibility

---

[102] Figueroa, op. cit., 221–223; Landau, "Term Limits."

[103] Indeed, the Chavez party suffered a significant loss of seats, and the loss of its two-thirds and even three-fifths majority. Two-thirds were needed to operate the reform rule!

[104] "Fact Sheet: Constitutional Amendment in Venezuela" January, 2009. US Embassy of the Bolivarian Republic of Venezuela. http://www.embavenez-us.org/factsheet/FS-Amend-F4-Eng.pdf.

(Article 6). More importantly, the Venezuelan Constitution was better designed in linking levels of change to each revision rule. Thus, here the decision of referring to the highest, or even middle level of change would have been textually supported. And, most importantly, the core of the same project of change was already introduced as "reform" before being arbitrarily redefined as "amendment" whereas Article 345 explicitly banned the re-introduction of a revised reform initiative in the same parliamentary session.[105]

Yet the Venezuelan Court proceeded to sustain the amendment, which was then ratified in a second referendum. It is important to note here that in 2004, before the first revision attempt, the most extensive and important court-packing scheme under the Bolivarian Republic was successfully implemented.[106] While there was an argument to be made for increasing the small size of the constitutional chamber of the Supreme Tribunal because of the increased workload, the new, ultimately majoritarian appointment structure,[107] and the possibility of annulling appointments indicated that it was political packing and disciplining that was intended. Whether so intended or not, the packed Supreme Tribunal was hardly an instance to go against the government's reform or amendment plans, even with the help of the clearly designed multi track structure. That structure was more openly threatened in Venezuela than in Colombia. Thus, while the strong Colombian Court chose to defend a merely implicit structure, thereby strongly re-enforcing it, the weak Venezuelan Court abandoned an explicit structure.[108] For the time being at least, the two higher levels of change became irrelevant in Venezuela, in violation not only of the rule system but also of the participatory ideology of the regime, that should have welcomed the convening of a new constituent assembly when its plans to reform were frustrated rather than retreating to what appeared as a lower rather than higher level of change.[109]

---

[105] In his excellent comparative analysis, Colon-Rios neglects these differences, and especially the difference two very different Courts made in the outcome. It is not right to say, however, that the two outcomes followed from generally different national interpretations of what the limits to amendment are.

[106] Gregory Wilpert/Carlos Escarra, "The Venezuelan Judicial System."

[107] As proposed, after three failed attempts at a two-thirds majority, a simple majority could appoint justices of the Supreme Tribunal. Ibid.

[108] I do not agree with Landau, "Term Limits," that constitutional designers should assume weak courts as in Venezuela and three other Latin American courts he considers, rather than a strong one as in Colombia. As far as I am concerned, and the negotiated cases confirm this, the insurance model tends to yield strong courts, whereas imposed populist models do not. I leave to the side, however, that given the unification of all the other powers, the Venezuelan Court would not have succeeded in stopping the amendment. See Figueroa, op. cit., 236.

[109] For a different evaluation of the Venezuelan case than mine, see Braver, "We, the Mediated People."

My hypothesis, admittedly based more on logic than on broad empirical evidence, is that without strong amendment review a multi- track structure plays a merely symbolic or expressive[110] rather than legal role. The Colombian–Venezuelan comparison is a preliminary empirical confirmation of the logical relationship of enforceable multi-track structure and amendment review. It works primarily because the codification of the multi-track structure was more explicit and better formulated in Venezuela than in Colombia, and yet the respective strengths of the two courts led to the contrary result we would have expected from constitutional text.

The structural importance of amendment review for multi-track structures is indeed difficult to dispute. But is amendment review justifiable and coherent under democratic regimes?[111]

JUSTIFICATIONS OF AMENDMENT REVIEW

It is of some interest that Carl Schmitt's conception was used in both Colombian and Venezuelan court decisions with opposite consequences.[112] This was undoubtedly an indication that his conception (as against his stated views on courts) was not only one of the earliest, but was probably the strongest so far justifying amendment review. There have been other attempts before and after,[113] in light of the countermajoritarian difficulty returning on a higher level, with the weakening of the "preservationist" claims made from Hamilton and Marshall to Hayek and Ackerman, oriented to a higher form of democratic legitimacy.[114] Whether any of these attempts could deal with the charge of juristocracy or *gouvernement des juges* avoided by Schmitt (though at a high price!) was another question.[115] Let me list the attempts at justification, in order of their strength (in my estimation), and briefly comment on them, starting with the weakest, and ending with those most influenced by Schmitt, the strongest so far.

---

[110] Albert, "Constitutional Handcuffs" for the idea of an expressive role of some constraint on the amending power. I agree with his stress only where strong courts are absent, or decline amendment review.

[111] Bernal, op. cit. usefully distinguishing between problems of meaning, justification and democratic legitimacy.

[112] Figueroa op.cit. 219f and 225ff; see Jacobsohn, *Identity* for India, making a similar point. The Constitutional Court in turkey also made a classical Schmittian argument, and we can assume his influence vis-à-vis the BVfG.

[113] For my earlier summary complemented here, see Multi-track.

[114] See Ackerman, *We the People* I for the fullest statement of this the preservationist case.

[115] Hirschl, *Towards Juristocracy*; Albert, "Nonconstitutional" and "Constitutional Handcuffs," 2009; Ergun Özbudun and Ömer Faruk Gençkaya, *Democratization and the Politics of Constitution-making in Turkey* (Budapest: Central European University Press, 2009). using the category of juristocracy.

1 *The Linguistic Attempt*

One long-standing argument, from nineteenth-century America to twentieth-century India, has relied on the supposedly plane meaning of the word "amend," notion that "to amend" accordingly means "to add to," "to modify," "to incrementally improve" and not to overthrow, destroy, revolutionize or create.[116] Taken alone this argument is not very convincing. According to a version, that partially anticipates my multi-level model, some constitutions (US states; France 1848; Spain 1978) thus use the term revision or even total revision when more radical alteration is allowed, and assign a special, even more democratic process to accomplish it.[117] However tenuously, the convention formula in US Article V. could even be interpreted this way.[118] But when it cannot rely on formalization[119] with respect to method of alteration and the relevant substance, the semantic argument runs into a lot of trouble. Does to amend mean to change a little of the text, while to revolutionize means to change a great deal of it? Obviously, very small textual changes could matter a great deal, while in many constitutions the elimination or replacement of many passages may matter little, in a constitutional sense. If we are to ever make sense of the difference between "amendment" and more radical forms of alteration, without supporting formal text, the linguistic or literal argument thus needs to be and is usually supplemented by one of the arguments below, many of which imply unwritten eternity clause(s).

2 *Natural Rights*

Natural law, or natural rights arguments, in effect limit not only the power to amend, but also the sweep of other arguments that would extend beyond

---

[116] Murphy; Viand and Brandon in Levinson ed. *Responding to Imperfection*; G. Austin, *Working a Democratic Constitution* (Delhi: Oxford, 2003).

[117] Murphy, op. cit., p. 177; P. Suber, *The Paradox of Self Amendement* (Peter Lang International Academic Publishers., 1990), p 229.

[118] The argument seems to go back to the 1930s and Selden Bacon. See Suber, pp. 210ff. and Vile p.195 More radically than Bacon's conception, it has been recently imagined that the US Article V. contains such scheme, by hierarchizing the four possibilities latent in the rule 1) governmental draft –(state) governmental ratification; 2) governmental draft – ratification by (state) convention; 3) draft by national convention – governmental ratification; 4) draft by convention – ratification by conventions. The scheme proposed by William F. Harris derives from what the founders indeed thought of the as the institution best representing popular sovereignty, namely the extra-ordinary convention. But as Justice Roberts pointed out in Sprague, the Constitution involves neither a hierarchy among the four possible models, nor assigns any substantive fields appropriate to the competence of each. See Harris, *The Interpretable Constitution* (Baltimore: Johns Hopkins University Press, 1992) chapter IV.

[119] What is called ex ante control by Dixon and Landau in "Constraining Constitutional Change."

the question of fundamental rights. In India, however, the evolution was in the reverse direction. In the early Golak Nath case, dealing with the issue of property rights, it was around a natural rights type of argument that the Indian Supreme Court sought to limit the power to amend.[120] The argument then was very loosely linked to codification by fastening on constitutional language in Article 13 that provided that no *law* shall abridge the fundamental rights, and on the abstractly defensible notion that constitutional amendments were laws.[121] However, as the later Indian Kesavananda Court recognized and declared, constitutional amendments are not "law" as understood in constitutional language whether in India or the USA. Beyond such unsuccessful attempts to piggy-back on codification, the natural rights argument maintains the superiority and the legal enforceability of fundamental rights, and their meta-right – that is for Walter Murphy, following the *Grundgesetz*, human dignity against all forms of legislation including constitutional amendments, with or without prior codification as in the German case. If this were right, undoubtedly the superiority would also be present in the case of the makers of original constitutions. Arguably, under liberal or democratic constitutions as in the USA, Germany, and India, to one extent or another, natural rights can be said to be institutionalized in the constitutional scheme. Once there is constitutional jurisdiction, review and enforcement, it becomes according to Murphy the duty of courts to enforce natural rights already institutionalized against the amending power. But it should be noted that this argument implies that all sections of the constitution dealing with rights, perhaps including their enforcement and protection, are protected by eternity clauses that would even limit a revolutionary legislator in principle. This could mean, as Joel Colón-Rios has pointed out,[122] that changing the contents of rights or even adding to them when other rights may be diminished (e.g., welfare rights vs property rights) would also be banned under an eternity clause.

3 *Normative Democratic Arguments*

Concerning these little needs to be said, because they have not played much of a role so far, except that here the natural law argument is extended beyond

---

[120] Jacobsohn, "An Unconstitutional Constitution? A Comparative Perspective." *International Journal of Constitutional Law* 4.3 (2006): 460–487.

[121] Austin, *Working a Democratic Constitution*, p. 197, and for the debate, as well as subsequent amendment and overrule passim. Recently, Walter Murphy repeated the same argument regarding any amendment that would restrict our 1st (Vile, op. cit., 196; Murphy, op. cit., p. 176 fn.40).

[122] *Weak Constitutionalism*, op. cit.

rights to cover the dimensions of the constitution that establish and organize political powers. Without the benefit of even the uncertain codification of rights as limits, Carlos Bernal-Pulido, for example, argues that fundamental presuppositions of deliberative democracy such as political rights, rule of law, separation of powers, when threatened or violated, supply a sufficient ground to declare constitutional amendments unconstitutional. Yet while the meaning of rights and the choice among them can be contested, this is even more the case for democratic institutions. Even in the debate around presidential term limits it could be, and was, effectively argued on both sides on the normative level, as a submission of the Venezuelan Embassy in the USA, focusing on the freedom of the electorate indicates, drawing on Hamilton in the *Federalist Papers*.[123] Thus Carlos-Pulido too needs to supplement this argument by historicist claims, concerning the dangers of hyperpresidentialism in Latin America, and specifically Colombia under Uribe and Venezuela under Chavez. Generally, the argument, as with all natural law types, again implies an eternity clause, even if for Colombia Bernal-Pulido mentions only the highest level of change in the constitution. Thus, it remains vulnerable to either the charge of juristocracy that excludes radical democratic alteration, or to the opposite one that on the level of replacement democracy is unprotected either from populism or its own paradox.

4 Functional Democratic Arguments

Closely related, functional arguments return to the origins of the notion of constitutionalism as it has been developed in America and France against the British notion of parliamentary sovereignty, expressed most famously by the septennial law in which a parliament greatly extended its own tenure. Deriving the differentiation of the constituent and constituted from Montesquieu, the idea is that one of the incumbent branches of government, or even all of them in combination, should not be able to extend their powers at one another's cost, or at the expense of the electorate. This idea was developed by Jefferson in the 1781 *Notes on Virginia*, in the *Federalist Papers* as well as by Sieyès, but it leads to a theory of limitation only where the rule of amendment resembles that of parliamentary sovereignty's simple majority by merely increasing the proportion of votes required for enactment. In that case a party, after a sufficiently great electoral victory, would be in the same position as the Westminster Parliament. Where an amendment rule required the cooperation of different branches, or,

[123] Hamilton in *Federalist*, no. 72; but compare Condorcet, "On the Principles of the Constitutional Plan."

as under federalism, different governments, the argument would lose some of its force. It would not lose all of it, however, because of the possibility, noted by Tocqueville, that a single party could predominate in all the branches and governments. In the case of an amendment rule involving popular participation, whether as initiation or ratification, the argument would lose even more of its power. Conversely, it could be said that where the argument retains its power it would potentially allow less change than even the natural rights claims. But functional arguments cut in two directions. While it is true that, in principle, almost all areas of the constitution could be used to favor incumbents, it is also true that constitutional adjustments may be required from the point of the functioning and even survival of the whole. While it is difficult to demarcate the area where constitutional change could be made easily without great risk, the functional perspective would likely insist on such a demarcation, but as always, even in the case of statutes, under judicial supervision and control.

5 *Historicist Arguments (Positive)*

Without the very tenuous link to codification (or a more explicit one as in the *Grundgesetz* Article 79–3), the idea that natural rights or deliberative democracy are absolutely entrenched is the mark of extreme dogmatic positions. It is neither philosophically nor legally plausible to introduce natural rights that appear as ordinary constitutional provisions as legal trumps versus the democratic process of the amending power today. Maurice Hauriou's supralegal constitutional principles,[124] that directly influenced Schmitt, represented an improvement in two respects. First, he historicized the conception by focusing on the long-term development of the normative structure of political communities. Thus, unlike the natural rights conception, he allowed change in what is to be protected. And second, he tried to go beyond a narrow rights orientation, compatible with a benevolent authoritarianism. As against a timeless, abstract and merely philosophical argument seeking to ground fundamental rights, he asked instead what are the meta- or supralegal constitutional principles that the French tradition maintained and developed in its rather many written constitutions, sometimes in a codified, but often in a merely implicit form. As Schmitt later, he took the famous unamendable republican government clause of the 3rd Republic (added: August 14, 1884) as a sign of the presence of constitutional principles, rather than as some have argued[125] the proof of the exclusion of other limits. Other principles, like those of the Declaration of the Rights of Man and Citizen which established the

---

[124] *Précis de droit constitutionnel* (Paris: Sirey, 1923), 1st ed.   [125] Vile, op. cit., 197.

principles of an individualist society but were not taken into the formal text of the Constitution of the 3rd Republic, have a similar, if not greater importance, according to his convincing argument.[126] Hauriou's stress on equality and publicity of taxation and that of the separation of powers between the adminis-tration and the judiciary do not carry the same conviction, and thus represent a danger sign for his mode of proceeding. Whereas natural rights perspectives established a definite domain worthy of the highest protection, one generally also distinguished in constitutions by their tables of rights, Hauriou's institutionalism simply goes shopping among principles deemed more and less important, respectively. However, what he successfully establishes is that there is such a thing as constitutional legitimacy whose principles are based on historical continuity that can be missed only by "the majority of authors hypnotized by a rigid conception of a written constitution."[127] The cost may have been a slow movement toward something like the basic structure doctrine with it attendant difficulties, including the idea of implicit "eternity."[128]

6 Historicist Arguments (Negative)

The historicist argument can also focus on what to avoid in a given country's constitutional tradition. Where there is a history of dictatorship, or "abusive constitutionalism" it is claimed that even without textual support, an apex court rightly judges amendments that imply the historical dangers and pit-falls should be unconstitutional.[129] Similarly, where there are institutions such as hyperpresidentialism, thus very close to the threshold of non- or semi- or authoritarian democracy, attempts to push it over that threshold by, e.g., removal of term limits should be invalidated by apex courts. Thus, in parlia-mentary democracies or even genuine systems of the separation of powers, as

---

[126] He did not argue for the absolute entrenchment of their mode of organization, only of their principles that would make the complete abolition of the relevant rights unconstitu-tional (298). The Schmitt of the Verfassungslehre follows him here *Constitutional Theory*, pp. 214–215.

[127] *Précis*, 297–298.

[128] This can be seen in a contemporary revival of an argument based on continuity and tra-dition, by G. Jacobsohn, which refers to Burke, but produces an argument very similar to Hauriou's earlier one. Jacobsohn affirms the basic structure doctrine whose ambiguities and political precariousness he is aware of, and explicitly recommends against relying on the Schmittian, sovereignty-based dimensions of the doctrine that could just as well be used to justify the other side. He is only right in the special context of India, where emergency government and attempts to limit amendments found themselves on different political sides. The Burkean attempt to defend the basic structure doctrine is entirely implausible, and leads to no determinate result of any kind. See "An Unconstitutional Constitution."

[129] Halmai, op. cit.

in the United States or even in France after de Gaulle, there is generally no problem with the re-election of prime ministers or presidents, while under strong presidentialism there is. Thus, the argument concedes its own lack of generality, and should admit that it depends on a decision by a court which category a given country may belong to. Yet the same argument can be made more general or even universal by shifting to one based on the fundamental paradox of democracy.

7 Paradox of Democracy: Militant Democracy and Judicial Review

Along with all other forms of political sovereignty, under classical assumptions, the democratic citizenry can use their powers to change not only political forms, but also popular sovereignty itself. As is well known, Carl Schmitt leveled this charge against amendment rules,[130] and recently both replacement and amendment have been linked to the possibility of "abusive constitutionalism."[131] Schmitt at least, eschewing reliance on courts, implied that militant democracy using exceptional or emergency powers is the only solution to the dilemma. Both the concept of commissarial dictatorship he used, and the actual role of exactly such a dictatorship ushering in full-fledged authoritarian rule in 1933 indicate that this form of supposed protection is as dangerous as the original problem. Thus, contemporary critics of abusive democracy reject it in its classical form. Yet militant democracy in the form of constitutional court administered party dissolution has its strong advocates today.[132] The idea is that parties that can be potentially agents of anti- or undemocratic deformation of democracy, should be dissolved before they can triumph in an election that would be the last one free and fair. More recent experience with such role of courts, in Turkey in particular where over twenty parties have been dissolved, many on spurious grounds, has thrown doubt on this method as well.[133] Yet the paradox of needing a form of correction against abuse that is itself dangerous or abusive arises only on the input side, by trying to eliminate the possibility of the problem arising in the first place. Arguably, constitutional review of amendments can deal with the same on the output side, by invalidating measures that can transform the constitution

---

[130] *Verfassungslehre*, op. cit.; Schmitt, *Legality and Legitimacy* (Durham, NC: Duke University Press, 2004).

[131] Landau, "Abusive"; Dixon and Landau, op. cit.

[132] (see Sajo edited volume; *Constellations*. Even Halmai?)

[133] H. Shambayati "The guardian of the regime: The Turkish Constitutional Court in comparative perspective." Ed. S. Arjomand *Constitutional Politics in the Middle East* (2007): 99–122.

in illiberal or undemocratic directions. Thus, amendment review becomes the functional equivalent of party dissolution, or militant democracy enforced by an apex court. I myself have made this point for the Turkish Constitutional Court's headscarf decisions in 2008, that, as against some critics, I found partially convincing and very much short of juristocracy.[134] Nevertheless, in Turkey the Court had constitutional texts to rely upon, arts. 1–3 of the Constitution as fundamentally entrenched by art. 4 (itself not self-entrenched). The same is true in Germany, another country of party dissolutions by the BVfG, under *Grundgesetz* Article 79 not yet actually used. In the absence of such textual support, the problems of identifying what needs to be protected by this functional equivalent of militant democracy remains unclear. Moreover, even in the presence of specifically protected texts, it is unclear when and if amendments to other articles of the Constitution become unconstitutional, as they must logically if the eternity clause is to make any genuine sense. Thus potentially the Constitution as whole or much of it may be "frozen" as I once argued, unless a consensual process "unfreezes" it.[135]

8 Basic Structure or Replacement

Abstractly, the difference between minor and major change makes sense only if we can identify what is essential about a constitution, what establishes its identity or its fundamental nature. This is what the basic structure doctrine articulated by the Indian Supreme Court evidently does, first, hesitantly during the Golak Nath case in 1967, then cleverly but emphatically, in spite of court packing, in the Kesavananda Bharati (1972) decision, and, finally, successfully reiterated and maintained through subsequent constitutional crisis and conflict.[136] The same argument, in essence, was revived by the Colombian Constitutional Court's "replacement doctrine," a Court that, in contrast to the one in India, had an arguably higher level rule to which to refer. Relying on a wide variety of sources, the Indian judges conceived the basic structure, both structurally and taxonomically.[137] Neither approach worked fully, as the structural claims remain either highly abstract or highly contestable, and because

---

[134] See Arato, "Unfreezing" and Ozbudun and Genckaya, op. cit.

[135] "Unfreezing." In Turkey, it takes 110 deputies to apply to the Constitutional Court for amendment review, thus "eternity" could be interpreted with respect to much of the Constitution as a consensus enforcing device.

[136] There was always a Schmittian side to this conception, apparently imported into India by the German scholar Dietrich Conrad, which I will neglect for the moment. Austin, *Working a Democratic Constitution*, pp. 201; 205 and elsewhere; 260.

[137] E.g., Jacobsohn, *Constitutional Identity*, pp. 139–140.

the taxonomic approach always winds up including more and more, potentially yielding, at a Court's own discretion, greater and greater jurisdiction to the same Court. While the amending practice of the Indian parliament was never fully subordinated to this doctrine, it is certainly the case that the Supreme Court acquired through it the ability to state, without any further recourse to anyone else, what the basic structure did and did not include. It may not be too much of a stretch to claim that for amending legislation the Court has become in effect a third (not necessarily the dominant) parliamentary chamber, which certainly in and of itself implies a fundamental change in the "basic structure" of the constitution of 1950. Similarly, where there was no eternity clause as in India, the introduction of an implicit eternity clause as in this doctrine also represents fundamental change.[138] Such changes established by a court involve serious legitimation problems. The Colombian Court, and subsequently the Turkish Constitutional Court, both show the links of the replacement doctrine to original constitution making already present in India. Accordingly, certain kinds of constitutional changes require exactly the same type of process as the original one that gave birth to the constitution itself. This idea is the one I articulated in the path of Jefferson, Condorcet and Arendt. It is least problematic where the original model is simulated by a track within the given amendment rule. It is more difficult to defend in instances where there is no such a track, as in India, and especially where the given constitution has been produced in a *coup d'état*, as in Turkey.[139] Thus, the basic structure or replacement doctrine needs a theory of the original constituent power to rely on.

9 *The Difference Between Constituent and Constituted Powers*

The arguments used so far can be strengthened if used in combinations of two or three approaches. Versions of several of them (1, 2, 6, 7 and 8) presuppose the strongest argument of all: the illegitimacy of merely constituted powers altering the most fundamental choices of the constituent power.[140] Distinguishing between original and derived constituent powers (namely the amendment rule), the argument explicitly returned in the decisions of the Constitutional Courts of India, Colombia and Turkey, and in a theoretical

---

[138] Halmai seems to treat all review of amendments as linked to eternity clauses, codified or implicit; op. cit.

[139] Note the Court's very language as in Turkey: See Arato, op. cit., as well as chapter 5 above.

[140] Only Jacobson, in his version of the historicist argument, warns against relying on the concept of sovereignty, that following Schmitt, he sees in two often incompatible version: the lord of the exception vs. the subject of the constituent power.

form in the argument for "weak constitutionalism" by Colon-Rios.[141] Derived from Sieyès, and before him English revolutionary thought, this form of analysis was developed both in France and Germany. But to my knowledge Carl Schmitt was the very first who applied exactly these concepts to the problem of unconstitutional constitutional amendments. Indeed, Schmitt has the merit of having first raised on the level of a rigorous theory the problem of amendment limitation, hence the doctrine of unconstitutional constitutional amendment. Everyone who bases amendment review on the theory of the constituent power, or on the distinction between original and derived constituent power follows in Schmitt's track, whether or not they derived the concept or the distinction from him directly.

Of all the alternatives, it is this theory that I wish to concentrate on, not only because it is still the strongest as against its competitors unless they assumed and absorbed it in their own arguments. For reasons that will be obvious, I wish to go beyond it, while preserving at the same time the stress on constitutional origins or foundations. Thus, I wish to focus on both Schmitt's achievement as well as the reason for the failure of his attempt. Since I have reconstructed and criticized this theory in detail in a previous work,[142] here a few points will suffice.[143]

According to Schmitt, the making of the constitution involves (or ought to involve?) the revolutionary act of a fundamental decision concerning the nature of a political regime, visible in preambles first and foremost, one that involves some of the major, but by no means all dimensions of a constitution that also contains mere constitutional laws.[144] Constitutional amendments can (legitimately) change constitutional laws, but do not (rightly) have the competence to alter the fundamental decisions, the essential part or the constitutional identity. Only a new exercise of the constituent power, in a democratic age the agent of the popular sovereign, can (legitimately) establish a new constitution. The constituent power is legally unlimited, however, and can (legitimately) establish any constitution whatsoever. It is also procedurally unlimited, meaning that whoever acts in the name of the constituent power, without being repudiated by the popular sovereign, can choose its own procedures.

---

[141] See also Y. Roznai's op. cit.; even as he comes around to a multi-track conception, the unlimited Schmittian constituent power he shares with Colon-Rios is still there in Roznai, "The Spectrum of Constitutional Amendment Powers" unp. where he finally discovers tiered or multi-track amendment structures in relation to unconstitutional constitutional amendments.

[142] Multi-track, op. cit.   [143] All drawn from *Verfassungslehre*.

[144] As argued in my 2011 piece, "Multi-track," op. cit. I consider this distinction parallel, but inferior, to Hart's distinction between the material constitution (the essential part) and the formal constitution that may contain much that is inessential.

As I explained elsewhere,[145] Schmitt's admittedly powerful conception runs into three ultimately insoluble problems, the What, the Who and the How. As to the first, he is less successful than Kelsen (who focused on the rules for rule making, interpreting and enforcing) in identifying what is essential in a constitution, and in the end gives us only various lists that either include too much or too little. While he notes that some constitutions like that of the 3rd Republic do identify unamendable provisions, following Hauriou he considers these to be only clues that there are many other unchangeable elements. After all, a republican government clause is potentially linked to many of the other features of the constitution, e.g., structure of government, elections and even rights. Arguably, in a large state, though not in France (though in the track of both Montesquieu and Rousseau), even federalism is arguably a precondition of republican form of government. As to the Who, on one level Schmitt adopts the mythological concept of the *pouvoir constituant* of the unitary people, in a move that has nevertheless impressed even some democratic theorists. In reality, however, he has two less mythological subjects in mind: the one enforcing the ban on illegitimate amendments, and the other as the one that legitimately makes the constitution in the name of the popular sovereign. Using a distinction justly famous, the first of these is the lord of the exception, the *commissarial* dictator, and the second the *sovereign* dictator.[146] Schmitt, who in his debate with Kelsen[147] rejected judicial review of even legislation, has never for a moment contemplated amendment review by a court, unlike the jurists who followed him in India, Colombia, and Turkey, for example. But what happens when the first subject tries to act in the name of the second, as it indeed happened during the collapse of the Weimar Republic? Or if the supposedly temporary sovereign dictator as in the Third Reich establishes its dictatorship as quasi-permanent? Given the mythical concept of the constituent power he relies on, as well as the procedural indeterminacy of the How, Schmitt could not, even if he wanted to (he did not!), exclude these possibilities, and in fact prepared the ground for both in the tract *Legality and Legitimacy*.[148] Note, however, that even these choices do not solve the question of the radical ambiguity of the procedural conception of Schmitt, who lists in *Verfassungslehre* at least four possible procedures used up till then historically, including the sovereign constituent assemblies, authoritarian plebiscites and even differentiated constitutional conventions.[149]

---

[145] Ibid.   [146] For these concepts, see *Die Diktatur* (Berlin: Duncker & Humblot, 1921).
[147] *Hüter der Verfassung* (Berlin: Duncker & Humblot, 1931).   [148] Op. cit.
[149] *Verfassungslehre*, op. cit. Those who use or rediscover Schmitt, either applaud the procedural indeterminacy, as does Colon-Rios; or fall into it like Bruce Ackerman.

These ambiguities of Schmitt, present even at his best, are very serious. Gary Jacobsohn rightly calls attention to the opposite consequences in India of focusing on the lord of the emergency (Mrs. Gandhi) and the equally Schmittian stress on the original constitution making act (the Supreme Court). Similarly, Figueroa perceptively notes the reliance on Schmitt's doctrine of the constituent power both by the Colombian Court that invalidated the amendment on term limits referring to the constituent assembly, and the Venezuelan Court that upheld the same provision and contented itself with a referendum even as the Constitution had the constituent assembly option. These difficulties that arise in contemporary contexts, should alert us to the great problems of relying on Schmitt's theory of the constituent power.

Not only conceptions explicitly derived from Schmitt are affected. Schmitt's notion of the radical difference between constituent and amending powers helps to interpret many of the other justifications of amendment review as implying extensive or limited, explicit or implicit eternity clauses. Logically, if such a clause is explicitly or implicitly assumed, then what is off limits to amendment cannot be revised short of a revolutionary transformation or replacement of the constitution. Revolution after all cannot be excluded, empirically at least, by any of the justifications of amendment review. Indeed, for Schmitt and some of the other lines of argument, revolutionary replacement could even be normatively justified if based on the identity of the *pouvoir constituant*, the unified people or the nation. Unfortunately, however, as I have repeatedly argued and tried to document, revolutionary replacement leads to constitutional democracy very rarely. As Condorcet rightly feared, eternity clauses make revolutions and *coups d'état* more rather than less likely.[150]

And yet, with all this said, Schmitt is the only main theorist who rightly maintains that the original constituent process is the ultimate reference point for judging the legitimacy (and perhaps also the legality) of amendment and replacement. Even Ackerman only used that reference point to judge the legitimacy of informal amendments, rather than the illegitimacy of formal ones. With a different type of constituent process in mind, the multi-stage post-sovereign paradigm, we are in the position to renew the emphasis on the constituent power as a guide. This means not only, as already argued, that the multi-stage, post-sovereign origin of the constitution has an elective affinity to multi-leveled, or tiered amendment rules, but that the later provide both a new type of justification for amendment review: to police the differentiation among the levels of amendment linked to a new conception of the constituent power.

---

[150]   R. Albert in "Constitutional Handcuffs."

Unfortunately, analysts even today tend to consider the multi-track constitution and the doctrine of the unconstitutional constitution separately.[151] As a result, they tend to either pronounce each a relatively weak defense against "abusive constitutionalism," i.e., using amendment or replacement to diminish democratic government, or one stronger than the other, mainly amendment review because of its greater flexibility and potential range. On the other side, amendment review without the multi-track conception, thus implying either implicit or explicit eternity clauses, is readily accused of juristocracy.[152] In my view, supported by cases such as South Africa and Colombia, and logically at least all the negotiated processes of constitution making, taken together the multi-track constitution and amendment review are stronger than either separately. Moreover, taken together, they address the charge of juristocracy[153] by leaving the highest level of change to an intensified form of democratic politics.[154] Instead of seeing this level as merely "expressive" or "symbolic" it becomes a legal one as long as amendment review operates in the hands of a strong court.

Granted, a multi-level structure would seem difficult to use as a justification of amendment review when it is established or perfected by a court in the first place. This happened in India where a new level, the basic structure, was added, and in Colombia, where the Court established a hierarchy of topics to be dealt with by the already present plurality of amendment procedures. With the implication of an eternity clause as in India, or even without it as in Colombia, such activism raises the countermajoritarian problem anew, on a higher level than before. Yet the prior existence of levels or plurality of amendment rules in the two countries helped to reduce the legitimation problems. Where there are clearly defined levels of constitutional change involving a plurality of rules, as in Spain, Bulgaria, and South Africa, and where the highest level is not eternity with its radical revolutionary implications, amendment review needs no further justification: it is a legal requirement of the procedural structure of the constitution whether explicitly provided for or not. The justification is as old as that of Hamilton and Marshall, but is now applicable to amendment rules, and not only mere statutes or lower-level legal acts. Just as previously illegal alteration by statute was banned in the name of the amendment rule provided for, so in the multi-track constitution, illegal amendment is prohibited by the existence of a higher rule of change.

---

[151] See the already cited articles of Albert, Landau, even Landau and Dixon. Now Y. Roznai, op. cit. seems to break with the pattern.

[152] Albert, "Nonconstitutional."   [153] The same Albert in "Constitutional Handcuffs."

[154] As Ackerman argued in op. cit., but focusing on informal paths!

As many constitutions today demonstrate it is wrong claim that constitutions cannot provide for their own replacement.[155] But by providing such rule in a multi-track structure a constitution bans replacement by amendment. This is a source of a new form of legality as well as legitimacy for amendment review under the doctrine of the unconstitutional constitutional amendment. When a constitution provides for replacement modeled on its own origins, as in Spain's new elections for a (constituent) parliament, Bulgaria's Grand National Assembly and Colombia's Constituent Assembly, the democratic legitimacy of amendment review is further enhanced.

But what about constitutions like the interim Hungarian one in 1989–1990 that do not have a multi-track structure, but rather a formally unlimited single rule of change? I have argued previously that the Constitutional Court in that country should have established its right of amendment review, blocking the road to a populist-authoritarian reversion.[156] As to justification, the negative historicist and functional arguments are both important here yet ultimately insufficient. According to the first, in a country with a recent dictatorship as Hungary it is legitimate for a Constitutional Court to deny efforts of authoritarian restoration. According to the second, the limitation of amendments was needed precisely in that country to close the process of open-ended constitution making with its majoritarian dangers. I myself have made this second argument, as well as the legal-textual one, that the four-fifths rule of change that established in 1994–6 a three-tiered structure should not have been removed by a two-thirds vote of parliament based on 52 percent of the popular vote.[157] Yet, on the level of a legitimacy considerations, it is more important still that Hungary was involved in a post-sovereign process of change, based on consensual practice in 1989 as well as between 1994 and 1996, and this generated a new pluralistic model of the constituent power linked not to an identity such as the mythical people, but to the inclusive plurality of the major forces of society deciding publically and consensually the identity of the constitution. There was a good argument to be made that the result of such a process, namely the interim constitution, should not be abrogated relying on one of its relatively minor components, the two-thirds single-chamber parliamentary

---

[155] U. Preuss, cited by Jacobsohn; Roznai, op. cit. even more emphatically!

[156] See, e.g., chapter 4 of *Post Sovereign*; Halmai, op. cit. We agree on the main point here, but our assessment of the post FIDESZ constitutional court is slightly different.

[157] Of course, it would have been better if this new rule was made for all future efforts at replacing the interim constitution rather than for that parliamentary session, and was self-entrenched, even though through an error it survived, and there is a good argument for implicit entrenchment in such cases. See Suber.

amendment rule linked to a highly disproportional electoral law.[158] Thus, it is the combination of arguments, historicist, functional, textual as well as the one based on a new conception of the constituent power, which would have legitimated the judicial invalidation of the FIDESZ Basic Law, if the Hungarian Constitutional Court had the courage to take the step.

POST-SOVEREIGN PROCESS, MULTI-LEVEL AMENDMENT AND THE POWER TO REVIEW

My thesis, in short, is that the post-sovereign process has an elective affinity to a multi-level amendment structure that is a form of justification for amendment review. Equally, such a process works only if enforced by amendment review by an apex court under the unconstitutional amendment doctrine. Such an enforcement would be based on two things: *legally*, on the multi-level structure whose differentiation should be preserved; and with respect to *legitimacy* on a new idea of constituent power. The thesis represents a synthesis of the insurance argument and the radical democratic one proposed earlier. A pure insurance model would culminate in an eternity clause, which could try to "forever" insure the lower-level forms of constitutional compromise by the negotiating parties. A pure radical democratic model focused on the act of foundation would probably resemble the "weak constitutionalism" of Colon-Rios where there is no virtue as such in constitutionalist forms of protection, and where the popular constituent power is ever ready to enter the political sphere in procedurally undetermined and unlimited forms.[159] The synthesis proposed here protects constitutionalist guarantees as well as leaving an opening to radical democratic politics.

---

[158] I made this point in historicist terms in "Post-Sovereign Constitution-Making in Hungary: After Success, Partial Failure, Now What?." *South African Journal on Human Rights* 26. Part I (2010). I think this may have been is the argument Kim Scheppele was also trying to make in "Unconstitutional Constituent Power" forthcoming in R. Smith and R. Beeman, *Constitution Making* (Philadelphia: University of Pennsylvania, 2015), but it was confused by the reliance on a Schmittian conception of the constituent power, that can be then arbitrarily applied to support what the author supports (e.g. the MDF-SZDSZ exclusionary pact of 1990 amending the constitution; as against the exclusionary effort of the FIDESZ government that had more votes to rely on then the two parties of 1990). See chapter 4 of *Post Sovereign*.

[159] It is another matter that Colon-Rios departs from the pure radical democratic model, when entertaining amendment review in Colombia, as a form facilitating the move to the higher level, the constituent assembly. Op. cit. In reality, such a move occurred in neither Colombia since 1991, nor even Venezuela since 1999. Guetemala). Thus, in practice, Colon-Rios also occasionally argues for an element of insurance.

David Landau has questioned whether my post-sovereign model is worked out for any other process than transitions from authoritarian rule.[160] Part of his own problem, I think, is that he has not systematically considered the mutually re-enforcing quality of the tiered conception, and amendment review.[161] But even as I insist on that combination there are other aspects of this criticism I must deal with. To answer him fully, especially in light of his own fears concerning the problem of replacement, I must turn to the question of the highest level in a multi-track conception.

Almost all recent scholarship agrees: eternity clauses are a serious problem from a democratic point of view. I note, that of my nine cases only revolutionary Tunisia has established such a clause strictly speaking, while supposedly federal Iraq and Nepal use only a quasi-eternity clause, namely consent of provinces to changes adversely affecting them, similarly to one provision in the US Article V (concerning equal Senate representation). Most interesting is the South African case where the interim Constitution indeed contained 34 such judicially enforceable clauses or principles, but where the final Constitution retreated to a three-fourths majority (plus the majority of the provinces) for articles deemed especially important. This rule was in effect South Africa's replacement rule, one without substantive limitations. Thus, it is fair to say that empirically, the post-sovereign or negotiated paradigm is not likely to produce eternity clauses. Normatively, in the spirit of the radical democratic argument, it seems to be the case that constitution makers do indeed tend to make their own original practice the criterion for the highest rule. Revolutionary constitution makers, for example, can and often do, since France in 1791, point to future extralegal revolutions as the most important context of radical change, and eternity rules or very difficult to amend constitutions represent a way of accomplishing this goal.[162] Post-sovereign constitution makers, however, acting within legal continuity, if they establish a replacement rule, do so within at least procedural legality. Thus, the Colombian Constitution made by a constituent assembly, established a new constituent assembly as the highest level of change, at least in the interpretation of the Constitutional

---

[160] Landau "Abusive," fn. 202. When making this criticism he neglects my attempt to introduce the multi-track model as a new, normatively desirable form of constitutionalism. But admittedly, I did not link the two paradigms sufficiently, or only on the level of legitimacy that is still inadequate. Here I am making a second effort.

[161] He did notice the connection, as already said, in his political article on "Presidential Term Limits," but did not argue the matter systematically, thus revising his earlier diagnosis of weakness of constitutional protections against abusive constitutionalism.

[162] Thus, the contradiction in the Constitution of 1791 within the text of the very difficult amendment rule. The Constitution of 1793, by adopting one of Condorcet's rules, corrected the error, of course in vain. Its amendment rule was never to be used.

Court. Given that the first constituent assembly was pronounced as sovereign, there was no attempt (unfortunately) to fully constitutionalize rules of election, procedure, and ratification for such a body. But in line with the earlier but failed attempt of the political actors in 1991 to limit the assembly, and to subject these limits to Court supervision, the constitution did allow the establishment of such limits on the Constituent Assembly,[163] giving jurisdiction over them to the Constitutional Court (Article 241f). Indeed, such rules were subsequently established on the statutory level.[164] Granted, given the earlier precedent, there was thus serious ambivalence concerning replacement even in Colombia, where a Constituent Assembly could have been established without the possible limitations, and where the relevant statutes could have been derogated from by new legislation. This ambivalence is relevant to the meaning and structure of the highest rule. Even when granted, that it should not be an eternity clause, it remains a question whether the highest instance should be sovereign and unlimited, as in Venezuela (Article 349), or post sovereign and subject to limitation?

There is a sharp division among the scholars dealing with the question, with the authors still under the influence of Schmitt on the one side and the more liberal ones on the other.[165] While the former fear juristocracy if the powers of replacement were limited, the latter think of even replacement as opening the door to abusive democracy, as in Venezuela and Hungary most recently. In line with my post-sovereign normative conception, I side, of course, with the latter, but wish to avoid undemocratic consequences or opening the door to revolution as the only model of complete change. Empirically, I note that, unlike Venezuela, no post-sovereign case produced an unlimited instance as the agent of replacement. But the idea of limitation does not solve all the questions regarding the nature of the highest rule. Several current scholars dealing with this question have indicated important choices in this area facing constitution makers. In Albert's terminology, should the tiers including the highest tier be comprehensive or restricted to only some issues? This is an important question that can be critically addressed to many amendment rules today, but it is not a difficult one to answer if legal replacement is to make sense at all. While it is indeed important in my view to treat all the intermediate levels of amendment as restrictive, and applying to specific constitutional domains, this logically cannot apply to the highest level, a replacement or

---

[163] Article 376: "By means of a law approved by the members of both chambers, Congress may stipulate that the people decide by popular vote if a Constituent Assembly should be called with the jurisdiction, term, and members determined by that same law."

[164] Figueroa, op. cit.

[165] With Albert, Colon-Rios, Roznai on one side, and. Landau and Dixon on the other.

total revision clause, unless we introduce an eternity clause by stealth for full replacement.[166]

More difficult are two puzzles proposed by Landau and Dixon,[167] that I think significant even as I do not fully agree with their analysis and especially their solutions. They ask two analytical questions, both of which are informed by different jurisprudential sensibilities. Should limitations on the highest rule be *ex ante*, by text, as civil jurists would prefer, or *ex post*, contained or incorporated in the power of a court to review, as common lawyers are likely to advocate. And second, reflecting the alternatives of natural law and positivism, should the limits of the highest rule be substantive or merely procedural?

Landau and Dixon consider both *ex post* and *ex ante* options to have serious weaknesses, but according to them *ex post* is more powerful because of the in-built limits of the extent of any codification and the greater flexibility of constitutional judges. In my view, as already indicated, the relative weakness of each is due, above all, to their separation. As the case of Venezuela showed, codification of amendment tiers is powerless without a strong court enforcing it. At the same time no court to my knowledge established a doctrine like basic structure or replacement without already relevant codification of tiers in place, even if limited (as in India) and not formally linked to specific domains (as in Colombia). I agree that invalidation by a Court can be more powerful, but without codification this implies eternity clauses whose democracy problem the authors are aware of. Moreover, the flexibility of constitutional judges is not necessarily served by indeterminacy, which raises the question of the limits of activism without any clear thresholds to consider its legitimacy. Where there are tiers, however, an apex court still retains the interpretive task and thus the flexibility, of determining to which level given amendments belong. Presidential re-election, for example, as we have seen, can be interpreted as a merely technical matter belonging to the lowest amendment tier (as in Venezuela), but also as a matter having to do with the fundamental quality of democracy (as in Colombia), and, I would add, could be even linked to the issues of the fundamental rights of citizens.

As to the choice between procedure and substance, unlike Dixon and Landau, on the highest or replacement level I would clearly opt for procedural review alone, as did South African constitution makers who chose not to

---

[166] To avoid misunderstanding, a rule like the South African three-fourths rule, is comprehensive. It is true, that only some issues require this procedure, but full replacement also does by implication. Three-fourths of the assembly is a replacement assembly, if having the support of over half of the provinces. While the two-thirds lower-level tiers are indeed restricted, the higher tier is able to dispose over all parts of the Constitution.

[167] "Constraining Constitutional Change."

absolutely entrench the previously unamendable principles of the earlier interim constitution. I already argued, and the Colombian and Turkish Courts did indeed note, that on the lowest and intermediate amendment tiers procedure and substance cannot be fully distinguished. Thus procedural review, allowed by these two constitutions, had to examine the substance of amendments to know if either the level of replacement (Colombia) or that of eternity clauses (Turkey) has been usurped. But this cannot be done on the highest level where there is no higher level still whose substance would not be available for alteration.[168] Only if there is an eternity clause could there be conceivably replacement that could usurp the right of revolution, assumed in the manner of the Turkish Court to be the only genuine replacement doctrine. Thus, having argued against eternity clauses, I reject the idea of substantive limits on replacement in the spirit of the Colombian Court. This does not mean, however, that I am forced to concede an unlimited and unlimitable constituent power under the cover of replacement.[169] Replacement can be limited procedurally both *ex ante* by establishing precise rules for the highest level, and *ex post* by these rules being strictly enforced by an apex court if the political branches choose to violate them. I am skeptical regarding the argument of Dixon and Landau concerning the weakness of procedural limits on the bases of the indeed sad Hungarian experience, where a two-thirds majority was attained and abused by one party.[170] This case shows only the weakness of weak procedures, namely a single-chamber qualified majority rule that can be relatively easily satisfied, as I warned from the early 1990s, by a strongly disproportional electoral rule. Indeed, in a setting of such an amendment rule, the possibility of ex post intervention by the Constitutional Court was greatly weakened.

Procedural rules in order to work against abusive replacement with sufficient legitimacy must be both relatively strong and operate on more than a single democratic channel. Admittedly, not all procedural rules in multi-track models

[168] Thus, the limitation to procedural review should be strictly adhered to in a case like the Colombian Articles 241–2 where the Court has a say on the activation of the highest track. Here substantive review would indeed be judicial abuse. Undoubtedly, judicial power could also be abused on the lower levels, as Figueroa was kind to point out to me. But restricting review on these levels to procedure alone cannot work, and certainly opens the door to formally legal forms of abusive constitutionalism where incumbents control their own powers.

[169] Roznai, "The Spectrum," 2f; 10ff. The article's argument, an example of a Schmittian doctrinaire attitude, flies in the face of many replacement rules that are indeed procedurally limited. No one claims of course that revolutionary replacement can be legally limited, but that is hardly the point for constitution makers today, who unlike Schmitt are attached to democracy.

[170] "Constraining Constitutional Change."

are satisfactory from this point of view. When the rules do not indicate the domains to which each rule is relevant, the lawyers of an Uribe or a Chavez (with the help of a weak court!) can claim that parliamentary supermajorities or referenda are alternative ways of representing the popular sovereign. Where the highest rule is required by very few domains, as Dixon and Landau rightly note even in the case of South Africa, the door is left open to abuse through amending other domains. Where the highest rule is only a qualified majority of legislatures as again in South Africa,[171] there is no obvious opportunity for enhanced forms of popular participation to fully legitimate the replacement of the constitution even if it was originally enacted a strongly democratic process.

In contrast, several, if not all of the successful cases of the post-sovereign model created an amendment rule involving the deliberate and potentially well-publicized election of a new constitution-making assembly, whether constituent or constitutional or formally ordinary. This should be a clue, that normative-logically if not unfortunately empirically, it is this approach that should have guided the makers of the amendment rule. The normative argument is the Jeffersonian-Arendtian one also insisted on by Ackerman, of preserving and institutionalizing the possibility of the founding experience and its high democratic legitimacy for future generations. Of my cases, only Spain, Bulgaria, and Colombia satisfied this desideratum, along with procedural limits for establishing such an assembly. As long as there is no ordinary legislature that is supposed to remain in place during the constitution-making process, it does not matter that in Spain two ordinary parliaments are provided for the enactment of "total revision," while in Bulgaria the term Grand National Assembly is used. Even in Spain, this is not a matter of merely introducing time, as Elster and the many who follow him argue, a claim relevant only when a single parliament must adopt a text in two or multiple "readings" separated by temporal criteria. What is at stake here rather is involving a new election in the process of constitution making, with the obvious option for popular debate of the proposal, a desideratum inherited from all versions of the multi-stage method, and even the quasi-revolutionary cases of Colombia and Tunisia that were preceded by important negotiations.

None of the existing amendment formulas that came out of inclusively negotiated processes are perfect. They could all be improved by introducing the dimension of double differentiation, fought for in amendment rules ever since Condorcet, but realized, with the exception of individual US American

[171] Albert, "Structure of Constitutional Amendments."

states, mostly on paper only.[172] Of all my cases, this feature is present only in Colombia. If electing new constitution-making assemblies should not mean absence of procedural limitation, then having to coexist with a law making legislature would be the most important such a limit. It is one that would help re-enforce the constitutional control of the procedures of the assembly by an apex court. While such a new formula, up till now played a significant role only in federal states, the Colombian case shows that there is no reason why unitary bodies politic could not adopt it if there is strong enough enforcement by an apex court. Here we notice a flaw inherent in the post-sovereign model, to the extent that it was developed in polities without legitimate and competitively elected legislatures. They cannot thus provide a model for a doubly differentiated amendment process. Under already existing democracies, the idea of post-sovereign constitution making could be further improved in this manner, and in Colombia and Venezuela it was, above all, the idea of a sovereign constituent power that in the end defeated the initially adopted model of double differentiation.[173]

Conclusion

The tension between constitutionalism and democracy has not always been a productive one, and the classical solution of referring to origins threatens to renew it on a level of amendment rules and their review. Since the power of amendment was the most important attempted solution of the conflict, it becomes even more difficult to resolve when amendments themselves are attacked in the name of constitutionalism. By combining the logic of insurance and radical democratic norms, the post-sovereign paradigm offers a new solution to the dilemma on this higher level. The key is a combination of a multi-track structure of amendment, along with amendment review. The elective affinity of the post-sovereign or inclusively negotiated method to multi track review admittedly does not imply empirical causality or even an inescapable form of covariance. Yet the empirical evidence in my admittedly preliminary analysis points to the significantly greater likelihood of the emergence of the

---

[172] e.g. in France; the two Latin American cases of Colombia in 1991 and Venezuela in 1999 indicate the main difficulty: the persistence of the sovereign theory of constitution making. Cf. Figureoa for this argument, op. cit.

[173] That defeat was re-institutionalized in the amendment rule of Venezuela, stating that "the existing constituted authorities shall not be permitted to obstruct the Constituent Assembly in any way." (Article 349). In Colombia (Article 376) provides both for the possibility of legal limits on the Constituent Assembly, and deprives Congress (rightly) only of its amending power for the duration. Thus the constituted powers are not deprived of enforcing limits on the Constituent Assembly, approved in a referendum.

linkage under the post-sovereign paradigm, than in revolutionary or reformist process when not informed by a strong logic of negotiations, as it was in Colombia and Tunisia. This claim, a hypothesis rather, should be further explored. What is crucial for me, however, and more important than mere empirical relationships, is the presence of two normative logics in the post-sovereign paradigm, the normative logic of insurance that follows from the plurality of necessarily uncertain actors in the comprehensively negotiated cases, along with the normative logic of institutionalizing the democratic post-revolutionary founding experience. Insurance moreover, unless it becomes overinsurance that can lead to a version of bankruptcy in the form of eternity rules and unchangeable constitutions, opens up a link to the founding experience through the institution of a suitably structured and enforceable rule of revision. While most of the post-sovereign negotiated cases produced such a rule, only some of them produced the multi-track rule open, though procedurally limited on the highest replacement level. While all these cases generated constitutional courts, only some explicitly established amendment review. Yet on the level of the normative logics of insurance and foundation it is that combination that best expresses the meaning of post-sovereign constitution making.

The combination does not mean putting an end to the adventures of the constituent power, but rather replaces the already deeply compromised, yet still influential Schmittian subject of such adventures by a pluralistic liberal as well as democratic *pouvoir constituant*.

Epilogue

Breaking the Link Between Revolution and Sovereign Dictatorship
The Case of the Russian Constituent Assembly

The adventures of the constituent power have been tightly linked to the modern history of great revolutions. The thesis of this book, assuming the continued likelihood of revolutionary change, is that revolution can and should be freed of the burden of sovereign constitution making, of the danger of sovereign dictatorship. The post-sovereign paradigm provides important clues how this can be done. But does not the same paradigm's promise to "domesticate" revolution imply a loss as well? In Hannah Arendt's evocative reconstruction,[1] modern revolutions from the American and French in the eighteenth century, to the Hungarian of 1956 (that I myself have directly experienced), involved the experience of high-level public participation as well the generation of new, direct democratic institutions: the sections, the councils, the councils of the Commune, the soviets, the anjomans,[2] the Räte, or the munkástanácsok (*pace* Arendt: *workers'* councils). Arendt's implicit thesis pointed to the fundamental paradox of revolution: almost universally creating forms of intense poltical involvement and participation, the logic of revolution seems to inevitably destroy these very forms.

While the post-revolutionary form I advocate did involve high levels of public participation in several countries, especially in Poland and South Africa, in none of the cases have direct democratic political forms played a major role.[3] The role of grass roots mobilization has been assumed by new movements

---

[1] *On Revolution* (New York: Viking, 1963), chapter 6.

[2] In Iran's "constitutional revolution" of 1905–6: see S. Arjomand, *The Turban for the Crown* (Oxford: Oxford University Press, 1988), pp. 38–39 for the mushrooming of new councils, associations and forms of local assemblies at that time. For their political role, see N. Sohrabi, *Revolution and Constitutionalism in the Ottoman Empire and Iran* (Cambridge: Cambridge University Press, 2011), pp. 365–380.

[3] Again there is an exception, in Poland, in the epoch of the first Solidarity of 1980–1981, when the idea of worker's control or self-management was important. After 1989, this idea was sacrificed to

of civil society and alternative publics that seemed to have been subjected to the traditional life-cycle involving mobilization followed by demobilization.[4] True, in Arendt's own analysis, forms of intense poltical participation seem to belong to a special revolutionary temporality (Walter Benjamin's *Jetztzeiten*), that is everywhere out of sync with the evolutionary time of consolidation. No succesful revolution seems to institutionalize these forms, whether Jefferson's wards or the later councils, that are bypassed or defeated either by new dictatorships as in France, and Russia or by forms of liberal constitutionalism as in America and Germany. But, in the time of revolutions at least, direct democratic experimentation seems to have a major presence.[5] Is there a third notion of time, beyond both Benjamin's theological and the historian's linear, developmental time, a time of institution building that potentially would allow the survival of direct democratic forms, and overcome the paradox of revolutions?

Admittedly, the question of the institutionalization of forms of direct democracy has barely come up in recent cases of regime transformation. As shown in the previous chapter, the post-sovereign model, at its best, has been able to institutionalize in amendment rules only its own mode of origin that in general relied on political society rather than grassroots institutions emerging from below. Nevertheless, I would argue that this model of constitutional change would, in principle, have a better chance of finding an important constitutional space for direct democratic forms, than the revolutionary alternative of sovereign constituent assemblies. It is perhaps renewed revolutionary experiments in the future, that have assimilated some of the lessons of post-sovereign constitution making that would have the best chance of combining the democratic experimentalism of classical revolutions, with the second Arendtian desideratum, the secure establishment of constitutional government.

To make this argument, I would like to show why the institutionalization of direct democracy is incompatible with the logic of classical revolutions. I wish

---

the mode of transformation involving radical privatization. But the grassroots syndicalist movement was no longer strong, at that time. For an early, untenably optimistic treatment of this possibility, see A. Arato, "The Democratic Theory of the Polish Opposition: Normative Intensions and Strategic Ambiguities" (1984) https://kellogg.nd.edu/publications/workingpapers/WPS/015 .pdf

4 Arato, *Civil Society, Constitution and Legitimacy* (Lanham: Rowman & Littlefield, 2000). chapter 2.

5 This seems to have been the case even in Tunisia recently. See B. Challand's forthcoming book, and the special issue of *Constellations* he edited: see: Challand, "Citizenship Against the Grain: Locating the Spirit of the Arab Uprisings in Times of Counterrevolution," *Constellations*, 20.2 (2013): 169–187.

to make this case not on the bases of general theoretical considerations, but by reconstructing the most important example perhaps, the dissolution in January of 1918 of the All Russian Constituent Assembly (*Uchreditelnoye Sobraniye*) that quickly led to the destruction of the democratic meaning of the council movement. I will point to what alternatives may have existed at the time, on the level of the constitution-making process, to establish a dualistic framework of representative and direct democracy, and will briefly refer to the German Revolution of 1918 to show how the combination did not have to remain merely an abstract utopia of many of the participants of both revolutions.

In its 100th anniversary year, it seems fitting to speak of the Russian Revolution, which, even to Marxists like Karl Kautsky and Rosa Luxemburg, "went wrong" with the Bolshevik dissolution of the constituent assembly, especially as it was not followed by the election of a new one.[6] As should be clear from my thesis, I do not agree with historians to whom this event represents a battle where constitutionalism and the sovereign constituent assembly were supposedly on one side, and executive dominance and usurpation of the constituent power on the other. I do agree with the judgment of Kautsky and Luxemburg, though I am skeptical whether new elections in themselves would have helped. In line with my conception I wish to depict another better road, one also not taken, based on a different conception than that of the sovereign constituent power that even these Marxist thinkers found no problem with.

The important story,[7] which used to be well known not only to Russian historians, but more generally on the Left, is briefly this.[8] With the collapse of the Tsarist government, all major revolutionary forces accepted and advocated the classical formula of provisional government and constituent assembly that had been demanded by many actors in the failed revolution of 1905. There was no disagreement on this question between the two contenders of the

---

[6] See R. Luxemburg, *The Russian Revolution* chapter 4 https://www.marxists.org/archive/luxemburg/1918/russian-revolution/ch04.htm; who misspoke concerning when the Constituent Assembly was elected; Kautsky, *The Dictatorship of the Proletariat* (1918) chapter 6 at: https://www.marxists.org/archive/kautsky/1918/dictprole/ch06.htm; the latter answered by Trotsky, *Terrorism and Communism* (1920) (Ann Arbor: University of Michigan Press, 1961).

[7] "The All Russian Constituent Assembly, together with the election which produced it" was "arresting episode" in the history of the Russian Revolution, even if a failure, according to the most serious historian of these elections, O. Radkey. See *Russia Goes to the Polls* (Ithaca: Cornell University Press, 1970; 1990), p. 77. In a new foreword to the book, the revisionist historian S. Fitzpatrick "translates" this to say that the assembly itself, and its dissolution, as against the elections, has "small historical significance."

[8] For the best descriptions see O. Anweiler, *The Soviets* (New York: Random House, 1974), pp. 208–218; Pipes, *The Russian Revolution* (New York: Knopf, 1990), pp. 537–550.

emerging system of dual power, the provisional government initially formed with the remnants of the last tsarist Duma, and the soviet organs based on the self-organization of the factories and the military forces.[9] Not only the constitutionalist right, but also all major left wing parties, the Bolsheviks and Mensheviks, as well as the left and right Social Revolutionaries supported the demand for a constituent assembly. Moreover, the great majority of Leftist parties and at least a strong minority of the Bolsheviks aimed at a political model of transformation combining parliamentary government, symbolized by the constituent assembly, and soviet grass roots democracy.[10] It is certain that many constitutionalist members of the provisional government sought a purely parliamentary system, but they were mostly willing to let a constituent assembly decide this question. The main disagreement between the Left and the provisional government, however, was about timing. Left-wing parties in and out of the soviets, wanted to elect the assembly as quickly as possible, to be able to replace a heteronomously formed provisional government. The latter, for both good and bad reasons, wished to delay. The good reasons had to do with the grave difficulties of organizing the first universal suffrage elections in such an immense country.[11] The bad ones were expressed in terms of the supposed impossibility of holding elections in a country at war, with insecure boundaries. In reality, what lay behind this rhetoric was the desire of the government and its external allies to settle the war question on their own, or to continue Russian participation even in the face of crushing defeats and devastation. The Bolsheviks, the most important peace party, tirelessly denounced the delay, and became advocates of electing and assembling the constituent assembly as soon as possible. Even at those moments when their slogan was "All power to the soviets" many Bolsheviks, possibly with the main exceptions of Lenin and Trotsky, saw no contradiction between a constituent assembly and that demand.[12]

[9] The worker, soldier and peasant soviets, both base and peak organizations repeatedly and emphatically called for the convening of a constituent assembly, from 1905 to 1917 and even beyond the Bolshevik insurrection. They almost invariably supported the formula of constituent assembly plus soviets. See Anweiler op.cit. 63 and passim. It was only the fully Bolhsevized soviet organizations that dropped this demand after the dissolution of the Constituent Assembly.

[10] Anweiler, op. cit., pp. 139ff; 142ff.

[11] Kautsky, *The Dictatorship*; but Radkey, op. cit., has serious doubts on this score, and focuses mainly on the desire to continue the war (pp. 92; 95–96). His comparisons to Germany and France, countries with many previous universal suffrage elections are not convincing, however.

[12] But Lenin even forced the temporary abandonment of "All power to the soviets" when he became pessimistic, after the failed insurrection of July, about his party's chances to dominate the grassroots, and the national soviet organs. He returned to it on the eve of the uprising when he realized that temporarily only the two capitals would count. Anweiler, op. cit., pp. 161–165; 169–176

After a failed Bolshevik uprising in July 1917,[13] the provisional government under the pressure of the Executive Committee of the Soviet, established a relatively early time table. Elections by universal including women's suffrage would be in November, and the Constituent Assembly would meet as soon as possible thereafter.[14] It was just 18 days before the projected elections[15] that the Bolsheviks launched their successful insurrection capturing executive power in the capital, Petrograd as well as the control of Moscow.[16] The pre-emption of the constituent assembly elections may or may not have been fully deliberate on Lenin's part.[17] It was in any case entirely consistent with his theory of such a body. I note that Zinoviev and Kamenev, two of the most important Bolsheviks after Lenin, voted against the insurrection in the Central Committee of the Party, with the argument that it was wrong to take power before the elections and the meeting of the Assembly. Their political model remained the formula supported by almost all the councils themselves, namely constituent assembly cum soviets.[18] Even Trotsky, who did not want a parliament to share political power as early as 1907, wanted to delay the uprising, until an impending All Russian Congress of Workers and Soldiers Soviets,[19] meeting in early November, called for

---

[13] The new calendar puts the Bolshevik insurrection to November 7, as against October 25 (as in "October revolution").

[14] Originally, elections were called for November 12; the opening session for November 28. Pipes, pp. 539–542. Radkey (4–5) speaks of adhering to the date of November 12 in some places, but not in many others, in an electoral period of three months overall. In some remote areas people were still electing after the assembly was dissolved?

[15] See, for example, the highly critical declaration of the Executive Committee of the Peasant Soviets that mentioned three weeks, having in mind perhaps the projected opening session. Anweiler 204; Pipes 539 says two weeks. But October 25 to November 12 in the old calendar is 18 days.

[16] A similar attempt at preemption was launched by the militants of the KPD or Spartakus, On January 4–5, 1919, 14 days before the scheduled elections to the National Constituent Assembly, in that case against the vote of the leaders who wished instead to participate in the elections. See P. Nettl *Rosa Luxemburg* (Oxford: Oxford University Press, 1969), p. 474ff.

[17] Pipes argues that it was consciously intended as such: p. 473; but he has a tendency to interpret the history after April as a Leninist conspiracy realized. Nevertheless Lenin wrote on October 23 in Report to the decisive sitting of the Central Committee: "It is senseless to wait for the Constituent Assembly that will obviously not be on our side..." *Selected Works* (Moscow: Progress, 1970), vol. 2, p. 446. On October 29, again to the Central Committee, Lenin argued that the Party could not wait for the Constituent Assembly "because there was only enough bread for a day [in Petrograd]"!! This point focused on disintegration of government under the dual power system.

[18] For Lenin's depiction of this conflict see: "Letter to Bolshevik Party Members" [October 18] ibid. 451–453 and "Letter to the Central Committee of the R.S.D.L.P. (Bolshevik)" ibid., 454ff.

[19] According to Pipes, who is hostile to the soviets as well as the Bolsheviks, a Congress illegally convened, and packed through highly disproportional electoral representation, pp. 474–476; see Anweiler op.cit., pp. 125; 176–181 for an alternative view, who shows that the Bolsheviks

it.[20] Lenin was successful, however, in arguing that the agreement of the Soviets, where the Bolsheviks now seemed to be closer to a majority, should be gotten retroactively, once the uprising was carried out and governmental power was secured.[21] Thus, he remained consistent regarding the primacy of executive power that must be achieved before any deliberations concerning the future form of government.

The insurrection whose legitimacy was retroactively confirmed by the (Second) Soviet Congress indeed succeeded in handing the full executive power to the *Sovnarkom* (Council of People's Commissars = government) at first composed of only Bolsheviks.[22] This decision of the Congress specifically mentioned the Constituent Assembly as the outer limit of the tenure of the new provisional government.[23] That very formulation represented the beginning of the last act of the drama of the Constituent Assembly. After an attempted delay, the Bolshevik government confirmed the project of its election by universal suffrage between November 12 and November 18.[24] As is very well known, the Bolsheviks lost the elections whose results were:

Party	Votes[2]	Percent	Deputies
Socialist-Revolutionary Party (SRs)	17,100,000	41.0	380
Bolsheviks	9,800,000	23.5	168
Constitutional Democratic Party (Kadets)	2,000,000	4.8	17
Mensheviks	1,360,000	3.3	18
Others	11,140,000	26.7	120
Total (turnout 48.44%)	41,700,000	100	703

could use the Petrograd and Moscow Soviets, where they had genuine majorities to organize the insurrection. He does not stress the illegality of calling the Second Congress, though harshly criticizes the Bolsheviks for confronting this supposedly supreme body with a fait accompli. Ibid., pp. 194ff.; 206f.

[20] Anweiler, op. cit., pp. 90–91.

[21] Pipes, pp. 483–484; he speaks of Lenin having had to compromise, but is entirely unclear why. In fact the resolution gave free hands to the leadership to decide the question of timing. See Lenin *Selected Works*, vol. II, p. 450.

[22] Pipes, pp. 499–500, initially even the Left Social Revolutionaries who insisted on a coalition government of all socialist parties refused to join. Lenin persuaded them, however, gave them control of five ministries and representation even in the Cheka and this led to a temporary alliance till the Brest-Litovsk treaty the Left SRs violently opposed.

[23] "Decision to Form the Workers' and Peasants' Government" Lenin, *Selected Works*, vol. II, p. 478. This was a decision of the Soviet Congress, possibly formulated by Lenin.

[24] In Petrograd it seems that voting started on the originally scheduled date of November 12, but elsewhere it was delayed for another week, or much longer. See Radkey, op. cit.

From the moment the outcome became known, the constituent assembly was under attack by the new government, depicting it as an institution only of the bourgeois revolution that was about to be transcended in the direction of soviet power and socialist policy.[25] In response, several parties. as well as the Peasant Soviet Congress, launched the slogan "All Power to the Constituent Assembly".[26] The Bolshevik answer was ferocious. At first the meeting of the Assembly was merely postponed, initially indefinitely. One party to be represented, the Kadets, was dissolved.[27] Some delegates were even arrested, and a demonstration supporting the Assembly was fired upon. When all this ran into strong opposition, the government allowed the Assembly to meet on January 18–19, 1918[28], but wished that it constitute nothing, pass no legislation at all, and demanded that a formula be adopted amounting to self-dissolution and transference of authority to the Congress of Soviets with its Bolshevik (and Left SR) majority.[29] When the Assembly majority refused, the Bolshevik and Left SR deputies walked out. This act, only apparently a reversal of the expulsion of the Gironde in 1793 from the *Convention Nationale*,[30] was followed by the forcible closing of the Assembly by troops loyal to the government. There were several subsequent efforts to reconstitute the Constituent Assembly, but they all failed in the face of repression, popular disinterest, internal splits among its adherents and counter-revolutionary manipulation. Meanwhile, in March of 1918, a Third Congress of Soviets, and in June the Fifth Congress, having fully

[25] Lenin Theses on the Constituent Assembly (December 24, 1917), vol. II, p. 506ff.
[26] Lenin Ibid. point 14; Pipes, op. cit., p. 544; Anweiler p. 216 who cites the Menshevik program: "All power in the state belongs to the constituent assembly." Note that in 1905 the Bolsheviks adhered to the same slogan. See *Two Tactics* p.465 that speaks of a "complete transfer of power to a constituent assembly."
[27] W. Rosenberg, *Liberals in the Russian Revolution* (Princeton: Princeton University Press, 1974), pp. 275–278. The voting totals of this party were especially high in Petrograd and Moscow, thus representing a potential challenge to the Bolsheviks.
[28] This took place most likely under the pressure of the Left SR's taken into government to help neutralize peasant self-organization; Pipes, pp. 536–537.
[29] Lenin, *Selected Works*, vol. II, pp. 526–527. The one area where this proposed and rejected resolution would have left some residual powers to the Constituent Assembly was the area of federalism.
[30] For this parallel see Arendt, op. cit., pp. 238–240; F. Furet, *The Passing of an Illusion* (Chicago: University of Chicago Press, 1999), pp. 68 and 71. It should be added that Bukharin apparently sought to repeat the history of 1793 more precisely, by recommending that the Bolshevik and SR minority form a revolutionary convention by purging the rest of the Constituent Assembly. The alternative was rejected by the Bolshevik leadership. See Anweiler, op. cit., pp. 213–214; Pipes, op. cit., p. 545.

absorbed an already rump Congress of Peasant Soviets,[31] proceeded to enact a constitution designed by the experts of the government.[32]

These events, like the purging of the Gironde in 1793, had cataclysmic effects on subsequent Russian history. Not only were there no free elections for more than eighty years, but, even more importantly, the immense majority of the population was made into first a potential, and then an actual enemy of the new regime at least in its formative period, most likely till the German invasion of 1941. As the purging of the Gironde was a coup against not only representative government, but also of Paris against France, so the dissolution of the Constituent Assembly was a devastating attack of people controlling the capital (and Moscow along with a few other cities) against Russia.[33] Initially at least, before the true reactionary color of the counterrevolution showed itself, the loss of peasant support and the turning of the Socialist Revolutionaries into enemies helped to fuel and intensify the civil war.

The great dangers, normative and strategic, of the dissolution of the Constituent Assembly have been repeatedly explained, not only by opponents of the Russian Revolution, but also its critical friends on the left, like Kautsky and Luxemburg. What has not, however, ever been thematized is the role of the constituent assembly form in the very unfortunate history of this type of representative organ in Russia. While clearly it was a dictatorship that destroyed the Constituent Assembly, its own logic too implied what Carl Schmitt called sovereign dictatorship.

Lenin at least had no doubt about this logic. His highly interesting early (1905) views[34] concerning constituent assemblies played an important role in his actions later. He based his conception on Marx, who in 1848 repeatedly

---

[31] Initially, the peasantry was organized in an active All Russian Congress of Peasant Soviets, parallel to the organization of workers and soldiers. When this organization was split, with its left dominated executive committee merging with that of the Congress of Workers and Soldiers Soviets, the peasantry was to lose its direct democratic form of participation, just as it subsequently lost its representation through the dissolution of the Constituent Assembly. Anweiler, pp. 204–206; XXX. The Peasant Soviet Congress dominated by the Bolsheviks continued to meet until finally absorbed in March by the Congress of Workers and Soldiers Deputies, and in June by the Soviets of Workers', Soldiers', and Peasants' Deputies in the new constitution. Pipes, pp. 536–537.

[32] Pipes, op. cit., p. 516.

[33] It proves nothing that under the existing conditions there was no rural mobilization on behalf of the assembly. The peasantry losing democratic rights became a serious matter when the burdens of the modernizing regime were put squarely on this class. The NEP too was probably a failure culminating in several crises, because the government remained illegitimate from the point of view of the peasantry.

[34] "Two Tactics of Social-Democracy in the Democratic Revolution," Selected Works, vol. I, pp. 465–471; 474–475; 495–496; 517.

criticized the Frankfurt Assembly for not exercising dictatorship, and not destroying the power of the Prussian government that remained in position to neutralize the representative body.[35] While highly critical of the actual policies of the contemporary constituent assembly in France, Marx considered it natural that the assembly exercised dictatorship through its general Cavaignac.[36] Lenin thought the context of 1905 in Russia sufficiently parallel to directly apply Marx's reflections to projects of liberals and some of the Left to elect a constituent assembly while the Tsarist government was still intact. Such a government would be able to control the elections, the procedures, the deliberations and the outcome of a constituent assembly.[37] Thus, he claimed that only an insurrection, establishing a provisional government provided the right context for electing a constituent assembly. It was this belief that allowed him to support a constituent assembly after the February revolution of 1917, when the likelihood of Bolshevik taking of power was remote, and, more importantly, to allow the elections after the insurrection of November when his party did control the executive. His belief, that a constituent assembly – its election, composition, deliberations and outcome – would express the will of the government in power remained constant. Nevertheless, it was this belief that was falsified by the elections of 1917–1918.

To save the hypothesis, Lenin followed by Trotsky, produced the following argument that confirms my reconstruction.[38] The reason according to them

[35] "The Crisis and the Counter Revolution" (1848) in Marx and Engels, *The Revolution of 1848–49. Articles from the Neue Rheinische Zeitung* (New York: International, 1972), p. 124: "Every Provisonal political set-up following a revolution calls for dictatorship, and an energetic dictatorship at that."

[36] *The Class Struggles in France 1848–1850* (NewYork: International, 1964).

[37] In 1905, admittedly, following the resolutions of the Third Congress of his party, Lenin conceptualized the control of a revolutionary provisional government in terms of guaranteeing that the elections be fair, and that the assembly be genuinely representative. *Two Tactics*, pp. 467–469. This rhetoric was very much inconsistent with the stress on dictatorship in the same essay, that forshadowed his later views on the topic (ibid., pp. 475, 493–494). By 1917, Lenin's conception of a constituent assembly was to fully shift in an authoritarian direction, with the legitimacy of the assembly (the electoral outcome, the procedures and activity) being defined by adherence to the class based logic and institutional outcome of the revolution. In other words he wished to assert the kind of control that in 1905 he suspected an intact tsarist government would have exercised. The link between the two conceptions was the definition of revolution in terms of one class replacing the domination of another. As long as he understood the revolution as bourgeois (pp. 487–488), he accepted the idea of "free and fair" as the criterion of legitimacy. Once the revolution became socialist or proletarian, this idea seemed to be obsolete.

[38] "Theses on the Constituent Assembly" op. cit., points 5, 6, 11, 15 and 16. The only serious historian of the elections, O.H. Radkey accepts the relevance of the Bolshevik argument, but also turns it against them. What if, he asks, the elections were held much later, when the revolutionary fervor was weakened, soldiers demobilized and the peasants became attached to the private property they initially gained? The decline of the SR depended, he argues, on how

why the Bolsheviks lost the election was because in the country as a whole their taking of power was still not sufficiently known. Moreover electoral PR lists were drawn up before the insurrection, as well as before the splitting of the Social Revolutionary party into Left and Right formations. According to this argument, had the elections been held later, on separated lists, the Bolsheviks and their (very temporary) allies, the Left SRs, would have gained the majority.[39] All this presupposed the thesis that whoever has executive power controls the elections to and the deliberation of a constituent assembly. Nevertheless, Kautsky and Luxemburg could still ask why not in that case have another election of a second constituent after the dissolution of the first[40], as did even France in 1792 when, after a new insurrection, the *Convention Nationale* was elected in the place of the Legislative Assembly. The answer of Lenin and Trotsky was that this was impossible during the civil war that commenced soon after the dissolution,[41] and that in any case the soviets were a superior and more democratic organ than the bourgeois constituent assembly.[42] Yet those who considered the (supposedly) direct democratic soviets to be an important achievement of the revolution did not have to accept this normative counterargument. Without perhaps knowing the Zinoviev and Kamenev case

much they could reorient their policy to defend the new property of their constituents. In any case, the peasant vote would not have gone to the Bolsheviks. In general, Radkey concludes that Russia, in spite of its history, "voted in favor of self government, while the Bolsheviks, although strong were not strong enough to govern 'by other than dictatorial means'. See *Russia Goes to the Polls* (Ithaca: Cornell University Press, 1970), pp. 75–77, 135. In a second edition he also in one place slightly sanitizes the latter phrase to "not strong enough to govern democratically, even if they so desired" (p. 115). It is this version implying perhaps reluctant dictators, who are really democrats, that his new editor, Fitzpatrick prefers (p. xiii).

[39] "It is only a pity that this knowledge was arrived at after one had been left a minority in the Constituent Assembly" Kautsky pointed out; op. cit. Pipes shows that the claim was moreover false, since even the several districts where the Left and Right SRs were on separate lists, the voters overwhelmingly opted for the Right SRs; op. cit., 541. Radkey shows that there were many alternatives for radical peasants on smaller lists, and only where soldiers agitated in their communities did the peasants (always a minority) vote Bolshevik.

[40] As even Lenin initially proposed: "Theses," op.cit.; In this text, Lenin, for one moment, called for electing a new Constituent Assembly, on the bases of an electoral rule provide by the new (Bolshevik dominated) Executive Committee of the Soviets: point 18. See Kautsky, op. cit.; Luxemburg, op. cit.

[41] Trotsky, *Terrorism and Communism*, p. 42ff.

[42] In the resolution drawn up by Lenin, for the Constituent Assembly to pass, new elections were no longer mentioned. This was the first text of the "Declaration of Rights of the Working and Exploited People" rejected by the Constituent Assembly before its dissolution. (January 16) *Selected Works* pp. 526–7. The second version, Article One of the Constitution of 1918 enacted in March no longer mentions even the Constituent Assembly. Finally, the Draft Decree on the Dissolution of the Constituent Assembly (January 19, 1918) dissolved the Assembly, on the bases of the earlier justifications, without further ado. ibid., 530–531.

against the insurrection, Luxemburg went on to fully develop the very important thesis[43] that the Soviets could remain democratic only in combination
with a freely operating representative assembly, but not in the context of a party
exercising dictatorship that made it its business to suppress all other parties as
well as the civil liberties needed for all democratic functioning.[44]

Today we no longer need to demonstrate the great foresight of Rosa Luxemburg's critique of the Russian Revolution. While the relationship of direct
democratic and representative forms remains unresolved to this day, what is
certainly well shown by history is that under one-party dictatorship both representation and direct participation become and remain a sham, with devastating
consequences for the unrepresented as well as the pseudo-participants. This
important problem is not the topic of this Epilogue. I have here only the more
limited purpose of showing that it was very unlikely that a constituent assembly
after the Bolshevik insurrection, under prevailing theoretical assumptions as
well as Russian conditions in 1917 and 1918, should generate either a reasonable
combination of representative and direct democratic forms, or any other form
of constitutional government. The problem, however, was not only with the
very real dictatorial aspirations of the Bolsheviks, but with the revolutionary
constitution making form itself as it was then understood.

---

[43] "The Russian Revolution": chapter 4 op.cit. The important idea of this type of dualistic
democracy has been long dormant. It was revived by Claude Lefort, reflecting on the Hungarian
revolutionary councils of 1956, in "the Age of Novelty," *Telos* (Fall 1976) # 29. We have come
up with a parallel conception of the "plurality of democracies" in Cohen and Arato, *Civil
Society and Political Theory* (Cambridge, MA: MIT Press, 1992).

[44] Admittedly, this position was not consistent with the slogan "All power to the Soviet(s)" that the
Spartacists adopted, following the Bolsheviks. Yet the national conventions and congresses of
the German Räte repeatedly resisted this slogan, and remained firm in their call for a constituent
assembly. See E. Eyck, *A History of the Weimar Republic*, vol. I (New York: Atheneum, 1970),
pp. 49–51; also P. Nettl *Rosa Luxemburg* (Oxford: Oxford University Press, 1969), pp. 464–
468. It is often claimed that once she rejoined her comrades, Luxemburg changed her mind
on the dissolution of the constituent assembly, since she came to strongly oppose calling the
German one. At issue, however, was the not unreasonable fear that in Germany the *Räte* would
be suppressed by a provisional government hostile to them that would control the assembly.
She herself continued to claim that in Russia the situation was different. There she feared and
predicted (rightly!) the instrumentalization and "the crippling" of the Soviets by the Bolsheviks,
with the repression of political life in the country. See P. Nettl, *Rosa Luxemburg* 433–435 vs
452–453. Even in her strongest polemics against the German assembly, Luxemburg considered
such a body as the possible terrain of political conflict between two ideas of the state. As a result,
in the end she spoke in favor of participating in the elections for the constituent assembly, a
proposal of the executive that was turned down by the founding Congress of the KPD. This
time, indeed reversing herself, she argued that it was the Russian example of dissolution that
did not apply in Germany. Reversing also an argument of Lenin, she claimed that precisely
because their majority socialist enemies were in power, the KPD should participate in the
elections, presumably to gain a vantage point. Ibid., 474.

Let me just once again restate the essentials of the form. 1. As in the doctrine of Sieyès and Schmitt, the constituent assembly is a complete and legitimate stand in of the constituent power of the people or the nation in "the state of nature." 2. As the latter, the assembly is under no constitutional rules, and is legally unlimited. 3. As there are no prior procedural rules, a constituent assembly has only the unworkable choice of deciding by unanimity, and the almost inevitable option of making decisions through simple majority. 4. Having electoral legitimacy, the assembly would supersede any previous provisional government produced by the means of an insurrection, and a new one would have to be in effect its own executive committee.

As long as Lenin's prediction concerning the relationship of executive power and constituent assembly was correct, that assembly would have indeed remained merely an expression and an organ of the new revolutionary government.[45] But it was not correct. The elections established an assembly where the Bolsheviks were in a minority. Without any form of pre-existing legal regulation, the Assembly with its new majority had electoral legitimacy, while at the same time the Sovnarkom had both the power and, in the eyes of the armed insurrectionary militants, revolutionary legitimacy. For the moment, the dual power so well described by Trotsky,[46] of provisional government and soviets reappeared, but this time in the form of representative vs. soviet government, the latter controlled by the Bolsheviks. Moreover this time the two slogans "All Power to the Soviets" and "All Power to the Constituent Assembly" implied two claims to sovereign dictatorship, as in Lenin's earlier conception of dual power, that did not correspond to the period between February and October when neither provisional government nor soviets claimed all the power. Between the two claimants of sovereign power it seemed only force could decide.[47] So let us put ourselves for the moment in Lenin's position. Having carried out a victorious insurrection, given his very specific short-term (end the war) and long-term (socialize the means of production) projects of change, was he supposed to hand over power to another majority under no

[45] This is shown by the behavior of the Bolshevik caucus in the Constituent Assembly, many of whose members opposed the dissolution, but fully played along with its scenario. Anweiler, op. cit., p. 212ff.; Pipes, op. cit., pp. 552–555 and first the best description see R.V. Daniels, *The Conscience of the Revolution* (New York: Simon and Schuster, 1969), p. 68.

[46] *The History of the Russian Revolution* (New York: Simon and Schuster, 1936), vol. 1, chapter 11. See also the contrasting views of Anweiler, op. cit., pp. 128–134 and Pipes, op. cit., pp. 323–326.

[47] The idea of two sovereigns aiming at dictatorships facing one another in a revolution, the origin of the idea of dual power, was already in Marx, who thought, however, in terms of the old regime facing the potentially new. As against Lenin, he resolutely took the side of the constituent assembly, and criticized it for not exercising sovereign dictatorship. See "The Crisis in Berlin" in *The Revolution of 1848–49*, p 150 and also pp. 31; 63; 122; and 126.

constitutional limitation? If another election was organized, and the Bolsheviks then lost again as remained likely, was he then to hand over all the power to another majority? And if he won a majority that second time, why would he not use the unlimited power to establish exactly the same type of regime that emerged through the Bolshevik practice, legitimated by a written constitution without constitutionalism similar to the document of 1918?

Has there not been the intention of a revolutionary dictatorship one might very well argue that the form of a constituent assembly could have been used to establish a new republic with representative institutions. But how would that be done? In any case, that very intention was part and parcel not only the Leninist idea of revolution, inherited from a phase of Marx's writings, but also his own ideas of revolution in the weakest, underdeveloped link as well as that of skipping stages of development or the acceleration of historical time. Dictatorship was also understood as inevitable in the face of the friend–enemy relations implied by both the real and the imagined counterrevolution.[48] A long and extended period of parliamentary government was incompatible with that aim, both ideologically and very likely in reality as well. The Bolsheviks were a minority, and if majority rule became the norm they might lose on all their issues. Assuming that some fundamental political role of the soviets needed to be preserved, as even Luxemburg thought, what was the guarantee that the Great Russian Constituent Assembly would any more preserve it than did, in their view, the Weimar National Assembly?[49] It may very well have seemed to Lenin that there was only a choice between a bourgeois republic or the dictatorship disguised as soviet rule, the latter incompatible with a constituent assembly whose majority was elsewhere. Thus, arguably, the legitimate interests of the mobilized minority could no more be reliably protected in Russia in a sovereign constituent assembly, than the economic interests of the Parisian sections who forced the purging of the *Convention Nationale*, or of the mobilized minority in India, where M.A. Jinnah wrecked another constituent assembly that was in the process of asserting its sovereignty.

I am not making a normative argument justifying Lenin, or Hébert and the Enragés, or Jinnah, all of whom contributed to incredible human hardship through their actions. Nor would I insist on a complete parallel among the

---

[48] Trotsky, *Terrorism*, p. 20ff. The counterrevolution was real enough, especially after but not only because of the Kadets who eventually supported it. But the counterrevolutionary aspirations of the other socialist parties were imagined, or constructed. If SRs joined counterrevolutionary efforts, it was with extreme reluctance, and because they were driven to it among other things by the dissolution of the Constituent Assembly.

[49] On this, see below.

cases. In particular, Lenin, who controlled the executive power, was in a good position to negotiate with the majority of the Constituent Assembly, as desired even by many Bolsheviks who were in favor of a broad coalition government. But what form would such negotiations taken and what would be their result when the Constituent Assembly could claim to be under no limits? What I will suggest is that the one important common lesson of all these constitutional crises, and especially that of Russia, is that there was a great need to find a third way between the triumph of the interests of the majority and the minority, between majority or minority imposition, between alternative and incompatible forms of Carl Schmitt's sovereign dictatorship.[50] And as we now know after the South African regime change, the Colombian constituent process and the Tunisian Revolution, all described in this book, that third way must be one that blocks any new force for filling the empty place of the pre-revolutionary form of power.[51]

So to partially paraphrase Lenin: What could have been done? As Renata Segura has stressed in several writings comparing Colombia and Venezuela, the key is the pre-assembly moment.[52] In the case of a revolutionary break, this moment has two components: the formation of an inclusive provisional government and the creation of rules for a constituent (constitutional!) assembly.[53] In the Russian case only the first of these issues came up, but it was very important. After the October insurrection, many parties in the Soviets as well as many Bolsheviks proposed and even demanded a genuine coalition government, including at least all the socialist parties.[54] While the Bolshevik claim that this was offered and rejected by all, except eventually and briefly the Left SRs, seems not to be in good faith,[55] the many walkouts of the other parties from the Bolshevik and Left SR majority soviets seem to confirm it. Yet such a coalition government could have united around many, if not all the socialist projects of the government. If coupled with joint control over the forces of violence, a coalition would have represented a guarantee against unilateral action such as the banning of individual parties (first the Kadets, the liberal

---

[50] Lenin thought of dual power as two dictatorships confronting one another, and undoubtedly he thought that exactly such a confrontation could be reproduced by the Constituent Assembly and the government in different hands. See the remarks on dual power in *Selected Works*, pp. 48ff and 55–56.

[51] Lefort, *Democracy and Political Theory*.   [52] See chapter 4 above.

[53] The third component, the formation of an apex court enforcing agreements seems to be relevant so far only to the post revolutionary scenario of central Europe and South Africa, but not to the more revolutionary one of Colombia and Tunisia. On this, see chapters 4 and 5.

[54] On the failed coalition attempts of 1917, and the relevant struggle within the Bolshevik Party, see Daniels, op. cit., pp. 63–66.

[55] Lenin, *Selected Works*, p. 485.

Constitutional Democrats, followed by all the others) and the dissolution of the Constituent Assembly. But on its own even this step may not have been enough to prevent the re-emergence of a destructive form of dual power with the formation of the assembly under majoritarian assumptions.[56] Perhaps the outcome would have been failure only, but under the circumstances that would have been bad enough.

Thus, the second dimension of the pre-assembly moment should have been comprehensive negotiations among the major parties producing procedural rules for a non-sovereign, i.e., limited constituent assembly. This would have taken the place of the one-sided Bolshevik declarations of "self-limitation," implying total surrender of power by the Assembly, which the government tried to unsuccessfully foist on that body before its dissolution.[57] Such rules could have involved voting by proportional representation, differentiation of the constituent assembly from other modes of power, making constitutional decisions at least by high qualified majorities, and ratification by organized bodies. Together, they could have removed the twin dangers of governmental domination of, and majoritarian imposition, on the part of the assembly. The first of these rules, PR, was realized in Russia, resulting in a constituent assembly where no single party could have the majority. But, admittedly, a coalition of SRs and Mensheviks could have achieved a dominant position in the body. If dealing with the very same issues, the conflict between government and assembly could have continued despite the participation of some of the same parties in both, as it did under the last phase of the pre October dual power system. Thus, it would have been all-important to formally separate the constituent from the other powers, and to confine the Constituent Assembly to and only to the task of constitution making. This was possible, by agreeing that for the period of constitution making, responsible government would be rooted not in the constituent assembly but in the soviets, whose Congress has been rightly described as itself a legitimate parliamentary body.[58] Such a double differentiation was incompatible with either of the two slogans, "all power to the soviets" or "all power to the constituent assembly." But it would

---

[56] Anweiler, op. cit., 133–134 rightly stresses that in the earlier period before October the inclusion of soviet-based socialist ministers in the provisional government did not mitigate the problems of dual power, I would add as long as the jurisdiction of the powers was not constitutionally regulated.

[57] Ibid., 525–527. This Declaration amounted to little more than a diktat to the Constituent Assembly, even if for a moment the Assembly was supposedly left to decide the principles of the Federation that it was forced to declare. That freedom could not be taken seriously under the circumstances.

[58] Anweiler, op. cit., p. 112.

have provided a solution to a problem that already concerned Sieyès and Condorcet, but was almost never solved under revolutionary conditions, namely how to introduce the separation of powers via double differentiation into the constitution-making process.[59] In addition, making constitutional decisions by high qualified majority would have forced both majority and minority to compromise on substance, as previously on procedures. In Russia, for example, under the conditions of high-level self-organization in factories, parts of the countryside, and military units, it is highly likely that the parliamentary parties, whose interest, of course, pointed to representative democracy, could have come to a dualistic compromise with the more radical parties speaking for the soviets. Actually, much of the assembly could have also agreed on some substantive issues like land reform, workers' control in the factories, and federalism. Indeed, the majority of the assembly though critical of the Bolshevik, was in favor of forms of direct democracy. An institutional outcome that found an important place for the soviets, would have been especially likely "under the shadow" of the ratification of a constitution by the lowest-level worker, peasant and soldier councils.[60] Certainly, the chances of a dualistic democracy that institutionalized and domesticated dual power would have been much higher than the preservation of direct democracy under the conditions of a one-party dictatorship.

---

[59] It was not solved in Tunisia under revolutionary conditions. In Iraq the attempt of the CPA to impose a caucus system for electing a provisional parliament failed, and in Nepal the re-call of a dissolved parliament led to very negative consequences. See chapters 2, 4 and 5 above. The one major exception in a revolution, was the making of the Weimar Republic, where under the appropriately titled interim constitution, concerning "temporary Reichsgwalt" (Eyck = "sovereignty"; Mommsen = "national power") the National Constituent Assembly gave itself the exclusive constitution making power (with limits concerning the territory of the states), but required all other laws to be approved by the States Committee [Staatenauschuß] that represented the parliaments of the states, elected more or less at the same time. See "Gesetz über die vorläufige Reichsgewalt" vom 10. Februar 1919 https://de.wikisource.org/wiki/Gesetz_%C3%BCber_die_vorl%C3%A4ufige_Reichsgewalt (accessed October 20, 2016) See E. Eyck *A History of the Weimar Republic* pp. 62–63; Mommsen *Weimar Democracy* 54–5. But here, the provisional government was responsible to the National Assembly, necessarily, since unlike in Russia the peak organizations of the councils no longer played a national role, after they repeatedly opted for the constituent assembly, and sovereignty was transferred by them to the latter.

[60] Such desirable and very possible form of ratification, resembling that by the town assemblies of Massachusetts and New Hampshire in the 1780s, was strikingly not utilized even for the passing of the Constitution by the Fifth Congress of Soviets in June of 1918. Nor was this form insisted on in Germany at the time, since there was a supposedly full transfer of sovereignty from the Congress of Councils to the National Assembly.

Let me consider an instructive example, which could be used to throw doubt upon the chances of incorporating some of the institutions of revolution under constitutionalism.[61] I have in mind the German Revolution of 1918, whose main political agents in the beginning were worker, soldier and even peasant councils, where their peak executive organizations and congresses opted for a constituent assembly rather than a republic of soviets (*Räterepublik*), and where the political dualism institutionalized by the National (Constituent) Assembly was not between parliament and councils, but, if at all then between the presidency and parliament.[62] Does this outcome indicate that the choice in Russia as well as Germany could only be between soviets and parliament? While there were many similarities between these cases, there were also important differences. The most important one was that the German developments occurred a year later, in full view of the developments in Russia, and where as a result the political idea of council democracy, whether monistic or dualistic, was widely discredited, or defeated. Before even the meeting of the National Assembly a large number of council movements linked to a variety of ideologies and programs were physically repressed. Moreover, on the level of the parties, not counting the small minority of the Spartacists or KPD that argued for "All power to the soviets" a slogan repeatedly rejected by the councils themselves, it was also a relative minority, the independent socialists or USPD, that repeatedly argued for a dualistic version with the primacy of the *Räte*.[63] The much larger majority socialists or MSPD along with the so-called bourgeois parties that were their coalition partners opposed any political role for the councils, and wished to abolish their peak organizations once the Constituent Assembly was in session.[64] The main unions moreover, much more powerful than in Russia, wished to limit even the economic role of workplace councils. In Russia, by contrast, there was little opposition on that latter score, and even more importantly all the socialist parties were friendly to the soviets and, with the exception of the top leadership of the Bolsheviks, could very easily accept

---

[61] Arendt does refer to this case, but only to show the incompatibility of parties and councils, and to seemingly reject constituent assemblies where parties are present and active. See op. cit., pp. 254 and 255.

[62] For a full discussion, see Mommsen, op. cit.

[63] See N. Reich, *Labor Relations in Republican Germany. An Experiment in Industrial Democracy* (Oxford: Oxford University Press, 1938), p. 29; Nettl, op. cit., p. 448.

[64] This may have been the background of Arendt's hostility to political parties as such supported by many absurd and wrong arguments (op.cit. pp 238ff.; 255–260), notwithstanding her adherence to a formula of constitutionalism cum councils. But there can be no modern constitutionalism linked to freedoms of assembly, association and press that eliminates political parties. It is simply not true that multi-partyism has the same logic as one party regimes.

the institutionalization of dualism that would favor their survival. Finally, while all provisional revolutionary governments in Germany were coalitions, before and after the elections for and the meeting of the National Assembly, nevertheless in the government responsible to that body the advocates of local and industrial democracy were weak. Thus, in summary, the position of the councils in the comparable stages of the two revolutions was much weaker in Germany than in Russia, before and not merely because of the election of the respective constituent assemblies.

And yet the Weimar National Assembly was capable of generating legitimate compromise, as it did on the issue of federalism that was formally parallel to the issue of direct democracy.[65] Amazingly enough, this willingness touched even the matter of the councils, at least after a strike movement moved the issue back unto the Assembly's agenda.[66] The final constitutional draft enacted a provision, Article 165, which could have become a focal point for expanding the powers of the councils. The article provided for[67] not only worker and

---

[65] Formally parallel, because local democracy and industrial democracy are themselves analogous, with one involving territorial, the other functional forms of autonomy and self-organization. Both require a federal form, and indeed all the peak council organizations in Russia as well as Germany were federations. Only Arendt, op. cit., pp. 237 and 259 seems to recognize this point, though she stubbornly and wrongly insists on the territorial nature of the councils, rejecting their economic role. Thus she would have considered Article 165 to amount to the depolitization of the councils, as against their institutionalization. Moreover, apparently forgetting her critique of the dilemmas of representation (pp. 229f.), she never seemed to realize that the (bad)bchoice between imperative mandate and unbound representation, supposedly soved by the direct democracy of grassroots councils, would return also for a council peak organizations, Congresses, Executives or whatever.

[66] Reich, *Labor Relations in Republican Germany*, p. 43. The first draft of the Constitution according to Reich neglected industrial democracy, but this omission was compensated for in the second draft, and its Articles 159 and 165.

[67] **Article 165**:

Workers and employees are called upon to participate, on an equal footing and in cooperation with the employers, in the regulation of wages and working conditions as well as in the economic development of productive forces. The organizations formed by both sides and their mutual agreements are recognized.

Workers and employees are granted, in order to represent their social and economic interests, legal representations in Enterprise Workers' Councils as well as in District Workers' Councils, organized for the various economic areas, and in a Reich workers' council.

District workers' councils and the Reich workers' council, in order to fulfil the economic tasks and to execute the socialization laws in cooperation with the employers, join District economic councils and a Reich Economic Council, in which the employers' representatives and other concerned circles also participate.

The district economic councils and the Reich economic council are to be organized in such a way, that all important professions are represented according to their economic

employee councils in all economic units (enterprises and districts) with important responsibilities in determining wages and working conditions, but united them in a peak organization of a National (Reich) Worker's Council. Even more importantly, the provision sought to establish A National Economic Council (*Reichswirtschaftsrat*), in principle a third parliamentary chamber, which was to approve and even propose economic legislation.[68] This body was to unite the Worker's Council and parallel organizations of other economic interests, like the employers, consumers and economic experts.[69] Admittedly, subsequent developments, agreements between the unions and the employers, and especially the Factory Council Law of late 1919, reduced many of these functions to a mere formality and, on the higher levels, to even less.[70] But this happened because of the opposition of the SPD and unions that would have had to play a major role to actualize the meaning of the provision, as well as the disinterest of the left that aimed at either a pure soviet system (Left of the USPD) or a party dictatorship a la Russe (KPD). My point here is not that a dualistic system could have been institutionalized and developed in

and social importance Basic law drafts of social-political and economic character are to be presented by the Reich government to the Reich Economic Council for approval, before they are presented to Reichstag. The Reich Economic Council is entitled to propose such law drafts. If the Reich government does not approve to such a draft, it has to present the draft to Reichstag, accompanied by an explanation of its diverting position. The Reich economic council is entitled to have one of its members represent the draft in the Reichstag.

Supervision and administration authority may be transferred to the workers' and economic councils within the area they are responsible for.

The regulation of consistence and tasks of the workers' and economic councils, as well as their relation to other bodies of self-administration is exclusively a Reich matter. http://www.zum.de/psm/weimar/weimar_vve.php#Fifth Chapter: The Economy.

[68] Reich, *Labor Relations in Republican Germany*, pp. 44–45; Mommsen, pp. 59–60. A similar body was recently established by statute, along with the South African Interim Constitution: the National Economic, Development and Labour Council (NEDLAC). See H. Klug, *Constituting Democracy* (Cambridge: Cambridge University Press, 2000), pp. 121–122. Such bodies have been established by statute in many European countries. But the Constitution of Slovenia has gone even further, in establishing a second chamber, called National Council that is in part (18 out of 40 deputies) an economic chamber with some significant powers. See: Constitution of Slovenia Articles 96–7. http://www.us-rs.si/media/constitution.pdf. These powers, including the ability to call for referendum and a suspensive veto, were reduced by amendment in 2013. The National Council had no role in constitutional amendments, a grave omission on the part of its original advocates.

[69] There were supposed to be district workers councils and economic councils as well. But only at the local or plant level were Workers Councils ever constituted, playing important but limited roles. See Reich, op. cit., chapters 5 and 6, especially 157ff.

[70] Mommsen, op. cit., p. 80; and Reich, op. cit., chapter 2.

the face of the opposition of most socialists in Germany or, for that matter, the Communists in Russia, but that it depended on radical socialists, in Russia the Bolsheviks or a Bolshevik-led coalition, as well as the activists of the council movements themselves, whether the constituent assembly could generate a viable, and normatively attractive, framework bringing together council self-government and democratic parliamentary representation.

Of course, even serious pre-constituent attempts at the formation of a coalition government and the initiation of negotiation and compromise may all fail, as they dramatically failed in India. There too, as in Russia, sovereigntist assumptions on both sides defeated the pre-constituent moment.[71] But now we have learned that such attempts can also succeed.[72] We cannot, of course, undo the consequences of the wrong turn of the Russian Revolution, embedded in Russia's past, but we can still preserve ourselves from such predictable disasters in the future. In that effort post revolution rather than classical revolutionary scenarios ought to be our guide.

For more than two hundred years, radical change has been under the star of the French Revolution. The Russian Revolution that continued and radicalized its great predecessor's logic has become an equally important model through most of the twentieth century. If anything, the consequences were now more devastating than before. While liberal thought came to reject both French and Russian revolutionary models,[73] it took the emergence of new forms of change from the 1970s to the 1990s to help conceive radical alternatives without the danger of classical revolutions. From the point of view of *post revolution*, constitution making and its failure have become visible as one of the main reasons for the authoritarian consequences of revolution. This can be seen studying the history of both French and Russian Revolutions. Even as revolutions continue in our time, learning the lessons of post-revolutionary changes of regime is one important way to guard these forms of radical transformation from their worst tendencies. As Condorcet

---

[71] See chapter 4 above.

[72] This is shown by the recent example of Nepal, where a Leninist party, the Communist Party of Nepal, or CPN (Maoist) showed that it could fully participate in a post-sovereign constituent process. See Chapter 4 above. I have had a chance to publically discuss this problem with PM Pushpa Kamal Dahal (Prachanda) after the elections, but before the meeting of the Nepal Constituent Assembly, in New York, on September 26, 2008. http://www.newschool.edu/news/archives/2008/20080915.aspx. For one of the many transcripts of both of our remarks on the internet, see http://z11.invisionfree.com/Kasama_Threads/ar/t280.htm. In this transcript at least his answers to me, that were quite satisfactory as well as knowledgable are not recorded. See Appendix below for what I said.

[73] See F. Furet, *Interpreting the French Revolution* (Cambridge: Cambridge University Press, 1982), part I.

imagined, revolution should be institutionalized and legalized rather than rejected altogether. Yet even he thought this possible only under constitutions, or when change occurs from one constitutional ("free") regime to another. The new paradigm of constitution making represents attempts to accomplish the same feat during the very foundation of constitutional government, during the transition from authoritarian to democratic rule. Post revolution and post sovereign constitution making are our best hope of humanizing the adventures of the constituent power that will inevitably continue for a long time to come.

APPENDIX (REMARKS ON SEPTEMBER 26, 2008, AT THE NEW SCHOOL
FOR SOCIAL RESEARCH, NEW YORK)

. . . . his excellency Prime Minister Pushpa Kamal Dahal, much better known as Prachanda, as I may refer to him if he permits, is the democratically elected head of government of the Federal Democratic Republic of Nepal. His party, the Communist Party of Nepal or CPN (Maoist), has received in an earlier election in 2008 roughly 30% of the votes and 38% of the seats, both pluralities, but not majorities in combined first [past-the-post] and proportional combined voting.

He is the first self-declared Maoist who has been chosen in democratic elections and parliamentary process, to head a coalition government, and, quite strikingly, since Lenin he is the first Leninist and perhaps revolutionary Marxist to head the executive power in the face of a democratically elected Constituent Assembly. As in the case of Lenin, who headed a coalition government narrower than Prachanda's, his party too is in the minority in the assembly, even though, in distinction from the Bolsheviks, it is the largest single party. Before asking him whether under any conditions he might wish to follow the actions of Lenin, who wound up dismissing the constituent assembly by force, it is well worth considering Prachanda's quite different constitutional situation.

Prachanda and the CPN (Maoist), clearly revolutionaries who have engaged in a long insurrection, do not come to power in a revolution whether internally or externally imposed. The national specificities characteristic of Nepal, the radical political transformation that took place in that country, belongs to the type of negotiated transition of regime change, first experimented in Spain in the 1970s, further developed in Europe in the late 1980s and 1990s and perfected in South Africa in the mid-1990s. The key elements of this process are civil society mobilization and pressure, negotiations among the major political actors, the creation of an interim constitution that brings provisional government under the rule of law and constitutionalism, and election of a constitutional assembly that is itself under rules, and is not sovereign in the sense of the classical European tradition since 1789 that is still assumed by all Russian revolutionaries.

Without underestimating the bravery and influence of insurrectionary activity of the CPN (Maoist) for over a decade or more that helped initiate the process, it remains hard to dispute that the transformation that led to today's constitutional assembly began with a negotiated agreement between that party, the CPN(Maoist) and Nepal's several liberal and reformist parties in 2005. (In New Delhi, actually). From that point on, the non-violent, broad-based civil society-based initiatives and movements culminating in the popular movement in 2006 that put an end to the King's dictatorship, were much more important than any insurrectionary activity. And even more crucial, the negotiation of an interim constitution by an eight party alliance squarely took Nepal out of the tradition of revolutionary transformations and established a Nepali version of a negotiated transition, that continues to this day.

Though there has been severe conflict and even bloodshed, what is even more remarkable is how the main political actors ultimately adhered to this chosen paradigm, repeatedly renegotiating it when new actors and new claims appeared without ever abandoning it. At the head of a revolutionary party that possesses its own insurrectionary forces and means of violence, I think Prachanda and his colleagues deserve special praise for self-limitation within such a peaceful regime change process possible.

The process I briefly described puts him and his government in a very different, though hardly less complex, constitutional situation than the one faced by Lenin in early 1918. The Nepali constitutional assembly is not a sovereign one, it is itself under constraining constitutional rules. It could and it already did change those rules but it requires two thirds majority to do so. But no party has more than 38%, and no two parties – even together have the two thirds needed to change the interim constitution.

This is not the situation in which Lenin found himself in early 1918. We will never know whether he dissolved the constituent assembly because he could not impose his will without a Bolshevik majority, or because he feared there was a majority of the peasant-based revolutionary party that could alone dominate the assembly and the process. We do not know how he would have acted in other words in Prachanda's place, especially since a minority of Bolshevik leaders were opposed to the action against the assembly. Prachanda also does not have the majority to impose his own constitutional ideals, but unlike Lenin he has more than the required one-third vote under the rules to stop any constitutional provision, or any draft as a whole from passing. He is in a position to work on a constitutional compromise on favorable terms to his side, but not to impose on the majority or even large minority any constitutional solutions that they cannot possibly accept.

If he is satisfied with that, he will not have to resort to Lenin's solution even if he wanted to, and was in a political-military position to be able to, and I doubt, as far as he is personally concerned, that he wants to or is in the political military situation to be able to.

So what kind of constitution will Prachanda and his party actually try to achieve, and what kind of constitution can they achieve? The party remains a radical party of the Left, yet following a social democratic strategy in many ways. Yet the kind of change Prachanda and his CPN(M) wish to lead is probably far more thorough and more far-reaching than any historical social democracy that was in power. Here I am certainly not any kind of expert, but I do believe Nepali society does need radical social and economic change, and the CPN(M) owes its support for having effectively represented it. But many who want that kind of change think in terms of decentralizing, federalizing, pluralizing previous state authority and for a left party the agency through which change can be achieved is always been through central state power. I see three areas where Prachanda will have to clarify, not only to us, but to himself and to the Nepali electorate, what he and his party are trying to establish: the structure of the state, the structure of government, and the structure of elections.

As to the structure of the state, almost everyone is now committed in Nepal to some kind of federalism in a previously centralized state. But what kind of federalism? Geographically or ethnically based? And with how many units? And how will the power of the center and the new units be distributed? Will the central state retain enough power to accomplish the changes the CPN(M) is committed to?

Regarding the structure of government: the amendments to the interim constitution produced a parliamentary structure with a weak president elected by parliament. It is to the significant credit to Prachanda that he democratically accepted the defeat of his party's candidate in elections for that position, for president. But now, will he be tempted to write in the new constitution popularly elected Presidents, either with or without significant powers, which in either case could become a threat to the democratic order under crisis conditions. On that we have the authority of the Marx of the 18th Brumaire. And yet in the new republic there must be a strong temptation to fill the empty place of the king with the figure of a democratic [?] leader. In India too there have been attempts, so far failures fortunately, to introduce presidential government with extra-ordinary powers. We see the results of such populism in some of the South American Andean republics that have made new presidential constitutions and processes and the results that should not be, and have not been so far, the models for Nepal's efforts.

Finally, still under the veil of ignorance is CPN Maoist's push for a system of pure proportional representation. As an unexpected gift of some opponents, the first past the post seats were increased, and it turned out that the CPN Maoists party took 30% of the votes and gets a pretty big surplus of seats, in such an Anglo-American type system. Prachanda in an interview now dreams of getting two-thirds in the next election, and perhaps 90% in the one after that. These are still traditional Leninist dreams. (Laughter) And I think he will find that if votes and elections are kept free and fair in a divided society like Nepal, where all reforms will have losers as well as winners, it will be tough to go over 40%. But under some electoral rules, even such a percentage could lead to two-thirds the seats, if not the votes. Prachanda must seriously consider whether he and his party should not return to principled position returned to under the veil of ignorance, i.e., proportional representation that will continue to allow, unlike first past the post, for the largest number of Nepali political forces to remain represented.

Undoubtedly, the audience would add other questions to these and it would certainly interesting to hear Prachanda speak about his plans for the constitutional assembly. But for now, welcome and congratulations, and may the political transformation of Nepal that has created a democratic constitutional republic continue with the same success as before.

References

A note on references: The following list refers only to the published sources, including published pamphlets, used for this research. References to other archival sources – including draft laws, bills, petitions, legal submissions, documents from the case files, interview transcripts, newspaper reports and other unpublished materials – appear in the footnotes of the individual chapters of this book.

Ackerman, Bruce. *The Future of the Liberal Revolution*. New Haven: Yale University Press, 1994.
  "The Rise of World Constitutionalism." *Virginia Law Review* 83, no. 4 (1997): 771–797.
  We the People, Volume 2: Transformations. Cambridge, MA: Harvard University Press, 2000.
  We the People: Foundations. Cambridge University Press, 1991.
Adams, W.P. *The First American Constitutions*. Lanham, MD: Rowman & Littlefield, 2001.
Adhikari, A. *The Bullet and the Ballot Box. The Story of Nepal's Maoist Revolution*. London: Verso, 2014.
Al Ali, Zaid. *The Struggle for Iraq's Future: How Corruption, Incompetence and Sectarianism have Undermined Democracy*. New Haven, CT: Yale University Press, 2014.
  "The New Egyptian Constitution: an Initial Assessment of its Merits and Flaws," *Open Democracy*, 2012.
  "Egypt's Third Constitution in Three Years: a Critical Analysis," *Constitutionnet*, December 20, 2013.
Albert, Richard. "Constitutional Handcuffs," *Ariz. St. LJ*, 42 (2010): 671–672.
  "Nonconstitutional Amendments" *The Canadian Journal of Law and Jurisprudence*, 22 (2009): 5–47.
  "The Structure of Constitutional Amendment Rules," *Wake Forest Law Review* 49 (2014): 913-at.
Amar, Akhil. "Popular Sovereignty and Constitutional Amendment." In Amar Akhil and Sanford Levinson, *Responding to Imperfection: The Theory and Practice of Constitutional Amendment*. Princeton, NJ: Princeton University Press, 1995, pp. 89–115.

Ambedkar, B.R. "Basic Features of the Indian Constitution" in V. Rodrigues ed., *The Essential Writings of B.R. Ambedkar*. New Delhi: Oxford University Press, 2002.

Anweiler, Oskar. *The Soviets: The Russian Workers, Peasants, and Soldiers Councils, 1905–1921*. New York: Pantheon Books, 1975.

Arjomand, Said Amir. *The Turban for the Crown*. Oxford: Oxford University Press, 1988.

"The Islam and Democracy Debate After 2011," *Constellations* 20(2) (2013): 302–303.

Arato, Andrew. "A magyar közjogi rendszer két súlyos fogyatékossága," *Magyar Hirlap* 1994, May 30.

Civil Society, Constitution and Legitimacy. Lanham, MD: Rowman & Littlefield, 2000.

"Civil Society Against the State: Poland 1980–81," *Telos* 47 (1981): 23–47.

Crisis of Parliamentary Democracy. Cambridge, MA: MIT Press, 1994.

"Democratic Constitution-Making and Unfreezing the Turkish Process," *Philosophy & Social Criticism*, 36(3–4) (2010): 473–487.

"Framed. America's 51 Constitutions and the Crisis of Governance. By Sanford Levinson. Oxford: Oxford University Press, 2012." *Constellations* 20, no. 3 (2013): 503–507.

"Good-bye to Dictatorships?," *Social Research*, 67(4) (Winter 2000).

"International Role in State-Making in Ukraine: The Promise of a Two-Stage Constituent Process," *German Law Journal* 16 (2015).

"Multi-Track Constitutionalism Beyond Carl Schmitt," *Constellations* 18(3) (2011): 324–351.

"Political Theology and Populism," *Social Research* 80(1) (2013).

"Post-Sovereign Constitution-Making in Hungary: After Success, Partial Failure, Now What?," *South African Journal on Human Rights*, Vol. 26, Part I, 2010.

"The Roundtables, Democratic Institutions and the Problem of Justice," In András Bozóki, ed. *The Roundtable Talks of 1989: The Genesis of Hungarian Democracy. Analysis and Documents*. Budapest: Central European University Press, 2002.

"Választás, koalició és alkotmány." In *Civil társadalom forradalom és alkotmány*. Budapest: Új mandátum, 1999, pp. 17–34.

Arato, Andrew & Jean Cohen. "Banishing the Sovereign? Internal and External Sovereignty in Arendt," *Constellations* 16(2) (2009): 307–330.

Civil Society and Political Theory. Cambridge, MA: MIT Press; 1992.

Arato, A. and Z. Miklosi "Constitution Making and Transitional Politics in Hungary." in Laurel E. Miller, and Louis Aucoin, eds. *Framing the State in Times of Transition: Case Studies in Constitution Making*. Washington: USIP, 2010, pp. 350–390.

Arato, Andrew and E. Tombuş. "Learning from Success, Learning from Failure: South Africa, Hungary, Turkey and Egypt," *Philosophy & Social Criticism*. 2013.

Arendt, Hannah. *On Revolution* New York: Viking, 1963.

Atkinson, Doreen. "Brokering a Miracle? The Multiparty Negotiating Forum," *South African Review* 7 (1994): 13–43.

Austin, Granville. *The Indian Constitution*. Delhi: Oxford University Press, 1999.

Working a Democratic Constitution: A History of the Indian Experience. Oxford University Press, USA, 2003.

Awad, Ibrahim. "Breaking out of Authoritarianism: 18 Months of Political Transition in Egypt," *Constellations* 20(2) (2013): 275–292.

"Postscript," *Constellations*, 20(2) (2013): 293–296.

Baduel, P. "Le temps insurrectionnel comme "moment politique". Tunisie 2011," *Revue internationale de politique comparée* 2/2013 (Vol. 20): 33–61.

Baker, Keith. *Inventing the French Revolution*. New York: Cambridge University Press, 1990.

"Sieyès" and "Sovereignty" In François Furet and Mona Ozouf, *A Critical Dictionary of the French Revolution*. Harvard University Press, 1989.

Bamyeh, Mohammed, and Sari Hanafi. "Introduction to the Special Issue on Arab Uprisings," *International Sociology* 344(4). (2015): 343–347.

Bastid, Paul. *Sieyès et sa pensée*. Paris, 1939.

Beaud, Olivier. *La puissance de l'état*. Paris: PUF, 1994.

Théorie de la Fédération. Paris: Presses Universitaires de France-PUF, 2007

Bensel, R. *Yankee Leviathan: The Origins of Central State Authority in America, 1859–1877*. New York: Cambridge University Press, 1990.

Bernal-Pulido, C. "Unconstitutional Constitutional Amendments in the Case Study of Colombia: An Analysis of the Justification and Meaning of the Constitutional Replacement Doctrine." *International Journal of Constitutional Law*, 11(2): 339–357.

Bernard-Maugiron, N. "Personal Status Law in Egypt." *Promotion of Women's Rights*. Egypt. 2010.

Bernhard, M. and J. Kubik. *Twenty Years After Communism: The Politics of Memory and Commemoration*. Oxford: Oxford University Press, 2014.

Bishara, M. *The Invisible Arab: The Promise and Peril of the Arab Revolutions*. New York: Nation Books, 2013.

Blackstone, W. *Commentaries on the Laws of England*. Chicago: University of Chicago, 2002.

Böckenförde, E.-W. 'Die verfassunggebende Gewalt des Volkes – Ein Grenzbegriff des Verfassungsrechts' in *Staat, Verfassung, Demokratie*. Frankfurt: Suhrkamp, 1991.

Bonime-Blanc, A. *Spain's Transiton to democracy*. Boulder, CO: Westview Press, 1987.

"Constitution Making and Democratization. The Spanish Paradigm" in Laurel E. Miller and Louis Aucoin, eds., *Framing the State in Times of Transition: Case Studies in Constitution Making*. Washington, DC: US Institute of Peace Press, 2010.

Boraine, A. *A Country Unmasked. Inside South Africa's Truth and Reconciliation Commission*. Oxford: Oxford University Press, 2000.

Bozóki, A. et. al. eds, *A rendszerváltás forgatókönyve*. Budapest: CEU Press, 2000.

The Roundtable Talks of 1989: The Genesis of Hungarian Democracy. Budapest: CEU Press, 2002.

Bracher, K.D. *The German Dictatorship*. New York: Penguin, 1970.

Braver, Joshua. "We, the Mediated People: Revolution, Inclusion, and Unconventional Adaptation in the Creation of Post-Cold War S. American Constitutions," *Yale Law School Doctoral Dissertation*.

Brewer-Carías, Allan R. *Dismantling Democracy in Venezuela: The Chávez Authoritarian Experiment*. Cambridge University Press, 2010.

Brown, Nathan J. "Egypt: A Constitutional Court in an Unconstitutional Setting." In J.O. Frosini and F. Biagi, *Political and Constitutional Transitions in North Africa*. New York: Routledge, 2015), p. 33.

Brown, Nathan J. and Clark Lombardi. "Islam in Egypt's New Constitution," *Foreign Policy*, December 13, 2012.

Buchanan, Allen. *Secession and Self Determination*. New York: NYU, 2003.

Calda, M. "The Roundtable Talks in Czechoslovakia" in Jon Elster, ed., *The Roundtable Talks and the Breakdown of Communism*. Chicago: University of Chicago Press, 1996.

Calhoun, John Caldwell, and Ross M. Lence. *Union and liberty: The political philosophy of John C. Calhoun*. New York: Liberty Fund Inc., 1992.

Canovan, M. *The People*. London: Polity, 2005.

Casanova, Jose "A spanyolországi demokratikus átalakulás tanulságai" in A. Bozóki, et al. eds., *A rendszerváltás forgatókönyve*, vol. VII. Budapest: CEU Press, 2000, p. 682.

Carré de Malberg, Raymond. *Contribution à la générale Théorie de l Etat*. Paris: Dalloz, 2004.

Challand, Benoît. "Citizenship Against the Grain: Locating the Spirit of the Arab Uprisings in Times of Counterrevolution," *Constellations*, 20(2) (2013): 169–187.

Childs, D. *The Fall of the GDR*. London: Longman, 2001.

Choudhry, Sujit, and Richard Stacey. "Semi-presidentialism as a Form of Government: Lessons for Tunisia," *Center for Constitutional Transitions*. 2013.

Christodoulidis, E. and S. Veitch "Reconciliation as Surrender: Configurations of Responsibility and Memory" in François Du Bois and Antje Du Bois-Pedain. *Justice and Reconciliation in Post-apartheid South Africa*. Cambridge University Press, 2008, pp. 9–36.

Cohen, Jean L. *Globalization and Sovereignty. Rethinking Legality, Legitimacy and Constitutionalism*. Cambridge: Cambridge University Press, 2012.

Cole, J. "Egypt's New Left Versus the Military Junta," *Social Research*, 79(2) (2012): 487–510.

Colon-Rios, J. *Weak Constitutionalism*. London: Routledge, 2012.

"Rousseau, Theorist of the Constituent Power" (forthcoming in 2017 in the *Oxford Journal of Legal Studies*).

Condorcet, N. *"Discours sur les conventions nationales"* [August 7, 1791] in *Oeuvres*, vol. X. Stuttgart-Bad Cannstatt, 1968. *Selected Writings*. Indianapolis: Bobbs Merrill, n.d.

Condren, Conal and Lawson, George. *Lawson: Politica Sacra et Civilis*. Cambridge: Cambridge University Press, 1992.

Cristi, Renato. "Schmitt on Constituent Power and the Monarchical Principle," *Constellations* 18(3) (2011): 352–364.

Davis, D. and M. le Roux. *Precedent and Possibility. The (Ab)use of Law in South Africa*. Capetown: Double Storey Books, 2009.

Derrida, Jacques. "Declarations of Independence," *New Political Science* 7(1) (1986): 7–15.

Dicey, Albert Venn. *The Law of the Constitution*, 8th ed. [1915].Indianapolis: Liberty Fund, 1982.

Di Palma, G. *To Craft Democracies: an Essay on Democratic Transitions*. Berkeley: University of California Press, 1990.

Dixon, R., and Landau, D. 'Transnational Constitutionalism and a Limited Doctrine of Unconstitutional Constitutional Amendment,' *International Journal of Constitutional Law*, (2015). 13(3): 606–638.

Dow, D. "The Plain Meaning of Article V." In Sanford Levinson ed., *Responding to imperfection: the theory and practice of constitutional amendment*. Princeton, NJ: Princeton University Press, 1995.

Du Bois, Francois and Du Bois-Pedain eds. *Justice and Reconciliation in Post Apartheid South Africa*. Cambridge: Cambridge University Press, 2008.

Du Bois-Pedain, Antje. "Communicating Criminal and Political Responsibility in the TRC Process" in Du Bois and Du Bois-Pedain eds. *Justice and Reconciliation in Post Apartheid South Africa*. Cambridge: Cambridge University Press, 2008.

Ebrahim, H. *The Soul of a Nation. Constitution Making in South Africa*. Capetown: Oxford University Press, 1998.

Elkins, Zachary, Tom Ginsburg, and James Melton. *The Endurance of National Constitutions*. Cambridge University Press, 2009.

Elster, Jon. "Arguing and Bargaining in Two Constituent Assemblies," *U. Pa. J. Const. L.* 2 (1999): 345.

   ed. *The Roundtable Talks and the Breakdown of Communism*. Chicago: University of Chicago Press, 1996.

   "Transition, Constitution-making and Separation in Czechoslovakia," *European Journal of Sociology* 36(1) (1995): 105–134.

   Ulysses Unbound: Studies in Rationality, Precommitment, and Constraints. Cambridge: Cambridge University Press, 2000.

   "Legislatures as Constituent Assemblies" in R. Bauman and T. Kahana eds. *The Least Examined Branch: The Role of Legislatures in the Constitutional State*. London: Cambridge University Press, 2006.

Elster, Jon, Claus Offe, and Ulrich K. Preuss. *Institutional Design in Post-communist Societies: Rebuilding the Ship at Sea*. Cambridge: Cambridge University Press, 1998.

Epstein, L., Knight, J., and Shvetsova, O. "The Role of Constitutional Courts in the Establishment and Maintenance of Democratic Systems of Government," *Law and Society Review*, (2001): 117–164.

Farrand, M. *The Records of the Federal Convention of 1787*. New Haven: Yale University Press, 1911.

Figueroa, Nicolás. "Counter-Hegemonic Constitutionalism: The Case of Colombia," *Constellations* 19(2) (2012): 235–247.

   A Critique of Populist Jurisprudence: Courts, Democracy, and Constitutional Change in Colombia and Venezuela. *New School Doctoral Dissertation*. May 2016.

Fossum, J.E. and A.J. Menendez. *The Constitution's Gift*. Lanham, MD: Rowman & Littlefield, 2011.

Forsyth, Murray. *Unions of States: The Theory and Practice of Confederation*. London: Burns & Oates, 1981.

Fox et al. "Lessons of the Colombian Constitutional Reform of 1991." In Laurel E. Miller and Louis Aucoin, eds. *Framing the State in Times of Transition: Case Studies in Constitution Making*. Washington: USIP, 2010, pp. 81–110.

Foyer, Jean. "The drafting of the French Constitution of 1958." in Robert A. Goldwin and Art Kaufman. *Constitution Makers on Constitution Making: the Experience of Eight Nnations*. No. 479. American Enterprise Institute for Public Policy Research (1988): 7–46.

Frank, J. *Constituent Moments.* Durham, NC: Duke University Press, 2010.

Franklin, Julian. *John Locke and the Theory of Sovereignty.* Cambridge: Cambridge University Press, 1978.

Friedman, Steven, ed. *The Long Journey: South Africa's Quest for a Negotiated Settlement.* Johnnesburg: Ravan Press of South Africa, 1993.

Fritz, C. *American Sovereigns: The People and America's Constitutional Tradition Before the Civil War.* Cambridge: Cambridge University Press, 2008.

Furet, François. *Interpreting the French Revolution.* Cambridge: Cambridge University Press, 1981.

 Revolutionary France 1770–1880. London: Blackwell, 1995.

 "Revolutionary Government" in F. Furet, and M. Ozouf, *A Critical Dictionary of the French Revolution.* Cambridge, MA:Harvard University Press, 1989.

Furet, François, and Mona Ozouf. *A Critical Dictionary of the French Revolution.* Cambridge, MA: Harvard University Press, 1989.

Gana, Nouri. *The Making of the Tunisian Revolution: Contexts, Architects, Prospects.* Edinburgh: Edinburgh University Press, 2013.

Garlicki, Lech, and Z. A. Garlicka. "Constitution Making, Peace Building, and National Reconciliation: The Experience of Poland." In Laurel E. Miller and Louis Aucoin, eds. *Framing the State in Times of Transition: Case Studies in Constitution Making.* Washington, DC: USIP, 2010, pp. 350–390.

Gauchet, M. *La revolution des pouvoirs.* Paris: Gallimard, 1995.

Gicherman, Jessica, "The judicial system in Venezuela & the lack of checks and balances" *University of Central Florida Doctoral Dissertation.* May 2012.

Gillespie, Michael Allen and Michael Lienesch, eds. *Ratifying the Constitution.* University Press of Kansas, 1989.

Ginsburg, T. *Judicial Review in New Democracies.* Cambridge: Cambridge University Press, 2003.

Ginsburg, T., Elkins, Z., & Blount, J. "Does the Process of Constitution-making Matter?," *Annual Review of Law and Social Sciences,* 5(5), 2009.

Glenn, J.K. *Framing Democracy.* Stanford, CA: Stanford University Press, 2001.

Gobe, E. and Salaymeh, L., "Tunisia's 'Revolutionary' Lawyers: From Professional Autonomy to Political Mobilization." *Law & Social Inquiry* 41, no.2, Spring 2016: 331.

Godechot, J. *Les Constitutions de la France depuis 1789.* Paris: Flammarion, 1995.

Griffin, Stephen M. *American constitutionalism: from theory to politics.* Princeton, NJ: Princeton University Press, 1998.

Grimm, D. "Das Risiko Demokratie." In Bernd Guggenberger, and Tine Stein, *Die Verfassungsdiskussion im Jahr der deutschen Einheit: Analysen, Hintergründe, Materialien.* C. Hanser, 1991.

 Sovereignty. New York: Columbia University Press, 2015.

Gueniffey, P. "Elections" In Furet, François, and Mona Ozouf. *A Critical Dictionary of the French Revolution.* Cambridge, MA: Harvard University Press, 1989.

Guha, R. *India after Gandhi: The History of the World's Largest Democracy.* Delhi: Pan, 2007.

Gunther, R. *Spain After Franco.* Berkeley: University of California Press, 1988.

Hajji, L. "The 18 October Coalition for Rights and Freedoms in Tunisia." *Arab Reform Initiative,* February 2007.

Halmai, G. "Unconstitutional Constitutional Amendments: Constitutional Courts as Guardians of the Constitution?" *Constellations* 19(2) (2012): 182–203.

Hamoudi, H. *Negotiating in Civil Conflict: Constitutional Construction and Imperfect Bargaining in Iraq*. Chicago: University of Chicago Press, 2013.

Harris, William F. *The Interpretable Constitution*. Baltimore: Johns Hopkins University Press, 1993.

Hart, H.L.A. *The Concept of Law*. Oxford: Oxford University Press, 1961.

Hauriou, Maurice. *Précis de Droit Constitutionel*. Paris: Sirey, 1923.

Hirschl, R. *Towards Juristocracy: the Origins and Consequences of the New Constitutionalism*. Cambridge, MA: Harvard University Press, 2009.

Hobbes, Thomas. *The Elements of Law, Natural and Politic: Part I, Human Nature, Part II, De Corpore Politico; with Three Lives*. Oxford University Press, USA, 1999.
  Leviathan, or the matter, form and power of a commonwealth, ecclesiastical and civil. New Haven: Yale University Press, 1907.

Hohmann, B. "Etappen des verfassungsrechtlichen Diskurses" In Guggenberger, Bernd, and Tine Stein. *Die Verfassungsdiskussion im Jahr der deutschen Einheit: Analysen, Hintergründe, Materialien*. C. Hanser (1991): 98–99.

Horowitz, D.L. *A Democratic South Africa?* Berkeley: University of California Press, 1991.

International Crisis Group [ICG]. "Nepal's Royal Coup: Making a Bad Situation Worse," ICG Asia Report 91. 9 February 2005.
  "Nepal: Obstacles to Peace," ICG Asia Report 57. 17 June 2003.
  "Towards A Lasting Peace In Nepal: The Constitutional Issues," Asia Report 99. 15 June 2005.
  "Popular Protests in North Africa and the Middle East (IV): Tunisia's Way," Report 106 April 2011.
  "Marching in Circles: Egypt's Dangerous Second Transition," Asia Report 35. August 2013.

Jacobsohn, G. "An Unconstitutional Constitution? A Comparative Perspective," *International Journal of Constitutional Law* 4(3) (2006): 460–487.
  Constitutional Identity. Cambridge, MA: Harvard University Press, 2010.

Jaffrelot, Christophe, ed. *A History of Pakistan and its Origins*. London: Anthem Press, 2004.

Jaume, L. "Constituent Power in France" M. Loughlin and N. Walker eds. *Paradox of Constitutionalism*. Oxford: Oxford University Press, 2007.

Jehlicka, P. et al. "Czechoslovak Parliamentary Elections 1990" in J. O'Loughlin et al. eds. *The New Political Geography of Eastern Europe*. London: Belhaven Press, 1993.

Jellinek, G. *Verfassungsänderung und Verfassungswandlun*. Berlin: O. Häring, 1906.
  Allgemeine Staatslehre. Berlin: Springer, 1920.

Jennings, Ivor. *The Law and the Constitution*. London: University of London Press, 1959.
  ed. *Constitutional Laws of the Commonwealth*. Oxford: Clarendon Press, 1957.

Johnson, D. "Beyond Constituent Assemblies and Referenda: Assessing the Legitimacy of the Arab Spring Constitutions in Egypt and Tunisia," *Wake Forest L. Rev.* 50, 2015: 1007–1032.

Jung, C. and I. Shapiro. "South Africa's Negotiated Transition: Democracy, Opposition, and the New Constitutional Order," *Politics & Society* 23.3 (1995): 269–308.

Kalyvas, Andreas. *Democracy and the Politics of the Extraordinary*. Cambridge: Cambridge University Press, 2009.

"Popular Sovereignty, Democracy, and the Constituent Power," *Constellations* 12(2) (2005): 223–244.

Kazin, Michael. *The Populist Persuasion. An American History*. New York: Basic Books, 1995.

Keay, J. *India: A History. Revised and Updated*. New York: Grove/Atlantic, 2011.

Kelly, Paul. *Locke's Second Treatise on Government*. New York: Continuum, 2007.

Kelsen, H. *General Theory of Law and State*. Cambridge, MA: Harvard University Press, 1945.

Khan, Y. *The great partition: The making of India and Pakistan*. New Haven: Yale University Press, 2007.

Khatib, L. "Political Participation and Democratic Transition in the Arab World," *U. Pa. J. Int'l L.*, 34 (2012):336–339.

Khokhosvar, F. *New Arab Revolutions That Shook the World*. London: Routledge, 2016.

Kis, János. "Between Reform and Revolution," *East European Politics and Societies* 12, no. 2 (1998): 300–383.

"A rendszerváltást lezáró alkotmány," *Népszabadság*, August 19, 1994.

Klein, Claude. *Théorie et pratique du pouvoir constituant*. Paris: PUF 1996.

Kolarova, R. and D. Dimitrov "The Roundtable Talks in Bulgaria." In J. Elster ed. *The Roundtable Talks and the Breakdown of Communism* (1996), pp. 178–212.

Koseki, Shoichi. *The Birth of Japan's Post War Constitution*. Boulder, CO: Westview Press, 1997.

Kotzé, Dirk. "The New South African Constitution." In M. Faure and J.-E. Lane, *South Africa: Designing New Political Institutions*. London: Sage, (1996), pp. 34–58.

Kouddous, Sharif Abdel. "What Happened to Egypt's Liberals After the Coup?," *The Nation*, October 1, 2013.

Klug H. *Constituting Democracy: Law, Globalism and South Africa's Political Reconstruction*. Cambridge: Cambridge University Press, 2000.

La Nauze, John. *The Making of the Australian Constitution*. Melbourne: Melbourne University Press, 1972.

Lambert, É. *Le gouvernement des juges* [1921 ed.]. Paris: Dalloz, 2005.

Laclau, Ernesto *On Populist Reason*. New York: Verso, 2005.

Landau, David. "Constitution-Making Gone Wrong." *Alabama Law Review* 923, 2013.

Landau, David., N. Feldman., B. Sheppard, and L.R. Suazo, *Report to the Commission on Truth and Reconciliation of Honduras: Constitutional Issues*. FSU College of Law, Public Law Research Paper, 2011.

Landau, David, and Rosalind Dixon. "Constraining Constitutional Change." *Wake Forest L. Rev.* 50 (2015): 859.

Landsberg, Chris "Directing From the Stalls? The International Community and the South African Negotiating Forum" in Friedman, Steven, Glenn Moss, Ingrid Obery, and Doreen Atkinson, eds. *The small miracle: South Africa's negotiated settlement*. Johannesburg: Ravan Press of South Africa, 1992.

Le Pillouer, Arnaud. *Les pouvoirs non-constituants des assemblées constituantes*. Paris: Dalloz, 2005.

Lerner, H. Making Constitutions in Deeply Divided Societies, Cambridge CUP, 2011.

Lefort, Claude. *Democracy and Political Theory*. Cambridge, MA: MIT Press, 1989.

"The Permanence of the Theologico-political?," *Democracy and Political Theory* (1988): 213–255.

Lenin, V.I. "Two Tactics of Social Democracy in the First Russian Revolution," *Selected Works* 1 (1975): 425–527.

Levinson, Sanford, ed. *Responding to Imperfection: the Theory and Practice of Constitutional Amendment*. Princeton, NJ: Princeton University Press, 1995.

Framed: America's 51 Constitutions and the Crisis of Governance. Oxford: Oxford University Press, 2012.

Levy, Leonard W. "Bill of Rights" in L.W. Levy ed. *Essays on the Making of the Constitution*, New York: Oxford University Press, 1969.

Lindahl, H. "Constituent Power and Reflexive Identity: Towards an Ontology of Collective Selfhood" in Martin Loughlin and Neil Walker, *Paradox of Constitutionalism*. Oxford: Oxford University Press, 2007.

Linz, Juan and Alfred Stepan. *Problems of Democratic Transition and Consolidation*. Baltimore: Johns Hopkins University Press, 1996.

Livius, Titus. *Early History of Rome*. London: Penguin, 1960.

Lijphart A. *Power-Sharing in South Africa*. Berkeley: IIS, 1985.

Llorente, F. Rubio "The Writing of the Constitution of Spain" in R. Goldwin and A. Kaufman *Constitution Makers on Constitution making*. Washington: AEI, 1988.

Locke, John. *Second Treatise of Government: An Essay Concerning the True Original, Extent and End of Civil Government*. John Wiley & Sons, 2014.

Loewenstein, K. *Volk und Parlament*. [1922]. Munich: Scientia, 1967.

Loughlin, Martin and Neil Walker, *Paradox of Constitutionalism*. Oxford: Oxford University Press, 2007.

Loveland, I. *By Due Process of Law? Racial Discrimination and the Right to Vote in South Africa, 1855–1960*. Oxford: Hart Publishing, 1999.

Ludwikowski, R.R. *Constitution-Making in the Region of Former Soviet Dominance*. Durham, NC: Duke University Press, 1996.

Machiavelli, Niccolo. *The Discourses*. Penguin, 1970.

Macpherson, C.B. *John Locke: Second Treatise of Government*. Indianapolis: Hackett Publishing Company, Inc. 1980.

Macumbe, J. "Electoral Processes and Procedures in Zimbabwe." In O. Sichone *The State and Constitutionalism*. Harare: Sapes Books, 1998.

Madison, J. (A. Koch ed.) *Notes of Debates at the Federal Convention of 1787*. New York: Norton, 1987.

Maier, Pauline. *Ratification: The People Debate the Constitution 1787–1788*. New York: Simon and Schuster, 2010.

Dissolution. Princeton, NJ: Princeton University Press, 1997.

Mamdani, M. "Amnesty or impunity? A preliminary critique of the report of the Truth and Reconciliation Commission of South Africa (TRC)." *Diacritics* 32(3) (2005): 33–59.

Maraval, J.M. and J. Santamaria "Political Change in Spain and the Prospects of Democracy" in G. O'Donnell and P. Schmitter *Transitions from Authoritarian Rule*. Baltimore: Johns Hopkins University Press, 1987.

Marbury, W. "Limitations upon the Amending Power." *Harv. L. Rev.* 33 (1919): 223.

Matynia, Eżbieta. "A demokrácia századvégi berendezkedáse, avagy a lengyel kerekaszta" in A. Bozóki, et al. eds *A rendszerváltás forgatókönyve*. Budapest: CEU Press, 2000.

The Roundtable Talks of 1989. *The Genesis of Hungarian Democracy*. Budapest: CEU Press, 2002.

Performative Democracy. Boulder: Paradigm Publishers, 2009.

Marks, Monica. "Women's Rights Before and After the Revolution" in Nouri Gana, *The Making of the Tunisian Revolution: Contexts, Architects, Prospects*. Edinburgh: Edinburgh University Press (2013), pp. 224–251.

Marx, Karl. *The Class Struggles in France 1848–1850*. New York: New World Paperbacks, n.d.

Marx, Karl. *The 18th Brumaire of Louis Bonaparte*. Wildside Press LLC, 2008.

Marx, Karl, and Joseph O'Malley. *Critique of Hegel's' Philosophy of right*. [1843]CUP Archive, 1977.

Marzouki, N. "From Resistance to Governance." In Gana, Nouri. *The Making of the Tunisian Revolution: Contexts, Architects, Prospects*. Edinburgh: Edinburgh University Press, 2013.

McCloskey, Robert G., *The American supreme court*. Chicago: University of Chicago Press, 2010.

McCormick, J. *Machiavellian Democracy*. Cambridge: Cambridge University Press, 2012.

McDonald, Forrest. *We the People: the Economic Origins of the Constitution*. New York: Transaction Publishers, 1991.

Mednicoff, David M. "A Tale of Three Constitutions: Common Drives and Diverse Outcomes in Post-2010 Arab Legal Politics," *Temp. Int'l & Comp. LJ* 28 (2014): 215.

Merkl, Peter H. *The Origin of the West German Republic*. New York: Oxford University Press, 1963.

Merone, F. and F. Cavatorta "The Rise of Salafism and the Future of Democratization" In Gana, Nouri. *The Making of the Tunisian Revolution: Contexts, Architects, Prospects*. Edinburgh: Edinburgh University Press, 2013.

Meyer, R. "From Parliamentary Sovereignty to Constitutionality: the Democratization of South Africa 1990–1994" in P. Andrews and S. Ellman eds. *Post Apartheid Constitutions*. Athens: Ohio University Press, 2001.

Michnik, A. *Letters From Prison*. Berkeley: University of California Press, 1985.

Miller, Laurel E., and Louis Aucoin, eds. *Framing the State in Times of Transition: Case Studies in Constitution Making*. Washington: USIP, 2010.

Möllers, Christoph. "We Are (Afraid of) the People: Constituent Power in German Constitutionalism" in M. Loughlin and N. Walker, *The Paradox of Constitutionalism*. Oxford: Oxford University Press, 2007.

Morris, Gouverneur. *The Diary and Letters of Gouverneur Morris: Minister of the United States to France*. Vol. 1. C. Scribner's Sons, 1888.

Moustafa, T. "Drafting Egypt's Constitution. Can a New Legal Framework Revive a Flawed Transition," *Brookings Doha Center Paper Series*. March 2012.

Mtisi, Joseph, Munyaradzi Nyakudya, and Teresa Barnes. "War in Rhodesia, 1965–1980" in B. Raftopoulos and A. Mlambo, *Becoming Zimbabwe*. Harare: Weaver Press, 2009, pp. 141–166.

Murray, Christina. "Negotiating Beyond Deadlock: from the Constitutional Assembly to the Court," *Int'l J. Legal Info.* 32 (2004): 322.

Murswiek, D. *Die verfassunggebende Gewalt nach dem Grundgesetz für die Bundesrepublik Deutschland.* Berlin: Duncker & Humblot, 1978.

Ndulo, M. "Zimbabwe's Unfulfilled Struggle for a Legitimate Constitutional Order" in Miller, Laurel E., and Louis Aucoin, eds. *Framing the State in Times of Transition: Case Studies in Constitution Making.* Washington: USIP, 2010.

Negretto, G. *Making Constitutions: Presidents, Parties, and Institutional Choice in Latin America.* Cambridge: Cambridge University Press, 2013.

Nelson, Brian A. *The Silence and the Scorpion: The Coup Against Chávez and the Making of Modern Venezuela.* Nation Books, 2009.

Neuman, L. and J. McCoy "Observing Political Change in Venezuela: The Bolivarian Constitution and 2000 Elections." *Carter Center Paper Series,* 2001.

Omri, M. "No Ordinary Union: UGTT and the Tunisian Path to Revolution and Transition," *Workers of the World: International Journal on Strikes and Social Conflict,* 1(7) (2015): 14–29.

Osiatinsky, W. "Poland's Constitutional Ordeal," *E. Eur. Const. Rev.,* 3(29), 1994.

Ost, D. *Solidarity.* Philadelphia: Temple, 1990.

Ottaway, M. "Democratic Transitions and the Problem of Power" *Wilson Center Occasional Papers.* Spring 2014.

Özbudun, Ergun, and Ömer Faruk Gençkaya. *Democratization and the Politics of Constitution- making in Turkey.* Budapest: CEU Press, 2009.

Ozouf, M. "Federalism." In Furet, François, and Mona Ozouf. *A Critical Dictionary of the French Revolution.* Cambridge, MA: Harvard University Press, 1989.

Palmer, R.R. *The Age of the Democratic Revolution I.* Princeton, NJ: Princeton University Press, 1959.

   The Age of the Democratic Revolutions II. Princeton, NJ: Princeton University Press, 1964.

Partlett, William. "Separation of Powers without Checks and Balances: The Failure of Semi-Presidentialism and the Making of the Russian Constitutional System, 1991–1993," *The Legal Dimension in Cold War Interactions: Some Notes from the Field.* Law in Eastern Europe Series. Leiden: Brill, 2012.

Pasquino, Pasquale. *Sieyès et l'invention de la constitution en France.* Paris, Éditions Odile Jacob, 1998.

Peeva, R. "A bolgár kerekasztal tárgyalások összehasolitó szempontból" in Bozóki, A. et al. eds *A rendszerváltás forgatókönyve.* Budapest: CEU Press, 2000.

Perkins, K. "Playing the Islamic Card: The Use and Abuse of Religion in Tunisian Politics." In Gana, Nouri. *The Making of the Tunisian Revolution: Contexts, Architects, Prospects.* Edinburgh: Edinburgh University Press, 2013.

Pickard, Duncan. *Lessons from Constitution-aking in Tunisia.* New York: Atlantic Council of the United States, 2012.

Preuss, Ulrich. "The Round Table Talks in the GDR" in Jon Elster, ed. *The Roundtable Talks and the Breakdown of Communism.* Chicago: University of Chicago Press, 1996.

Przeworski, A. *Democracy and Market: Political and Economic Reforms in Eastern Europe and Latin America.* Cambridge: Cambridge University Press, 1991.

Quint, Peter E. "The Constitutional Law of German Unification." *Md. L. Rev.* 50 (1991): 475.

Ramaphosa, Cyril. "Negotiating a new nation: reflections on the development of South Africa's Constitution." *The Post-Apartheid Constitutions: Perspectives on South Africa's Basic Law.* Johannesburg: Witwatersrand University Press, 2001.

Revkin, M. "Egypt's Constitution in Question." *Middle East Law and Governance,* 5(3) (2013): 343.

Richet, D. "Revolutionary Assemblies" In Furet, François, and Mona Ozouf. *A Critical Dictionary of the French Revolution.* Cambridge, MA: Harvard University Press, 1989.

Rickard, Carmel. "The Certification of the Constitution of South Africa" in Andrews, Penelope, and Stephen Ellmann, eds. *The Post-apartheid Constitutions: Perspectives on South Africa's Basic Law.* Johannesburg: Witwatersrand University Press Publications, 2001.

Robertson, Claire "Contesting the Contest. Negotiating the Election Machinery" in S. Friedman and D. Atkinson eds. *The Small Miracle.* Johannesburg: Ravan, 1994.

Roellecke, G. "Dritter Weg zum Zweiten Fall." in Guggenberger, Bernd, and Tine Stein. *Die Verfassungsdiskussion im Jahr der deutschen Einheit: Analysen, Hintergründe, Materialien.* C. Hanser, 1991.

Rosanvallon, P. *Le Peuple Introuvable.* Paris: Gallimard, 2002.

Rousseau, Jean-Jacques. *[Considerations on] The Government of Poland [1771–1772].* Indianapolis: Hackett, 1985.

  Natural Law and Society. Chicago: University of Chicago Press, 1942.

  The Social Contract: & Discourses. No. 660. J.M. Dent & Sons, 1920.

  Letter to Beaumont, Letters Written from the Mountain, and Related Writings, vol. 9. UPNE, 2013.

Roznai Y. "Unconstitutional Constitutional Amendments – The Migration and Success of a Constitutional Idea." *American Journal of Comparative Law,* 61(3) (2013): 657–719.

Roznai, Y. and Yolcu, S. (2012) "An Unconstitutional Constitutional Amendment – The Turkish Perspective: A Comment on the Turkish Constitutional Court's Headscarf Decision," *International Journal of Constitutional Law,* 10(1): 175–207.

Russell, P. *Constitutional Odyssey,* 3rd ed. Toronto: University of Toronto Press, 2004.

Sachs, Albie. The Politics of Accommodation: Constitution-making in South Africa: A Lecture. *National Democratic Institute for International Affairs,* 1998.

Said, Edward. *From Oslo to Iraq and the Road Map: Essays.* New York: Vintage, 2004.

Sarakinsky, Ivor. "Rehearsing joint rule: The Transitional Executive Council." S., Friedman, D., Atkinson,(Eds), *South African Review* 7 (1994).

Sarotte M.E. 1989. *The Struggle to Create a Post-War Europe.* Princeton: Princeton University Press, 2009.

Scheppele, K. "Unconstitutional Constituent Power" in R. Smith and R. Beeman (eds.), *Constitution Making.* Philadelphia, PA: University of Pennsylvania Press, 2015.

  "Constitutional Negotiations. Political Contexts of Judicial Activism in Post-Soviet Europe" in S.A. Arjomand (ed.), *Constitutionalism and Political Reconstruction.* Leiden: Brill 2007.

Schiemann, J. *The Politics of Pact-making: Hungary's Negotiated Transition to Democracy in Comparative Perspective.* London: Palgrave Macmillan, 2005.

Schlink, Bernhardt. "Deutsch-deutsche Verfassungentwicklungen im Jahre 1990." In Guggenberger, Bernd, and Tine Stein. *Die Verfassungsdiskussion im Jahr der deutschen Einheit: Analysen, Hintergründe, Materialien.* C. Hanser, 1991.

Schmitt Carl. *Verfassungslehre.* Berlin: Duncker & Humblot, 1928.

The Leviathan in the State Theory of Thomas Hobbes. Chicago: University of Chicago Press, 1996.

Political Theology. Chicago: University of Chicago Press, 1985.

Die Diktatur. Berlin: Duncker & Humblot, 1928.

Segura, Renata, and Ana María Bejarano. "¡Ni una asamblea más sin nosotros! Exclusion, Inclusion, and the Politics of Constitution-Making in the Andes," *Constellations* 11(2) (2004): 217–236.

"Deepening Democracy via Constitutional Change." *Contrasting Colombia and Venezuela. Ponencia presentada en el taller LASA-Mellon Foundation." The gap from parchment to practice: Ambivalent effects of constitutions in democratizing countries.* Washington, May (2013): 28–29.

Shambayati H. "The Guardian of the Regime: The Turkish Constitutional Court in Comparative Perspective" in Arjomand, Said Amir, ed. *Constitutional Politics in the Middle East: With Special Reference to Turkey, Iraq, Iran and Afghanistan.* London: Bloomsbury Publishing, (2008), pp. 99–122.

Sieyès, E.J. *Écrits politiques.* Basle, Switzerland: Gordon & Breach, 1994.

Skinner, Quentin. *The Foundations of Modern Political Thought.* Cambridge: Cambridge University Press, 1978.

Hobbes and Republican Liberty. Cambridge: Cambridge University Press, 2008.

Skocpol, Theda. *States and Modern Revolutions.* Cambridge: Cambridge University Press, 1979.

Skowronek, S. *Building a New American State.* New York: Cambridge University Press, 1982.

Smolenski, Jan. "Semi Federalism: The Principles and Implications of the Making of the 1780 Constitution in Massachusetts," *The New School for Social Research,* unpublished seminar paper, 2015.

Sohrabi, Nader. *Revolutions and Constitutionalism in the Ottoman Empire and Iran.* Cambridge: Cambridge University Press, 2011.

Sólyom, L. "The Role of Constitutional Courts in the Transition to Democracy With Special Reference to Hungary" in Said Amir Arjomand, ed. *Constitutional Politics in the Middle East: With Special Reference to Turkey, Iraq, Iran and Afghanistan.* London: Bloomsbury Publishing, 2008.

"A jogállami forradalomtól az EU csatakozásig. Az alkotmányfejlődés keretei" in L. Majtényi and Z. Miklósi (eds.), *És mi lesz az alkotmánnyal.* Budapest: Eötvös Károly Intézet, 2004, pp. 15–16.

Snellinger, Amanda. "The Production of Possibility Through an Impossible Ideal Consensus as a Political Value in Nepal's Constituent Assembly," *Constellations* 22(2) (June) 2015: 233–245.

Stein, E. Czecho/Slovakia. *Ethnic Conflict, Constitutional Fissure, Negotiated Breakup.* Ann Arbor, MI: University of Michigan Press, 1999.

Stepan, A. "Tunisia's Transition and the Twin Tolerations," *Journal of Democracy*, 23(2), 89–103, 2012.

Suber, P. *The Paradox of Self-Amendment*. New York: Peter Lang, 1990.

Taagepera, R. and M. Shugart. *Seats and Votes*. New Haven, CT: Yale University Press, 1989.

Tadros, M. *The Muslim Brotherhood in Contemporary Egypt: Democracy Redefined or Confined?* London: Routledge, 2012.

"The Muslim Brotherhood's Gender Agenda: Reformed or Reframed?," *IDS Bulletin*, 42(1) (2011): 88–98.

Tagapeera and Shugart. *Seats and Votes: The Effects and Determinants of Electoral Systems*. New Haven, CT: Yale University Press, 1989.

Tavana, Daniel L. "Party Proliferation and Electoral Transition in post-Mubarak Egypt," *The Journal of North African Studies* 16(4) (2011): 555–571.

Teitel, R. *Transitional Justice*. Oxford: Oxford University Press, 2002.

Templin, W. "Die Diskussion über the Verfassungsentwurf des Runden Tisches" In Guggenberger, Bernd, and Tine Stein. *Die Verfassungsdiskussion im Jahr der deutschen Einheit: Analysen, Hintergründe,Materialien*. C. Hanser, 1991.

Thompson, L.M. *The Unification of South Africa*. Oxford: Clarendon Press, 1960.

Tilly, Charles. *From Mobilization to Revolution*. Reading, MA: Addison and Wesley, 1978.

Touraine, A. et al. *Solidarity: the Analysis of a Social Movement: Poland, 1980–1981*. Cambridge: Cambridge University Press, 1983.

Trotsky, Leon. *The Russian Revolution*, trans. by M. Eastman. New York: Simon and Schuster, 1936.

Terrorism and Communism. Ann Arbor, MI: University of Michigan Press, 1961.

Tugal, C. *The Fall of the Turkish Model*. London: Verso, 2016.

Van Tonder, J.J. "The Salient Features of the Interim Constitution" in M. Faure and J.-E. Lane, eds, *South Africa. Designing New Political Institutions*. London: Sage, 1996.

Van Zyl, Paul. "Dilemmas of Transitional Justice: the Case of South Africa's Truth and Reconciliation Commission," *Journal of International Affairs*, 52(2), Spring 1999.

Varol, O. "The Military as the Guardian of Constitutional Democracy," *Colum. J. Transnat'l L.* 51 (2012): 547.

Vásárhelyi, M. "A tárgyalások nyilvánossága, a nyilvánosság tárgyalása" in A. Bozóki et al. eds "A rendszerváltás forgatókönyve v. VII." In Vile, M.J. C., *Constitutionalism and the Separation of Powers*. Indianapolis: Liberty Fund, 1998.

Von Gierke, Otto Friedrich. *Natural Law and the Theory of Society: 1500 to 1800*. Boston, MA: Beacon Press, 1957.

Wagner-Pacifici, Robin. *What is an Event?* Chicago: University of Chicago Press, 2017.

Waldron, J. *The Dignity of Legislation*. Cambridge: Cambridge University Press, 1999.

Weber, Max. *Economy and Society I*. Berkeley: University of California Press, 1987.

Wheare, K.C. *Federal Government*. London: Oxford University Press, 1963.

Constitutional Structure of the Commonwealth. Oxford: Oxford University Press, 1960.

Whelpton, John. *A History of Nepal*. Cambridge University Press, 2005.

Wiechers, Marinus. "Namibia's Long Walk to Freedom: the Role of Constitution Making in the Creation of an Independent Namibia" in Laurel E. Miller and Louis Aucoin, eds., *Framing the State in Times of Transition: Case Studies in Constitution Making*. Washington, DC: USIP, 2010), pp. 81–110.

Williams, Damian. "Nepali Constitution-Making After the Revolution," *Constellations* 22(2) (2015): 246–254.

Wood, Gordon S. *The Creation of the American Republic, 1776–1787*. UNC Press Books, 2011.

Zeghal, Malika. "Competing Ways of Life: Islamism, Secularism, and Public Order in the Tunisian Transition," *Constellations* 20(2) (2013): 254–274.

Zemni, Sami. "The Extraordinary Politics of the Tunisian Revolution: the Process of Constitution Making," *Mediterranean Politics* 20(1) (2015): 1–17.

"From Socio-economic Protest to National Revolt: the Labor Origins of the Tunisian Revolution" in Nouri Gana, *The Making of the Tunisian Revolution: Contexts, Architects, Prospects*. Edinburgh: Edinburgh University Press, 2013.

Zweig, E. *Die Lehre von Pouvoir Constituant*. Tübingen: J. C. B. Mohr, 1909.

Index

absolutism, 18, 24, 26, 58–65, 82n105, 93–94, 103, 163, 167. *See also* dictatorship; *specific countries, topics*

Ackerman, Bruce, vii, 108, 112, 120–124, 124n68, 132–133, 132n90, 144, 151, 170, 259–260, 293, 311, 408

Al-Ali, Zaid, 276n53, 351

Albert, R., 388n78

Ali, Ben, 336, 339, 339n222, 347, 348

Amar, Akil, 121n54, 121n58, 123, 125n70, 132–137, 132n90

Ambedkar, B. R., 308, 309

amendment, 2n2, 4, 7n25, 132, 368, 370, 385, 386t; Arendt on, 378n50; Bulgaria and, 231; Colombia and, 313; consociationalism and, 251; convention and, 154; Czechoslovakia and, 213, 215, 222; democracy and, 399–400; elective affinity and, 408; entrenchment and, 4n9, 8; France and, 380; freezing and, 251; GDR and, 222, 223; Hungary and, 207, 209, 330, 383; inclusion and, 388; informal, 5n13; Iraq and, 383; judicial review, 389–397; juristocracy and, 413; justifications of, 397–411; legitimacy and, 416; limitation, 406; linguistic argument, 398; Locke on, 65, 65n64; multi-track structure, 129, 389, 390, 392–397, 409; natural rights and, 398–399; Nepal and, 383; normative argument, 416; parliamentary sovereignty and, 400; pluralism and, 388; popular sovereignty and, 330n191; post-sovereign model, 330n191, 383, 386, 408, 411–417, 420 (*see also* post-sovereign model); power of, 78, 79, 411; routes, 128n78; Russia and, 387; Schmitt and, 397, 403, 406–408; South Africa and,

383, 388; Tunisia and, 343, 345; U.S. and, 122, 123, 124, 146, 380; Venezuela and, 317, 387, 414. *See also specific countries, topics*

antinomy, ix, xiii, 27, 37, 55, 112; federation and, 140–144, 154, 157; France and, 88, 96, 106, 162–180; Locke and, 75–76; revolution and, 253; Schmitt and, 139, 142, 143; Sieyès and, 88n118, 161, 164, 168, 174–175, 177; sovereignty and, 75, 109–112, 111n23, 122, 131, 141, 143, 144, 151; spatial, 125; theory/practice, 162; USA and, 106, 132n88, 141–144, 153–159, 174, 181

apartheid, 7, 233, 239, 244–246, 252, 255, 256n242, 257

Arendt, Hannah, xii, 14n48, 14n49, 17, 259, 261, 378; amendment and, 378n50; authority and, 14, 17; constitutionalism and, 31, 157n154, 266, 435n64; democracy and, 436n65; political participation, 420; republicanism and, 18; revolution and, 171n202, 260n7, 264, 419; Sieyès and, 54, 95; small republics, 154, 157, 168; sovereignty and, 31, 107–108, 108; state of nature and, 157, 171n202; USA and, 80, 107–108, 157; Venezuela and, 381, 381n62

Argentina, 158, 253

Aristotle, 31n98, 45n1

Articles of Confederation, 117, 120, 124, 142–143

Austin, Granville, 299, 305, 307

authoritarianism. *See* dictatorship

Azad, Maulana, 308

Bacon, Selden C., 126

Baker, Keith, 54

Bastid, Paul, 160

Bejarano, Ana Maria, 313, 318

Hungary, viii, 194, 251, 365n4; amendment rule, 207, 209, 330, 383; Bulgaria and, 230; Communist Party, 205–206; Constitutional Court, 207, 247; EKA, 204, 206; elections and, 205, 208; FIDESZ, 203, 209, 385, 411n158; interim constitution, 206, 209, 213, 252; majority rule, 415; National Round Table, 205; parties, 207, 208, 209; Poland and, 204–210; post-sovereign model, 372, 410; Round Table, 205, 210, 212, 216, 240, 243n198, 329; South Africa and, 235, 241–243, 252

ideology, 16, 20, 34, 36, 101–104, 431. *See also specific types, topics*
imputation, theory of, 28–29, 56
India, xi, 257, 269, 284; basic structure doctrine, 8, 329, 388, 405, 409; Cabinet Mission Plan, 298, 300, 301, 305, 309; Colombia and, 298; Constituent Assembly, 300, 304, 305, 306, 307; Dalits, 308; double differentiation, 294, 296, 306, 328, 329; elections, 307n127; eternity clause and, 405, 409; France and, 305, 307; Golak Nath case, 399, 404–405; Government of India Acts, 296; Hindus, 300, 308; Independence Act, 299, 300, 304, 306; legitimation and, 296, 405; Muslims, 300, 301–302, 303, 308; Nepal and, 284–285; parties, 299–303, 305–307; partition, 299, 304, 308; provincial assemblies, 307; replacement doctrine, 405; revolutionary reform, 295–310; Sikhs, 302; socialism, 308; South Africa and, 309; sovereignty, 298, 299, 310; Supreme Court, 247, 404–405; USA and, 306; Venezuela and, 298
insurance model, 314, 344; benefits of, 367–368; constitutionalism and, 366–377, 373t, 374t, 381 (*see also* constitutionalism); eternity clause, 411; France and, 378; guarantees for, 370; Hungary and, 372; interim constitution and, 371; judiciary and, 368, 369, 396; levels of, 375, 375t, 376, 377; political form, 372; post-sovereign model, xii, 366, 411, 418; round table countries and, 376; South Africa and, 371
interim constitutions, 383; convention and, 175–181; Egypt and, 358; GDR and, 213, 224; Hungary and, 209, 213; insurance and, 371; Iraq and, 273–274, 385; multi-stage and, x; Nepal and, 384, 385; Poland and,

213, 385; revolution and, 434n59; Sieyès and, 176–178, 179; South Africa and, 235, 385. *See also specific countries*
international law, 25, 26, 61, 93, 234n171, 376
Iran, 260n7, 265, 275, 350n274
Iraq, 210, 257, 267, 269, 274; amendment rules and, 383; Constitutional Committee, 285; CPA and, 274; elections and, 274; eternity clause and, 412; final constitution, 275; interim constitution and, 273–274, 385; Nepal and, 289–290; parties in, 274, 275; post-sovereign process, 276; round table, 293n83; SCIRI and, 276; TAL, 274, 276
Islam, 341, 348–350, 356, 359. *See also specific countries, topics*

Jacobsohn, Gary, 402n128, 408
Japan, 21, 22, 22n67, 274
Jaume, L., 176n215
Jefferson, Thomas, xii, 79, 86, 178n221, 179, 378, 379, 400
Jellinek, G., 5n13, 123, 259
Jinnah, M. A., 302, 303, 309, 431
Jouvenel, Bertrand de, 14, 15
judiciary, 8, 376; amendment rules and, 413; constitutional courts and, viii; democracy and, 403–404; elections and, 331; entrenchment and, 368; insurance model and, 368; juristocracy, viii, 78, 391, 413; jury concept, 166; Locke and, 64n63; Schmitt and, 403; sovereign dictatorship and, 330. *See also specific countries, topics*

Kalyvas, Andreas, viii
Kant, Immanuel, 78n95, 85
Kautsky, Karl, 421–423, 428
Kelly, Paul, 74
Kelsen, Hans, 3–10, 13, 19, 29, 33, 102, 263, 407
Kis, Janos, 187n4, 195, 208, 262
Klein, Claude, 96
Klug, Heinz, ix
Kohl, Helmut, 225
Kojève, Alexandre, 14n48

Laclau, Ernesto, xiii
Landau, David, 331, 398n119, 412, 414, 415, 416
large N studies, viii, 327n185, 366n4, 371n28
Latin America, 158, 159, 174n212, 253, 254, 293
Lawson, George, 61–63, 66, 70, 71
Lefort, Claude, xiii